010 publishers, Rotterdam 2004

Jan Middendorp

Dutch Type

To Catherine

Acknowledgements

This book was born out of curiosity. Letterforms have fascinated me since childhood, but I did not get involved with them professionally until the late 1980s, when I began working as a self-taught graphic designer. I gradually realized that I had a natural preference for text faces by Dutch designers: Hollander, Caecilia, Quadraat, Thesis. I could relate to their confident modernity; I liked the way they avoided both the somewhat affected traditionalism of many contemporary American typefaces and the blandness of the Helveticas of this world. Having worked as a performing arts critic in a previous life, I turned back to writing and started interviewing the people whose typefaces I was so intrigued by. Those first meetings were crucial, as the generosity of the type designers I approached, their readiness to share their views and let me in on the tricks of the trade, allowed me to deepen my knowledge of methods, techniques and historical references.

When work on this book began, literature on contemporary Dutch type design in particular consisted mostly of scattered articles and a few books of limited scope, mostly out of print. Substantial books by or about Bram de Does, Gerrit Noordzij, Helmut Salden and Gerard Unger have come out since. For the history of the Dutch type founding trade, *Dutch typefounders' specimens* by John A. Lane and Mathieu Lommen became an invaluable reference work. But my main source, at least for the contemporary half of the book, remained the interviews and informal conversations with type designers, lettering artists and, occasionally, people involved in the business of producing and selling type. Between 1997 and 2003 I spoke with Jeroen Barendse, Anthon Beeke, Donald Beekman, Hermanus Berserik, Onno Bevoort, Peter Biľak, Evert Bloemsma, Frank E. Blokland, Erik van Blokland, Petr van Blokland, Jelle Bosma, Thomas Castro, Wim Crouwel, Gerard Daniëls, Bram de Does, Rudy Geeraerts, Henk Gianotten, Julius de Goede, Luc(as) de Groot, Marianne van Ham, Rudo Hartman, Akiem Helmling, Eyal Holtzman, Boudewijn Ietswaart, Bas Jacobs, René Knip, Hartmut Kowalke, Jan Kuiper, Paul van der Laan, Henk van Leyden, Lida Lopes Cardozo, Martin Majoor, Roelof Mulder, Gerrit Noordzij, Peter Matthias Noordzij, Martijn Oostra, Ootje Oxenaar, Nele Reyniers, Martijn Rijven, Donald Roos, Just van Rossum, Alex Scholing, Piet Schreuders, Elmo van Slingerland, Fred Smeijers, Bas Smidt, Erik Spiekermann, Swip Stolk, Joost Swarte, Gerard Unger, Peter Verheul, Chris Vermaas, Max Velthuijs, Mark van Wageningen, Martin Wenzel and Ad Werner. I held dialogues by phone and e-mail with Jacques Le Bailly, Maurice Blok, Jeanne de Bont, Melle Broeksma, Aad van Dommelen, Andrea Fuchs, Max Kisman, Peterpaul Kloosterman, Henk Lamers, Catelijne van Middelkoop, Sander Neijnens, Christoph Noordzij, Albert-Jan Pool, Pim Pootjes, Pieter van Rosmalen, Loek Schönbeck, Ko Sliggers, Jan Tholenaar and Rudy Vanderlans. I am grateful to Denise Brand-Balis and Chris Brand's children, as well as Ingeborg Kurpershoek and Liesbeth van Trigt for sharing their recollections.

Many people have supported *Dutch Type* throughout. I especially want to mention Françoise Berserik, Esther Cleven, Henk Gianotten, Karin van der Heiden, Jan de Jong, Jan Keijser, Max Kisman, Dick Maan, Gerrit Noordzij, David Quay, Huug Schipper, Erik Spiekermann, Jan Willem Stas, Rick Vermeulen, Marc Vlemmings, Wouter Vos and my publisher, Hans Oldewarris at 010.
The original idea was to make a Dutch and an English version of *Dutch Type*. Financial limitations made it necessary to focus on one edition only, and so I wrote the book in English. My knowledge of that language has proved sufficient for writing a book, but too limited to do so without help. I am extremely grateful to Andy Crewdson who commented on most of the articles, and to the publisher's editor, John Kirkpatrick, who patiently corrected the final draft of the whole thing. Both have not only pointed out grammatical errors and stylistic inconsistencies, but have also intercepted a few embarrassing factual flaws. Single chapters were reviewed by Matthew Carter, Gregory Ball, Stephen Westcott and Kent Lew. Others have given precious advice regarding parts of the contents: Frank E. Blokland, Henk Gianotten, Dick Maan, Mike Parker, Gerard Unger and Peter Verheul. While all these people have contributed to the quality of the writing, any errors or omissions are entirely my responsibility.
This book could not have been compiled without the cooperation of the type designers in providing visual material as well as typefaces, many of which are as yet unpublished. I am grateful to them, and to the companies that made available typefaces or gave permission to show samples from their publications: Bankiva Groep, Uitgeverij De Buitenkant, Dutch Type Library, The Enschedé Font Foundry, the Font Bureau, FontShop Benelux, The Foundry, Heineken, Eiichi Kono, LettError, Linotype Library GmbH, LucasFonts, Uitgeverij Van Oorschot, OurType, Philips Company Archives, Rosbeek Printers, Tetterode (formerly the Amsterdam Type Foundry), Total Identity, Trip Producties/Mecanorma, Typotheque, Underware, (URW)++ Design & Development GmbH, Visualogik.
Additional material was provided by De Beyerd, Haags Gemeentearchief, Haags Gemeentemuseum, Museum van Communicatie, Museum Meermanno, NAGO, Nederlands Architectuur Instituut, Plantin-Moretus Museum/City of Antwerp and Museum Rijswijk. Special thanks to Johan de Zoete and Andrea Roosen at the Enschedé Museum, to Dingenus van de Vrie at the Museum Boijmans Van Beuningen, to Marja Bosma and Len van den Berg at the Centraal Museum, to Mechteld de Bois at the Drents Museum and to Astrid Balsem, Jos Biemans, Mathieu Lommen and Joke Mammen at the Amsterdam University Library (UvA); we are especially grateful to this institution for renouncing the usual reproduction rights.
Much of the material came from private collections, notably those owned by Martijn F. Le Coultre, Allaert Creutzberg, Peter Enneson, Dick Maan, Hans Oldewarris and Jan Tholenaar. For providing

reproductions and other material I would like to thank Hugo De Blieck, Henze Boekhout, Peter and Conchita van der Linde, Martin Majoor, Piet Schreuders, Sander Pinkse, and Snoeck/Ducaju. The Stichting 'Het Archief van Jurriaan Schrofer' granted permission to show that designer's work.

This book has been in the making since 1997. There are a few good reasons for this long incubation period. Among other things, preparation was interrupted by another book, commissioned by Stroom hcbk, the contemporary arts centre of the City of The Hague. Researching and writing 'Ha, daar gaat er een van mij!' ('Hey, there goes one of mine!') between 2000 and 2002 has helped me immensely in getting a broader view of Dutch typographic design and its context. I also want to thank FontShop Benelux (the Dutch-Belgian subsidiary of the FontShop network) and its principal Rudy Geeraerts for trusting me with the editing and design of many of their publications on type and typography since 1998. As the editor of their magazine Druk (1999 – 2002) I was in a privileged position to commission articles from Dutch and foreign type designers and pick their brains about their craft.

Dutch Type has grown over the years, as did the body of work of the type designers involved. Bart de Haas and Peter Verheul have shown incredible patience and flexibility throughout the process. I have written far too much; thanks to Bart's dexterity and good taste, and Peter's relentless work on his typeface Versa all the words fit in and the mass of text is agreeably readable. Peter has honed and expanded Versa until it was perfect for the book. To me, this collaboration has been proof of how important type can be for the success of a work of graphic design.

Finally, a special thank you to the lady to whom this book is dedicated. As on previous occasions, my partner Catherine Dal has not only put up with it all, but has also been my informal assistant in various stages of the project.

Yet I am sure that in spite of her dedication, my obsessiveness and the help from many friends, the book still has enough flaws to justify a few admonishing remarks. I sometimes envy software developers: not only are they better paid, it is also taken for granted that their product does not work well until the first patches and updates can be downloaded from the internet. I cannot be sure if and when there will be a version 1.2 of this book. But I invite readers to participate in making the next version better by actively visiting the website dutchtype.org.

Ghent, 23 January 2004

Contents

infés

neats

Gerrit Noordzij, sketch
for a bold roman and italic.

Introduction: type, culture and identity

The reputation of the Netherlands as one of the world's design phenomena has taken on almost mythical proportions. Foreigners who have only read about it in trade magazines may be disappointed on their first visit. While design and architecture journalists like to portray the Netherlands as a place where every corner has been visually optimized under the scrutiny of uncompromising specialists, the reality is less glamorous. Shopping streets in Holland are as heavily polluted by red and yellow global identities as anywhere else. There have been as many architectural blunders. Newspapers and books are often superbly made but just as often mediocre or ugly – more or less like anywhere else. It may be true that there is a certain design consciousness among the Dutch; but pub lettering is better in Britain, sign-painting is more creative in Venezuela or Egypt, and design shops are bigger in Spain. So why is the Netherlands special?

One aspect of Dutch design culture that is invariably mentioned in literature on the subject is the special commitment of government bodies to quality and innovation; the courage of politicians and civil servants to accept unusual, even radical solutions. Among the most cited examples are the banknotes, stamps and telephone directories of the 1970s and '80s; the corporate identities of the PTT (Post, Telephone and Telegraph Service) and the Dutch Railways; and the more recent identity of the Dutch police with its dapper red and blue stripes.[1] Besides the talent of the designers involved, there have been two decisive factors in bringing this about. One is the presence of intermediaries with practical sense, vision and taste in positions where they could make a difference; and the other, perhaps more significant factor is a political and civil culture that allowed these people to obtain that position, and keep it, in spite of – or even because of – their unorthodox views.

Although it is always hazardous to speculate about 'national character', this openness to innovation may be a result of historical factors. The Netherlands is a small nation with big neighbours, and has been occupied by Spanish, Austrian, French and German forces. Throughout its history, the sea has been an ally as well as a threat. It is a country of many religions and convictions, each of which has (or used to have) its own network or 'pillar' of affiliated public service organizations. These peculiar conditions have fostered a practical attitude. The Dutch tend to give a lot of credit to the man with the best plan – not necessarily the person with the best political connections or the cheapest solution.[2] This is helped by the fact that there is not a strong sense of hierarchy; the Dutch do not easily take orders and talk back to those who give them.

An outsider's view

The American Alston W. Purvis, who for eleven years taught graphic design at the Royal Academy of Fine Arts in The Hague[3], sketched a penetrating portrait of the Dutch in his introduction to his book *Dutch Graphic Design 1918–1945*. As an outsider, his view is more objective than that of the present author, who was born and raised in The Hague. Here are a couple of quotes from Purvis's text.

'Twenty-seven percent of the land is below sea level, and from as early as the twelfth century this generated a perpetual need to sustain an intricate network of dikes, bridges, aqueducts, dams, windmills, and canals. ... To a large extent, the very existence of the Dutch depended on their mastery of natural forces, and for this reason perfection, exactness, computation, order and planning for the future have all become part of the Dutch consciousness. On a less positive side, this has also resulted in an unyielding and sometimes exasperating recalcitrance. But their success in

▲ The 'Sunflower' or fifty guilder banknote designed by R.D.E. 'Ootje' Oxenaar with Hans Kruit, 1982. Discontinued when the Euro was introduced in 2002.

▲ Corporate identity for the Dutch police by Studio Dumbar, 1993.

1 The banknotes were designed by R.D.E. 'Ootje' Oxenaar, who at the time was also head of the PTT/KPN Art & Design department, and by Jaap Drupsteen, a designer who has become famous for his pioneering television work. The numeral standard stamps and the telephone directories were designed by Wim Crouwel. The 1978 corporate identity of the PTT was developed by Total Design and Studio Dumbar; in 1989 Studio Dumbar did the restyling. The Dutch police was styled by Dumbar in 1993. The Dutch Railways were restyled in 1970–71 by Tel Design.

2 This is less true today than it was in previous decades. Oxenaar once remarked that his Art & Design department was 'in the business not of making profits but of spiritual well-being'. Due to global competition, European bureaucracy and short-term management, the margins within which designers operate have narrowed; the discontinuance of KPN Art & Design in 2002 (the management of KPN – the privatized PTT – judged it an unnecessary expense) was seen by the design community as a very bad sign indeed.

3 Hereafter this school will mostly be referred to as the Royal Academy, or KABK (Koninklijke Academie van Beeldende Kunsten).

▸ An order of 20,000 kilos of
type leaving the Amsterdam
Type Foundry, c. 1910.

▾ Martin Wenzel: an utterly
new E (from the experimental
FUSE alphabet Schirft), 1993.

defying their neighbours' belligerence, the unpredictable weather and the North
Sea has only fortified their conviction that struggle, diligence, and confidence can
conquer all. It has also helped to produce a unique sense of national unity, self-
assurance, tolerance, and pride.'
'A Dutchman delights in an energetic debate and, seldom reticent, will usually de-
fend his values with reason, spirit, persistence, and intellect. Indeed, he is not averse
to giving his opponent a stern and sometimes didactic admonishment. … An obsession for perfection helps complete the sketch of the Dutch identity. The Dutch are
averse to improvisation, to the non-essential and the arbitrary, and they have a distinct proclivity for simple logic and basic common sense. They are constantly seeking an unambiguous and unpretentious visual language.'[4]

Identity and style

So much for national character. But when it comes to graphic design, have these
traits (on which other authors concur) also resulted in a national style or method?
One thing that almost all Dutch designers have in common is their pragmatic attitude. As Purvis notes, Dutch designers are no great theorists; in their writings they
mostly tackle practical matters. What they are interested in is whether something
works, how it works and why. When it comes to defining a view of design in more
abstract terms, the tone is often sloganeering rather than philosophical.
This shared attitude has not led to a common style in graphic design. For some time
during the 1960s and '70s, when the functionalist creed reigned supreme – advocat-
ing objectivity, clarity and simplicity – graphic design began to look more or less the
same all over; but this happened on a global level. Before and after that brief period
of relative homogeneity, graphic design in the Netherlands has had almost as many
faces as there have been designers. In Max Kisman's words, the Dutch style 'is the
style of styles. There is a pluriformity which is unique to Holland.'[5]

Type culture

For a community of designers driven by pragmatism, individualism and perfectionism, type design seems a natural specialization. It should be added that, besides
craftsmanship and perseverance, a certain mercantile talent is also a great asset,
today as in the days of Johannes Enschedé I or Nicolaas Tetterode. While punchcutters and type designers used to be independent individuals selling their products
to one or more foundries, today many Dutch type designers run their own digital
type foundry.
Erik Spiekermann has often said that the Netherlands is the country with the highest density of type designers per square kilometre, and that is probably true. What
is more significant is the quality of the work and the impact it has on the global
type community. Dutch type designers have helped in setting new standards for the
emerging technology of desktop typography. They have done so by insisting on the
one principle that their predecessors Sjoerd Hendrik de Roos and Jan van Krimpen
agreed on: that new technologies need new letterforms. Revivals are not completely
out of bounds (although some of the best known Dutch type designers never made
any) but designing original alphabets is generally seen as a more worthy endeavour
by far. There may be a certain romanticism in that ambition, but there are also very
practical reasons. Designing type is a conventional discipline by nature: an utterly
new E cannot be recognized as an E, whereas any shape that has a roof and walls can
be seen as a house. To be able to take a step forward within the strict conventions of

reading, and perhaps arrive at a solution that 'the old fellows' (as Frederic Goudy called them) might never have thought of, it is necessary not to look at immediate models and only take into account a general idea of what a letter looks like.

Writing is a good way of doing this. Some critics claim that the Dutch practice of using the written letterform as a point of reference for type design unavoidably leads to nostalgic or old-fashioned type designs, but the opposite is true. Writing is the least restricted way of making letters, even when informed by formal training. The limitations are only in the mind and the hand, while they are in the software when designing on-screen, or in the geometry when constructing letterforms.

These are ideas that most type designers in the Netherlands – especially those who make text type – will agree on. Paradoxically, this predilection for original forms has led to the design of typefaces that have certain traits in common. Many are recognizably Dutch – not necessarily because of similar details but because of a general feel, of characteristics that can only be described in commonplace terms such as sturdy, open, clear, unadorned. In addition, some faces that originate from the same school, notably Gerrit Noordzij's teachings in The Hague, also betray an influence of the same 'hand' in their construction.

Type and lettering

So where does this leave the pluriformity that Kisman speaks of? Does his characterization also apply to type design? That depends on how that discipline is defined. As the present book shows, there has been a staggering diversity of custom-made letterforms in the Netherlands from the moment when graphic design slowly began to evolve as a separate discipline – around 1890. Most of these belong to the category that would now be called 'display type'; they were drawn, painted or constructed as part of a graphic layout. Of course, these letters are not part of the great tradition of practical Dutch book faces. Alphabets by Theo van Doesburg or Chris Lebeau are outsiders in relation to the lineage that connects designers such as Bram de Does, Gerard Unger or Fred Smeijers to the craftsmen of the sixteenth and seventeenth centuries. Some have said that the fanciful or geometric lettering by graphic designers and architects is not 'real' type design; but then what is 'real' type?

If graphic design is a generic term for combining text and visuals to create a message that can be read in one way or another, then any representation of the alphabet that graphic designers can use as a tool is type. Sometimes the most beautifully made text face just won't do the job – what is needed may be a spectacular display font, or even 'bad' type.

In the days of metal type and the early days of phototypesetting there used to be a clear distinction between text faces and jobbing faces or display type (the beautiful Dutch term is *smoutletter*). There were even separate systems for the two genres, as they were used in different ways. Today, digital typography has changed all that. Not only can text faces be scaled to poster size, and vice versa – they are also marketed the same way and have similar pricing.

Desktop typography has also changed the status of type design. Before the advent of desktop computers, letterforms that had been made for personal use normally remained 'private' – unless some type manufacturer saw an opportunity and decided to produce it. Processing the design of a typeface into a marketable industrial product was an enterprise of considerable scope and cost. Today, the distinction between an alphabet made for personal use and a font that others can work with is blurred. Everyone has a computer and simple type design software is cheap. When

4 Alston W. Purvis, *Dutch Graphic Design 1918–1945*, New York 1992, pp 3–5.

5 Quoted by Peter Biľak in 'Contemporary Dutch graphic design: an insider/outsider's view', in HD. *New Dutch graphic design*, ACTAR, Barcelona, 2001

Adobe published the source code to its Type 1 PostScript font format in the late 1980s, the means to produce professional type became generally available. Every graphic designer interested in letterforms can now be a type designer.

This is a reason for looking back at the development of Dutch type in the twentieth century with different eyes. Yesterday's lettering artists might have been designing type today; sometimes their alphabets do become part of today's toolbox. The Foundry in London has produced fonts based on experimental alphabets by Bart van der Leck, Theo van Doesburg and other leading figures of early Modernism. The Font Bureau in Boston published *Brok*, a digital font based on a 1925 poster by Dutch designer Chris Lebeau; the incomplete set of characters in that poster was extrapolated into a complete font with enough sensibility to be able to think of the typeface as Lebeau's. In this way, lettering artists and typographers posthumously have become what they virtually were but could not be called: type designers.

Although the mainstream of Dutch type design concentrates on sophisticated text faces, there is a growing interest in the lettering work of artists and architects from the 1920s to '60s. They are a source of inspiration to designers such as Joost Swarte, Max Kisman and René Knip. Some younger designers, like Paul van der Laan or Pieter van Rosmalen, are inspired by both currents. Today's scene is pluriform indeed.

What this book is not

This book aims to give a comprehensive survey of Dutch type design from today's perspective. As there is an obvious continuity from the early days of printing to the current practice, a historical prologue was judged to be necessary. In that first chapter I have briefly sketched the first centuries of type production in the Low Countries (that is, Flanders and Holland), focusing on those figures who have inspired type designers of the twentieth and twenty-first centuries. I had no ambition to write a definitive short history of early Dutch printing and punchcutting, and I hope that my summary will lead readers to take up the works of the real specialists in that field – their titles are listed in the bibliography.

The subsequent section, an overview of type design and lettering of the first part of the twentieth century – roughly up to 1970 – might be mistaken for a history of Dutch graphic design from a specific point of view. That is not my intention. Typographers and graphic designers have not been included for their significance as organizers of the printed page, but for the letterforms they have proposed. This implies that some renowned designers – the names of Hendrik Nicolaas Werkman, Otto Treumann and Gert Dumbar spring to mind, representing three generations of 'modernism' – are not discussed, despite their compelling approach to the *use* of type.

A note on typographic terminology

I have not tried to develop a watertight method of type description or categorization for this book. I assume that most readers are familiar with the conventional categorization of the roman, but whenever I use terms like 'oldstyle' or 'transitional' I do so with some reserve, and usually try to specify why I think a typeface could be thus labelled. When I use terms from the Vox/ATypI classification, their meaning is usually explained. More often than not, I use common-sense descriptive terms such as monolinear sanserif, slab serif or cursive script. I trust that the meaning of my haphazard terminology will be made clear by the context.

Early type design and printing in the Low Countries

The city of Haarlem boasts two statues of the mythical inventor of printing, Laurens Janszoon Coster. One is in front of the Enschedé building on the industrial site of Spaarnwoude, this one on the main square (Grote Markt).

▸ Among the strongest evidence that Haarlem did indeed have a tradition of early printing is a series of fragments of popular schoolbooks printed with unknown, primitive types; these strips were twined into strings to be used in bookbindings or for tying folders. These undated fragments are from the archives of the Haarlem Great Church or Cathedral, and preserved in the Haarlem City Library.

The Netherlands and the invention of moveable type

For centuries Dutch schoolchildren have been taught that the inventor of printing was a Dutchman. According to a persistent Dutch tradition, a Haarlem citizen named Laurens (or Lourens) Janszoon Coster developed the technique of printing with moveable metal type between 1423 and 1440, years before Gutenberg printed his *magnum opus*, the 42-line Bible.

Coster is not the only non-German who has been claimed to have invented printing. Nicolas Jenson, the French printer and innovative punchcutter who worked in Venice from around 1470, was praised as the inventor of 'the magnificent art of the book' in the imprints of certain works he published. In the Low Countries, a similar claim was made by one Johannes Brito of Bruges in 1477. In Britain, William Caxton, who practiced the craft in that same Flemish city from 1475, was long believed to have invented printing. Finally, there are documents in the legal archives of Avignon, France, which lend some weight to the nomination of a printer called Walfogel. But Coster's is a different case.

The Dutch, being the stubborn people that we are, especially where our reputation in technological matters is at stake, managed to build up the Coster myth over several centuries. Eventually the Haarlem printer was believed to be Gutenberg's only serious competitor. Coster and his workshop were pictured by famous artists and praised by Italian historians; his ingenuity became a source of pride and confidence for the Dutch in general and for the Haarlem printing business in particular. In the nineteenth century, theatre pieces about the printer of genius were staged in Paris, Antwerp and London. In Haarlem, massive Coster festivals were organized in fierce competition with the Gutenberg centennial celebrations in Germany; on Haarlem's main square a bronze statue was installed in 1856 that is still there today. The Coster celebrations of 1923 were an occasion for Jan van Krimpen to visit Haarlem and meet Johannes Enschedé, who commissioned the typeface *Lutetia* from him almost on the spot. As late as 1947 the Coster hypothesis was taken seriously enough to be used for badgering the Germans, who had occupied Holland for five nightmarish years: a book entitled *Coster – niet Gutenberg* (Coster – not Gutenberg) set out to demonstrate that the reputation of the Mainz printer was nothing but the result of a systematic German propaganda campaign which had practically started in 1460.

Present-day historians are convinced that printing with moveable type can only have been invented in Mainz. There is little doubt that Gutenberg and his right-hand man, Peter Schoeffer, were responsible for the new craft's first masterpieces. There is evidence that Gutenberg, who had fled his native Mainz around 1430, carried out his first experiments in Strasbourg before 1440. So where does this leave Laurens Janszoon Coster? In truth, he was probably concocted. His name does not appear in writing until 1588, and there is a lack of formal evidence for a printer of that name having existed. The Coster legend is mainly a fascinating piece of cultural history: four hundred years of historical research, forgery, ardent patriotism and political strategy, resulting in a virtually indestructible myth.[1]

Some elements of this whodunnit have remained unsolved. There is a group of rather crude early editions printed with moveable type, called *prototypography* but often referred to as 'Costeriana', whose age and provenance have never been established with certainty. These works were printed with primitive types that, while of unknown origin, were clearly based on a Dutch style of handwriting. Fragments from these prints have been found in the bindings of books known to have been made by a Haarlem bookbinder who is mentioned in connection with Coster in the 1588 chronicle in which his name first appears. There is also some fascinating circumstantial evidence. After the sacking of Mainz in 1462, German printers, and with them the new technology, swiftly spread across Europe. But in the Netherlands a lot of printed matter from the second half of the fifteenth century seems to have been printed with means more primitive than those available in neighbouring countries. This could be an indication that the inventor of moveable type was, after all, a Dutchman. What else could have been the reason for the Netherlands being relatively slow in adopting the new, more sophisticated technology?[2]

Whether or not it was based on fact, the persistence of the myth has yielded a considerable advantage for Dutch printing and typography. It has helped to stimulate and keep alive the interest in books and their conception. Haarlem's fame as one of the printing capitals of Europe was based on the Coster legend; it boosted the self-confidence of its most renowned printing office, Johannes Enschedé en Zonen. So even if Coster was a mere phantom, his influence on the pride and feeling of superiority of Dutch printers and punchcutters has been considerable.

Printers and punchcutters

From the outset, book production was a supranational, pan-European trade. Printers travelled, carrying their equipment with them; books which were forbidden in one country were printed elsewhere and then illegally imported; there was vigorous international competition among printers and type founders. Latin was the scientific and religious *lingua franca* used throughout Europe, which made it even easier for books to travel across borders.

With the continent being in constant political turmoil, the fates of states and regions shifted rapidly. A region's political or economic domination usually coincided with that country's leadership in arts and sciences. As for type design and book printing, the Low Countries (the Netherlands plus the northern half of Belgium) were at the forefront in the late sixteenth and seventeenth centuries – an era in which painting and architecture flourished as well.

Until the founding of Belgium in 1830, the history of the northern Netherlands was closely tied to that of Flanders, currently the Dutch-speaking part of Belgium. The economic boom in the Low Countries began in Flanders in fourteenth-century Bruges, a thriving textile city and a centre of European trade, where Italian bankers opened the very first stock exchange. A hundred years later, nearby Ghent was the most prosperous European city north of Paris, as well as the place where the new art of oil painting was explored. The sixteenth century – the Baroque period – was the golden age of Antwerp: for a short time it was the continent's foremost trade and financial hub, as well as a centre of arts, architecture and printing. But in 1588 the closure of the Antwerp port by the Spaniards put an abrupt end to prosperity. About half of the population left the city and many artists and intellectuals fled to Amsterdam. Having got rid of its main competitor, Amsterdam entered its age of Rembrandt – a period when the northern Netherlands became a leader in the field of book production.

Although Flanders was economically superior until the end of the sixteenth century, printing was in fact introduced in the North and the South in exactly the same year: 1473. Or to be more precise, this is the year from which the first dated examples of printing with moveable type – from Utrecht and Alost (Aalst) – have been preserved. As we noted, the English businessman William Caxton printed his first works in Bruges in the 1470s. Around 1500 the eastern city of Deventer was the country's main printing town, thanks to the presence of schools and fairs. In the first decades of the sixteenth century, when Antwerp reached its economic peak, that port city became one of the European capitals of printing.[3]

The first type designer, or punchcutter, of any significance in the Low Countries came from Rotterdam and worked in both Delft and Antwerp. Henric Pieterszoon called himself Henric die Lettersnider, or letter-cutter. He was active from around 1490 until his death in or around 1517.[4]

Prof. H.D.L. Vervliet, the Flemish authority on early printing, describes Lettersnider as 'the symbol of the advancing specialization and rationalization of the printing trade'. He continues: 'Before him, a printing house was a vertically integrated organization: from the selection of the text and the raising of funds, through punchcutting, type-founding, composition, correction, printing, to selling the final product, everything happened under one roof, was carried out by one man or by one group. [...] In about 1480–1490 specialists began to appear. The first to break loose from the power of the traditional pattern was also the most advanced technically:

Matrices of a textura type by Henric Pieterszoon Lettersnider ('Letter-cutter') have been preserved to date in the Enschedé collection. It is probably the only latin typeface that has been available for an uninterrupted period of four centuries.

Prologus

j. Verba Ecclesiastae/ filii David/ regis Jerusalem. Vanitas vanitatum/ dixit Ecclesiastes: vanitas vanitatum/ et omnia vanitas. Quid habet amplius homo de universo labore suo/quo laborat sub sole? Generatio praeterit/ et generatio advenit: terra autem in aeternum stat. Oritur sol/ et occidit/ et ad locum suum revertitur: ibique renascens/ gyrat per Meridiem/ et flectitur ad Aquilonem: lustrans universa in circuitu pergit spiritus/ et in circulos suos revertitur. Omnia flumina intrant in mare/ et mare non redundat: ad locum/ unde exeunt flumina/ revertuntur ut iterum fluant. Cunctae res difficiles: non potest eas homo explicare sermone. Non saturatur oculus visu/ nec auris auditu impletur. Quid est quod fuit? ipsum quod futurum est. Quid est quod factum est? ipsum quod faciendum est. Nihil sub sole novum/ nec valet quisquam dicere:

1 The earliest source is *Batavia* (1588) by Adriaen de Jonghe [Hadrianus Junius], which tells the tale of a workman named Johannes who stole Coster's material and took it to Mainz. The Coster question is thoroughly examined by Lotte Hellinga-Querido and Clemens de Wolf in *Laurens Janszoon Coster was zijn naam*, Haarlem 1988 – a critical study published by Joh. Enschedé en Zonen, the same firm that fuelled the Coster myth for centuries. But did Gutenberg's invention really define moveable type as we know it? As shown in a BBC Open University programme of 19 November, 2001, 'using computer software, Blaise Aguera y Arcas and Paul Needham analysed Gutenberg's work to try and identify the tools he used to create them. To their surprise, they discovered every letter was different, casting doubts on his methods.' (cf. the OU website, still active in summer 2003: www.open2.net/ renaissance2/doing/ gutenberg.html.) Their thesis is discussed in James Mosley's new introduction to the Hyphen Press reprint of Harry Carter, *A View of Early Typography*, London 2002, pp 11–12.

2 Speculations about this hypothesis were made by Gerrit Noordzij in one of my interviews with him.

3 D.B. Updike, *Printing Types*, vol. I, Cambridge 1951, pp 94–95; H.D.L. Vervliet, *Post-incunabula*, The Hague/Boston/London 1979, pp 4–5; H. de la Fontaine Verwey, 'The Netherlands Book', in Hellinga, *Copy and Print in the Netherlands*, Amsterdam 1962.

4 M.H. Groenendaal, *Nederlandse drukletters*, Amsterdam 1960, p 10; Updike (cit.) p 97.

ABCDEFGHI KLMNOP RST V XYZ Æ

ABCDEFGHI LMNOPQRSTV

a b c d e f g h i l m n o p q r s ſ t u v x y

œ Œ ff ij œ ß ſt &

Joos Lambrecht's remarkable
upright italic. Alphabet as
shown in H.D.L. Vervliet's
*Sixteenth-century Printing Types of
the Low Countries.*

Totten Leſer Saluut.

Ick ſchaems my der plompheyt, datmë in onʒen landen ʒo menyghen menſche vindt, die ons nederlantſch duutſch of vlaemſche ſprake, in Romeynſcher letteren gheprentt, niet gheleʒen in cã, ʒegghen dat hy de letteren niet en këot, maer het dijnckt hem latijn of griecx te weʒen. Dit ouer ghemerct ende want ic dit boucxkin in Romeynſcher letter (die allen anderen vlaemſchen letteren, in nettigheden ende gracyen te bouen gaet) gheprentt hebbe, ende noch meer ander ʒin hebbe (metter gracye goods) in ghelijcker letter te druckene, ʒo hebbic hier den Romeynſchen A. b. c. by gheprentt, op dat een yghelick, de ʒelue uader by ʒaude moghen ʒien ende leeren kenné, om alʒoo te meerder affeccye ende ioſten totter ʒeluer te cryghen. Ghelijc wy ʒien dat nu de walen ende franchoyʒen doen, die daghelicx haer tale meer doen drucken in Romeynſcher, dan in Baſtaertſcher letteren.

ABCDEFGHIJKLMNOPQR
ABCDEFGHIKLMNOPQR
STUWXYZ.
STVWXYZ

Cabcdefghiklmnopqrſstvuwxyzʒ&.
a b c d e f g h i k l m n o p q r ſ s t u v u w x y z &.

the type-cutter and type-founder. It was he who broke through the unity of conception, execution and distribution which was characteristic of the incunabula period.
In the Low Countries – and here we were in the lead – the individual who brought
this about was Henric Lettersnider.'[5]

It is important to realize that Henric's typefaces did not look like Jenson's or Griffo's
– the letterforms which have become the prototypes for today's roman and italic
book faces. At the time of the incunabula (the editions produced during the first
decades of printing) the dominant type of formal handwriting in northern Europe
was blackletter, also known as gothic, or broken script. Gutenberg's 42-line Bible
was set in a typeface cut to closely resemble the local variety of broken script, called
textura quadrata, with characteristic rectangular shapes. The common blackletter in
the Netherlands and Flanders was rather similar. Reproductions in metal type of this
kind of handwriting were regarded as the appropriate typeface for books in the vernacular (the people's language) even well after the Italian and French romans had
begun their triumphal progress.

Lettersnider based his type on the hand used by the Brothers of the Common Life,
whose prolific output of manuscripts had been extremely influential over the previous decades. This local version of the textura is also known as *Netherlandish Gothic*.
Variations of Lettersnider's fonts, as well as those by his son, Cornelis Henricszoon,
were to be commonly used until the end of the sixteenth century. Missals and other
religious books continued to be set in this kind of type up to the twentieth century.
The matrices of one of Lettersnider's types passed from one foundry to another and
finally ended up in the well-preserved Enschedé collection. It is probably the only
typeface which has been available continuously for more than 400 years.

Roman or gothic?

In our time, the issue of typographic readability frequently leads to heated discussions. Many recent typefaces have been accused of lacking legibility: from *Futura* and
Helvetica to the entire Emigre library. For those concerned with innovation, it is perhaps a comforting thought that these legibility debates are as old as printing itself.
In sixteenth-century Northern Europe, blackletter was – to paraphrase a famous
quote from Emigre's Zuzana Licko – what people read best because it was what they
read most (and, it may be added, what they wrote). But although blackletter types
were to be printed and read for centuries to come, some printers began to promote
the use of roman type as early as the 1530s.

Probably the first to publicly criticize the typographic preferences of Dutch and
Flemish readers was Joos Lambrecht of Ghent, one of the early masters of printing
and punchcutting in the region. Lambrecht [6] wrote the first dictionary of the Dutch/

[^] To demonstrate the clarity of
the roman, Lambrecht showed
a blackletter type next to his
own Pica Roman.

[^] Preface to the *Refereynen int
Vroede, int Zotte, int Amoureuze*
(1539) by Joos Lambrecht of
Ghent, in which the author
launches an emotional plea
in favour of 'Roman' types.

[^] Many years after roman script
had replaced blackletter in
Latin and French texts, printers
continued using blackletter for
texts in the vernacular. A work
by Arnoldus Vinnius, a Leyden
professor of law, published in
1659 by Daniel Elsevier, discusses Roman law in Latin and
gives certain legal terms in
Dutch – using a textura similar
to those cut by Christoffel
van Dijck.

nam, ut recte plerique respondent, non proponitur in
specie *d. l. ult.* institor, qui cum aliquo contraxit, aut
se institorio nomine obligavit, sed qui tantum profes-
sus est, esse penes mensam præponentis certam sum-
mam pecuniæ: ex cujusmodi nuda scriptione, ad fidem
mensæ protestandam, om *credit* van de tafel te
onderhouden / mirum non est, si post mortem
præponentis conveniri non possit. *Costal. in d. l. ult. &
ad l. 1. §. est autem. 17. de exerc. act.* Ubi tamen refert,
aliud placuisse Curiæ Parisiensi, eamque censuisse, in-
stitores non recte conveniri ex iis contractibus, quos
nomine institorio inierunt, sed in dominos actionem

ᴂ. Æ.A.B.C.D.E.F.G.H.I.K.L.M.N.O.P.Q.R.S.T.
V.X.Y.Z . a.b.c.d.e.f.g.h.i.k.l.m.n.o.p.q.r.ſ.s.t.v.u.x.y.z.
&.ct.ã.é.í.ó.ũ.ñ.j.æ.ę.œ.ç.ſſ.ff.ʽ.(.q̃.ſi.fi . 1.2.3.4.5.6.7.8.9.0ʹ
â.ê.î.ô.û.fl.ſl.q́.ff.ſ.   In principio erat verbum,& verbum.
&c. Amen dico vobis,ego ſum vitis vera. & pater meus agri-
cola eſt . Omnem palmitem in me non ferentem fructum,tol
lit : & omnem qui fert fructum, purgat , vt copioſiorem fru .
ctum afferat . Manete in me & ego in vobis . Iam vos mundi
eſtis propter ſermonem quem . ᴂ ...

◂ Double Pica Roman (*Ascendonica*)
cut in 1563 by François Guyot for
the Plantin foundry. It was
extremely successful, making
appearances in works printed in
Portugal, Japan and Mexico
(Vervliet 1968, pp 248–249).

▾ Ameet Tavernier, 2-line Pica
Roman (*Ascendonica*), c. 1551.
Though not a world-wide success like Guyot's Double Pica,
Tavernier's roman was used in
many European cities, from
Copenhagen to Lisbon. As late
as 1712 it was used by a printer
in Ghent.

Flemish language, published a collection of 'wise, crazy and amorous' poems, some of which were regarded as heretical, and eventually had to flee to Germany due to his conversion to Protestantism.[7] Lambrecht was an enthusiastic promoter of innovative type design. He cut a number of handsome roman typefaces, which he had difficulty selling to other printers, and a remarkable upright italic of which he remained the sole user.[8] He was not very fond of gothic types (although he cut a graceful French-style blackletter type himself),[9] and tried to persuade his fellow-countrymen to accept roman as the standard letter. Here is his text on the subject, published as a preface to his *Refereynen int Vroede, int Zotte, int Amoureuze* (1539):

> I am ashamed about the uncivilized attitude of so many people in our country, who are unable to read our low-Dutch or Flemish tongue when printed in Roman type, saying that they do not recognize the letters, and that it seems Latin or Greek to them. Having noticed this, I have printed this booklet in Roman type, which surpasses all other Flemish letter-forms in clarity and grace, and I intend (by the grace of God) to print more in the same letter; therefore I have printed here the Roman alphabet so that every one can see it and get acquainted with it and develop more affection and sympathy for it. Just as we see now that the Walloons and the French are having their own language printed in Roman rather than Bastardic (Blackletter) typefaces more and more every day.[10]

Lambrecht's plea would not result in immediate acceptance of the roman face for texts in Dutch. The language and its literature belonged to the lower classes; the court and nobility spoke French and, later, Spanish; scholars and clergymen communicated in Latin. Printing the vernacular in regional blackletter was in a way a matter of maintaining the cultural identity. However, roman and italic types were an important object of research and experimentation in sixteenth-century Flanders.

Growing self-confidence; the types of Tavernier

Joos Lambrecht was not the period's most productive or important type-cutter, but he may have been the most original. It was Lambrecht who taught the art of cutting punches to Ameet Tavernier, an apprentice printer from French Flanders. Tavernier moved to Antwerp, where he became a member of the artists' guild in 1556 and printed his first book the following year. Together with François Guyot, his competitor in Antwerp, Tavernier changed the face of roman and italic type in the Low Countries. Thanks to his work, 'the rather old-fashioned typography of a culturally out-of-the-way province gave way to a Renaissance book of the highest standard, but with some national characteristics clearly marking it off from its French, German or Italian counterpart,' wrote Vervliet.[11]

DETERMINADO.   37

91 Dixo me, Tu en lo primero
      Huye el Pais amoroſo,
      Do el Señor es liſongero,
      El Plazer ſiempre engañoſo,
      Y el Engaño verdadero.
   No es de razon natural,
      El que no teme eſte mal,
      D'el qual el guſto he perdido,
      Y à el no ſoy admitido
      Solo en ſer mi nombre tal.

5 Vervliet, *Post-incunabula* (cit.), pp 5–6.

6 H.D.L. Vervliet, *Sixteenth-Century Printing Types*, Amsterdam 1968, p 61.

7 Ibid., p 25.

8 Ibid., pp 312–313.

9 Ibid., p 151.

10 Ibid., pp 312–313. My translation. I have transcribed the Flemish original as follows:
    Ick schaems my der plompheyt, dat men in onzen landen zo menyghen mensche
    vindt, die ons nederlantsch duutsch of vlaemsche sprake, in Romeynscher letteren
    gheprentt, niet ghelezen en can, zegghend dat hy de letteren niet en kendt, maer het
    lijkt hem latijn of griecx te wezen. Dit over ghemerct ende want ic dit boucxkin in
    Romeynscher letter (die allen anderen vlaemschen letteren, in nettigheden en
    gracyen te boven gaet) gheprentt hebbe, ende noch meer ander zin hebbe (metter
    gracye godts) in ghelijckcker letter te druckene, zo hebbic hier den Romeynschen Abc
    by gheprentt, opdat een yghelick, de zelve daer by zaude moghen zien ende leeren
    kennen, om alzoo te meerder affecye ende ionsten (gunsten?) totter zelver te
    cryghen. Ghelijc wij zien dat nu de walen en de franchoyzen doen, die daghelicx haer
    tale meer doen drucken in Romeynscher, dan in Bastaertscher letteren.

11 Vervliet, *Sixteenth-Century Printing Types* (cit.), p 29.

Being at the centre of the north European trade network, Antwerp was an ideal place to sell type. Tavernier's faces spread as a consequence. By 1550 they were the standard types in the Netherlands, and ten years later they could be found in England, Scotland, Scandinavia, Germany and the Iberian peninsula. They had a surprisingly long life: as late as the eighteenth century, his types show up in typefounders' specimens. Tavernier's types differ from the designs made by his famous French contemporaries – like Garamond and Granjon – in that they are sturdier and have a larger x-height. He thus 'paved the way for the bold, though more graceful, design of Van den Keere and the robustness of Dutch type in the later seventeenth century.'[12] In other words, Tavernier's designs were the first step toward what Fournier would call *le gout Hollandais* (literally: 'the Dutch taste'), that pragmatic and economical style which has been rediscovered and reinterpreted by present-day Dutch designers from Gerard Unger to Fred Smeijers.

The versatile talent of Hendrik van den Keere

It is generally accepted that products of a new technology in its first stages mimic those of previous technologies. Only later do they take on characteristics appropriate to the new technical possibilities and constraints. Early typographical textura or blackletter faces, such as Henric Lettersnider's (c. 1505), were designed to resemble handwritten models. A few decades later, a young punchcutter from Ghent took a different, more rational approach. Hendrik van den Keere the Younger (born c. 1540) set to creating letterforms with the talent of an aesthetically gifted technician. Fred Smeijers has written: 'If the French punchcutters dominated the scene in the sixteenth century, Hendrik van den Keere was one of the few north European punchcutters whom one can consider in the same breath. He is their equal in output, in skill, and style, too.'[13] Vervliet calls him 'the best letter-cutter of the Low Countries in the sixteenth century.'[14] Son of the printer Hendrik the Elder, the young Van den Keere (also known as Henri du Tour) may have learnt the art of making type from Tavernier; Mike Parker, who studied Van den Keere's work at the Plantin-Moretus Museum in 1958–1959, is convinced that he was apprenticed to Granjon in the 1560s.[15] Very few works printed by Van den Keere the Younger have been identified, so he seems to have specialized in type design early on. In 1568, he began working as a freelance punchcutter for one of the first printers in Europe who worked on an industrial scale: Christophe Plantin in Antwerp.

◄ Hendrik van den Keere's Two-Line Double Pica Roman (*Canon Romaine*, c. 45 pts.), c. 1570. The specimen was photographed in the Plantin-Moretus Museum by Fred Smeijers, who used this type as a model for his *Renard*. *All Plantin reproductions: courtesy Plantin-Moretus Museum/City of Antwerp.*

▲ The first blackletter cut by Van den Keere for Plantin, c. 1570; described in the inventories as 'Gros texte Flamand de Henri du Tour'. (Vervliet 1968, pp 114–115)

⬘ Civilité types were modelled on Gothic cursive handwriting. The genre was 'invented' in the 1550s by Robert Granjon and marketed as a nationalistic French alternative to the successful Italics. This well-made Civilité used by several Flemish printers has been attributed to Van den Keere. (Vervliet 1968, pp 206–207)

Born in Tours, France, Plantin had moved to the Flemish port city in his twenties, and in 1550 became a member of the Antwerp Guild of Saint Luke as a book printer. At the time, Antwerp was the most important cultural centre north of Paris, and its book trade flourished. 'Of the 150-odd printing-offices in the Netherlands between 1500 and 1540, sixty were in Antwerp,' writes de la Fontaine Verwey.[16] After a difficult start, the newcomer Plantin soon surpassed the competition in quality and output. By 1565 he had seven presses working; at the height of his career he had twenty-two. In 1570 Van den Keere became Plantin's main supplier of punches. This was the same year that his prolific French colleague Robert Granjon went back to Paris after a seven-year sojourn in Antwerp, and the year in which François Guyot died. It was also during this period of great prosperity that Plantin moved to a building on the Friday Market, preserved to this day as the Plantin-Moretus Museum.

Van den Keere was to work for the great Antwerp printer for only twelve years, as he died prematurely from a leg injury in 1580. In that brief period he cut dozens of types which, through the international success of his patron's publishing enterprise, became known to readers and printers across Europe.

Van den Keere, writes Vervliet, was 'constantly aiming at letters that were not too complicated and that would not be choked with ink'.[17] His Small Pica Textura was enormously successful in the late sixteenth century, when blackletter was still common in Dutch printing: Plantin sold it to dozens of printers, especially in the northern Netherlands. Van den Keere's clear and open blackletter style lent itself perfectly to the design of small-size typefaces for use in bibles. He cut texturas in Bible, Minion and Nonpareil sizes, roughly comparable to 8, 7 and 6 pt. respectively. Van den Keere's texturas 'governed the development of Black Letter in the Netherlands in times to come, from Christoffel van Dijck's up to the last century'.[18]

To today's typographers, Van den Keere's achievements in blackletter design can only be of marginal interest. But his roman typefaces have stood the test of time. For centuries they remained secreted in the repository of the Antwerp Plantin-Moretus Museum, although a few of them were also preserved in the Enschedé collection. Following the research at the Museum by Mike Parker, Hendrik Vervliet, Harry Carter and others in the 1950s, his faces have been rediscovered as milestones in typographic development. Recently, his work has inspired new digital faces by Fred Smeijers (who also wrote about Van den Keere's working method in *Counterpunch*), Frank E. Blokland and Tobias Frere-Jones. The latter took Van den Keere's work as a starting point for *Poynter Oldstyle*, a newsface developed at the Font Bureau with the support of the Poynter Institute for Media Studies as part of the *Readability Series*.

Like the texturas, Van den Keere's romans are open and unadorned; although building on the French Renaissance style of Claude Garamond they are heavier and slightly more condensed. One of their main features, the large x-height, was inspired at least in part by economic motives. Granjon, when working for Plantin, received instructions to shorten the descenders and ascenders of the sets of Garamond types, so that they might be cast on bodies smaller than the original ones. This required less lead for production, and saved space on the printed page. Being his successor at Plantin's, Van den Keere was asked to cut many more of these adaptations or re-workings of existing alphabets in his client's collection. These adaptations, as well as Van den Keere's original types, may be regarded as precursors of the later 'thrifty' Dutch style.[19]

Extensive research done in the Plantin-Moretus Museum has made it clear that his legacy is unique. The Van den Keere collection comprises a staggering amount of original punches and matrices – some 40 sets – as well as bills, correspondence, account books and posthumous inventories, amounting to 'the earliest detailed picture that we have of a working type foundry'.[20]

In the northern provinces, the typefounding trade made a much slower start. When the City Council of Leyden set up a printing press in 1577, they bought their types in Flanders, ordering two fonts from Van den Keere who had established a virtual monopoly by then. However, the ongoing religious wars in the southern provinces made life increasingly difficult for Protestants like Hendrik van den Keere and his family. When the Spanish conquered Ghent in 1584, four years after Hendrik's early

ABCDEFGHIKLMNOPQ RSTVXYZabcdefghijklm nopqrsſtuvxyzÆæ&ct&ffffifi fflflœſſſiflſſiſtʒ áàâ áçéééèëçíìì îïñőóòōþ ꝑ ꝑ ꝙ ꝙ ꝗ ꝗ ŕřŭúùûü 1234567890,.'!?;:(-¶

▲ Van den Keere's Paragon Roman (Reale Romaine, c. 1576). This showing is from Vervliet 1968, based on matrices in the Plantin-Moretus Museum.

▼ The same typeface as shown in Plantin's Folio Specimen, c. 1585.

Reale Romaine.

Anachar. Scytha. Aiebat ſe mirari quī fieret, vt Athenienſes qui prohiberent mentiri, tamen in cauponum tabernis palàm mentirentur . Qui vendunt merces, emuntque lucri cauſa, fallunt quemcunque poſſunt, quaſi quid priuatim eſſe turpe, fiat honeſtum, ſi publicè facias in foro. At in contractibus maximè fugiendum erat mendacium. Sed tum maximè mentiuntur homines, quum maximè negant ſe mentiri.

12 Ibid, p 30.

13 Fred Smeijers, *Counterpunch*, London 1996, p 128.

14 Vervliet, *Sixteenth-Century Printing Types* (cit.), p 30.

15 Parker & Melis, *Inventory of the Plantin-Moretus Museum Punches and Matrices*, Antwerp 1958; Parker, Melis and Vervliet, *Typographica Plantiniana II. Early Inventories of Punches, Matrices, and Moulds in the Plantin-Moretus Archives*, Antwerp 1960. A study based on these publications by Mike Parker, presenting evidence that Van den Keere was in fact Granjon's apprentice, has remained unpublished.

16 H. de la Fontaine Verwey, in Wytze Gs Hellinga, *Copy and Print in the Netherlands*, Amsterdam 1962, p 23.

17 Vervliet, *Sixteenth-Century Printing Types* (cit.), p 47.

18 Ibid., p 32.

19 H.D.L. Vervliet and Harry Carter, *Type Specimen Facsimiles 2*, London 1972, p 7.

20 Vervliet, *Sixteenth-Century Printing Types* (cit.), p 31.

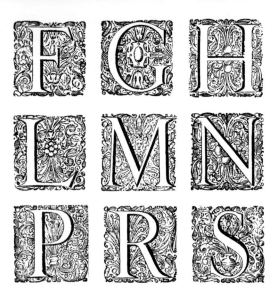

death, his children left for London and later established themselves in the northern Netherlands. Van den Keere's former foreman caster, Thomas de Vechter, who had acquired part of his master's matrices and tools from his widow, also moved to the North: he set up shop on the premises of Christophe Plantin's Leyden branch. This printing office, founded by Plantin himself and taken over by his son-in-law Frans van Raphelingen (Raphelengius), also possessed punches and matrices cut by Van den Keere. In the 1590s, Raphelengius commissioned three new exotic typefaces from the De Vechter foundry, which may have been cut by Van den Keere's son-in-law, the cartographer Judocus Hondius.

With their material and know-how inherited from Van den Keere and Plantin, the Flemish typographers in Leyden – political refugees, to some extent – laid the basis for what, in an astonishingly short time span, would become the leading type-founding and printing industry of Europe. The typefaces they had brought with them (fonts by Van den Keere, Tavernier, Granjon and Pierre Haultin) [21] were a deter-mining factor in the development of the influential Dutch style in type design.

The 'Golden Age' of Dutch printing. The Blaeu house

In the seventeenth century, several factors combined to bring about the 'Dutch mir-acle', a golden age during which the arts, sciences and printing all flourished in the Northern Netherlands. The Republic had become Europe's dominant seafaring na-tion, a position that was strengthened by the closure of the Antwerp port. Besides being freighters to the western world, the Netherlands also profited from a climate of relative religious freedom, offering room for ideas and writings that in other countries were censored or deemed heretical. Dutch printers were fearless and oft-en unscrupulous: not only did they print Bibles, original scientific and philosophi-cal treatises and atlases, they also produced numerous unauthorized reprints – 'pirate' editions of foreign best-sellers. It has been calculated that during the sev-enteenth century more books were printed in the Republic of the Netherlands than in all other countries put together. Most of these editions were produced for foreign markets.

The two printing/publishing houses whose names have become synonymous with seventeenth-century Dutch printing are Blaeu – father and son – in Amsterdam, and the Elsevier dynasty, founded in Leyden by a former employee of Plantin, and com-prising several independent firms in Leyden, Amsterdam and elsewhere.

▲ Ornamental initials no. 22 in the Enschedé collection, origi-nating from the Blaeu foundry.

▼ The flourishing of type design and printing in the Northern Netherlands was preceded by another art of the letterform: mannerist calligraphy.
The greatest Dutch writing mas-ter of the era was Jan van den Velden (1568–1623), whose *Spieghel der Schrijfkonste* (Survey of the art of writing, 1605) contains samples of his handwriting adapted for print by engravers. Gerrit Noordzij has written that this type of calligraphy is the purest expression of the man-nerist attitude, which 'creates its own little cosmos amidst the chaos'. (*Letterletter* 14, 1996)

The Blaeus' fame rests mainly on their world atlas, generally regarded as the century's most beautiful publication of its kind. Begun around 1630 by Willem Blaeu, it was completed by his son Joan in the 1660s, and published in Dutch, Latin, French, German and Spanish. But the bulk of the Blaeus' production had little to do with this enormously ambitious enterprise. The Blaeus seem to have made most of their money by printing missals, Jesuit writings and other works of devotion for Catholic clients – an activity which was not greatly appreciated by the predominantly Protestant inhabitants of Amsterdam.

The Blaeu printing shop had a type foundry attached to it, but relied on outside suppliers for matrices. In the early years, most of these came from Nicolaes Briot, a goldsmith from Gouda who had set up a type foundry in Amsterdam in the early 1620s. According to John E. Lane, an expert on seventeenth-century Dutch printing types, Briot was 'a very important but hardly known typecutter'.[22] He was one of the first in Holland who, independently of the Flemish heritage, cut original typefaces. Apart from an article by Lane on his Hebrew types, very little information about Briot is available. Type historian Charles Enschedé reports that arguments arose between Blaeu and Briot about the latter's practices. Briot was reported to have cast types for third parties from matrices which Willem Blaeu had commissioned for himself. Irritated by the moonlighting, Blaeu refused payment: typeface exclusivity was already an important issue in the seventeenth century.[23]

After Briot's death, the Luther foundry in Frankfurt became Blaeu's main supplier of matrices; Willem Blaeu travelled to that city at least once a year to visit the booksellers' fair. In the following decades, Joan Blaeu took over his father's business and new Dutch typefaces were added to the foundry's collection, possibly cut by Bartholomeus Voskens and Christoffel van Dijck, to whom we shall return later. All type was cast exclusively for the Blaeu office's own use; Thomas Marshall, agent to Dr. John Fell of Oxford, complained to his patron that Blaeu refused to sell any types to other printers or typefounders.[24]

Joan Blaeu died in late 1673, less than two years after the fire that destroyed his newly-built printing office. His widow put both the stock of books and the type foundry up for sale. On 7 May 1678 the readers of the *Oprechte Haerlemse Courant* (the era's main daily newspaper) were informed that the Blaeu letter-foundry was to be continued by Dirk Voskens and Johannes Adamsz. The advertisement summed up the available typefaces in detail. 'Anyone desiring letter to be cast in these matrices is requested to apply to the aforenamed, and shall be well served.'[25]

The Voskens family

Dirk Voskens was the son of Bartholomeus Voskens, who had formed a partnership with his brother Reinhard in 1641 'to produce punches, matrices and the equipment essential to a type foundry, which they propose to establish'.[26] After this partnership had been dissolved, Bartholomeus made a name for himself in Amsterdam as an able typefounder and a punchcutter of mostly Fraktur types – a kind of blackletter based on the German equivalent of the chancery script. In 1662 or thereabouts Bartholomeus made an attempt to establish himself in Hamburg; a type specimen issued in that port city by 'Bartholomeus Voskens, Schrift-schneyder und Giesser' can be dated around 1665. It is probable that Voskens returned to Holland soon afterwards, since in early 1670 Thomas Marshall wrote to Dr. Fell that he had made a journey to Amsterdam to confer with the city's best-known typefounders; 'where I quickly understood [that] last winter had sent Van Dijke & Voskens, the two best Artists in this Country, to their graves. Both have left sons, with whom I treated.'[27]
Reinhard Voskens, who had moved to Germany around the same time as his brother, established himself as a typefounder in Frankfurt. For several years he continued to bring in trained workmen from Holland, to the indignation of the Frankfurt founders Fievet and Luther, who filed a complaint against him in 1665. The dispute must somehow have been settled, for some years later we find Reinhard Voskens offering typefaces cut and cast by himself. When he died, his business was bought by

21 Some of these types, it must be said, had found their way to Dutch printers at an earlier stage.

22 'een zeer belangrijk maar nauwelijks bekend lettersnijder', e-mail to the author, March 2002.

23 Charles Enschedé, *Typefoundries in the Netherlands*, Haarlem 1978, pp 112–113.

24 Ibid., p 73n.

25 Ibid., p 115.

26 Douglas C. McMurtrie, *The Brothers Voskens and Their Successors*, Chicago 1932.

27 Ibid.

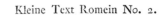

Kleine Text Romein No. 2.

Vult tamen tibi Iuftinianus , ut ifte curator præfte folemne jusjurandum apud Præfectum urbi, vel Præfidem, quo edicat omnia fe re-EeDEFGHIKLMNOPQVRSTVWVXZ : ABC ₢GHIKLMNOPQuRSTVWXYZ,..:

Kleine Text Curcyf No. 2.

Eo mifit Rex Suecus Theodoricum Falckenburquum, adminiftratoris adjuturum conatus; Joa neid inerat eommeatus,& rei tormentariæ Mag deburgum euravetr ABCDEFGHIFKL MNOPQ RSTVUWXYZ Æ jasis ſt ſtw

Kleine Auguftyn Romein.

Tardius aliquanto moleftiufque cum OR AN-GIO acta res eft. Is enim recua fcripferat, Hollandis , Zelandifque atque Burgundis Præfctum defignaret quando fe hifce prefecturis ce hijklmnopq ſstvuw ABCDEFGHI ABCDEFGHIKLMNOP Q STVUXYZÆ

Kleine Auguftyn Curcyf.

Æadem, is admonenti Gubernatrici ut abiret Amftelodamo,non modo non a paruerit, fed etiam Miſſuma Gubernatrice Turrium a fecretis pri urbe Protinus abfcendere,non Exaudito Re-ΛABCDE FGHJI KLM MNOP

Johann Adolf Schmidt, who continued the Frankfurt establishment until 1685 and then moved it to Amsterdam. Schmidt specialized in the cutting of Hebrew and other oriental types, but also cut some good romans, 'with an eye on the English market,' Stanley Morison wrote.[28]

By then, having acquired most of the material from the Blaeu foundry, Dirk Voskens had established himself as one of the city's most distinguished typefounders – his former partner Adamsz having set up shop independently. Like his father, Dirk Voskens was highly esteemed as a punchcutter; there is however no certainty as to which typefaces are actually his.

After his death in 1691, several type specimens were issued by his widow and sons. These documents do not mention types cut by Dirk Voskens; the specimens refer to 'typefaces which can be bought from the widow of Dirck Voskens (and sons)'. In later specimens, some typefaces appear that have been signed with 'B. Voskens sculpsit' or 'Gesn. door B. Voskens'. This is Dirk Voskens' son Bartholomeus the younger. Enschedé calls him 'an expert punchcutter' who 'added some excellent new types to the stock of the foundry'.[29] All in all, the Latin types which can be identified as being genuine Voskens creations are precious few. Most importantly, the body of work of Dirk Voskens, who is usually considered to have been the greatest talent of the family, can only be guessed at.[30]

After the death of Voskens' last partner Clerk, the firm was put up for public sale. The bulk of the material was bought by one Adam Mappa, who re-established the foundry in Rotterdam. As his firm failed to flourish, he left for New York, where his material was offered for sale in 1794. Mappa's material was bought by Binny & Ronaldson, the first successful American type foundry, which later changed hands many times, eventually becoming MacKellar, Smiths & Jordan. The firm was absorbed by the American Type Founders Company in 1892. Dutch punches or matrices may or may not have been part of the ATF's heritage; apparently no serious research has been done about this connection.[31]

The Elsevier dynasty and Elseviromania

Although there were other Dutch printers and publishers in the seventeenth century who were equally accomplished, the fame of the Elsevier family has taken on mythical proportions. From the early eighteenth century, a genuine *Elseviromania* took possession of bibliophiles throughout Europe. There was even a period when some of their editions were 'worth their weight in gold'.[32] According to romantic novelists, no erudite's library was complete without a shelf of 'priceless little Elseviers'. These popular 32mo classics, less than 15cm tall, were miniature forerunners of our pocket books. Yet, according to the engraver and type designer S.L. Hartz, the Elsevier editions 'only represent the average printing of their era, and in several of their productions do not even approach the best done by others.'[33]

Writing around 1900, when the Elsevier book still enjoyed great popularity, Charles Enschedé described the craze with some reserve. 'It was not enough to allow them their surpassing merit as printers, they were supposed to have been peerless typefounders as well.'[34] French book-lovers especially raved over the typographic superiority of 'les Elzévirs'. The types used in the books became so popular that a whole class of type was named after them. To this day, the term *Elzévir* is used in French for typefaces which have the characteristic open counters (*gros œuil*) of the Dutch style;

many French-speaking writers even put the entire category of Renaissance-inspired romans under this heading.[35]

In fact, there is not one single style of Elsevier typography; nor was the famous Elsevier printer's mark – the tree with the *Non Solus* emblem – an absolute guarantee of quality. Not all members of the Elsevier dynasty were as attentive to book design as Abraham or Bonaventura in Leyden, or the perfectionist Daniel Elsevier in Amsterdam; some left the printing to local printers of dubious skill.

Christoffel van Dijck

It was long assumed that most of the Elsevier fonts came from a single Dutch source. Charles Enschedé wrote: '... when, in 1878, Alphonse Willems announced that the Amsterdam punchcutter and letter-founder Christoffel van Dijck had supplied the types for the Leyden press and type foundry, Van Dijck at once acquired a popular reputation.'[36]

In reality Van Dijck played only a marginal role as a supplier of type to the Leyden office. Charles Enschedé has shown that of the 51 fonts belonging to Johannes Elsevier in 1658 only two or three were cut by Christoffel van Dijck; most other types had been bought at the Luther foundry in Frankfurt. In Amsterdam the situation was different. Daniel Elsevier, too, used many fonts bought from Luther, but he was in contact with Van Dijck and probably bought types from him during his lifetime. After Van Dijck's death in 1669, Daniel Elsevier bought most of the type material from the stock and thus came into possession of the punches and matrices of the type designer who in his lifetime was regarded by many as the best of his trade.

Although his name (spelled alternatively as Van Dyck or Van Dijck) sounds distinctly Dutch, we learn from his marriage announcement that Christoffel was born in what is now Germany – in Dexheim, not far from Frankfurt. He must have come to Amsterdam shortly before 1640, when he was recorded to be working as a journeyman goldsmith (for non-English speakers: a journeyman is an assistant, one step up from 'apprentice'). Another official document from the 1640s mentions his profession as typefounder. During his first decades as an independent craftsman and businessman, Van Dijck was often in financial trouble. He set up a type foundry in a rented house on the Bloemgracht (Flower Canal) in 1647, but merely two years later was forced to give up his possessions to his creditors. However, he managed to deposit much of his furniture and tools with neighbours and friends before the inventory was made. From 1650, his business began to prosper, and an inheritance from his parents in 1652 secured his financial position. Throughout the 1650s and 1660s business must have gone on satisfactorily.

Van Dijck died in 1669; his only son Abraham, also a punchcutter and typefounder, survived him by less than three years. In April 1673, a newspaper advertisement was published in which the entire inventory of the workshop was put up for auction; as we saw, most of it was bought by the printer and bookseller Daniel Elsevier. After Daniel's death in 1680, his widow put the foundry up for public sale. The type specimen issued by the widow Elsevier announcing the sale in March 1681 was an impressive overview of the punchcutter's body of work; but the sale never took place, possibly because the widow died that very month.

That famous 1681 type specimen (> p 13) gives a perfect idea of what distinguished the style of Christoffel van Dijck from that of his predecessors. The specimen's headline suggests that it consists solely of 'types which have been cut by the Late Christoffel van Dyck', but there are also some typefaces by Garamond, Granjon and Van den Keere. The Van Dijck types however, cut almost a hundred years after the French and Flemish ones, stand out. As Max Caflisch wrote, 'the contrast between the hairlines and the main strokes is more pronounced in the types of Van Dijck, the serifs are almost imperceptibly cupped, the capital letters are more powerful .... The typeface in general appears to have been cut more sharply, and have a more accentuated effect.'[37] On the whole, the effect is that of clarity, openness, economy and 'blondness', as Gerard Unger likes to say.

Ascendonica Romein and *Cursyf* as shown in the 1768 Enschedé specimen. The roman is almost certainly by Van Dijck, the italic may be atttributed to him with some certainty. Cf. John Dreyfus (ed.), *Type Specimen Facsimiles*, London 1963, p 17 and John A. Lane, notes to *The Enschedé type specimens of 1768 & 1773*, pp 54–55.

Ascendonica Romein.
Fr. Gros Parangon Romain.
Engl. Double Pica Roman.
Hoogd. Doppel Mittel Text Antiqua.

Quod quifque in ano eft, fci unt. Sciunt Id qui in Aurum Rex reginæ dixerit : Sciunt in Æ ABCDEFGHIKLMN ([§†?✠℮ ABCDEFGHIKLMNO

Ascendonica Cursyf.
Fr. Gros Parangon Italique.
Engl. Double Pica Cursiv.
Hoogd. Doppel Mittel Text Cursiv.

Cathedralium , Monasteriorum, ac omnium & singulorum beneficiorum, electivorum rerularium siFris ABCDEFGHKLMNOPQRS.

28 Stanley Morison in his draft for an introduction to the English edition of Enschedé's *Typefoundries*. Now in Enschedé (cit.), p 422.

29 Enschedé (cit.), p 116.

30 In 1994 Boston's Font Bureau published *Meno* by Richard Lipton; in the 1995, 1997 and 2001 catalogues, its wonderfully baroque italic is reported to have been based on 'Dirk Voskens' work in seventeenth-century Amsterdam'. My request to the designer to comment on this description led to a brief discussion via e-mail with Mike Parker, the type historian who wrote the font descriptions. Finally, Mike Parker suggested that it might be safer to attribute the original model or models to 'an unknown punchcutter from the Dutch school'. Parker pointed out that Meno italic makes use of exaggerated 'beaked' serifs which 'C.H. Griffith popularized ... by picking the 14 point Stempel italic [of the Original-Janson] as the model for Linotype Janson – those serifs greatly simplify the problems in fitting an italic to the constraints of the Linotype matrix. Sometime after that the italic was attributed to Voskens around Linotype, wrongly or rightly I do not know.' (e-mail to the author, June 2003)

31 Information supplied by Andy Crewdson.

32 Enschedé (cit.), p 63.

33 S.L. Hartz, *The Elseviers and their contemporaries*, 1955, p 43. Cf. essays by Hoftijzer and Lankhorst in Dongelmans et al., *Boekverkopers van Europa*, Zutphen 2000.

34 Enschedé (cit.), p 63.

35 This confusing terminology – and, perhaps, the foreign reference – may have been an incentive for Maximilien Vox to propose his *nouvelle classification* in 1954 and come up with neologisms such as *Humanes* and *Reales*.

36 Enschedé (cit.), p 80.

37 Max Caflisch, 'Christoffel van Dijck, an outstanding punchcutter', in *Type*, vol. 1 no. 1, Spring 1997, p 7.

ABCDEFGHIJKLMNOPQ
RSTUVWXYZ&ŒÆÇ
abcdefghijklmnopqrstuvw
xyz ff ffi ffl fi fl æ œ ç
1234567890.,:;'!?——-([

ABCDEFGHIJKLMNOPQ
RSTUVWXYZ& ÆŒÇ
abcdefghijklmnopqrstuvw
xyz ff ffi ffl fi fl æ œ ç
1234567890.,:;'!?——-([

The subsequent vicissitudes of the Van Dijck material have been carefully traced by type historians as a succession of inheritances, mergers and sales resulting in the survival of one single italic typeface in the Enschedé collection. It is a story that illustrates how punches and matrices passed from foundry to foundry through the centuries and ended up either in a museum or in the melting-furnace.

In mid-1681 the punches and matrices were bought by Joseph Athias, a Jewish bookseller and printer of Spanish-Portuguese birth who became famous for having printed and smuggled into England tens of thousands of English Bibles. What followed was a rather successful attempt by the Amsterdam typefounding establishment, led by Dirk Voskens and others, to undermine Athias's ambitions. Masters and journeymen agreed by covenant that it was forbidden to buy Van Dijck matrices from Athias, or enter his services. Consequently, Athias found himself lacking workmen for several years and was unable to meet his clients' orders. He was heavily in debt to the widow Schippers, a printer and bookseller who had been one of his partners in the English Bible business, and was forced to give her half the type foundry. After the death of these co-owners, Athias's son sold his half of the foundry to the widow Schippers's daughter; that family sold most of the establishment to Jan Roman in 1755. In 1767 the material was put up for public sale and was purchased by the country's two largest type foundries: Johannes Enschedé in Haarlem and Ploos van Amstel in Amsterdam. After Enschedé acquired Ploos van Amstel in 1799, most of the latter's types were sold as scrap metal. As typographic fashions changed drastically in the early nineteenth century, the same would happen to all of Van Dijck's matrices and punches still in Enschedé's possession. Apart from three blackletter types, only his *Kleine Text Curcyf* made it into the twentieth century. It was as a roman companion to this sole survivor that Jan van Krimpen would design his most elegant typeface, *Romanée*.

The Van Dijck revivals

Throughout the centuries, Van Dijck's faces have been praised for their regularity and simple elegance. Joseph Moxon, one of the earliest pundits of typography, wrote favourably about them in his *Meckanick Exercises*. And in 1925 Stanley Morison wrote that '[although] his typefaces are not as important to the historian as those of Garamond, they are certainly more beautiful.' [38]

As typographic advisor to Monotype, Morison asked Jan van Krimpen to act as consultant on the design of *Monotype Van Dijck* as part of his revival programme. Although Van Krimpen was one of the programme's harshest critics, he grudgingly complied. Van Krimpen was convinced that the roman model Morison had chosen from the Enschedé catalogue could not have been a genuine Van Dijck. Van Krimpen settled on a typeface used in 1671 for the first edition of *Herscheppinge*, Joost van den Vondel's famous translation of Ovid's *Metamorphosis*, printed by Daniel Bakkamude. This clear, open face became the model for Monotype Van Dijck roman.

When Monotype Typography reissued Van Dijck as a digital font in the mid-1980s, selling it in one package with the *Poliphilus* and *Blado* revivals, it was quite disappointing. Van Dijck, like many Monotype typefaces converted from the hot metal library, looks thin and powerless when used in normal text sizes. [39] The Berthold revival, made under the scrutiny of Günther Gerhard Lange, is much better.

The one Van Dijck revival that was newly designed as a digital typeface family – and certainly the most versatile of all – is very recent, and of Dutch origin. Under the supervision of Frank E. Blokland, Gerard Daniëls of The Hague drew DTL *Elzevir*, a Van Dijck-based typeface completely adapted to the qualities of digital typesetting and present-day high-quality printing.

ABCDEFGHIJKLMNOPQ
RSTUVW YZ
ABCDEFGHI KLMNO Q
RSTUV XYZÆ
abcdefghijklmnopq
rstu wxyz &ſſt ſhſl

Alphabet from Ovid (Amst, Ab. de Wees) 1761 with sorts from Enschede's specimen Tardius
aliquanto etc.

The unprecedented fonts of Miklós Kis

Most of what we know about the Voskens family comes from the writings of a Transylvanian who trained at their workshop.[40] Born in 1650, Miklós Kis (pronounced *Kish*; the christian name is usually internationalized as Nicholas) travelled to Holland when he was thirty years old. He came to Amsterdam with a precise mission: the Calvinist bishop Tofeus had ordered him to have the Hungarian Bible printed at Daniel Elsevier's office, and supervise corrections. When this proved impossible (Daniel Elsevier had died one month before Kis' arrival – and perhaps the bishop failed to come up with the funds needed), Kis decided to take on the job himself. He spent some months as an apprentice printer or compositor in the Blaeu printing office, and soon afterwards entered the Voskens workshop as an apprentice punchcutter. He showed a remarkable talent in cutting type. In less than three years he seems to have learned all there was to know about the craft. In his autobiographical notes (*Mentség*, 1698) he wrote: 'My master's father cut beautiful German types but no Latin ones. My master cut rather good roman and rotunda [gothic] types, but did not manage very well at cutting italics, which he left to me.'[41]

Kis also quoted his master as saying that he would never have agreed to teach his craft to any Dutchman for fear of competition; when Kis set out as an independent punchcutter in Amsterdam instead of travelling back to Hungary, Voskens complained that printers began avoiding him and instead went to Kis for their types. This was reported to Kis in later years by a Dutch professor who, according to Kis, added 'They used to say that you excelled all the Dutch in the art of cutting letters.'[42]

In 1684, only four years after beginning his apprenticeships in printing and punchcutting, the self-willed Kis had started printing his first Hungarian Bible, set in his own typefaces, at the office of the Amsterdam printer Olofsz. Kis continued printing religious texts in the following years, but also started promoting himself as a punchcutter. From 1687 this was his only occupation. A type specimen from around 1686 has the following text at the foot: 'Anyone who desires to have strikes or punches for these types may address the aforenamed master dwelling in Amsterdam on the Achterburgwal opposite the Swan brewery ...'

Kis's types are admirable indeed, especially when taking into account that he made them so shortly after he had learnt to cut punches. John E. Lane wrote about them: 'They are even more impressive in their conception (what we would now call their design) than in their execution. His italics in particular are among the finest of the century, and seem to have been more widely used and more influential than his romans.'[43] György Haiman, Kis's biographer, makes some interesting technical comments about these italics. When comparing them to their immediate predecessors and contemporaries, one notices a number of deviations from the traditional calligraphic model. There is a rationalilty to them which was quite new: the characters are slanted at a uniform angle; the strokes end in a clear-cut horizontal. Equally remarkable is the way the italics harmonize with the romans.[44]

The Amsterdam type specimen shows a consistency and unity that was quite unique at the time. While other specimens listed types by several punchcutters, Kis's is probably the first to show the work of one single designer. This was because his business did not include typefounding; it was limited to selling his designs, as unjustified matrices (strikes) or justified matrices. Kis's catalogue is also one of the first instances of a body of work in which the fonts in different sizes do not look like so many individual typefaces, but are clearly derived from a single unified concept of what type should look like.

In his later Amsterdam years, from 1687 to 1689, Kis was at the height of his punchcutting career. He worked for clients in England, Poland, Sweden, Germany, Armenia and Georgia. One of his biggest and most prestigious customers was Cosimo de' Medici, Grand Duke of Tuscany; from 1691 Kis's types began to appear in Florentine printings. In the autumn of 1689 Kis set out for his native country, taking with him several thousand copies of the Amsterdam Bible and Psalter. He left some sets of matrices in Amsterdam and deposited a complete range of them at a foundry in Leipzig, apparently hoping to sell them. With the remaining fonts of type – those

Miklós Kis came to Amsterdam to have a Hungarian Bible printed by Daniel Elsevier. He ended up printing it himself, with new typefaces cut for the purpose. The only copy of the 1683 title page is preserved in the library of Koloszvár, the capital of Transylvania (now Cluj in Romania).

38 Quoted in Caflisch (cit.), p 11.

39 The PostScript fonts were based on the Monophoto Lasercomp data, which in turn were the result of a large-scale conversion of Monotype's phototypesetting fonts. Deterioration had begun with an earlier hasty adaptation from the original metal type to photocomposition, in which 'some aspects of the change in technology were not fully acknowledged'. (*The Monotype Recorder – New Series*, no. 10, 1997, p 27)

40 That is, if the anonymous 'master' in Nicholas Kis's writings is indeed Dirk Voskens. Harry Carter was the first to point out that Voskens was the most plausible candidate, and other specialists concur. Kis's biographer György Haiman voiced some doubts, because Kis's type design does not show 'the influence of a single master'. John E. Lane wrote to me: 'Haiman's doubts are pseudo-science. [...] Kis's information about the size of his master's type foundry could hardly to refer to any other foundry, and there is no other possible father and son punchcutter in that particular period.' (e-mail, March 2002, my translation)

41 Enschedé (cit.), p 131, György Haiman, *Nicholas Kis*, San Francisco 1983, p 47.

42 Enschedé (cit.), p 131.

43 John E. Lane, Mathieu Lommen, *Dutch Typefounders' Specimens*, Amsterdam 1998, p 51.

44 Haiman (cit.), pp 41 – 65.

Dominus ille omnium liberrimus, ſumme bonus ſumme potens ſumme ſapiens,in quem nulla cadit mutatio aut converſionis obumbratio, a quo per quem in quem omnia,in quo nos etiam vivimus movemur & ſumus. mmmenelanann

Dominus ille omnium liberrimus, ſummè bonus, ſummè potens, & ſummè ſapiens, in quem nulla cadit mutatio vel converſionis obumbratio ; à quo per quem in quem omnia, in quo nos etiam vivimus movemur & ſumus. Adfligi

which were not lost during his extremely difficult journey – he set up a new printing and publishing house in Transylvania. He set out on an ambitious educational programme, hoping to get the people in his country to read and learn. However, due to his modern views on education, publishing and spelling, he made many enemies, some of whom even threatened his life. The positive result of this was that Kis felt forced to write his 'Apology' (*Mentség*, 1698), the only autobiographical work of a seventeenth-century punchcutter and one of our main sources on some aspects of the Amsterdam printing trade.

For centuries Miklós Kis was largely forgotten, both in Hungary and in the West. However, the types he left in Leipzig did survive. They came into possession of the Ehrhardt foundry, which around 1720 issued a specimen showing a large range of Kis types. Through several takeovers, the matrices eventually ended up at the Stempel Foundry, who bought them in 1919 as *Renaissance-Holländisch*. Stempel, knowing that the ancient Ehrhardt foundry had dealt with a Leipzig-based Dutch punchcutter named Janson, reissued the face as *Original-Janson Antiqua*, upon which Hermann Zapf based his revival for Linotype called *Janson* in 1951. Monotype also issued their own revival of these faces, called *Ehrhardt*, in 1937. In the same period, the American foundry Mergenthaler Linotype published C.H. Griffith's *Janson*.

The Janson-Ehrhardt question was resolved in 1954 when Harry Carter and George Buday published an essay proving that the designer of the types was in fact Miklós Kis.[45] Since then, several essays on Kis's work have been published, as well as the aforementioned book by György Haiman, which contains numerous facsimiles of Kis's Hungarian publications and some large-format enclosures with reproductions of specimens.

The English connection: Joseph Moxon and John Fell

The first person to write in technical detail about the art of printing and typefounding was the Englishman Joseph Moxon. His *Mechanick Exercises* began as a series of booklets for skilled artisans, and were later compiled into a printing manual published in 1683. Having grown up in Delft as the son of an English printer, Moxon was well informed on Dutch type design and was a great admirer of Van Dijck. Moxon cut a number of Dutch-style faces himself and issued the first English type specimen. In the *Mechanick Exercises* he wrote very favourably of punchcutting in Holland, with special praise given to the most recent output: 'Since the late made Dutch-Letters are so generally, and indeed most deservedly accounted the best, as for their Shape,

▲ Miklós Kis, detail from the Amsterdam type specimen (c. 1687). This specimen is probably the first to show the work of one single designer.

▶ Original specimen of the Fell Types, 1695.
Bodleian Library/DTL Collection

▶ 'English Roman' and 'English Italick' are Dutch types bought for John Fell in Amsterdam; the 'English' in the name refers to the size – approx. 12pt Didot. Stanley Morison has attributed the types to Christoffel van Dijck. It is a known fact that in c. 1670 Fell's agent Thomas Marshall bought matrices from Christoffel's son Abraham van Dijck; but these were not necessarily types cut by Van Dijck Sr.
Bodleian Library/DTL Collection

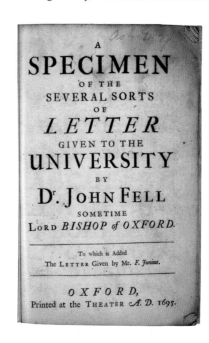

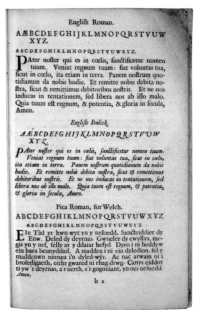

consisting so exactly [of] Mathematical Regular Figures as aforesaid, And the commodious Fatness they have beyond other Letters, which easing the eye in the Reading, renders them more Legible; As also the true placing of their Fats and Leans, with the sweet driving them into one another, and indeed all the accomplishments that can render Letter regular and beautiful, do more visibly appear in them than in any Letters cut by other People: And therefore I think we may account the Rules they were made by, to be the Rules of true shap'd Letters.' [46]

Moxon's high opinion of Dutch type was shared by Dr John Fell, Dean of Christ Church at the University of Oxford, who was responsible for establishing a learned press there. With the help of his agent Thomas Marshall – whose reports to Fell provide invaluable information on the Dutch printing trade – he purchased a large quantity of matrices, punches and types from Amsterdam type foundries. This material was bequeathed to the University after his death.

Some of the 'Fell types', as they have come to be known, may have been cut by Van Dijck or Voskens; there are others of an earlier date which were probably cut by Robert Granjon.[47] The Fell types are certainly the oldest punches and matrices surviving in Britain. Recently, DTL's Frank E. Blokland researched the Fell types and created DTL Fell, a digital font family based on some of them.

The house of Enschedé: Fleischman and Rosart

Although Dutch type remained in great demand for some decades, especially in England, its quality deteriorated after 1700. Bartholomeus II Voskens and the Cupy family were the only punchcutters of some standing who were still creating new types. Most other typefounders depended on the old punches and matrices they had in stock. Thomas James, an Englishman who came to Holland in 1710 to buy type, wrote none too kindly about his experiences: '... there's hardly such a thing as an honest man to be found; they all live by buying and selling ...'.[48]

It would take a German punchcutter and a Coster-inspired printer from Haarlem to bring some creative drive back into the typefounding trade.

The career of the punchcutter, Joan (or Johann) Michael Fleischman, is recounted by the printer, Johannes Enschedé, in a fine piece of corporate copywriting – the introduction to the famous type specimen published in 1768, only months after Fleischman's death.[49] Born near Nürnberg in 1707, Fleischman (whose name must originally have spelled Fleischmann) had a natural talent. As an apprentice punchcutter he made such quick progress that within a few years he was able to improve on his master's stock by cutting new characters. Before completing his apprenticeship he decided to quit and travel west, intending to go to France and England via Holland. He worked for a year at the Luther foundry in Frankfurt, 'hiding his expertise in punchcutting', and arrived in Amsterdam in November 1728. The next year he joined the foundry of the booksellers Alberts and Uytwerf in The Hague, where he first began working as a punchcutter. Uytwerf moved the business to Amsterdam and Fleischman followed, remaining in his service until 1732. From that year on he worked as an independent punchcutter, one of his main clients being the Amsterdam printer Rudolf Wetstein. After Rudolf's death, his son renovated the type foundry and even put out a type specimen featuring several Fleischman designs, but less than a year later he sold the Wetstein foundry to the Haarlem printers Izaak and Johannes Enschedé, father and son.

Thus in 1743 the Enschedés, who already owned one of the country's most renowned printing offices, came into possession of a well-equipped foundry and a stock of alphabets which were 'among the most desirable types of the day',[50] and secured for themselves an exclusive contract with the man who created them. The transaction would result in a lifelong partnership with Fleischman and helped Enschedé establish itself as the premier type foundry in Holland.

From 1748 Fleischman also worked for other foundries, such as Weyer (the successor to Uytwerf) and Ploos van Amstel. However, during their 25-year business relationship the bulk of his punches were cut for Enschedé – some 100 alphabets in all,

45 Harry Carter and George Buday, 'The Origin of the Janson Types: with a note on Nicholas Kis', in *Linotype Matrix* 18, March 1954; cf. Horst Heiderhoff, 'Zur Rehabilitierung der Nikolaus Kis' in *Die Original-Janson-Antiqua*, Frankfurt 1983.

46 Quoted in Haiman (cit.), p 40.

47 Colin Clair, *A History of European Printing*, London/New York/San Francisco 1976, p 291.

48 Quoted by Stanley Morison in Enschedé (cit.), p 428.

49 Facsimile: *Proef van Letteren welke gegoten worden...*, Haarlem/Amsterdam 1993.

50 Lane and Lommen (cit.), p 62.

Enschedé's Roman no. 65 and Italic no. 66, cut by Fleischman. This specimen is from *Fleischman on punchcutting*, by Frans A. Janssen. Set and printed by Bram de Does, who borrowed the Fleischman type from Enschedé. A publication of De Does's Spectatorpers, 1994.

FLEISCHMAN 12-POINT (D)
ROMAN NO. 65 AND ITALIC NO. 66

The following specimen gives a complete survey of Enschedé No. 65 and No. 66 available to the printer of this book.

ABCDEFGHIJKLMNOPQRSTUVW
XYZ&ÆŒÄÇÉÈÊËÓÖÜŁŚŢŤŻŽIJ
abcdefghijklmnopqrstuvwxyzijſ
æœ ct fb ff fi fl fh fk ffi ffl fb fh fi fl ſſ ſt ß ffi ffl
áàâäāą ć č ç é è ê ë ē ę ſ ì ï ï ĭ ł ń ó ò ô ö õ q̃
ú ù û ü ũ ŭ ṡ ṣ ṭ ź ž
.,;:!?*-—()[]/§† ❨ 1234567890
ABCDEFGHIJKLMNOPQRSTUVWXYZ
ÆŒÄÉÈÊËÖÜ

ABCDEFGHIJKLMNOPQRSTUVW
XYZ& ♂ ♀ ♀ Æ Œ Ä Ç É È É Ë Ö Ü IJ
ABCDJFMNPQR
abcdefghijklmnopqrstuvwxyzbvwijſ
æœ ct ff fi fl ffi ffl ſb ſh ſi ſſ ſt ß ſſi
á à ä ā ç è è ë ē ę ſ ì ï ï ï ñ ó ò ô ö õ q̃ q̧ q̃ ú ù û ü
.,;:!?-()[]*

▾ Anthropomorphous initials of
the kind that inspired Anthon
Beeke's women's alphabet
(> page 134). This alphabet was
cut for Enschedé c. 1750 by
Johannes Enschedé's friend
Cornelis van Noorde.

⊻ Title page of the 1768 Enschedé
specimen, of which a splendid
facsimile was published in 1993
by the Enschedé Museum,
the Enschedé Font Foundry
and De Buitenkant Publishers.

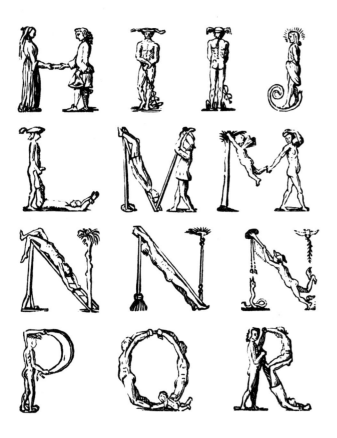

including Latin, Greek, Arabic, Armenian, Malaysian and blackletter. The most complex of all was a set of types for polyphonic music notation, which took him about two years to complete. He set a record by cutting 'the smallest type to be found in all Europe', the *Non Plus Ultra* or *Diamant Romein*, followed later by a blackletter type of the same size (c. 4p Didot).[51]

Fleischman's virtuosity in punchcutting was virtually unparalleled; his Diamant romans, music fonts and scripts were held in awe by his contemporaries for their sheer brilliance. Yet in typographic history, his name has never had the same resonance as that of his contemporaries Pierre Simon Fournier and John Baskerville. As Lane writes, 'his style of roman and italic has not appealed to twentieth-century tastes.'[52] Like Baskerville and Fournier, Fleischman designed letterforms which presage the 'modern', rationalist style of the late eighteenth and early nineteenth centuries. The serifs are almost straight; the contrast is vertical rather than diagonal; the overall image is more sparkling than that of the Renaissance and Baroque styles. This 'transitional' character is most obvious in the romans, with the italics still being strongly influenced by seventeenth-century models.

Although the twentieth century has been rather indifferent to Fleischman's work, he also had admirers. Stanley Morison wrote favourably about Fleischman in the opening essay of *Type Specimen Facsimiles*. Fleischman's typefaces, he wrote, vaguely follow the proportions and principles of the scientifically designed Romain du Roi, but Fleischman's are more idiosyncratic: 'As a whole, Fleischman's fonts represent the first personal, individualist interpretation of Roman and Italic.'[53] Paul Renner, the designer of *Futura*, praised Fleischman's work in his 1922 book *Typografie als Kunst* for which he also used a picture of Fleischman as frontispiece. His typeface *Renner Antiqua* (Stempel, 1939), although it has a strong calligraphic (and almost 'gothic') flavour, owes some of its features to Fleischman.[54] Renner's arguments for a revaluation of Fleischman found little response. The first serious Fleischman revival was commissioned in 1992 by Frank E. Blokland of DTL. He approached the German designer Erhard Kaiser, who based his design on several Fleischman samples in the Enschedé specimens of 1806, 1825 and 1953. *DTL Fleischmann* consists of two distinct series based on separate models, one meant to be used for large point sizes, the other for text sizes (> p 198).

Fleischman's work has been recently noticed in the United States as well. In the late 1990s, both Matthew Carter and the Hoefler foundry designed custom magazine typefaces inspired by Fleischman's designs. Jonathan Hoefler designed *Mercury* for *Esquire*; a text version of the font was made by Tobias Frere-Jones. This family is used by a number of newspapers in California and elsewhere. Carter's Fleischman-inspired *Fenway* was commissioned as part of the 1998 redesign of *Sports Illustrated*. About the latter, Carter wrote: 'I have always admired the small sizes of type cut by Johann Michael Fleischman for the Enschedé foundry, particularly an 8-point newspaper type of 1745, one of the first for that purpose. (I had studied Fleischman's punches when I was an intern at Enschedé in 1956.) Fenway Roman is not a historical revival, such as DTL Fleischman is, but I am very conscious of Fleischman as a mentor when struggling with legibility and spatial economy in type. The Italic, on the other hand, was influenced more by Fleischman's contemporary, Jacques-François Rosart, whose italics are less steeply inclined.'[55]

Rosart and son

Having acquired the Wetstein foundry in 1743, the Enschedés felt they immediately needed new fonts. Their ambition was to issue a specimen set wholly in types of their own. So they looked for another supplier besides Fleischman who could provide them with larger typefaces, which were not Fleischman's *forte*. Right there in Haarlem they found their man: a Belgian named Jacques-François Rosart who specialized in titling types and ornaments.

Rosart had not been happy when the Enschedés opened their foundry. He was a self-taught punchcutter who had come from Belgium to seek his fortune in Holland and

Fleischman's Galjart or Bourgeois roman (c. 8pt) from 1745, one of the first typefaces specially designed for newspapers, inspired Matthew Carter's Fenway roman.

Rosart's shaded titling capitals remained in use up to the 1970s.

FENWAY

VIDI IMPIOS SEPULTOS qui etiam cum adviverent in loco sancto erant et laudabantur in civitate quasi iustorum operum. Sed et hoc vanitas est. *Etenim quia non profertur cito contra malos sententia absque ullo timore filii hominum perpetrant mala.*

J. F. ROSART.

had set up shop in Haarlem only three years earlier. The formidable competition of the Enschedés left him no other choice but to work for them. The Enschedés were rather critical of the large types that Rosart had previously made and so commissioned new ones – seven sizes of roman titling capitals, along with two Greeks.

Though his connection with Enschedé must have brought him some prestige, the competition from their foundry eventually ruined his business. In 1746 his house on the Spaarne canal was put up for public sale; in 1750 he had to borrow a considerable sum of money. He also agreed to sell matrices and punches to an Amsterdam foundry. 'To sell punches', wrote Baudin and Hoeflake, 'is equivalent to giving up all the rights and depriving oneself of all possible profits from a typeface. That Rosart resigned himself to doing this argues a pressing need of money.' [56]

In the 1750s, we find him again doing business with Enschedé, but his position remained a difficult one. 'They were often pitiless towards [him],' write Baudin and Hoeflake. [57] The Enschedés's delight over Fleischman's work only made them more critical of Rosart's. There were occasions, though, when he made them quite happy: 'When he presented them with his *Financière* [a new kind of script type to go with his equally innovative music font], they showed themselves delighted. Both with the idea and the result. They bought strikes.' [58] But to Rosart's dismay, they did more: they took the idea to Fleischman, who cut two Financières which, of course, exceeded Rosart's in elegance and regularity.

By then Rosart had updated his style. Charles Enschedé wrote that some of his new romans and italics seemed exact copies of Fleischman's, but his 1978 editor Harry Carter does not agree: 'Rosart had less sure an eye than Fleischman for an evenly proportional alphabet and for the optically-even slope of an Italic; but he had more natural grace, though he too had ugly mannerisms.' [59] Rosart was also more sensitive to fashion than Fleischman, and perhaps more of an inventor. His *Financière* was unprecedented, as was his solution for music notation. His shaded capitals have become classics, and were still used by book designers in the 1970s.

Having tried for years to coexist with the increasingly ambitious Enschedés and their adoration of Fleischman, Rosart finally left for Brussels in 1759. Here he set up a type foundry with the support of the local (Austrian) government. In 1761 he issued his first type specimen, dedicating it to his patron, Duke Charles of Lorraine. In its introduction he made a point of stating that he had set up a type foundry in Haarlem three years before the Enschedés and that their fame was in part owed to him, having cut so many of their fonts. 'Now that I find myself under the patronage of H.R.H. I hope to show the whole of Europe proofs of my capacity.' [60] His Brussels workshop prospered. Rosart acquired an international reputation, exporting to France, Holland and Germany. His second Brussels specimen, issued in 1768, contains as many as 75 typefaces and a large number of fleurons, almost all cut by Rosart himself. The foreword is, again, rather spiteful towards Enschedé. [61]

51 Max Caflisch, *Typographische Monatsblätter* 5/2000, pp 1–2.

52 John E. Lane, Introduction and notes to *Proef van Letteren* (cit.), p 30.

53 John Dreyfus (ed.), *Type Specimen Facsimiles* I, London 1963, p XIV; reprinted in: Morison, *Letter Forms*, 1996, p 26.

54 Christopher Burke, *Paul Renner. The Art of Typography*, London 1998, p 163.

55 Carter in an e-mail to Andy Crewdson, published on Crewdson's website *Lines & Splines*, which was discontinued in 2002.

56 Fernand Baudin and Netty Hoeflake, *The Type Specimen of Jacques-François Rosart*, Brussels 1768, Amsterdam/London/New York 1973, p 21.

57 Ibid., p 11.

58 Ibid.

59 Enschedé (cit.), p 251. D.B. Updike was extremely critical of Rosart, reviewing his 1768 specimen with sarcasm in *Printing Types*, vol. II, Cambridge/London 1962, pp 40–41.

60 Baudin and Hoeflake (cit.), p 29.

61 Ibid., pp 30–31.

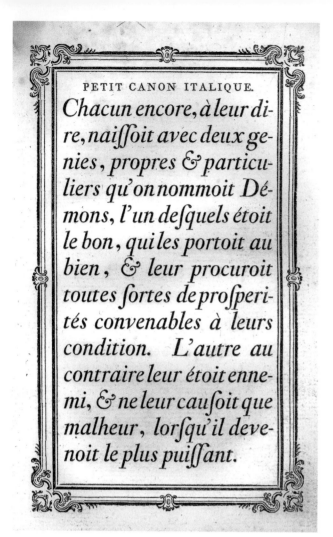

Two styles of italics by Jacques-François Rosart. The Cursyf is a narrow, sixteenth-century-style calligraphic italic. His Italique is more similar to the Romain du Roi and to the italics cut by Fournier and other French punchcutters of the eighteenth century. DTL collection.

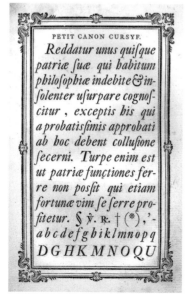

In their foreword to the facsimile of Rosart's 1768 specimen, Baudin and Hoeflake note that there is a considerable difference in style between the earlier types as published in the 1761 Brussels specimen – mostly conceived in Haarlem, in the Dutch fashion – and the newly cut types in the extended edition. This is especially evident in the italics. Rosart's new *Italiques* have been cut in the French mode of the time, influenced by the seminal *Romain du Roi*. They are hybrids of the cursive and the sloped roman and, like Fournier's italics, are precursors of the style perfected by Bodoni, Walbaum and Didot – 'modern face'.

In 1764 Rosart had been able to resume contact with Enschedé. The Dutch foundries were no longer his competitors – due both to the distance and to the patronage of the Austrian government – and, as Baudin and Hoeflake wrote, 'it would have been pleasant as well as profitable for him, one may well imagine, to sell his strikes abroad, and above all to Enschedé.'[62] Another motive for renewing the contacts with Haarlem was his eldest son Matthias, whose well-made textura was shown in Rosart's 1768 specimen and for whom the father may have hoped to find a job in Holland. We do not know if Matthias Rosart ever worked for Enschedé, but in 1768 we find him in Amsterdam as a supplier of strikes to several foundries. He later set up shop as an independent typefounder, and after Jacques-François's death in 1777 continued to sell both his father's and his own types.

The nineteenth century: a Dark Age?

In the history of type design, the nineteenth century is often described as a Dark Age in which the great Renaissance and Baroque traditions represented by Griffo, Garamond and Van Dijck all but dissipated; a period in which the virtuosity and speed of new reproduction techniques, as well as the advent of mass advertising, spawned excesses of ornament, affectation, kitsch and nonchalance. It is true that the nineteenth-century experiments were not always tasteful – as shown by the staggering output of typefaces which were shaded, back-slanted, condensed and extended to the extreme, turned inside-out or otherwise deformed – but the taste for novelty also enriched the language of typography immensely. Sanserif ('grotesque') and slab serif ('egyptian') were invented during this period; more generally, the nineteenth century may be seen as the period which gave birth to the display or headline typeface. The abundance of title pages looking like circus posters and spiky, dazzling text faces has fed the common notion that by 1890 typography 'had digressed into a vapid clutter'[63] and quality was non-existent; yet in the Netherlands the 1870s and 1880s also yielded industrially produced books that were well-bound and well-printed on paper that still looks good today.

Type production in the Netherlands – a province of revolutionary and Napoleonic France from 1795 to 1813 – was governed by French and, later, English influences. The development of native type designs ground to a halt. No new Latin text faces would be cut until Sjoerd de Roos's 1912 *Hollandse Mediaeval*. An even graver consequence, from the historian's point of view, was the drastic decision by most foundries to melt down the types of past centuries in order to make room (and furnish metal) for the new, fashionable types. Due to one fatal decision at Enschedé, the original materials of many sixteenth- and seventeenth-century types were destroyed: 'All the punches and matrices crossed out in this inventory were broken up and the copper sold in June 1808 as being of the least possible use to the foundry.'[64]

Enschedé versus Tetterode

The Enschedé foundry in Haarlem had little competition during the first half of the century. Its acquisition, in 1799, of the Ploos van Amstel foundry, its main competitor, had brought typefounding in Amsterdam to a halt. The first serious attempt at setting up a competing foundry in the Dutch capital was made in 1837, when Kornelis Elix bought what was left of the eighteenth-century foundry and printing office

Bruyn/Eyben. Elix set out to renew the 'rich, but outdated' Bruyn/Eyben collection by buying matrices in London and Paris. He also hired Jean Baptist De Passe, a Belgian punchcutter who had been a foreman to the Didots in Paris. Kornelis Elix's early death in 1845 put an end to the enterprise. De Passe had already left in 1841 to start his own foundry with his financial partner Menne. In 1843 they issued an ambitious type specimen, largely of type from the former Brussels foundry Lejeune; as John A. Lane wrote, the specimen 'must have given the firm of Joh. Enschedé something of a shock'.[65] However, due to De Passe's untimely death the following year, De Passe & Menne never became a serious competitor to the Haarlem foundry. The company existed for another decade, but was then sold off to a Rotterdam merchant who had, a few years earlier, directed his attention to typefounding: Nicolaas Tetterode.

Tetterode had begun his typefounding career by buying the Broese foundry in Breda in 1851; the acquisition of De Passe & Menne gave him the possibility to relocate to his native Amsterdam. He quickly expanded his company, which in due course would become Enschedé's sole competitor.

However, Enschedé did not always play the game according to Tetterode's moral standards. In the 1840s, a new electrochemical process called electrotyping had been introduced for making copies of metal objects. It soon became common practice, both in Europe and the United Stated, to make electrolytic copies of existing typefaces. Enschedé first used the system to make its own version of an English typeface which the manufacturer had refused to sell them, and soon stopped cutting new punches altogether, relying solely on the competitors' designs. The system of copying types was not illegal in the Netherlands – there simply weren't any copyright laws for type design, as is the situation in the United States and other countries today. But Tetterode was outraged. In 1861, he published a remarkable pamphlet entitled *De tegenwoordige stand van het lettergieters bedrijf* (The present state of the typefounding trade) in which he denounced these practices. 'Among other things,' he wrote, 'we imported a series of English Egyptian types, and shortly thereafter the firms of Enschedé, De Passe & Menne, and Oomkens, Van Bakkenes & Damsté made themselves master of my ethical privilege. The generally accepted principle was that this robbery fell under the heading of loyal competition.'[66] The piracy did not prevent Tetterode from expanding further. One of the firm's specializations was 'foreign faces': as the Dutch had important colonies in the East Indies, there was a large market for Buginese, Battak, Javanese, Chinese and other fonts. Some of these types were cut in-house by Louis Catherine, who worked for Tetterode from 1852 to 1866. Enschedé meanwhile continued its copying practices and ceased to be a force of any importance in the innovation of type. The firm regained some of its prestige after Charles Enschedé became director in 1887. Charles Enschedé was not a mere businessman, but took great interest in the history of printing and typefounding. He laid the foundations for the Enschedé Museum, which still exists today, and compiled several historical studies, the most important of which being *Fonderies de caractères et leur matériel dans les Pays-Bas du XVᵉ au XIXᵉ siècle* (1908). This book aroused international interest in the foundry's history and the unique collection of types it had – despite the earlier liquidations – been able to preserve. At that point, however, the company created by Tetterode and incorporated as Lettergieterij 'Amsterdam' (Amsterdam Type Foundry) in 1892, had long taken the lead in the Dutch typefounding trade.

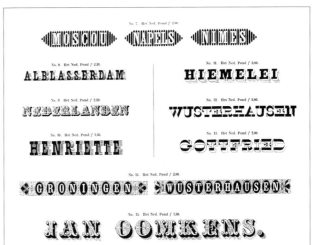

˄ One of the first type specimens issued by Nicolaas Tetterode, then still based in Rotterdam (early 1850s). *Collection Jan Tholenaar.*

˄ Display types available at the Van der Veen Oomkens type foundry, established in Groningen in 1843. Many of the types were 'genuine English types'. When the firm closed in 1894 after a series of takeovers, the inventory was taken over by Enschedé (cf. Lane/Lommen, pp 256–257). This specimen: c. 1844. *Collection Jan Tholenaar.*

New technologies

The nineteenth century, the age of industry, was also the century in which mass media and advertising were invented. A series of breakthrough inventions allowed for a new, mass-oriented typography to develop alongside traditional letterpress printing. Lithography and the production of large stamping dies (used for book covers) relied on the manual skill of craftsmen who drew fantasy letterforms by hand. With the mechanical production of wood type, facilitated by the invention of

62 Ibid., p 31.

63 Alston W. Purvis in *A Century of Posters*, Blaricum 2002, p 9. The view that mechanization in the nineteenth century led to 'a fall from grace' was challenged by Robin Kinross in his *Modern Typography*, London 1992, pp 25–34.

64 Ernst Braches, 'The Scheffers Type' in *Quaerendo* vol. 20 no. 4, 1990, p 267n.

65 Lane and Lommen (cit.), p 251.

66 Ibid., p 22.

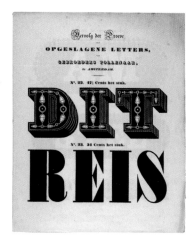

▲ Having bought the De Passe & Menne foundry in Amsterdam in 1856, Nicolaas Tetterode simply continued using his predessor's type specimens, replacing De Passe & Menne's name by his own.
Collection Jan Tholenaar.

▶ 'Opgeslagen kapitalen', metal display capitals mounted on blocks, as sold by the foundry of the Amsterdam brothers Tollenaar, c. 1840.
Specimen in the collection of the Amsterdam University Library (UvA), LPBR 48.

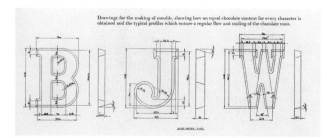

▲ A nineteenth-century Clarendon in a twentieth-century adaptation as chocolate letters. A lot of planning has gone into the development of these letterforms, as the characters' weights must be, and look, as equal as possible from A to Z in order to avoid conflicts in the family.

the pantograph in 1834, it became possible to manufacture large, bold alphabets – mainly for billboards – which weighed a fraction of metal letters. A different kind of billboard type was produced by small foundries such as that of the Tollenaar Brothers in Amsterdam. They manufactured 'mounted letters' (*opgeslagen letters*), large metal type cast from woodcut originals, and mounted on wooden or leaden blocks. Most of these titling alphabets were uppercase-only, and many were heavily decorated in the *faux-classique* manner which was so popular throughout the nineteenth century. Although some of these forms may have been created in-house, they relied heavily on the theatrical egyptian, grotesque, latin and ornamented letterforms developed in Britain, France and elsewhere.[67]

The most important challenge that the traditional type foundries faced, was the advent of hot-metal typesetting machines. In the course of a few decades, Linotype machines would become the standard equipment for the typesetting of newspapers and magazines. For the Amsterdam Type Foundry as well as Enschedé, this meant that the market for foundry-cast metal type was suddenly shrinking. Enschedé was first and foremost a typesetting and printing company, but the Amsterdam foundry needed to find new markets. It exported type to the East Indies and South Africa, and extended its collection of display types, the kind that the Linotype machine couldn't make. In the home market, it expanded its activities as a supplier of printing equipment and hot metal typesetting machines; in 1914, the company would become the Dutch agent of Intertype line-casting machines. New typefaces, acquired in the late nineteenth and early twentieth centuries, came from American, Britain and German foundries. With electrotyping, making a duplicate of an existing face was easy, and for lack of regulations, many European foundries did so without asking permission. The Amsterdam Type Foundry bought the reproduction rights to faces like Caslon, Cheltenham and Tiffany from ATF and other American foundries at prices as low as $150 – tariffs which they more or less established themselves. This practice was to change when, in 1907, the company hired S.H. de Roos as a graphic artist. De Roos in due time became the Amsterdam foundry's typographic conscience and in 1912 provided it with the first original Dutch text face created for over a century, the generically named *Hollandse Mediaeval* ('Hollandsche' in the pre-war spelling: 'Dutch Oldstyle'). With Sjoerd de Roos begins the story of modern Dutch type design.

Chocolate Clarendons

The only typically Dutch adaptation of nineteenth-century display letterforms is one that continues to surprise visitors to the Netherlands, and confirms once more that peculiar Dutch obsession with type: the chocolate letter, of which millions are sold each year towards the first week of December. This art form was described at length by the Dutch historian of typography G.W. Ovink, who wrote a serious (though subtly tongue-in-cheek) account of the history and technology of the Dutch chocolate letter for the London magazine *Typographica* in 1958.[68] Letters in almond-cake and chocolate are a traditional, personalized present on the occasion of the St. Nicholas or *Sinterklaas* feast, celebrated each year on the 5th of December (the American name 'Santa Claus' for Father Christmas probably derives from 'Sinterklaas'). 'The presentation of letters on St. Nicholas is already mentioned in the early nineteenth century,' wrote Ovink, but it was only from around 1890 that solid chocolate letters began to be made. Initially the type used was sanserif, or 'bamboo letters' as they were called; since the 1930s, a Clarendon-like pseudo-egyptian has become the norm. Ovink mentioned the existence of several contemporary, experimental chocolate letter designs which, unfortunately, do not seem to have survived.

67 Lane and Lommen (cit.), pp 21 – 26, pp 108 – 112 and pp 251 – 252.
68 G.W. Ovink, 'Dutch Chocolate Letters', *Typographica* 15, pp 26 – 32.

Reinventing tradition

Sjoerd Hendrik de Roos, binding for *De tors: in zeven zangen* by C.S. Adama van Scheltema, 1924.

'Nieuwe Kunst': type as decoration

Although brief and rather limited in output, the 1890s decorative movement was the hinge between two contrasting phases in typography: the anonymous, commercially driven book and magazine production of the mid to late nineteenth century, and the modern printed work which – while acknowledging the constraints and properties of mass production – reflects a personal, critical view of how a text may be organized and presented.

In the Netherlands, the 1890s movement – whose existence almost coincides with the activities of William Morris's Kelmscott Press in Britain – is known as *Nieuwe Kunst* ('New Art') [1]. Although the words mean the same as Art Nouveau, the artists of the Nieuwe Kunst never had much affinity with the graceful, seductive manner of artists such as Mucha and Van de Velde, champions of the curly 'whiplash' line. The movement's view of ornamentation and illustration was never light-hearted or frivolous: it was laden with symbolic meanings, spiritual concepts and high ideals.

Ever since it became a subject of historiography, 1890s Dutch book decoration has been described as a crucial contribution to what has been called 'the renaissance of the book'. Yet at the same time the artists of the Nieuwe Kunst were accused of having misunderstood the nature of the book by giving priority to decoration over typography, neglecting the basic principles of letterforms and the arrangement of type. [2] In his seminal dissertation *Het boek als Nieuwe Kunst* (The Book as New Art, 1973), Ernst Braches has tried to analyse the output of the book artists of the Dutch *fin de siècle* from the opposite point of view – theirs. Braches has outlined the complex ideas which inspired these artists to reinvent, as it were, the art of the book. The philosophy of the Nieuwe Kunst (the sum of many individual views) is a puzzling amalgam of disparate ideas and theories: socialism, symbolism, anarchism, theosophy, [3] as well as an uncompromising view of what makes a crafted product a real work of art. For the 1890s movement the organizing force of book design is decoration, not typography, because ornament and illustration are the elements that add beauty and spirituality to a book that would otherwise be a mere functional object. One of the main characteristics of the movement's mature phase was the notion that true, divine beauty can only be achieved by means of abstraction; an abstraction attained by following the mathematical laws rooted in nature itself. Hence the notion of 'system-based design' (*ontwerpen op systeem*), a method which was developed by the architect-designers J.L.M. Lauweriks and K.P.C. de Bazel and took squares, circles and triangles as the organizing elements of ornament. [4]

Although Braches' book dilates upon the complicated motives of the movement and its individual artists, analysing the symbolism of decorations and the ideas underlying structural decisions, it fails to trace a consistent view of the letterform. The erratic lettering of many books and posters of the 1890s suggests that such a view was indeed lacking. Yet several artists linked to the movement made investigations in type design; and some developed convincing lettering styles in later years.

New text types for new illustration techniques

In 1892, a group of Amsterdam artists rediscovered the crude power of woodcut, cutting three diplomas for a booksellers' organization: a defining moment. [5] From that date onwards, woodcut became the central technique of Nieuwe Kunst book decoration: the only reproduction technique which (unlike copperplate, etching or lithography) 'presses its lines into the paper just like type, and can be printed simultaneously with type.' Thus J.F. van Royen, who also noted a kind of conceptual merit besides the technical compatibility: '... its character goes towards synthesis. It is ...

◄ G.W. Dijsselhof, drawings for a sanserif text face, 1898. *Gemeentemuseum, The Hague*.

▼ G.W. Dijsselhof, lowercase alphabet cut in a breadboard, 1896. *Gemeentemuseum, The Hague*.

unable to focus on the details of reality.' Woodcut hints at reality, while other graphic arts aim at representing it – which book illustration does not need to do.[6] The book artists of the Nieuwe Kunst were dissatisfied with existing text faces – mostly polished and weakened Didot-style and Caslon types – which did not go well with the the sturdiness of their woodcuts. Correspondence between contemporary publishers and authors suggests that the designers J.B. Smits, C.A. Lion Cachet and A.J. Derkinderen all had the ambition to design a book face. Yet the most striking and best documented example is the research conducted by the artist G.W. Dijsselhof (1866 – 1924).

Dijsselhof had produced one of the finest samples of the new art of the book in 1894 with *Kunst en Samenleving*, Jan Veth's adaptation of *Claims of Decorative Art* by Walter Crane. The book was decorated with powerful ornaments executed in woodcut. Dijsselhof remained dissatisfied with the text type of the interior. Between 1892 and 1898 he made a series of attempts at designing a book face. Three types, *Klei*, *Hei* and *Wei* ('Clay', 'Heath', and 'Meadow'), are mentioned in early twentieth-century overviews by the well-informed authors Stols and Veth. Yet it remained unclear which type was which until in 1972 Ernst Braches published an essay examining Dijsselhof's alphabets.[7] In a letter from October 1896 Dijsselhof mentions two alphabets, of which 'one is too light and the other too bold so that I have named the one the *hei* and the other the *klei* type and I now intend to cut a third kind between the two which might be called the *wei* type.' The Gemeentemuseum in The Hague possesses three wooden boards in which Dijsselhof cut a series of letterforms, as well as two proof sheets in which these designs are tested by means of a reduced lithographic print. It is evident what the maker had in mind: an open, readable typeface, sturdier than most contemporary fonts and with an obvious artistic approach. Yet these alphabets are still somewhat naive attempts; irregularly spaced and with hesitant protrusions in the place of serifs. But the research continued. A design for a sanserif drawn by hand, dated 1898, shows remarkable progress in Dijsselhof's understanding of the letterform. The characters are less meagre and the designer is testing different widths and experimenting with the spacing. The design looks remarkably original: a humanist sanserif avant la lettre. 'We can call this typeface the Wei type,' wrote Braches, 'provided we remember that this name was given half jokingly by Dijsselhof in the autumn of 1896 to something which did not yet exist.'[8]

Dijsselhof's book face was never finished; nor were similar projects by contemporaries. The quest for a heavier, slightly more decorative book face would not be over until, towards 1907, new typefaces like the *Grasset* type and *Nordische Antiqua* hit the market. Finally in 1912 Sjoerd Hendrik de Roos, a son of the Dutch decorative movement, presented his *Hollandse Mediaeval* – a very mature typeface that combined the arts and crafts sensitivity of the 1890s with a new-found consciousness of typographic conventions and history.

1 The term 'Nieuwe Kunst' was introduced by L. Gans in a 1960 dissertation.

2 Ernst Braches, *Het boek als Nieuwe Kunst*, Utrecht 1973, pp 2 – 4.

3 The Theosophical Movement, founded by Helena P. Blavatsky (1831 – 1891), postulates that the universe is an organic whole – alive, conscious and divine – governed by laws of nature that are the result of intelligent forces.

4 Braches, *Het boek als Nieuwe Kunst* (cit.), pp 105 – 113.

5 The three diplomas were cut by G.W. Dijsselhof, C.A. Lion Cachet and Th. Nieuwenhuis.

6 Jean François van Royen in a 1919 article quoted in G.H. Pannekoek, *De verluchtiging van het boek*, 2nd ed., Rotterdam 1927, pp 4 – 7.

7 Ernst Braches, 'Bookfaces by G.W. Dijsselhof in the 'nineties', *Quaerendo* II, 1, 1972.

8 Braches, 'Bookfaces' (cit.), p 39.

◄ H.P. Berlage, initials used in the *Gedenkboek* published in 1895 at the opening of the Lacoa Bay Railroad (Pretoria); part of a complete alphabet that was also used for the magazine *Architectura*.

▼ Alphabet by J.L.M. Lauweriks, published in J. van Leeuwen's *Letterboek*, 1907.

◄ The principle of geometric construction results in a disastrous lowercase alphabet by Van Leeuwen (in *Letterboek*, 1907).

► Invoice of De Bazel & Lauweriks studio (1895). The document's heading sums up the firm's activities as 'architecture, furniture, decorative painting, woodcuts, posters, etc.'. Printed from the original block, the invoice was included in a 1925 portfolio of woodcuts by K.P.C. de Bazel for which Lauweriks wrote the introduction.

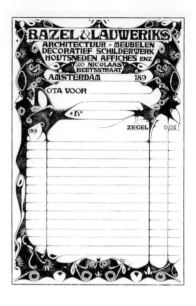

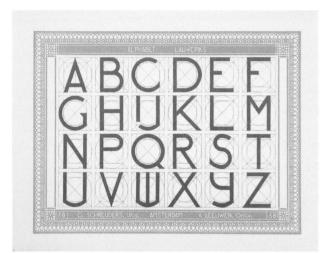

Intuitive forms and mathematics

If we have some documentation about the attitude of the Nieuwe Kunst artists towards text type, we remain in the dark as to their view on letterforms in general. In the book art of the 1890s, the lettering is part of, and subservient to, ornament and illustration; but it is unclear whether their forms were a subject of reflection or discussion. The discrepancy between the quality and precision of the illustrations and ornaments – by artists such as Dijsselhof, Berlage, Lion Cachet, Van Hoytema – and the rather primitive and naive character of their lettering is puzzling. For some of them, it was a matter of time: R.N. Roland Holst, Chris Lebeau and – of course – De Roos were among the artists who developed accomplished alphabets in later decades.

Remarkable and peculiar contributions to the development of letterforms were made by the architects related to the Nieuwe Kunst. H.P. Berlage, who was to become the country's most influential architect during the first decades of the twentieth century, made a name for himself in the 1890s as a book, magazine and poster designer. Yet there is something dilettantish about most of his graphic work; his hand-drawn letterforms are often amorphous and unsteady. The 1895 initials shown above are among his most confident lettering work.

K.P.C. de Bazel and J.L.M. Lauweriks explored several styles of ornamented lettering in the mid-1890s; after 1895, when they embraced the esoteric rationalism of theosophy, they began experimenting with geometrically constructed letterforms. Two of their alphabets – a sanserif by Lauweriks and a very similar seriffed alphabet by De Bazel – are included in a classic manual published in 1907: *Letterboek* by the artist-craftsman K. van Leeuwen, who was best known as a furniture designer.[9] Van Leeuwen, who was also a teacher at the Vâhana course headed by Lauweriks and De Bazel, wrote that 'harmonic unity in the alphabet must be obtained with the help of geometric figures, so that the letterform rests firmly on positive data.' The alphabets by Lauweriks and De Bazel, as reproduced (and redrawn) by Van Leeuwen, shown a certain artificiality which is due precisely to the exaggerated fidelity to the underlying squares and circles. Lauweriks would solve the problem by going one step further: from 1911 onwards, he conceived a radical style of constructed type with only straight lines, made of typesetter's brass rule (> p 68 – 69)

In Van Leeuwen's own alphabets, the rationalist principle becomes not just a guideline but a dogma. All letters are tied down to the grid, and when this proves impossible, the dilemma is solved by adding yet another circle. This treatment does a lot of harm to the lowercase characters especially. Van Leeuwen's publication reveals some of the problems of the Nieuwe Kunst in dealing with letterforms and shows, in a way, how this generation could produce both a Wijdeveld and a De Roos.

'Books of beauty'

In the 1910s, the 'decorative' or Nieuwe Kunst movement branched out into two distinct developments. One was headed by architects and designers whose work comprised anything from buildings and interiors via textile and furniture to posters and books. Within this current, the group known as the Amsterdam School developed the most influential and most controversial typographic work in a style which may be filed under Art Deco. This development will be dealt with on page 66 ff.

The other group, more loosely linked to the decorative movement, was a small circle of rather purist typographers. Their leading figure was Sjoerd Hendrik de Roos. Having learnt the trade in an arts-and-crafts environment, De Roos re-educated himself as a book typographer and gradually incorporated the principles of classical typography into his work to create something distinctly contemporary. In doing so, he inspired a number of colleagues who, in some cases, eventually became his rivals or successors: Jan van Krimpen, Charles Nypels, Dick Dooijes.

In the first decades of the twentieth century, het *Schoone Boek* ('the Book of Beauty') became the generic Dutch term for bibliophilic and other tastefully made books. Some were printed in small numbers by private presses, but many books made with industrial means were also regarded as 'beautiful'. Contrary to the dominant view during the 1890s, the aesthetic quality was not necessarily judged by the technique used, or the handmade feel of a book; this acceptance of industrial production methods for quality work marks the emergence of the designer as a key figure in book production.

In historical studies of Dutch graphic design much importance is given to five key figures whose work has defined the neo-traditionalist strand in twentieth-century Dutch typography and who have even been nicknamed 'the Great Five'.[10] As type is our concern here, separate articles will be dedicated to the two type designers among them, Sjoerd Hendrik de Roos and Jan van Krimpen. Although the remaining three – Jean François van Royen, Charles Nypels and Alexander Stols – never designed type, their activities as typographers, writers and printer-publishers fostered the development and propagation of new type and typography.

Five views of the book page

Two books designed by Sjoerd de Roos are generally seen as the starting point of modern typography in the Netherlands: *Kunst en maatschappij* (Art and Society) from 1903, a collection of William Morris essays, and the 1907 *Drukkersjaarboek* (Printers' Yearbook). Some have argued that the Morris book still has a strong Art Nouveau flavour, and that only the *Drukkersjaarboek*, with its clear, unadorned pages, shows a truly new approach.

De Roos's achievements as a typographer did not go unnoticed; in addition, his writings began to have some influence in the printing world. By the end of 1911 he had already published more than 100 articles in the trade press, many of which were reviews of foreign publications on typography.

One of the indicators of a renewed interest in well-made books was the creation by two poets of a small publishing company called De Zilverdistel in 1910. The initiative soon became the one-man venture of the writer P.N. van Eyck, who was joined in 1913 by J.F. van Royen, a lawyer, art lover and book collector. Under Van Royen's artistic direction the work of De Zilverdistel entered a new, more ambitious phase. Jean François van Royen (1878–1942) was an idealist who, like De Roos, firmly believed that beautiful, harmonious and well-made things would contribute to the spiritual well-being of mankind. In a famous 1912 article he fulminated against the

RONSARD
LES SONNETS
POUR HELENE

PARIS
LA CONNAISSANCE
MCMXXIV

Charles Nypels learnt his typographic skills as a trainee at the Amsterdam Type Foundry, where Sjoerd de Roos was his mentor. Ronsard's *Les sonnets pour Helène* (Paris, 1924) is one of many books designed by Nypels for which De Roos drew initials and vignettes. The typeface used is De Roos's Erasmus Mediaeval.

9 K. van Leeuwen, *Letterboek voor den teekenaar en ambachtsman*, Bennekom 1907.
10 cf. Mathieu Lommen, *De grote vijf*, Zutphen 1991.

Imprint of two books designed
and printed by Jean François van
Royen: *Suster Bertken* (De Zilver-
distel, 1918) and *In den Keerkring*
by the poet P.C. Boutens
(Kunera Pers, 1941–1942).
Both are set in Pissarro's
Disteltype.

State Printing Office, whose publications he called 'ugly, ugly, ugly – thrice ugly – ugly in typeface, ugly in typesetting and ugly in paper.' [11] A few years later, he acquired a position which enabled him to change the face of public services in the Netherlands by setting examples. As aesthetic consultant of the Dutch PTT (Post, Telephone and Telegraph service) he became the originator of that remarkably progressive design policy of Dutch institutions which would largely persist until today. Van Royen's greatest importance lies in these professional activities as a mediator between artists and their public. But the books he realized as a typographer and printer with De Zilverdistel, and subsequently the Kunera Press, are among the most peculiar examples of purist twentieth-century book design in the Netherlands. At the PTT, Van Royen showed remarkable open-mindedness, inviting radical artists such as Paul Schuitema and Piet Zwart to design stamps and publications; but as a publisher and book typographer he was an utter traditionalist.

De Zilverdistel became the Netherlands' first private press when Van Royen acquired an Albion hand press in 1914. He had prepared this step by ordering two typefaces for exclusive use: one – *Zilvertype* – from De Roos; the other – *Disteltype* – from Lucien Pissarro, the son of the painter Camille Pissarro and the owner of the Eragny Press. Van Royen's involvement in these projects was intense. Zilvertype is possibly De Roos's most harmonious roman. Pissarro's typeface, based on the Carolingian miniscule, is more problematic; it is very picturesque, and hardly suitable for setting an entire book. De Roos often worked for Van Royen, drawing initials and titles for his publications and giving informal artistic advice. After this collaboration had come to a halt, Van Royen designed his own lettering which, as Mathieu Lommen wrote, 'betrays the hand of the amateur'. [12]

Van Royen's style, modelled on late fifteenth-century incunabula, and his production method (using a hand press in a time when Futurists and Constructivists sang the praises of the machine) were not appreciated by everybody. Jan van Krimpen did not mince matters when, twenty-two years old, he reviewed De Zilverdistel's early products in a 1914 article. He accused Van Royen of snobbery, and argued in favour of modern production techniques and contemporary typefaces. Although Van Krimpen's piece contained some praise for Hollandse Mediaeval, De Roos reacted sharply in an article published a month later. He recommended that the young Mr. van Krimpen educate himself 'in knowledge and insight'. [13]

This polemic was the start of a relationship which remained tense until the end. Not only did De Roos and Van Krimpen become rivals, working for the two competing Dutch type foundries, their tastes and personalities were also incompatible. The vast differences between them were laconically summarized in an article by G.W. Ovink: 'De Roos evidently was the socialist arts-and-craftsman who, together with his contemporaries in the SDAP (the Social-Democratic Party), hoped to achieve a just, peaceful and happy society, full of beautiful people and things; Van Krimpen was a sharp man of letters with an aristocratic attitude, who took satisfaction when a fine text had been neatly laid out or when the illusive letterform had once more been captured in a way that allowed civilized people to read more easily and more agreeably.' [14]

Charles Nypels (1895–1952) was the complete opposite of Van Krimpen. Whereas the latter was an uncompromising, even blunt Calvinist Northener, Nypels was a bonvivant with a Latin spirit. Born and raised as a printer's son in the southern border town of Maastricht, he was fluent in French and Dutch, as well as the Limburg dialect. According to a poet friend, he practiced eloquence 'like a spiritual circus artist'. [15]

When Nypels was sent to the Amsterdam Type Foundry as a trainee in 1914, Sjoerd
de Roos became his mentor. Thanks to De Roos, Nypels became an accomplished
printer and publisher; he was to remain a faithful disciple and friend all his life.
Among the pre-war neo-traditionalists Nypels distinguished himself by his fresh
and intuitive approach; his use of colour and illustration and his choice of typefaces
were less orthodox, as was his view of page layout. Throughout his career as a typographer, printer and publisher, Charles Nypels remained an advocate of contemporary Dutch type design, using the typefaces of both De Roos and Van Krimpen to
great effect.

Nypels's younger friend Alexander Stols (1900–1973) came from a very similar background: he, too, was the son of a Maastricht printer. Stols belonged to the small
artistic circle of which Nypels was the central figure and which was heavily influenced by the aestheticism of the French writer J.-K. Huysmans – especially his novel
A rebours, the bible of dandy book lovers. Nypels was instrumental in showing Stols
the way to typography and 'books of beauty'. At 22, Stols began his activities as a
typographer-publisher. Under the imprint A.A.M. Stols he was to publish more than
1000 books in less than four decades, becoming the most prolific one-man publishing company in the country.

Charles Nypels supervised the first publications designed and composed by Stols
together with his brother Alfons (A.A.J.) Stols, a partner in the family printing firm
Boosten & Stols. The two brothers would remain creative partners for many years.
Alexander Stols has written about himself that he was initially influenced by De
Roos and later by Van Krimpen. As a publisher, he gave numerous design assignments to the latter but also worked with many younger and less established artists
and typographers including Helmut Salden, Theo de Haan, Bertram Weihs and
Gerrit Noordzij. One of Stols's most impressive achievements was *Halcyon*, a splendid quarterly typographic magazine in portfolio form which was published in four
languages between 1940 and 1942. Sjoerd de Roos, who had retired as head of the
Amsterdam Type Foundry's design department, was a regular contributor both as
author and typographer; the first issue contained a specimen of his uncial *Libra*. The
Halcyon double issue 9/10 (1942) was mostly devoted to De Roos's work. Stols himself
contributed a brochure about De Roos's private press, which was in fact a chapter
from his book on De Roos's life and work, published the following year by the
Amsterdam Type Foundry.[16]

Alexander Stols left the Netherlands in 1951 for Ecuador on an assigment as a typographic specialist for UNESCO. From 1956, he worked in Mexico, where he was adviser and typographic designer to the Escuela Nacional de Artas Gráficas and the
publishing firm Fondo de Cultura Economica. In 1960, he was joined by a young
Amsterdam designer named Boudewijn Ietswaart, who became his assistant. Although now largely forgotten, Ietswaart was one of the most talented lettering
artists of the postwar Dutch scene. Ietswaart's work will be dealt with on page 109.

CERVANTES

DON
QUICHOTTE
I

LES ÉDITIONS DU BALANCIER · LIÉGE
MCMXXIX

11 Quoted in Paul Hefting, *PTT Art & Design*, The Hague 1992.

12 Mathieu Lommen, *De grote vijf*, Zutphen 1991, p 8.

13 Ibid., pp 11–12.

14 G.W. Ovink, 'Anderhalve eeuw typografie in Nederland', in *Anderhalve eeuw boek-
    typografie 1815–1965*, Nijmegen 1965, p 380.

15 Jan Engelman in *In Memoriam Charles Nypels*, Amsterdam 1953, p 7.

16 C. van Dijk, *Alexandre A.M. Stols 1900-1973*, Zutphen 1992.

A pioneer: Sjoerd Hendrik de Roos

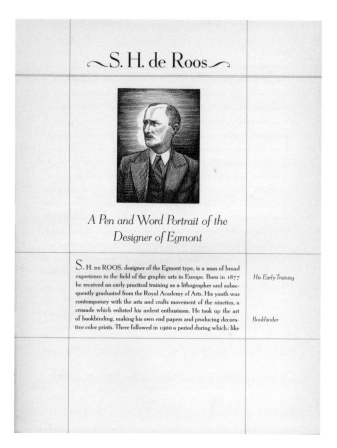

~S. H. de Roos~

A Pen and Word Portrait of the
Designer of Egmont

S. H. DE ROOS, designer of the Egmont type, is a man of broad
experience in the field of the graphic arts in Europe. Born in 1877
he received an early practical training as a lithographer and subsequently graduated from the Royal Academy of Arts. His youth was
contemporary with the arts and crafts movement of the nineties, a
crusade which enlisted his ardent enthusiasm. He took up the art
of bookbinding, making his own end papers and producing decorative color prints. There followed in 1900 a period during which: like

His Early Training

Bookbinder

Page from the brochure
announcing the Egmont
typeface. Intertype Corporation,
Brooklyn, New York, 1936.

Sjoerd Hendrik de Roos has been called 'the first professional typographic designer in the Netherlands'.[17] He created the first original Dutch book face since the days of Fleischman. He was a pioneer in bridging the gap between the ideals of the arts and crafts movement and the reality of modern book production. Yet the significance of his type designs today is purely historical. His great romans – *Hollandse Mediaeval*, *Zilvertype* and *De Roos Romein* – have virtually disappeared, as have the display alphabets he drew without much conviction. Ironically, of all the typefaces he was involved in, the one which has been embraced by today's designers is *Nobel* – a derivative design produced to please his employers in a style to which he had no particular affinity.

Born in 1877, Sjoerd de Roos was the son of a socially committed artisan-shoemaker who left his native Friesland for Amsterdam. After elementary school, Sjoerd became an apprentice at a lithographic plate manufacturer. During the evenings he frequented an art school and, upon reaching the age of eighteen, enrolled in additional morning classes – before the working day – at the Rijksacademie (State Academy). Young De Roos admired the work of architects such as Berlage, De Bazel and Derkinderen, with whom he shared a strong social idealism as well as an interest in typography and book design. In 1900 he became part of that circle when he landed a job as assistant draftsman and designer at Het Binnenhuis, the workshop for furniture and applied arts created by Berlage and others. At the time, De Roos still aspired to be a painter, and in 1903 he took part in a small group show of 'socialist artists'.

That same year he received his first major assignment as a book designer. Significantly, the book was a translation of essays by William Morris (*Kunst en Maatschappij*). The printer who produced the Morris book was Berend Modderman, the owner of the Amsterdam firm Ipenbuur & Van Seldam and one of the great proponents of innovative book design. Having recognized De Roos's talents, Modderman commissioned him to design one of his own publications – the 1907 *Drukkersjaarboek* (Printers' Year Book). De Roos's choice of type in both books is significant. For the Morris, he chose the *Grasset* type by the French architect and painter of that name; the *Drukkersjaarboek* was set in W. Zachrisson's *Nordische Antiqua*. Both are rather round and dark in colour, unlike the Didot derivates which had been in vogue for the last half century. His own Hollandse Mediaeval, issued a few years later, would have the same qualities.

The *Drukkersjaarboek*, generally regarded as the first modern book in the Netherlands, is a wonder of simplicity and taste. The only fanciful element on the regular, clear text pages are De Roos's meticulously ornamented art nouveau initials; but printed in tangerine and warm grey, they are just right. De Roos also contributed an article to the book. In this piece entitled 'American typesetting' he expressed his admiration for the restrained style developed in the United States by designers and printers such as Bruce Rogers and Will Bradley; he argued that their work was superior to the

JAC.VAN LOOY GEDICHTEN

German typography that was so popular and influential in the Netherlands. With this article and the design of the book, De Roos established himself as an emerging protagonist in the young movement of typographic innovation.

Sjoerd de Roos at the Amsterdam Type Foundry

Introduced by Modderman, De Roos was hired by the Amsterdam Type Foundry, formerly N. Tetterode, as artistic consultant in June 1907 – a dream come true. One of his first assignments was the design of the Cheltenham specimen, a 70-page book with dozens of fictitious examples of the typeface in use. The critic J.W. Enschedé – a member of the family which ran the competing foundry, but not a partner in it – wrote: 'These pages display such craftsmanship in their layout, arrangement and colour combinations that they must appeal to everyone who understands what a good influence this foundry has on the modern Dutch book.'[18] Also in 1907 the Amsterdam Type Foundry presented De Roos's first typeface: the *Bilderdijk Initialen*, an ornamental alphabet based on the six initials drawn for the *Drukkersjaarboek*.

De Roos's tasks at the Type Foundry were manifold. He was an in-house designer of typefaces, type specimens and other forms of promotional printed matter; he advised on foreign typefaces to be bought and adapted; he was also appointed librarian of the magnificent Typographic Library, built as part of the 1913 extension of the factory and designed by one of De Roos's idols, the architect K.P.C. de Bazel. The first text face which De Roos completed was a rather complex one: a Javanese alphabet, simply called *Nieuw Javaans* (1908–1909), to add to Tetterode's large collection of oriental scripts. The island of Java was the political centre of the Netherlands' largest colony, the Indonesian archipelago. In cooperation with two specialists – P.J.W. Oly for the linguistic aspects and Jan Wesselius for the engraving – De Roos created a fluent, rhythmic script which was more harmonious than the existing Javanese fonts. Apparently the users – those who, unlike De Roos, spoke and wrote Javanese – found the alphabet quite satisfactory.

De Roos's view on type and the Hollandse Mediaeval

From 1907 onwards, De Roos published dozens of articles on printing and typography. His most extensive early comment on the state of type, appearing in 1908, was 'De tegenwoordige drukletter' (Printing types today). In this piece, he summed up the properties of a good book face, emphasizing that practical usability must come before aesthetic considerations. Clarity and regularity are crucial. The designer should not concentrate too much on the shape of single characters, because adult readers do not stop at each letter: 'The eye does not have that much time; we slide over the lines and simultaneously with the letter scan the whole word.'[19] In a concise historical survey, De Roos criticized the nineteenth-century fashion of thin, high-contrast Didot-like types. He praised William Morris's pioneering typographic

⬛ AMERIKAANSCH ZETWERK ⬛

Het is een betreurenswaardig feit, dat onze hollandsche boekdrukkers zoo ijverig bij de duitsche buren ter schole gaan, tengevolge waarvan ons nederlandsch smoutwerk een beslist duitsch karakter draagt. Toch zij het verre van mij, te willen beweren, dat het duitsche materiaal niet veel bruikbaars heeft en vooral in den laatsten tijd, nu door het werken van bekende leidende kunstenaars als Otto Eckmann, Peter Behrens, Heinz König, Otto Hupp en Heinrich Wieynk, kunstvol ontworpen typen op de markt worden gebracht en de meer moderne eischen van vlakversiering ook op de drukkunst worden toegepast. Het uitsluitend volgen van duitsche voorbeelden, — en dan meestal niet de beste — is een gevaar voor onze inheemsche boekdrukkunst te achten. Deze staat nog niet op een hoog peil in vertoont nog bij lange na niet een zoo opgewekt leven als de andere gebruiks- kunsten, die de hollandsche inzendingen op de tentoonstelling te Turijn en ook onlangs die te Milaan de hoogste onderscheidin- gen deden verwerven. Wat hier op typografisch gebied in moderne opvatting gemaakt wordt, getuigt behoudens enkele uitzonderin- gen, nog van eene slechts oppervlakkige navolging, niet door- dringende in principes, die heden ten dage te ambachts- en nijverheidskunst beheerschen. Dat de Duitschers reeds verder zijn dan wij, wie zou het betwijfelen? Dit is te danken aan den invloed van het werk van Morris, maar ook van dat der Amerikanen, wier superioriteit door de Duitschers zelf wordt erkend.

De kunst van den boekdrukker is bij uitstek eene van overweging

1   1

17 Jan P. Boterman (ed.), *Sjoerd H. de Roos, typografische geschriften*, The Hague 1989, p 39.

18 Quoted in Lane and Lommen, *Dutch typefounders' specimens*, Amsterdam 1998, p 27.

19 'De tegenwoordige drukletter', in *Sjoerd H. de Roos, typografische geschriften* (cit.), p 82.

work but criticized his *Golden Type*, which the Amsterdam Type Foundry sold as *Kloosterschrift*. 'There is no doubt', he wrote, 'that the typeface has certain decorative qualities, but also, and especially in the serifs, a certain self-consciousness (*'iets gewilds'*), which can be a possible reason for its limited usefulness as a book face.'

He went on to discuss the *Grasset* type, which he had himself introduced in the Netherlands in his design of the 1903 Morris book; he confessed that he was no longer as happy with the Grasset as he had been a few years earlier. It was not regular enough, it caused a certain fatigue, and perhaps its French origins were too obvious; in short, 'this type is not the book face we desire.' Two more new foreign typefaces are mentioned as having great merits: *Nordische Antiqua* and *Cheltenham*. The concluding paragraph, although somewhat cryptic, contained a promise: 'The rapidly shifting current of the times and, consequently, the changing insights will determine which typeface will manage to survive the era of its creation. Let us hope that this may be the case with the long – and still – awaited Dutch book face.' [20]

It was, of course, De Roos himself who would design this long-anticipated new Dutch roman. On New Year's Day 1912, the Amsterdam Type Foundry presented his *Hollandse Mediaeval*, or Dutch Mediaeval (*Hollandsche Mediaeval* in the early spelling). The small broadsheet announcing the type caused a sensation in the printing world. In an article published that same week, the graphic artist R.N. Roland Holst praised the type's harmony, beauty and usability. J.F. van Royen wrote about its square construction, 'steering clear of later narrow typefaces, which were notably chosen by the Elzeviers in the seventeenth century'.[21] Van Royen pointed out that the new face's 'prototype' was to be found in the typefaces cut by Jenson in Venice in the 1470s, with their 'look of unsurpassed harmony'. 'Yes, De Roos's choice is significant and good. It shows us his longing for the right principles that a typeface must meet.' De Roos, too, wrote an article about his creation: a down-to-earth and modest piece which, in simple terms, explained the principles of type design to an unspecialized audience. A good typeface, he wrote, should be well-made and businesslike, 'free of exaggerated ornamentation' which would unnecessarily 'draw attention to the shape of a single character'.[22]

This last phrase can be read as criticism of the generation of which De Roos was a product: the book artists of the 1890s for whom the letterform was yet another means to decorate the page. De Roos was probably the first – at least in Holland – to describe the letter as a reading tool, designed according to rational and what we would now call functional or ergonomic principles.

The Hollandse Mediaeval's success was immediate and total. During the first years it was adopted by a number of high-profile publishers – a clear signal to the country's printers. By the 1930s, virtually every printing office in the Netherlands used Hollandse Mediaeval. Because of its ubiquity it was famously used for clandestine publications during the 1940–1945 German occupation: a pamphlet set in Hollandse Mediaeval could never be traced back to the printer who made it.[23]

In spite of De Roos's claims to rationality, his first roman still has many decorative elements. Its cupped feet, the little serif on the crossbars of t and f, the curly italic: there is much in Hollandse Mediaeval that is reminiscent of Art Nouveau. It was for these mannerisms that Jan van Krimpen, initially an admirer of De Roos, came to dislike his style.

There were other factors which stood in the way of perfection. One of the constraints most loathed by early twentieth-century type designers was the standard line (*Normallinie*) introduced by the German typefounders Genzsch & Hense and later

Over boekkunst en de Zilverdistel
(The Hague, 1916) was the
manifesto of De Zilverdistel,
a literary publishing company
which Jean François van Royen
turned into a private press.
The booklet was the first
publication set in Zilvertype,
designed by De Roos under
Van Royen's scrutiny.

adopted by Linotype and Intertype. The anglophile Sem Hartz described it as 'one of those wonderful Teutonic inventions, whereby the letter is tied down on a Procrustean bed,'[24] and De Roos, in a letter to Van Royen, referred to it as 'that dumb Prussian standard line'.[25] Thanks to the standard line – which prescribes the maximum height of the descenders for a particular point size – typesetters could combine different typefaces and still get them perfectly in line. Types of smaller point sizes could easily be combined with larger ones by adding standard incremental point-size leads. The drawback was that the units that had been established were unsuited to the classic roman letterform; the descenders were virtually amputated. Another constraint was enforced on the italic: the Intertype line-casting machines which the Amsterdam Type Foundry supplied needed the italic to be of the same width as the roman. All of De Roos's pre-war typefaces have suffered from these technical requirements. All, that is, except two: *Zilvertype* and *Meidoorntype*, both created for private presses.

Zilvertype and Jean François van Royen

On the strength of the Hollandse Mediaeval, Jean François van Royen asked De Roos to design a new typeface for his bibliophile publishing company, De Zilverdistel. Even though the type was produced by the Amsterdam Type Foundry, the usual technical constraints did not apply because this face was made as handset type only, in one size, for a specific client. The development of Zilvertype has been extensively documented in Jan Boterman's book *Zilvertype corps 15*. In addition to notes, sketches and proofs, the book contains the correspondence between designer and client, from the early contacts in 1914 to the 1916 release of the Zilverdistel pamphlet *Over boekkunst* (On the art of the book), in which the typeface was first used.

In his article on the Hollandse Mediaeval typeface, quoted above, Van Royen had clearly outlined his views on type design. He believed that type is ideally based on the handwriting of its own time; but as the present way of writing lacked style and grace, a different model had to be chosen. Van Royen agreed with De Roos that the best model to be guided by was the pioneering typeface developed by Jenson in 1470s Venice. So Zilvertype, too, was to be based on the Jenson type. It turned out that Van Royen had very specific ideas on how the new face should look; early on he made it clear to De Roos that he intended to be an active client and that the typeface was to be created in 'complete collaboration'.[26] Judging from the correspondence with De Roos, his involvement with the development of Zilvertype was so intensive that it might be justifiable to credit him as co-designer.

Having freed himself, just for once, from the formal straightjacket imposed by the Type Foundry's system, De Roos could now draw a more faithful interpretation of his early Renaissance model. Most importantly, the descenders were now almost the same length as the ascenders. The typeface had oldstyle numerals instead of the lining figures prescribed for the Type Foundry's own faces. Theoretically De Roos could now also have drawn a narrower, 'humanist' italic, but for financial reasons no italic was commissioned. In many ways, Zilvertype is an improved version of Hollandse Mediaeval – and that is how De Roos saw it.[27] But the many subtle improvements – several of which were suggested by Van Royen – have made Zilvertype a very different face from its predecessor: lighter in colour, simpler, less ornamented and on the whole more modern. In this sense Zilvertype precedes the more businesslike book faces which Jan van Krimpen designed a decade later.[28] Produced as an exclusive, custom-made typeface, the use of Zilvertype remained limited to five books.

¶OVER BOEKKUNST.
DE ZILVERDISTEL WIL BOEKKUNST GEVEN. ¶IN DEZE VERSCHIJNT HET BOEK ONS ALS EEN EENHEID, WELKE HET BUITEN HAAR niet bereikt en die het nochtans, wil het een kunstwerk zijn, bereiken móet. Deze eenheid is die van geest en materie, bepaald door de uit het begrip 'boek' af te leiden wetten en door het karakter van den geschreven inhoud. Vrucht eener kunstarbeid, is het boek in dit saamtreffen van geest en materie een nieuwe schepping, een nieuwe persoonlijkheid, die door de volmaaktheid van haar lichaam te beter de volmaaktheid van haar innerlijk doet erkennen. Als zoodanig moet het in de eerste plaats voor de constitutieve vereischten der soort eene technisch en aesthetisch op het volmaakte gerichte verwer-

2

20 *Sjoerd H. de Roos, typografische geschriften* (cit.), p 92.

21 Quoted by A.A.M. Stols in *Het werk van S.H. de Roos*, Amsterdam 1942, pp 20–23.

22 'Ter inleiding van een nieuwe boekletter', in *Sjoerd H. de Roos, typografische geschriften* (cit.), p 109.

23 Dick Dooijes, *Mijn leven met letters*, Amsterdam 1991, p 37.

24 Sem Hartz, *Essays*, Aartswoud/Amsterdam 1992, p 27.

25 'lamme Pruisische normaallijn'. Jan P. Boterman (ed.), *Zilvertype corps 15*, Amsterdam 1994, p 114. Nevertheless some have claimed that the Standard Lining System was an American invention; cf. D.B. Updike, *Printing Types*, Cambridge 1951, vol. 1, p 35.

26 *Zilvertype corps 15* (cit.), p 59.

27 'Een herschepping van mijn eersteling', *Zilvertype* (cit.), p 43.

28 Cf. the comments by Jan P. Boterman in *Zilvertype* (cit.).

De Roos as typographer and lettering artist

Although working for and with the perfectionist Van Royen did cause De Roos occasional moments of irritation, there was enough common ground for further collaboration. De Roos's skills complemented Van Royen's rather modest artistic talents: De Roos was a master craftsman, whose ornamental constructions – be it for title pages, packaging or a guilded leather mantlepiece at Tetterode – were of dazzling perfection. He later contributed numerous initials and ornaments to publications printed by Van Royen. These hand-drawn embellishments were classic or even romantic in style, which is probably how Van Royen wanted them.

In some of De Roos's other work, such as the wrappers and stamping dies made for the Rotterdam publisher Brusse, there was a development towards a more modern aesthetic. For the bindings of a series of classics translated by the poet Boutens, De Roos even drew a thin sanserif alphabet, combining it with striking geometric ornaments. These books are among his very best works as a typographic designer; but they were rare moments of abstraction in a body of work dominated by the floral forms which were favoured by the Nieuwe Kunst.

Ella Cursief, Erasmus and Grotius

Sjoerd de Roos had won the Amsterdam Type Foundry new respect as a supplier of sophisticated type, yet the firm's interests would always be strictly commercial. Whenever the market demanded typefaces of a certain kind, the Type Foundry would comply. *Ella Cursief* (1916) was based on the lettering one would find in a ladies' magazine or on a soap box of the era: bourgeois art nouveau, monolinear, curly, neither fish nor flesh. De Roos's assistant Dick Dooijes wrote: 'This typeface ... was apparently meant to convey a playful gracefulness. This was not in keeping with the personality of the designer, who was not inclined to frivolousness.' [29] Yet the alphabet was well drawn and its stiff elegance must have appealed to the taste of the day: it had a decent success.

De Roos's next typeface was *Erasmus* (1923), a lighter variety of Hollandse Mediaeval, followed by a bold or semi-bold called *Grotius* (1925). Stylistically, Erasmus/Grotius was a step back from Zilvertype: its undulating forms recall some of De Roos's older lettering for title pages; the tension achieved in Zilvertype was abandoned.

Grotius was not presented as 'Erasmus semibold', although it clearly had the same construction. The main reason for this was probably commercial. In a 1931 edition of the Type Foundry's newsletter *Typografische Mededeelingen*, Grotius was not only recommended as 'a semi-bold to be used with Erasmus', but also as a 'type full of character' for jobbing work. The Type Foundry's marketing people evidently hoped for a cross-over effect, opening up the growing market for advertising types to a design originally made as a book face.

Het markante contrast der letters en de grote nauwkeurigheid ervan
GAF EEN RUSTIG BEELD

◄ Sjoerd de Roos's Ella Cursief (1916) was based on a type of commercial lettering that was popular in the 1910s.

▼ Nobel (1929) was an adaptation of Berthold Grotesk, giving a 'modernist' treatment to a nineteenth-century-style original. Broadside showing the details of the revision, c. 1929. *Amsterdam University Library.*

▲ Egmont (1934–1935), designed by De Roos but largely drawn by Dick Dooijes. An idiosyncratic variation on the concept of 'modern face'.

Meidoorntype, Nobel and Egmont

From 1926 onwards, Sjoerd de Roos ran his own private press, the Heuvelpers (Hill Press), named after the small hill near Hilversum village on which his house was built. Typesetting and printing were done by his son, S.H. de Roos, Jr. The type he designed for the press in 1927 is called *Meidoorntype*. It recalls contemporary German lettering and printing types, notably *Koch Antiqua* (1923): a strong diagonal stress, a certain angularity, capitals of the same height as the ascenders, a faux-mediaeval feel. Although the single characters look rather eccentric, Meidoorntype is a surprisingly pleasant text face. As an assignment to himself, it may have been a compensation for the market-oriented work De Roos was asked to do at Tetterode.

As noted earlier, *Nobel* (1929) is not an original De Roos design. It was an attempt to keep up with changing tastes by cleverly adapting an existing face. Bauer had released its ground-breaking *Futura* by Paul Renner in 1926; the Amsterdam Type Foundry wanted to offer something similar in reply to the demand for modernist and 'machine-like' letterforms. De Roos was asked to rework Berthold Grotesk, giving it something of a Bauhaus touch. In this way, the firm capitalized on its recent acquisition of a substantial interest in the Berlin type foundry H. Berthold AG.[30] The re-design, conceived by De Roos but executed by Dick Dooijes, is remarkable indeed. By changing a limited number of key elements, De Roos and Dooijes managed to create an attractive hybrid. Neither ever came to regard Nobel as a personal achievement. Yet it was one of the Type Foundry's most successful type families: it became the standard sanserif in many small printing shops and was still widely in use by the 1960s. It was, however, reviled by post-war functionalists such as Wim Crouwel, who preferred the industrial straightforwardness of nineteenth-century sanserifs like Akzidenz Grotesk, of which Nobel was a picturesque parody in their eyes .

The typeface which followed Nobel is arguably De Roos's most original and most peculiar book face. It, too, was designed to fill a gap. The Amsterdam Type Foundry did not have a text typeface in the 'modern face' category. Instead of adapting an existing typeface, De Roos chose to invent his own variant, leaving most of the drawing work to Dooijes. *Egmont*, although it has the strong vertical stress and the thin straight serifs of a Didone, is by no means a revival of any of the main historical families in that class – Didot, Bodoni or Walbaum. Dooijes himself has pointed out where its main incongruity lies. At the joints of the stem and the serif, the verticals are slightly bent, as if mimicking the movement of a calligrapher's pen. The paradox is that the overall construction of Egmont is based on the classicist pointed pen, whereas the curvature at the joint is typical of the broad-nibbed pen.[31] There is also an odd incongruity between the extreme length of the ascenders and the shortness of the descenders. Due to these unusual solutions, Egmont could not be regarded as

Nobel Antieke Corps 60

ABGJKMM L.A.
ABGJKMM Berthold
NPRSUVW L.A.
NPRSUVW Berthold
ZÄÜ&?2679 L.A.
ZÄÜ&?2679 Berthold
astvwzáàâä L.A.
astvwzáàâä Berthold
æå ÆŒ L.A.

29 Dick Dooijes, *Over de drukletterontwerpen van Sjoerd H. de Roos*, Zutphen 1987, p 40.

30 Lane and Lommen (cit.), p 29.

31 Dick Dooijes, *Over de drukletterontwerpen … (cit.), p 48.

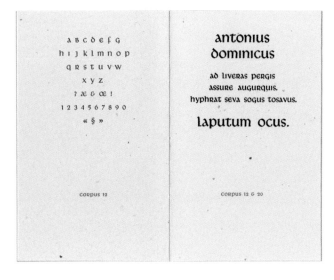

the Amsterdam Type Foundry's Bodoni; and before long the Type Foundry decided to market a traditional Bodoni acquired from Berthold alongside Egmont.

Unlike earlier romans by De Roos, Egmont came with both lining and oldstyle figures, but most European catalogues show only the lining figures. In the USA Egmont was brought out circa 1936 by the Intertype Corporation. The American specimen shows sets of small caps, swash initials and special ligatures not featured in the European catalogues, as well as a series of decorative initials drawn to match the typeface by George F. Trenholm.

Eccentric uncials

Since the mid-1920s there had been ongoing speculation in European typographic circles about the possibility of a 'universal alphabet' which, by abandoning the distinction between upper- and lowercase, would make texts simpler to write, more true to speech and somehow more democratic. Bauhaus-affiliated designers such as Herbert Bayer and Jan Tschichold designed single alphabets based on the lowercase, while from France A.M. Cassandre contributed *Peignot*, mainly based on uppercase forms. Sjoerd de Roos hated this kind of typographic showmanship and was strongly opposed to what he jokingly called 'anti-capitalism'.

When De Roos was challenged to design his version of a single alphabet, he went back to an ancient script: the pre-Carolingian uncial. *Libra* was the outcome of a lettering assignment given to De Roos by J.F. van Royen in 1937 for a monument to the artist Jan Toorop in The Hague. De Roos's uncial-like letterforms for this project delighted all the parties involved. A few months later De Roos reworked the design into a complete new typeface. Although De Roos had hoped for Libra to embark on a literary career, his employer saw other possibilities for it. Libra was promoted as an advertising typeface, and in order to enhance its potential the type foundry offered optional fonts with long ascenders or descenders. Libra sold well on both ends of the spectrum. It found its way into commercial jobbing work, but was also used for literary and historical texts; some volumes of poetry were set entirely in Libra, which was definitely too much of a good thing. Not surprisingly, Libra became a huge success in Ireland, where a renewned national consciousness was taking shape.[32]

If Libra seems to be a pastiche – a 'parody' without satirical intent – of a historical model, *Simplex* takes that model into modernity. A monolinear, sanserif uncial is an interesting concept, and Simplex is impeccably drawn, consistent, and a little crazy. According to Dooijes's autobiographical *Mijn leven met letters* (My life with type), it was he who made the drawings for Simplex and its semi-bold. He never seems to have realized that the typeface was in some way quite special, and admitted to having worked on it half-heartedly. 'From the start, it seemed like a strange fabrication … and that is what it was.'[33] Wim Crouwel agreed, and dismissed Libra as well: 'They are modish products by someone who had no affinity with the modern movement.'[34]

De Roos Romein

After the Nazis defeated the Dutch army and occupied the Netherlands in May 1940, recession hit the printing world. Tetterode had to downsize. In order to prevent his assistant Dick Dooijes from being fired, Sjoerd de Roos requested early retirement. After Dooijes had taken over his position as artistic adviser, De Roos dedicated more and more time to landscape drawing. He did not, however, abandon type design altogether. Two years after the war, in 1947, his seventieth birthday was celebrated with the presentation of a new typeface, *De Roos Romein*. It had been the Amsterdam Type Foundry's chief project during the war years, and was the foundry's first roman produced without the constraint of the 'standard line'.

If De Roos's previous romans were all to some extent based on the Jenson model, his last and possibly finest typeface took Garamont's work from circa 1530 as its point of reference. De Roos Romein is not a revival; with its subtly angular, oval forms and slender, slightly cupped serifs it is a personal, contemporary interpretation of the Renaissance model. The typeface is narrower than its predecessors,

Reinventing tradition

A B C D E F G H I J K L M N O P Q R S T U V W X Y Z

which suits the italic especially well. In 1951 a semi-bold version was added to the De Roos family, which also contained an attractive alphabet of titling capitals.

De Roos dedicated the last years of his life to drawing; when visitors brought up the subject of typography, he did not seem interested. When De Roos died in April 1962, his younger friend Sem Hartz wrote a touching and lucid obituary for a yearbook published in Haarlem, the city where they both lived. Writing about the influence of socialist ideals on De Roos's life and work, Hartz concluded: 'It is a peculiar fact that this shoemaker's son managed to put into practice the crux and the essence of the social revolution better than many famous foreigners. William Morris was an example to him; I doubt whether De Roos ever realized that he has managed to do for our country what his idol was never able to accomplish for his.'[35]

De Roos today

In light of his key role in the development of Dutch typography, it is amazing how little resonance De Roos's work has in the collective consciousness of today's designers. 'His track has gone lost,' said Huib van Krimpen, who completely omitted De Roos from the 1986 second edition of his *Boek*, the Dutch bible of typography – simply because he 'did not think of him'.[36] More recently, publications by Dick Dooijes and Jan Boterman have reached a small number of type enthusiasts. On the whole, De Roos's work seems to be regarded as outdated and largely irrelevant.

The present lack of availablity of his typeface confirms this. The only typeface connected with De Roos which is readily available – in two high-quality versions – is Nobel. The first type designer to take it up was Tobias Frere-Jones, who digitized Nobel in 1993 for his then employer, the Font Bureau in Boston. He had noticed Nobel (as well as *Reiner Script*) in an old Tetterode type catalogue sent to him by a Dutch friend, designer Chris Vermaas. Almost simultaneously, a German student at the Arnhem Academy, Andrea Fuchs, proposed digitizing the typeface to her teacher Fred Smeijers. Their version was eventually published by the Dutch Type Library. Being based on different models (the foundry Nobel was repeatedly modified over the years), the two versions differ in many respects.

While production of De Roos's romans was discontinued, perhaps even before 1970, Libra was produced for phototypesetting by Tetterode's German partner Linotype. It was later licensed to Bitstream, who carries it as a digital headline face. Simplex was reissued by a foundry called Type Revivals, which has even registered the name as a trademark and distributes through Agfa/Monotype (Creative Alliance). Agfa/Monotype also supplies Hollandse Mediaeval, but only in two weights, with no italics. Finally, a revival of Egmont was made by the New York designer Dennis Ortiz-Lopez for *Family Life* magazine. Although part of his version is quite faithful, he took liberties by redesigning the italic and inventing a condensed version. In an e-mail to the author Ortiz-Lopez made it clear that it had not been his intention to make a faithful revival. 'I recreated it based on the general look of the samples provided. If it comes close to the original, it is pure serendipity.'[37] Ortiz-Lopez has now made his Egmont commercially available.

Fortunately, the original Egmont, Hollandse Mediaeval, Libra et al. are not dead yet: their foundry type incarnations are cherished by private presses in the Netherlands and elsewhere. In these circles De Roos's types are still in demand.

La guerre est
quelque chose d'absolument mauvais,
une entreprise stupide
* * *
Il n'y a pas un seul but qui vaille
que l'on fasse la guerre. Ou plutôt, il n'y
en a qu'un: détruire la guerre elle-même,
la supprimer à tout jamais,
la rayer de l'histoire
des peuples

Jules Romains dans:
Les Hommes de Bonne Volonté

◄ Page from the 1951 specimen of De Roos Romein. The Jules Romains quote, possibly chosen by Dick Dooijes, is telling: 'War is something absolutely wicked, a stupid enterprise. There is not a single goal worth waging war over. Rather, there's only one: destroying war itself, erasing it forever from the history of nations.'

↕ Open titling capitals of De Roos Romein, 1951.

▾ Title page of the 1951 De Roos Romein specimen.

Enkele toepassingen van

onze nieuwe series

DE ROOS ROMEIN

en

DE ROOS CURSIEF

N.V. LETTERGIETERIJ ‹AMSTERDAM›
VOORHEEN N. TETTERODE

32 Koosje Sierman, 'De Libra van S.H. de Roos, een uitmiddelpuntige' in *TYP* vol. 2 no. D, July 1988.

33 Dick Dooijes, *Mijn leven met letters*, Amsterdam 1991, p 33.

34 Wim Crouwel, 'Onderkast in Nederland' in *Bulletin Drukwerk in de Marge*, 18 (1990), p 34.

35 'Sjoerd Hendrik de Roos', in *Jaarboek 1962*, reprinted in Sem Hartz, *Essays* (cit.), p 23.

36 Quoted by Koosje Sierman in 'Libra, een uitmiddelpuntige' (cit.). Sierman points out that the first edition of Huib van Krimpen's *Boek* (1966) did mention De Roos Romein, so the omission cannot have been completely unintentional.

37 E-mail, August 1999.

Display types for the Amsterdam Type Foundry

Although the Amsterdam Type Foundry had won respect with its new typographic course under Sjoerd de Roos, selling new typefaces was not exactly the firm's core business. Usually referred to by its founder's name, Tetterode, the firm dealt in machinery: printing presses, typesetting machines, machines for folding, cutting, glueing and binding. As such, it built up a virtual monopoly in the Netherlands in the decades between 1920 and 1960. This is one of the reasons why most of its typefaces became best-sellers: almost every small printer used their machines, and they were the sole supplier of typefaces for them. Although De Roos was an idealist, the management's view of type was strictly commercial. Huib van Krimpen wrote: 'Tetterode's tactics, well learned from the German foundries in the pre-war days, were simple and effective. Roughly once every year or eighteen months a new typeface – preferably a jobbing face – was brought out, usually in the form of a special offer, and sold to the majority of Dutch printers, particularly smallish shops. Thus, a short-lived fashion was created, and after a year or a year and a half, the design was no longer popular, the type was worn out, and a new one was launched to take its place.'[38]

Many of these display faces were foreign designs which were re-released under a different name: the American Type Founders' *Empire* became *Iris*, *Stanley/Titantipo* from Wagner & Schmidt became *Hercules*. But the Amsterdam Type Foundry also ordered new types from in-house designers as well as Dutch and foreign independent artists.

An early display face cut for the firm was *Das Antieke*, presented in 1920 as 'the advertising type par exellence'. In *Dutch typefounders' specimens*, Lane and Lommen describe this typeface as having been acquired from the German foundry Wagner & Schmidt.[39] Contemporary sources, though, call it a 'modern Dutch typeface' and mention Pieter Das as its designer.[40] Almost forgotten today, the Dutch illustrator and lettering artist Pieter Das established himself in Germany around 1910, where he set up shop working for clients in industry and retail. In 1914, when Germany was

▲ Pieter Das, cover of the February 1917 issue of *De Bedrijfs-reklame*, the trade magazine of the advertising sector. The issue contains a richly illustrated article about Das's work. Das's ad for a Hague bookshop shown right was published in that issue.

▶ Pieter Das, brochure for Philips electric stoves (c. 1920). *Reproduced with kind permission from the Philips Company Archives.*

⬚ Das Antieke as shown in an Amsterdam Type Foundry specimen. *Jan Tholenaar collection.*

▸ Indépendant by G. Colette and J. Dufour (c. 1930) was produced by Etablissements 'Plantin' S.A., the Amsterdam Type Foundry's Belgian subsidiary.

De zeer bijzondere eigenschappen der "Indépendant" verleenen haar een speciale geschiktheid voor de markante reclame-drukwerken 123

ABCDEFGHIJKLMNOPQ
12345RSTUVWXYZ67890

▾ Succes (Success in English-speaking countries), another display face designed in the Type Foundry's drawing room, was partly based on Das Antieke. The open capitals were also known as Lux Capitals. *Amsterdam University Library (UvA), LPBR 405*

▾ Savoy (c. 1936) was the third display face drawn under De Roos's supervision which took Morris Fuller Benton's Broadway as a starting point. Two earlier derivates, Bristol and Carlton, had been released in 1929.

about to enter the Great War, he returned to the Netherlands, where he set up his own advertising studio in Soest. He was one of the first Dutch commercial artists to abandon the painterly arts-and-crafts advertising style and communicate more directly, creating attractive combinations of powerful type and witty illustrations. His influences are distinctly German. His bold lettering and illustrations sometimes mimic Lucien Bernhard's Plakatstil; some of his lettering echoes the *Berthold Block* typeface published in 1908. As one of the first Dutch exponents of this new, striking style, Das was soon successful, boasting clients such as De Bijenkorf department store, the Utrecht Trade Fair, Philips electric appliances and Verkade biscuits. In several advertisements and folders from around 1917, Das used hand-lettering which is almost identical to the font which the Amsterdam Type Foundry released three years later under the designer's name.[41] In 1928 the foundry brought out *Succes* (*Success* in English-speaking countries), a typeface drawn under the direction of Sjoerd de Roos, which is an updated and extended version of Das Antieke, retaining the informality of its wobbly outlines.

Sjoerd de Roos seems to have complied rather reluctantly with the growing demand for fashionable display faces. *Ella Italic* (1916) was an early example of a short-lived alphabet for advertising. Ten years later Art Deco was ubiquitous and Morris Fuller Benton's *Broadway* (ATF) was its quintessential typeface. In 1929, The Amsterdam Type Foundry presented two new faces based on Broadway: *Bristol* and its inline variant *Carlton*; both were drawn by Dick Dooijes under De Roos's somewhat uninterested supervision. In the early 1930s a shaded variety, *Savoy*, was added to the series. The foundry's 1950s specimens show that this variant briefly survived the Second World War, but Bristol and Carlton went missing in action. Dooijes, in his survey of De Roos's types, gracefully skipped the threesome, although they were more drastic redesigns than *Nobel* was of *Berthold Grotesk*.

The Type Foundry also hired foreign designers to draw jobbing types. Its Brussels subsidiary Établissements Plantin contributed *Indépendant* by G. Colette and J. Dufour (c. 1930). Like its constructivist contemporaries, Indépendant plays with squares and circles, but it does so in a charming rather than a radical manner: it is high-street aesthetics rather than Bauhaus radicalism. It was shown in Ruari McLean's *Manual of Typography* as a typeface 'with some built-in illegibility'.[42]

Tschichold's first typeface

A constructivist typeface from a more prestigious source was *Transito* by Jan Tschichold, his first published typeface. Transito came out in 1930, when Tschichold was at the height of his constructivist period. His book *Die Neue Typographie* had come out two years earlier; his famous proposal for a single-case 'universal alphabet' dates from 1929. Transito, a stencil alphabet in upper- and lowercase, has obviously taken clues from Josef Albers's *Kombinationsschrift* (1925–1931). As Transito was freer and less reductive in its choice of elements than the Kombinationsschrift, Tschichold was able to solve certain details in a more elegant and charming way. In many respects Transito is also similar to Paul Renner's *Futura Black* (1929). One cannot help wonder if, for Tschichold, Transito was a contribution to constructivist research, or an opportunity to cash in on the sudden popularity of 'New Typography'.

Transito, like Indépendant, had a short life. In the first type catalogues which the Amsterdam Type Foundry published after the Second World War, such as the English/Swedish-language *Choice of Modern Type* (c. 1951), there is not a trace of either. In the Tetterode archive at the Amsterdam University Library there is a folder con-

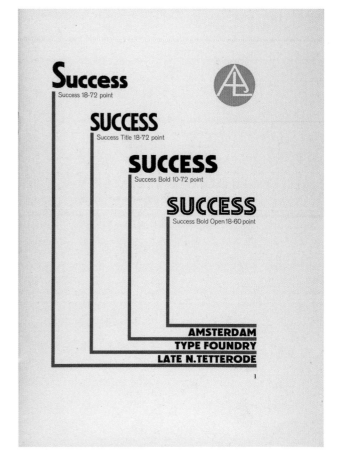

1

38 'Type design in the Netherlands and the Influence of the Enschedé Foundry', *Fine Print*, vol.15, no. 4 (1989).

39 Lane and Lommen (cit.), p 166.

40 A.A.M. Stols, *Het schoone boek*, Rotterdam 1935, p 57; M.H. Groenendaal Jr., *Drukletters*, 3rd printing, Haarlem 1944, p 119.

41 Jan Feith, 'Over Pieter Das', *De bedrijfsreklame*, vol. 2, no. 1 (1917). Guus Bekooy et al., *Philips Honderd. Een industriële onderneming*, Zaltbommel 1991, p 53.

42 Ruari McLean, *Manual of Typography*, London 1980, p 45.

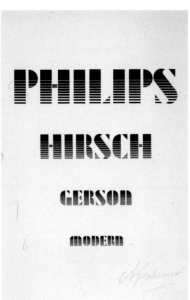

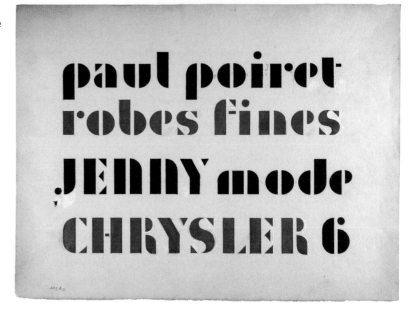

▸ Jan Tschichold, drawings for
Transito (c.1929). Signed on the
back: 'Tschichold'.
*Amsterdam University Library (UvA),
De Roos Collection, folder 203.*

◂ Sketches (probably by
Dick Dooijes) for Transito
Versierd ('Transito Decorated',
1937). The proposal was
rejected. *Tetterode archive of
the Amsterdam University Library
(UvA), LPBR 806.*

▾ In 1936 the Amsterdam Type
Foundry produced Flex, from
drawings by George Salter.

Jan zonder Vrees

Stefan Schlesinger, poster for
an Amsterdam cinema theatre,
1930s.

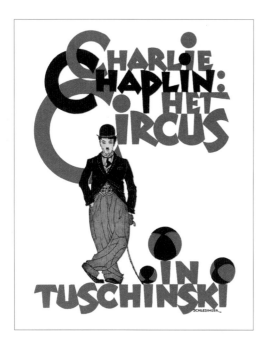

taining designs for a typeface which was (provisionally) called *Transito Decorated*. This variety of Transito – in which the characters are filled with horizontal, graded lines – appears to have been proposed by Dick Dooijes, but many of the sheets are marked with the annotation 'rejected'. Apparently, the typeface was never brought to completion.[43]

Tschichold was not the only important international designer from whom the Lettergieterij Amsterdam commissioned a font. In 1936 the foundry produced *Flex*, from drawings by George Salter. Salter (1897–1967) had made a name for himself in Berlin as a stage designer and commercial artist but fled to New York in 1934. Salter's numerous book jackets for Alfred A. Knopf stand out for their expressive hand-drawn type. Considering the designer's reputation, *Flex* is disappointing. It suggests that each letter is made of an ingeniously bent ribbon; but what could have been an intriguing play with the third dimension is stiff and unconvincing. It is by no means up to Salter's lettering work, and soon disappeared from the catalogues.

Stefan Schlesinger: a lost talent

Stefan Schlesinger (1896–1944) was one of about a dozen graphic artists from Germany and Austria who emigrated to the Netherlands in the interwar period. He was a commercial artist rather than a typographer: a master letterer who could capture virtually any style with grace, verve and unmatched precision. This was a combination unseen in the Netherlands, where Art Deco lettering was, all in all, a rather stiff affair and where liveliness was often confused with carelessness. The Amsterdam Type Foundry released two display types by Schlesinger, the second of which – *Rondo*, released posthumously – became a bestseller. Yet both were ultimately unsatisfactory, as they do not fully reflect the brilliance of the letterforms Schlesinger invented on a daily basis. Had Stefan Schlesinger survived World War II, he might have become one of the prominent type designers of the 1950s and beyond.
Born in Vienna, Stefan Schlesinger briefly worked as an architect, but soon found he had more affinity with illustration and lettering. He became an intern in Julius Klinger's famous Atelier für Plakatverziechnis ('Workshop for poster design'). Klinger's style, characterized by energetic draughtsmanship and great feeling for communicative imagery and letterforms, left an indelible mark on Schlesinger; in the foreword to his 1939 lettering book Schlesinger paid tribute to his master, 'who was the first to open my eyes to the possibilities hidden within the letter'.[44]
Schlesinger met his Dutch wife Anna Kerdijk in about 1923 in the Masonic lodge Vertrauen ('Trust') in Vienna, of which he was a founding member. Having moved to Amsterdam in 1925, they co-founded two Masonic lodges; both worked hard to increase an awareness of art and beauty within the Dutch Freemasonry.[45]

◄ Stefan Schlesinger, cover for a season's catalogue, Metz & Co. department store, 1927.

▼ Stefan Schlesinger, packaging for Van Houten's instant pudding (1940). The lettering was done in hand-drawn 'glyphic' capitals, which Schlesinger used as a kind of 'corporate alphabet' for Van Houten.

▽ Schlesinger's drawings for a Van Houten cherry liqueur chocolate box (1939) and an instant dessert package show the kind of script lettering that his typeface Rondo (> pp 53 and 91) was based on.

43 Lane and Lommen (cit.), p 239.

44 *Voorbeelden van moderne opschriften voor schilders en tekenaars*, Amsterdam 1939, p 2.

45 Van Dam and Van Praag, *Stefan Schlesinger*, Abcoude 1997, pp 21–23.

▾ Stefan Schlesinger, packaging design for writing paper of the Van Gelder paper factory, 1932.

▾ Page from Schlesinger's lettering book published in 1939.

▸ Stefan Schlesinger, Saranna. Design for an unpublished typeface, 1940–41. Sketch in the Trio Printers archive, *City Archive, The Hague.*

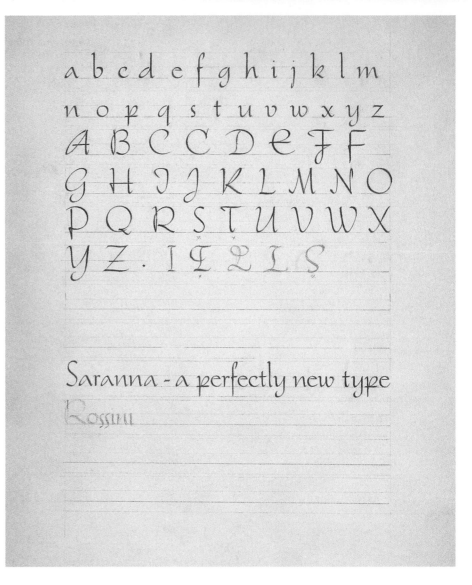

Schlesinger soon received design assignments from high-profile clients. Metz & Co. was (and still is) an exclusive department store specializing in textiles and furniture, whose suppliers at the time included the Wiener Werkstätte. From 1926 to 1931 Schlesinger designed the firm's stationery and packaging, labels, advertisements and brochures. Playful yet restrained, stylish yet light-hearted, Schlesinger's lettering must have captured the spirit of 1920s radical-chic to perfection.

Circa 1927 Schlesinger began working for the chocolate factory Van Houten. This collaboration resulted in countless splendid designs – logos, advertisements, showcards, packaging. Many were purely typographical; some carried humorous illustrations or simple decoration. Lettering styles varied, but one alphabet of sanserif capitals with flared terminals – predating *Optima* and *Pascal* – stands out, and can be regarded a kind of corporate typeface for Van Houten.[46] It is likely that this work by Schlesinger influenced other lettering artists using similar details, such as Helmut Salden, Theo Kurpershoek and Jan Vermeulen (> page 104 ff).[47]

Another important client of Schlesinger's was the printing firm Trio in The Hague, famous for the typographic experiments done in its composing room by Piet Zwart. From 1932, its director was Frits Kerdijk, brother of Schlesinger's wife Anna. Kerdijk, a book lover and author as well as a manager and engineer, commissioned his brother-in-law to design the company's logo, stationery and goodwill publications; this work, too, amounted to a kind of corporate identity avant la lettre.

PUBLICITÉ DU SOIR
Holland en België

◄ Stefan Schlesinger, Hidalgo (1940) and Rondo (1948). Originally called Figaro, Hidalgo was renamed after Monotype announced the release of their typeface of that name. Rondo was begun by Schlesinger and finished by Dick Dooijes.

▼ Cover of the 1939 lettering book, 'Samples of modern lettering for signpainters and draughtsmen'.

Figaro/Hidalgo and Rondo

Work on Schlesinger's first printing type began in 1939 and was completed the next year. The assignment must have been the Amsterdam Type Foundry's idea: for Schlesinger to propose a revival of a nineteenth-century billboard type would have been an uncharacteristic move. A nineteenth-century 'Italienne', with exaggeratedly thick top and bottom strokes, the typeface was initially named *Figaro* because it was to resemble the masthead of the French newspaper with that name. As English Monotype was developing a very similar typeface, also called Figaro, the name of Schlesinger's face was changed to *Hidalgo*. The main thing that can be said about Hidalgo is that it is well-made – it shows Schlesinger's craftsmanship, but none of his fantasy and wit. The typeface was briefly successful, but was largely forgotten after 1950.[48]

Rondo, the other typeface Schlesinger designed for the Amsterdam Type Foundry, was definitely his initiative. For years, Schlesinger had used variants of an attractive, very legible round cursive in his Van Houten packaging designs. When he proposed to the Amsterdam Type Foundry that he design a script type based on this lettering style, it was decided that Rondo should be an unconnected script. As Kurt Löb wrote, this idea suffered from an intrinsic contradiction: 'for commercial and technical reasons the Rondo concept – originally a script of rhythmically joint letters – was made to function as a printing type with completely separated characters.' Although the designer may have had some doubt – a letter to the Tetterode management suggests that he had some trouble convincing himself that Rondo was going to be 'a good and usable type'[49] – the typeface quickly took shape in the first months of 1941. However, anticipating trouble because of anti-Jewish measures from the occupying German authorities, Schlesinger proposed that Dick Dooijes act as a co-designer. With his consent, Dooijes worked on to complete the typeface after Schlesinger had been deported to the Nazi camp Westerbork in the summer of 1942, his wife joining him voluntarily. During his internment at Westerbork, Schlesinger continued to supervise the work from a distance, and even received permission to leave the camp twice for working visits to Amsterdam.

In September 1944, Schlesinger and his wife were sent to the Theresienstadt camp; despite attempts by friends and colleagues to get them released, they were transferred to Auschwitz where they died in the gas chambers in early October 1944.

The murder of Schlesinger cut short a career full of promise. Several plans for type designs were interrupted. In the archive of the Trio printing firm (City Archive, The Hague) there are drawings of *Saranna*, an upright script which seems to solve the Rondo paradox – to maintain a rhythm without connecting the letters – in a more natural way. Other typefaces mentioned in Schlesinger's 1941 notes (*Oriol* and *Imper*) seem to have disappeared without a trace.[50]

Rondo was released in 1948, and became the most popular of the script faces published by the Amsterdam Type Foundry in the post-war period. *Rondo Bold* was licensed to Mecanorma for production as dry transfer lettering and became part of Mecanorma's digital type library in the early 1990s.

46 Kurt Löb, 'Deutschsprachige Gestalter als Emigranten', in *Philobiblon*, vol. 33, no. 3, September 1989, pp 180–183.

47 Dozens of original Schlesinger designs for Van Houten have been preserved by chance. Hans Oldewarris – the publisher of the present book – found them in a waste container when he went to photograph the factory after the firm's bankruptcy.

48 For some years during the war, Hidalgo was forbidden by the occupying Nazi forces for a complex reason: a German satiric magazine called *Der ware Jacob*, which used an Italienne as headline face, turned out to have been edited by a Jewish writer in the 1880s, so the Italienne was banned as being 'Hebrew'. The fact that the designer of Hidalgo was also Jewish did not have anything to do with this. Reported in Van Dam and Van Praag, *Stefan Schlesinger* (cit.), p 91.

49 Letter dd. 31 May 1941 in the Amsterdam University Library. 'Nu ik mij weer in dit onderwerp heb ingewerkt, geloof ik wel dat de RONDO een goede en bruikbare letter zal worden.'

50 Van Dam and Van Praag, *Stefan Schlesinger* (cit.), p 95.

Jan van Krimpen's modern traditionalism

Izaak Enschedé was admitted journeyman compositor in the Haarlem printers' guild on the twentyfirst of June; and it is from that day that his firm reckons its jubilees and centenaries. It is probable that, like most compositors at that time, he did much of

Izaak Enschedé was admitted journeyman compositor in the Haarlem printers' guild on the twentyfirst of June; and it is from that day that his firm reckons its jubilees and centenaries. It is probable that, like most compositors at that time, he did much of his work at home, and it is not

Izaak Enschedé was admitted journeyman compositor in the Haarlem Printers' guild on the twenty-first of June; and it is from that day that his firm reckons its jubilees and centenaries. It is probable

Izaak Enschedé was admitted journeyman compositor in the Haarlem printers' guild on the twentyfirst of June; and it is from that day that his firm reckons its jubilees and centena-

Izaak Enschedé was admitted journeyman compositor in the Haarlem printers' guild on the twentyfirst of June; and it is from that day that his firm reckons its jubilees and centenaries. It is probable that, like most compositors at that time, he did much of his work at home

Jan van Krimpen's Italics, printed by Bram de Does in *Romanée en Trinité: Historisch origineel en systematisch slordig* (1991). From top to bottom: Lutetia, Romanée, Romulus, Cancellaresca Bastarda, Spectrum.

Jan van Krimpen was an uncompromising typographer, lettering artist and type designer. In his formative years he was influenced by Sjoerd de Roos, fifteen years his senior, but soon distanced himself from the decorative element in De Roos's work, and at times wrote critically about his typefaces. Their relationship would always be an uneasy one; this was enhanced by the fact that they worked for the two competing Dutch type foundries. Yet they had one important goal in common: both men wanted to design new alphabets for a changing technology. Although Van Krimpen was a friend of Stanley Morison, he disapproved of the revival programme Morison established at Monotype. He felt that the idea of recreating the types of past centuries for use in mechanical typesetting was a fallacy. Apart from one revival project he was involved in as a consultant – *Monotype Van Dijck* – all his typefaces were new and original designs. Van Krimpen was among the first to take a fresh look at the proportions and details of Renaissance letterforms, and incorporate them in faces which were classical in approach but had a distinctly contemporary and rational look.

Born in 1892, Jan van Krimpen studied to be a draughtsman and teacher at the Academy of Art in The Hague. As a student, he developed an interest in literature and became friendly with the Dutch poets of the so-called 'generation of 1910', including Jan Greshoff and J.C. Bloem. His love of poetry naturally led to an interest in the form of the book; he obtained a German translation of Edward Johnston's *Writing & Illuminating, & Lettering* and began practicing lettering, calligraphy and bookbinding. His earliest lettering appeared in *De Witte Mier* (The White Ant), a small magazine directed by Greshoff. In 1912 he collaborated with Sjoerd de Roos on a book jacket for Brusse Publishers in Rotterdam. He perfected his understanding of letterforms by studying the Italian writing masters of the sixteenth century and in 1917 began publishing self-designed volumes of poetry by his literary friends. It is significant that, after having set the first two books in *Hollandse Mediaeval*, Van Krimpen replaced De Roos's typeface with *Caslon* – a simpler and lighter face – by the time these publications became somewhat institutionalized under the series title Palladium.

Thanks to his work for *De Witte Mier* and his friendship with Greshoff, Van Krimpen became acquainted with Jean François van Royen, the lawyer and typographer who in 1920 obtained a key position as aesthetic consultant to the Dutch PTT (Post, Telegraph and Telephone service). Van Royen recognized his talent as a lettering artist and in 1923 commissioned him to design the lettering of two series of postage stamps issued to celebrate Queen Wilhelmina's silver jubilee. Thus the quality of his work was brought to the attention of Enschedé en Zonen, the Haarlem company which had printed all the Dutch postage stamps since 1866. When Van Krimpen visited Haarlem in November 1923 for the opening of an exhibition in honour of Laurens Janszoon Coster, the mythical inventor of printing, he was approached by Johannes Enschedé, who suggested that Van Krimpen should design a new type for his firm. This was, as John Dreyfus wrote 'an opportunity which Van Krimpen was eager and able to take. ... He already possessed a perfectly clear idea of the type design which he wanted to produce: he promised to proceed at once with a drawing for Dr. Enschedé which showed exactly what he had in mind.'[51]

Lutetia and the hand of the punchcutter

Enschedé liked the sample – a fragment from a French poem – that Van Krimpen had drawn to illustrate his idea. Van Krimpen set to drawing a full character set for the roman, which he finished towards mid-1924. The alphabet was seen by Van Royen, who decided that the new typeface should be part of the Dutch contribution to the 1925 Exposition Internationale des Arts Décoratifs et Industriels Modernes in Paris, which he was curating. He urged Enschedé to get on with production and Van Krimpen swiftly drew the italics. Punches were cut for a 16-point size of the type; unfortunately, production was not finished in time to set all the Dutch printed matter for the Paris exhibition in it. The typeface was only used for a catalogue of Dutch art, but there still seemed to be reason enough to call it *Lutetia*, the Roman name for Paris. On the same occasion Van Krimpen exhibited a selection from his Palladium series, as well as some examples of his calligraphic writing. Both his typographic work and the new typeface met with wide admiration, and he was awarded a *grand prix*.

Lutetia was experienced by Van Krimpen's contemporaries as something genuinely new and fresh, and it is easy to see why. Although it is based on Renaissance characteristics, the combination of roundness, clarity and simplicity is distinctly modern; the fine serifs, very slighty cupped, suggest a forward movement. It was a very different typeface from other romans in the same style – the ubiquitous Caslon or the newly revived Garamond. The italic, too, was original. It was inspired by sixteenth-century chancery scripts, but it was not a revival like Frederic Warde's *Blado*, modelled on the Arrighi italic (a chancery script adapted for print). As Van Krimpen wrote [52], he based the italic on his own handwriting, which he had recently reformed after studying the Italian writing masters. Lutetia's italic is somewhat wider and more legible than Blado; however, it is still too narrow and too distinctive to work really well as a companion to the roman.

There are considerable differences between the preliminary sketch presented in late 1924, and the finished version of Lutetia. Of course the design must have involved a learning process, which is hard to trace in retrospect because no drawings of the first stages of production have been preserved. But there was also another force at work that continued to have a strong impact throughout Van Krimpen's type designing career: the insight and skills of P.H. Rädisch, Enschedé's punchcutter. Rädisch was one of the last masters of a craft which began to disappear in the early twentieth century, with the advent of mechanical punchcutting. In fact, Enschedé was one of the last foundries in western Europe where punchcutting was a task performed manually, and Van Krimpen's types might never have reached the same perfection and brilliance had his drawings been copied directly into working drawings

51 John Dreyfus, *The Work of Jan van Krimpen. A record in honour of his sixtieth birthday*.
   Joh. Enschedé en Zonen, Haarlem/W. de Haan, Utrecht 1952, p 7. It has been pointed
   out that Van Krimpen firmly 'directed' the contents of this book and that many of
   Dreyfus's words are probably based on Van Krimpen's opinions.

52 *On Designing and Devising Type*, The Typophiles, New York 1957.

CCEEFFGGLLQ Qeehhiijjmmnnss88??!!..,,;;::()()--""''[][]

ABCDEFGHIJKLMN
OPQRSTUVWXYZ

◄ Lutetia: characters modified in 1928 on the request of the Carnegie Institute of Technology in Pittsburg. In each pair, the left-hand character is from the original version of Lutetia.

◄ In or around 1930, sets of 48 and 36 point Lutetia capitals were worked over with a burin by Rädisch, Enschede's punch-cutter, resulting in Lutetia Open.

▼ Curwen Press initials, 1929.

for pantographic production. Having learned his craft in Leipzig and at the German Reichsdruckerei in Berlin, P.H. Rädisch complemented Van Krimpen's drawing skills by cutting punches of astonishing acuteness and clarity. Although Van Krimpen's drawings were very precise, they needed to be interpreted in order to create optically correct fonts in smaller point sizes – which Rädisch did faultlessly. Their collaboration began when both men were in their early thirties and continued until Van Krimpen's death in 1958, resulting in 'a team of unusual effectiveness', as John Dreyfus wrote. Rädisch had strong opinions on how a typeface should look – witness the modifications he kept making to Sem Hartz's *Emergo* (> p 96). Yet there was always something odd about the way Van Krimpen showed his appreciation for the man who gave his types their finishing touch. He seldom mentioned Rädisch's name, and even when Van Krimpen paid direct tribute to him – as he did in the postscript to *On Designing and Devising Type* – Rädisch remained an anonymous craftsman, 'the punchcutter of the House of Enschedé'. For Van Krimpen, the designer was the mastermind; the punchcutter 'may be replaced without noticable difference in the result'. 'Consequently,' he wrote in a posthumously printed essay, 'I can understand the opinion that there is no need to mention this auxiliary hand's name.' [53]

Lutetia improved

Lutetia was welcomed by the international typographic community as a remarkable endeavour, but the appreciation was not unconditional. In *The Fleuron* 5 (1926) Stanley Morison hailed it as being 'a new type, underived from any historic predecessor or school' and 'exceedingly handsome'. Yet he also criticized certain details, such as the sloped bar on the lowercase e (possibly an influence from Hollandse Mediaeval which, unlike Lutetia, was modelled on Jenson's type) and the exaggerated width of the capital E. Bruce Rodgers praised Lutetia's combination of 'strength with delicacy, grace with dignity'. [54] But when he bought Lutetia for his press he replaced the lowercase e, m and n with letters from a Caslon font. A more drastic modification to the typeface was made in 1928, when the printer Porter Garnett of the Carnegie Institute of Technology in Pittsburgh chose it for the monumental catalogue of the Frick Art Collection. Garnett proposed a number of changes which Van Krimpen readily agreed to because, as he wrote later, he would have made similar changes had he been given the opportunity to do so. For the Carnegie version about twenty characters and punctuation marks were redesigned. The new E and F were narrower and their middle bar was lowered; the vulnerable long tail of the Q was shortened; the dots on i and j, hovering high over the stems towards the right, were lowered and centred; h, m and n became wider and more in harmony with the whole. Although most of these changes were distinct improvements, neither Enschedé nor Monotype – which began to produce the face in 1928 – saw reasons to incorporate them into the retail version of Lutetia.

Van Krimpen at Enschedé

Following Lutetia's successful Parisian debut, Jan van Krimpen was engaged as a full-time employee by Enschedé to supervise further production of the typeface. He was not only hired as a type designer and type consultant; the firm also wanted to make use of his skills as a typographer, author and specialist in book production. He was to design type specimens with the firm's historical type collection, help produce issues of the firm's monthly publication and provide advice on printing orders. In his letter of appointment, Johannes VI Enschedé expressed his high hopes that the

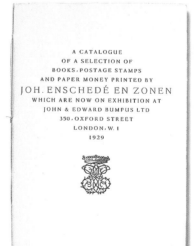

A CATALOGUE
OF A SELECTION OF
BOOKS, POSTAGE STAMPS
AND PAPER MONEY PRINTED BY
JOH. ENSCHEDÉ EN ZONEN
WHICH ARE NOW ON EXHIBITION AT
JOHN & EDWARD BUMPUS LTD
350, OXFORD STREET
LONDON, W. I
1929

Catalogue of an Enschedé exhibition at John & Edward Bumpus Ltd., London 1929. Cover design by Van Krimpen.

Reinventing tradition

ΕΥΑΓΓΕΛΙΟΝ ΚΑΤΑ ΙΩΑΝΗΝ
Ἐν ἀρχῇ ἦν ὁ λόγος, καὶ ὁ λόγος ἦν πρὸς τὸν Θεόν, καὶ Θεὸς ἦν ὁ λόγος. Οὗτος ἦν ἐν ἀρχῇ πρὸς τὸν Θεόν. πάντα δι' αὐτοῦ ἐγένετο, καὶ χωρὶς αὐτοῦ ἐγένετο οὐδὲ ἕν ὃ γέγονεν. ἐν αὐτῷ ζωὴ ἦν, καὶ ἡ ζωὴ ἦν τὸ φῶς τῶν ἀνθρώπων. καὶ τὸ φῶς ἐν τῇ σκοτίᾳ φαίνει, καὶ ἡ σκοτία αὐτὸ οὐ κατέλαβεν.

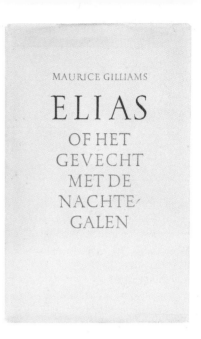

MAURICE GILLIAMS

ELIAS
OF HET
GEVECHT
MET DE
NACHTE-
GALEN

▲ Antigone, of which Van Krimpen wrote in 1956: 'If it is any good at all ... it must be a matter of sheer luck.' (*On Designing and Devising Type*, p 33)

▶ Hand-lettered dust jacket for Meulenhoff publishers, Amsterdam 1936.

arrival of Van Krimpen would create new possibilities to 'create a beautiful book' in the true Enschedé heritage.[55] These expectations were fulfilled: during the Van Krimpen years Enschedé regained international fame as a printer and publisher of splendid books in the classical tradition.

Although Van Krimpen's position in Haarlem was comparable to that of Sjoerd de Roos at the Amsterdam Type Foundry, there were huge differences in the way they functioned within the company. De Roos was forced to comply with the caprices of the Tetterode management and marketing department; Van Krimpen moved on a level of equality with Enschedé's directors and was, to a large extent, his own master. He accepted design assignments from other publishers at will and in later years decided, without consulting the management, to limit his working day at the firm to the morning hours. There was a certain presumptuousness in his behaviour which irritated some directors; but he would remain in Enschedé's service until the day in 1958 when, aged 66, he died of a stroke on his way to work.

Typefaces of the 1920s

True to his literary roots and his vocation as a 'modern classicist', Van Krimpen would never lower himself to designing display types. But he was no enemy to decoration, as shown by his hand-lettering for book covers. Many times he even indulged in mannerist ornamentation, as long as he could convince himself that it served to present the contents in an attractive and tasteful way. None of his typefaces, though, shows a similar degree of frivolousness. The titling alphabets produced for hand-setting in the 1920s are elegant, yet stern.

The beautiful *Lutetia Open* was made as an alphabet to be used for titles and initials in a monthly magazine printed at Enschedé. It was produced under Van Krimpen's direction by P.H. Rädisch who engraved a white line in the 36 and 48 point sizes of a single set of Lutetia capitals. Towards 1930 it was decided to produce matrices from this type and release it as a commercial typeface.

The *Open Capitals* (*Dubbel Augustijn Open Kapitalen*, 1927) were to serve the same purpose as Lutetia Open, but are different in conception: the inline was carved without breaking through the letterform, and the result is a pure outline. Van Krimpen possibly based his work on an 1885 sourcebook of Roman inscriptions.[56] Twenty-five years later, the Bauersche Schriftgießerei released a rather similar typeface: Max Caflisch's *Columna*. Van Krimpen was furious. When Caflisch protested that he had not even been aware of the existence of the precedent, Van Krimpen became somewhat milder, writing that the design must have been 'a case of unconscious inspiration by a forgotten example'.[57]

◀ Lettering of the parchment spine of a memorial book for the paper trading company Brandt & Proost, printed by Enschedé in 1943.

53 Quoted by John Dreyfus in the introduction to *A letter to Philip Hofer on Certain Problems Connected with the Mechnical Cutting of Punches*, Cambridge/Boston 1972.

54 Quoted by Dreyfus in *The Work of Jan van Krimpen* (cit.), p 23.

55 Koosje Sierman, 'De Enschedese jaren van Jan van Krimpen 1925–1958' in *Adieu Aesthetica & Mooie Pagina's!*, The Hague/Amsterdam/Haarlem 1995, p 23.

56 Aemilius Hübner's *Exempla scripturae epigraphicae* from 1885, cf. *Adieu Aesthetica & Mooie Pagina's!* (cit.), p 37.

57 *On Designing and Devising Type* (cit.), p 39.

◄ Sketch of Romanée, 1928.

▸ Jan van Krimpen, title page designed with Romanée, 1932.

▾ Romanée specimen, c. 1968. Design by Sem Hartz, typography by Bram de Does.

THE POEMS OF
M ★ A ★ R ★ Y
QUEEN OF SCOTS
TO
THE EARL OF
BOTHWELL

HAARLEM
JOH. ENSCHEDÉ EN ZONEN
1932

A set of initials, custom-designed for the Curwen Press in 1929, was omitted from Dreyfus's 1952 book. Perhaps the alphabet was judged to be too marginal for inclusion in this overview. Being Van Krimpen's most decorative printing type, it does deserve some attention. Its story, researched by John A. Lane, was published as a note to the 1990 Dutch edition of *On Designing and Devising Type* prepared by Huib van Krimpen, son of Jan. The initials were commissioned from Van Krimpen by Herbert Simon and Harry Carter, who were, respectively, director and typographic adviser to the Press and visited Enschedé in 1928. Apparently, the initials were produced in two sizes, executed both as line blocks etched in zinc and mounted on lead bodies and as electrotypes etched in copper.[58]

A remarkable face from the 1920s is a Greek type named *Antigone*. Walter Tracy has called it 'one of the best of Van Krimpen's designs'.[59] It was meant to be part of a larger project, a complete set of characters and symbols for mathematical text books, which was supervised by the famous physic H.A. Lorentz, who lived in Haarlem. After Lorentz's sudden death in 1928 the project was abandoned, but Antigone, its 'by-product' – Van Krimpen's words – was released separately. Despite the designer's reservations, Antigone enjoyed a brief success. Having been used in a famous Homer edition, Antigone became the quintessential typeface for Greek literature to several generations of Dutch students. Van Krimpen later judged the typeface to be too hastily made and too calligraphic; in contrast, he made his *Romulus Greek* resemble a roman face as closely as possible.

Romanée and the Van Dijck heritage

The famous type specimen book issued by Enschedé in 1768 included several types attributed to the great seventeenth-century punchcutter Christoffel van Dijck. A few decades later however, many of Enschedé's baroque types were melted down to make way for contemporary fashions. In Van Krimpen's time the only Van Dijck type of which matrices had been preserved was the *Great Primer Italic* (*Kleine Text Curcyf No. 2*) – 'perhaps the finest of all surviving italics', according to Stanley Morison. In 1928 Van Krimpen designed a new roman as a companion to this italic. The type was named Romanée, after the fine wine (a Bourgogne) which was served at a meal held in an English country inn to celebrate the completion of the typeface.

Romanée was based on the proportions of the lost typeface shown in the 1768 specimen as *Kleine Text Romein No. 2*, and as a consequence is slightly darker than Van Krimpen's other romans. But it was by no means a revival. Instead of reproducing printed samples, Van Krimpen drew it afresh; under Rädisch's sharp burin it became a clean-cut modern-looking roman. As Van Krimpen wrote in 1957, it lacked the 'carelessness' of the seventeenth-century faces, and precisely for this reason was a failure as a companion to the original Van Dijck italic.[60] Ultimately, Van Krimpen agreed with Morison's verdict in *The Fleuron*: 'The two are not mated'. Twenty years

ROMANÉE

ROMEIN & CURSIEF

KLEINKAPITALEN

SIERKAPITALEN

LETTERGIETERIJ
JOH. ENSCHEDÉ EN ZONEN
HAARLEM / HOLLAND

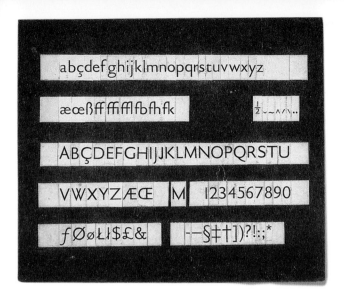

◄ Soot proof of the unpublished
Romulus sanserif, late 1930s.

▲ Romulus roman and its unusual
italic (or sloped roman), 1937.

▼ Romulus specimen, c. 1962.
Design by Sem Hartz,
typography by Bram de Does.

later he designed an upright italic for Romanée. It is a very original and personal design, and rather conspicuous next to the roman, but once one gets used to the combination the two work well together and the overall effect is of harmony, elegance and legibility.

Meanwhile, Monotype made plans to revive the Kleine Text Romein No. 2. Van Krimpen was called in as a consultant and, although he was no fan of revivals, complied – perhaps as a service to Morison, or because he was, as Tracy wrote, 'in no position to oppose the plan'. He had come to doubt whether the typeface Monotype wanted to use as a model was indeed the work of Van Dijck. After further study he proposed to use a different original: the typeface of Vondel's translation of Ovid, printed in Amsterdam in 1671. Helped by a small number of punches cut by Rädisch, production was completed by Monotype. Van Krimpen appeared to be happy with the results, which in a letter to Monotype he called 'very satisfactory indeed'. But writing about his typefaces in 1957 he stressed that his role in the creation of *Monotype Van Dijck* had been chiefly advisory, calling the typeface 'a doctored adaptation of a seventeenth-century Dutch face'.[61]

The Romulus project

The next typeface was a joint venture between Monotype – represented by Stanley Morison – and Enschedé. Van Krimpen wanted to name it Epiphania, but Monotype's publicist Beatrice Warde came up with a more down-to-earth name: *Romulus*. As she said, 'If he was not a good Roman: who was?'[62] Maybe the name was also a little ominous. Brought up by a she-wolf, Romulus and Remus, the founders of Rome, did not grow old in harmony: Remus was killed by his twin brother.

The Romulus project was an ambitious experiment which, had it succeeded, would have resulted in one of the most complete typeface families to date. The series was to consist of a roman and an italic, a semi-bold and semi-bold condensed, a Greek typeface, and four weights of a matching sanserif. While today the concept of a family consisting of a serif type with its sanserif companion is common practice, it was a revolutionary idea at the time. Van Krimpen designed all nine varieties and added a tenth, *Cancellaresca Bastarda*; Rädisch cut punches for at least one weight of each font. Yet the project was not completed as planned and several faces were never published. The Romulus series turned out a somewhat dysfunctional family.

The Romulus roman is vintage Van Krimpen – a continuation of the principles underlying Lutetia and Romanée, but in a more rational, cooler mood. The italic, on the other hand, is a famous example of how an interesting theory can lead to a dubious decision. In 1926 Stanley Morison had published an article entitled 'Towards an Ideal Italic' (*The Fleuron* 5) in which he argued that the best companion to a roman type is not the conventional calligraphic italic, which stands out too much, but a sloped version of the roman that follows its design as closely as possible. The per-

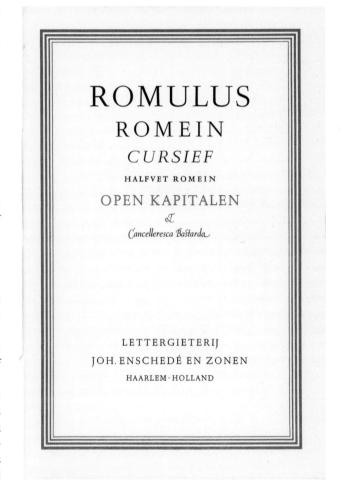

58 Van Krimpen, *Over het ontwerpen en bedenken van drukletters*, Amsterdam 1990, pp 155–163.

59 *Letters of Credit* (cit.), p 106.

60 *On Designing and Devising Type* (cit.), p 41.

61 Ibid., pp 42–44.

62 Ibid., p 52.

CANCELLERESCA BASTARDA

CORPS 20 No 6918   MINIMUM 5,25 KG

TYPOGRAPHY MAY BE DEFINED AS THE ART OF rightly disposing printing material in accordance with specific purpose; of so arranging the letters, distributing the space and controlling the type as to aid to the maximum the reader's comprehension of the text. Typography is the efficient means to an essentially utilitarian and only accidentally aesthetic end, for enjoyment of patterns is rarely the reader's chief aim. Therefore

A B C D E F G H I J K L M N O P Q R S T U V W X Y Z
Æ Œ À Ä Å Ç É È Ê Ë Ñ Ö Ø Ü
A B D H J K L M N P Q R V W Z
a b c d e f f g h b i j k l m n o p q r s t u v w x y y z ÿ
æ œ á à â ä å ç é è ê ë í ì î ï ñ ó ò ô ö ø ú ù û ü
fb ff ffi ffl fh fi fk fl ß ct ct st st gg gj gy ll tt $ £ & ct
1 2 3 4 5 6 7 8 9 0 . , '' „ " : ; ! ? -])

Romulus Greek: a Greek typeface designed to resemble a roman as closely as possible.

ΓΔΘΛΞΠΣ
ΦΨΩΔΖΣ
ΦΩΞϕϕΨ

fect italic, according to Morison, was a slanted roman. Van Krimpen was impressed by his friend's arguments and designed the Romulus italic according to these principles. A few years later both men had to admit they had been wrong: the sloped roman did not work very well. Van Krimpen had in fact been, as the Dutch say, more Catholic than the Pope; for when Morison designed his *Times New Roman* in 1931–32 he did not apply his own dogma and made a rather Didot-like italic.

From the onset Van Krimpen and Morison had planned a tertiary font: a script type, possibly based on the Italian chancery italic. In a letter Morison proposed 'the creation of a script whose nature shall partake of cursive and formal qualities – in a word, your new script type will have to be a *cancellaresca bastarda.*' [63] Van Krimpen was delighted with this programme and worked it out admirably: *Cancellaresca Bastarda* became one of his most outstanding designs. It was a very complex typeface, too. Van Krimpen felt that he could not make a natural-looking script on the same body as the corresponding roman; he developed a scheme to cast the fonts on larger bodies, using extra leading to align the script with the roman when used in the same setting. Thus the 16 and 20 point Cancellaresca align with leaded settings of 12 and 16 point Romulus. Another remarkable feature of Cancellaresca Bastarda is the huge number of alternate characters: more than a hundred swash characters and ligatures were added to the alphabet.

Problematic family members

Opinions differ on whether Romulus Greek is a good typeface. John Dreyfus, writing under Van Krimpen's scrutiny, called it 'most pleasing'. The bibliographer Philip Gaskell, who judged the earlier Antigone to be 'a poor thing', found Romulus Greek 'far worse': 'it contains half a dozen characters so unsightly as to catch the eye wherever they appear.'[64] Van Krimpen's aim was to keep the differences between the Latin and Greek alphabets to a minimum, giving some shapes that are usually calligraphic a more 'roman' look. As Gerrit Noordzij summed up in his critique of the Romulus project, 'he underestimated the cursive character of the Greek minuscule'. The semi-bold and its condensed version are not totally successful either. When drawing the semi-bold Van Krimpen carefully calculated the widening needed to give the same openness to a bolder weight, but this resulted in a face that looks too wide and (as Walter Tracy wrote) 'sprawls in a most ungainly way'.[65] The condensed semi-bold is a much more plausible variety; it is very readable and was used by an English publisher to set a prayer book.

The most fascinating aspect of the Romulus project is the sanserif, which was designed and cut in four weights. Van Krimpen has written that he regretted the fact that these designs were cut manually, not mechanically – for in the case of a sanserif he advocated the neutralizing effect of the engraving machine. The main reason why it was never completed was apparently Morison's growing dislike of sanserifs in general. As it is, the typeface must be judged by the 12 point test fonts cut by Rädisch, with which proofs were made at Enschedé. (> p 58) It is mainly the proportions between the capitals and the lowercase, as well as the relationship between form and counterform in the bolder weights which would have needed important adjustments. Gerrit Noordzij has argued that the Romulus Sans could never have succeeded because Van Krimpen did not understand the nature of the sanserif. Only if Van Krimpen had realized that the essence of the sanserif is a diminished contrast between thick and thin, Noordzij wrote, would it have been possible for him to design a good bold weight by extrapolation.[66]

Haarlemmer and Spectrum

Haarlemmer was commissioned in 1938 as a custom-made type for a Bible edition to be published by the bibliophiles' association Nederlandse Vereeniging voor Druk- en Boekkunst. The budget was very limited, and it was therefore decided that the type should be made to work with an existing Monotype keybar layout – which essentially meant that the widths of the characters were fixed. This constraint proved too much for Van Krimpen, who came to regard Haarlemmer as a total failure and possibly directed John Dreyfus towards his harsh judgement of it in *The Work of Jan van Krimpen*. 'The roman was far too dazzling, and the italic a good deal too wide.'[67] Some thirty years later Walter Tracy wrote that 'the design had more promise than John Dreyfus's account of it suggests', adding that a number of minor changes would have set things straight. Be that as it may, the Bible project was interrupted by the Second World War and the Haarlemmer typeface was abandoned. Monotype did, however, produce at least one preliminary weight of the font, and it certainly was not a total failure. A 1996 booklet printed with the provisional typeface, acquired by the bibliophiles' association which originally commissioned it,[68] shows that although it has flaws in contrast and adjustment it is potentially harmonious and certainly original. It also shows that Van Krimpen's next text face, *Spectrum*, was to a large extent a continuation of Haarlemmer.

Spectrum was designed in 1941 – 43, initially as a Bible typeface for the Utrecht publishing house Het Spectrum. The idea may have been suggested by their typographic adviser, Charles Nypels, who also supervised the development of Haarlemmer for the Vereeniging voor Druk- en Boekkunst. The typeface was intended for use on Monotype machines; Monotype would be asked to produce a larger series for use in Het Spectrum's wide range of publications. When communications with England were resumed after the war (during which Monotype had mainly been active as a weapons manufacturer) the firm was unwilling to spend so much energy on a series for a single client. Het Spectrum was persuaded to relinquish its rights to the type

abcdefghhijklmnopqrſttuvwxyyÿze&æœ̨1234567890.,;!?s
ABCDEFGHIJ KLMNOPQRSTUVWXYZ
ÆŒ&&

do you
want to
learn
dutch?

Yes, of course you do.
Perhaps you want to go to
Holland next holidays.
Than it's fine to speak
and understand dutch
like a native.
That's not impossible.
With the Crown-Method
you read already a novel
within four months.
Just send us your name and
address on a postal card.
In return, we will send you
the first lesson at no
obligation to you.
Write that card today!
CROWN-METHOD
785 LOW SQUARE
DETROIT 21
MICHIGAN

63 John Dreyfus, *The Work of Jan van Krimpen* (cit.), p 39.

64 *Adieu Aesthetica & Mooie Pagina's!* (cit.), p 45.

65 *Letters of Credit* (cit.), p 111.

66 Gerrit Noordzij, *De actualiteit van het Romulus projekt*, self-published brochure, 1992.

67 *The Work of Jan van Krimpen* (cit.), p 35.

68 The Haarlemmer matrices were probably scrapped, but c. 1990 Monotype declared they were prepared to manufacture new matrices. Jan Keijser, the chairman of the Vereniging voor Druk- en Boekkunst, bought a set of Haarlemmer matrices for his Avalon Press. The publication referred to is J.M.A. Biesheuvel, *Angst*, Nederlandse Vereniging voor Druk- en Boekkunst, 1996.

▶ Of all of Jan van Krimpen's typefaces, only Spectrum was adapted for photo-typesetting, and
then for digital technology.
The showing is from a 1958
Enschedé specimen designed by
Will Carter and Jan van Krimpen.

▾ The forthcoming digital version
of Van Krimpen's Bible face,
Sheldon.

design to Enschedé, and in 1950 it was decided that the Spectrum typeface would be
completed under its original name as a joint venture of Enschedé and the Monotype
Company. Spectrum is different from Van Krimpen's other romans. It is stronger in
contrast, though not as strong as Haarlemmer; it has a larger x-height, and its serifs
are more prominently wedge-shaped.

Walter Tracy called Spectrum 'the most practical of Van Krimpen's book types'. It has
in fact become the only Van Krimpen typeface which continued to enjoy popularity
among publishers and designers. It survived the changing technologies, was made
avaible for phototypesetting and was part of the first generation of digital PostScript
fonts. This also had its drawbacks. Like Bembo, Van Dijck and other Monotype originals, it was reproduced without acknowledging the impact of the new technology
on the sharpness of the letterform – resulting in an image which is too meagre
when used in sizes smaller than, say, 12 point.

Typefaces with a purpose

Sheldon was the third type commissioned from Van Krimpen for a Bible project, and
the first one to be actually used for that purpose. It was designed in 1947 for the
Oxford University Press for use at 7 point only. In Van Krimpen's day it was common
practice, when creating metal type for setting small-size Bibles, to fit an existing
design on a smaller body by drastically reducing the descenders of g, j, p, q and y,
thus creating space-saving type without having to change the ascenders or the capitals. Van Krimpen's solution was different: he started afresh, drawing a lowercase
alphabet with a generous x-height, placed more or less centrally on the body with
short yet well-developed ascenders and descenders and low capitals.

Between 1944 and 1958 Van Krimpen was a member of a committee which was to
propose a series of standard alphabets for use in street signs, signage, nameplates
and other public lettering. The committee, to which G.W. Ovink and Sem Hartz also
belonged, was initially created to formulate alternatives to the DIN alphabets imposed by the German occupying forces. After the war the group went on to develop
two typefaces which were presented as NEN 3225; namely a sanserif which owes much
to the *Johnston Underground* alphabet and *Gill Sans*, and a roman typeface which clearly bears the signature of Van Krimpen. This NEN 3225 Romein has all the qualities of
a regular book face, and is similar in shape and colour to Haarlemmer and Spectrum.
It is in every aspect an unlikely signage alphabet, boasting fineries such as fh, fb, tk
and ffl ligatures, an ampersand and a long-tailed Q. Not surprisingly, its use remained very limited. The sanserif, on the other hand, was more widely adopted and
found its way to the street signs of a number of cities, including Amsterdam (> p 296).
There were several more projects during the post-war era for which Van Krimpen
designed new alphabets. Among them was at least one alphabet meant for advertising and packaging – a realm new to Van Krimpen. The client was Amstel Beer – now
a subsidiary of Heineken, then its main competitor. Van Krimpen drew the name of
the product, which was then incorporated in a white-and-red circle to form the
beer's logo. He also designed an alphabet 'consisting of capitals of a somewhat different structure than those with which the word Amstelbieren is formed'.[69] In the
subsequent decades, the alphabet – a typical Van Krimpen roman – was implemented by other designers in packaging, advertising, glasses, enamel signs and much
more; it was gradually modified, losing its unique literary feel and becoming more
like a regular display type.

THE COMPLETE ROMAN ALPHABET

ABCDEFGHIJKLMNOPQRSTUVWXYZ
ÆŒ&
abcdefghijklmnopqrstuvwxyzæœfiflffifflff
1234567890   .,:;-!?''(*†‡§[£$ƒ—
1234567890 (F990)   /(S121)   % (S8416)
ÁÀÄÂÅÃÉÈËÊÍÌÏÎÓÒÖÔØÕÚÙÜÛÇÑ
áàäâåãéèëêíìïîóòöôøõúùüûçñ
ß ij fbfhfkfj

THE COMPLETE ITALIC ALPHABET

ABCDEFGHIJKLMNOPQRSTUVWXYZ
ÆŒ&
abcdefghijklmnopqrstuvwxyzæœfiflffifflff
1234567890   .,:;!?''([§   1234567890 (F991)
ÁÀÄÂÅÃÉÈËÊÍÌÏÎÓÒÖÔØÕÚÙÜÛÇÑ
áàäâåãéèëêíìïîóòöôøõúùüûçñ   ß ij fbfhfkfj

DTL Sheldon
Regular *Italic*

Although Van Krimpen was not a letter-carver, he did design several signs and gravestones which were executed by craftsmen. His largest assignment in this field was the lettering of the National Monument on the Dam square in Amsterdam, designed by J.J.P. Oud to pay homage to the victims of the Second World War. Oud's curved wall was covered with three text fragments – almost a thousand letters which were cut in the travertine stone by J.M. Veldheer, a Haarlem stonemason with whom Van Krimpen had worked before. The timing was irresponsibly short, and there were some technical mishaps, but when the monument was inaugurated in 1956 it met with general approval. Van Krimpen was disappointed; he wrote to the architect saying that he found the result ugly.

Van Krimpen's typefaces now

Walter Tracy admired the originality and refinement of Van Krimpen's type designs, but the final verdict in *Letters of Credit* is rather harsh. 'None of [his typefaces] has achieved full admittance to that select list of types that are known to be effective in the practicalities of everyday printing. The reason is this. Each of the types, when closely examined, has a feature – amounting, in my opinion, to a defect – which has diminished its chance of unqualified welcome into the printer's typographic resources.' As to the cause of these defects, Tracy writes that Van Krimpen 'was not ruled by the designer's sense of "fitness for purpose" when he was designing a type'. He 'thought like an artist, not like a designer'.[70]

One might wonder whether it would be legitimate to amend the 'defects' Tracy refers to – small numerals in one case, too narrow an italic in another – in a critical revival of Van Krimpen's designs. Following Van Krimpen's own logic, a revival would be out of the question; it would be a better idea to design new typefaces in the same vein, as Gerrit Noordzij has done with his (as yet unpublished) *Remer*. On the other hand, Van Krimpen is much closer to us than, say, Van Dijck was to him; so an 'improved' digital version may be seen as a continuation of the typeface rather than its revival – a well-deserved second chance for some great designs with obvious flaws which can now be amended more easily than four or five decades ago. Recently the two main Dutch independent type foundries, The Enschedé Font Foundry (TEFF) and Dutch Type Library (DTL), have begun producing digital versions of three of Van Krimpen's romans.

The first was DTL *Haarlemmer*, produced by Frank E. Blokland after Van Krimpen's original drawings and published in 1995. Van Blokland's initiative raised some eyebrows among his peers in the Netherlands, because the typeface is known to have been regarded as a failure. In a special issue of *The Monotype Recorder* that DTL produced in 1996, Blokland recapitulates the two best-known opinions: the negative verdict in Dreyfus's book, probably prompted by Van Krimpen's own disillusionment, and the more positive view of Walter Tracy, quoted above. Blokland argues that producing – one can hardly speak of 'reviving' – the typeface on the basis of the drawings, without the constraints of the unit system, was in fact a very legitimate thing to do. He also analyzes Haarlemmer as being 'in essence ... the prototype of Spectrum'.[71] For DTL *Haarlemmer*, Blokland explains, he interpreted Van Krimpen's drawings in much the same way that Rädisch, his punchcutter, interpreted them in his punches. The scanned drawings were converted to outlines, then 'given a face-lift'. In the roman 'weight and contrast, form and adjustment were considerably improved.' DTL's rather drastic reworking has resulted in a very well-made typeface: pleasant to read, even in colour and still recognizable as Van Krimpen's. The roman, however, seems to be closer to what the digital Spectrum should have been than to what the metal Haarlemmer ever was.

In 1996 Van Blokland designed a sanserif companion as a corporate face for the Boijmans Van Beuningen Museum. *Haarlemmer Sans* translates the proportions of the seriffed roman into a readable, contemporary humanist sanserif.

Thanks to Blokland's extensive collaboration with Monotype, as well as his close contacts with Huib van Krimpen (the son and heir, who died in 2002), DTL has been able to embark on a Van Krimpen project which will include the production of two more typeface families. Frank E. Blokland presented DTL *Romulus* – including the odd

In the early 1950s Van Krimpen designed a logo and an alphabet for Amstel Beer.

▾ Jan van Krimpen, numeral stamps for the Dutch PTT, published in 1946.

69 From a letter from Amstel to Van Krimpen, quoted in *Adieu Aesthetica & Mooie Pagina's!* (cit.), p 88.

70 *Letters of Credit* (cit.), pp 101 and 120.

71 Frank E. Blokland, 'Jan van Krimpen's Haarlemmer Type', in *The Monotype Recorder*, New Series, vol. 9, pp 29 – 32.

but characteristic sloped roman – during the DTL FontMaster Conference in November 2003. Sheldon, the large x-height bible face, is being produced at the moment of this writing.

While Monotype held the copyrights to its versions of Lutetia, Romulus and Sheldon, and the Haarlemmer copyrights reverted back to the Van Krimpen estate, the rights to Romanée lay solely with the Enschedé Type Foundry and passed on to its new incarnation, The Enschedé Font Foundry, founded by Peter Matthias Noordzij. Design of the PostScript version of the much-loved Romanée began in 1995, when Noordzij and Fred Smeijers digitized it for inclusion in the TEFF library. An early version of it was used for a book about Van Krimpen – *Adieu Aesthetica & Mooie Pagina's!* – designed by Martin Majoor and published that same year. Production of the full family has slowed down since, but is being continued by the TEFF studio. A release date has not yet been announced.

Other original Enschedé types

The year 1925, when Jan van Krimpen was hired by Enschedé to supervise the production of his *Lutetia*, was the beginning of a new era for the Enschedé Type Foundry. Before Lutetia, no original book faces had been issued since 1761. In the first decades of the twentieth century, Enschedé acquired several German and French typefaces which they often published under a new name: *Römische Antiqua* (Gensch & Heyse, 1888) became *Bradfort*; *Helga* (F.W. Kleukens for Stempel, 1912) became *Olga*. Huib van Krimpen wrote: 'There are many more designs, undistinguished and unnamed, in the foundry specimen book of 1932. If the matrix numbers are any indication, all of them were obtained in the early 1920s.'[72]

With Lutetia, Enschedé embraced the modern-classic Van Krimpen aesthetic, which would bring the Type Foundry and the printing office fame and fortune in the years to come. At the same time, however, the firm worried about the success of the Amsterdam Type Foundry's Hollandse Mediaeval, followed by Erasmus in 1923, and felt it had to compete. In December 1925, only months after Lutetia's appearance as a ravishing debutante, Enschedé presented a somewhat clumsy text face called Nassau. Its original name was Grotius; but as this name had already been claimed by the competition for De Roos's bold version of Erasmus, the type was renamed at the last minute. Designed by D. Scholten, a draughtsman at the company from around 1910 until his premature death in early 1940, Nassau lacks the qualities of both De Roos's and Van Krimpen's work. It mimics certain traits of Hollandse Mediaeval, notably those that had been dictated by the Amsterdam Type Foundry's Intertype system and the standard line: the f without overhang, the short-tailed g, the wide italics; there were no technical reasons for these expedients at Enschedé, but they do make Nassau look like a less gifted cousin of Hollandse Mediaeval.

The Enschedé Museum possesses a second typeface which, according to the files, was made by Scholten. It is a set of 36 point sanserif outline capitals in Art Deco style, which were probably meant to be used as initials. The alphabet exists as a set of matrices; no proofs could be found and there is no evidence that the font was ever released.

Another member of the Enschedé drawing office was André van der Vossen (born 1893). Van der Vossen's preferred medium was woodcut. The documents he created for the Dutch PTT, from charters to greeting cards and postage stamps, are powerful combinations of illustration, ornament and lettering. His *Houtsneeletter* (woodcut type) which Enschedé issued in 1927, was based on his informal lettering. The alphabet was produced in two sizes only – 12 and 18 point – and, as Huib van Krimpen wrote, 'the type's usefulness is, of course, extremely limited.'[73] Yet the *Houtsneeletter* is a rare and convincing rendering in metal type of Expressionist woodcut lettering; its legibility, despite its quirkiness, still stands out. It remained in production as foundry type until the 1970s.

DOOR HET OPHEFFEN VAN HET GILDEWE-zen moesten op den duur ongeschoolde krachten de werkplaatsen binnengaan: door het langzaam maar toch gaandeweg overheerschen van 't machine-wezen, moest langzaam aan de oude sleur wijken en moesten door de steeds aanzwellende behoefte aan drukwerk, de drukkerijen zich omzetten in industrieele ondernemingen. 1234567890

DOOR HET OPHEFFEN VAN HET GILDE-wezen moesten op den duur ongeschoolde krachten de werkplaatsen binnengaan: door het langzaam maar toch gaandeweg overheerschen van het machine-wezen, moest langzaam aan de oude sleur wijken en moesten door de steeds aanzwellende behoefte aan drukwerk, de drukkerijen zich omzetten in industrieele ondernemingen. 1234567890

^ Nassau (1925), designed by D. Scholten, was probably produced to compete with Sjoerd de Roos's Hollandse Mediaeval.

> D. Scholten also designed an alphabet of outline initials that was never produced as a typeface. *Enschedé Museum.*

v André van der Vossen, Season's greetings for the year 1927 of the Dutch PTT. Set in his Houtsneeletter (black print), combined with woodcut.

72 Huib van Krimpen, 'Type design in the Netherlands and the Influence of the Enschedé Foundry', in *Fine Print*, vol. 15, no. 4, 1989.

73 Ibid.

Manifestations of the new

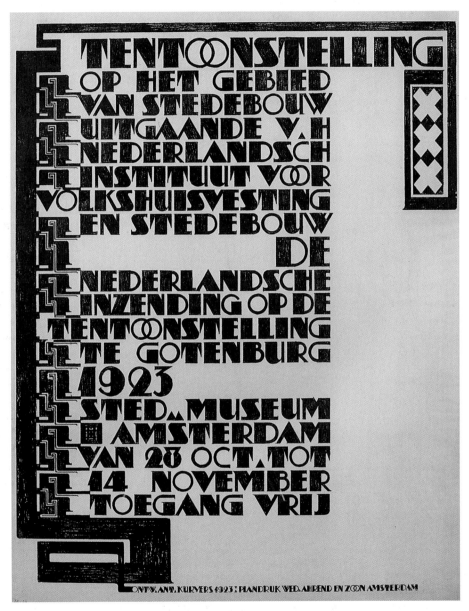

Anton Kurvers, poster for an architectural exhibition at the Amsterdam Stedelijk Museum, organized by the Dutch Institute for Public Housing and Urban Development, 1923.

Exploring the new

It would be convenient – and it has been tried – to describe Dutch graphic design between the World Wars as a bipolar development. This would result in a clear-cut dichotomy: the bookish approach of 'new traditionalists' like De Roos and Van Krimpen on the one hand versus modernist radicalism, represented by *De Stijl* and Dutch Constructivism, on the other.[1] However, at the time when these two groups were developing their contrasting views, there was a third current which is much harder to pinpoint. Various names have been proposed for this tendency, but Art Deco – a term which was not coined until the late 1960s[2] – seems to be the most persistent and comprehensive. I will use it here for want of a better word, describing a widely diverse body of work by dozens of artists. Art Deco is not completely separated from the modernist avant-garde: the lines are blurred and there have been mutual influences. Modernist experiments – e.g. those involving geometric shapes – were preceded and/or followed by more decorative exercises in a similar direction.

The last part of this chapter deals with the avant-garde, from De Stijl to Constructivist Typo-photo, and these movements' view of type. First I will focus on the architects and designers which I have tentatively labelled Art Deco, some of whom developed a consistent body of rather extravagant letterforms. None of them made printing types – let alone book faces – although some alphabets have posthumously been issued as digital display typefaces.

The typographic output of these artists has often been treated as a marginal phenomenon; an anomaly or an extravagance. Yet during the 1920s and '30s, Art Deco was not marginal: it was the mainstream. This becomes all the more evident when taking into account the run of printed works. More often than not, the products of both traditionalist typographers and modernists were either limited editions or specialized publications intended for a small group of subscribers or clients. In large-circulation books and periodicals, as well as posters and advertising, the preferred style was almost invariably some sort of Art Deco, or a watered-down hybrid derived from it.

Although it has remained a hazy concept, Art Deco might be interpreted as a continuation of Art Nouveau (and its local manifestations, called Jugendstil, Modernismo or Sezession). If Art Nouveau had had two distinct manifestations – the lush, curvilinear style of Brussels, Paris and Barcelona versus the more rational, geometric constructions of Vienna, Glasgow and Amsterdam – Art Deco took elements from both but gravitated towards the relative simplicity of the latter. It also incorporated design elements from exotic and ancient cultures such as Mayan, Egyptian and Indonesian art. Letterforms often hesitated between the geometry proposed by the international avant-garde, and the joyous seductiveness of commercial lettering. Art Deco was not a movement; it was a style, or a mixture of styles, even a fashion. Much like today's (or yesterday's) postmodernism, it was a combination of high art and street art, of individual play with form and mass production.

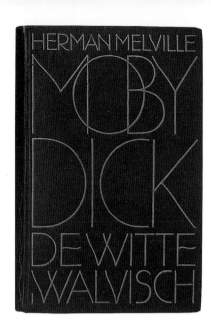

◁ Jan de Bruijn, cover for a boy scouts manual, 1924.

▷ J.B. Heukelom, book cover (1929). Heukelom was a designer and woodcutter as well as an influential teacher at the Amsterdam Quellinus School.

▽ Titus Leeser, book cover, 1929. Leeser was best know for his illustrations and cover designs for children's books.

Considerable research on Art Deco letterforms still waits to be done.[3] Some of the best lettering has been designed by commercial artists who, precisely because they were commercial, have largely been overlooked by design historians. It would be an interesting exercise to map the lettering from the 1920s and '30s and compose a typology of letterforms; but that would be the subject of a different book. I have chosen to present a limited number of designers who have each created a consistent body of work and who, had they had today's technology at their disposal, might have joined the ranks of type designers.

◁ P.A.H. Hofman designed book jackets and posters (as well as stained-glass windows) in a wide range of decorative styles. His lettering for Simon Vestdijk's novel *Narcissus op vrijersvoeten* (1938, facsimile 1987) is among his most experimental works.

▷ The designer and writer Piet Marée was unashamedly populist, and is widely known for his do-it-yourself books and books on modern transport. Although his work is beautifully made and at times quite interesting, he was never taken seriously by design criticism. Detail from a book cover, c. 1935.

1 'Modernism' has become the generic term used, especially in English-language literature, to designate the international avant-garde of 1915–1935 as well as its continuation and institutionalization in post-war functionalism (aka 'Swiss Style' or 'International Style'). At the time, artists and authors preferred other notions, from Mondriaan's 'New Imaging' (*Nieuwe Beelding*) to Van Doesburg's rather bombastic 'those who carry the quadrate'.

2 The term became widely accepted after the publication of Bevis Hillier's *Art Deco of the Twenties and Thirties* in 1968. In the Netherlands, Hans Oldewarris subtitled his 2003 exhibition of Wijdeveld's typographic work 'Art Deco design on paper'.

3 Dutch architectural lettering from the Art Deco period is discussed in Kees Broos, *Architekst*, Eindhoven 1989.

Wendingen and Art Deco

In the Netherlands, the most extreme form of Art Deco typography was known as *Wendingen style* or *rule tendency* (lijnenrichting), a graphic style which was firmly rooted in the architecture of the Amsterdam School. The person who took the ideas and aesthetics of this group to the printed page was Hendrik Th. Wijdeveld (1885–1988), the founding editor of the magazine *Wendingen*.[4]

Wijdeveld's view of typography and letterforms has often been identified with one expedient which was particularly scorned by traditionalists and modernists alike: his tendency to construct type and ornament with compositors' brass rule, the way an architect would use bricks to make a relief on a wall. This was, however, only one of many techniques Wijdeveld used. Throughout his career – spanning more than seven decades – he adopted a wide range of styles and techniques, often meticulously drawing letters by hand.

Hendrik Wijdeveld's typographic inventions were greatly inspired by the work of J.L.M. Lauweriks. The linear typography that Lauweriks produced in 1905–1920 is of special interest here. Having developed a system-based design method with the architect K.P.C. de Bazel in the 1890s (> p 36), Lauweriks took these ideas to a new level of experimentation in the design of the magazine *Ring*, which he published in Düsseldorf (Germany) in 1908–1909. On the front page, the magazine's title was constructed with what looks like machine-typed uppercase O's, or rings. In the interior, sanserif type was combined with stern, rigid ornamentation made with typesetters' rule. Lauweriks later used type and ornamentation constructed by the same method in invitation cards, school certificates and other printed matter designed both during his German period and after his return to Amsterdam in 1916.

While in the neighbouring countries the Great War was raging, cultural life went on more or less as usual in the neutral Netherlands. In 1916 the Amsterdam society Architectura et Amicitia began making plans to publish a new magazine. The members of the organization, which included not only architects but also artists, artisans and civil servants, had decided that Holland needed a magazine which discussed

◄ G.J. Langhout & J.F. Staal, Facade of the Telegraaf building, Amsterdam (1928–1930): a concrete version of Wijdeveld's 'rule typography'.

◄ J.L.M. Lauweriks, folder for the Quellinus School. (c. 1918).

◄ One of Lauweriks's earliest experiments with constructed type. (1913).

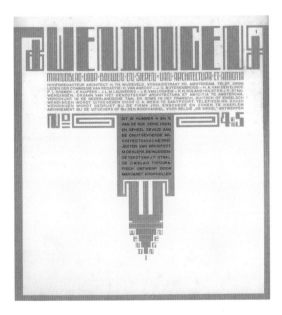

architecture in connection with the other arts. Although Lauweriks took part in the preparatory meetings, he could not be persuaded to be involved in the magazine itself. It was the flamboyant Wijdeveld who became 'the soul of the project'[4]. He came up with a name – *Wendingen* meaning 'turns' or 'changes' – and became the new review's editor-in-chief and 'art director' (a term which had yet to be coined). Unlike *De Stijl*, publication of which began almost simultaneously, *Wendingen* did not publish manifestos or polemics; its theme issues were richly illustrated presentations of a wide variety of subjects, including not only architecture and design but also painting, sculpture, theatre, masks, advertising, and natural phenomena such as crystals and shells.

Designed ten years after Lauweriks's *Ring*, *Wendingen* took over both its typographic principles and its oriental looks (notably visible in the Japanese binding technique). Titles as well as ornamentation were constructed with brass rule; as in *Ring*, the text typeface was a wide nineteenth-century Grotesque (*Brede Antieke*). Wijdeveld made no secret of this influence: *Ring* was repeatedly mentioned as a source of inspiration, and Lauweriks was invited to design the cover of the first issue of *Wendingen*.

Although the design of the *Wendingen* interior was flexible enough to allow for slight variations, it remained greatly unchanged during the thirteen years of the magazine's existence. The opposite is true of the cover designs. Each *Wendingen* cover was a work of art in its own right, reproduced with graphic techniques such as lithograph and woodcut. Although the designers did not receive a fee, the country's best known artists, designers and architects were happy to contribute; *Wendingen* came to be regarded as a prestigious showcase. The magazine was a platform for a young generation of architects, several of whom conceived cover designs in the typical '*Wendingen* style', making elaborate constructions of angular type and ornaments, either drawn with a ruler or composed with compositors' material. Among those who most faithfully represented this style were the architects Margaret Kropholler, J.F. Staal, W.M. Dudok, and Wijdeveld himself. Other designs, however, were much more exuberant, ranging from the painterly work of Jan Sluyters to the mystic black and white lithographs of Roland Holst and Toorop. The bulk of the *Wendingen* covers is somewhere in between, often combining hand-drawn lettering with simple ornamentation or illustration. Among the artists contributing covers in this manner are Samuel Jesserun de Mesquita, Willem Hendrik Gispen, Anton Kurvers and Tine Baanders. Finally, there have been only two cover designs which directly referred to the international modernist movement: a 1929 design by Vilmos Huszár (who also drew the first logo of the magazine *De Stijl*) and the most famous of all, the 1921 cover of a Frank Lloyd Wright issue by the Russian constructivist El Lissitzky.

Many *Wendingen* covers were designed by architects who were part of, or showed an affinity to, the Amsterdam School. W.M. Dudok designed the cover of this 1924 special issue about his masterpiece, the City Hall in Hilversum, where he was director of Public Works. Influenced by Frank Lloyd Wright, Dudok later switched to thin monoline alphabets for the lettering of his corporate buildings.

^ H.Th. Wijdeveld developed his *Wendingen* typography using alphabets constructed with typesetter's brass rule – as shown in this 1924 title page.

▸ In his three-dimensional designs – shops, exhibitions stands and pavilions – H.Th. Wijdeveld used seductive letterforms that were a far cry from his rigid *Wendingen* type. Blue Band showroom, Amsterdam 1924.

4 Martijn F. le Coultre, *Wendingen 1918–1932*, Blaricum 2001, p 33; see also: Hans Oldewarris, *H.Th. Wijdeveld, Art Deco design on paper*, The Hague/ Rotterdam 2003.

Wijdeveld's books and posters

Wijdeveld's versatility and innovativeness as a typographic designer have often been overlooked. During his apprentice years at the office of the architect P.J.H. Cuypers, Wijdeveld had been influenced by Cuypers's neo-Gothic style, as is shown by his first lettering projects – two memorial stones for churches. His graphic designs in the years just preceding *Wendingen* are hand-lettered and decorated in an ornate Art Nouveau-like manner. In complete contrast with these decorative layouts he created a remarkable series of letterpress-printed theatre posters, arranging sanserif type and typesetting material in stern rectangles. In some designs of the *Wendingen* years, there is not a trace of angular letterforms or rules. The gorgeous booklets in the *Pauw Serie* (Peacock Series, c. 1919) have title pages on which the type has been replaced by elegant hand-drawn vignettes, placed almost on the edge of the page.

In 1925 Wijdeveld resigned as editor-in-chief of *Wendingen*, and two years later left the editorial board. He kept true to the *Wendingen* style in some – but not all – of his graphic work. For the Amsterdam Stedelijk Museum he designed a few posters in which he combined standard grotesque capitals with letterforms constructed from brass rule. In a 1931 poster for a Frank Lloyd Wright exhibition in the same museum, the constructed lettering was apparently replaced by specially cast type from the Enschedé firm in Haarlem, which sponsored the event by printing the poster free of charge. If this is true, it means that Wijdeveld is the only Dutch designer of this tendency whose letterforms were actually made into type – although probably not a complete alphabet.[5]

Der geesten gemoeting (*Encounter of the Spirits*) by J.W. Schotman (1927) is generally regarded as Wijdeveld's typographic masterpiece. The orientalism which also characterized *Wendingen* is very appropriate in this collection of texts on Chinese signs, and has resulted in a fine work of typographic art: angular constructed ornamentation and lettering, arranged asymmetrically and partly printed in gold; Japanese binding; and a splendid slipcase which is closed with two pieces of ivory.

Wijdeveld's post-1930 designs for print – his own books as well as his brochures for the artistic community he founded, Elckerlyck – are fine examples of lucid, modern typography, but entirely made with standard type. Only in the 1960s – aged about 80 – did Wijdeveld turn to lettering again. The editor and the art director of the underground magazine *Hitweek*, Willem de Ridder and Anthon Beeke respectively, persuaded Wijdeveld to draw a headline for one of their issues; Wijdeveld happily recreated a new variation on one of his most outrageous lettering styles of the 1920s. In the same period, he did a poster for an exhibition of his own work at the Stedelijk Museum that looks almost like a self-parody.

Among the most intriguing works in the extensive Wijdeveld collection of the Netherlands Architecture Institute (NAi) is a set of four sketches of unpublished

◄ Two of the four sheets in the Wijdeveld archive of the Netherlands Architecture Institute showing experimental alphabets. Although the sheets are not signed, the appearance of variations on Wijdeveld's monogram (a square within a circle) strongly suggests that the designs are his. Date unknown.

Hitweek, founded by Willem de Ridder and Peter J. Muller, was a magazine that broke all the rules – including those of 'functionalist' typography. In 1966 De Ridder and art director Anthon Beeke invited H.Th. Wijdeveld, aged 81, to design the headline of the New Year issue (30 December 1966) announcing the Dutch blues band Cuby & The Blizzards.

▼ Wendingen, a digital font by Christian Küsters, 1998.

alphabets. They are undated; judging by their style, they could be from around 1930, but since some of the test words appearing in the sketches refer to *Wendingen*, they might date back to the mid-1920s. A signature is also lacking, yet they are 'signed' with variations of Wijdeveld's monogram – the square within the circle – and therefore are very likely to be indeed his. The alphabets bear no resemblance to the *Wendingen* 'line lettering'; they are all stencil alphabets that may have been inspired by Josef Albers's 1926 Bauhaus alphabet or his 1931 *Kombinationsschrift*. Constructivist principles – notably the construction based on squares, quarter circles and triangles – have been adopted in a playful way, trying out alternate forms for each character. These letters precede Jurriaan Schrofer's investigations of minimal letterforms (> p 124) by three decades or so, but the results are similar.

Wijdeveld became the longest-living Dutch artist ever. He remained a keen self-promoter until the end, drawing up endless plans for a catalogue of his life's work which never materialized. When asked to contribute a cover illustration for the Wijdeveld issue of *Forum* edited in 1975 by Hans Oldewarris, he made impeccable separate drawings for each of the colours. When Wijdeveld was 102, a book about his work was published; it was entitled 'My First Century' (*Mijn eerste eeuw*).

In 1998, London-based designer Christian Küsters brought out a font called *Wendingen*, based on Wijdeveld's rule lettering, as part of his Acme Fonts library.

5 Le Coultre and Purvis, *A century of posters*, Blaricum 2002, p 44. Asked by the author, Le Coultre mentioned a conversation with an old typesetter at Enschedé as his source of information about the specially cast type.

◄ Chris Lebeau, poster for the
Willem Brok art gallery,
Hilversum. Lithograph made
from a woodcut, 1919.
*Collection S.S.K., Drents Museum,
Assen.*

▲ Chris Lebeau, alphabet
designed for embroidering,
1908.
*Collection S.S.K., Drents Museum,
Assen.*

Chris Lebeau, cover of
De Bedrijfsreklame, a trade journal
on advertising, January 1920.
The alphabet used is similar to
the one in the Amsterdamsche
insurance policy (opposite
page). The issue is entirely
devoted to the work of Lebeau.

The monumental letterforms of Chris Lebeau

During the forty-odd years of his professional activity, Chris Lebeau (1878–1945) worked as a textile and glass designer, stage and costume designer, illustrator, painter and graphic designer. What is most impressive about his versatile body of work is 'the unmatched perfection he managed to attain in each of these disciplines' – thus his biographer, Mechteld de Bois.[6] Although graphic design and typography were never his main occupation, Lebeau made numerous book jackets, posters and official documents, as well as commercial catalogues and packaging. Most of this work was hand-lettered, sometimes amounting to hundreds of meticulously drawn letters for one assignment.

Chris Lebeau trained at the Amsterdam Quellinusschool and the Rijksschool voor Kunstnijverheid (State School of Applied Arts), both of which were rooted in the 1890s aesthetic movement. Here, much attention was given to the design of ornaments on a geometric pattern – a system-based, rhythmic design method developed in about 1895 by the architects De Bazel and Lauweriks and soon accepted more widely. In 1898–1899 Lebeau frequented a weekly design course, set up by these two architects in collaboration with an organization called Vâhana Lodge. The contact with De Bazel left an indelible mark on Lebeau's work.[7]

Lebeau soon made a name for himself as a textile designer and specialist of 'batik', the Indonesian technique of painting textiles using greases. In 1900 he designed the binding of Louis Couperus's novel *De stille kracht*, one of the very few book bindings ever executed in batik. He became a supplier to Het Binnenhuis, the Amsterdam furniture shop linked to the Nieuwe Kunst movement, and to the linen manufacturer Van Dissel & Zonen. He designed his first printed matter for Van Dissel: a series of catalogues advertising his own textiles. From 1914 to 1917 Lebeau was the in-house designer of the country's most innovative theatre company, Eduard Verkade's Die Haghespelers, designing stage sets, posters and booklets in a wide array of modes – from lush decoration to sobre monumentality.

The lettering of Lebeau's early graphic designs owed much to Art Nouveau aesthetics. In the printed matter made for Van Dissel textiles he often used monoline capitals, sometimes adorned with small curls – the kind of letter that may have inspired Sjoerd de Roos's *Ella Cursief*. During the period with Verkade he began experimenting with outrageous forms, sacrificing legibility for theatrical effect, but sometimes reverted to simple, sculptural sanserifs.

Towards 1920 Lebeau's graphic work began to show strong influences of the Amsterdam School. Although he seldom practised the *Wendingen* technique of building letters with brass rules, his letters (invariably capitals) always have a strong architectural character. His favourite stylistic expedient was a heavy horizontal stress, produced by giving one of the strokes – usually the bottom horizontal – exaggerat-

Chris Lebeau, proposals for generic postage stamps (3 cents and 1 cent), submitted as part of a limited entry competition organized by the Dutch Post, Telephone and Telegraph Service (PTT), 1920.

Following the 1920 competition, which he did not win, Lebeau was invited to design an airmail stamp. This design, issued in 1921, was later adapted for general use in many values and remained in print for twenty years.

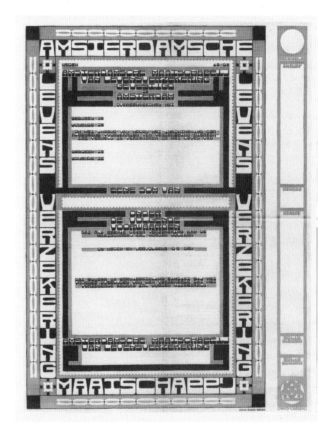

FB\BROK\ABC DEFGHIJKLMN OPQRSTUVWXYZ

◄ Elizabeth Holzman (Font Bureau) based her Brok font (1995) on the poster which Chris Lebeau designed in 1919 for the Brok gallery (opposite page).

▼ Chris Lebeau, insurance policy for the Amsterdamsche Maatschappij van Levensverzekering, c. 1920.

ed weight. With true constructional logic, the letterform was treated as a plastic shape that must rest firmly on its built-in plinth.

One of the earliest designs in which Lebeau made use of this typical style of lettering was a poster, made after a woodcut, for the opening of the Willem Brok art gallery in 1919. The powerful portrait of a bearded man looking through his fists is jammed in between two blocks of black, heavy type. All the texts, including the names of the two dozen artists represented by Brok, are hand-drawn in the same alphabet. The Brok poster has been repeatedly reproduced in books on Dutch design, and was noticed by type designer Elizabeth Holzman at the Font Bureau, Boston. She completed and digitized the alphabet in 1995 with sufficient respect and sensibility for the resulting font to be regarded as Lebeau's design. Font Bureau recommends the use of negative leading to 'reduce the white stripes that separate lines to the slender size of those that separate letters, bringing out the dark and blocky shapes.' [8]

During the 1920s Lebeau used similar alphabets for numerous design jobs. In some cases his medium was woodcut; other designs were engraved or lithographed. One of his most remarkable works is an insurance policy for the Amsterdamsche Maatschappij van Levensverzekering. Like most of Lebeau's graphic work, the design is filled to the brim. The front of the policy is painstakingly lettered, the small print on the back is printed in a sanserif metal typeface. The company's typists were given precise instructions to type the client's data symmetrically and centred in the blank spaces left between the equally symmetric printed text blocks. Perhaps the impracticality of this work was a kind of sweet revenge on Lebeau's part: at a preliminary meeting with the company's management he had voiced his objections against insurance, which he found to have a negative effect on people's sense of responsibility.[9]

Lebeau's predilection for decoration over functionality could lead to very impractical proposals indeed – as in a 1920 limited competition for postage stamps. His design for a generic 1-cent stamp was derided in a very personal attack by the critic H. Hana: 'The fact that you have continued to participate in the pathetic showing-off of modern half-wits, who try to distinguish themselves by mutilating our letterforms into silly, daft little shapes, is a symptom of the sickness of your artistic abilities.'[10] In spite of the criticism, Lebeau received an assignment for an airmail postage stamp the next year. His comparatively simple design featuring a stylized pigeon was later used for a large series of generic stamps which remained in use for twenty years. Apart from stamps, Lebeau made a number of designs for the Dutch PTT, including publicity material and a greeting telegram.

The letterforms used by Lebeau in the 1920s were not limited to the heavy, square forms discussed above. A poster designed for the Utrecht trade fair has a perfectly readable sanserif, as do some (but not all) of his *ex-libris*. The solemn mourning card

6 Mechteld de Bois, *Chris Lebeau 1878–1945*, Assen/Haarlem 1987, p 9.

7 For the Vâhana lodge and the mathematic principles of design, see Ernst Braches, *Het hoek als Nieuwe Kunst*, Utrecht 1973 (to be reprinted: Amsterdam 2003).

8 The Font Bureau, *Type Specimens Third Edition*, Boston 2001, p 203.

9 De Bois, *Chris Lebeau* (cit.), p 149.

10 De Bois, *Chris Lebeau* (cit.), p 151.

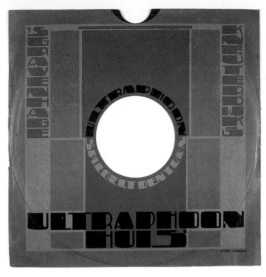

◀ Chris Lebeau, record sleeve for the Ultraphoonhuis record shop in The Hague, 1920s.

▶ Chris Lebeau, mourning card for K.P.C. de Bazel, 1923. Although Lebeau mastered many styles, he remained a faithful pupil – even an epigone – of De Bazel in his woodcuts throughout his career.

issued in 1923 at the death of his master, K.P.C. de Bazel, is lettered in a condensed monoline sanserif.

From the late 1920s onwards, Lebeau concentrated more and more on painting and drawing. After the Nazis occupied the Netherlands in 1940, he became a supplier to the resistance. He was a master forger, falsifying documents with such perfection that the Gestapo was unable to differentiate them from the real items. Lebeau was arrested in 1943 and was imprisoned after refusing to sign a declaration stating that he would refrain from illegal activities. He kept on working when in captivity, drawing numerous portraits and designing diplomas. In May 1944 he was transported to Dachau concentration camp, where his condition was worsened by his refusal to give up his strict vegetarianism. Chris Lebeau died of exhaustion in early April 1945, a month before the final collapse of the Nazi regime.

Amsterdam alphabets: Anton Kurvers and the Bridge type

Educated as an architect, Anton Kurvers (1889–1940) was closely connected to the Amsterdam School, but was never involved in the kind of large-scale town planning projects that Berlage, De Klerk or Kramer took on. Kurvers worked as a painter, decorator, designer and graphic artist and became deputy head of the Public Works office in Amsterdam.[11] He is best known for the postboxes and the postage stamp machine he designed for the Dutch PTT (commissioned by J.F. van Royen) and a postbox for the Amsterdam City Bank (Gemeentegiro). He was also a prolific designer of books and posters. In this printed work he explored a limited number of constructed letterforms, some of which were based on the hand-lettered captions in his architectural sketches. These alphabets are typical of the Amsterdam architectural school: part geometry, part decoration; defying typographic tradition; original and unorthodox, sometimes to the point of being illegible.

The most famous alphabet the Amsterdam School has produced is one whose maker has remained anonymous: the *Amsterdam Bridge Type* (*Brugletter*), made by or for the Public Works department. Amsterdam boasts around 600 bridges and sluices, most of which have a name. Somewhere around 1930 it was decided that all bridges with names were to have identical cast steel nameplates, attached to the railings on either side of each bridge. The steel alphabet of capitals designed for this purpose consists of typical engineers' or architects' letterforms (that is: with no typographic refinements) in a style related to certain letters on Amsterdam School buildings. The designer Piet Schreuders, who was asked in 1989 to supervise the letterspacing of bridge names made with newly cast Brugletters, researched the alphabet and hypothesized that it might have been drawn by the architects Kramer or Van der Mey.[12] I would say that Anton Kurvers is a more likely candidate. Not only did he

◀ Anton Kurvers, book cover (1921). Some of the letters used for this series of technical handbooks recall the Amsterdam Bridge Type (e.g. E, R and S in the lower block).

▼ Anton Kurvers's carefully constructed lettering of book covers and posters makes use of a limited number of alphabets. The letterforms on Schorteldoek's technical manual *Het uitvoeren van gebouwen* (Executing buildings, c. 1920) are similar to the lettering in Kurvers's architectural drawings.

work at the Public Works department, he also designed book covers using letters which have various traits in common with the Brugletter.

Around 1992 the bridge typeface was digitally revived by Amsterdam-based designer René Knip, working at Studio Anthon Beeke. In early 2003, Argentinian type designer Ramiro Espinoza released a rather literal adaptation of the bridge alphabet called *Mariabrug*.

Rotterdam designers: Jongert, De Koo and Gispen

Like Chris Lebeau, Jac. (Jacob) Jongert (1883–1942) was a child of the 1890s aesthetic movement: he was a student of R.N. Roland Holst, one of the outstanding poster and book designers of that generation, and later worked as Roland Holst's assistant. While Roland Holst's socialist ideals made him shy away from commercial work and concentrate on cultural and political assignments, Jongert managed to reconcile idealism with an interest in industry. In his writings he advocated sensible collaboration between artists and businessmen. One of Jongert's long-time clients was the Rotterdam coffee, tea and tobacco manufacturer Van Nelle, for which he created an ever-evolving corporate identity.

While Jongert's early work was made in a rather painterly style related to 1890s aesthetics, he soon evolved towards a more functionalist approach. He was enthusiastic about the ideas of the avant-garde; as head of the decorative arts department of the Rotterdam Art Academy he invited Piet Zwart, one of the movement's spokesmen, to become a teacher. Although Jongert himself never became a full-blooded avant-gardist, his later advertising and packaging designs for Van Nelle show influences of various modernist tendencies. His use of primary colours, strong contrasts and simple forms owes much to the constructivist idiom; occasionally he used photographs in a way that recalls 'Typo-photo' as practiced by Moholy-Nagy, Zwart, Schuitema and others.

Throughout this stylistic itinerary Jongert researched letterforms to match his shifting views of ornament and colour. A 1930 sourcebook by N.J. van de Vecht[13] shows three alphabets by Jongert. One, from 1914, is a set of somewhat mannered classical capitals. The other two are sanserif alphabets, a geometric uppercase and a lowercase, both from 1929. Drawn with ruler and compass, they have the quirkiness of Renner's earliest sketches for *Futura*. The lowercase is charming but impractical; Jongert does not seem to have pursued it any further. The uppercase is similar to the straightforward sanserif capitals with which he lettered most of the display material and packaging for Van Nelle in the late 1920s and early 1930s. Unlike Zwart and Schuitema, who began using ready-made typographic material in the name of efficiency and objectivity, Jongert remained the craftsman who drew each single letterform by hand. This

Jac. Jongert, sanserif alphabets (1929). Published in N.J. van de Vecht, *Onze letterteekens en hun samenstelling* (The signs of our alphabet and their construction, Rotterdam 1930).

11 Van Dam and Van Praag, *Amsterdam gaf het voorbeeld*, Abcoude 1996, p 47. Other architects of the era who experimented with letterforms in their designs include H.P. Berlage, J. Crouwel, G.Th. Rietveld, P.L. Kramer, M. de Klerk, J.M. van der Mey, J. Duiker, D. Greiner and F.A. Warners. Cf. Kees Broos, *Architekst*, Eindhoven 1989.

12 Schreuders, *Lay In – Lay Out*, second edition, Amsterdam 1997, p 83.

13 N.J. van de Vecht, *Onze letterteekens en hun samenstelling*, Rotterdam 1930, pp 76–77.

telefoon

◄ Jac. Jongert designed an ever-
evolving corporate identity for
the Rotterdam coffee, tea and
tobacco manufacturer
Van Nelle, with the characteristic sanserif lettering seen on this
metal storage box, c. 1930.

▲ W.H. Gispen, lettering for the
PTT phone booths by the architect L.C. van der Vlugt, 1931.

► Nicolaas P. De Koo, poster for
Phoenix Beer, c. 1924.
Martijn F. Le Coultre Collection.

▼ Nicolaas P. De Koo, brochure
for the City of Rotterdam, 1924.

allowed his work to retain a certain spontaneity and a painterly quality; it also made him more flexible. 'By drawing his letters,' wrote Dick Maan, 'he could extend, heighten and condense them at will without disturbing their rhythm – a strategy that digital typography has made common practice today.'[14]

Nicolaas P. de Koo (1881–1961) worked in a similar vein as Jongert, but his output was less adventurous and lacked Jongert's conceptual tendencies. Although educat-ed as an interior designer at the Amsterdam State School for Applied Arts, De Koo mostly worked in graphic design. Among his clients were the City of Rotterdam and the Phoenix Brewery. He had a long-lasting working relationship with the Dutch PTT, for which he designed numerous letterbox posters and other printed matter. De Koo's posters, booklets and folders are very consistent in style. He absorbed cer-tain principles of modernism without abandoning his arts-and-crafts roots; this resulted in compositions that were attractive and fresh, tightly structured but never coldly perfect. De Koo frequently used variations on the same letterform: Futura-like geometric sanserifs of his own design. The fact that virtually all his lettering was hand-drawn allowed him to play with the letterforms and occasionally modify them into illustrative elements.

The alphabets used by Willem Hendrik Gispen (1890–1981) were similar to De Koo's: geometric sanserifs with a human touch. Graphic design was but a sidetrack of Gispen's career. Throughout the 1930s, '40s and '50s he was one of Holland's leading industrial designers, producing revolutionary steel-tube furniture and lamps in his own factory. Some of his best-known graphic work was made to promote his own designs, such as the famous poster for Giso lamps. Yet as a graphic designer he also had outside clients. The fact that he was regarded as somewhat of a lettering spe-cialist is illustrated by the assignment he received to design the lettering of the well-known phone booths by the architect L.C. van der Vlugt (1931).

Fré Cohen, graphic chameleon

The work of Fré Cohen (1903–1943), the most prolific female designer of pre-1940 Holland, is appealing and charming. Her numerous book jackets, magazine covers, brochures, and vignettes are well-made, lively, often colourful and stylistically con-vincing. What is bewildering about her production – the result of a little over fifteen years of professional activity – is its diversity. Expressionist illustration, arts-and-craftsy linocut, photomontage, in-your-face constructivism, *Wendingen* rule typogra-phy, architectural ornament: Cohen happily alternated between all these modes and did not seem to have a preference for any particular one. The quality of her

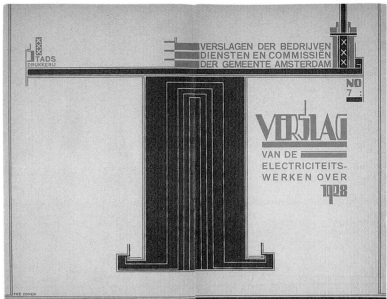

Fré Cohen explored a variety of styles in her designs for the City of Amsterdam.

▲ Programme of a study trip to Holland of the German equivalent of the National Trust (1928); 1928 year report of the Electricity Authority.

▸ Leaflet to promote the use of electrical kitchen appliances: 'The electric breakfast is always on time!', 1931.

↕ Brochure promoting the Amsterdam harbour and airport, 1931.

hand-lettering is uneven. At times it is awkward and hastily executed, usually it is adequate and in some cases it is a perfectly executed expression of Art Deco eclecticism.[15]

Cohen started out as a self-taught designer, drawing occasional advertising material for the cable factory where she worked as an office clerk. On the strength of this work she was hired by a socialist publisher as a designer-cum-administrator. An opinionated, petite woman, she had to overcome scepticism in the composing and printing room, and was sometimes embarassed by her lack of technical insight. She therefore enrolled at the Instituut voor Kunstnijverheidsonderwijs (Institute of Applied Art Education), where she studied part-time from 1924 until 1930, while her professional design career was already taking off. Initially her main client was the AJC, the Workers' Youth Association, of which she was a member. For this nationwide organization she designed dozens of covers for brochures, songbooks and plays, as well as posters and advertisements. While she became one of the favourite designers of the socialist movement – with many trade unions among her clients – she also offered her services to capitalism: she designed magazine covers for the advertising trade press and packaging for an appliances manufacturer. For three years she was an in-house designer at the City printing office, which continued to be an important client after she had become an independent designer in 1931. Her work for the City of Amsterdam included not only books and brochures, but also a corporate identity avant la lettre for the City Bank (Gemeentegiro). Being Jewish, Cohen had to go into hiding in May 1942, two years into the Nazi occupation. A year later, after many relocations, she was tracked down by the Dutch ss, but escaped imprisonment by swallowing a lethal pill.

Fré Cohen was 'never a major innovator' (Purvis)[16]: she followed trends rather than setting them. This also applies to her alphabets. Yet precisely because of her reluctance to limit herself stylistically and her lack of an artistic programme, her letterforms are an eloquent catalogue of the wide array of possibilities available to her contemporaries. They also show that, in spite of the heated debates and ardent pamphlets that seemed to invariably accompany that era's artistic choices, it was nonetheless acceptable for a talented designer to put on a style like an overcoat.

14 Dick Maan, 'Zo moet de wereld zijn', Druk 008, Spring 2001, p 24.

15 The most comprehensive overview of Cohen's work is Van Dam and Van Praag, Fré Cohen 1903–1942, Abcoude 1993.

16 Alston W. Purvis, Dutch Graphic Design 1918–1945, New York 1992, p 56.

De Stijl, Constructivism and the New Typography

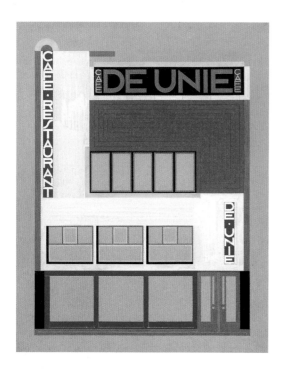

During the war of 1914–1918, and partly as a result of it, a radical view of the arts took shape in several European countries. Although this avant-garde had many local names, mostly evoking change and simplicity, it was in essence an international movement which is now generally referred to as Modernism, or the historical avant-garde. Modernism was a drastic reaction to the devastating experience of the war and to the nineteenth-century values and attitudes of 'the old Europe' which were perceived as the war's underlying cause. In numerous manifestos and programmes the past was bid farewell and the future embraced. 'There is no longer any way out for Europe. Centralization and prosperity, spiritual and material individualism was the foundation of the old Europe. In that it has caged itself. It is falling to pieces. We observe this calmly. We would not want to help even if we could. We do not want to extend the life of this old prostitute.' [17] Thus wrote Theo van Doesburg in a 1921 issue of *De Stijl* (The Style), the magazine he founded in 1917 and whose contributors included the painters Piet Mondriaan (also known as Mondrian), Vilmos Huzsár and Bart van der Leck and the architects Gerrit Rietveld, Jan Wils and J.J.P. Oud. *De Stijl* magazine appeared under Van Doesburg's editorship until 1928; a final commemorative issue was put together after his death in 1931.

Although the magazine itself never sold more than about three hundred copies, *De Stijl* was the Netherlands' most influential contribution to the international modernist movement. Rejecting figuration and narrative, it called for simplicity and objectivity, using elements of pure form and colour 'to construct an ideal "model" for a new world through furniture, sculpture, interior design and architecture'. [18] De Stijl's foundations lay in painting; Piet Mondriaan's post-1920 paintings – carefully balanced constructions of squares and rectangles in primary colours, separated by firm black lines – are among its lasting icons. Yet Mondriaan was not alone; he had arrived at his uncompromising style through a series of exercises in abstraction carried out in 1917–1919 in 'a symbiotic relationship' [19] with three other painters initially associated with De Stijl – Van Doesburg, Huszár and Van der Leck. The architects and designers of De Stijl took these ideas into other realms. Gerrit Rietveld designed his famous furniture, as well as a number of houses of which the Schröder house in Utrecht (1924) stands out as one of the most innovative housing projects of its time. J.J.P. Oud and Van Doesburg, among others, also put De Stijl ideas into practice in imaginative architecture and interior design.

Some of these projects, such as the famous Café De Unie by Oud (Rotterdam, 1924, reconstructed in 1985), or shops by Rietveld, featured attractive lettering in a semi-geometric Deco style. Yet the most innovative expression of De Stijl typography is to be found in the works of those Stijl-affiliated artists who made designs for print.

Alphabets by Huszár and Van der Leck

The contribution of De Stijl to graphic design and typography has been quantitatively modest; but the radical solutions it proposed have remained relevant to date. *De Stijl's* first remarkable piece of graphic design was the magazine's original masthead. It was an abstract woodcut composed of black rectangles, over which the words DE STIJL were drawn in fragmented square capitals. In his foreword, Van Doesburg mentioned the painter Vilmos Huszár as the designer of the vignette; it is generally assumed that Huszár also drew the lettering, which was subsequently used by Van Doesburg for the magazine's stationery. [20]

^ Drawing of the Rotterdam Café De Unie by Jacobus Johannes Pieter Oud, who also designed the integrated lettering. Built in 1924–1925, the building was bombed in 1940 and reconstructed on a different location in 1985. Gouache, c. 1924. *Oud Collection of the Netherlands Architecture Institute*

▸ The first cover design of *De Stijl* magazine, used from 1917 through 1920, carried an abstract image by Vilmos Huszár. He probably designed the lettering as well.

Vilmos Huszár (1884–1960), a Hungarian living in Holland, was active as a painter, interior designer, graphic designer and commercial artist. Although his contribution to the earliest editions of De Stijl were crucial, his relationship with the magazine was soon disrupted after heated conflicts with Van Doesburg. He had relations with the international Constructivist movement and worked with Piet Zwart; this led to an increased interest in graphic design. In his graphic work Huszár continued his exploration of rectangular, constructed letterforms but seldom, if ever, returned to the fragmented, mosaic-like forms of the Stijl logo. He designed an alphabet of indented square characters which he used, in various forms, throughout the 1920s: in a 1922 bookplate, in his stationery for the Bruynzeel wood factory and on his well-known cover for the 1929 Diego Riviera issue of *Wendingen*. In 1926, when commissioned to design a full-fledged advertising campaign for the cigarette brand Miss Blanche, his approach was less radical. His stylized yet seductive portrait of a female smoker (based on an existing vignette) was accompanied by hand-drawn varieties of a sanserif which owed as much to nineteenth-century grotesques as to geometry. A short article by Huszár in the magazine *i-10* (which was to some extent the successor to *De Stijl*) shows how much manual work was involved in the Miss Blanche campaign. Each billboard was designed individually, taking into account the quality of the architecture as well as other aspects of the site. 'The lamp-post in front of the building was incorporated in my composition,' wrote Huszár of one particular piece of lettering.[21] In several posters from the late 1920s, Huszár freely combined his square alphabet with this type of more conventional sanserif lettering.

While Huszár seemingly lost interest in the logic of the Stijl logo, similar 'decomposed' forms were the essence of the lettering designed from 1919 onwards by Bart van der Leck (1876–1958). Van der Leck never embraced pure abstraction; one of the reasons why he broke away from De Stijl only a few months after its inception was his reluctance to subscribe to what he felt was a dogmatic and limiting approach.[22] In Van der Leck's post-1920 paintings, figurative images are 'broken down' to form compositions of straight and diagonal lines and blocks; yet a residue of the original figure or object is always palpable. Van der Leck was convinced that painting needed to be anchored in day-to-day reality; he also wanted his art to have a place in that reality, and for several years almost entirely abandoned painting for interior and industrial design.

Unlike Huszár, Van der Leck did not adopt a different, more accessible idiom when applying his art to advertising. His famous poster for the Batavier Line (1915) used the same Egyptian-style human figures that inhabited his paintings. As soon as he had developed his fragmented forms in painting, they appeared in poster designs as well, combined with typographic constructions made along the same lines. This was an obvious choice when designing a poster for his own exhibition at an Utrecht gallery; it became problematic when in 1919 he was invited to submit a proposal to

Vilmos Huszár, campaign for
Miss Blanche cigarettes, 1926.
Each of the hand-painted
billboards was designed
individually, acknowledging
the properties of the sites
– including the lamppost in
front of the wall.

17 Purvis (cit.), p 25.

18 Paul Overy, *De Stijl*, New York 1991, p 9.

19 Ibid., p 55.

20 Els Hoek (ed.), *Theo van Doesburg*, Utrecht/Otterlo/Bussum 2000, pp 209–211.

21 Republished in Arthur Lehning and Jurriaan Schrofer, *i-10, de internationale avant-garde tussen de twee wereldoorlogen*, The Hague 1963 (2nd printing 1974), pp 72–74.

22 cf. Bart van der Leck, *Lezing* (1957) in Van Kooten (ed.), *Bart van der Leck*, Otterlo 1994, pp 130–131. Van der Leck's stylistic development is discussed in the essays by Cees Hilhorst and R.W.D. Oxenaar in this book, pp 143 ff.

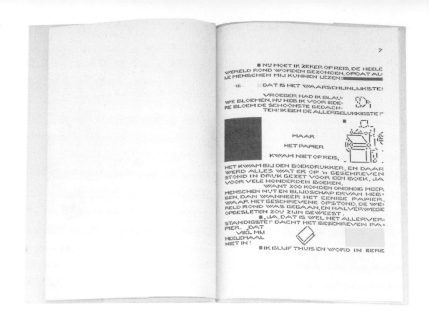

▾ Bart van der Leck's poster design for Delfia vegetable fat (1919) was rejected by the management of the Nederlandse Olie Fabriek. This gouche is said to be the last of twelve designs for the poster (Le Coultre/Purvis 2002, p 35).
Martijn F. Le Coultre Collection.

▸ Bart van der Leck, *Het vlas* by Hans Christian Andersen, 1941. The text was completely hand-lettered in Van der Leck's fragmented alphabet.

Bart van der Leck, packaging for Metz & Co. department store, early 1950s.

the Delft Salad Oil Factory (NOF). Van der Leck made several designs based on the same fragmented figure showing, in all probability, a moustached man holding (or selling?) a bottle of Delfia vegetable fat. The lettering follows the same logic as the image: capitals are spliced into blocks and lines along horizontals, verticals and diagonals. The board of directors was not ready for such a degree of abstraction: Van der Leck's design was rejected and the poster never printed.

In the lettering of the Delfia poster (which in fact precedes the 1920 exhibition poster), some of the characters are suggested rather than represented, which makes it difficult to read. In his later typographic work, Van der Leck solved the problem by further simplifying the letterform until he achieved an alphabet of square capitals constructed with straight and diagonal lines. He remained true to these forms for decades. In the early 1940s he was asked to illustrate a new translation of Hans Christian Andersen's fairytale *The flax* (*Het vlas*). He decided to design the typography as well, by meticulously hand-lettering the text. Despite the difficult circumstances of the early war years, the resulting booklet was a beautifully printed, idiosyncratic masterpiece in which the images and the text formed an inextricable unity.

Van der Leck's most important commercial client throughout the 1930s and again in the early 1950s was the Amsterdam luxury department store Metz & Co. His work for Metz first allowed him to apply his art to public spaces: the firm commissioned him to design shop interiors, colour schemes for the company's fabrics, and carpets based on his paintings. In 1952, already in his seventies, he redesigned the company's packaging. The charming grey boxes and paper bags were hand-lettered using a thin version of his alphabet.

In 1996, The Foundry in London released a digital typeface called *VanDerLeck* as part of its *Architype* series. The forms are inspired by Van der Leck's lettering, notably of *Het vlas*, but although it is a well-executed tribute, it is difficult to think of the design as Van der Leck's. The forms have been rigorously cleaned up, thereby losing the spontaneity and vulnerability of the original.

The elastic alphabet of Theo van Doesburg

Of the artists linked to *De Stijl*, it was its founder, Theo van Doesburg (1883–1931)[23], who developed the most influential and provocative view of typography.

In 1919 Van Doesburg drew an alphabet as a tool to express the typographic ideas of *De Stijl*. Although he was always extremely critical of Wijdeveld and *Wendingen*, the typeface shows some influences of Wijdeveld's brass rule style. Van Doesburg drew a modular alphabet of simplified capitals on a grid of 5 × 5 squares. It was not made for legibility: some characters, especially the K, R and X, are so unconventional that they must have been problematic (and annoying) to many readers. Van Doesburg

BOND VAN REVOLUTIONNAIR-SOCIALISTISCHE INTELLECTUEELEN

◁ The square letterforms of Van Doesburg's modular alphabet could be adapted at will to form 'justified' lines, as in the 1919 logo for the 'League of Revolutionary-Socialist Intellectuals'. *Centraal Museum, Utrecht.*

▷ Theo van Doeburg, book cover for *Klassiek, Barok, Modern,* Antwerp 1920.

▽ Van Doesburg's alphabet as issued by The Foundry, London (Architype Van Doesburg, 1996).

allowed for slight variations of the basic forms when necessary, and often used condensed or extended versions in order to 'justify' lines that were unequal in length. It has been suggested that the varying widths were created by changing the squares of the 5 × 5 grid into upright or oblong rectangles.[24] That is not quite correct, because this would have resulted in a deformation of the stems, creating a difference in thickness of the horizontals and the verticals (as with electronic scaling).[25] Van Doesburg's lettering is always monoline, even where the letters are narrowed down to almost half their width. In fact, he used his alphabet in a way that was neither systematic nor aesthetic, redrawing the letters at will. This allowed him to adopt the alphabet in regular design jobs.

One such job – his largest – was an assignment from the Amsterdam trading company Hagemeijer & Co. During the second half of 1919 Van Doesburg worked almost exclusively for this firm, designing a large set of stationery, a poster which was never printed and a 'CASSA' (cash desk) sign. Some of these designs were made solely with the Van Doesburg alphabet, apparently hand-drawn; others use an existing grotesque typeface ('antieke') combined with monograms of his own design.[26]

One of the best-known designs made with the grid alphabet is his logo for the League of Revolutionary-Socialist Intellectuals; it is a typical example of how the widths of his letters could be adapted to form a justified rectangle. The logo was used, together with a monogram, on letterheads, envelopes and a manifesto. In early 1920 Van Doesburg took part in a competition for the cover design of *Klei* (Clay), a trade magazine of brick manufacturers. Van Doesburg used a beefed-up version of his alphabet for the masthead, but although this block-like lettering was fitting to the task, the design was not selected. Van Doesburg subsequently refused to take part in an exhibition of the entries.[26] The Centraal Museum in Utrecht possesses another unexecuted design which is even more intriguing: a large working drawing of the words LETTERGIETERIJ AMSTERDAM (probably about 1919). As it is not very likely that the foundry commissioned a nameplate in constructivist style, this design may have been part of a campaign on Van Doesburg's behalf to introduce himself to the firm as a type designer.[27]

In January 1921, *De Stijl* appeared in a new layout. Van Doesburg and Mondriaan had redesigned the cover, replacing Huszár's logo with a new masthead that consisted of standard sanserif type. The words DE STIJL were superimposed over two large bold capitals printed in red: NB, i.e. Nieuwe Beelding ('new imaging') – Mondriaan's motto for the movement. The layout – a daring combination of symmetry and asymmetry – was highly appreciated by Tschichold, who reproduced a postcard designed in the same style in *Die Neue Typographie*, praising it as an early example of new typography: 'a pure typographic style using only type, space and colour.'[28]

That same year Van Doesburg settled in Weimar, home of the Bauhaus. Although the school's director Walter Gropius shied away from hiring the boisterous Dutchman, Van Doesburg gave several lectures, as well as a 'Stijl course' which was attended by Bauhaus pupils and staff. His geometric approach appealed greatly to some students and young teachers, who were less taken with the romantic and esoteric approach of Bauhaus teachers like Johannes Itten. It seems very possible that Van Doesburg's presence in Weimar contributed to the radicalization and rationalization of the Bauhaus curriculum. It may have been a personal triumph for Van Doesburg that his students began designing posters using his alphabet.

In subsequent years, Van Doesburg abandoned hand-lettering for ready-made type. He wrote and designed visually challenging 'cubist poems' which were published

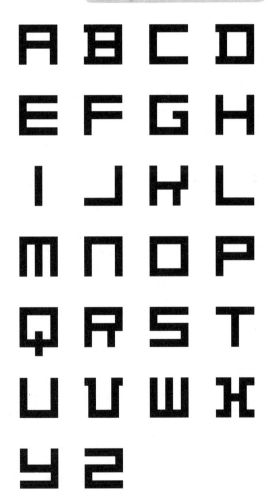

23 Van Doesburg's real name was Christian Emil Marie Küpper. He renamed himself after his stepfather Theodorus Doesburg (without 'Van'), who may also have been his biological father.

24 Kees Broos, *Mondriaan, de Stijl en de Nieuwe Typografie,* Amsterdam/The Hague 1994, p 12.

25 Donald Beekman's *FF Beekman* (1999, p 268) is a case in point: based on principles similar to Van Doesburg's, it allows for electronic scaling, deforming the verticals.

26 This example and the following: *Oeuvrecatalogus Theo van Doesburg* (cit.) pp 244–263.

28 Jan Tschichold, *The New Typography,* transl. Ruari McLean, Berkeley/Los Angeles/ London 1998, pp 58–59.

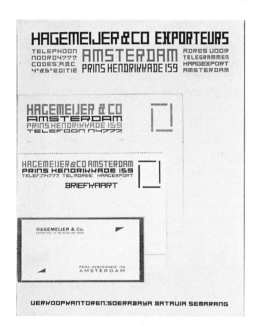

◀ Theo van Doesburg, proposals for the use of his alphabet on a magazine cover (1920) and in
▶ a nameplate for the Amsterdam Type Foundry (1919?). *Centraal Museum, Utrecht.*

▼ Theo van Doesburg, stationery for Hagemeijer & Co, 1919. *Centraal Museum, Utrecht.*

▼ Van Doesburg's alphabet for l'Aubette in Strasbourg, as digitized by The Foundry, London (Architype Aubette, 1996).

in *De Stijl* under the pseudonym I.K. Bonset (an anagram of ɪᴋ ʙᴇɴ sᴏᴛ, 'I am crazy'). Van Doesburg's alter ego became the editor of a new magazine called *Mecano*, which published Dadaist contributions by the likes of Tristan Tzara, Hans Arp, Kurt Schwitters and Francis Picabia. If the 1921 cover of *De Stijl* was the prototype of modernist 'new typography', then *Mecano*, launched merely a year later, was post-modernism avant la lettre, combining an eclectic array of foundry type with found images from technical catalogues as well as original art. There was a sense of fun and anarchy about *Mecano* which was taken to new extremes in a series of wild posters and programmes for the Dada shows that Van Doesburg organized with Schwitters in early 1923.

Van Doesburg returned to his grid-based alphabet once more in 1926–1928, when working on L'Aubette in Strasbourg. L'Aubette was an eighteenth-century military building which had been converted into an enormous entertainment complex. Van Doesburg had been invited to take part in the project by Hans Arp and Sophie Taeuber-Arp, to whom it had originally been assigned; he soon took charge. L'Aubette was described by Van Doesburg as the long-awaited *Gesamtkunstwerk* (total work of art) of the movement: 'the first realization of a programme which we have cherished for years'.[29] Apart from breathtaking colour schemes for the walls, ceilings and floors of several halls, Van Doesburg designed numerous accessories, from neon lettering and signage to ashtrays and invitation cards. For these items he used a modified variant of his alphabet, allowing for a limited use of diagonals. This resulted in a more legible and 'user-friendly' lettering style. Apart from one more cover design for yet another magazine (*Art Concret*, 1930), Van Doesburg's activities as a graphic designer were over. In the last years before his early death in a Swiss sanatorium, he mainly concentrated on interior design, architecture and painting.

Van Doesburg's original alphabet and his typeface for L'Aubette have been issued in The Foundry's *Architype* series as *VanDoesburg* and *Aubette*. Both are cleaned-up yet respectful revivals; their main drawback is that they have fixed a form which, in the hands of the original designer, was made to change continually.

Zwart, Schuitema and Kiljan: towards uninteresting type

In 1928, the German typographer Jan Tschichold published *Die Neue Typographie*. In his rather schoolmasterly way Tschichold explained the motives and methods of the typographic avant-garde. As we saw earlier, he mentioned the experiments of De Stijl as one of the catalysts of innovation; the book even took its epitaph from Mondriaan. In turn, Dutch designers like Piet Zwart and Paul Schuitema approved of Tschichold's standpoint and embraced his notion of a 'new typography'.

The role of these designers – the torch-bearers of early Dutch Functionalism [30] – in the development of type design and lettering is marginal at best. However, their view of typography has had a lasting influence on twentieth-century design in the Netherlands and abroad – precisely because of the way in which they aimed to achieve 'crude legibility' with sparse means. This approach represents the antithesis of Art Deco: it aimed at radically omitting all that was aesthetic, ornamental or deliberately 'beautiful' in favour of 'pragmatic organization'.

Born in 1885, Zwart was trained as a craftsman, draughtsman and architect; his early work consisted of textile, furniture and interior designs in a style that showed affinity with the Amsterdam School. In 1918 or thereabouts, having met Vilmos Huszár and

Jan Wils, Zwart became interested in the ideas of the avant-garde. His earliest typographic work was the stationery he designed for Wils, to whom he was an assistant for two years. From 1921 to 1927 Zwart worked for H.P. Berlage, the most influential Dutch architect of the era.

Zwart's earliest typographic experiments follow the architect's logic. His 1920 furniture designs for the Bruynzeel factory (for which Huszár supplied the colour schemes) are lettered in a square alphabet similar to the letterforms that Wijdeveld, Huszár and Van Doesburg were designing at the time. At 36, Zwart landed his first graphic design assignment – a series of advertisements and stationery for the flooring company Vicker's House. He made a hand-lettered poster, using constructed square letters combined with a sanserif fat-face of his own making. A similar fat-face alphabet can be found in the Church of Christ Scientist (The Hague, 1926), a Berlage project for which Zwart designed the interior. By then, however, Zwart had begun using existing compositors' material in his designs for print.

In 1923, Zwart was hired by the Nederlandse Kabelfabriek (NKF) to design the cable factory's advertisements in the trade press. His very first piece was a meticulously hand-drawn composition, more or less in the Amsterdam School style. But, as Zwart told Kees Broos: 'I was still not finished with it when the magazine had already come out. So I realized that this was not a very good way to work and plunged into typography. ... I actually learned about typography from an assistant in the small printing company where the monthly magazine on electro-technology was being produced. ... I began making sketches and then during lunch hour with that young man tried to figure out how we could produce these things ... that's how it came about. I have had to learn the typographic craft from scratch like that.'[31]

Between 1923 and 1933, Zwart made 275 NKF advertisements, acting as his own copywriter, playing with visual puns and alliterations. He began to refer to himself as a 'typotekt' (a contraction of 'typographer' and 'architect') who built pages with type, lines and photos. He embraced photography as an integrating element of the composition because of the dynamic tension between the flatness of the type and the dimensionality suggested by photography. Among his best-known works produced with this technique (for which Moholy-Nagy coined the term 'Typo-photo') are the NKF catalogues, brochures for the PTT and the covers for a series of cinema books.

Zwart had precise ideas on which typefaces were best suited for photo-typography. His most extensive essay on the subject is 'van oude tot nieuwe typografie' (from old to new typography – no caps, of course), a text written for a brochure he edited and designed for the printing firm Trio.[32] It is a passionate plea for no-nonsense typefaces or, in Zwart's words, uninteresting type. 'we want typefaces that are more business-like; advertising demands brutal legibility. for the time being, the "grotesque" best answers this requirement .... although there is a senseless, unrestrained prolif-

29 Quoted in Overy, *De Stijl* (cit.), p 179.

30 *Dutch Constructivism* – stressing the formal aspects of their 1930s work – is also a commonly used term. A notion used at the time is *Nieuwe Zakelijkheid* ('zakelijk' meaning 'business-like', 'pragmatic' and 'objective').

31 Kees Broos, *Piet Zwart 1885–1977* (cit.), p 38 (my translation); see also Alston W. Purvis, *Dutch Graphic Design 1918–1945* (cit.), p 66. Zwart, of course, uses 'typography' in the strict sense of composing and printing with metal (or wood) type.

32 The brochure remained in the proof stage and was not published until 1994, when it was inserted in Kees Broos's book *Mondriaan, De Stijl en de Nieuwe Typografie*.

eration of the number of typefaces, due to variations on and 'improvements' of existing types, an elementarily functional, scientifically grounded letterform has not yet been made. therefore new typography is forced to make do with the simplest, least decorated, most pragmatic typefaces: a few grotesques and some old-style faces. in any case those types are to be avoided that have a self-conscious, personal, peculiaristic character; their pretentiouness is contrary to the essence of typography; *the less interesting the typeface, the more typographically usable.* a typeface is less interesting when it has fewer historic residues and is more of a product of the exact, tense spirit of the 20th century. every era has had its typical, characteristic typeface, ours still has to create its own "particular" faces. these letterforms will have to be based on physiological-optical constraints – not on individualistic considerations and predilections.'

Zwart's brothers in arms in his struggle for an objective, functional typography were Paul Schuitema and Gerard Kiljan. The three designers had independently developed similar ideas when they met in the mid-1920s. They began to operate as a kind of avant-garde design troika, signing manifestos together and participating jointly in exhibitions. In 1930 Gerard Kiljan started up a department of advertising design at the Art Academy of The Hague, and invited Paul Schuitema to become head teacher. This collaboration resulted in the first functionalist design school in the Netherlands, showing a strong affinity with the Bauhaus. Gerard Kiljan's body of work is rather limited (although it includes pioneering designs for postage stamps, a telephone and an ergonomic lemonade bottle); he saw himself first and foremost as a teacher. Schuitema, on the other hand, was one of the most influential graphic designers of the interwar period.

Trained as a painter, Schuitema soon switched to advertising – a field which he felt offered him more significant possibilities to express the spirit of the times. He made some of his most outstanding work for two related commercial clients, the P. van Berkel meat company and the (Van) Berkel scales and cutting machine factory. Yet, like Zwart, he was also active in leftist circles and made cover designs for socialist magazines. Like Zwart, Paul Schuitema developed his own variant of Constructivism, combining type – often set diagonally – and photography. It is interesting to see how this modernist work was preceded by a short phase in which Schuitema was influenced by the colourful mainstream of Art Deco design. His earliest showcards and packaging labels for Van Berkel are hand-lettered in a charming style which is a far cry from his later, more radical work but already possessed its clarity and compositional quality. Many years later, somewhere in the 1950s, Schuitema returned once more to lettering. He produced a poster showing a juxtaposition of two alphabets: a set of black 'grotesque' capitals, printed over a geometric alphabet in red.

As late as 1971, Schuitema summarized his view of type and typography in an unpublished text written on the occasion of his grandson's birth. 'To me, the letter was no more than a thing for reading that had to be used in a clear, straightforward and unadorned way. A manner of speaking without rhetorics or frills, but flexible enough in its appearance to be able ... to distinguish texts of primary importance from secondary ones.' The lively yet pragmatic typography that Schuitema envisaged required resourcefulness, scrupulousness and economic thinking, 'formulating problems as lucidly and clearly as possible at all times'.[33]

Throughout the 1930s, '40s and '50s, Kiljan and Schuitema trained several generations of industrial, interior and graphic designers at the Hague Academy of Arts. Type was never a priority in the curriculum: their functionalist view of type was not very stimulating to those who had an interest in letterforms. Elsewhere at the Academy, however – in the department of Drawing and Painting – other teachers were developing contrasting views, thus laying the foundation for what would become, from 1970 onwards, the 'Hague school of letters'. That other lineage is sketched on pp 102–103.

▲ Although Paul Schuitema rejected any form of 'charming' lettering in the 1930s, his early designs show some influence of fashionable Art Deco alphabets.

▼ Towards the end of his life, Schuitema went back to exploring letterforms in a rather playful way. His experiments resulted in this double alphabet, issued as a poster in the 1960s.

Gerard Kiljan, hand-lettered leaflet for Junker & Ruh kitchen stoves (c. 1927). In his post-war years, Kiljan returned to lettering design. The Kiljan estate contains some unpublished sketches for typefaces.

---

33 From the archive of Dick Maan, a former student of Schuitema.

Manifestations of the new

Metal type: the final years

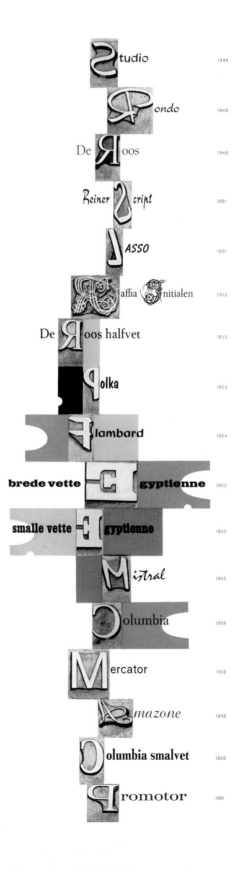

Studio   1946

Rondo   1948

De Roos   1948

Reiner Script   1951

LASSO   1951

Raffia Initialen   1952

De Roos halfvet   1953

Polka   1953

Flambard   1954

brede vette Egyptienne   1955

smalle vette Egyptienne   1955

Mistral   1955

Columbia   1956

Mercator   1958

Amazone   1958

Columbia smalvet   1959

Promotor   1961

Type stock of the Amsterdam Type Foundry, as shown in a 1960 advertisement. Detail from a design by Harm Hagedoorn.

The Amsterdam Type Foundry after 1945

Memorial book for the 100th anniversary of the Amsterdam Type Foundry/N. Tetterode, designed by Dick Elffers, 1951.

The beginning of the Second World War had signalled the end of the De Roos era at the Lettergieterij 'Amsterdam' voorheen N. Tetterode (Amsterdam Type Foundry). De Roos stepped down as head of the drawing department in favour of his assistant Dick Dooijes, who had a young family to feed. After a few years, Dooijes gained the company of G.W. Ovink, a book historian who would become one of the country's outstanding specialists on the history of printing, and took the position of Tetterode's artistic adviser. Immediately after the liberation, the Tetterode company continued its international expansion. The firm established an American import office in New York in 1948. Amsterdam Continental Types & Graphic Equipments Inc. went on to sell foundry type from other firms as well, including Berthold and Enschedé. In that year, the Amsterdam Type Foundry boasted that its types were available 'from Ireland to New Zealand, from Finland to Chile'.[1] According to a 1951 commemorative book, its production capacity at that point could only be surpassed by the American Type Founders (ATF), a company with which Tetterode had a close working relationship. The Amsterdam Type Foundry had subsidiaries in Brussels, Paris, New York and Jakarta (Indonesia).

A market for scripts

In the immediate post-war years, design and advertising were imbued with a newly found optimism and informality. In the design of books as well as posters a painterly and loose kind of illustration was combined with hand-drawn romans and scripts. At the Amsterdam Type Foundry, it was felt that the printing trade needed 'brisk jobbing types';[2] many of the display faces made during this period were scripts of some sort.

The first typeface of this kind produced after 1945 was *Studio* by A. (Dolf) Overbeek, who was head of the studio of the Vada printing firm and around 1948 became graphic adviser to De Arbeiderspers, a major publishing and printing house. Dolf Overbeek (1905–1969) was an authorative and demanding taskmaster, as well as the designer of prize-winning books and calendars. He was not fond of experiments and preferred conventional no-nonsense typography to fancy modernisms. Annoyed by bad typeface combinations, he analysed the compatability of faces of different catagories and designed the 'Letter Organ' – a kind of scientific type table – which prescribed exactly which combinations to use, and which to avoid.[3] Considering what a stern man he must have been, Studio (1946) and its companion bold face, *Flambard* (1954) are surprisingly undogmatic and unorthodox. They look like sign-painting done with a flat brush. Studio proved very readable in small sizes, and was even used as a text face in literary publications. Too regular and upright to be called scripts, Studio and Flambard were initially listed as display types, and later as *manuaires* – an in-between category of the Vox classification, adopted by the Type Foundry in its specimens from the late 1950s onwards.

Metal type: the final years

REINER SCRIPT

A B C D E F G H I J
K L M N O P Q R
S T U V W X Y Z †
a b c d e f g h i j k l m n o p q r s
t u v w x y z th tz sj tt ß e s t
1 2 3 4 5 6 7 8 9 0

STUDIO

A B C D E F G H I J
K L M N O P Q R S
T U V W X Y Z &
a b c d e f g h i j k l m n
o p q r s t u v w x y z ?!
1 2 3 4 5 6 7 8 9 0

FLAMBARD

A B C D E F G H I J
K L M N O P Q R S
T U V W X Y Z &
a b c d e f g h i j k l m n
o p q r s t u v w x y z ?!
1 2 3 4 5 6 7 8 9 0

▸ A. Overbeek, Studio (1946) and its accompanying bold face, Flambard (1954); two types in the *manuaires* catagory that were judged regular and readable enough to set entire books in.

◂ Imre Reiner's Reiner Script (1951), the quirkiest of the many script faces that the Amsterdam Type Foundry issued in the post-war decades.

▾ Imre Reiner, working drawing of Reiner Script, 1951. *Tetterode Archive of the Amsterdam University Library (UvA).*

Imre Reiner and Reiner script

In 1948, the Amsterdam Type Foundry published *Rondo*, a typeface begun by Stefan Schlesinger and completed, after Schlesinger's death, by Dick Dooijes (> pp 50 and 91). But apparently the demand for scripts was great enough for more fonts to be ordered. *Reiner Script*, which came out in 1951, is probably the most whimsical typeface ever published by the Amsterdam Type Foundry. It was designed by the Polish artist and typographer Imre Reiner, who worked as a book designer for clients in many countries, including the Netherlands. In 1949 the Amsterdam Type Foundry issued his *Primula Ornaments*, a set of informal ornaments that seem to have been drawn with a broad-nibbed pen. Reiner Script, based on Reiner's own handwriting, has similar characteristics. Reiner Script was quite successful and was frequently used in book design and advertising throughout the 1950s and 1960s. Some thirty years later, Tobias Frere-Jones of the Font Bureau in Boston, felt 'attracted by its free-form structure and unique texture'.[4] He made a digital revival, relying on handset proofs of the original Reiner Script, and adding over twenty ligatures 'for flexibility and variety in headlines'. He also drew a new boldface to accompany it. Both fonts are beautifully made, respectful interpretations of the original, although the Bold especially lacks some of the quirkiness of Reiner's design.

Henk Krijger, cover of the 1956 Best Book Designs Catalogue.

De bestverzorgde vijftig boeken van het jaar 1956

Henk Krijger and Raffia Initials

One of the most meticulous typographers of the 1950s was Henk Krijger (1914–1979), who was also a painter, sculptor, illustrator and writer. Krijger belonged to progressive Protestant circles and tried hard to outline the possibilities of an experimental 'Christian art'. In his best books he combined well-wrought, mildly modern typography with vivid, realistic illustrations that sometimes show influences of Picasso's figurative work. He hand-lettered his book jackets with painstaking precision: his letterforms and vignettes lacked the nonchalance of many of his contemporaries, but retained their liveliness in spite of their perfection.

1 *Grafische mededelingen* 5 (1948), quoted in John A. Lane and Mathieu Lommen, *Dutch typefounders' specimens*, Amsterdam 1998, p 33.

2 *Dutch typefounders' specimens* (cit.), p 33. A chapter of this book, Mathieu Lommen's 'A history of Lettergieterij "Amsterdam" voorheen N. Tetterode (Typefoundry Amsterdam) 1851–1988' is an important source of information on the subject.

3 'Letterorgel' shown in Aldus, *Allemaal Flauwekul*, Amsterdam 1989, p 83.

4 The Font Bureau, *Type Specimens Third Edition*, Boston 2001.

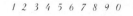

a b c d e f g h i j k l m n o p q r s t u v w x y z

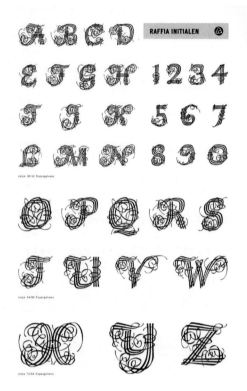

His alphabet of initials, *Raffia Initialen* (1952), was an impressive tour de force. Each of the capitals and figures is made of three parallel strokes, whose extremities are bent and curled in the way way that real raffia, or packaging ribbon, may behave. If there is one typeface which represents the 1950s version of mannerist calligraphy (> p 20), this it it. Raffia's forms are echoed more than once in Krijger's lettering work and ornaments – as in the vignettes for a 1957 novel, or the double page made for a 1961 *liber amicorum* – but the typeface itself possesses a virtuosity and sheer delight in form which he has rarely displayed elsewhere.

Raffia is the only typeface which Krijger completed. At least twice – in a newspaper interview and in an article he wrote [5] – he mentioned his plans for text typefaces for the Amsterdam Type Foundry which remained stuck in the design phase because he found no immediate function for them. Krijger even published the names of these unfinished types: *Bourdon, Bambu, Tarquinia*.[6] Although his daughter remembers these plans, there is no trace of his unpublished type designs in the Krijger estate. Given his unmistakable talent for type design, this is very unfortunate indeed.

More scripts; the types of L.D.H. Smit

In 1955 the Amsterdam Type Foundry bought Roger Excoffon's *Mistral* (1953), which became very successful and was followed in 1964 by the same designer's *Choc* (originally published by Olive in 1955). Furthermore, the ATF's *Dom Casual* was released under the name *Polka* in 1954.

The company management felt that the market for scripts was not yet saturated: there was room for a more elegant face, perhaps to compete with Günther Gerhard Lange's *Boulevard*, released by Berthold in 1955. *Amazone* was presented in 1958: 'simple but graceful; connected but with no kerning.'[7] The beautifully executed – but perhaps a little too well-behaved – typeface was designed by Leonard H.D. Smit (1917 – 1986), an in-house designer with the firm. Although Smit had been employed since 1949, Amazone was his first original typeface; it had been years in the making. As it did not kern – that is, no part of any character protruded from the body – it was easier to cast and to handle than other connected scripts; yet its joints looked as natural and well-fit as those of other, more vulnerable fonts.

Amazone survived the swift technological changes of the 1960s, '70s and '80s. It was licensed to Bitstream, who re-released it as a digital font. Unfortunately, its forms were 'cleaned up' in a rather banal way and some of its most charming features, such as the lowercase 't' which referred directly to contemporary handwriting, were lost in the process.

Smit designed three more typefaces. *Promotor* (1960), a wide Bodoni-like display face was based on a nineteenth-century 'Alsacienne' of which matrices were in the Foundry's possession. It was followed by a boldface companion, *Orator* (1961). W. Pincus Jaspert wrote that Smit's design 'has some similarities to *Craw Modern* [published by ATF in 1958] but is more rounded and has less variation in stress between thick and hair-line strokes.'[8]

The last type by Smit was *Revue* (1969), a bold display type produced for the Foundry's new FilmLetter system. FilmLetter fonts were sets of photographic positives on film, 'complete with alignment and spacing guides'.[9] Titles could by 'typeset' by applying the separate characters to self-adhesive transparent sheets. The system was no serious competition for Mecanorma's and Letraset's transfer sheets and soon disap-

Revue

ABCDEFGHIJKLMNOP
QRSTUVWXYZ
abcdefghijklmnopqrst
uvwxyzæœijß&
1234567890£$!?/.,:;-*«)

Mecanorma Orator

ABCDEFGHIJKLMNOP
QRSTUVWXYZ
abcdefghijklmnopqrst
uvwxyzæœijß&
1234567890£$!?/.,:;-*)

◂ Orator (1961), Promotor's bold-face companion, was licensed to Mecanorma for production as transfer sheets; in the 1990s Mecanorma issued a PostScript version. Not to be confused with the typewriter font of the same name.

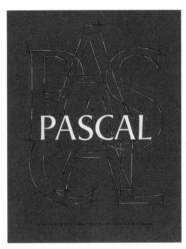

P ★ Een moderne variant op de klassieke Bodoni-serie voor breedlopende slagregels met een pittig horizontaal accent

Promotor

In onze tijd vraagt de typografische ontwerper dikwijls om letters die een duidelijke horizontale of verticale werking hebben. Vooral onder de schreefloze soorten zijn lettertypen te vinden met een breed en sterk horizontaal geaccentueerd beeld. Een letter met overeenkomstige werking was echter tot dusver in het Bodoni-type niet te vinden. Om in deze leemte te voorzien werd de Promotor ontworpen, uitgaande van traditionele vormen, maar modern in zijn detaillering en vooral in zijn werking. De Promotor wordt geleverd in de corpsen 16, 20, 24, 28, 36 en 48, en vertoont in al die verschillende grootten hetzelfde heldere en contrastrijke beeld. Dit maakt de letter zo bij uitstek geschikt voor vele uiteenlopende soorten werk. Op gladde zowel als op ruwere

peared; the typeface was equally short-lived. For some time, Smit worked on the adaptation of typefaces for use on phototypesetting systems, until illness forced him to give up his job at the Foundry in 1976.

Foreign text faces: Columbia and Pascal

One of the Type foundry's most disappointing experiences in the post-war years was the production of *Columbia* (1949–1956). This text face, which could be labeled 'transitional' – that is, in between baroque and classicist –, was designed by the American Walter H. McKay. According to Dick Dooijes one of Tetterode's directors discovered the preliminary designs of Columbia during a working visit to the United States. The Type foundry needed a low-contrast workhorse typeface as a successor to *Hollandse Mediaeval*. Both the 1927 *Garamont* and the recent *De Roos Romein* had proved too elegant for that purpose; an informal request to the lettering artist and typographer Helmut Salden to design a new face had yielded no result. The management ordered that Columbia be produced at the Amsterdam Type Foundry under Dooijes's supervision right away. This greatly annoyed Dooijes, as it meant that the plans to develop his *Bronletter* – a one-weight bible face – into an all-purpose roman under the name *Nieuw Romaans* were brushed aside.[10] Production dragged along for seven years, the laborious transatlantic correspondence being the main reason for the slowness of the process, and huge amounts of money were spent. After countless drawings has been made, rejected and remade, the final version was a typeface that was uncommonly common and lacked personality. Columbia never became the commercial success its advocates had hoped for.

Possibly the Type Foundry's most sophisticated text face was *Pascal* (1961), the first typeface by José Mendoza y Almeida. Mendoza had worked with Maximilien Vox, whom Dooijes greatly admired, and Roger Excoffon before setting up shop as an independent designer. Pascal, based on experiments carried out by Mendoza's father in 1943[11], is a 'glyphic' face: it has subtly flared extremes instead of serifs, suggesting forms used in letter-carving. In a letter[12] Mendoza described it as 'a reaction of "Latin sensitivity" to "Swiss" monotony', referring to the new sanserifs of the time, Helvetica and Univers. The Type Foundry probably saw it more as a timely answer to Hermann Zapf's *Optima*. But if Optima has the round forms of a Roman inscriptional letter, Pascal is narrower and, despite its Latin temperament, has a certain coolness to it.

▴ Promotor (1960) by Tetterode's in-house designer Leonard Smit was based on a nineteenth-century 'Alsacienne'.

◂ Type specimen for Pascal by José Mendoza y Almeida (1961); this specimen was designed by Mendoza with Gérard Blanchard.

▾ Columbia by Walter H. McKay, produced at the Amsterdam Type Foundry between 1949 and 1956.

Columbia heeft alle eigenschappen, die
EEN BIJ UITSTEK PRAKTISCH TY
Corps 12 – no. 3253 – minimum 7 kg

Columbia heeft alle eigenschappen, die
EEN BIJ UITSTEK PRAKTISCH TY
Corps 12 – no. 3267 – minimum 4 kg

Columbia heeft alle eigensch
Corps 16 – no. 3255 – minimum 8½ kg

Columbia heeft alle eigencha
Corps 16 – no. 3269 – minimum 5½ kg

Columbia heeft alle eig
Corps 20 – no. 3256 – minimum 8½ kg

Columbia heeft alle eige
Corps 20 – no. 3270 – minimum 6½ kg

5 Article in *Drukkersweekblad en Autolijn*, Christmas Issue 1961, p 78.

6 Mentioned in a 1973 review in *The Globe and Mail* (information supplied by Peter Enneson, who researched Krijger's work with the cooperation of Nienke Krijger).

7 Advertisement of the Amsterdam Type Foundry in *Drukkersweekblad en Autolijn*, Christmas Issue 1958.

8 *The Encyclopaedia of Typefaces*, fourth edition, 1970.

9 Lettergieterij Amsterdam, *Internationale catalogus van drukletters*, Amsterdam [1968], p 140.

10 Dick Dooijes, *Mijn leven met letters*, Amsterdam 1991, pp 52–53.

11 Introduction to the Pascal type specimen, Lettergieterij Amsterdam, 1961.

12 Letter to Mathieu Lommen, cf. *Dutch typefounders' specimens* (cit.), p 36.

The ambitions of Dick Dooijes

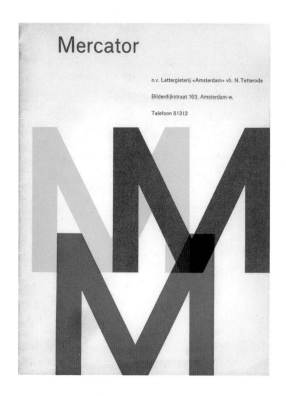

Specimen of Dick Dooijes's
Mercator 'and related sanserifs',
c. 1968.

Dick Dooijes (1909–1998) was a tireless organizer and cultural manager: a board member of several cultural organizations, a member of the Amsterdam city council for the Social-Democratic party and, from 1968 onwards, director of the Rietveld Academy in Amsterdam. Of all the post-war type designers in the Netherlands, he was the most prolific writer. He published over a dozen books and booklets and numerous articles about type and typography – and about himself. He even wrote a typographic autobiography, entitled *Mijn leven met letters* (My life with type). But when assessing Dooijes's position as a type designer and a cultural figure, one should be sceptical of the rather self-satisfied way he portrayed himself in his writings.

Judging by the presence of his work in today's digital market, Dooijes's importance as a type designer is marginal at best. His two major type families, *Mercator* and *Lectura*, are unavailable; the typeface which comes closest to a Dooijes revival is an unauthorized digitization of Lectura named *Leighton* by Paul Hickson (Red Rooster, 1993). Yet it would be unjust to pass over him in silence as Max Caflisch did in a 1989 overview of Dutch type design.[13] Dooijes was, at a certain point, the country's most prolific type designer; during the 1960s Mercator and Lectura were virtually the only contemporary text faces in their category available to those printers who depended on the Amsterdam Type Foundry for the supply of their equipment and type. Lectura especially is well-made, pleasing and rather original.

Apprenticeship

Dick Dooijes owed both his position and the development of his skill as a type designer to Sjoerd de Roos. Dooijes was seventeen when he met De Roos, already a well-known type designer and typographer, who was married to a cousin of his mother's. Apparently impressed by his nephew's drawing skills, De Roos hired him as his assistant and apprentice at the Amsterdam Type Foundry (Tetterode), where he was senior designer and draftsman. During the working day young Dooijes was introduced to the principles of typography and type by the foundry's engravers and the head of the in-house printing office. In the evenings he took drawing courses at the Instituut voor Kunstnijverheidsonderwijs (Institute for Applied Arts Education). For fifteen years Dooijes shared De Roos's sombre office. A small window in the office opened onto the Type Foundry's Typographic Library. In that splendid room designed by the architect De Bazel, Dooijes spent considerable time researching and cataloguing books and receiving visitors. Although rather aloof at first, De Roos did become a mentor of sorts to him. He introduced him to Edward Johnston's *Writing & Illuminating & Lettering* and involved him in the preparation of the 1926 'fifty best books' competition.[14]

In the late 1920s Dooijes started taking part in the design of new typefaces as an assistant draftsman. Among the first designs he worked on were *Bristol* and *Carlton*, based on Morris Fuller Benton's *Broadway*. The acquisition and adaptation of Broad-

▾ After the Nazis had arrested Stefan Schlesinger, the original designer of Rondo, Dick Dooijes continued production of the typeface. The bold weight, finished after Schlesinger's death, was developed by Dooijes from Schlesinger's sketches.

▸ Bristol (1929) was one of three display faces drawn under De Roos's supervision based on Morris Fuller Benton's Broadway.

Es elegante el Rondo Gordo

Corps 36 – no. 3121 – minimum 11½ kg

▴ Dick Dooijes, Hebrew alphabet as reproduced in his typographic autobiography *Mijn leven met letters* (1991), with the characters in the wrong order.

way had been a purely commercial decision in which De Roos had little or no say. 'My critical sense had not yet matured,' wrote Dooijes, 'and it did not weigh heavily on my artistic conscience to help embellish [these] modish pieces of rubbish with little serifs and shadings. ... This whole business had nothing to do with Art Deco; there was no attempt whatsoever at stylistic innovation.' [15] Dooijes was also involved in the production of *Nobel*, another derivative design reluctantly undertaken by De Roos.

The first newly designed type family to which Dooijes made a considerable contribution was De Roos's *Egmont*. Starting from the designer's sketches of the basic forms and details, Dooijes made pencil drawings of each character. These drawings were used as models for manually engraved stencils from which punches were cut for different sizes by a pantographic machine. The numbers are impressive: for a full-fledged family such as Egmont (5 styles), 970 drawings had to be made. [16]

Hebrew alphabet and Rondo

The first original typeface Dooijes designed was for a script he could not read. The management of the ever-expanding Tetterode firm had discovered market potential in the young Israeli nation which began to take shape in Palestine: a Hebrew face was called for. Not only did Dooijes study historical literature about Hebrew writing, he also ordered newspapers to be sent from Palestine. Having noticed the frequent use of serifless type in newspaper headlines, he drew a sturdy, geometric sanserif. According to my Israeli sources [17], Dooijes's approach was quite innovative, perhaps a bit naively so. Most of his solutions are quite plausible, although somewhat oversimpliflied; the most complex characters have visual inconsistencies, apparently because Dooijes did not know what liberties he could take.

Production of the typeface was begun, but contacts with potential clients became impossible after the outbreak of the Second World War. Dooijes's *Hebreeuws* disappeared and its drawings were not recovered until the Tetterode collection was acquired by the Amsterdam University Library around 1990.

After Hitler's army occupied the Netherlands in 1940, the printing industry went into crisis. Sjoerd de Roos, foreseeing hard times at the Type Foundry, saved his assistant's job by requesting early retirement for himself. Dooijes now became designer-draftsman and head of the library. He also made his debut as a book designer with a publication about his mentor, *Het werk van S.H. de Roos* by A.A.M. Stols (a brief survey of De Roos's work, published by Tetterode in 1942). Book design was to remain part and parcel of Dooijes's activities at Tetterode. Dooijes developed his own no-nonsense style of laying out type catalogues, the first of which was praised in 1947 by the British trade magazine *Paper & Print*: '... a really handsome type specimen book'. [18]

One of his wartime tasks was the supervision of a new type design by Stefan Schlesinger, the brilliant calligrapher and commercial artist whose *Figaro* (later renamed *Hidalgo*) had been quite successful in the previous years. Schlesinger's script *Rondo*,

13 Max Caflisch, 'Some peaks in type design in the Netherlands' in *Gravisie 14*, Utrecht 1989.

14 Most biographical details are taken from *Mijn leven met letters* (cit.).

15 Ibid., pp 28–29.

16 Ibid., pp 30–31.

17 I asked type designers Yanek Iontef and Eyal Holtzman for their opinions.

18 *Mijn leven met letters* (cit.), p 67.

omvangrijke teksten die op een klein oppervlak gezet moeten worden toch een goede leesbaarheid te geven.

Het type bevindt zich nog in een experimenteel stadium, nog niet alle lettervormen voor verschillende vetheidsgraden zijn getekend, gegraveerd en gegoten. Daarom moest voor de kolommen die gezet werden uit de cursief en de vette soort een wonderlijke tekst worden samengesteld uit de weinige letters die beschikbaar waren.

Dit is de gebruikelijke gang van zaken bij de uitvoering van een nieuw letterontwerp. Men kan zich uit een dergelijk stuk zetsel reeds een goed oordeel vormen over hetgeen bereikt zal kunnen worden. Door zulke proefnemingen kan worden vastgesteld of de ver-

brusse abonnee benoembaar nabeurs neusbeen saus rebus brigges rigoreus meegeren ou boogbrug gebrom graumann surgeon sarong sobbing signe bibberig gironummer onbego minimuminbreng abuis bain graaf barones sir senior ruim gebrom rumoer neurien men brusse abonnee benoembaar nabeurs neusbeen saus sierro brigges rigoreus meegeren ou bonus boogbrug gebrom gra boemerang surgeon serge sar signer gissing unerring bibbe onbegonnen minimuminbren noir marius senior ruimer mo

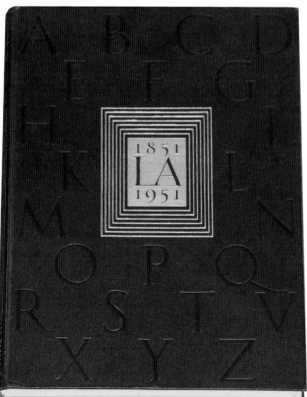

based on one of his styles of hand lettering, still needed a lot of work. Several versions of the lowercase drawn by Schlesinger were tested until, in 1942, Schlesinger was captured by the Nazis. With Schlesinger's consent, Dooijes finished Rondo and drew its bold weight. The latter became one of the most popular display types of the 1950s and 1960s, and was in great demand for the shopfronts and packaging of butchers, bakers and confectioners.

After 1945; Bronletter versus Columbia

In 1946 Dooijes enrolled for a course given by the writing master and typographer Henri Friedlaender. Friedlaender, a German Jew, had been working in the Netherlands since the early 1930s and had escaped the Nazi terror by going into hiding. His career and influence are examined in greater depth on pages 100 – 101. For Dooijes, Friedlaender's classes were an eye-opener: 'More than the years with De Roos, the weeks with Friedlaender have made me realize what creating letterforms is really about. ... In printing type, it is crucial that a clear and harmonious image is created, possibly in any combination of characters. ... If one has good control over the pen, which Friedlaender tried to impart to us, this harmony originates naturally while writing.'[19]

The course prepared Dooijes for what gradually became a strong ambition: to design a roman typeface. His first chance to do so came when a printer of religious books, Gooi & Sticht, ordered a Bible type. *Bronletter* (Source Type) was to replace a German face which was no longer available because the factory that produced it had been bombed. The typeface was meant for use at 7 pt only, and was therefore given a generous x-height and little contrast between thick and thin. Dooijes has called Bronletter 'a crucial project' which gave him his first opportunity to 'test in practice my vision of what a text type should be'.[20]

The type was delivered to the client in late 1949 and remained in use until the advent of phototypesetting. Although it does not look like a very confident design, Dooijes proposed expanding it into a complete family (working name: *Nieuw Romaans*). Having progressed considerably, in consultation with Tetterode's artistic adviser G.W. Ovink, the process was abruptly brought to a halt when one of the directors chanced upon an unpublished American typeface, *Columbia* by Walter H. McKay which he thought was fit for the job. Adding insult to injury, Dooijes's superiors assigned the supervision of Columbia's production to him. Forty years later, Dooijes still wrote bitterly about this episode. As described on page 89, the American typeface became a commercial fiasco. Dooijes never felt sorry about this: it eventually gave him the chance to develop his Lectura.

Mercator, a neutral sans

Despite his predilection for classical romans, Dooijes's first large type family was a sanserif. In the late 1950s the success of the Type Foundry's Nobel had waned. The influence of Swiss typography had aroused an interest in nineteenth-century grotesques, and new designs based on these earlier models were developed abroad. Tetterode possessed a wide array of matrices of grotesques (called *Antieken* in the foundry's specimens) but these designs were too disparate to form a proper series. Dooijes was asked to design a neutral, straightforward sanserif to complement the old grotesques. The first weights of Mercator were made available in 1958. It is unclear at which point Dooijes became aware of the German and Swiss designs based on the same principles: *Neue Haas Grotesk* (later called *Helvetica*), *Univers* and *Folio* were

NIEUWBOUW

Het eikenhout dat ik gebruik brandt
veel feller dan welke houtsoort ook
en daarom wordt elze- of dennehout
AAN DE BEPALING VAN EEN

Corps 28   no. 3613   minimum 11¾ kg

Corps 12   no. 3608   minimum 7 kg

À cette page
il faut donner
MUSIQUES

El anatema lanzado aquí sobre
Anatole France es el del espí-
MUESTRA EL ESCENARIO

Corps 14   no. 3609   minimum 7¾ kg

Corps 36   no. 3614   minimum 13¾ kg

abcdefghijklmnopqrstuvwxyz&1234567890
ABCDEFGHIJKLMNOPQRSTUVWXYZ

◄ Dick Dooijes, Mercator Light
(Mercator Mager, c. 1959).
Mercator was the Amsterdam
Type Foundry's answer to
Univers and Neue Haas Grotesk/
Helvetica; but Dick Dooijes and
G.W. Ovink probably began
researching the nineteenth-
century grotesque as a possible
model some time before these
typefaces were published.

▼ *Een vacantie reis revue* ('A vacation
travel magazine'), specimen of
Dick Dooijes's Contura, 1965.

all published in 1957, and it is highly likely that by then work on Mercator was well under way.

Dooijes and Ovink agreed that early nineteenth-century types were a good starting point for the new typeface. Decades later, Dooijes explained: 'I think that the idea underlying the geometric sanserif is based on a misunderstanding. What the eye requires cannot always be accomplished with a rule, triangle and compass. ... It seemed important to me to look for forms which were more optically pleasing and which would make it possible to draw more freely.'[21] Designed independently of any specific model, Mercator differs in look and feel from its contemporaries. Its narrowness and rather wide letterspacing make it stand out. It is less refined than Univers; and although many of its ideas recall Helvetica, it has details which give it a certain individuality: the open c and s, the straight angle at which the eye of the a departs from the vertical, and the Q with its bent tail.

Mercator was issued as a typeface for hand-setting and hot metal composition, as well as a headline face for filmsetting. Piet Zwart, always an advocate of no-nonsense type, admired the typeface and called it 'the first Dutch sanserif on an international level'.[22] Mercator was briefly successful; in the 1980s, a few styles were made available for photosetting. After the advent of desktop publishing Dooijes hoped for a revival of the complete family in digital form, but nobody volunteered. Perhaps Mercator was simply not special enough.

Contura and Lectura

The publication of *Contura* (1965) was seen by Dooijes as a secret personal triumph. This outline face – which unlike earlier open capitals by Van Krimpen and Caflisch also contained a lowercase alphabet – was based on the shapes of the Bronletter. Dooijes revelled in the idea that the management accepted Contura without realizing that, hidden within it, was the same design they had once rejected. But perhaps it stayed too close to the original roman to become a successful display type. It lacks vigour, and its outlines are drawn so mechanically that in narrow stems, or in places where strokes meet or intersect, a clotted effect is visible.

Lectura, published in 1969, was a more ambitious enterprise. Its concept dates back to 1962 when Dooijes and Ovink, in view of the Columbia debacle, discussed the desirability of a new book face to be added to the Tetterode type library. It was decided that the new roman be produced with new technologies in mind. In 1964 Dooijes visited Intertype, the British supplier of Tetterode's line-casting machines, which had begun developing its own phototypesetting system. Work on the typeface progressed simultaneously in Amsterdam and Maidenhead (near London).

The working name of Dooijes's new roman was *Van Dijck*, after the Dutch punchcutter by that name. In his introduction to the first specimen, Ovink also mentioned the Voskens family and Nicholas Kis as references. Dooijes summed up the creative

19 *Mijn leven met letters* (cit.), p 47.

20 Ibid., pp 51–52.

21 Mathieu Lommen, *Letterontwerpers*, Haarlem 1987, p 24.

22 *Print*, 1964, quoted in *Mijn leven met letters* (cit.), p 85.

lectura medium

abcdefghijklmnopqrstuv
wxyzæœfiflß
ABCDEFGHIJKLMNOPQR
STUVWXYZÆŒ
1234567890
&ƒ$£§†()[]!?¡¿%‰
.,:;-——''""·‹›«»*

process in an unpublished typescript, writing about himself in the third person.
'As a prototype, he chose the work of his seventeenth-century fellow Amsterdammer, and he tried in many sketches to seek out the essence of the forms of Christoffel van Dijck's types. During this activity, his own approach gradually arose out of
the ancient foundation. It was never his intention to copy the three-hundred-year-
old Amsterdam type, and as he continued to work, the distance from the prototype
became greater and greater.'[23] Like Van Krimpen's Romanée, Lectura was not meant
to be a Van Dijck revival, but a personal, contemporary interpretation. It is Dooijes's
best design by far.

Lectura is similar in colour to Times New Roman. It is also related to Times in the
way the bold weight, with its increased vertical stress, relates to the regular. But its
feel is very different, very 1960s; the italic is especially spirited, and surprisingly pretty. In the 1980s, Lectura was digitized for the Linotron 202 system; an adaptation for
Linotronic 300 was made later. Two variants (bold condensed and bold condensed
italic) were digitized for PostScript, but never released.[24]

Swan songs

In 1968, the year in which Lectura was announced, Dooijes was invited to become
director of the Gerrit Rietveld Academy. He decided that he was indeed ready to leave
the company where he had worked for forty-one years. Recently there had been
conflicts with the management about administrative and financial matters; Dooijes
was also slightly bitter because he had realized that some of his typefaces – notably
Rondo and Mercator – could have made him a lot of money had he been a freelancer, while as a regular employer he was not entitled to royalties. Tetterode had
done little to compensate for this.

Dooijes remained director of the Rietveld Academy until 1974. After his retirement
he was active as a writer, publishing a volume of articles, a book on Dutch pioneers
of typography and the 'rather superficial autobiography' (Mathieu Lommen's description[25]) mentioned earlier. Dick Dooijes died in 1998.

Not only did Lectura mark the end of Dooijes's career as a type designer, it was also
the Amsterdam Type Foundry's swan song. Tetterode merged with a large paper distribution company in 1963 and became Bührmann-Tetterode. After moving to new
premises in 1981, the casting of metal type continued on a limited scale, but in 1988
these activities were taken over by the Fundición Tipográfica Neufville in Barcelona.
From 1984 onwards Tetterode was the exclusive Dutch distributor of Linotype's ana-
log and digital typesetting systems, and as a consequence also distributed the Linotype fonts for these systems. After the introduction of PostScript in 1985, Tetterode's
type specialist Henk Gianotten became a pioneer and evangelist of PostScript technology, as well as Linotype's Dutch ambassador; he was a public figure in the printing world, much the way Ovink and Dooijes had been in earlier decades. Licenses for
the production of digital fonts from designs made for the Amsterdam Type Foundry
were sold to several manufacturers, including Bitstream, URW, Elsner+Flake, and
Linotype. The Dutch Type Library (DTL) obtained the rights to digitize most of the
firm's Dutch type designs.

In 2002, Tetterode stopped its activities in type distribution to fully concentrate on
its core business as a supplier of workflow hardware for printing firms. The year
before, Linotype Library in Germany honoured Gianotten, who has since retired, by
naming a new typeface after him.

Sem Hartz, professional gentleman

Sem Hartz (1912–1996) described himself as 'a designer and engraver, mostly of postage stamps and banknotes, sometimes of books and dust-jackets'. Portraits – notably of the royal family – were his speciality. Usually he worked from his own sketches, cutting the engravings directly in steel or copper. For the letters and figures on most of his stamps he relied on the skill of Jan van Krimpen because it was, in Hartz's words, 'the best lettering one could possibly get'.[26]

In early 1940, when working on a set of Luxembourg stamps, Hartz agreed to do some of the type and figures himself. 'The result was so terrifying,' he wrote, 'that I was shocked.' After several more attempts, he got 'so fascinated that lettering became a sort of obsession. Borrowing Edward Johnston's book on *Writing & Illuminating, & Lettering* I began to study written letter forms.' This was the beginning of a modest career as a type designer, resulting in two text typefaces, *Emergo* and *Juliana*, and a few titling alphabets. But Hartz's biggest achievements lay elsewhere: as 'Royal Engraver'; as consultant and ambassador to the Enschedé firm; as a teacher and writer; and, last but not least, as a professional gentleman.

Born in 1912 the son of an artist and a musician, Sem Hartz studied engraving at the Amsterdam Rijksacademie (State Academy) and joined Enschedé in 1936 as an apprentice engraver. While his precision and pragmatism made him a perfect craftsman, his natural flair, witty conversation and flawless English allowed him to move in circles to which none of his Enschedé colleagues had access. He represented Enschedé – a printer of banknotes and stamps to several governments – in international projects, and even travelled to Indonesia with the company's president to discuss a series of stamps with President Sukarno. Being the kind of anglophile who would travel to London to get his shoes repaired, he had many friends in British typographic circles.[27] He gave lectures at the Double Crown Club and the Wynkyn de Worde Society and contributed to the Penrose Annual. The Brits loved his naughty stories and appreciated his sportsmanship – he had been a boxer, loved sailing and was a keen amateur hunter. They also loved his off-hand demonstrations of virtuosity: 'When the occasion is less formal and more relaxed, Sem may produce a diamond or steel from his pocket and, while chatting, decorate a tumbler, or a window pane, with his own or his host's initials, or a sailing-ship. I often wonder how many pub-keepers up and down England have realized that their premises have been enriched in this way, or have appreciated it.'[28] As it is safe to assume that Hartz was a bigger star in England than in his own country, it is a mere act of justice that his most successful typeface, Juliana, was first shown in a British publication – the 1958 *Penrose Annual* – and was used in a number of best-sellers in the most English of pocket book series – the Penguins.

Sem Hartz, postage stamps featuring engraved portraits of Queen Juliana (1948) and her three eldest daughters (1946). For the lettering, Hartz relied on the skills of Jan van Krimpen. Hartz would later confess that Van Krimpen had made a much better deal with the PTT, earning up to ten times as much as Hartz on the same stamp. (Lommen, *Letterontwerpers*, p 34)

23 *Dutch typefounders' specimens* (cit.), note on p 36.

24 information provided by Henk Gianotten, who supervised the conversion of Tetterode's typefaces (e-mail to the author, 3.2.2003).

25 Mathieu Lommen in *Dutch typefounders' specimens* (cit.), p 31 n 56.

26 This quote and the following: Sem Hartz, *Essays*, Aartswoud/Amsterdam 1992, p 9. This book was a personal initiative of Bram de Does, who printed it on his own Victoria platen press, set in Emergo (borrowed from Hartz).

27 These and other details are reported by Ruari McLean in 'Our Sem', his contribution to *S.L. Hartz in de grafische wereld*, The Hague 1969.

28 Ibid., p 49.

After Sem Hartz had decided to withdraw Emergo, originally produced at Enschedé, it became the standard typeface of Hartz's private Tuinwijkpers. The showing below is reproduced from the collection of Hartz's essays printed and co-published in 1992 by Bram de Does, who borrowed the font from Hartz for that occasion. When Sem Hartz passed away in 1996, the Emergo font was bequeathed to Jan Keijser's Avalon Press in Woubrugge.

ABCDEFGHIJKLMNOPQRSTUVW
XYZJRÆŒ&ÄÅÇÉÈÊËÏÑÖØÜ
abcdefghijklmnopqrstuvwxyzij
æœáàâäåçéèêëíìîïñóòôöøúùûü
1234567890ctfbffffifflfhfifjfkflgy
1234567890.,:;''„"!?--()[]§†‡⁺

ABCDEFGHIJKLMNOPQRSTUVWXYZ
ÆŒJ&ÇÉ1234567890

ABCDEFGHIJKLMNOPQRSTUVWXYZ
ÆŒ&ÄÅÇÉÈÊËÏÑÖØÜQUQuRT
abcdefghijklmnopqrstuvwxyzÿ
1234567890.,:;''„"!?-()[]ctfbfffifflflfjflfhfk
æœáàâäåçéèêëíìîïñóòôöøúùûü

Detail from 1954 season's greetings, set in Emergo and printed at the Tuinwijkpers. On the back of the card is a complete Emergo specimen.

As usual rather late, T. & S. Hartz
send you their best wishes for
1954

The Emergo typeface

The German occupation (1940–1945) was a decisive period in Hartz's career. The events, he wrote, 'spelled the end of my work as a designer of stamps. To pass the time I tried my hand at punchcutting with Van Krimpen's punchcutter, P.H. Rädisch, an exacting taskmaster. For a long time, I had toyed with the idea of having my own press for letterpress printing …. Punchcutting soon put into my head the idea that my own type would make the products of the press perhaps poorer things but even more mine own.'[29] Being Jewish, he was soon forced to go into hiding. He used his skills to falsify official documents for the resistance, and to illustrate clandestine publications. In the last year of the war, 1944, Hartz started work on the design of the typeface which would become *Emergo*, making his first sketches on scraps of wallpaper in his hiding place.

His drawings for Emergo were amazing. Being used to executing minute engravings for postage stamps, Hartz made the designs at actual size. Jan van Krimpen, Hartz's boss at Enschedé, admired the drawings and bought them for the firm. '… I now had the expert assistance of our able punchcutter. But as there were only the rather rough small drawings to work from, I had to finish the punches myself – the drawings, even after being blown up, were not of much use to the punchcutter.' This is what Hartz wrote for *Printing & Graphic Arts* in 1954;[30] in an interview with Mathieu Lommen, three decades later, he was more precise, and a little less diplomatic. 'During the war Van Krimpen wrote me a terrific letter about the Emergo, about those little drawings at actual size: "You, for one, understand what this work is about. Not like De Roos …" He probably thought that nothing would ever come of it: I am not known for my tendency to complete things. When the drawings were done, I told him: "Now what more do I have to do about them, Jan?" After having been bent over them for forty-five minutes, he replied: "Well, I have always had to do it all by myself, too." After the war I engraved the basic letterforms and left the rest to Rädisch. Rightaway Rädisch said: "This is absolutely hopeless," and kept making changes. After four and a half years of fighting with him and making new engravings over and over again, I told him: "Now if you won't touch my typeface any more, and just make it technically sound, I'll give you one of my father's paintings." [Louis Hartz was a well-known painter – JM] I knew he wanted that very much. He accepted the proposal. And I had my typeface.'[31]

During the process, proofs had been made available for review to colleagues and friends. Stanley Morison wrote to him in July 1948: 'I have a very agreeable impression from my inspection of your roman and italic. The proportions of the former so closely resemble those of the Aldine-Bembo that I can hardly fail to be pleased. The weight is what it should be.' And in August 1949: 'I am very pleased to see the progress that has been made with your Emergo type. The roman now looks extremely well, mellow, flowing and supremely well cut. The italic is, to my mind, very pleasantly rational.'[32] When Enschedé published a preliminary specimen of the newly cast 12 point Emergo, Hartz's debut was praised by critics – John Dreyfus among them. However, the typeface was never brought out.

Hartz in conversation with Lommen: 'Jan van Krimpen had drawn the Spectrum typeface during the war and wanted it to be produced in order to sell it. He evidently didn't like the idea of Monotype publishing my Emergo as well. As I wanted to avoid a clash with him at any cost, I decided to withdraw Emergo. In retrospect I don't regret that, for the Tuinwijkpers now has its own type.'[33]

ABCDEFGHI

A PRELIMINARY SPECIMEN OF

abcdefghijklmn

JULIANA, A NEW TYPE FACE

JKLMNOPQR

FOR LINOTYPE COMPOSITION

opqrstuvwxyz

DESIGNED BY S. L. HARTZ

STUVWXYZ

Juliana: for export only

In 1951 the printer James Shand introduced Hartz to his friend Walter Tracy, who was head of the department for type development at Linotype England. Shand suggested that Linotype should invite Hartz to design a new book face. Hartz submitted drawings of a few characters in the autumn of 1952; trial characters were cut, cast and proofed. Tracy wrote: 'It was evident that they had the style of sixteenth-century Italian types, which was what we were seeking; but at the same time it was clear that the proportions of the letters one to another would need revision.'[34] This was not surprising, writes Tracy, because Hartz was used to working in 'final size' as he had done with the Emergo drawings. This time he had been asked to draw letters 6 to 7 cm high. Production advanced slowly, as Linotype gave priority to the production of fonts which had 'immediate export value', such as oriental types; but the project was kept alive and in early 1958 the first sizes of the Juliana typeface were presented in the *Penrose Annual* alongside an article by Hartz. Later that year all the sizes of the new typeface were introduced.

Hartz later described how he went about designing his first typeface for a linecasting machine. The types made for Linotype and Intertype machines often had 'an ugly, too wide italic' because the widths of both styles needed to be the same. It occurred to him that there might be 'a solution which nobody had apparently thought of before. Of course, you have to do it the other way around: to start with the difficulty of the italic, and adapt the roman afterwards. The result was not too bad. It is simply a case of learning what a machine can do and making sure you have your way.'[35]

The *Penrose* article is a series of considerations triggered by working on Juliana, a process which, as Hartz suggests, had given him considerable worries. The piece challenges 'the widespread misconception that the types we use owe everything to writing and calligraphy' and focuses on the role of the punchcutter. 'The crux of the matter is that type is not pen-written characters, but sharply-cut letters.' He fulminates against the 'artsy-craftsy' lettering of German masters, and accuses Excoffon's *Mistral* of being a useless and illegible novelty, concluding that '… the only valid reason for designing a new type nowadays seems to be a type with some specific purpose, without bothering about writing or whether it is contemporary or not. Beauty and contemporariness are not things that can be designed into a type; they can come only of their own accord. The Juliana design is simply an attempt to make a rather narrow and space-saving type, as legible as possible.'[36]

Juliana became quite successful in Great Britain. Precisely for the qualities mentioned by Hartz, it was used for numerous Penguin books. Yet the matrices were never produced at the height required for use on Dutch Linotype machines; therefore, the elegant collection of literary essays with which Juliana was presented to the Dutch typographic world in 1959 was also its last appearance in a book made in Holland. In 2003 David Esser, a student of the Type & Media course at the Royal Academy in The Hague, presented a digital version of Juliana as a graduation project.

Capital gain

Having withdrawn Emergo, Hartz would never again design a text face for Enschedé. The firm did, however, publish two display alphabets which were 'signed' by him, *Molé Foliate* and *Panture*. The extent of Hartz's involvment in the making of Molé Foliate is not totally clear. Released in the 1960s, the typeface was a revival of an old titling font by the Paris founder Molé. Johan de Zoete, curator of the Enschedé

29 Sem Hartz, *Essays* (cit.), p 10.

30 The piece was reprinted in *Essays* (cit.), pp 9 – 10.

31 *Letterontwerpers* (cit.), p 35. Van Krimpen wrote to Hartz on 24 March 1945, six weeks before the liberation: 'I am so happy with what you sent me because it makes me realize that finally there is someone in the Netherlands who approaches typographic letterforms in the same way as I do. It is easiest for me to express this by quoting the late Frederic Warde. "But as long as we work with the arbitrary signs of the alphabet, we shall be dependent on the past and – like the Greek vase makers – we shall derive our finest effects from the subtle personal variations on a traditional style and shape." – And that you are that someone makes it a double pleasure to me.' (letter in the Hartz archive of the Museum Meermanno, The Hague; my translation. The letter is also full of warnings against the Amsterdam Type Foundry and its director, whom Van Krimpen does not mention by name but calls 'an arch deceiver' ('aartsbedrieger'); apparently Hartz had told Van Krimpen that he considered negotiating with Enschedé's competitor.)

32 Quoted by F. Mayer in *S.L. Hartz in de grafische wereld* (cit.), p 69.

33 *Letterontwerpers* (cit.), pp 36 – 37. The Tuinwijkpers (named after Tuinwijkstraat, the street in Haarlem where Hartz lived) was the private press he installed in his home in the early 1950s. Its first publication was a 16-page booklet containing three ancient love songs, set in Henric de Lettersnider's textura from Enschedé. For several years no other books were published, although Hartz did print single sheets, such as the season's greetings which his friends usually received 'rather late'. It was not until he had found a partner – C. van Dijk, the author of the biography of Alexander Stols – that the press's output became more regular.

34 W. Tracy in *S.L. Hartz in de grafische wereld* (cit.), p 46.

35 *Letterontwerpers* (cit.), pp 39 – 40.

36 *The Penrose Annual* 1958; reprinted in *Essays* (cit.), pp 11 – 19.

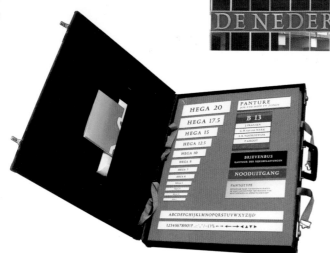

Museum, recalls that it was another engraver-designer at Enschedé, Pieter Wetselaar, who was greatly responsible for completing and cutting the sophisticated, nostalgic alphabet of capitals. 'Wetselaar actually cried when he saw that all the credits went to Hartz,' says De Zoete. Apparently there were more craftsmen like him – the names of Staphorst and Nijhuis are mentioned – who anonymously contributed to work for which the stars at Enschedé took the credits.

Panture, on the other hand, is obviously a Hartz design; a contemporary face with classical proportions and pronounced serifs. It was designed for Pantotype, a system developed by Enschedé for the mechanized engraving of metal and plastic plates for signage and lettering. The system was introduced circa 1971, at a time when Enschedé felt the need to diversify and explore new technologies. Shortly after, the firm hired a young, aspiring type designer named Gerard Unger; he, too, was asked to design an alphabet for the new system. The two Pantotype faces were presented together in a 1973 brochure. Unger's Pantotype face, called *Markeur*, was his first typeface, and is a sanserif in upper- and lowercase. Hartz's Panture – a caps-only classical roman – is an admirable anomaly among post-war signage alphabets. Panture was preceded by a rather similar alphabet Hartz designed in the mid-1960s for the Netherlands Bank: a typeface which was used for all lettering, signage and name-tags in the bank's Amsterdam headquarters. It was, in fact, a more complex design than Panture because the letters had to be engraved in several different techniques. Hartz designed the steel letters on the gates, a stencil alphabet for painted letters and a series of matrices for mechanic engraving. He also wrote instructions for spacing the alphabet when engraving new names.

Talent and genius

On the whole, Sem Hartz's types are well-made, elegant and, especially in the case of Juliana, very adequate alternatives to other modern classics, such as Jan van Krimpen's. If they lack anything, it is spirit and character; in that sense they are the opposite of their maker. In his short article on 'our Sem', Ruari McLean recalled Oscar Wilde's famous dictum, as reported by Gide: 'Do you want to know the great drama of my life? It is that I have put my genius into my life; all I've put into my works is my talent.' To this, McLean added: 'It is just possible that this is also true of Sem Hartz.'[37] Whether or not Hartz silently agreed we do not know; but coming from one of his best friends in his beloved England, this is a poignant and challenging observation.

---

37 Ruari McLean in *S.L. Hartz in de grafische wereld* (cit.), p 50.

Painters and penmen

Willem Sandberg, *scheursel* (tearing) from *Piet Zwart, Sleutelwoorden*, a book Sandberg made in collaboration with Jurriaan Schrofer, 1967.

Hand-lettering: a new tradition

W·STARK

HISTORIA
DE LA ECONOMÍA
EN SU RELACION
CON EL DESARROLLO
SOCIAL

FONDO DE
CULTURA
ECONOMICA

Boudewijn Ietswaart, cover for
*Historia de la economía en su relación
con el desarrollo social* by W. Stark.
Mexico, FCE, 1961.

Dutch book design in the 1950s and '60s showed a growing sense of quality. Publishers called in typographers, not only for bindings and dust jackets, but also for the design of the interiors. Much of this work was done by 'enlightened traditionalists' [1] who advocated harmony, simplicity and classic romans for body type, but were open to innovations and would not shy away from an asymmetric page layout. As most printing offices had only a small collection of display types – let alone large romans to harmonize with the interiors – it was a logical step for the designers of book jackets to draw their own letters.

If lettering for books and magazines in the 1920s and '30s often used constructed, geometric letterforms, this changed after the Second World War. It is hazardous to speculate about the psychological effects of the Nazi occupation; but after 1945 there somehow seems to have been a craving for reassuring, more traditional forms, and a regained appreciation of the human touch. Constructivism and typophoto were abandoned for a more painterly approach to graphic design. The mechanical-looking lettering that dominated pre-war high-circulation publications made way for a style that was less rigid, yet strongly rooted in tradition – a more personal kind of lettering based on writing and calligraphy. Some artists, such as Willem Rozendaal and his pupils, created highly personal, loose interpretations of traditional letter shapes. Others drew painstakingly precise alphabets, using the same forms over and over again, so that they were in effect type designers taking commissions from themselves. Each designer invented his or her own variations on renaissance and classical roman, humanist sanserif and italic.

This post-1945 development actually began just before the war, and was heavily influenced by the influx of graphic designers from Germany and Austria who had fled the Nazis. Among the German-speaking figures whose contribution changed the face of Dutch typography were Susanne Heynemann, Helmut Salden, Bertram Weihs and Henri Friedlaender.

Henri Friedlaender, writing master

Henri Friedlaender (1904 – 1996) was the son of a Jewish father and an English mother; he left Germany for Holland in 1932 because it had become increasingly difficult for him to find work due to the economic crisis and growing anti-semitism. On a recommendation from Sjoerd de Roos, he found a job as typographic adviser at Mouton printers in The Hague. Friedlaender had learned typesetting and printing while working at printing shops throughout Germany; at Klingspor in Offenbach he had worked under Rudolf Koch, who stimulated his interest in letterforms. He believed in subtle, inconspicuous typography and was not an admirer of 1930s Dutch book design, which he found mechanical and rigid. As soon as he had settled in the

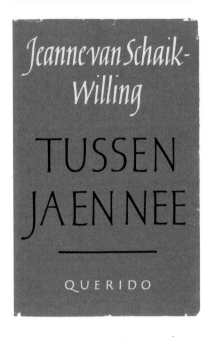

Netherlands, he began teaching. At Mouton he set up a typography course for apprentice typesetters; this resulted in the publication of a book entitled *Typographisch ABC* (1939), which has been called 'the first typographic textbook of any importance in the Netherlands'.[2]

Immediately after the war – during which he had been in hiding for three years in a garden shed near his house – Friedlaender began giving classes in writing and typography in The Hague and Amsterdam. Among his students were professional typographers such as his fellow expatriate Otto Treumann, Dick Dooijes of the Amsterdam Type Foundry, and Huib van Krimpen, son of Jan. In The Hague his students included several aspiring artists: the poet-publisher Jan Vermeulen from Leyden and three students of painting from the Hague Academy of Fine Arts, Hermanus Berserik, Jenny Dalenoord and Bertram Weihs.

In the brochure of the Typography and Book Design course he gave in Amsterdam, it was made clear that the classes were not meant for amateurs, but for people who had some knowledge of printing and typesetting. Moreover, it was 'very advisable that the participants have taken earlier courses in calligraphy or at least frequent the letter writing classes which are given parallel to this course.'[3] The distinction between 'writing' and 'calligraphy' is not without importance. Like his master Rudolf Koch, Friedlaender had a certain disdain for the mannerisms of calligraphy, and preferred a more commonplace attitude towards letterforms.

Twenty-odd years later, his approach to writing as the foundation of typography would be echoed in the teachings of Gerrit Noordzij, who started up an ambitious type and lettering programme at the Hague Academy in 1970. Noordzij claims that everything – typography, type design, civilization itself – starts with writing; and to this day, writing has remained a fundamental skill in the typographic curriculum in The Hague. Noordzij himself has pointed out Friedlaender's importance for the letter-friendly climate at the Hague Academy, notably through his influence on the teachers of the painting department.[4]

In 1950, Friedlaender decided to emigrate to Israel. Shortly before he left The Netherlands, work had begun on a Hebrew type for the Amsterdam Type Foundry. The design of the typeface was continued from a distance; it would take another eight years before it was ready for publication. Friedlaender's *Hadassah* type was released in 1958.

1 'Enlightened traditionalists': Gerard Unger's term (in an e-mail to the author).

2 Reinold Kuipers, *Gerezen wit*, Amsterdam 1990, pp 44–47.

3 Quoted in Kurt Löb, *Exil-gestalten*, Arnhem 1995, pp 130–131, an important source of information about Friedlaender's Dutch period.

4 Ibid., p 302.

Hague hands: Rozendaal and his students

◄ W.J. Rozendaal, leaflet for the fiftieth anniversary of the Residentieorkest (The Hague City Orchestra), 1954.

▼ Bertram Weihs, poster for Simon Carmiggelt's book *Poespas*, 1954. *Museum Rijswijk.*

▼ Piet van Trigt, a teacher of calligraphy and lettering at the Hague Academy, also worked for the PTT as a typographer and lettering specialist. He personally supervised the placement of his lettering for the Dutch post offices and sometimes corrected the spacing on site.

The post-1945 situation at the Academy of Fine Arts in The Hague (which became the 'Royal Academy of Arts' or KABK in 1957) was rather peculiar. There were two separate departments where one could train to be a graphic designer, but neither regarded the training of students for this occupation as its main task.

The Department of Advertising Design (Reclame-ontwerp), headed by Gerard Kiljan and Paul Schuitema, was a Bauhaus-like, interdisciplinary design school, where book design and text typography were no priorities. In spite of the department's name, few students aspired to be commercial artists; many felt that doing work for ad agencies was close to selling one's soul to the devil. Graduates from the post-1945 period ended up in a wide variety of jobs: photographer, exhibition designer, toy designer, director of TV shows.

At the Drawing and Painting Department, the atmosphere was completely different. Its most charismatic and influential teacher, Willem Rozendaal (1899–1971), had worked as a graphic artist as well as a designer of glass and porcelain before the war; he had also been the assistant of the architect Hendrik Wijdeveld. Although his students trained to be painters, Rozendaal kept urging them to be realistic – and preferably a little cynical – about the possibilities of making a living as an artist. In his opinion, artists should also be artisans with a broad repertoire of practical skills. Rozendaal had been appointed as a teacher of book illustration and decoration, but his courses encompassed anything from typography and writing to reproduction techniques and mechanical typesetting. As a result, many of Rozendaal's former students found work as illustrators and graphic designers. Their style is often immediately recognizable: Rozendaal's own witty, expressive drawing style, combined with idiosyncratic, improvised lettering, was a hard influence to get rid of.[5]

One teacher at the Hague Academy bridged the gap between the Departments of Painting and Advertising. Piet van Trigt, a meticulous calligrapher and typographer, taught lettering to fine art students as well as aspiring designers. Van Trigt was also a designer at the Royal Dutch PTT, taking care of key aspects of its corporate identity: he designed the lettering of the post boxes, and personally supervised the placement of the word POST in his own large *Clarendon*-like capitals on the post offices. In 1960, he was instrumental in having Gerrit Noordzij appointed as a teacher of writing at the Academy. After Van Trigt's unexpected death in 1970, Noordzij took over his job as well, and started up his seminal 'letter programme' for art and design students.[6]

Bertram Weihs and Hermanus Berserik

Although Willem Rozendaal was an enthusiastic teacher of all aspects of book design, his work as a lettering artist was average at best. Apparently he was aware of this. It was he who advised his students to enroll in Henri Friedlaender's writing classes in 1945–1946. A few years later he invited former student Bertram Weihs to join the department as a teacher of writing and calligraphy. Born in Austria in 1919, Weihs had come to The Hague, where he had relatives, in 1938 – the year Hitler occupied his native country. He was to complete his studies and pursue a career as a commercial artist, but became a designer of book jackets and a cartoonist instead. His art school training had provided him with a basic insight into letterforms; Friedlaender's teachings had deepened his knowledge. Weihs's classes at the Academy were disciplined and methodical, taking the students from one historical style to the next, writing endless lines until a natural flow appeared.[7]

Painters and penmen

◀ During the 1950s and '60s,
Jan Kuiper designed dozens of
book covers for the publisher
Boucher in The Hague. Among
them were almost forty tiny
bound volumes in Boucher's
aphorism series.

◀ Nacieron (Jan Kuiper and
R.D.E. Oxenaar), vignette for the
international Philips magazine
Direct Export Digest, 1955.

Bertram Weihs was a teacher at the Academy for less than a decade. An incurable
melancholic, he gradually shut himself off from the world, was hospitalized, and
took his own life in 1958.

One of Weihs's close friends was another Rozendaal student, Hermanus Berserik
(1921–2002). Berserik became one of the most prominent exponents of the Hague
school of figurative painting. He consciously made little distinction between the
'free' work he created as an artist, and the 'applied' work of his illustrations for
books and advertising, and allowed one to influence the other. His best-known
achievement as a designer is a large series of book covers made between 1954 and
1962 for the Ooievaars ('Storks'), one of the earliest Dutch series of pocket books.
Sometimes Berserik used typeset titling for lettering the jackets, but mostly he drew
his own nonchalant but well-proportioned letterforms. Berserik's method, developed as a teacher at the Hague Academy, of creating letters using counterforms cut
out of paper, was described by Gerrit Noordzij as something of an eye-opener.[8]

Jan Kuiper and 'Ootje' Oxenaar

Jan Kuiper (1928), a student of Rozendaal and Weihs in the 1950s, is still active as a
painter in the Northern Netherlands. For him, Weihs was 'the initiator of the post-
war letter tradition at the Hague Academy'. During the 1950s and '60s Kuiper worked
as an independent designer of book jackets and posters, combining his baroque
pen drawings with eclectic hand-lettering.

For some years, Kuiper's business partner was R.D.E. 'Ootje' Oxenaar (1929), with
whom at one point he ran a studio called Nacieron. In the mid-sixties Oxenaar
became one of the country's most prominent designers: he was head of the Dutch
PTT's Art and Design department, and simultaneously designed a large number of
banknotes. In the first series – a portrait gallery of Dutch 'heroes' from the past –
certain traits of the sarcastic, cartoon-like style of his master Willem Rozendaal are
still visible. In the banknote designs, Oxenaar used a cool, anonymous sanserif, yet
in most of his posters and book covers he adopted a wide array of lively letterforms.

▲ R.D.E. Oxenaar, poster for the
Gemeentemuseum, The Hague
1966.

▲ Jan Kuiper, vignette for the
Boucher bookshop, ca. 1960.

▶ Hermanus Berserik is best
known for his realist, often
humorous illustrations.
Some of the covers of
the Ooievaar pocket book
collection were purely
typographic.

5 Cf. Jan Middendorp, '*Ha, daar gaat er een van mij*', Rotterdam/The Hague 2002, pp 30–35.

6 Information supplied by Liesbeth van Trigt and Gerrit Noordzij.

7 Cf. *Gerezen wit* (cit.), pp 166–177; S. Carmiggelt, foreword to *Bertram: Bijna zonder woorden*, Amsterdam 1956; W.J. Rozendaal, 'Bij de afwezige: Bertram Weihs', in *Bertram
Weihs, Grafisch Werk*, The Hague 1959. Additional information supplied by Jan Kuiper.

8 Gerrit Noordzij, *De handen van de zeven zusters*, Amsterdam 2000, pp 158–159.

Helmut Salden, the perfectionist

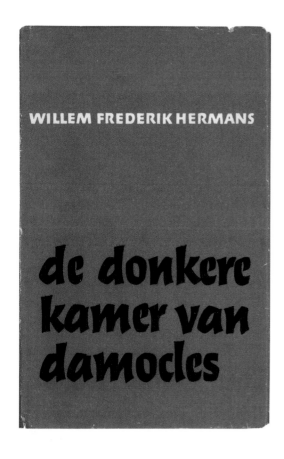

Of all the typographers and lettering artists working in Holland who specialized in the design of books and book covers, Helmut Salden (1910–1996) was probably the most conscientious and certainly the most prolific. Salden was one of the many anti-Nazists who were forced to leave Germany after Hitler's takeover in 1934. After a prolonged stay in Mallorca, where he took part in the resistance against Franco, he was captured but managed to escape. He arrived in the Netherlands in 1938.

Salden's background was modernist; his teacher of advertising design and photography at the Folkwangschule in Essen was Max Burchartz – a member of the Ring neuer Werbegestalter, an association of radical designers. In Holland, Salden became the assistant of Piet Zwart, one of the Dutch members of the Ring. Dissatisfied with this collaboration, Salden soon set up shop as a freelance book designer. During the German occupation, he was arrested and sentenced to death for resisting military service. Thanks to the persistent efforts of his Dutch girlfriend, who sent samples of his work to Göring's headquarters, he was granted reprieve and was imprisoned in Germany. In 1946 he returned to the Netherlands, where he resumed his work as a book designer.[9]

Many of Salden's 1930s and '40s book jackets have modernist traits: strong contrasts between black, white and coloured forms; a frequent use of bold, sanserif or slab serif hand-lettered type; use of lowercase only. Yet in other instances he experimented with the traditional letterforms – roman capitals, inventive scripts and italics – for which he would become famous. He continued to design book jackets as well as book typography for almost five decades, working for many different publishers: Stols, Querido, De Arbeiderspers, Contact and – the one-man firm for which he did his most outstanding work – Van Oorschot.[10]

Helmut Salden seldom, if ever, used existing typefaces for his book cover designs. He continuously invented new variations on the letterforms to which he was attracted. His scripts are marvellous, and never the same. Although they are strongly calligraphic, they were not written but drawn – each form was meticulously filled in with

▲ Helmut Salden, dust jacket for *De donkere kamer van Damocles* (The dark room of Damocles) was printed in different colours; this is the 6th printing, 1963.

▶ Salden's stylistic development can be illustrated by these two cover designs for the same book, from 1940 and 1965 respectively.

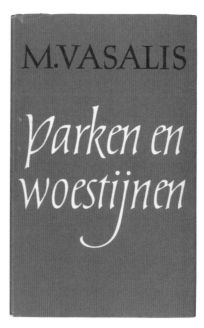

Painters and penmen

E. BRETON DE NIJS
TEMPO DOELOE
FOTOGRAFISCHE DOCUMENTEN UIT HET OUDE INDIË
QUERIDO

India ink and, if necessary, corrected with process white, just like the more constructed roman and sanserif forms. For the famous india-paper editions of the Russian Library published by Van Oorschot, he 'wrote' the names of the authors in powerful narrow italics. His paperback covers for the popular columnist Simon Carmiggelt were different each time, with expressive lettering made to match the title. But there were also recurring letterforms, which Salden drew and redrew hundreds of times with astonishing precision, or (in a few cases) had reproduced photographically to be able to paste up single letters. For Van Oorschot's extensive Stoa series he used a sturdy slab serif that shows great affinity to *Palatino* by Hermann Zapf, a type designer whom Salden much admired. This alphabet also appeared on many other jackets, providing dozens of books, designed for different publishers, with an unmistakable Salden signature. Another of his favourite letterforms was a bold 'glyphic' or incised – a roman with flared terminals rather than serifs.

While as a book designer Salden followed the principles of restrained, 'invisible' typography, he took a much more non-conformist attitude when lettering bindings or wrappers.[11] In some cases lettering was integrated with illustration; type became image and colour. His monograms and vignettes, too, took the letterform to a more autonomous level. He must have drawn hundreds of them, for authors, publishers, printers, magazines, colleagues and friends as an endless variety of sensuous curves, entangled or intersected to form a unique sign.

Although Salden's works – the total amounting to around a thousand books – can be found on every bookshelf in the Netherlands and have always been much admired, he never generated a following. Possibly his work was seen as too personal, or too German: very few Dutch designers ever felt the urge to emulate him. In Britain, Michael Harvey was aware of Salden's work early on. He wrote to Mathieu Lommen: 'I have admired Helmut Salden since 1957, when I was beginning to design my first book-jackets. His work had such a contemporary feeling: his letterforms were so lively and at the same time beautifully shaped. I found them very refreshing after working at typically English lettering ... which was in comparison so classical and backward-looking. To escape from this I shamelessly copied Salden's letters, and to this day I can still see his influence in some of my letters ...'[12]

Helmut Salden never designed a printing typeface, although he must have made more than one attempt to do so. A request from the Amsterdam Type Foundry to design a book face, made circa 1950, met with little enthusiasm on Salden's part. Yet it is not unlikely that he did start working on a text face as early as this. In or just before 1964 Salden received an assignment for a book face from the Dutch government. Pencil drawings of the alphabet were shown in a 1964 exhibition and were published in a 2003 monograph on Salden.[13] Yet the project was never brought to completion. This may in part be due to the quick succession of technological changes in the printing world; but in his succinct contribution to the Salden monograph, Gerrit Noordzij ventured a different hypothesis. Perhaps Salden was not very interested in designing a text typeface because his work was too elegant: '... the subtle result would have been lost in the mass of the body text. Salden can only come close to his ideal in a short text. He invented the culture of the book jacket for that purpose.'

Salden died in 1996. None of his alphabets have been made into typefaces to date. DTL's Frank Blokland has informally announced his plans to digitize a Salden alphabet, but no concrete steps have been taken. To this day, Salden has remained the greatest unpublished modern type designer in the Netherlands.

Gontsjarow

OBLOMOW

G.A.VAN OORSCHOT AMSTERDAM

a.koolhaas
vanwege
een tere huid

9 Katja Vranken, 'Biografische schets' in *Helmut Salden. Letterontwerper en boekverzorger*, Rotterdam 2003; C. van Dijk, *Alexandre A.M. Stols 1900–1973*, Zutphen 1992, p 303.

10 Mathieu Lommen, *Helmut Salden 1910–1996*, Amsterdam 1998; Dick Dooijes, introduction to *Helmut Salden* (catalogue), Nijmegen 1965.

11 Cf. Mathieu Lommen, *Helmut Salden* (cit.), p 9.

12 From a 1989 letter quoted in Lommen, *Helmut Salden* (cit.), p 23.

13 *Helmut Salden. Letterontwerper en boekverzorger* (cit.), pp 99–100; pp 109–110.

The natural talent of Susanne Heynemann

When Henri Friedlaender gave his typography classes in Amsterdam in 1946–1948, his assistant was a young German woman named Susanne Heynemann (1913). Having left Berlin for the Netherlands in 1939, Heynemann had been in love with books all her life. She had learnt typesetting as a voluntary worker in a Berlin printing shop and as soon as she set foot in Amsterdam continued her informal apprenticeship with local printers. During the early war years, she taught herself calligraphy, borrowing lettering books at the Public Library. She had an amazing natural talent. In 1944 she published her first book, a small volume of ten calligraphed Emily Dickinson poems. In the summer of 1945, only months after the Nazi defeat, she began designing book jackets for the Amsterdam publisher Querido, working wonders with the limited materials available. She met Charles Nypels, who began to regard her as his pupil, sharing with her his long-time experience as a printer, typographer and publisher. She later did some of her best work for the Stichting De Roos, an association of book lovers which was created as a tribute to Sjoerd de Roos, and which produced limited-edition bibliophile editions.

Heynemann worked for Querido for almost a decade. When her husband was appointed professor in Groningen, she was hired by J.B. Wolters (later Wolters-Noordhoff), a major publisher of educational books in that city for whom she continued working until 1983, the year she turned 70. At Wolters she contributed to a radical change in style, which transformed the company's output from greyish schoolbooks to sophisticated didactic works of exemplary typographic clarity. For book covers, Heynemann continued to combine hand-lettering with typeset texts.

Although her stylistic choices as a lettering artist were not unlike Salden's – an alternation of spirited scripts, classically-inspired romans and more contemporary styles – Heynemann's work showed a freer attitude. Being a lively, somewhat chaotic woman, her lettering has an intuitive, improvised feel, and an unmistakable cheerfulness. Although she was capable of creating attractive and original display typography as well as structuring complex contents, she never seems to have theorized about either. A catalogue published in 1998, with texts by Heynemann and former colleagues, is for the most part a charming but rather superficial collection of 'Memoirettes': disjointed, sometimes pointless recollections and truisms which do not reveal the thinking behind her remarkable body of work.[14]

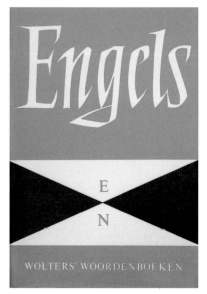

▶ From 1956 onwards Heynemann worked for J.B. Wolters, one of the country's largest publishers of educational books. She brought about a drastic facelift of the company's output, exemplified by her dust jackets for the Wolters dictionaries, c. 1975.

▼ Susanne Heynemann, book jackets for Querido publishers: *De ingewijden* by Hella Haasse (1957); *De maand Mij* by Catharina van der Linden (1959). By the time these books were published, Heynemann had already left Querido.

Jan Vermeulen, poet and typographer

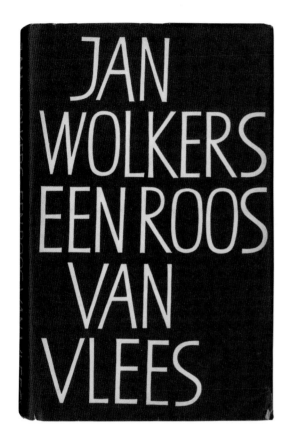

Jan Vermeulen, born in 1923, was a man of letters in every sense. Literature was his first love, and he aspired to be a poet for years. He was the (largely unpaid) secretary and editor of the poet Gerrit Achterberg and helped A.A.M. Stols run his publishing company in the immediate post-war years. He was best friends with Jan Wolkers, Holland's most controversial novelist, with whom he had a life-long working relationship as the designer of his books.[15]

From 1947 to 1949 Vermeulen was assistant to Henri Friedlaender, who sharpened his understanding of letterforms and typography and provided him with enough technical baggage to embark on a splendid career as a book designer. Like Helmut Salden, Vermeulen's approach to typography was two-sided: while he designed unorthodox and challenging book jackets, he was a modern traditionalist when working on the interiors of books.

Although Vermeulen continued to produce high-quality typography until his death in 1985, his most impressive book jackets date from the 1960s. The lettering quickly evolved from elegant romans and sanserifs with a distinctly hand-drawn feel to a more radical style using modified versions of existing sanserif types. His Jan Wolkers book jackets illustrate this development perfectly. On a formal level, there is a world of difference between the slightly sloped, calligraphic capitals of 1963's *Een roos van vlees*, the red-and-green day-glo condensed gothic of *Turks Fruit* (1969), or the pink-on-denim dot matrix letters (probably hand-drawn) of the 1971 *Werkkleding*. Yet these very diverse solutions are evidently the product of one mind: sharp, communicative, and completely in tune with the contents of the books. For a brief period Vermeulen was a partner in a studio called Adviesbureau voor Visuele Kommunikatie ('Consulting Agency for Visual Communication' – a tongue-in-cheek take on functionalist pretensions), which was actually run by his former student Julius de Goede, who did virtually all of the work (> p 257). In later years he co-designed his book covers with his wife, Marlous Bervoets; at that point, hand-lettering had long been surpassed by phototypesetting and, later, digital type.

Throughout the 1970s and '80s Jan Vermeulen taught typography at the Arnhem Academy of Arts. He was a charismatic teacher, who held erudite monologues about aspects of design and culture, and convinced his students that typography and letterforms should be lively. His dictum 'a straight line is a dead line' was taken as a guideline by Evert Bloemsma, the first Arnhem graduate to design typefaces for digital technologies.

Jan Vermeulen, book jackets for *Een roos van vlees* by Jan Wolkers (1963), collected poems by C.S. Adama van Scheltema (1961) and Wolkers's *Werkkleding* (1971).

14 *Susanne Heynemann, typografe*, The Hague/Groningen 1998.

15 Jan Wolkers, Hans van Straten et al., *Leven in letters. Over Jan Vermeulen*, Arnhem 1992; Julius de Goede, *Gedachtig aan Jan V.*, self-published brochure, Utrecht 1993.

Painterly alphabets: Theo Kurpershoek and Nicolaas Wijnberg

The Amsterdam painters Theo Kurpershoek and Nicolaas Wijnberg practised a realism not unlike the work of Hermanus Berserik and other Hague artists. Both were accomplished craftsmen who had been educated at the Amsterdam Grafische School.

Nicolaas Wijnberg (born 1918) trained as a colour lithographer. When the publisher Geert van Oorschot hired him to design low-budget book jackets, Wijnberg proposed producing the wrappers on a lithographic press, drawing each colour directly on the stone. Consequently, all Wijnberg's early dust jackets for Van Oorschot are original lithographs. The lettering was, naturally, done by hand. Wijnberg developed a range of playful lettering styles which had little to do with the sophisticated pseudo-typography of Helmut Salden – his colleague at Van Oorschot – but were just as beautifully done and fitted in seamlessly with his delightful illustrations. Wijnberg also made dozens of theatre posters, notably for the Nederlandse Comedie, a one-time Dutch equivalent of the Comédie Française. In a period when poster designers were increasingly influenced by the hard-edged, sanserif Swiss style, Wijnberg's work was remarkable because of its expressive illustrations and exuberant lettering, reminiscent of Polish theatre posters.[16]

While Wijnberg treated letterforms with casual nonchalance, Theo Kurpershoek (1914–1998) studied and created them with the utmost scrupulousness. His training at the Graphic School had equipped him with an elementary knowledge of the trade, but as a typographer and lettering artist he was self-taught – his great examples being the English writing masters: Johnston, Fairbank, Gill. When Susanne Heynemann left Querido in 1954, Kurpershoek became the publisher's 'house typographer'. In daily practice this meant that, besides the book covers he designed with his 'joyous pictural talent', he was entrusted with the design of the interiors.[17] The great care and restraint with which he carried out this task paid off immediately: in the 1955 edition of the yearly 'best book' competition, seven out of the 50 prize-winning book designs were his. Several times Kurpershoek redesigned the 'Salamanders', Querido's successful series of pocket books. Acting as art director, he often commissioned illustrations from artist friends; in these cases, the lettering was usually his. Other Salamander covers featured his own painterly illustrations, some of the best of which carried only hand-drawn type combined with simple, modern ornamentation or colour planes.

Between 1960 and 1965 Kurpershoek did some of his best lettering for the dust jackets of Querido's hardcover editions. He often drew similar letterforms: classically proportioned titling capitals, sometimes equipped with small serifs, other times with the widened terminals of a glyphic typeface.

▾ Theo Kurpershoek, dust jacket
 and paperback cover, both 1966.

▾ Nicolaas Wijnberg, dust jacket
 for a novel in Van Oorschot's
 Witte Olifant series, 1964.

▾ For a 1963–1965 edition of
 Kafka titles, Kurpershoek used
 a handdrawn alphabet of
 sanserif capitals, combined
 with Kafka's drawings.

▾ Nicolaas Wijnberg, dust jacket
 for a volume of poems, 1959.

Boudewijn Ietswaart's unnoticed brilliance

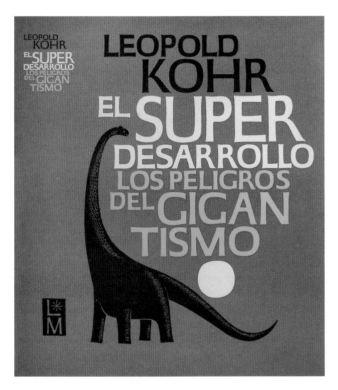

One of Kurpershoek's students was a brilliant lettering artist named Boudewijn Ietswaart (born 1936), who started working for Querido shortly after graduation. Ietswaart's lettering skills, which encompassed many different styles, technically surpassed his master's. In 1960, Ietswaart was called to Mexico as assistant to the publisher-typographer A.A.M. Stols on a UNESCO mission. Stols wrote about him: 'Seldom have I met anybody who had so many skills. He was able to draw anything he wanted, type as well as illustrations, and had mastered techniques such as woodcut, engraving and etching. He had a flawless taste …' [18] (Stols was mistaken about the graphic techniques: Ietswaart denies he ever did any engraving or etching.) [19]

Although Ietswaart's hand-lettered book jackets are among the best of their genre, most of his work has remained unknown in his own country. In the early 1960s he lived in Mexico, where he married Ingeborg Kurpershoek, the daughter of his former teacher and a designer in her own right. His main clients were the publishing house of the Universidad Nacional Autónoma de México (UNAM) and the Fondo de Cultura Económica; for both clients, Ietswaart designed dozens of book jackets, delicately illustrated and impeccably lettered. From 1964 until 1970 the couple lived in Barcelona, Spain, where Ietswaart worked for several publishers, including Luis Miracle, Editorial Joventud and the Bertelsmann book club. For a short period during the 1970s, he was a freelance designer in Amsterdam, then went back to Latin America. During the last decades of his career Ietswaart abandoned lettering and graphic design to specialize in scientific and didactic illustration.

When working in editorial design in the 1960s, Ietswaart designed at least one complete alphabet, an interesting wide lowercase sanserif which he used for a series of economic textbooks. Among his other favourite styles was the seriffed roman with strong vertical stress ('modern face'), of which he invented numerous variants. Yet none of these alphabets was ever issued as typefaces; they were simply drawn over and over again for each job.

⌃ Boudewijn Ietswaart, dust jacket for *El superdesarrollo: los peligros del gigantismo* by Leopold Kohr, Barcelona. Editorial Luis Miracle, 1965.

▸ Cover of the Mexican edition of Miguel Covarrubias's *The Eagle, the Jaguar, and the Serpent: Indian Art of the Americas*. UNAM, 1961.

▸ Ietswaart designed a sanserif lowercase alphabet for a series of textbooks on economy, published by the Fondo de Cultura Económica, Mexico, 1962.

16 Nicolaas Wijnberg, *Van de hoed en de rand*, Venlo – Antwerp, 1997, pp 92 – 100.

17 A.L. Sötemann, *Querido van 1915 tot 1990*, Amsterdam 1990, pp 123 – 124. Additional information supplied by Ingeborg Kurpershoek.

18 C. van Dijk, *Alexandre A.M. Stols* (cit.).

19 Information provided by Boudewijn Ietswaart.

A lost art?

Throughout the 1950s, hand-lettering was the rule rather than the exception in Dutch poster and book cover design; in the early 1960s, under the influence of the 'Swiss school' and because new technologies became available, many designers abandoned custom lettering for ready-made typefaces.

The modernist roots of Elffers and Bons

In the work of Dick Elffers, one of the country's leading post-war graphic designers, this development is evident. Before World War II, Elffers (1910 – 1990) worked as an assistant to the two main exponents of Dutch constructivism, Paul Schuitema and Piet Zwart. Yet he ultimately rejected the modernist claim to objectivity, embracing an expressive, painterly style. In his posters of the 1940s and '50s, Elffers combined colourful, almost childlike imagery with informal hand-lettering. Between 1959 and 1962, his preferred typeface was a blown-up typewriter letter – an original solution at the time. Towards 1965 Elffers, like many of his peers, shifted towards a Swiss-style hard-edge approach and the use of standard sanserif type.

Jan Bons (1918), whose theatre posters for Studio and De Appel have become modern classics, was also a child of the modernist movement. Having trained, very briefly, with Kiljan and Schuitema at the Hague Academy and with Hajo Rose in Amsterdam, he rejected modernist dogma and adopted a very personal, loose style that breathes total freedom and creative joy. Illustration and text form an inseparable whole in his designs; the lettering may vary from sturdy sanserifs to cut-out or torn letters and hasty scripts – each of them designed or written for the occasion. Jan Bons seldom used off-the-shelf type, and continued to make new letters even for his most recent designs for De Appel (2000). In this last series of posters for this Hague theatre company he used a stencil alphabet that was one of his most complete and consistent in a long series of self-invented letterforms.

Max Velthuijs's monthly posters for the Jazz in Pepijn series (c. 1979) were made with simple means: completely hand-drawn and printed in black on regular office stock.

Max Velthuijs: from advertising to children's books

Max Velthuijs is a special case. Born in 1923, Velthuijs has acquired worldwide fame in recent decades as the author and illustrator of children's books featuring friendly characters such as Frog and Crocodile. During the 1950s and '60s, however, he did art work for large advertising agencies as well as book covers and posters for arts institutions. Most of this work featured his highly personal, elegant hand-lettering. His scripts are delightful. A series of low-budget jazz posters, done in the late 1970s for a small Hague theatre called Pepijn, was completely lettered by hand, with the headline 'Jazz in Pepijn' drawn as an elaborate construction in a different style each month.

Whith the passing of the years, Velthuijs abandoned graphic design and lettering and specialized in illustration and storytelling. The typographic design of his book covers has been taken over by his publishers' in-house studios. When a publisher occasionally asked him to do the lettering himself, he happily complied.[20]

A brief renaissance

Among the designers who still use custom lettering is Max Kisman, whose tribute to the designer Jan Bons makes use of casually hand-drawn type rendered as a digital out-line image, 2002.

With the advent of transfer sheet type and photocomposition, hand-lettering all but disappeared from book cover design. The dominance of the 'Swiss style' – which recognized only a few sanserif typefaces as legitimate – curtailed the creation of handmade letterforms even further (replacing them occasionally by constructed geometric forms). Informal – often meaning amateurish – lettering continued to be the preferred technique for laying out underground magazines and posters, but in editorial design prefabricated letters became the norm. The most interesting exceptions to this rule will be dealt with in subsequent chapters.

During a short period in the 1980s a small group of young typographers – notably pupils of Gerrit Noordzij such as Peter Matthias Noordzij, Peter Verheul and Luc(as) de Groot – went back to inventing new variations on traditional letterforms for single assignments. As soon as the technology became available to store and reproduce those letters on a desktop computer, these letterforms were made into fonts; the distinction between lettering and type design virtually disappeared.

20 Information supplied by Max Velthuijs, 2000.

Torn type by Sandberg

stedelijk museum

Willem (or Wil) Sandberg (1897–1984), who signed his designs with his last name only, was a unique figure in the Dutch cultural world. Sandberg worked as a full-time designer until he was appointed deputy director of the Amsterdam Stedelijk Museum in 1938. He became a wartime hero as the central figure – and only surviving member – of a resistance group that in 1943 burnt down the municipal office of records to frustrate the administration of the Nazi government. After the liberation in 1945 Sandberg became director of the Stedelijk; he was also the driving force of the new artists' and designers' organization GKF.[21]

Sandberg was an unorthodox cultural manager who turned his museum into a lively interdisciplinary meeting point and personally designed most of its catalogues and posters – hundreds of them –, providing the museum with a unique corporate identity. For this, he closely collaborated with the City Printing Office, communicating his ideas with tiny sketches which he often made during meetings. Sandberg loved the Printing Office's collection of wood poster types which he used for book covers and posters, printed on rough materials such as brown wrapping paper.

Sandberg also designed his own letterforms which, like the materials he preferred, were 'a bit rough'. They were not drawn or constructed, but torn out of coloured paper. 'The tearing's something I've always done, because you get so much more lively edges that way. I don't care for clean outlines.'[22] Sandberg liked to refer to his torn letters and words as *tekens* ('signs'), putting them in the same category as his other abstract or figurative *scheursels* ('tearings'). These signs appeared in several publications which Sandberg wrote or edited: an homage to Piet Zwart; two books of autobiographical notes entitled *Nu* ('now') and *Nu 2*; and a series called *Experimenta Typographica* in which Sandberg assembled texts by himself and others that refer to his obsessions: art, the vulnerability of civilization, health and sickness, the role of the creative individual in society and history.

Sandberg's torn letters are usually variants of conventional letterforms, whose improvised character and ragged edges give them an unmistakable signature. One style which Sandberg was particularly fond of was the stencil alphabet: he created letters resembling stencils by pasting up separate torn-out letterparts. Sandberg used an alphabet of such stencil-like capitals for his most monumental assignment: the lettering on the walls of the Waterlooplein (Waterloo Square) metro station in Amsterdam, 1977.

◄ Willem Sandberg designed hundreds of catalogues for the Amsterdam Stedelijk Museum. Only a few of them – like this 1954 catalogue of the exhibition '9 jaar' – carry his characteristic 'torn' type.

◄ The lettering of the Amsterdam underground station Waterlooplein (1977) was based on Sandberg's torn letters. The word Waterloo is repeated several times, and the outlines of the letters vary slightly.

◄ Stencil lettering from *Experimenta Typographica 4*, 1981.

21 Ank Leeuw-Marcar, *Willem Sandberg, portret van een kunstenaar*. Amsterdam 1981; Leonie ten Duis and Annelies Haase, *The World must Change*, Amsterdam 1999.

22 Bibeb, *Sandberg*, Nijmegen 1969, p 7.

Functionalism and geometry

Wim Crouwel, exhibition catalogue designed with constructed, custom-made letterforms, 1960.

Functionalism and the grid

The Dutch movement, or mode of operation, that in the 1960s became known as 'functionalism', was in many ways a continuation of the research carried out by the pre-war pioneers of functionalist graphic communication. For more than a decade after 1945, Dutch graphic designers largely ignored this modernist heritage. The leading figures of the pre-war movement – Schuitema, Kiljan and Zwart – remained active throughout the 1950s but their output was small and had little impact on the development of the profession. The teachings of Schuitema and Kiljan in The Hague were of invaluable importance to individual students who in turn became teachers and designers (as well as photographers, writers, television directors, etc.); but these pupils lacked the charisma and the vigour to bring Dutch rationalist design back to the fore. Besides, the 1950s in Holland did not provide an ideal climate for innovation. It was a period of restoration and middle-class tastes; advertising and graphic design were expected to be reassuring and friendly – painterly, craftsman-like and colourful.

Towards 1960, the climate changed. The Nieuwe Zakelijkheid – a democratic and functionalist approach to building which had started around 1920 and was resumed after the war – appealed greatly to a younger generation of graphic designers. Their main influence, however, was the International Style of graphic design, which in Holland was mostly referred to as Swiss Style or Swiss Typography.

Switzerland – which had remained neutral during both World Wars – was the only country in Europe where functionalist graphic design had been able to transcend its initial experimental phase and develop into a national visual language. Designers such as Karl Gerstner, Josef Müller-Brockman and Max Bill proposed a reductive, unadorned graphic design that aimed for objectivity and efficiency. Their purist ideals did not exclude a strong sense of beauty. Swiss design managed to obtain maximum aesthetic effect by the simplest means: black-and-white photography, unjustified, homogeneous blocks of sanserif text, a conscious use of white space as a compositional element and the grid as a guiding principle. Towards the end of the 1950s, the Swiss 'school' even gave birth to its own typefaces: *Helvetica/Neue Haas Grotesk* by Max Miedinger and *Univers* by Adrian Frutiger. Swiss typography became the International Style when its principles were adopted in the United States, where the soil had been prepared by Bauhaus-affiliated German designers who had fled there in the years preceding the Second World War.

In Holland, the Swiss were greatly admired by many designers. But not many were inclined to emulate them, let alone appropriate their principles and procedures in order to develop a Dutch, pragmatic version of the functionalist working method. For this achievement, all credits go to the two graphic designers who, in 1963, co-founded Total Design: Benno Wissing and Wim Crouwel.

The pragmatism of Benno Wissing

Born in 1923, Benno Wissing trained as a painter at the Art Academy in his native city of Rotterdam. After 1945 he became active in the Rotterdam art world, co-founding a cultural centre which united artists, architects and film-lovers. Later he was a member of the Liga Nieuw Beelden (League of the New Image) which advocated the integration of architecture, art and design. When travelling through Eastern Europe, Wissing had become aware of the relativity of modernist ideals: 'I visited Yugoslavia. That made a tremendous impression on me ... The confrontation with the bare necessities of life was so terribly direct, that I soon understood that there were more elementary things than the whole elementarism of the functionalists in Holland after the war.' [1]

From 1949 to 1966 Wissing worked as a designer for the Boymans Van Beuningen Museum in Rotterdam. His posters were only sparsely illustrated; he let the typography do most of the work, choosing freely from the large and diverse collection of display faces at the City Printing Office. From the outset his approach to structuring information was very systematic; even his earliest posters and catalogues, when he was an absolute beginner, show an underlying grid. Occasionally, Wissing seems to have designed his own letterforms: a narrow face based on ovals and circles for a Henry Moore exhibition (1953), two-tone lettering constructed with triangles and squares for a Frank Lloyd Wright poster (1952). By the time he began working for the industrial sector, around 1958, his typographic work had evolved into a straightforward, clear style which used the grid as a basis for a dynamic layout. In 1962 Wissing teamed up with interior designer Kho Liang Ie for his biggest assignment so far. He was invited to design the directional signs for the interior of the new Schiphol Airport. A period of intensive research resulted in a solution which was to become a shining example of rational signposting. Illuminated signs – using *Akzidenz Grotesk*, with no capitals except for the gate numbers – were attached to the ceiling, so that passengers would not block each other's view. All decisions were made for pragmatic, not ideological reasons. The one question Wissing and Ie had asked themselves was about why nervous, hasty passengers managed to lose their way in other airports and how this could be prevented at Schiphol. [2]

The founding of Total Design

During the preparation of the airport project, Wissing became involved in the creation of the first multi-disciplinary large-scale design studio in the Netherlands. Its name was a programme in itself: TD Association for Total Design. Wissing's creative partners were Friso Kramer, an industrial designer, and Wim Crouwel who, like Wissing, had designed numerous trade fair stands and exhibitions but was mainly regarded as a graphic designer. Total Design took its cues from similar design firms in Switzerland, Britain and the United States. Like its models, Total Design would take up large projects which involved many disciplines and specializations, distributing the various aspects of the work among several teams. The approach to design projects was systematic and, more often than not, modular. 'Friso, Wim and I had seen very quickly that, in dealing with large projects, a number of things had to be normalized so that the arrangement of information could be more easily programmed, and more time would be available for handling intrinsic problems. If there were to be variations in the final product we preferably searched for variations within a modular system, so that mutual relationships, inter-connection, clustering and related industrial production would not need follow-up care. The principle was applicable in architecture, industrial design and graphic products. That's the history of the birth of the grid! A cuckoo in the nest?' (Benno Wissing in 1983) [3]

One of Total Design's most systematic and most thoroughly researched typefaces was conceived by Wissing: the alphabet for the Rotterdam events venue Ahoy' (1970). The two other designers on the team were Hartmut Kowalke and Josephine Holt. Apparently, much of the actual research and design work was done by Kowalke, a young German designer who had been 'discovered' by Wissing while presenting his graduation project at the Ulm Academy. The Ahoy' alphabet was not the first modu-

◄ Wim Crouwel's famous poster for the 1968 Vormgevers (Designers) exhibition at the Stedelijk Museum. The grid that Crouwel had been using for his designs of the museum's catalogues became the poster's central theme as well as the guideline for the alphabet that was drawn for it.

▲ Benno Wissing, poster for a Frank Lloyd Wright exhibition at the Ahoy' centre, organized as part of the 1952 centennial celebrations of the Rotterdam Academy of Arts and Technical Sciences. Wissing used a specially designed alphabet of constructed letterforms; the triangles and squares refer to basic shapes in Wright's work.

1 Kees Broos, *Ontwerp: Total Design*, Utrecht 1983, p 7.

2 Cf. Dingenus van de Vrie (ed.), *Benno Wissing*, Rotterdam 1999, pp 64–65; see also: Ben Bos, 'An interview with Benno Wissing' in Crouwel and Bos, *Benno Wissing*, Amsterdam 1993.

3 From a long letter to Kees Broos, who was then preparing Total Design's twentieth anniversary book: Broos 1983 (cit.), p 11.

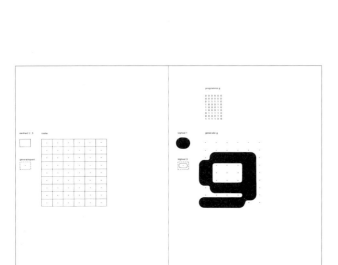

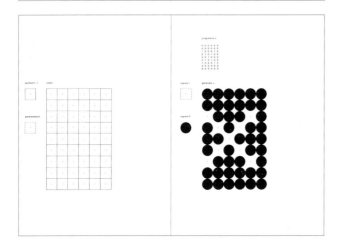

lar or grid-based alphabet conceived at Total Design: more examples will be shown below. But in this case, the use of the grid was based on purely functional considerations. The Ahoy' is a large, flexible space for sport, concerts and exhibitions that can accommodate audiences from a few dozen up to over 10,000. Initially the signage was conceived to be equally flexible. Several audience mobility programmes were tested in a transparent scale model. A system was proposed to electronically create variable texts by making individual lamps light up to form letters. Hence the idea to use simple, matrix-based letterforms, for which several models were tested with on-off (1-0) schemes. While the illuminated news trailer (*lichtkrant* in Dutch) was the original model for this proposal, the resulting typefaces were presented as the outcome of a process which took into account 'the possibility to produce letterforms in all kinds of ways, without a loss of characteristics.' All alphabets were based on a 6 by 9 grid; by varying the 'signal' for each unit or pixel (square, circle or ellipse), it would be possible to generate different typefaces or styles. The signal could be 'chosen according to the circumstances and is not limited to any particular shape or colour, size or dimension.' [4] Unfortunately the electronic signalling system proved too expensive; eventually the signage was produced with conventional fixed signs. But the matrix-based lettering was retained, resulting in letterforms which were rather unusual and immediately recognizable.

Modular structuring and grids remained the trademark of Total Design's output throughout the 1960s and '70s – from interior projects to logos and single letters. The 'authorship' of the grid has often been credited to Wim Crouwel, who was nicknamed 'the system general'. In 1980, Emil Ruder paid the ultimate tribute, writing 'If the typographic grid started with the Bauhaus, the movable grid with Karl Gerstner, then the total grid can be attributed to Wim Crouwel.' [5] For those involved in TD, it has always been clear that grid-like systems were the outcome of a group process; if there was one 'system ideologist' within TD, it was Wissing rather than Crouwel. Nevertheless, of all the founding partners of Total Design, Wim Crouwel probably had the most complex attitude towards rationalizing and structuring design.

Wim Crouwel and Dutch Calvinism

This poster for a 1957 exhibition by the French artist Fernand Léger is one of Wim Crouwel's best known early posters. The letterforms were drawn as a typographical interpretation of Léger's work.

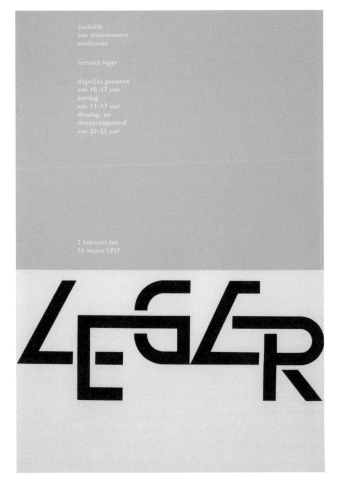

Wim Crouwel (1928) is from Groningen, the northern Dutch province known for its down-to-earth mentality and ethic of hard work. He trained as a painter, but was soon attracted by the ideals of the Nieuwe Zakelijkheid movement in design and architecture – *zakelijk* meaning both 'objective' and 'businesslike', or 'no-nonsense'. In 1951, he moved to Amsterdam to take evening classes at the graphic design department of the IVKNO or Instituut voor Kunst Nijverheids Onderwijs (Institute of Applied Arts Education; later the Rietveld Academy). Significantly, his typography teacher was Charles Jongejans, who had been a student of Schuitema and Kiljan at the Hague Academy. In the daytime Crouwel designed exhibition stands for a specialized firm. Occasionally he worked for Dick Elffers, one of the most successful graphic designers in post-war Holland. Elffers had been assistant to both Paul Schuitema and Piet Zwart, but had abandoned the dogmas of modernism and moved on to a more painterly approach.

During this period Crouwel first made contact with Swiss typography. In 1952 he met Karl Gerstner; he met Gérard Ifert and Ernst Scheidegger the following year. 'Crouwel was impressed', Hugues Boekraad wrote, 'by the strategically structural approach, by the daring and clear typography and by the minimalism of the formal elements they used.' [6]

The formal solutions proposed by the Swiss designers provoked in Crouwel a kind of 'shock of recognition'. His affinity with their sense of order, their aesthetics of the elemental, was not merely professional. It touched on a very personal internal paradox. 'I have such a compulsion to create a certain order in everything,' he confided to Max Bruinsma (*Items* magazine) in 1993 [7]; colleagues at TD have caught Crouwel cutting the slices of cheese on his sandwiches into exact squares. But there is also a flamboyant, almost dandyish side to him: for decades he has been driving British sports cars such as MG, AC and Morgan, he wore tailor-made suits as soon as he could afford them and is an admirer of expressive works of art and design which have no relation whatsoever to the functionalist principles he has advocated so enthusiastically for the past 40 years. At 24, he made dynamic abstract drawings which betray his admiration for the work of Alexander Calder and Ben Nicholson, with many lush curves and a precise balance between solid and feathery forms. The costume designs he did at the age of 26 for a production of *Peer Gynt* by Theater, a company from Arnhem, were downright sexy.

Why did Crouwel renounce this more joyful, sensuous aspect of his talent when he turned to the grid? His purist attitude can be traced back, at least in part, to the influence of Calvinism, that typically Dutch, stern brand of Protestantism. 'I am a functionalist who has had too much trouble with aesthetics!' said Crouwel in the *Items* interview – an analysis he has made on other occasions too. When I asked him if it wasn't the other way around, that perhaps he was, also, an aesthetician who was

4   *Geprogrammeerde belettering Ahoy'*, Amsterdam 1970, an internal publication issued by Total Design. Additional information provided by Hartmut Kowalke.

5   In Helmut Schmidt, *Typography today*, Tokyo 1980, p 74. See also Huygen and Boekraad, *Wim Crouwel – Mode en module*, Rotterdam 1997, p 15.

6   Hugues Boekraad, 'Lines. About the designer Wim Crouwel', in *Affiche* 7, September 1993, p 58. Dutch version published, with modifications, in Huyghen and Boekraad 1997 (cit.).

7   Max Bruinsma, 'Wim Crouwel interview' in *Items* 5/6, December 1993 (with English translation in supplement).

Catalogue of an exhibition of work by the painter Edgar Fernhout at the Van Abbe Museum, Eindhoven, 1963. The letterforms were inspired by the vertical brush strokes Fernhout used in his abstract landscapes. The same lettering was used for the poster but in different, more earth-like colours.

Exhibition catalogue for the Stedelijk Museum, Amsterdam (1964), designed with a constructed variation on a condensed grotesque. Crouwel had used a similar letterform much earlier, in the 1957 Hiroshima poster (cf. *Wim Crouwel Alphabets*, 2003, pp 40–41).

bothered too much by Calvinism, he answered, 'Exactly. It certainly has to do with a Calvinist background, with that kind of morality which forbids you to abandon a path once taken. ... Being consistent with oneself was always a principle which I held in extremely high regard. It would happen to me that I established a certain line, a system or grid, and when designing things that were based on it, realized that the result would be better or more beautiful if I deviated from that line; I forced myself not to do so because I thought being consistent throughout the project was more important than the success or beauty of a single part. Sometimes it was hard to forgive myself. Rather silly, if you think about it.' [8]

As Hugues Boekraad has pointed out [9], it is difficult to interpret Crouwel's position and body of work without taking into account the self-image he has projected in his writings and earlier interviews. There is little doubt that he is the single most influential graphic designer in post-war Holland, and has been instrumental in turning the Netherlands into a laboratory of rational graphics. But while he has always tended to present himself as a straightforward embodiment of post-war modernism, filtering out inconsistencies, the real picture is more complex.

In the *Items* interview, Crouwel summed up his functionalist ideals: '... Certainly, there is a social vision behind it. The primary thing that fascinates me about Functionalism is its spirituality. My guiding principle is that in a certain sense design must order things, in order to provide people with the greatest possible clarity. Their spiritual development, and raising society to new levels, is served by this form of normality, this no-nonsense simplicity of Functionalism.' [10] Yet as a designer of telephone directories, corporate identities, catalogues and posters, Crouwel has not always limited himself to the purest, simplest and most 'normal' solutions. There was sometimes a touch of madness to his method, hidden in uneasy colour schemes, in hazardous juxtapositions of abstract forms, type and imagery.

More importantly (at least for our purpose) there were the letterforms he invented: type that was not a variation on the rational grotesques he admired and used almost exclusively (mainly Akzidenz Grotesk and Univers), but display faces which, although being based on a grid, were also highly unusual, quirky and personal.

Wim Crouwel and type design

Crouwel wrote in 1980: 'Experimental typography and functional typography are, up to a certain point, opponents of each other. Experimental typography is not only reflecting a cultural pattern, but gives primarily a self-reflexion. As soon as we carry out experiments in order to improve a certain typographical solution, that means as soon as we do research, we cannot speak of experimental typography; experimental typography never results in a solution for a certain problem.' [11]

Typefaces are, of course, the bricks of any typographical solution. In 1950s Holland, the advocates of modernist typography found it hard to get hold of typefaces which had the neutrality they wanted. The Amsterdam Type Foundry had a virtual monopoly in the printing world, and the firm's only sanserif typeface with modernist aspirations was *Nobel* – that hybrid reworking of *Berthold Grotesk*. 'We hated Nobel', says Crouwel, 'because it was a characterless piece of trash, a bad copy of *Futura*. We would have liked to have used the original Berthold Grotesk. We tried to find samples of Akzidenz Grotesk. But the publisher, Bauersche Gießerei, only had very limited distribution in the Netherlands because the Amsterdam Type Foundry controlled the market. For small jobs I used to cut out single letters and glue them in position – I have done that in certain posters for the Van Abbe Museum. I had discovered Akzidenz Grotesk when collaborating with Gérard Ifert on a large exhibition presenting the United States' Marshall Plan to the Dutch public. Ifert worked for the United States Information Service in Paris. They used big rubber stamps of Akzidenz, typographic stamps with which they printed their displays. I could not afford to buy one of those sets, they were completely hand-made and frightfully expensive; but on some occasions I was able to borrow them.' [12] So in the late 1950s, Helvetica and Univers came as gifts from the gods. Crouwel used Univers for many jobs, including the Dutch telephone directory, which he redesigned with Jolijn van de Wouw in 1977, setting the listings in lowercase only.

Functionalism and geometry

◀ Crouwel's lettering of the 1970 Claes Oldenburg exhibition at the Stedelijk Museum recalled that artist's large, soft objects.

◀ As a present for Oldenburg, Crouwel designed a complete alphabet based on the lettering of the poster and catalogue. The alphabet was digitized by David Quay for The Foundry in 2003 (> p 123).

As early as 1957 letterforms appeared in Crouwel's designs (notably his posters and catalogue covers for the Van Abbe Museum in Eindhoven) that did not come out of the typecase but were hand-drawn. They were simplified letters, constructed from squares, triangles and circle segments – legitimate heirs, as it were, of Josef Albers's *Kombinationschrift*. Most of these faces have remained incomplete. They were meant for a single occasion, and consequently only those characters needed for a particular name or title were drawn. There is the word 'olanda' designed on a 4 × 7 grid for the Dutch entry in the 1960 Venice Biennale; and a slightly more complex variation for a Jean Brusselmans exhibition that same year. The most subtle of these is a type drawn in 1963 for the poster and catalogue of an exhibition by the painter Edgar Fernhout. It is built on a grid of four rows: two for the x-height, one for the ascenders and one for the single descender of the g. Its main elements are rectangles and quarter circles, but Crouwel opened up the strict geometry of the basic grid by cutting off the short segments at an angle. Crouwel: 'The Fernhout typeface referred to the way in which Fernhout painted. He used a little flat brush with which he painted short rectangular strokes, one next to the other. That way of organizing the painting appealed to me. But of course I departed from it and drew those letters my way, so that only Fernhout specialists realize that there is a connection.'[12]

Total Design: logotypes and alphabets

Once Crouwel had entered the realm of corporate design with Total Design, type design took a different course. This need for original letterforms is obvious when thinking about corporate identities and trademarks. At times, TD took a fundamentalist approach to the logotype by setting it in Helvetica capitals, as was done with the TD logo itself – much to the merriment of their critics. Symbolic pictograms were often created in the geometric style which one identifies immediately with that period and with TD (and their peers abroad). TD's twentieth anniversary book says: 'The reduction to basic forms and strict stylization was prompted … by the stipulation of an optimally broad application and by recognizability under negative circumstances.' Soon, however, literally everybody started doing logos with circles and triangles, and recognizability was reduced to a minimum. This prompted TD to reintroduce more legible and playful trademarks.[13]

Logotypes spelling out the brand names were often drawn by hand as well. PAM and Calpam by Wissing; Intradal, a stylized rendering of handwriting with the broadnibbed pen, by Crouwel; ARC, based on a grid of hundreds of circles, by Ben Bos. Although 'designing complete alphabets never was an ambition of TD'[14], some of their most successful custom letterforms were extended into larger series, or corporate typefaces. The alphabet by Benno Wissing and Harmut Kowalke for the Rotterdam Ahoy' exhibition venue has been dealt with in the previous pages. Crouwel's logo for Al Futtaim Electronics in Dubai was made into a double alphabet

Intradal

abcdefghijklm
nopqrstuvwxyz
1234567890

▲ Total Design (Bram Engelse), alphabet for the Onze Lieve Vrouwe Gasthuis, an Amsterdam hospital, 1979.

▲ Wim Crouwel's lettering for the Intradal logo (Total Design, 1975) is a constructed form derived from writing with the broad-nibbed pen.

8 Conversation with Wim Crouwel.

9 Huygen and Boekraad (cit.), pp 46–57.

10 Bruinsma, 'Wim Crouwel interview' (cit.).

11 Crouwel in Helmut Schmid, *Typography today* (cit.), pp 18–25. I quote the English text as published.

12 Conversation with Wim Crouwel.

13 Broos 1983 (cit.), pp 19–22.

14 Ibid., p 22.

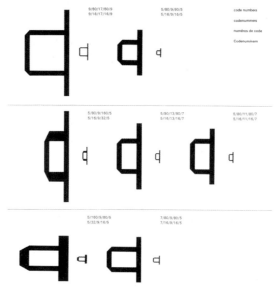

of lowercase Latin letters and arabic characters, with outline versions of both. Ben Bos designed an alphabet for the Randstad temping agency (> p 123). Another alphabet derived from a one-word lettering project was *Oldenburg*. For his poster announcing an exhibition of Claes Oldenburg at the Stedelijk in 1970, Crouwel conceived a typeface that recalled that artist's large, soft objects. As a present for Oldenburg, a personal friend, Crouwel drew a complete alphabet based on these forms.

◄ Page from the New Alphabet booklet showing the bold, condensed and extended variants with their respective 'code numbers'.

◄ Cover of the booklet announcing the New Alphabet, published in the Kwadraatbladen series of the printer Steendrukkerij de Jong, 1967.

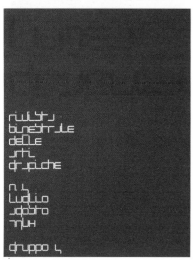

◄ The cover of the Italian magazine *Linea Grafica, rivista bimestrale delle arti grafiche* (1968) was probably the only commissioned design Crouwel made with the New Alphabet.

▼ Digital version of Crouwel's New Alphabet in three weights, The Foundry, 1997.

New Alphabet

In TD's fourth year, Crouwel made the national headlines with a typeface he had developed as a personal project. The *New Alphabet* was made public in October 1967 in an issue of the Kwadraatbladen, the series of square-format goodwill publications edited by Pieter Brattinga for the Hilversum printer Steendrukkerij de Jong. The 20-page quadrilingual brochure contained a detailed 'Proposal for a new typeface that, more than the traditional types, is suited to the composing system using the cathode-ray tube.' The publication of the New Alphabet was a sign of the times. The graphic world had seen a fast transition from the world of metal type to that of phototypesetting, from mechanics to type reproduction at the speed of light. In his introduction, Crouwel argued that traditional alphabets '[whose] letters are individually designed with meticulous care' belong to an era in which typesetting, too, was a task performed by hand, allowing for subtle corrections and subjective interventions. With the advent of new technologies, Crouwel wrote, it had become necessary to create new letterforms that were better suited to these new developments.[15] Crouwel's solution was, to put it mildly, unorthodox. The New Alphabet was drawn on a variable grid of a minimum of 5 by 9 units; the basic form of these units was square, but the system allowed for horizontal and vertical scaling. All the variables (number of units, number of scan lines per units, relative x-height) were to be represented in a five-number code. This scientific-looking system was a clear sign that Crouwel's proposal was intended for a high-tech world which had not even been fully realized: although the moon landing had yet to take place, the New Alphabet brochure already carried a picture of an astronaut floating in space, printed in a futuristic-looking line screen.

The letterforms Crouwel had devised were equally unconventional. The typeface was a single alphabet with no capitals; it was rectangular, constructed with just horizontal and vertical lines, with 45-degree sheared corners. About half the characters were clearly recognizable, the others looked so unfamiliar that one would have to learn to read them anew. Crouwel says he did not invent these peculiar characters in order to create something astounding or controversial. 'I simply wanted to make a consistent alphabet on the basis of that grid of squares. I did not want any cluttering of vertical stems and did not find a solution within the conventional structure of the characters. So I began researching the past, looking for alternative signs with which

Functionalism and geometry

I could replace the conventional forms. One could have made them up, but I wanted them to have some kind of footing in the history of type.'[16] The technical drawings of the typeface were done by hand, without the help of any mechanical or electronic device, by Crouwel's father, who had worked as a retouching artist at a lithographer's workshop.

The New Alphabet raised a lot of dust. In late 1967 it got more newspaper coverage than Total Design had received in its first four years. Crouwel had obviously intended his alphabet to be speculative, deliberately opting for an extreme proposal that was open to debate. 'I think I have always inclined not to bother too much about things that have been developed through tradition. It's good to create a breakthrough and then see how you can adjust it.' But many of Crouwel's peers thought his proposal went too far and wasn't realistic. Gerard Unger, who had himself begun researching the correlation between letterforms and technology, published *A Counter-proposal*, also in the Kwadraatblad series. He proposed creating new letterforms which, although adapted to the particular demands of the new technology, were firmly rooted in tradition: 'One should find new subtleties for the old forms, which can be reproduced well by the new machines.'[17] Which is exactly what he went on to do in the following decades.

In 2001, type designer Evert Bloemsma re-evaluated the New Alphabet in the light of subsequent developments. He wrote that 'Wim Crouwel's New Alphabet can be regarded as the last attempt to maintain the correlation between the means of production (digital imagesetter, electronic page layout) and the result (the letterform). After more than thirty years it stands out as the most consistent demonstration of the idea of the oneness of modern tools and their products.'[18]

Fodor and the Stedelijk: type as grid

Crouwel continued experimenting with grid-based letterforms. He had become interested in crystallography and saw parallels between regular crystal structures and the 'on and off' dot patterns generated by means of early computer technology. At the same time, Crouwel made a series of photographs of pre-digital bitmap type: vernacular lettering with roof-tiles and bricks. These preoccupations led to several typographic experiments.

In 1968 the Stedelijk Museum – for which Crouwel had designed most of the printed matter since the early 1960s – presented an exhibition of graphic and product designers. The 'Vormgevers' poster has become a classic, 'probably the Crouwel poster that was most often reproduced in design literature,' according to Hugues Boekraad, who wrote that it represents 'the most essential image of design from Crouwel's point of view'. Its most striking feature is that the grid is made visible – the same grid used in his designs for the Stedelijk Museum catalogues. It is taken as a starting point for a new, experimental letterform (but more practical than the New Alphabet). The construction of the characters, writes Boekraad, 'becomes the core of the design'.[19] The alphabet was never developed beyond the word *Vormgevers* until the London-based Foundry offered to digitize it, and created the *Stedelijk* font.

One of Crouwel's most interesting alphabets is the one he created for the small Fodor Museum. For the cover of the museum's bulletin he conceived a basic design in two colours which was to be overprinted in black for each issue. To save money on typesetting, the black text was 'set' on an electric typewriter which Crouwel had at his disposal at the Stedelijk (it came with a typist). Crouwel liked the contemporary look of the square typeface, and also the idea that the monospaced characters formed both horizontal and vertical lines. This was made visible by a regular pattern of pink dots on the orange background. The characters f o d o r and the numerals were created on top of this grid. What could have been a straightforward modernist construction became quite a remarkable typeface through a simple but brilliant intervention. By breaking through the outlines and counters of each character with rounded notches, Crouwel at once created a computer-style, 'futuristic' feel and a forward movement which refers to formal writing and the traditional typefaces derived from it. A complete corporate alphabet was developed from the principles used in the fodor logotype: an admirable hybrid indeed.

▾ In the catalogues for the Fodor Museum, Amsterdam (1973 – 1977), the body text was set by means of a conventional monospace typewriter. The grid based on the proportions of the typewriter face was taken as a starting point for the hand-drawn Fodor alphabet.

▾ Crouwel's Fodor alphabet was digitized in 1997 by The Foundry and published as Fodor.

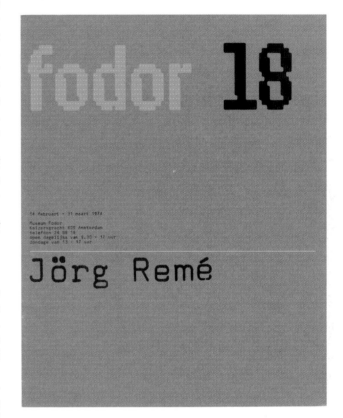

15 Wim Crouwel, *New Alphabet*, Hilversum 1967. English text quoted as published.

16 Conversation with Wim Crouwel, 1999.

17 Gerard Unger, *A counter-proposal*, Hilversum [1968].

18 Evert Bloemsma, 'Balance, Avance, Cocon', in Van Rixtel and Westerveld (eds.), *Letters*, Eindhoven 2001, p 77.

19 Huygen and Boekraad (cit.), p 332.

Hamburgifons

affilare tipologia onore teologia canale parallelepipe canale traente continente grafologia trotterellare citofono noleggiare pioppella film incognita politecnico fotocopia attaccare cancet concetto girata aereo carreggiata galleggiante proiettile cofano recitare tecnologia litigio filarello grafico contrapporre alterare alligatore lettera italiano poi oggetto poliglotta tinteggiare longilineo

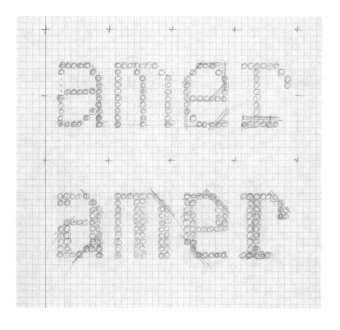

Foundry Gridnik

Light Regular **Medium Bold** Over de feestviering van 1823 kan ik niet medespreken; maar dit kan ik getuigen, dat die van 1856 niet geweest is eene openbaring van nationale eenheid, maar van de goedhartigheid eener provincie-stad, welke zich er over verheugde dat een harer oudste en geachtste ingezetenen voortaan rustig sterven kan, zonder te scheiden te hebben van zijn bekend stokpaard.

From Olivetti to stamps

Around 1974 Crouwel was invited by the Italian manufacturer Olivetti to design an alphabet for electric typewriters. He found himself in good company: Olivetti had simultaneously commissioned a typeface design from Josef Müller-Brockmann, the leading figure in Swiss typography, as well as Perry A. King and Herbert Lindiger. As shown by the Fodor project, Crouwel was interested in typewriter typography. He was convinced that typewriters demanded a totally different kind of letter design than typesetting and had expressed his annoyance when IBM released a system with variable widths, which made typewriting look like printed matter.

After various possibilities had been sketched, including seriffed and monospaced characters, with and without contrast, Crouwel proposed a monoline sanserif with three widths, which Olivetti named *Politene*. Not unlike the New Alphabet, the basic form is a rectangle, with 45-degree corners. In close-up, the type has some subtle typographic features, such as rounded corners and terminals set at slight angles.

While Crouwel, Müller-Brockmann and the others were developing their fonts, the interest in electric typewriters began to wane in favour of more flexible electronic systems. By the time the faces were completed, Olivetti had no need for them any more. The firm had decided not to issue the machine for which they were intended. For Crouwel this had one advantage: the copyright to the typeface went back to him. In that same period Crouwel was commissioned to design the standard numeral stamps for the Dutch PTT (published from 1976). He drew a special version of the Olivetti Politene design, consisting solely of the word 'nederland' and the numerals to indicate the value.

The 1997 and 2003 re-releases

Since the early 1980s, young graphic designers have used photocopied versions of the New Alphabet, often replacing its less readable characters by alternatives of their own devising. British designer Peter Saville 'quoted' the type on his album cover for Joy Division's *Substance* and the 12" single *Atmosphere*. This brought Crouwel's 1960s experiments to the attention of a new audience; but it also gave an unfaithful representation of his ideas. After the advent of PostScript would-be type designers began issuing illegal and modified digital versions of Crouwel's types. When David Quay of The Foundry in London approached Crouwel with a proposal to revive the New Alphabet and some other type designs as part of The Foundry's Architype series, Crouwel hesitated, as the fonts had never been meant to be used by third parties. He finally consented, realizing that an authorized revival would give him an opportunity to help put an end to bootlegging and set the record straight.

Fodor and *Stedelijk* are pretty straightforward reissues of, respectively, the Fodor alphabet and the 1968 Vormgevers design. Quay and Freda Sack have added a few characters, such as quotes, brackets and the $ and £ signs, but without extending the

à b c d p q r s

é f g h t ü v x

i j k l w :yz

m ;no ?-ˇ¸;!

acht

rare

a set

vie

One of the complete alphabets developed at Total Design by a designer other than Crouwel or Wissing was the *Randstad* typeface designed in 1969–1970 by Ben Bos and Zdena Srncova. The alphabet was based on the formal principles of the logo, a constructed abstract sign with 45° angles. The lowercase alphabet derived from it came in two versions: a normal and a dot matrix version. According to Ben Bos (in an e-mail to the author) both alphabets were used only sparsely in internal publications of the company, which has now become The Randstad Group: 'one of the largest temporary and contract staffing organizations in the world' (2003 website). Although the logo has remained in use to date, the company has never adopted the Randstad alphabet as its corporate font, using Helvetica and later Frutiger instead. In 2003, San Francisco-based Dutch type designer Max Kisman set out, with Bos's consent, to ditgitize the alphabet, adding an uppercase and many accented characters and other glyphs. The font is as yet unpublished.

▾ Foundry Catalogue, the 2003 digital version of Crouwel's alphabet for Claes Oldenburg.

alphabets into complete character sets with diacritics. The same goes for the New Alphabet, which was carefully reproduced with all the idiosyncrasies and 'illegible' characters of the original. Crouwel's original *Proposal for a New Alphabet* included the possibility of extended and condensed varieties, which on paper seemed less satisfying as graphic forms than the core version, constructed around a square. It is, naturally, the square that has been taken as starting point for the Foundry revival, which consists of three weights.

The most commercially successful of The Foundry's Crouwel faces is *Gridnik*, based on the Olivetti and postage stamp designs. 'I still had piles of technical drawings for the face,' says Crouwel, 'so reproducing the forms was comparatively easy. But as the typeface had been designed for a typewriter with three standard widths, it took some time to fix the spacing.' Gridnik (the new name was thought up by Sack and Quay) is the one Crouwel revival which has been conceived as a complete text typeface. There is a single font, simply called Gridnik, which is a more or less faithful revival of the original alphabet, with added accents and other diacritics. The other version is called *Foundry Gridnik*; it is a family of four weights (light, regular, medium, bold) which Quay developed from the original design under Crouwel's supervision. Crouwel is happy with the result. 'I'm even using it on my own typewriter,' Crouwel admitted to me a few years ago. By this he meant that he had installed the face on his Macintosh. Having retired from his position as director of the Boymans Van Beuningen Museum in Rotterdam in 1993, Crouwel had returned to being an independent designer and consultant. Still active at 75, he uses the computer as a supplemental tool – leaving the actual studio work to others.

In 2003, international public attention for Crouwel's work reached new heights. He was the guest of honour at the first edition of Grafic Europe, an international conference which took place in Barcelona, and lectured to a full house at the celebrations of the International Society of Typographic Designers (ISTD) in London which, like Crouwel, turned 75 that year. A well-illustrated book introducing Crouwel's alphabets was conceived by David Quay, with interviews by Kees Broos. A visually stunning book about the New Alphabet was produced as a thesis by the young Italian designer Paolo Palma. Towards the end of the summer The Foundry announced a new digital Crouwel typeface: *Foundry Catalogue*, based on the 1970 alphabet for Claes Oldenburg. With Catalogue, one of Crouwel's most idiosyncratic and humorous typographic designs has become available to today's graphic designers.

catalogue

soft solid soft outline

Jurriaan Schrofer: alphabets made to measure

Jurriaan Schrofer (1926–1990) was one of the most original individuals of post-war Dutch graphic design. He was as much a philosopher as a typographer, and towards the end of his career naturally gravitated towards pure art – art made with letterforms and text.

A son of the painter Willem Schrofer, Jurriaan had been fascinated by type and lettering since childhood. Through his father he met the typographer and lettering artist Helmut Salden; Schrofer would never forget Salden's criticism of the decorated letterforms he had drawn for a school project about China.[20] As a law student, he took part in theatre projects and became interested in cinema; he moved to Amsterdam, hoping to become a film director. He was soon introduced to the modernist heritage, meeting artists such as Cas Oorthuys, Dick Elffers, Emmy Andriesse and Piet Zwart. In the 1950s he was assistant to Dick Elffers, and began designing books and book covers. He landed a job at Meijer Printers, for whom he created a famous series of type specimen books with colourful covers showing compositions made with single characters from book faces. A collaboration with photographer Ed van der Elsken, *Een liefde in Saint Germain des Prés* ('A love affair in Saint Germain des Prés', 1955) was a masterpiece of book design, as well as a brilliant and intense view of existentialist Paris. He designed some of the finest examples of a typical post-1945 genre, the corporate photo book.

Around the same time, Schrofer began experimenting with constructed letterforms, of which his 1954 advertisement for a paper company is an early example. His interest in philosophical matters led him to more fundamental questions. What is the minimum number of basic elements with which a typographic idiom can be created? Is it possible to find a single formal principle with which all sign systems can be described? This was the starting point for an intensive personal investigation into minimalist alphabets, built out of elementary shapes (mostly squares and quarter circles). There was, of course, an historic dimension to this research. It was in many ways a continuation of the experiments carried out by the Bauhaus typographers

internationale avantgarde 1927-1929 i10 stedelijk museum amsterdam 18-10-18-11 '63

catalogus 344

△ One of the first showings of a Schrofer alphabet constructed with basic shapes – square and quarter circle. Catalogue for an exhibition based on an anthology of the 1920s magazine *i10* which had been edited by Schrofer and Arthur Lehning, 1963.

◁ Among Schrofer's typographic experiments in the 1950s was a series of type specimens for Meijer Printers: the covers were compositions made with single characters from the classic typefaces shown in the catalogues. LP stands for *Letterproef*: type specimen.

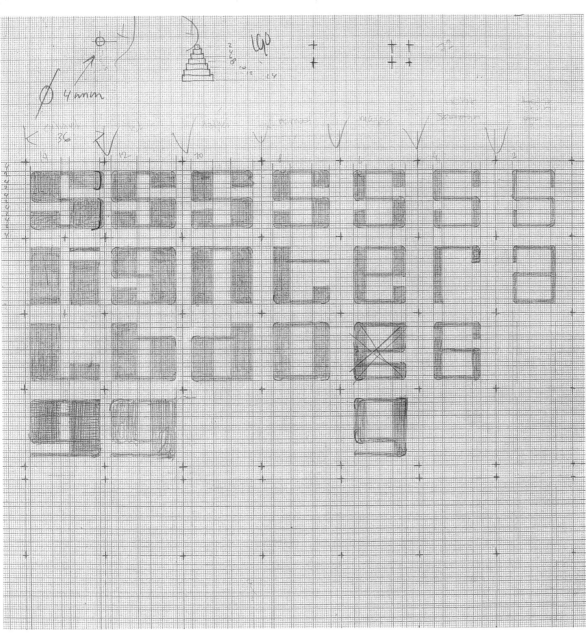

◄ For Schrofer, each assignment could become the starting point of an intensive investigation into letterforms. Having been commissioned to design a commemorative stamp for the International Labour Organization (IAO, 'Internationale Arbeids Organisatie') Schrofer developed a family of alphabets of increasing weight, in order to build up the letters IAO with small type forming waves on the minute surface of the stamp. *Museum of Communication, The Hague.*

▼ The printed stamp, 1969.

▼ Custom dry transfer sheets were ordered for producing the stamp's working drawings.

Josef Albers and Herbert Bayer. It was therefore very appropriate that the first 'public' application of a fundamental Schrofer alphabet was the cover of *i10, de internationale avant-garde tussen de twee wereldoorlogen*, an anthology of the 1920s arts magazine i10 edited by Schrofer and Arthur Lehning.

Schrofer made several attempts to create complete typefaces – one of which was wittily called *Sans serious* – but this was never his goal. 'Is it necessary', he wrote, 'to make complete alphabets with upper- and lowercase, figures, diacritrics and seriously adorned with a name, when the aim is merely a formal investigation into basic recipes?' [21] Schrofer's domain was never the design of typographic alphabets, to be used by other designers, but always the creation of letterforms 'made to measure' as part of his own designs of – mainly – book covers and postage stamps. He created a rectangular alphabet as the basic element of his ever-changing covers – each based on the same grid but coloured differently – for a series of scientific books, 'Les textes sociologiques' from Mouton Publishers. He made sophisticated pixel-based letters, all drawn by hand, and experimented with photographic screens as a means of distinguishing simplified letterforms from the background. He created logotypes built from custom-made letterforms, based on rectangular grids.

In the early 1960s, Schrofer began his long-time working relationship with the Dutch Post, Telephone and Telegraph Service (PTT). One of his most remarkable assignments for this client was the 1965 diary, in which poems by Jan G. Elburg and

20 Bibeb, *Jurriaan Schrofer*, Nijmegen 1972, p 3.

21 Jurriaan Schrofer, *Letters op maat*, Eindhoven 1987, p 2.

◄ Composition based on the word Rijkspostspaarbank (State Post Savings Bank), designed for an annual report, c. 1970.

► In his booklet *Letters op maat* ('Type made to measure', 1987), Schrofer presented many of his experimental alphabets from the 1960s and '70s. The booklet was part of a series of goodwill publications edited by Wim Crouwel for Lecturis Printers, Eindhoven.

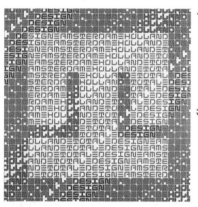

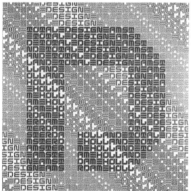

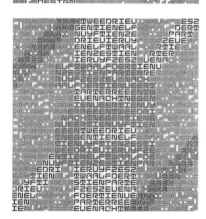

◄ The initals TD (Total Design) formed with the words *total, design, amsterdam* and *holland* set in a constructed alphabet drawn by Schrofer.

↕ A similar system was used for the numerals indicating the floors at the Ministry of Culture, Recreation and Social Work in Rijswijk (one example shown) and the Post Bank in Leeuwarden, both produced in 1974.

single words taken from them were used as illustrations, printed in large, deformed type. Working for the PTT enabled Schrofer to further develop his typographic research. An apparently simple assignment like the postage stamp celebrating 50 years of the International Labour Organization (ILO) in 1969 was welcomed as an excuse for developing an extremely complex typographic construction. Schrofer drew a series of alphabets of increasing weights, which he then had produced as custom-made dry transfer sheets. With these sheets, he 'typeset' the Dutch name of the organization – *internationale arbeiders organisatie* – in a undulating pattern of bolder and lighter characters, in which the initials IAO stand out.

In 1972 Schrofer accepted the invitation to join the management of Total Design. His new position as senior designer of Holland's leading studio for corporate design did not stop him from embarking on ever more experimental typographic projects. The numerals used for indicating the floors at the Ministry of Culture, Recreation and Social Work in Rijswijk as well as the Post Bank in Leeuwarden (both 1974) were matrixes of small, coloured, square characters which spelled out the numbers 1 to 10. A similar principle was used for a telecommunications building in Utrecht. The 1983 Total Design book quotes a short statement by Schrofer about his types: 'It's not about whether they are original or beautiful or suited for the computer. They even gradually become more illegible, but I am not interested in that now.' [22] This is a remarkable attitude for someone who, at that point, was supposed to represent the country's sternest exponent of objective functionalism.

Over the years, Schrofer's work became simpler and more poetical. He began cutting letterforms – of a slightly more conventional alloy than his earlier type – out of paper and cardboard; some of his designs were executed in steel. In each of these later works light plays a central role: the types' outlines are cut into a monochrome surface, and the letters are only visible through the reflections of front and back lighting on the subtly protruding and receding surfaces. A collection of twelve three-line poems by J.C. van Schagen was published as a booklet (*Ik ga maar en ik ben*, 1984) in which the texts were reproduced as black-and-white photos of Schrofer's cut-outs. This type of work culminated in a number of large-scale three-dimensional projects. For a college in Zwolle, a suspended steel Möbius ring was created which carries a poem by Jan G. Elburg. Red lamps were used to backlight a text incised in the steel arch of the Heerlen library (mid-1980s). To Schrofer, his work had not fundamentally changed: 'The character of graphic design does not change because, in spite of space and size, the text is the image and the image is the text.' [23]

In 1988, two years before his untimely death, Schrofer presented a major exhibition at the De Beyerd arts centre in Breda. *Onvolmaakt geheugen* ('Imperfect Memory') was a labyrinth of texts cut out in long sheets of paper which hung from the ceiling. It was a monumental final chord in a body of work in which the letterform had always had a central role – without ever producing printing types for general use.

Functionalism and geometry

Functionalism for the masses: Ad Werner

Ad Werner, outline version of Rochetta, a typeface designed for exclusive use in the women's magazine *Margriet*, c. 1980.

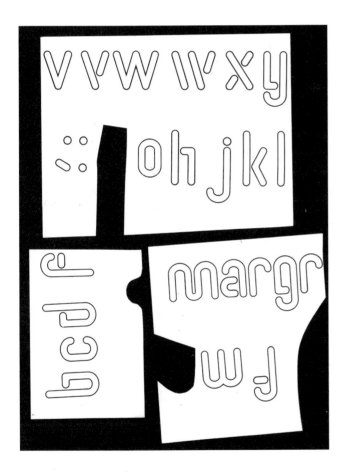

Few post-war Dutch type designers have been as prolific and omnipresent as Ad Werner (1926); and few have remained as anonymous. With his logotypes, alphabets and magazine and poster designs he was one of those rare one-man bands whose impact on the graphic outlook of the country in the 1970s and '80s rivalled that of large studios such as Total Design and Tel Design. Thanks to the success of his Mecanorma transfer sheet typefaces – the best-known of which has the very Dutch name *Dubbeldik* ('double-fat') – his presence abroad has also been considerable. Yet he was never granted much recognition by his peers, nor by design critics. As a graphic designer, Werner was an outsider. Instead of meeting with colleagues, he preferred to hang out with his friends in Amsterdam social-democratic circles. He seldom received assignments from museums, literary publishers and other strongholds of highbrow culture, but he did design the hugely popular women's weekly *Margriet*, a much-publicized Bible-in-instalments, the Succes diary and the corporate identity of the HEMA chain of department stores. His aesthetic views share certain characteristics with Crouwel's and Schrofer's: a delight in new and simple forms, a preference for geometry and grids, an optimistic view of modernity. But he is wary of intellectualism and conceptual thinking. Ad Werner is a pragmatic, street-wise problem solver. A smart operator, but also someone who perfectly captured the spirit of the times and managed to give it an undiluted expression that was acceptable to a wide audience.

Werner grew up in his father's printing shop in the green village of Wassenaar, where he learned typesetting as a child. He was fascinated by the printing trade and very keen on drawing, so the nearby Art Academy in The Hague was a logical choice for his education. In the late 1940s, the masters of Dutch modernism Gerard Kiljan and Paul Schuitema taught 'advertising' here. To the young Werner (he was barely 17 when he entered the school) the Bauhaus-like curriculum was 'not uninteresting' although, as he recalled more than fifty years later, functionalist theories were 'a nightmare' to him. 'I just wanted to draw singing tea-kettles with rays around them, and for the Konijnenburg firm [a family name meaning 'rabbit hill'] a couple of rabbits that ran really, really fast.' Once he had finished his studies he started his own advertising studio on the first floor of the family printing house, and offered his services to the tradespeople of the high-class residential village. 'I had taken a correspondence course which told me exactly how to go about it. You get on your bike, you whistle a tune while you enter a shop and happily announce: 'Good morning, Mr Van Buren, I have come to sell you a trademark.' And it damned well worked! I could supply them with everything they wanted: logotype, letterheads, envelopes, I had unit prices for each item. All this changed when I met a writer who said to me: "Ad, things are never going to work out for you this way. If you really want to be somebody in your life, you must go to Amsterdam." The next morning I packed my little cardboard suitcase and took the train, to apply for a job with a firm that seemed kind of interesting to me. From that day on I designed film posters for Keeman & Co.' [24]

Despite his modernist training, Werner's style and technique as a poster designer were rather romantic. He painted his first poster, for Cocteau's *La belle et la bête*, literally on the canvas. But from the start he had a feeling for trends: both his dramatic illustrations and the decorative hand-lettering are perfect products of their time. According to Werner, his former teacher Paul Schuitema was furious when he heard

22 Broos 1983 (cit.), p 21.

23 Jurriaan Schrofer, *Zienderogen*, Amsterdam 1988, p 39.

24 All quotes based on interviews with Ad Werner.

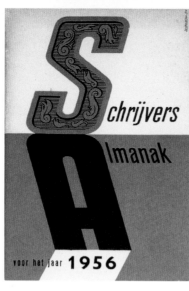

◄ Paperback cover of the 1956
Writers' Almanac.

◄ Ad Werner, poster for the
Amsterdam showings of the
Douglas Sirk film *Sleep My Love*,
c. 1949.

► Lettering for a supermarket
poster, 1950s.

▸ Ad Werner drew over a dozen
constructed alphabets, of which
this nameless 1979 design is one
of the most complex.

▾ The Dubbeldik alphabet was
originally designed for the
bindings of a Bible in instalments (the last volume of which
is lacking in the copy shown
here). Published in 1972 as a
lowercase-only typeface by
Mecanorma, it became hugely
successful as a font for dry
transfer lettering.

↯ One of its best-known uses
was the masthead of the weekly
national hit parade.

aaaabbbbccddddeeee:
FFgghhiiyyyyjkklllm;
mnnnooppqrrrsssst;
tuuuvvwwxxyyzz:

de nederlandse top 40

17e jaargang nr 16   18 april 1981

no. 1 trofee
alarmschijf
nationaal produkt

ALS HET OM MUZIEK GAAT, IS... K-TEL SIMPLY THE BEST !!

Auteursrecht uitdrukkelijk voorbehouden.   Gehele of gedeeltelijke overname in welke vorm dan ook alleen
na schriftelijke toestemming van de Stichting Ned. Top 40. tel. 035 - 231 647, postbus 706, 1200 as hilversum

DE NEDERLANDSE TOP 40 IS SAMENGESTELD DOOR DE STICHTING NEDERLANDSE TOP 40 UIT GEGEVENS VAN HANDEL EN INDUSTRIE

deze week	vorige week	Titel - Artist - (Producer) / Componist - Label & bestelnummer - Distributiemij	aantal weken	deze week	vorige week	Titel - Artist - (Producer) / Componist - Label & bestelnummer - Distributiemij	aantal weken
1	1	**VIENNA** - ultravox (ultravox/plank) currie/cross/cann/ure - 102 905 - ariola	6	21	28	**AND LOVE GOES ON** - earth, wind and fire (maurice white) white/white/dunn/enz. 9521 - cbs	3
2	6	**ANGEL OF MINE** - frank duval & orchestra (frank duval) duval/maloyer - 6 12949 - rca	4	22	26	**IK HEB 'N TRUCK ALS M'N WONING** - henk wijngaard (limpens)/hoes - 3115 - telstar	4
3	2	**DON'T STOP THE MUSIC**, yarbrough and peoples (simmons/ellis) simmons/peoples/ellis - 6170 024 - phon.	8	23	—	**'T IS MOEILIJK BESCHEIDEN TE BLIJVEN** - p. blanker (davis/klaris/blanker) idem, 103 044, ar./fl.	1
4	3	**IN THE AIR TONIGHT** - phil collins (phil collins/hugh padgham) collins - 79 198 - wea	9	24	29	**MORNING DEW** - long john baldry (heydon) donson/rose - 1a 006 86329 - emi rec.	2
5	8	**WITHOUT YOUR LOVE** - roger daltrey (jeff wayne) billy nicholls - 2002 022 - polydor	5	25	15	**LEILA** - dolly dots (de bois/v. asten) idem - 18.473 - wea	8
6	4	**SHADDAP YOU FACE** - joe dolce (dolce/mckenzie) dolce - 102 947 - ariola	7	26	14	**STARS ON 45** - stars on 45 (j. eggermont)/m. duiser - 141 708 - cnr	13
7	9	**ONE NIGHT AFFAIR** - spargo (david/lafour/spargo) driessen - 1417 - ineico	5	27	30	**HET IS EEN WONDER** - linda williams (goya/v.d. laar) v.d. laar/de wit - 18 499 - wea/ttr	3
8	11	**MISTER SANDMAN** - emmylou harris (brian ahern) pat ballard - wb 17 758 - wea	4	28	39	**PUNTJE D'RIN PUNTJE D'RUIT** - de slijpers (e. muenze/m. dreier/j. hoes) idem - 3202 - telstar	2
9	12	**JEALOUS GUY** - roxy music	5	29	17	**SHINE ON** - l t d	11

Designed several decades ago, Werner's logotype for Quick, a Dutch brand of sports shoes, was recently revived by the company's new management.

▼ Custom-made dry transfer sheet of the corporate typeface for the Succes stationery firm. The company also published the Succes diaries which Werner designed with specially made display alphabets.

⌄ Outline version of Paperclip, the only typeface besides Dubbeldik that Werner published for dry transfer lettering, c. 1974.

about the turn that his pupil and fellow-villager's career had taken. It seems that Schuitema even went to Amsterdam to have a chat with the management of Werner's indirect client, The Tuschinski Cinema – to no avail. For five years, Werner designed posters for Amsterdam cinemas, over a hundred in all.

From the mid-1950s Ad Werner worked as a freelance designer. He became acquainted with the Amsterdam in-crowd of left-wing politicians and journalists and was a member of the Amsterdam Journalists' Cabaret (cabaret being a typically Dutch brand of satirical musical theatre). One of his teammates in that group was Hedy d'Ancona, who would later become Minister of Culture for the socialist party, the PvdA. In 1972, d'Ancona and Wim Hora Adema, the initiators of Man-Vrouw-Maatschappij (Man-Woman-Society), got him involved in the founding of the feminist magazine *Opzij*.

By then, Werner had made a name for himself in several areas. He designed trademarks and printed matter for large and small enterprises, from the HEMA department store to the bed shop Bröring, for which he also designed the interior. He created logotypes for several hospitals. He was an important supplier to a group of famous entertainers who had been part of the legendary Lurelei company, designing publicity material as well as stage sets for the comedy shows and musicals starring Jasperina de Jong, Gerard Cox and Frans Halsema. Moreover, his Studio Werner did a lot of editorial design for De Geïllustreerde Pers, one of the country's largest publishers of weeklies, monthlies and illustrated books in instalments. It was in the context of these editorial assignments that most of his typefaces were conceived.

One of the publisher's most ambitious projects was a full-colour illustrated Bible in weekly instalments, to be saved in plastic binders. For these binders Werner invented a graphic form which also worked as a sales trick. On the spines, like a logo, the text 'd e b ij b e l' was printed in gold – one letter for each book, so the title would not be complete until all the volumes had been purchased. The typeface he drew for this purpose – a bold two-lane lowercase, constructed from circle segments and lines – was incredibly hip, considering the contents. Werner decided to develop the design and produce a complete alphabet. *Dubbeldik* was published in 1972 as a Mecanorma transfer sheet typeface and became a minor hit worldwide. The face turned out to be an ideal tool for cooking up instant logos, suggesting a wide range of contemporary connotations, from science fiction to corporate cool. It was even used for the giant numbers on the hangars at the Charles De Gaulle airport in Paris.

Mecanorma issued a second display type, called *Paperclip*, which gained a certain fame among art directors and architects. After that, Werner decided not to design any more fonts for general use, but only make type on demand. 'Those Mecanorma letters were all over the place,' says Werner, 'but the royalties were negligible. Every time I saw *Dubbeldik* in use, I said to myself: hey, I've made another half guilder. I realized there was much more to be earned from designing type if you sold it directly to the clients.' Werner thought up a clever system: instead of selling the copyrights of his designs, he leased them out at a substantial yearly rent. Both his headline alphabet for the women's weekly *Margriet* (named *Rocchetta* after the village in northern Italy where he built his self-designed second home) and the types for the Succes diaries remained in use considerably longer than the clients had envisaged. They earned their designer better revenues than many typefaces that were marketed on a large scale. *Dubbeldik* is a case in point: although it has been available as a PostScript font for over a decade and can be found on shop-fronts and letterheads all over Europe, it has never yielded royalties of any significance.

Werner designed numerous theatre posters as well as album covers for a group of well-known Dutch entertainers. This poster for Jasperina de Jong and Eric Herfst (1980) was designed with Werner's typeface Zero, which existed in at least three weights but was never made publicly available.

▸ Zero's lightest weight was used for the Werner family's 1974 season's greetings.

▾ Nameless alphabet used in false perspective on an album cover, 1981.

◂ Type design for the Teletext pages of the BUMA copyrights organization, 1970s.

▾ Werner designed a constructed 'logotype' for the jackets of a translation of Freud's complete works, published between 1979 and 1993 by Boom Publishers.

No other Werner typeface has been issued in digital format. When they were designed in the 1970s and '80s, Werner and his assistants drew each alphabet by hand and multiplied them – if necessary – by camera. For use in layouts, characters were cut out of negative films or repro proofs and pasted in position. The types that were leased to publishers, such as the *Succes* typeface, were made reproducible by ordering custom-made transfer sheets produced for exclusive use by the publishers' in-house production studios.

Several Werner types have remained nameless; some have never even been used. Among those that did get a name and some kind of career, *Zero* is one that stands out. It is simple and straightforward, a lowercase face based on a rounded square. But it has some remarkable features which make it more interesting than the typical late '70s home-baked geometric alphabet. It had two weights, bold and semi-bold; possibly there were others that were lost. The semi-bold is the most balanced. It was used in certain publications by De Geïllustreerde Pers. The bold is more experimental: several characters exist in two widths or two distinct variants, and there is an unusual alternation of straight and round angles. If *Zero* had been perfected and released as a digital font around 1990, when Neville Brody, Zuzana Licko and others presented similar geometric faces, it might have enjoyed a discrete success.

It is possible that Werner's unpublished fonts will eventually be re-released in digital format; his sons, who have taken over the studio, have played with the idea. A font called *Bröring,* based on Werner's logo for the furniture shop of that name, is waiting to be completed.

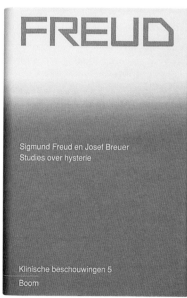

Functionalism and geometry

A typographic counterculture

Swip Stolk, airbrushed lettering
for a genealogy of the
Knijnenberg family, 1973.
The rabbit letters – referring
to the family name, which can
be translated as 'rabbit moun-
tain' – read *Stamboom*, the
Dutch word for 'family tree'.

Form follows fun

By the mid-1970s, the 'functionalism' which Total Design had practised and promoted in the Netherlands for over a decade reigned supreme. In 1976 the PTT introduced two designs by Wim Crouwel which were distributed in millions of copies: a set of eleven numeral postage stamps, and the new phone book, set in lowercase *Univers*.[1] Following the example of Total Design and their Hague equivalent Tel Design, numerous smaller studios were now specializing in functional corporate design. Companies, public services and even cultural organizations across the country had their printed matter laid out in the cool, impersonal 'Swiss style'. Graphic design education in Dutch art schools was dominated by the functionalist creed. But its ubiquity also bred resistance. A kind of typographic counterculture took shape. Young artists, writers and designers published small-scale magazines in which provocative content was presented in an irreverent form, mixing in elements related to commercial art, street culture ('vernacular') and the history of design and typography. Launched between 1965 and 1980, magazines like *Hitweek*, *TIQ*, *Aloha*, *Tante Leny Presenteert*, *Furore*, *De Enschedese School* and *Hard Werken* differed from each other in many respects, but their form had one thing in common: an individualistic, libertarian approach to design and type which indicated that beyond the orthodoxy of functionalism there was a wealth of possibilities – and more fun to be had. Posters and 'house styles' designed by Swip Stolk, Anthon Beeke and Gielijn Escher suggested the same.

This chapter is only partly written in the past tense. All of the artists mentioned – except for Martin Kaye, who is no longer with us – are still making significant work today and are still busy exploring new approaches to text and image. Today, as twenty years ago, their work is an antidote to the soporific clichés of so-called no-nonsense typography – the derivatives of functionalism that abound in today's corporate design.

▲ *Hard Werken* from Rotterdam was a typical product of the late 1970s. While the magazine was soon discontinued, the design collective of the same name became an innovative force in Dutch graphic and theatre design.

▶ *Hitweek* (1965–1969) was more than a music magazine. Talking openly about sex, drugs and rock'n'roll it was the magazine that heralded youth culture. Designed by the editor Willem de Ridder, with such maverick graphic artists such as Anthon Beeke and Swip Stolk, *Hitweek* presented politically incorrect typography like this *Wendingen*-inspired lettering, combined with photos that shocked parents all over the country.

≯ *TIQ*, a competing, more artsy magazine from The Hague, existed for less than two years (1967–68).

Swip Stolk's expressive type

In the mid-1960s, Swip Stolk (1944) was one of the few young designers in the Netherlands to question the hegemony of 'Swiss typography' as practised and promoted by firms like Total Design. 'My expressive style and urge for innovation,' Stolk said, 'were at odds with the ideas of Wim Crowel.'[2] A brilliant illustrator, Stolk chose to quit the Rietveld Academy (Amsterdam) after a few months because his teachers could not believe he had actually done his assignments himself – and because he hated their authoritarian attitude. Unable to work for a boss, he soon became an independent designer. For a brief period during the late 1960s and early 1970s he teamed up with Anthon Beeke (1940), in whom he found – as he called it – 'an ally and sparring partner'.[3] While Beeke went on to create his Studio Anthon Beeke, the individualist Stolk has largely remained a one man band, hand-picking clients who were willing to give him the freedom he needs and with whom he could establish a long-lasting relationship.

From the outset, Swip Stolk created his own letterforms, or modified existing ones to fit seamlessly with his exuberant, imaginative style. He designed several series of numerals for the inventive calendars he made for a printing company and drew constructed lettering for several commercial clients. He created a psychedelic-looking typeface called *Ström*, after the ficticious art patrons *Ström & Gatsy*, invented by the artists Willem de Ridder and Wim T. Schippers. The typeface was used in a 1965 poster in *Hitweek*, the magazine designed by De Ridder and Beeke, to which Stolk contributed regularly. All Stolk's early lettering was meticulously executed by hand, using many techniques including pen and pencil, gouache and airbrush.

His one corporate alphabet was made for the VARA, a left-wing public television channel. Backed by TV director René Coelho, Stolk designed a striking corporate identity built around the image of a rather fierce and macho rooster – a tongue-in-cheek reference to that old metaphor of socialism, the new dawn. The cocky imagery was accompanied by a typeface of capitals called VARA *Bold* that was used for printed matter as well as on-screen texts and the lettering of a large studio set. To underline the ironic monumentality of the house style, VARA Bold had 'a lower serif twice as thick as the upper one'. There was no other typeface, according to Stolk, which 'when … placed in text blocks presented [such] a powerful, compact image.'[4]

In his work for the Groningen Museum, his main client throughout the 1990s, Stolk has frequently used customized type, subtly (or not so subtly) deforming off-the-shelf type. Since the mid-1990s he has found a new, international audience. He designed the well-known logo of *Dutch* magazine, as well as the identity of its recent German spin-off *D*. He has contacts with fashion photographers and art directors around the globe, who commission him to invent contributions to their glossy magazines. One of his latest achievements is *Swip*, a new 'coded' typeface that was presented in the first issue of the international magazine *Stile* (> p 309).

Swip Stolk's VARA alphabet was part of an innovative corporate identity for the broadcasting organization of the same name, 1978.

---

1 Crouwel designed the phone book with Jolijn van de Wouw.

2 Han Steenbruggen (ed.), *Swip Stolk, Master Forever*, Groningen/Ghent 2000, p 39.

3 Ibid., p 41.

4 Ibid., p 44 (Stolk's estimation is a little generous; it is more like 1.6 times as thick.).

Anthon Beeke: re-humanizing the alphabet

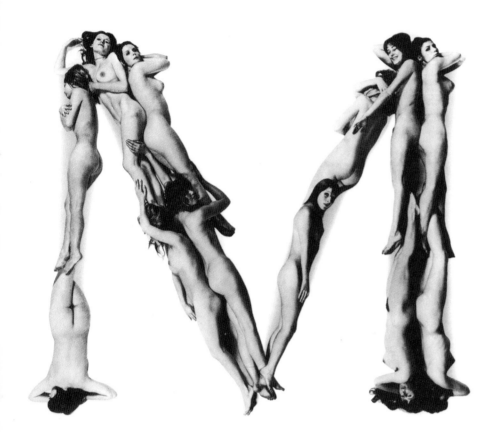

When Wim Crouwel published his proposal for a *New Alphabet*, many of his peers were perplexed, amazed or downright angry. Anthon Beeke (1940), amused rather than annoyed, reacted in his own inimitable way.

While Crouwel had dehumanized the alphabet, creating forms which were conditioned by the limitations of machines, Beeke wanted to make it as human as possible. Inspired by mediaeval and mannerist antropomorphic letterforms, he invited a dozen young women to Geert Kooiman's photography studio and created a set of titling capitals with their naked bodies. When asked if the alphabet was based on an existing classic face, Beeke replied that a set of Baskerville capitals had been the model.[5] Beeke's *Alphabet* was issued in 1970 by Steendrukkerij De Jong & Co as a portfolio of 30 black-and-white plates in their Kwadraatblad series – the same series that had featured Crouwel's proposal. The portfolio included a reportage of the sessions made by a second photograher, the late Ed van der Elsken.

In late 1970, Beeke briefly joined Crouwel's Total Design before creating his own Studio Anthon Beeke and making a name for himself as a designer of provoking and highly original posters, books, magazines and corporate identities. Type design was never part of the Studio's mission; but two designers hired by Beeke during the 1990s made use to their own letterforms in their graphic work. Se the chapters on René Knip (> p 270) and Ko Sliggers (> p 276).

5   Conversation with Anthon Beeke.

Piet Schreuders: making the old look new

One of the harshest and wittiest critics of Crouwel and his fellow-travellers was the founder and editor of *Furore* magazine, Piet Schreuders (1951). A self-taught graphic designer who studied Dutch language and literature, Schreuders contested the claims to objectivity and universality of post-war functionalism, calling it 'a style like any other'.[6] His own writings show what kind of design he was fascinated by: he wrote about street signs, American newspapers and advertising, and cartoon lettering. His research into American paperback cover art yielded a seminal publication, *Paperbacks USA*, translated into English as *The Book of Paperbacks* (1981).[7]

Schreuders's own graphic work has been criticized as being 'nostalgic'; but it would be fairer to say that Schreuders has often managed to create fresh images with elements from the past – including forgotten typefaces. His one-man magazine *Furore* has appeared irregularly since 1975; the magazine covers a wide range of subjects, feeding mainly on the idiosyncratic detective work carried out by Schreuders and a few like-minded artists and writers into obscure details of the history of cinema, music, comic strips, commercial art, literature, etc. While made with simple means and on a tiny budget, the early *Furore* issues managed to avoid the anarchic look of punk fanzines and looked like a kind of hand-made, informal *New Yorker* magazine. Schreuders's choice of typefaces was an eye-opener to many aspiring designers in the late 1970s and early 1980s. He was a fervent promoter of *Gill Sans*, the typeface used for the original masthead as well as headlines. His fascination for Americana led him to researching the typefaces of American newspapers and films, as well as the types and lettering of Oz Cooper. Lacking the possibilities to make his favourite alphabets into workable fonts, he recycled some historical typefaces by copying, cutting and pasting single letters. In this respect his work was related to that of the 'designers' of today's digital revivals, but with simpler means and without the ambition to improve or recreate typefaces.

Schreuders's motives for his unorthodox choice of type relate to content rather than form. 'The type is a means to create a certain atmosphere, to help the text come

▲ In his magazine and book designs, Piet Schreuders often 'revived' forgotten or unknown typefaces by photographic means. This issue of the *Poezenkrant* (Cat Newspaper) was made with copies of the *Los Angeles Times* headline face, 1977. The official name of the typeface is Sans Serif Medium Condensed.

▸ In his one-man magazine *Furore*, founded in 1975, Schreuders made use of a wide range of typefaces, often reproduced by copying, cutting and pasting. Many of these types were practically illegal in the functionalist design that was the norm in the 1970s and early 1980s.

Schreuders researched a style of shop window lettering in Amsterdam and The Hague which he called Spiegelletter (Mirror Type). In 1987 Schreuders designed a few record covers for The Gangbusters with a letterform derived from the Spiegelletter.

across in a specific way. Being the editor as well as the designer, I want to make the content as accessible as possible: the typography is there to open up the content.'[8] Given Schreuders's interest in popular culture, it is not surprising that he has also documented type in public spaces. From 1976 onwards he took a series of photographs of shop windows letterd in a 'typeface' which Schreuders has called *Spiegelletter* (Mirror Type). The lettering was the work of one or more unidentified firms active in Amsterdam and The Hague during the 1950s and '60s, who used a combination of metal foil and red or blue paint to apply their self-designed letterforms. These letters were apparently cut on the spot with the help of a ruler, and are therefore constructed with straight lines only, to interesting effect.[9] In 1987, Schreuders used the principles of the Mirror Type – including the false perspective – for the hand-lettering of record covers for a band called The Gangbusters. Schreuders also researched the Amsterdam Bridge Alphabet (> page 74). In 1989 he was invited by the City of Amsterdam's Department of Hydraulic Engineering to supervise the spacing of letters for new bridge signs. He documented his work on the alphabet with an article published in the short-lived magazine *Qwerty*.[10]

Since the advent of the Macintosh, Schreuders's one-man studio has become fully digital. In 2003 Schreuders was elected Art Director of the Year for his work on the VPRO radio and television guide. Apart from having made a number of glyphs and ligatures for *Cooper Oldstyle* for the new edition of *Lay In – Lay Out*[11], he has not ventured into digital type design. That, he says, is work for specialists.

6 Info about the anti-functionalist discussion in Huygen and Boekraad, *Wim Crouwel, Mode en module*, Rotterdam 1997; also in Piet Schreuders, *Lay In – Lay Out en ander oud zeer*, Amsterdam 1997.

7 Piet Schreuders, *The Book of Paperbacks: A Visual History of the Paperback Book*, London 1981.

8 Interview with Piet Schreuders, 1999.

9 'Letters van glas' in *TYP A*, November 1986, reissued in *Lay in – lay out* (cit.), pp 69 – 76.

10 'Amsterdamse ezelsbruggen. Het ijzeren alfabet van Publieke Werken', in *Qwerty* vol. 2 no. 2, 1990. Republished as 'Letters van ijzer' in *Lay in – lay out ...* (cit.), pp 80 – 85.

11 The new glyphs were digitized by Loek Schönbeck, the designer of the typeface Elyade (cf. p 305).

Piet Schreuders: making the old look new

Joost Swarte's universe

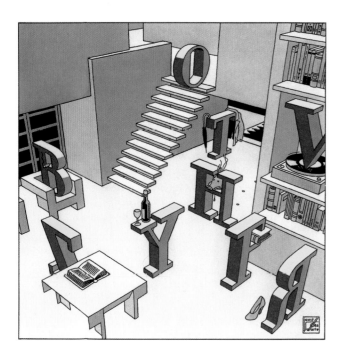

▲ Joost Swarte, *Letters op hun gemak* ('Letters relaxing'), drawing for the weekly *Vrij Nederland*, 1986.

▶ Booklet about Swarte's work for the Randstad employment group, 2002.

Unlike Piet Schreuders, Joost Swarte (1947) never participated in the functionalism-and-ugliness discussion. He did not have to: his characters inhabited a galaxy of their own, to which Total Design's system generals had no access – although perhaps they sneaked in after hours.

Swarte's mother is of Flemish descent, while his father's family was from Groningen in the northern Netherlands. His personality and work reflect the contrasting traits of this mixed heritage – the sober rationality of the north versus the Belgian sense of the absurd and the fantastic. Both for Joost and for his brother Rieks Swarte, a well-known theatre director and set designer, this combination has led to an idiosyncratic sense of humour as well as a liking for mental adventure and invention.

Joost Swarte trained at the Eindhoven Academy of Industrial Design to be a graphic or industrial designer but became a cartoonist instead. This decision was directly related to the Dutch design climate in the late 1960s. Although he admired the professionalism of designers like Benno Wissing, he found that the dominance of functionalist principles had a limiting effect: 'Design became something very essentialistic, almost dogmatic. Comic strips allowed me to tell my own story. Everything was possible, every image, every typeface, the whole story: I was my own master.'[12]
So Swarte created private worlds full of wacky characters, absurd situations, revealing perpectives, newly invented buildings and furniture – 'total design' indeed.

Like other Dutch and Belgian cartoonists of his generation, Swarte was heavily influenced by the drawing style of Hergé (Georges Remi), the Belgian creator of the character Tintin (aka Tim). He found that Hergé's 'clear line' (*klare lijn*) suited him well – it enabled him to draw architecture and objects with analytical simplicity and precision. It is exactly this meticulous attention to detail which often lends such an irresitably comic quality to his drawings. Like Hergé's work, Swarte's cartoons are hugely popular in southern Europe; in France, he has had several exhibitions, and many of his best book projects have been developed in collaboration with his Paris publisher Futuropolis.

Over the years, Swarte has developed a lettering style that is completely in tune with his timeless cityscapes and interiors, informed by a multitude of influences. His earliest lettering – for a hit parade he issued weekly in his teens – was done in a psychedelic style which owed much to the headlines of the magazine *Hitweek*. The headlines of his first self-published magazine, *Modern Papier*, were often modelled on the lettering of pre-war American comics. At college, the calligraphy classes of Margaretha Paulsen were seminal. 'She taught me to write a Mediaeval script, and made me aware that there were norms for sanserif, too. But she was also the kind of person who would say: "Now please put down your pens and look out the window. You won't see a beautiful sunset like this very often."'[13] In the 1970s, Swarte discovered the modernism of De Stijl and Bauhaus, and the playful work of late Italian Futurism.[14] He was even more attracted to the lettering styles of the avant-garde's eclectic contemporary – Art Deco. He admired the Amsterdam School and the magazine *Wendingen* with its ever-evolving cover art by artists and architects. Encouraged by the craftsmanship and the hand-made quality of these examples, Swarte has created his personal typographic universe, borrowing elements from every imaginable source. As Steven Heller wrote, 'a tapestry of twentieth-century influences as viewed through the lens of a visionary'.[15]

Swarte's respect of and fascination for the past has not made him a revivalist. 'A young artist must grow out of the past to build up a solid background,' he told Heller. 'But one must find one's own way out of nostalgia, and stop looking too

much over the shoulder.' In his article on Swarte, Heller also quotes Art Spiegelman,
former editor and publisher of *Raw*, the magazine that introduced Swarte's work to
the American public. 'He has a refined visual intelligence wedded to a sense of
humour and history. He experiments within a tradition, and is always trying things
that are so daring yet made so simple that by the time they are accomplished it looks
so easy that it belies the courage involved.' [16]

Swarte's typography – if we may call it that – is not the work of a type designer who
simply uses his own typefaces. It is more closely related to the advertising headlines
drawn by commercial lettering artists in the 1920s to 1950s: the forms of individual
letters are carefully balanced in order to form words and lines that are harmonic and
convincing and still look playful and effortless. This means that each word and each
combination of characters may be individually designed and spaced. As a case in
point Swarte likes to cite the logo of Hero, a manufacturer of canned food and soft
drinks, drawn by the Austrian Wilhelm Engel in 1928. Two types of letters – a light
monoline and a heavy modern face – are mixed in perfect balance, with a delightful
'r' that mimics the shape of an opened tin can. Naturally, Swarte could not resist
quoting the Hero alphabet (of which several more characters have been designed) in
a headline, extending the incomplete alphabet with new letters. But this is a pastiche: quite funny, but not his best work by far. There are other instances in which
the principles of the Hero logo are taken in a more personal direction – as in the
word *Articulado* for a book published in Spain.

The recent posters for the National Youth Theatre Day (Nationale Jeugdtheaterdag)
show a similar combination of letterforms: heterogeneous yet consistent and balanced. 'JEUGDTHEATERDAG' is a virtually impossible word to make look attractive
and youthful, and yet that is exactly what Swarte has managed to do: one could hardly think of a more functional typography. The 2000 poster also deserves closer
attention for the way in which the individual letterforms have been designed and
placed to interact with each other. Swarte is convinced that this approach to letter-

articulado

The 1928 Hero logotype by
Wilhelm Engel is a classic in
Dutch design. The ashtray
shows an attempt by an anonymous designer to create new
letterforms based on the same
principle. Many of Swarte's
lettering works, in which he
balances light and heavy
strokes, were inspired by the
Hero logo.

12 Ewan Lentjes, 'Joost Swarte, bricoleur typographique', in *Items* 6, December
    2001/January 2002, pp 28–37.
13 Interview with Joost Swarte, 2003.
14 Paul Hefting, 'Te veel om op te noemen. Notities over het werk van Joost Swarte',
    in Joost Swarte, *Plano*, Amsterdam 1987.
15 Steven Heller, 'Past Perfect. The lettering of Joost Swarte' in *U&lc*, vol. 26 no. 2,
    Fall 1999, pp 16–19. Heller seems to prefer the term 'Moderne' to Art Deco.
16 Ibid.

ABBCDEEFFEA
GHIIJKKLLMN
NNNOOPQRS'S'ぅ
TTUVWXYZ!?.:;
AA
012345-/ ⊓⊓
67891()×:;[]

ABCDEFGHIJKLMNN:
OPRSTUVWYZ OEE

UN PORTE-MONNaie
PLⓔiN deſ ProBLèMeſ

UN PORTe-MoNNaie
PLⓔiN de ProBLèMeſ

ing 'has been underexposed by design history while a lot of possibilities still lie ahead.' [17]

Almost all of Swarte's letterforms are based on the elemental graphic forms of square, triangle and circle. In some cases, like the lettering of a poster for the exhibition 'Maitres de la Bande Dessinée' (2001), these shapes are combined to form quirky constructions, as if forming legible characters merely by chance. But in spite of their obvious artificiality, Swarte's letters somehow look natural; their geometry doesn't prevent them from being friendly, human and communicative. This is partly a result of their playfulness, of the obvious delight that their maker has had in inventing new expressions of the age-old forms. But it is also due to a very conscious balancing of the conventional and the unusual, of black and white – moving and changing the letters until the counterforms assume a life of their own.

Because of Swarte's method of carefully designing each word or line of text, it never made much sense to him to distil complete typefaces from his lettering. There are a few exceptions. In about 1974, shortly after publishing his first collection of cartoons, Swarte drew a complete alphabet with strong Art Deco features: a high contrast sanserif, it is a bit like a narrow *Broadway* (M.F. Benton's typeface). It is of historical interest, but still a far cry from the mature Swarte alphabets.

Some have been given names. *Cinco*, as the name suggests, is an alphabet of capitals based on an underlying structure of five bars of equal width; it is equipped with vari-

A typographic counterculture

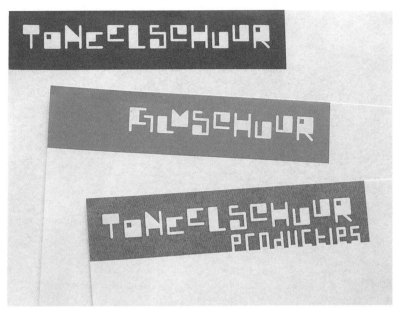

◀ Letterheads for the Haarlem theatre *De Toneelschuur*, 2003.

▶ Opened in early 2003, the Toneelschuur's new space was built according to drawings made by Swarte; he also created the lettering for the building's facade and signposting. *Photo: Henze Boekhout.*

▼ Cover for *Jopo in Mono*, a CD project created with singer-songwriter Fay Lovsky, 1992.

able serifs which have been tailored to work well with Swarte's method of contextual spacing and kerning of characters. The typeface designed for The Magnificent Seven, a show orchestra, is rather similar, although the grid is less strict. As in most of Swarte's faces, the S (which comes in three varieties) accounts for the most outrageous forms; 'the S is the alphabet's dissonant,' says Swarte.[18]

In April 1995 Swarte's long-time client, the Haarlem theatre De Toneelschuur, gave him the assignment of a lifetime: he was asked to design a new theatre building, to be built on the premises of the old Enschedé printing works and type foundry in the city centre. Although Swarte had designed three-dimensional structures before and had drawn hundreds of imaginary buildings, designing a major architectural work was an absolute first; therefore Mecanoo architects from Delft were called in to help Swarte realize his dream. The result was a theatre space that is unorthodox, colourful, happy, and remarkably functional. Following the opening in early 2003, a leading weekly hailed it as 'Holland's most beautiful theatre'.

Naturally, Swarte also designed the theatre's signage and corporate identity. The alphabet he conceived for the new Toneelschuur building once again reveals his fascination for the architects' alphabets of the pre-war era. It takes the linear letterforms explored by Lauweriks, Wijdeveld and Van Doesburg (> pp 68–82) into a new area. The Toneelschuur alphabet is constructed on a two-by-three grid, and built with rectangles, lines and a few 45° diagonals. This structure allows for bolder weights to be constructed at will by simply varying the thickness of the strokes, whereby the counters diminish accordingly. The use of contrast is deliberately inconsistent: sometimes the vertical strokes have all the weight, sometimes the horizontals. As legibility was of minor importance in the lettering of the theatre, the display version could be treated as an image; there is a text version built on a three by five grid that is more legible. With the Toneelschuur alphabet, Swarte has confirmed once more that, as a designer of 'non-typographic' letterforms, he has an unusual ability to think up radical proposals without ever becoming snobbish or deadly serious.

17 Interview with Joost Swarte, 2003.

18 Lentjes (cit.), p 32.

Martin Kaye: obsessed by the alphabet

◄ Martin Kaye, page from *Facade AlphaBets et Cetera*, 1985.

▼ Alphabet for tiles, proposed to the Sphinx ceramics factory in 1986 but never produced.

▼ Double page from Kaye's *Alphabet Index*; and a 1980s poster with type cut out of red film.

Martin Kaye was one of the many self-taught designers to make posters reflecting 1970s subculture. But Kaye was different. Born in London in 1932, he became an apprentice sign-painter at fifteen and at twenty travelled to Japan to learn the fine points of silk screening. He tried in vain to embark on a career as a fine artist and in 1968 left London for Amsterdam, where he became a fulltime silkscreen printer. His home was Paradiso, the former church that had been converted into the city's most famous rock music venue and cultural centre. Here Martin Kaye worked as in-house printer from 1972 until 1983, designing some 2000 posters for concerts and other events at the Paradiso, and printing them in limited runs, usually around 120–180 copies. He often used rainbow printing (*irisdruk* in Dutch) to create spectacularly coloured posters with just one or two impressions. His workshop at Paradiso, where he usually worked at night, became somewhat of a tourist sight. Kaye – a hippie by nature – distributed his posters personally, preferring sellotape to glue and friendly shop windows or bars to anonymous walls.

Kaye was fascinated by letterforms. When he died in 1989 he left an inventory of 60,000 known alphabets, partly collected from old and recent type specimen, partly just letter names scribbled down. A group of friends created a foundation, the Martin Kaye Alphabet Index and Library, to administer this inheritance. A book entitled *Facade AlphaBets et Cetera*, published in 1985 by De Buitenkant in Amsterdam, gives an impression of the way Kaye lived with letters. The book is an eclectic collection of display alphabets and poster designs, with sparse comments about the technicalities of letterforms. Many of the alphabets shown are redesigns of existing typefaces; others are new forms drawn by hand or cut out of red masking film. Plans for a second book remained in the preparation stage because of Kaye's untimely, violent death.

Kaye's body of work is problematic in that originality does not seem to have been relevant to him. In his posters he freely combined typographic constructions with existing photography, found illustrations and band logos. The result worked admirably in the crowded Amsterdam streets and certainly had a voice of its own. Yet it is often difficult to ascertain whether a design was based on his own ideas, or an adaptation of someone else's invention – such as an album cover – tailored to the sign-painter's taste. This also applies to his lettering. Kaye's alphabets are well-made and communicative; but as type designs they have had little or no impact.[19]

19 Sources for Martin Kaye include: Jan de Jong, preface to *Facade AlphaBets et Cetera*, Amsterdam 1985; Hub. Hubben, 'De brutale posters van Martin Kaye', *Volkskrant*, 2 November 1985; Robin Blom, 'Hippie, posterworkaholic en letterkundige', *Algemeen Dagblad*, 3 May 2003; additional information supplied by Peter and Conchita van der Linde, Amsterdam.

Printing types
for a changing technology

Font disk for the Bobst filmsetter, containing eight styles of Trinité by Bram de Does, 1982. Less than ten years later, the system had become obsolete; a completely new Post-Script version of Trinité was produced by Peter Matthias Noordzij and issued by The Enschedé Font Foundry.

Chris Brand: the power of the pencil

Chris Brand, cover design
of the writing manual *Ritmisch
schrijven* (Rhythmic writing),
c. 1955.

Chris Brand is often thought of as the designer of one single typeface: *Albertina*, which made its debut in 1965. He in fact designed several more alphabets, but most remained unpublished, and only Albertina has become a widely distributed digital font family. Brand's typefaces have not been trailblazing contributions to the development of Dutch type, yet in the Netherlands his work is probably the purest example of the calligraphic approach to type; besides, his influence as a teacher and as co-author of several writing books should not be underestimated.

Born in 1921, Chris Brand never received any formal training. Being from a poor family, he was forced to find work immediately upon leaving elementary school. But his interest in letterforms was keen even then. As a young boy he copied the headlines of the daily *Utrechts Katholiek Dagblad* with a pencil – the instrument which would remain his favourite tool all his life. A fellow-singer in the choir of the Utrecht Cathedral, Harrie Schültz, became his teacher and mentor. He gave young Chris free lessons in formal writing and stimulated him to take a teacher's diploma in calligraphy, which Brand obtained in 1940. Schültz also introduced him to a calligraphic society where he became acquainted with the history of lettering. Seeing Edward Johnston's work in an issue of *Zeitgemäße Schrift* was – as his friend and colleague Geert Setola wrote in 1996 – 'a revelation: genuine calligraphy and true typography in one and the same person!'[1] He went on to teach himself 'by reading books and copying letterforms'; Brand himself quotes De Roos, Van Krimpen and Helmut Salden as examples.[2]

In 1950 Chris Brand became a teacher at the St. Joost Academy in Breda, where he would teach formal writing, type design and typography for 36 years. He was an extremely committed teacher, motivated by the unorthodox way in which he had himself acquired his knowledge and skills. Those students whom he regarded as exceptionally talented were invited to his home to talk, eat and drink, and study letterforms. Yet unlike other teachers of type design and writing, such as Gerrit Noordzij, he never imposed his views on letterforms on his students and, stylistically speaking, never gained followers.

His most influential didactic work is a set of publications about the teaching of writing. Together with Ben Engelhart (pseudonym of J. de Rijk) he wrote and designed educational books such as *Naar beter handschrift* ('Towards a better handwriting', 1954) and *Ritmisch schrijven* ('Rhythmic writing', late 1950s). Brand contributed to the creation of a writing method for elementary schools based on Alfred Fairbank's proposals for italic handwriting, specified in an official publication which he designed, *Handschrift voor het lager onderwijs* (1958), and another book written with Engelhart but published under the names of De Rijk and Buursma: *Het normschrift* (c.1959). Due to a lack of enthusiasm among educators, the italic Normschrift ('standard writing') which Brand, De Rijk and others proposed was never generally introduced.[3]

Having married the Belgian Denise Balis, Brand lived in Brussels from 1948 to 1953. Here he established himself as an independent graphic designer and calligrapher, working for clients such as Lannoo – a major Flemish publisher – and the Plantin-Moretus Museum in Antwerp. He struck up a special relationship with the Belgian Royal Library 'Albert I' and with Herman Liebaers, its flamboyant director. Liebaers was one of the first to not only recognize Brand's talent, but also give him prestigious lettering assignments. Brand designed the Library's emblem, as well as the lettering on its facade, and calligraphed a charter by the emperor Philips II which he would always regard as one of his best works. It seems to have been while working on this commission that the thought occurred to him that from this kind of formal italic writing it must be a small step to type design.

▲ Chris Brand calligraphed the charter *Par le Roy* for the Belgian Royal Library during his Brussels years (early 1950s). Brand wrote several writing manuals with Ben Engelhart (pseudonym of J. de Rijk). Cover of *Naar beter handschrift* (Towards a better handwriting), 1954.

▶ Cover design for the Belgian publisher Lannoo, 1958.

▾ Lettering of the facade of the Belgian Royal Library 'Albert I', for which Brand also designed the logotype.

Monotype Albertina

In 1958, having moved to Breda, Brand started working on what was to become *Albertina*, a typeface for which he chose as models, or guides, the examples of English and Italian type and lettering to which Herman Liebaers had shown him the way in the Brussels Royal Library. While working on the typeface, Brand soon felt he lacked the support of a production house such as Enschedé or the Amsterdam Type Foundry, companies 'where there is a technical staff and where it is possible to make proofs'. He visited Jan van Krimpen, who was not of much help. He went to seek advice from Dick Dooijes, the most prolific Dutch type designer of the moment. 'I often spoke with him about Albertina. He thought it had a lot of character, and urged me to complete it.' [4]

What had been a spontaneous enterprise soon became an assignment. In the 1950s and '60s it was still crucial that the typesetting system for which a typeface was being produced be taken into account in the design. The Amsterdam Type Foundry, where Dooijes was type director, used the Intertype system which, like Linotype, did not allow for characters such as f to overhang, i.e. to exceed the width of the body; italic characters were supposed to be designed at the same width as their roman counterparts. Brand wanted a face with a traditionally typographic look, with narrow italics and overhangs. Although initial proofs were made at the Amsterdam Type Foundry, the design was refused for technical reasons by its aesthetic consultant, G.W. Ovink. But at Monotype, Stanley Morison was enthusiastic and decided in favour of production. With Monotype's system, most of Brand's design decisions could be respected. It was, however, a long process from Brand's pencil drawings through the Monotype drawing office to the finished product. It was decided that the new face was not going to be produced for metal typesetting, but was to be one of the first types designed with the new phototypesetting technology in mind. Monotype did not always reproduce Brand's drawings as faithfully as they could have. Most importantly, the Monotype studio did away with the subtle inward curves of the verticals,

1 Geert Setola, speech at the opening of the exhibition *Chris Brand, Letterontwerper en typograaf*, Breda, 8 March 1996 (typescript in the Brand archive).

2 Computer-printed cv, corrected in Brand's handwriting, copy in the Brand archive, NAGO, Amsterdam.

3 Cf. Ernst Braches, *De tragedie van NEN 2296*, 1984.

4 Mathieu Lommen, *Letterontwerpers*, Haarlem 1987, p 47.

The catalogue for the 1966 Stanley Morison exhibition in the Royal Library, Brussels, and the Museum of the Book, The Hague, was the first book set in Monotype Albertina. Design: Fernand Baudin.

Postcard showing Albertina. Monotype Corporation, c. 1966.

Monotype commissioned Brand to design the Coptic face Draguet for the printer Orientaliste, 1969. The Hebrew face Zippora (1970) remained unpublished.

ⲁⲃⲅⲇⲉⲍⲏⲑⲓⲓ̈ⲕⲗⲙⲛϣⲟⲡⲣⲥⲧⲩ ϥⲭⲯⲱϭϧϧⲃ⳽⳽ⲝⳉⳃⳁ אבגדהוזחטיכלמנסעפצקרשתדםוך ךׅ —!?:;'ʼ,·*0987654321

During his lifetime Chris Brand drew hundreds of monograms and vignettes for relatives, friends and clients.

turning them into straight stems and thus taking away some of the face's elegance and optical sophistication.

The new typeface was named Albertina in honour of the Belgian Royal Library 'Albert I'. Appropriately, the first book for which the new face was used was a joint publication of the Royal Library and the Museum of the Book in The Hague – a catalogue for an exhibition on Stanley Morison, who had insisted on using the font for this book. The catalogue, designed by Fernand Baudin, has an unusual appendix: after 40 pages of plates related to Stanley Morison's career there follows a one-page specimen of Albertina, plus two reproductions of Brand's drawings for the typeface. Chris Brand's favourite tool was a 5H pencil, which he also used for designing his printing types. His hand-drawn characters had the precision of working drawings; Fernand Baudin has written that he was perhaps the only type designer who worked in this way.[5] Brand also used this method in class. 'This meant: back to basics,' says René Knip, who was a student at the Breda Academy in the early 1980s. 'Trust your own hand, your own eye. You drew four-centimetre-high characters. No need to ink them, they would obtain their blackness when photographically reduced.'[6]

Published and unpublished typefaces

Although Albertina was not an immediate success, Brand's name was now widely known. In 1965 he redesigned the masthead of *De Volkskrant*, a large newspaper which at the time still bore a Catholic signature. The original masthead was set in Metropolis Bold, which Brand called 'an ugly Roman Catholic typeface'. He subtly restyled it into a logo which proved virtually timeless; yet Brand himself did not like being associated with it too much. While the paper changed considerably – it is now the country's main left-of-centre daily – the masthead remained unaltered until in 2002 it was redesigned even more subtly by David Quay.

After Albertina, Brand designed one more typeface for Monotype: *Draguet*, a sturdy Coptic face which was published in 1969. The design was for a single client: Orientaliste, a printing office in Leuven (Belgium) which specialized in non-Western typesetting and was in the process of switching from Linotype to Monotype. 'A fantastic assignment,' Brand said in an interview with Mathieu Lommen. 'I had many conversations with a priest named Draguet, who was a specialist in Coptic and provided me with copies of Coptic handwriting. I began to draw the alphabet proceeding from my ideas about the position of the pen when writing an uncial – for that is what Coptic is.'[7] Having been produced as matrices for hot-metal typesetting, *Draguet* was later made available as a typeface for photocomposition.

Some years later Brand designed another non-Western typeface: *Zippora*. The idea to make a Hebrew font came to him when admiring the metal lettering of the Israeli Pavilion at the 1958 World Expo in Brussels, designed by George Him. He loved the Hebrew letterforms, but had very little to go by when designing the alphabet; he let

abcdefghijklmnopqrstuvwxyzßæœç
ABCDEFGHIJKLMNOPQRSTUVWXYZÆŒ$£
11234567890!?†.,:;"·——-»«*()[]/§&℮I1234567890
ABCDEFGHIJKLMNOPQRSTUVWXYZÆŒ

abcdefghijklmnopqrstuvwxyzßæœç
ABCDEFGHIJKLMNOPQRSTUVWXYZÆŒ$£
11234567890!?†.,:;"·——-»«()[]/§&℮I1234567890*

abcdefghijklmnopqrstuvwxyzßæœç
ABCDEFGHIJKLMNOPQRSTUVWXYZÆŒ$£
11234567890!?†.,:;"·——-»«*()[]/§&℮I1234567890

abcdefghijklmnopqrstuvwxyzßæœç
ABCDEFGHIJKLMNOPQRSTUVWXYZÆŒ$£
11234567890!?†.,:;"·——-»«()[]/§&℮I1234567890*

abcdefghijklmnopqrstuvwxyz
ABCDEFGHIJKLMNOPQRSTUVWXYZ
!?.,:;„""'·-/-+†/§»«()[]&*1234567890
æœfffifI flcb chckßçáàâäéèêëíìîïóòôöúùûüÆŒÇ£$ÄÉÈÊËÖÜ

abcdefghijklmnopqrstuvwxyz
fbfffhfifjfkflffifflßÆŒæœ&℮
11234567890.,:;„""'·!?»«——-///()[]§*†‡+x=%¶&·©
ABCDEFGHIJKLMNOPQRSTUVWXYZ
ABDEFGHIJKLMNPRTUVWXYZ,
*áàâäçďèèêïíïñóòôöøúùûüæ*gg
ÁÀÂÄÇĎÉÈÊËÍÎÏŁ£ÑÓÒÔÖØ$ÚÙÛÜ

himself be guided by the generic principles of calligraphy. 'One doesn't know what the characters mean, nor what they sound like. You have nothing to hold on to. Yet this does have its advantages because familiarity may undermine critical thinking. I think the result is quite sensual and in Israel people were extremely pleased with it.'[8] Zippora was finished in 1970, but was never produced as a font; it was first used (in photographic reproduction) on the cover of a 1984 catalogue of the Israeli artist Dani Karavan for the De Beyerd museum in Breda.

Delta and Delta grotesque; Denise

Between 1965 and 1969 Brand worked on a typeface called *Delta*, which had been conceived for line-casting (Linotype or Intertype). He had no commission to design such a face but taking assignments from himself had become a habit. 'I wanted to know what kind of misery you encounter when designing a printing face for a line-casting machine. The italic, for instance, is usually too wide and it is impossible to create overhangs, which accounts for the f being a disaster. ... Delta had to be different from Albertina, which is why it is more open and wider.'[9] Delta is beautifully drawn; its shapes are less angular than Albertina's, its curves more luscious.

As his fellow teacher Geert Setola said in a speech about Brand: 'Letters are feminine. He approaches them, he touches them. And as soon as he does, they come alive with a sensitivity and a sensuality and a grey hue against which you'd want to trade the deepest crimson and the purest socialist morning red. In his eyes and his hands a Garamond becomes a French farmer's daughter and a Baskerville an English nursemaid.'[10]

In retrospect, Delta could have been quite successful as a hybrid text or headline face for advertising. It compares favourably to similar modern classics issued by ITC and Letraset in the 1970s; in this perspective, it was perhaps ahead of its time. What made it all the more interesting is that it was one of the first typefaces after Jan van Krimpen's *Romulus* to be designed as a family with both a seriffed and a sanserif variant. *Delta Grotesque* is, however, not the kind of humanist sans one would expect from one of the country's great writing masters. Like Dick Dooijes's *Mercator*, designed in 1958, the Delta sanserif is a variation on the nineteenth-century grotesque – Helvetica's pretty but somewhat chubby cousin. The typeface was drawn in one weight only, which Brand occasionally used for monumental lettering. 'If you'd want to make such a family commercially interesting, you'd have to draw at least 18 to 21 weights. To be able to accomplish such a vast task, I should have resigned as a teacher.'[11]

Chris Brand felt that teaching was his true vocation. But after hours, he drew letter-forms almost on a daily basis. Many of these found their way into title pages, book-plates, or monumental lettering assignments; others were limited to only a few characters and became monograms. In self-designed season's greetings he occa-

5   Fernand Baudin in *Chris Brand*, Brussels/Breda 1996.

6   René Knip, interviewed by the author.

7   Lommen, *Letterontwerpers* (cit.), p 48.

8   Interview in *De Volkskrant*, 8 March 1996.

9   Lommen, *Letterontwerpers* (cit.), p 49.

10 Geert Setola, speech at the opening of the exhibition *Chris Brand*, Antwerp, 22 May 1996 (typescript in the Brand archive).

11 Lommen, *Letterontwerpers* (cit.), p 49.

ABCDEFGHIJKLMNOPQRSTUVWXYZ

hamburgerfions

ggafcijl / ———.

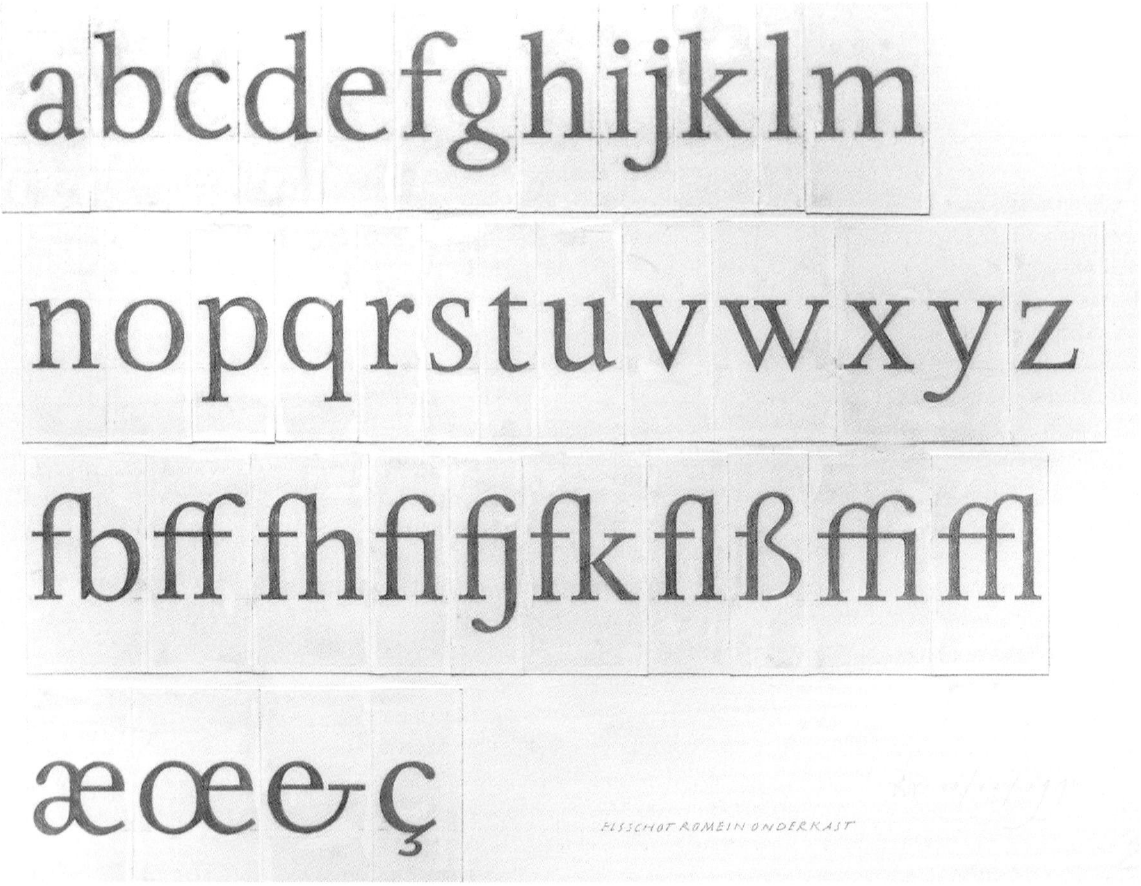

abcdefghijklm

nopqrstuvwxyz

fbff fhfifjfk flß ffi ffl

æœ&ç

sionally presented the alphabets he was working on. One such typeface was *Denise*, a rather upright italic named after his wife. Denise was drawn as an extensive one-weight set, complete with ligatures, accented characters and swash capitals. Of all Brand's typefaces, Denise is closest to his written italics; yet it is not a script font, as its details – especially in the uppercase characters – are definitely those of a book face. In a cv written by Brand himself, Denise is marked as having been 'released in 1983'. This must be taken to mean 'first shown in 1983', as the typeface was never produced.

In the Brand estate there is another unpublished design: a study for an alphabet of titling capitals called *Maurits Capitals*, dated 1988. Maurits is a glyphic typeface, with widened terminals instead of fully grown serifs; although it looks confident and mature, it was never taken any further.

The Elsschot project

In 1988 the daily newspaper *NRC Handelsblad* – *De Volkskrant*'s main competitor – commissioned four graphic designers to pitch a basic design for a weekly full-colour insert. One of the four competitors, a former student of Brand named Henry Cannon, decided to submit a proposal based on a specially designed typeface and asked Brand to present a preliminary study. Having received positive feedback from the editors, Brand continued with his design and drew a complete typeface which he named *Ennercee* (pronounced as 'Ennersay', which is how the Dutch say NRC).[12] When a new editor-in-chief came into office, plans for the weekly magazine were abandoned, to be revived only a decade later – using Bram de Does's *Lexicon* as text typeface.

Brand did not abandon his new typeface. He made drawing after drawing – a few thousand in all – , designed several weights of the serif text face, and completed the family by adding a sanserif companion. He renamed the typeface *Elsschot*, after the Flemish novelist whose sparse and sarcastic style he greatly admired. Elsschot is a departure from his earlier typefaces, which were all based on the diagonal stress of the broad-nibbed pen. As Frank E. Blokland and Antoon De Vylder noted in a broadsheet presenting the Elsschot drawings, both the serif and sans varieties show traces of the flexible pen, i.e. they have a vertical contrast, although not as pronounced as *Didot* or *Walbaum*. In structure, Elsschot is closest to 'transitional' faces such as Fleischman's or Baskerville's. The sanserif has more contrast than most faces of its kind; Brand clearly wanted to create a humanist sans and the result is not unlike, say, Fred Smeijers's *Quadraat Sans* which was conceived around the same time. Elsschot was first presented in the form of drawings at exhibitions that took place in Breda and Antwerp in 1996. Although the overall design would still need corrections before being fit to publish, Elsschot and its accompanying sanserif stand out as a remarkable and accomplished type family.

DTL Albertina, the digital version

The original Monotype Albertina never took off. Its fate was that of several other new faces published in a turbulent period of short-lived technologies: it fell between two stools. The face was produced for the Lasercomp typesetting machine in the early 1980s, but Brand was not happy with the result. He said he would like to propose corrections to compensate for the flare effect of photocomposition, but Monotype would not let him. 'In the Netherlands there is not a single printing shop that offers Albertina. The Morison catalogue is the only Dutch-language book set in this typeface. It is a great deficiency for a book designer not to be able to use his own typeface.'[13]

Brand would, in fact, never get that chance; but he did witness, and contributed to, Albertina's rebirth under a luckier star. Somewhere around 1993 the Flemish book designer Antoon De Vylder came up with the idea of digging up Albertina for a book he was to design for the Royal Library of Belgium, the institute which had given the typeface its name when it was still called Royal Library 'Albert I'. When contacted, Monotype appeared not to have any plans to digitize the face. De Vylder presented the idea to Frank E. Blokland of the Dutch Type Library (DTL). When the latter compared the Monotype version to the original drawings, he concluded that the drawings were superior by far. In the hands of the Monotype drawing office, the design had become more rigid. Blokland: 'Certain details, such as the tapering of the verticals, had disappeared from the Monophoto version. It was therefore decided to take the drawings, and not the published fonts, as a starting point.'[14] From the onset, Brand himself was involved in the revival of Albertina. He made meticulous pencil drawings for several new weights, such as the semi-bold and its italic. As Chris Brand was extremely pleased with the results, DTL was given *carte-blanche* for the production of the fonts.

Shortly after its rebirth, Albertina was chosen as the official face of the Royal Library in Brussels. In 1998, after consulting (URW)++ in Hamburg, the European Union selected the typeface as its corporate typeface after a series of tests. The availability of a Greek version (drawn by Brand himself) was one of the deciding factors. A Cyrillic version was released in 2001.

Brand did not live to witness the international success of his life's work. In late 1998, he was diagnosed with cancer. After a short illness, he died in late December of that year.

The digital Albertina was produced by the Dutch Type Library from 1994 onwards, and was based on Brand's original drawings plus additional drawings made by Brand for this purpose.

DTL ALBERTINA CAPS

ABCDEFGHIJKLM
NOPQRSTUVWXYZ
'&ŒÆÇØ'
([{1234567890}])
ABCDEFGHIJKLMNOP
QRSTUVWXYZŒÆ
ÇØÁÀÂÄÃÅÉÈÊË Ñ
ÓÒÔÖÚÙÛÜŸ
!?.,-$£¥¢§¶†©%#@

24/29

DTL Albertina

Italic Medium *MediumItalic* **Bold** **Bold-Italic** αβγδεζ ηθικλμν αβγδε ηθικλμν αβγδε ηθικλμν абвгед *абвгедж*

12 Frank E. Blokland and Antoon de Vylder, *Chris Brand & Willem Elsschot*, Breda/Antwerp 1996.

13 Lommen, *Letterontwerpers* (cit.), p 48.

14 Interview with Frank E. Blokland, 1999.

Gerrit Noordzij, teacher & master of crafts

The widely-acclaimed 'Haagse letters' (Hague types), which have been produced by young designers since the mid-1980s, would not have been created without the teachings and the work of Gerrit Noordzij. Not only have his theories on the contruction of letters helped to shape his students' thinking, these ideas have also left their mark on the form of their typefaces. Paradoxically, none of Noordzij's own type designs had been published until The Enschedé Font Foundry (TEFF), run by his son Peter Matthias Noordzij, concerned itself with their fate in the 1990s.

Born in 1931 in Rotterdam, Gerrit Noordzij started out in 1948 as a 17-year-old bookbinder's apprentice. Most of the bookbindery's output consisted of mass-produced bindings. Young Noordzij often found fault with the stamped lettering. 'So I thought', Noordzij recalls, 'let's do something about those letters.'[15] With his intuition as chief guide and helped by his astounding ability, Noordzij gradually developed a flawless feeling for typographic detail.

In 1954, on the advice of an acquaintance, he approached the renowned publisher-typographer Alexandre A.M. Stols, who then gave him an assignment for no less than eight book covers. In October of that year, Stols left The Hague for Latin America on a UNESCO assignment, hoping to be able to manage his publishing activities at a distance. 'Stols said to me: now you will also have to take care of the typography. I asked him what that was, and he replied: oh, I am sure you'll find out.' The lettering of the bindings and wrappers for these books was usually done by hand. Noordzij's very first book jacket, for *Achter de bergen* by the poet Ed Hoornik, showed him to be a sensitive craftsman. It was a symmetric all-capitals design, in a style which showed affinity with Jan van Krimpen's most simple lettering.

In 1956 Noordzij was hired by the Amsterdam publishing house Querido, where he stayed for two years. Working for one of the country's most prestigious literary publishers enabled Noordzij to learn about all the aspects of book design and production in a short timespan. During the year 1959 the Noordzij family lived in Germany, his wife's country of origin, where Noordzij enjoyed a brief success as a freelance graphic designer.

The following year Gerrit Noordzij was offered the job of his life. He was hired by the Royal Academy of Arts in The Hague as a teacher of writing. After the death of his colleague Piet van Trigt in 1970, he became the director of the writing and lettering programme at the graphic design department – a position he would hold until his retirement in 1990. He balanced his teaching job with a multi-faceted career as an independent book designer, lettering artist, author and letter carver. From 1978 onwards he designed virtually all of the book jackets for the G.A. van Oorschot publishing house in Amsterdam. Those covers were the chief breeding ground for his typefaces, of which he remained the sole user for a couple of decades. His type designing activities were supported by a clear but unconventional theory of the letterform. These ideas led him to experiment with writing lessons for children at the local primary school (his own sons Christoph and Peter Matthias among them) and to conceive and present a TV course in calligraphy for Teleac – the Dutch 'television university' – for which his former student Frank E. Blokland wrote the textbook and which aired in early 1991.[16]

A simple invention

Noordzij's classes at the Royal Academy have produced several generations of 'Hague' typographers and type designers. The persuasiveness of his teachings rested on two factors: his virtuosity as a craftsman, and the theoretical model he developed in the 1960s and '70s. Noordzij's theory of the written word possesses an unmistakable elegance and has an advantage over other theories in that it can immediately be put into practice – with the broad-nibbed or the pointed pen, with a brush or a chisel, but also when designing by computer. Not only did Noordzij's students face a teacher who promoted his 'simple invention'[17] with much enthusiasm and humour, but also a master craftsman who could create an impeccable line, curve or letterform with each instrument. In his reaction to the present chapter Noordzij pointed out another reason for his 'success as a schoolmaster': his commitment to his students. 'If I could not reach a student with a certain approach, I would search for weeks, day and night if necessary, until I had found a way to get through.'[18]

His ideas on letterforms have best been synthesized in a 1985 booklet entitled *De streek. Theorie van het schrift.* The book was based on an earlier English-language publication, *The stroke of the pen* (1982). The choice of the term *schrift*, 'writing', is significant for a publication aiming to be an introduction to all letterforms, including printing types. Noordzij's axiom – his 'dogma', wrote Robin Kinross[19] – is that there is no essential difference between handwriting and typography. For Noordzij, typography is 'writing with prefabricated letters'. Throughout the centuries there have been type designers who referred to writing as the main source of inspiration for printing types – Bodoni posed with a pen, Jan van Krimpen based some of his italics directly on his handwriting. Yet Noordzij was the first to speculate about the consequences of this relationship in a way that challenges most conventional assumptions about the structure and classification of letterforms. The fact that his tone in writing is often abrupt, even pedantic, may have put off some of his readers; his ideas are no less original for this. Moreover, those willing to enter his world – a world in which the 'I', armed with an impressive arsenal of facts and expertise, invariably knows best – are immersed in a merrily splashing stream of ideas, bon-mots and swipes at established scholarship.

Gerrit Noordzij *The stroke of the pen*

◂ Noordzij's first book cover design, made for the publisher A.A.M. Stols in 1954.

⯇ Gerrit Noordzij, book jacket for Insel Verlag, 1960.

▴ *The Stroke of the Pen* (1982) outlined Noordzij's theory of the letterform, which was first presented in 1970 and was further developed in the 1985 Dutch-language book *De streek* and in his one-man magazine *Letterletter* (1984–1996).

15 Quotes are taken from interviews held with Gerrit Noordzij in 1998–99, unless otherwise noted. This article is based on many sources including Mathieu Lommen and Peter Verheul, *Haagse letters*, Amsterdam 1998; Mathieu Lommen (ed.), *Het primaat van de pen*, The Hague 2001; and the writings of Gerrit Noordzij listed in the bibliography.

16 Frank E. Blokland, *Kalligraferen, de kunst van het schoonschrijven*, Utrecht 1990. Peter Verheul contributed a chapter on glass engraving.

17 *Een eenvoudig verzinsel*: literally 'something simple which I made up'.

18 Gerrit Noordzij in an e-mail to the author, 2003.

19 Robin Kinross, 'Type as critique' in *Typography Papers* 2, Reading 1997, pp 77–88.

abc ✳ ✳ cn

translation   *expansion*

▲ Noordzij's analysis of the letter-form is based on the principle of contrast – the distribution of thick and thin along the strokes. 'Translation' is the contrast produced by the broad-nibbed pen: an oblique vector projected on a path. Expansion is the contrast produced with a pointed pen, whereby increasing the pressure makes the two halves of the pen part, thus causing a gradual thickening of the stroke. Translation is a diagonal type of contrast; expansion is vertical. Typefaces can be designed with one of these extremes in mind, or as a mixture. The fact that the 'space' of possible letterforms within this scheme is a continuum is illustrated by Noordzij's cube.

▼ Noordzij's cube is a way of analysing letterforms without putting them into separate categories. It ranges variants of one character along three axes: the kind of contrast (z), increasing contrast (x) and diminishing contrast (y).

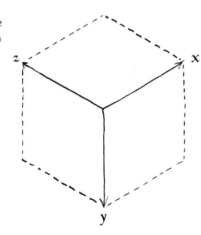

The theory

In Noordzij's analysis of the letterform, the contrast between thick and thin strokes is crucial. According to Noordzij, this contrast can only be described systematically by looking at its origin in writing. This is what Noordzij calls the 'primacy of the pen'. Briefly summarized, Noordzij's theory amounts to the following.

The shape of the letter is composed of one or more straight or bent strokes. The character of the stroke betrays the instrument with which it was made. A stroke produced with a pencil looks different from one made with a broad-nibbed pen or flat brush, or one made with a pointed pen. The main difference lies in the distribution of thick and thin – the stress or contrast.

When using a broad-nibbed pen, the stroke is formed by a moving 'frontline' whose length equals the width of the pen. That little line hardly changes direction: the angle of the pen on the paper is constant. This creates a pronounced diagonal contrast. The stroke can be at a right angle to the pen's front: it is then at its widest. Or it can be in line with the front: then it is thin, almost as thin as the pen's metal. So in the winding dance which brings forth the letterforms, the stroke of the pen is determined by that little line describing a path across the paper's plane surface. In mathematics, such a movement – whereby a vector is projected on a path – is called *translation*. Hence Noordzij's name for this type of contrast: translation.

While the broad-nibbed pen or quill was the writing tool par excellence in the Middle Ages and the Renaissance, writers in the Classicist era picked up the pointed pen. Now the difference between thick and thin was not created by a shifting frontline, but by widening the pen itself. The two halves of a pointed pen recede when pressure is applied; this makes the line thicken. The term which Noordzij coined for this phenomenon is self-explanatory: expansion.

Gerrit Noordzij has created a two-axis model for classifying the construction of written letterforms as well as typefaces. One corresponds with the difference between translation and expansion. The transverse axis corresponds with a second dichotomy: cursive versus interrupted writing. This difference roughly boils down to the question of whether or not the pen is lifted between strokes while making a letterform. This movement, the interruption of the stroke, is another crucial aspect of the construction of the letter.

These simple principles provide the student, typographer or type designer with a set of tools which allows almost every kind of letter – except for those composed of extremely exuberant shapes or purely mathematical constructions – to be analysed. Noordzij has emphatically recommended his model as an alternative to conventional type classifications, such as the complicated scheme created by Maximilien Vox. Such classifications have many shortcomings. They are fixated on details, lack flexibility and produce a multitude of categories which do not provide any true insight into the construction of letterforms. Noordzij's model is simpler and less rigid; as he himself points out, it not only takes into account those typefaces that already exist, but also provides a tool for creating forms that do not exist yet.

Noordzij also claims to have demonstrated that the sanserif as a separate category is a fabrication. The so-called sanserif, he wrote, has been derived from the roman by reducing the contrast between thick and thin; therefore the word 'sanserif' had better be avoided. 'What we are talking about is letterforms with the lowest possible contrast, and that is what I would like to call them.'[20]

Open though it is, Noordzij's model is, of course, also rather normative. It focuses on a certain kind of typeface and – as the work of some of his former students shows – encourages the creation of type designs which fit into the scheme. Typefaces which do not adhere to it (such as a high-contrast or geometric sanserif) can only be regarded as either 'wrong' or irrelevant.

In the course of the 1970s and '80s, Noordzij found an international forum for his ideas. He first summarized his theory in 1970 in a seminal article in *The Journal of Typographic Research* (which later became *Visible Language*).[21] Later he aired his opinions at the congresses of the Association Typographique Internationale (ATypI). Yet at the time his ideas seemed of little consequence to daily practice: those were the days of readability research and experimental computer faces; singing the praise of pen and brush as the road to a better understanding of letterforms seemed eccentric at best. In retrospect Noordzij's position was very valid indeed. Now that the desktop computer has become everyone's type design tool, writing and typography, handicraft and machine-made multiplication have gradually fused together into one process controlled by a single individual. This was possible because of the way a digital typeface is described: by means of vectors – the digital manifestation of the stroke. 'Thus, the traditional distinction between handwriting and printing type has been exposed,' wrote Noordzij triumphantly, 'as an obstacle that hampers a creative approach to writing.'[22] 'Writing' meaning, again, all forms of writing, also – or especially – typography.

The fact that his ideas now appeal to an international audience was underlined by the 2000 reissue as a book of the fifteen issues of *Letterletter*, a publication he edited from 1984 to 1996. Initially published by the ATypI, production was later taken over by The Enschedé Font Foundry. Unfortunately the book edition, issued in Vancouver by Hartley & Marks, left much to be desired. This was remarked by several participants in an international internet discussion about *Letterletter* which took place in 2002 but faded after a few months of heated debate.

Teaching

When shaping his 'letter programme' at the Royal Academy, educating type designers was by no means Noordzij's main concern. 'Learning to see' was what it was all about – not just letterforms, but forms in general. In Noordzij's words: an artist makes spots, or stains; true art lies in making good stains – in selecting the right form. 'When using letters, this problem becomes compact and surveyable,' said Noordzij, 'and one can easily do it again. To a student of painting who has drawn an A, it is not so discouraging to be told to try again, and pay attention to this or that. You can do that three or four times a day without giving him the idea that you're wrenching his life's work from his hands.'

One useful expedient was furnished to Noordzij by a fellow teacher at the Academy, the painter-designer Herman Berserik: he taught his students to create letterforms by means of counterforms made with torn pieces of paper. This 'negative' or inversed approach of the letter was echoed in several of Noordzij's writings about form, counterform, and 'word image'.

During the first years in which Noordzij's letter programme took shape – the early and mid-1970s – none of his students chose to embark on a type designing career. It was only around 1980 that his classes began to be populated by young talents who would form the first generation of 'digital' type designers: Petr van Blokland, Jelle Bosma, Noordzij's sons Christoph and Peter Matthias Noordzij, Frank Blokland, Albert-Jan Pool; joined, a few years later, by Just van Rossum, Luc(as) de Groot, Erik van Blokland and Peter Verheul. All of them were permanently influenced by Noordzij's ideas.

'When asked how I could attract so much promising talent to my programme at the Academy in The Hague,' Noordzij wrote in *Letterletter* 14 (1996), 'I answered: "I do not attract talent, I make talent because I am a teacher."' One makes talent – Noordzij told me – by maintaining a climate which challenges students to enter into a dialogue and join forces to make up new solutions. In all fairness it should be pointed out that Noordzij had some exceptional students. The success of Noordzij's type classes would not have been as phenomenal without the computer knowledge of Petr van Blokland, the organizational capacities of Frank Blokland or the irrever-

ATypI/Association Typographique Internationale/committee on education and research

Editor Gerrit Noordzij Langstraat 11 4176 BC Tuil The Netherlands 04185 1306

LetterLetter I Winter 1984-1985

Iets nieuws is niet oud genoeg

Tuilse apokriefen

kom mok

▲ Slate cutting using letterforms similar to the typeface Ruse. 'Something new is not old enough'.

▲ First issue of *Letterletter*, a publication edited and designed by Noordzij which was distributed to the members of the ATypI between 1984 and 1996.

▲ Illustration from the didactic calendar *Letters kijken*, showing the relationship between counters and spacing, 1994.

20 Gerrit Noordzij, *De staart van de kat*, Leersum 1988, p 99.
21 'Broken Script and the Classification of Typefaces', in *The Journal of Typographic Research*, vol. 4, no. 3, 1970.
22 'Een eenvoudig verzinsel' in *Haagse Letters* (cit.), p 9.

ent fantasy of Just van Rossum and Erik van Blokland – to mention just four talents whose 'making' was largely based on their own merit. At the same time Gerrit Noordzij's example has been more compelling than he would like to admit. The goal of his lessons was to educate students who would grab the tools from his hands in order to do their own thing. This has indeed happened, but in many cases the results have shown patently Noordzij-ish traits.

Types for private use

Gerrit Noordzij has worked as a teacher, historian, writer, photographer, biblical scholar, draughtsman, graphic artist, calligrapher, stonecarver, bookbinder, typesetter and graphic designer. Yet it is type design which is at the heart of most of his work. It is the theme of most of his essays; his graphic works – whether books, posters, stamps or inscriptions – are usually centred around self-designed letterforms. In all, Noordzij has probably designed two dozen alphabets which have been, or could be, further developed as complete typefaces. It is therefore all the more remarkable that until age 68 he remained an unpublished type designer: *Ruse*, his first published typeface, was released by The Enschedé Font Foundry in 2000.

The main reason for this paradox is a paradox in itself: Noordzij never saw himself as a type designer in the strict sense – i.e. a provider of typefaces to others. Noordzij only designed alphabets because he wanted to use them in his designs. 'I have made all my typefaces because I needed them,' he wrote. 'I have never made an effort to publish my faces. ... those who want to see my typefaces must look at the books I produced.' [23] In the 1970s and '80s, Noordzij did make a few attempts to get his type designs produced, negotiating with Linotype, Monotype and Berthold. His main motive was a personal one. He depended on composing machines for typesetting the body texts of the books he designed; in order to use his own types, they needed to be made available for these machines. The Noordzij typeface which came closest to being produced as a font for phototypesetting was *Rembrandt*, which was to be used for the *Rembrandt Bible* designed by Noordzij for Het Spectrum publishers. However, production by Monotype 'proceeded at such a terribly slow speed that I finally decided to set the work in [Van Krimpen's] *Spectrum*. When Adobe released the Type1 source code, I could finally produce my own typefaces. I have never used any other typographic material since.' [24]

Although it wasn't until 1990 that Noordzij was able to set body texts in his own typefaces, he did find a way to produce lettering for book jackets without having to draw each letter by hand. He devised his own low-tech photosetting system, using a modified enlarger and home-made photographic matrices produced from drawings with regular 35mm b/w film. The alphabets produced with this system found their way into the book cover designs for Van Oorschot and other publishers. When in the early 1990s the Macintosh finally provided him with his own type production and typesetting system, Noordzij immediately began using his typefaces for setting body text as well. *Tret* was used in the texts published by the theatre group Hollandia, both Ruse and Tret were used in several non-fiction books published by De Buitenkant and others; *Remer* – formerly *Rembrandt* – was first used as a text face in *Arti et Urbi* published by the Boymans-Van Beuningen Museum.

When trying to map out Noordzij's body of type designs, one is faced with an unusual phenomenon: the designer is reluctant to finalize or fix his typefaces. Changing ideas may lead to different shapes, to new names. Old designs which have been shown in early publications about his types have now vanished: *Dutch Roman* and *Batavian* seem to have been swallowed up by later designs or simply cancelled. Noordzij's way of working makes it unneccesary to keep precise accounts; the typefaces themselves were also subject to continuous change, whenever Noordzij's graphic design practice called for it. 'In my own workshop,' Noordzij wrote to me, 'it may occur that a typeface is changed five times a week in order to make it fit better to my typography.' In this sense, working with the desktop computer has a lot in common with the handicraft of old – it is more flexible than any mechanical or photographic typesetting system.

Many of Noordzij's typefaces originated in his cover designs for the publisher Van Oorschot. Some were never developed beyond the book, or the series, for which they were conceived.

◀ Hand-lettered cover for K. Ruys's *Een afgedragen huid* (1986).

▼ From the late '70s to the early '90s Noordzij used the same alphabet for all his cover designs for books by the Dutch writer A. Koolhaas. The typeface did not evolve beyond the phase of Noordzij's self-made photographic matrices and has remained nameless.

▾ Cover for a 1993 non-fiction book, designed with Tret.

Ruse, the first published typeface

Noordzij's type designing activities have always evolved from his daily practice as a typographic designer. This is also reflected in their given names – real 'workshop names', as Noordzij calls them.

The story of Ruse is a case in point. Noordzij's client, the publisher G.A. van Oorschot, asked him to design the jackets of the paperback editions of its renowned Russian Library. Now the original india paper edition of this series is somewhat of a monument in modern Dutch typography – Helmut Salden's masterpiece. Understandably, Noordzij wanted his design to move away from Salden's well-known dust-jackets with their hand-drawn lettering based on italics written with the broad-nibbed pen. He therefore took the pointed pen and drew a thin, cursive letterform with a vertical (expansion) contrast, which made its first appearance on the cover of Gontcharov's *Oblomov*. Having made a digital version of the italic for use on the Russian Library cover, Noordzij quickly made a roman companion while preparing *LetterLetter* 9, the Bodoni issue, circa 1989. He further developed the font over the years. The typeface was simply given the name of the book project it was part of: *Rus* (Dutch for Russian). Subsequent versions were called *Rus-A*, *Rus-B*, etcetera. By stopping at *Rus-E*, Noordzij arrived at a name which has a meaning both in French and English. It is also an amusing coincidence that the dictionary gives the Dutch word 'streek' (central to Noordzij's theory of writing) as a possible translation of the word 'ruse'; but in this case, in its meaning of 'trick'.

Having been designed for titling, Ruse turned out to work well in small sizes, too, although a slightly fleshier version was needed for that purpose. Noordzij wrote about the typeface: 'Ruse comes out of my handwriting. I have transferred the rhythm of the written word onto the typeface: all emphasis lies on the white forms which keep the black ones in place. … The theoretical product which I have distilled from my pieces of scrap paper, has now proved its use as a practical tool in posters, cartography and magazines. As for book production: I have been able to test Ruse in poems as well as scholarly publications and catalogues.'

When Peter Matthias Noordzij decided to publish Ruse as part of his Enschedé Type Foundry, it took him a while to convince his father to also design a bold version. This was the beginning of a phase of remarkably productive breeding. Published in early 2000, Ruse has grown into an extremely extended family. It comes in eleven weights or, as its maker calls them, *contrast values*. Each has four kinds of figures and a special font for ligatures; each version consists of a roman, an italic and small caps. The family which started out as a single light italic font for titling now consists of 154 fonts.

More new faces

Of the other text faces which Gerrit Noordzij has developed in the past ten years or so, Tret is likely to be among the first ones up for publication. It was conceived when a book cover with a long title called for a condensed titling face. According to Noordzij, Tret's compact proportions have much in common with those of the Fraktur; like this gothic predecessor it works well with little leading. Noordzij used it in several large book projects, including a Bible translation for the Nederlands Bijbelgenootschap (Dutch Bible Association). The overall impression of a text set in Tret is one of regularity and balance, but the individual letterforms are idiosyncratic, cheeky and unlike any other design. Tret is certainly one of the most original and playful Dutch book faces of recent years.

One of the volumes in the paperback edition of Van Oorschot's Russian Library for which Ruse Italic was originally designed.

Sketches for Tret, a typeface which Noordzij drew in order to be able to fit a long title on a book jacket in a large point size. Tret also proved very readable in small text sizes and was subsequently used for a Dutch bible edition, the *Bijschrijfbijbel* of the Nederlands Bijbelgenootschap (1992).

23 e-mail to the author, 2002.
24 Ibid.

Nine type designs developed by Gerrit Noordzij between c. 1980 and today. Apart from Ruse, all of the typefaces are as yet unpublished, although the designer has used most of them in the publications he designed and typeset. The specimens were made by Noordzij especially for this book.

Besides Tret and Ruse, Gerrit Noordzij has recently shown four new roman alphabets: *Remer*, *Ruit*, *Algerak* and *Sudum*. Remer is his Opus No. 1, Noordzij's first fullfledged typeface which was developed over several decades. A continuation of the typeface shown in about 1980 as Dutch Roman, it shows an affinity to the faces of Jan van Krimpen, notably *Spectrum*. It is Remer's clear italic – a spirited humanist cursive coming straight from Noordzij's confident pen – which makes it stand out from Van Krimpen's work. *Kadmos*, a Greek italic based on the same proportions, illustrates what Noordzij wrote about 'the cursive character of the Greek minuscule' in his essay on Van Krimpen's *Romulus* (> p 61). Recently, Sudum was developed as a narrower, sturdier variant of Remer. As the contrast is more conventional and the overall design more compact, Sudum is the most promising text face of the two.

Like Remer, Algerak originated in Noordzij's book cover designs. It has many traits in common with Remer, although it has a slightly more pronounced stress and thicker, wedge-shaped serifs. Hoping to get more information about Noordzij's motives and sources, I asked him what he thought were the main differences between the two designs. His laconic reply was typical: 'They look different.'

Ruit is a special case. It was designed especially for *Letterletter* 11, a special issue on the serif, and made to illustrate the provoking thesis that the fifteenth-century Venetian roman (notably Jenson's) was in fact a variant of the Burgundian Textura. To prove his point Noordzij designed a roman typeface with lozenge-shaped serifs (hence the name: *Ruit* = lozenge or diamond) much like the terminals of a Textura written with a broad-nibbed pen, and showed it alongside a facsimile of a Jenson page. While Ruit started out as what Noordzij calls a 'theoretical finger exercise', it has recently been developed into an exented family of text faces.[25]

A few other Noordzij typefaces seem to have been made chiefly as an illustration of one of his theories. *Burgundica* is a 'broken script', the kind of typeface often referred to as 'gothic' or 'blackletter', although in Burgundica's case a typographically more precise term would be *gothic cursive* or *bastarda*. The typeface is a result of Noordzij's research of the origin of Fractura – usually identified with Germanic tradition, but situated by Noordzij in fifteenth-century Bruges when it was under Burgundian rule. Burgundica is the name he has given to an elongated version of the script, also developed in the Southern Netherlands, that was the most popular book hand during the hey-day of Burgundy. Noordzij's typeface of the same name is simply a digital version of this script.

Apex and *Semantor*, finally, are italics without romans; both look like very regular, hand-written humanist cursives. They seem to be meant to prove Noordzij's axiom quoted above, but in fact undermine it. Because if these cursives – handwriting which has been rid of accidental details – persist in looking like handwriting, then perhaps for a typographic italic something more is needed.

Although most of Noordzij's 'official' typefaces have been mentioned here, the list of his type designs is by no means complete. In the Van Oorschot book jackets alone there are several alphabets he has repeatedly used; it is certain they sit on one of his disks, or have been preserved as photographic matrices, but they still lack a name and are probably unfinished.

Peter Matthias Noordzij and his team at The Enschedé Font Foundry are busy digitizing several more of his father's type designs. Then Gerrit Noordzij will finally be to the world what he has in fact been for a lifetime: one of the Netherland's most versatile type designers.

Algerak

1 CUSTODI ME DEUS QUONIAM SPERAVI IN TE 2 dicens Deo Dominus meus es tu bene mihi non est sine te 3 sanctis qui in terra sunt et magnificis omnis voluntas mea in eis 4 multiplicabuntur idola eorum post tergum sequentium non litabo libamina eorum de sanguine neque adsumam nomina eorum in labiis meis 5 Dominus pars hereditatis meae et calicis mei tu possessor sortis meae *6 lineae ceciderunt mihi in pulcherrimis et hereditas speciosissima mea est 7* benedicam Domino qui dedit consilium mihi insuper et

Tret **Tret**

1 CUSTODI ME DEUS quoniam speravi in te 2 dicens Deo Dominus meus es tu bene mihi non est sine te *3 sanctis qui in terra sunt et magnificis omnis voluntas mea in eis 4* multiplicabuntur idola eorum post tergum sequentium non litabo libamina eorum de sanguine neque adsumam nomina eorum in labiis meis 5 Dominus pars hereditatis meae et calicis mei tu possessor sortis meae 6 lineae ceciderunt mihi in pulcherrimis et hereditas speciosissima mea est **7 benedicam Domino qui dedit consilium mihi insuper et noctibus erudierunt me renes mei** *8 pro-*

Ruse *Ρυσια*

1 Custodi me Deus quoniam speravi in te 2 dicens Deo Dominus meus es tu bene mihi non est sine te 3 sanctis qui in terra sunt et MAGNIFICIS OMNIS VOLUNTAS MEA IN EIS *4 multiplicabuntur idola eorum post tergum sequentium non litabo libamina eorum de sanguine neque adsumam nomina eorum in labiis meis*

Apex

1 Custodi me Deus quoniam speravi in te 2 dicens Deo Dominus meus es tu bene mihi non est sine te 3 sanctis qui in terra sunt et magnificis omnis voluntas mea in eis 4 multiplicabuntur idola eorum post tergum sequentium non litabo libamina eorum de sanguine neque adsumam nomina eorum in labiis meis

5 Dominus pars hereditatis meae et calicis mei tu possessor sortis meae 6 lineae ceciderunt mihi in pulcherrimis et hereditas speciosissima mea est 7 benedicam Domino qui dedit consilium mihi insuper et noctibus erudierunt me renes mei

Burgundica

1 Custodi me Deus quoniam speravi in te 2 dicens Deo Dominus meus es tu bene mihi non est sine te 3 sanctis qui in terra sunt et magnificis omnis voluntas mea in eis 4 multiplicabuntur idola eorum post tergum sequentium non litabo libamina eorum de sanguine neque adsumam nomina eorum in labiis meis 5 **Dominus pars hereditatis meae et calicis mei tu possessor sortis meae 6 lineae ceciderunt mihi in pulcherrimis et hereditas speciosissima mea est 7 benedicam Domino qui dedit**

Ruit **Ruit**

1 Custodi me Deus quoniam speravi in te 2 dicens Deo Dominus meus es tu bene mihi non est sine te 3 *sanctis qui in terra sunt et magnificis omnis voluntas mea in eis* 4 multiplicabuntur idola eorum post tergum sequentium non litabo libamina eorum de sanguine neque adsumam nomina eorum in labiis meis **5 Dominus pars hereditatis meae et calicis mei tu possessor sortis meae 6 lineae ceciderunt mihi in pulcherrimis et hereditas speciosissima mea est 7** *benedicam Domino qui dedit consilium*

Remer *Καδμος*

1 Custodi me Deus quoniam speravi in te 2 dicens Deo Dominus meus es tu bene mihi non est sine te 3 sanctis qui in terra sunt et magnificis omnis voluntas mea in eis 4 multiplicabuntur idola eorum post tergum sequentium non litabo libamina eorum de sanguine neque adsumam nomina eorum in labiis meis 5 Dominus pars hereditatis meae et calicis mei tu possessor sortis meae 6 LINEAE CECIDERUNT MIHI IN PULCHERRIMIS

Ruse *Ρυσια*

1 Custodi me Deus quoniam speravi in te 2 dicens Deo Dominus meus es tu bene mihi non est sine te 3 sanctis qui in terra sunt et magnificis omnis voluntas mea in eis 4 multiplicabuntur idola eorum post tergum sequentium non litabo libamina eorum de sanguine neque adsumam nomina eo

Sudum **Sudum**

1 CUSTODI ME DEUS quoniam speravi in te 2 dicens Deo Dominus meus es tu bene mihi non est sine te 3 *sanctis qui in terra sunt et magnificis omnis voluntas mea in eis* 4 multiplicabuntur idola eorum post tergum sequentium non litabo libamina eorum de sanguine neque adsumam nomina eorum in labiis meis **5 DOMINUS PARS HEREDITATIS MEAE** et calicis mei tu possessor sortis meae 6 lineae ceciderunt mihi in pulcherrimis et hereditas speciosis-

25 Gerrit Noordzij (intr. Max Caflisch), 'Die Schriftentwürfe von Gerrit Noordzij', in *Typographische Monatsblätter* no. 2, 1994, pp [9] – [16].

The perfectionism of Bram de Does

The most remarkable thing about Bram de Does's career is that he became a type designer in the first place. He had been working as a book designer for twenty years when, in 1978, his employer Enschedé unexpectedly invited him to design the typeface that would become *Trinité*. At that precise moment, De Does was on the verge of giving up his career as a typographer and become a full-time farmer in biodynamic horticulture. 'It took me a week to think it over. Then I said to Nora, my wife: I think I am going to change the course of my life. I am going to accept. In fact, it was something which, unconsciously, I had always wanted to do.' [26]

Bram de Does (born 1934) was introduced to the printing trade in his father's workshop, a local printing office in the east of Amsterdam. After leaving secondary school he considered enrolling in the music conservatory – he had begun playing the violin at eleven – but found it difficult to make up his mind. So he set to work in the family printing shop where at eighteen, without any formal training, he designed, composed and printed a type specimen. He chose to attend a managers' training course at the Amsterdamse Grafische School (Amsterdam Printing Trade School). What he wrote about this course is typical of his later attitude as a typographer and book designer. '[During the typography classes] we were subtly invited to work in a "modern" and "fresh" manner and by all means avoid symmetry. I soon rebelled against such a foolish principle imposed on us and started setting symmetrical texts with nicely spaced small capitals. I needed to be so obstinate to gain a sense of self-esteem in that small community. I still have the feeling today that, by thinking along these lines, I have remained an exception in the big world, too. Apparently this well suits me.' [27]

During his training he discovered his affinity for two typefaces used in a specific way: '*Romanée* and *Bembo*, printed in letterpress – phototypesetting did not exist yet – on slightly tinted, slightly coarse stock. It was a love at first sight which has never left me.' [28]

In 1958 De Does was hired by Joh. Enschedé en Zonen, where Jan van Krimpen still ruled with an iron fist. 'I heard wild stories about what an obnoxious, hot-tempered man he was. My world collapsed, because in my wide-eyed idealism I had expected to enter an aesthetic paradise where everybody would be friendly and merry.' [29] He would never meet Van Krimpen; the great man died unexpectedly, two months after De Does joined the firm.

Soon printing and publishing great books stopped being a top priority at Enschedé. As De Does saw it, 'the company had become mainly a printer of banknotes and stamps.' [30] In 1962 De Does left to work with the Querido publishing house, but was convinced the next year by Enschedé's art director Sem Hartz to return to the Haarlem printing-house. De Does's new job consisted mainly of supervising the work of other designers; additionally, he designed annual reports, commemorative volumes and type specimens. De Does designed books for other clients apart from

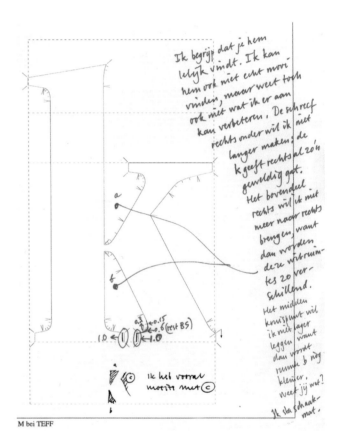

M bei TEFF

Ikarus printout with written comments by Bram de Does, explaining the difficulties with the counters of the character k (1999). The typeface is the bold condensed version of Lexicon, made as a headline face for the newspaper NRC Handelsblad.

De Does's comment ('I can understand that you find it ugly. I find it ugly too. … I am checkmated.') is typical of the dialogues he has conducted over the years with Peter Matthias Noordzij (The Enschedé Font Foundry), who has produced the digital versions of his typefaces.

◄ *Typefoundries in the Netherlands*, published in 1978, was De Does's typographic masterpiece. It was the last book completely produced by letterpress at the Enschedé printing house.

▼ Bram de Does, cover of an Enschedé type catalogue for which he also designed part of the interior pages, the other designer being Wim Bloem, c. 1959.

Enschedé – including himself. In 1961 he published a booklet issued by his own 'private press', Spectatorpers. The actual printing was done during the evening hours in his father's shop. De Does bought a single weight of Jan van Krimpen's Romanée for the purpose. The publication, a small volume of poems, was selected as one of the year's 'best book designs'. That honour was bestowed on him on many occasions, sometimes for regular commercial editions, sometimes for books printed on the Spectatorpers, the most recent one being the specimen *Kaba ornament* (2002).

Changes at Enschedé; the 'Typefoundries' book

In the 1970s Enschedé developed a renewed interest in its own history and in publishing. Now De Does could try his hand at designing beautiful books for Enschedé as well. The one masterpiece from this period that stands out is the dazzling *Typefoundries in the Netherlands*, Harry Carter's adaptation of *Fonderies de caractères* (1908) by Charles Enschedé. Published in 1978, *Typefoundries* has become a monument in Dutch printing and publishing. It is the last book that Enschedé ever printed completely by letterpress – which is the reason why De Does has jokingly called it 'an excunabulum'.[31] The book is a history of Dutch type up to 1900, based on the extensive collection of original types, punches, strikes and matrices conserved at the Enschedé Museum. All text samples in the book have been set in original or recast hand types; the body text was composed by hand in Romanée. During printing, De Does meticulously controlled every aspect of the process. He personally wrote the recipe for the paper, insisting that it be produced in his presence, and persuaded the Enschedé management that the entire book be printed by one and the same person in a specially equipped room. The result is a volume of breathtaking perfection.

As for the Enschedé Type Foundry, the Van Krimpen years had definitely been its final era of glory. No new typefaces had been made for decades; any type that Enschedé needed for its typesetting and printing business was obtained from Monotype, the supplier of its hot-metal typesetting machines and, from 1967 onwards, of the Monophoto Filmsetter.

The transition from metal type to photosetting was a gradual process at the firm. Hot-metal machines remained in use for another decade alongside the Filmsetter; besides, these first-generation photosetters were still constructed according to the trusted Monotype matrix system. In some cases the new system lacked certain characters, and this provided De Does with an opportunity to try his hand at type design. With the help of Enschedé's last punchcutter, Henk Drost (1932–1998), De Does developed a system for making photographic matrices for new characters with great precision.[32] In 1967, the year Monophoto entered the composing room, De Does cut a photosetting version of Van Krimpen's *Cancellaresca Bastarda* for his own pleasure, reproducing the characters directly from the original drawings.

26 Interview with Bram de Does.

27 Mathieu Lommen, *Bram de Does*, Amsterdam 1999, p 6. A reworked version of this essay was published (in Dutch and English) in Lommen (ed.), *Bram de Does, typographer & type designer*, Amsterdam 2003. All references are to the earlier version.

28 Bram de Does, *Romanée en Trinité*, Amsterdam/Aartswoud 1991, p 7.

29 See note 26.

30 Mathieu Lommen, *Bram de Does* (cit.), p 7.

31 Ibid., p 10.

32 Ibid., p 19.

▾ Specimen of the Autologic version of Trinité, 1982. The cover illustration underscores one of Trinité's most original features: the fact that it comes in three different extender lengths.

ᵥ Working drawing of Trinité, 1980. Marked: 'First proof'.

Trinité: functionally swinging

The steps which led to Trinité, De Does's first typeface, have been extensively documented in a handsome booklet, *Romanée en Trinité: Historisch origineel en systematisch slordig* ('Romanée and Trinité: Historically original and systematically sloppy'), written, designed and partly printed by letterpress by De Does.

In 1978 Enschedé was in the process of replacing its Monophoto typesetters with second-generation photosetting machines from the Swiss company Bobst Graphic (later Autologic). When the Swiss firm proposed reissuing Van Krimpen's Romanée as part of its type library, the Enschedé management consulted De Does, who strongly advised against it. In a lengthy letter he argued that Romanée is not one single design, but a series of different cuttings for each point size. Reducing the face to a single master font for photosetting would be a hazardous affair, with the possible result of a 'miserably meagre and contrasted' typeface. What De Does feared most of all, but did not mention in his letter, was that Romanée would be ruined by a careless, uninformed redesign. This had been the fate of *Monotype Bembo*, his other favourite typeface, which in the transition from metal to film had been reduced to a mere shadow of its original self. 'Wouldn't it be better, and even simpler,' De Does wrote, 'to commission a new typeface, especially designed for photocomposition?' [33] Although it had not been his intention, the Enschedé management promptly invited him to design the new typeface himself.

De Does worked on Trinité from 1979 to 1982. In the previous years he had collected many ideas for optimizing typefaces in order to obtain greater harmony and legibility, but had never seriously considered drawing new, original shapes. It took him a year to define his guiding principles, and develop a working method. 'I had no real experience at type design, so I had to invent things from scratch. I knew more or less what I wanted, but lacked the drawing expertise. I had always paid close attention to the shapes of the more exceptional characters [in existing typefaces], such as g, k and a; but had never studied very carefully what an m or n looked like, although those two are possibly the most important characters of any alphabet. So I began by photographically blowing up prints of the typefaces I liked: Bembo, Joanna, but also very small bible types, in order to study the spacing and proportions.' [34] Throughout the design process, Romanée – and, to a lesser extent, Bembo – remained a reference. 'One thing I like about these designs is that the uppercase characters are considerably lower than the ascenders. I also knew that I wanted to use several different extender lengths.' Trinité's name refers to the fact that the final font family had three variants, each with a different length of ascenders and descenders, while retaining the same width.

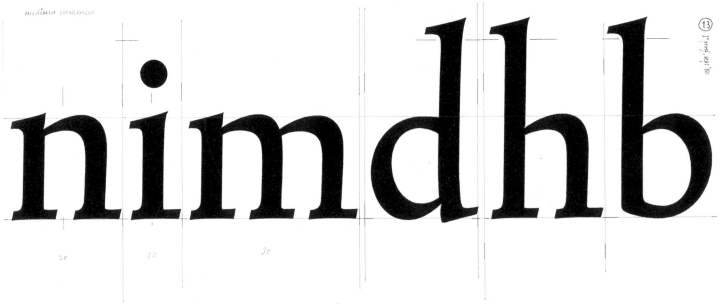

De Does formulated a long list of design principles for an ideal text face, including well-defined formal solutions and proportions. He distinguished four categories 'which are perhaps applicable to any kind of human production: *functionality* for the user (in the case of type this is legibility), *harmony*, *practical economic applicability* for the manufacturer (the foundry and the compositor) and finally *originality*.'[35]

Being a musician at heart, De Does had long been fascinated by the concept of harmony in type design. He was convinced that the coherence of the printed page had never been more powerful than in the first decades of the craft – the time of the incunables. 'Somehow, early Renaissance pages present a stronger, more regular overall image. I discovered two factors which contribute to that impression: the fact that characters are subtly slanted, and that the serifs are slightly longer towards the right.'[36] He therefore decided to give Trinité's characters a similar angle (1° for characters with a top serif – b h i k l m n –, slightly more for a d t, less for j p r) and to draw firm, calligraphic foot-serifs which are asymmetric and suggest a forward flow. The coherence of the words on the page was also enhanced by what De Does called 'functional swing': there is not a single straight line in Trinité. The result of these considerations was a typeface that, according to its designer, owes much to Romanée but unlike Van Krimpen's type is 'systematically sloppy' (*systematisch slordig*).

The fourth category of De Does's considerations, *originality*, seems to have been the most problematic. Being extremely self-critical and pragmatic, De Does will not easily tolerate interesting details for the sake of individuality. So, just as Trinité's liveliness and swing had to be functional and systematic, its originality needed to be justified by historical precedents. 'I think that many of the details I used for legibility and harmony can be considered *original*. Most of these details date back to the Renaissance, some are rooted in a later era. However, at the moment when I introduced them, they were not sufficiently available in my direct surroundings and on the composition equipment that I had at my disposal at Enschedé. Introducing them anew at a point when they had gone lost for me was, I think, a form of originality. One could call it *historical originality*.'[37] What De Does did regard as genuinely new were some practical features, such as the ad hoc ligatures formed automatically by certain pairs, the subtle difference between the two widths (Trinité Condensed is only 8% narrower than its Wide) and the three lengths of extenders.

In spite of its maker's efforts to objectify its qualities, there is an aesthetic aspect to the typeface that none of De Does's principles seems to account for. Trinité is probably the most elegant and handsome face created in the Netherlands in the past half century; an unmatched tool for lending a sense of sophistication to a design. This, of course, limits its possible uses: applying Trinité in a sales brochure would be, as the Dutch expression goes, like a flag on a mud barge. It took its designer some time to realize that his creation was not the universal tool he had envisaged. 'I had been convinced that, by following my principles of harmony, I would attain a certain objectivity which theoretically would allow Trinité to replace most other typefaces. When a group of colleagues asked me if I'd use Trinité for a newspaper, I said: sure, there are some weights – such as Medium Condensed 1 – that are rather similar to, say, Walter Tracy's *Times Europa*. They totally disagreed. I must now admit that they may have been right: perhaps it is a little pretentious for an ordinary paper.'[38]

Digital Trinité

Trinité was published as an Autologic typeface – licensed from Enschedé – in 1982. In the Netherlands it was immediately embraced by renowned book designers such as Guus Ros, Harry Sierman and Karel F. Treebus. Yet its use remained sparse, mainly because only two typesetting companies carried it.

Bram de Does left Joh. Enschedé en Zonen in 1988. By the end of the decade the printing company was ready to give up its activities as a publisher of books as well as typefaces. Its typesetting office had switched to the Linotronic digital system, keeping on the Autologic APS 153 only for Trinité. As Trinité was an important asset to the firm, the management took steps to have the typeface digitized by Linotype. Having seen the first results, De Does grew increasingly worried and discussed the problem with Peter Matthias Noordzij, the designer of PMN *Caecilia*. Noordzij convinced him

Hnhphp
fififlflggee

nor vexed its uncomplaining
He draw theim all qujckly of
best gummachy fluzzecxly
Head Illuminated print draw Ecchos by
fly qujck from vexed hussugs bazzyg

fi fj fl fb fh fk
fi fj fl fb fh fk
fi fj fl fb fh fk
fi fj fl fb fh fk
fi fj fl fb fh fk
fi fj fl fb fh fk
fg jg gg gj gy
fi fj fl fb fh fk

33 Bram de Does, *Romanée en Trinité* (cit.), p 15.

34 See note 26.

35 Bram de Does, *Romanée en Trinité* (cit.), pp 17–20. When proofreading this article, De Does proposed adding a few extra explanations: '*harmony* (for the aesthete), … and finally *originality* (because otherwise there is no use in making the thing).'

36 See note 26.

37 Bram de Does, *Romanée en Trinité* (cit.), p 20.

38 See note 26.

abbcddeffgghhiijjkkllm
noppqqrstuvwxyyz

*abbcddeffgghhiijjkkllm
noppqqrstuvwxyyz*

Lexicon has two variants:
the dictionary version with very
short extenders, and a version
with extenders of a more
conventional length.

that digital fonts could be produced for PostScript using the Ikarus-M system and on De Does's recommendation received an assignment from Enschedé to digitize the entire series of about 1600 characters.

When Enschedé showed no intention of marketing the typeface other than by selling composing service, Peter Matthias Noordzij proposed the creation of a new, small-scale digital type foundry. Led by Noordzij himself, this new company – The Enschedé Font Foundry (TEFF) – was to continue the activities which had begun in 1743 with the acquisition of the Wetstein foundry by Izaak and Johannes Enschedé. After publication as a PostScript font family in 1992, Trinité became one of the standard typefaces used in contemporary Dutch book design.

Lexicon: the improbable second typeface

In 1983, the year after the original version of Trinité was published, De Does held a lecture at a meeting of the typographic association ATypI. The lecture was in part a reply to those colleagues who had asked him when his next typeface would come out. There would be none, De Does announced: he would not be able to make any other style of typeface than the Renaissance-inspired Trinité. 'I do see in Trinité certain details that need improvement. It would in fact make sense to me to work on this in another typeface, but almost everyone would find it had remained the same typeface. Many designers think the same of Jan van Krimpen's romans.' [39]

Although the digitization of Trinité by Peter Matthias Noordzij allowed him to improve some of the details – increasing the lowercase italic by 2%, removing some optical corrections which had been necessary for photocomposition, improving the shape of individual characters – De Does began to be increasingly uneasy about several of its features, which he now saw as imperfections. 'In mixed composition the italic is too upright to really stand out from the roman. And Trinité is so little contrasted that it is extremely sensitive to anomalies in the printing process. As soon as the printing is too black, you get blobs which completely disturb the harmony.' [40]

In 1989, when the digital Trinité had yet to be produced, De Does was unexpectedly given an opportunity to try something new. Bernard C. van Bercum, the designer of the twelfth edition of Van Dale's *Dictionary of the Dutch Language*, a three-volume national monument, wanted to test Trinité for use at 7pt. De Does offered to design an e and a with larger eyes for better legibility, but then changed his mind. 'A week later I asked Van Bercum if Van Dale would like the idea of using a new typeface that would be designed specially for the dictionary. He said that the editors would probably not be ready for such a big change. So I proposed that we should make a test page, free of charge.' [41]

De Does began the *Lexicon* design process by studying anew the prints of metal typefaces he had made in 1979 at the start of the Trinité design, 'especially the very small point sizes such as *Angelus*, a 4.5pt bible type from Monotype, and one of Granjon's c. 7pt Gaillarde roman from 1570; I made a rough sketch with annotations for improvements.' [42] The first rough drawings were made with a felt-tipped pen, photographed, and then reduced to enable judgement of the overall design.

Peter Matthias Noordzij and Bram de Does had developed an excellent working relationship by then. They prepared a provisional font and a test page. The editors were happy with the result and, after comparing the new face to several alternatives, decided to go for it. Between December 1989 and October 1992, De Does made hundreds of working drawings which were digitized with Ikarus software by Noordzij.

The first version of Lexicon was optimized for legibility and contrast at the point sizes used in the Van Dale dictionary, which came out in 1992. It took another three years for the family to be ready for publication as part of the TEFF library. An excellent type specimen, designed by Marie-Cécile Noordzij, was published in 1997. Lexicon has two variants: the dictionary version with very short extenders, and a version with extenders of a more conventional length. More than Trinité, Lexicon has the qualities of a workhorse typeface. With its supple legibility in small point sizes and low resolution, it was described as having 'all the qualities to become the new *Times*'. [43] This point was proven when Lexicon was selected as the new headline and

Printing types for a changing technology

Relative units in machine composition all characters have a *set width* calculated in relative units; these increments are not standard like *points* but relate to the typesize in question; the unit is calculated by deviding the typesize *em* into vertical bands; for ex-

Relative units in machine composition all characters have a *set width* calculated in relative units; these increments are not standard like *points* but relate to the typesize in question; the unit is calculated by deviding the *typesize em* into vertical bands; for ex-

Relative units in machine composition all characters have a *set width* calculated in relative units; these increments are not standard like *points* but relate to the typesize in question; the unit is calculated by deviding the typesize *em* into vertical bands; for ex-

Relative units in machine composition all characters have a *set width* calculated in relative units; these increments are not standard like *points* but relate to the typesize in question; the unit is calculated by deviding the typesize *em* into vertical bands; for ex-

◄ Marie-Cécile Noordzij, double-page spread from the Lexicon type specimen, 1997.

▲ First sketches of Lexicon, with photographic reductions made to judge the typeface at small point sizes, November 1989.

39 Bram de Does, *Romanée en Trinité* (cit.), p 21.

40 See note 26.

41 Ibid.

42 De Does, 'De ontwikkeling van de Lexicon' manuscript, 1999, quoted in Mathieu Lommen, *Bram de Does* (cit.), p 24.

43 Mathieu Lommen, 'Bram de Does', in *Typokalender*, Nuth 1995 (reproduced in the *Lexicon* specimen, Amsterdam 1997).

Voor 20 miljoen aan diamanten geroofd
Voor 20 miljoen aan diamanten geroofd

Voor 20 miljoen aan diamanten geroofd
Voor 20 miljoen aan diamanten geroofd

text face for the Netherlands' most prestigious evening newspaper, NRC *Handelsblad*. Making Lexicon suitable as a newspaper face according to the specifications given by the NRC's art director proved a time-consuming task. Lexicon was – literally – replacing Times, and the newspaper wanted to preserve a similar overall look while solving a series of technical problems. Like many other newspapers, NRC *Handelsblad* had received complaints about its legibility after the advent of advanced typesetting equipment in the mid-1990s. The increase in reproduction quality, at both the pre-press and printing stages, made Times look too thin; an increase in point size brought some relief, but was uneconomical. In London, Dave Farey and Richard Dawson were working on the new, workflow-savvy *Times Millennium*, but it was clear that *The Times* would not lease the new font family to other papers. The designers of NRC *Handelsblad* chose to adopt an existing typeface as the new text face and chose Lexicon 'because it best answered the high requirements regarding readability and economy'. [44] Probably Lexicon's elegance was also taken into account: it makes the highbrow NRC *Handelsblad* stand out from other dailies which use Martin Majoor's *Scala* or one of Gerard Unger's pragmatic news faces.

For the text font, Matthias Noordzij provided an unmodified middle weight of the short-extender version with new kerning pairs adapted to the newspaper's CCI digital typesetting system. For the headlines, a new version of Lexicon bold was designed in which some qualities of Times Bold were preserved; Lexicon Headline is darker,

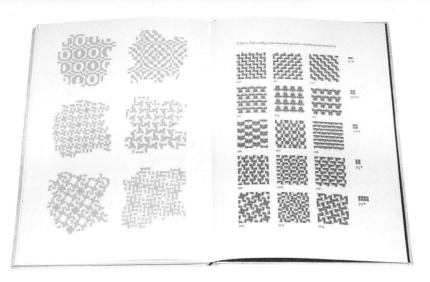

◀ De Does's book *Kaba Ornamenten*, printed by letterpress in 2002, shows how to make elaborate decorations with the two Kaba Ornaments.

▼ Enlarged reproduction of the Kaba Ornaments, produced as foundry type for De Does's private press, Spectatorpers.

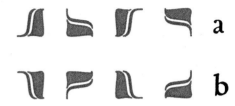

Tabel 6. Formaties van 4 Kaba ornamentjes met symmetrische eigenschappen

v2mm	v1m▼	v1m	v4	v2▼	v2	v1▼
41	45	49	61	73	77	81	89	98
42	46	50	62	74	78	82	90	99
43	47	51	63	75	79	83	91	100
44	48	52	64	76	80	84	92	101
		53	65			85	93	102
		54	66			86	94	103
		55	67			87	95	104
		56	68			88	96	105
		57	69				97	107
		58	70					
		59	71					
		60	72					

narrower and richer in contrast than the standard Lexicon Bold. The result works well but, as Peter Matthias Noordzij admits: 'It is not a typeface we would ever have made without the NRC assignment.' [45]

Spectatorpers and Kaba Ornament

From 1986, when the Spectatorpers became a full-fledged private press established in the designer's home in the village of Aartswoud (and later in Orvelte), De Does produced several bibliophilic books of stunning perfection which received national and international awards. These books often concerned type and typography. *The Steadfast Tin Soldier of Joh. Enschedé en Zonen* by Ernst Braches (1992) is a bibliography of the roman no. 6 in the Enschedé collection, which was long attributed to Peter Schoeffer (Johann Gutenberg's assistant) but is now thought to originate from the offices of the sixteenth-century printer Peter Quentell. The book was not only designed and printed by De Does; he even marbled the end leaves himself. *Essays* by Sem Hartz (1992), set in Hartz's *Emergo*, is a splendid tribute to the man who convinced De Does to give Enschedé a second try. *Fleischman on punchcutting* (edited by Frans A. Janssen, 1994) is a transcription of an unpublished text from the Ploos van Amstel legacy which Janssen has attributed to Johann Michael Fleischman, the first great punchcutter of the Enschedé type foundry. *Adieu Lettergieterij Enschedé* (1993, with the punchcutter Henk Drost) was a typographic epitaph for the type foundry.

In 2002 a book came out which describes what may be regarded as De Does's third typeface: the *Kaba Ornament*. Kaba Ornament is a set of only two forms, an asymmetric abstract form and its mirror image, which De Does had cut by Henk Drost and cast as foundry type at Enschedé. Kaba can be used as a single ornament, e.g. at the beginning of a paragraph; but its construction also allows for complex structures to be built. De Does's Kaba booklet is a manual of how to use symmetry and asymmetry to make these elaborate constructions, but like most of De Does's writings it is also a frank and witty account of his motives and methods for inventing something new. It is an autobiographical type specimen, as it were.

Bram de Does was the first Dutch type designer to be the subject of an extensive television documentary: in the Spring of 2003, Dutch nationwide TV broadcast the film *Systematisch slordig* ('Systematically sloppy'), produced by De Kazerne, a small publishing house and design studio, with the help of a new foundation, Stichting Nieuwe Letters. A major book about De Does by Mathieu Lommen and John Lane, co-edited by the publisher, Jan de Jong, was presented in Haarlem in October 2003.

44 Paul Steenhuis, 'Lexicon, een degelijke letter met een zwierig trekje', in NRC Handelsblad, 23 July 2001.

45 Peter Matthias Noordzij in conversation with the author.

The pragmatism of Gerard Unger

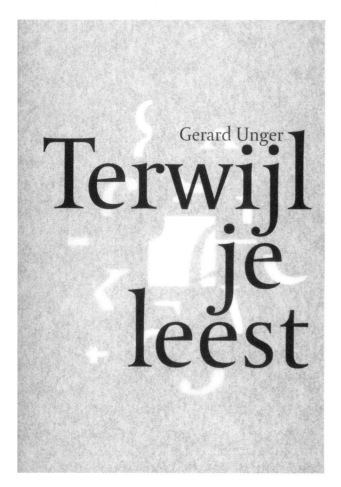

Gerard Unger (1942) has been called 'the prince of Dutch letters'. For years he was a conspicuous monument in the type landscape: he was the only Dutch designer whose typefaces were published on a regular basis. Then with the advent of the Macintosh generation he was joined by younger colleagues who, in certain cases, are also his competitors. Unger wouldn't want things to be otherwise: he welcomes new challenges like gifts from heaven.

Best of both worlds

Unger made his entry into the Dutch typographic world in an era of polarization. In the 1960s, when he studied at the Gerrit Rietveld Academy, one had to make choices. You were either a traditionalist or a modernist; you made symmetrically laid-out books and hand-lettered posters and book jackets, or you opted for the Swiss style with heavy-contrast photos and sanserif type. At the Rietveld such differences led to some rivalry between two teachers of graphic design: the modernist Charles Jongejans (who called himself a 'typotekt', just like Piet Zwart) and the sensitive painter-typographer Theo Kurpershoek. Like all students, Unger was supposed to choose, but he did not – he wanted the best of both worlds. Fascinated, he studied what he calls 'the gigantic reservoir of the European typographic tradition'. With the same eagerness he learned about the latest developments in phototypesetting and computer typography.[46]

His interest in type and design had been aroused years earlier. As a high school student he had copied letterforms from the sourcebook *Drukletters* (Printing Types) by M.H. Groenendaal, and leafed through the luxury editions in his father's well-equipped library. For some time, his father had been head of the publicity department of the Algemene Kunstzijde Unie (General Rayon Union) in Arnhem – which allowed young Gerard Unger to get acquainted with the work of a designer like Otto Treumann, who designed the company's magazine.

After graduation, Unger landed a job at Total Design. Although he only stayed for about six months, it took a long time before Wim Crouwel's influence began to wear off. For years Unger was under the spell of TD-style functionalism, attracted by the simple straightforwardness of their solutions. Gradually Unger realized that Crouwel's designs owed their visual power less to the functionalist formula than to Crouwel's artistic talent, 'his unfailing feeling for proportions and colour'.[47] After Total Design, Unger worked for a while at an advertising agency – which at the time was an unusual decision for a typographic designer.

Beginnings: Markeur and M.O.L.

In 1972 Unger landed two new jobs: he became a part-time teacher at the Rietveld Academy and was hired by Enschedé in Haarlem to work two days a week. He was asked to design a typeface for the Pantotype, a pantographic engraving system for

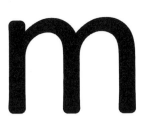

signs which the firm had developed in order to diversify the type foundry's activities. Producing typefaces for Pantotype was also a way to provide work for Henk Drost, the firm's last punchcutter. Sem Hartz designed *Panture* (1971), an alphabet of roman capitals. Unger's typeface, *Markeur* (1972), was the sanserif alternative.

With this, his first professional typeface, Unger outlined the approach which would characterize all his later projects: to respond to the given technical constraints by designing a letterform which solves the problem in a very practical way, yet is 'formally sophisticated'. [48] There is a striking discrepancy between Unger's working drawings (now in the Enschedé Museum) and the final product. As the forms were engraved with a rotating chisel, the corners were rounded. To avoid the effect this would have of making the terminals look too rounded-off, they were slightly widened. In the drawings the stems are clean-cut at a right angle, making Markeur look like a modernized *Optima*. The rounded terminals of the engraved letters give them a considerably different, more industrial look.

Unger's second typeface, M.O.L. (1974), shares a number of characteristics with Markeur. Designed in collaboration with a working group led by Pieter Brattinga for the Amsterdam metro, M.O.L. is also a sanserif signage alphabet. It, too, has rounded angles, but for different reasons. Many of the signs in the metro – white text on a blue background – are illuminated from within, which results in rounded halos forming around the letterform. M.O.L. is rounded throughout in order to improve legibility; this also enhances the consistency of the alphabet in front-lit and back-lit signs.

In 1974 Unger joined the ranks of what then could be seen as the jetset of type design: the small group – perhaps half a dozen people worldwide – who designed typefaces for the latest digital typesetting technology. He was offered a freelance contract with Dr. Ing Rudolf Hell GmbH in Kiel (later Linotype-Hell AG), a company which manufactured the Rolls-Royce among digital typesetting machines. The agreement with Hell was to last for almost fifteen years. It put Unger in an enviable position, allowing him to create an impressive range of innovative yet instantly recognizable typefaces, well paid and in relative freedom. The freedom he enjoyed was partly a result of the fact that to the hardware manufacturer, typefaces were only a by-product: Rudolf Hell's technocrats regarded type designers as humans of a special breed – as artists whose work should not be unduly interfered with.

For Unger, the main disadvantage of the contract was the relative invisibility of his work. The fonts, which in the early days of digital technology were platform-dependent, were only available to users of the expensive Hell typesetting equipment. It was thought largely unnecessary to publicize the typefaces or their maker. Unger compensated for this lack of exposure by regularly giving lectures and writing articles and books. In the Netherlands he was to participate in several projects of high visibility such as stamps, telephone books and – more recently – the national road signage.

Demos, Praxis and Flora

Unger's early type designs were strongly determined by the limitations of the new technology. *Demos*, his first typeface for Hell, was tailored to work with the cathode ray tube typesetter, a first-generation digital composing machine which required each character to be drawn on a rather coarse grid. Unger felt challenged by these constraints and drew a typeface with short, solid serifs and little contrast between thick and thin. Some of Demos's features were loosely inspired by De Roos's

⌃ M.O.L., the signage alphabet of the Amsterdam metro, designed by Unger in collaboration with a working group led by Pieter Brattinga, 1974.

⌄ Cover of *Terwijl je leest* ('While you read'), Unger's extensive essay on the pragmatics of type design and typography, 1997.

⌃ Unger's first typeface *Markeur* was designed for Enschedé's Pantotype engraving system. A comparison between a working drawing of the lowercase m and the final result shows how the corners were rounded by the rotating chisel, 1972.

46 Quotes are taken from conversations with Gerard Unger, 1996–2002. This article was based on many written sources as well, notably Unger's own writings as listed in the bibliography, the type descriptions on his website gerardunger.com, and the extensive monographs by Max Caflisch in *Typographische Monatsblätter*.

47 Unger in conversation with the author.

48 Robin Kinross in 'Technology, Aesthetics and Type', in *Eye* no. 3, 1991, pp 36–41.

▶ Unger's logo proposal for
a Dutch government body,
made in 1981, showed letterforms similar to his typeface
Flora.

▼ New version of Demos, 2001.

▼ Flora (1984); Hollander (1983).

Demos

Regular *Italic* **Bold** ***Italic*** Hebben onze
ouders, toen zij in 1823 medejubelden op
het vierde eeuwfeest der uitvinding, zich
aangesteld als eene kudde; volgden wij
zelve hun voorbeeld, toen wij in 1856 het
standbeeld hielpen onthullen, – dit kan
voor onze kinderen geen reden zijn, zich
onder een anderen vorm op nieuw als
eene kudde te gedragen.

Flora

Regular **Bold** De bakersvertelling van Junius
omtrent den kuijerenden grootvader, die op
eene wandeling in den Haarlemmer Hout
uit beukenschors een alfabet voor zijne kleinkinderen sneed, heeft, voor zoover ik mij
herinneren kan, nooit elders dan in de
kinderkamer gehoor gevonden.

Hollander

Regular *Italic* SMALL CAPS **Bold** Hij is
geen afgekoeld dweeper, geen scepticus
geworden idealist, geen *esprit revenu*,
zooals de Franschen zeggen, maar een
warm gebleven omgekeerde, een
ongeloovige opgevuld met bekeeringsijver, een apostel in de huid van een
renegaat, en daardoor meestentijds een
fanfaron de radicalisme.

Hollandse Mediaeval, which to Unger was a kind of primeval typeface: it had been the type used for many books he had read as a young boy. He based Demos's wide, chunky silhouette on De Roos's type, as well as some of its details, like the short-tailed, one-eyed g. Demos was newly digitized in 2001 in cooperation with the font production company Visualogic in 's-Hertogenbosch, who also sell it.

Demos was joined by two related fonts: *Praxis,* a sanserif (1977), and *Flora,* an italic sanserif (1984). There are strong family ties between the three typefaces, but Unger chose not to underscore that by giving them similar names. 'It is one of the typographer's pleasures to find interesting combinations of disparate faces. I don't want to prescribe anything to the user and therefore have consciously unlinked the members of the family. I later did the same with *Swift* and the sanserif, *Argo.*'

Flora, created in 1982–'83, was named after his daughter, who was born in 1983. While Demos and Praxis march across the page like Flemish workhorses, Flora is something quite different. Maybe this is partly a result of technological innovation: it was the first typeface designed with outlines using the Ikarus system. Ikarus was developed by URW's Peter Karow in 1974 and adopted at Hell from 1976 onwards.

Flora has the natural curves of a humanist italic, but at the same time lacks serifs as well as contrast. It is almost upright, like Eric Gill's *Joanna* and Jan van Krimpen's *Romanée* Italic. Unger initially made Flora for his own use; the typefaces evolved from his experiments with ballpoint and felt-tipped pen calligraphy. When Max Caflisch, Hell's typographic consultant, suggested the addition of a script face to the Hell library, Flora was waiting in the wings. Flora was originally designed as a display type but turned out to be well suited for setting short, informal messages. At the time of its release it was absolutely unique, though during the past twenty years 'humanist sanserif italic' has become a rather common genre (cf., among many others, *Lucida Sans, Legacy Sans* and *Scala Sans*). Yet Flora, more innovative and personal than most, has remained something of a milestone.

Besides his type designs for Hell, Unger worked on a series of prestigious assignments for Dutch companies and institutions. With the designer Pieter Brattinga he developed three experimental typefaces for dot matrix printers manufactured by Philips Data Systems. Assisted by Chris Vermaas he drew a new set of numerals for the famous telephone books that Wim Crouwel and Jolijn van de Wouw had designed using Univers. He designed the lettering for the standard postage stamps by artist Peter Struycken, featuring a computer-generated portrait of Queen Beatrix, as well as the new guilder coins by Bruno Ninaber van Eyben. All these activities culminated in 1974 when he received the H.N. Werkman Prize for his typographic work and for 'the way in which he has been able to reconcile typography and technology'. The award was a timely conclusion to the first phase of Unger's career, which had been dedicated almost entirely to solving problems caused by low resolution and other teething troubles of the emerging typesetting technologies.

Rediscovering the Dutch tradition

With the introduction of the Laser Digiset in the early 1980s, Hell replaced the coarse cathode ray tube technology with sophisticated laser beams, and pixelated letterforms with smooth outlines. The new technology paved the way for *Hollander.* Unger began drawing it in 1979, eager to finally design something with more subtlety and refinement than his rather hefty Demos/Praxis family.

Hollander was Unger's first historically inspired typeface. Unger: 'Certain books from seventeenth-century publishers in Utrecht, Leyden and Amsterdam possess a remarkable typographic brilliance. The typefaces used, cut by Christoffel van Dijck and possibly by Dirk Voskens, have a rather large x-height and are both open and robust. I have tried to translate that clarity into a modern concept by adopting the proportions of these seventeenth-century types and perhaps also their atmosphere, while the details are of course very Ungerian and contemporary.' Unger has written that the typeface reflects the horizontality of the Dutch landscape: 'Hollander is one of my designs to reflect the inescapable Dutch horizon. The horizontal part of the curves are stretched, the resultant gentle arches combining with the large serifs to assist the letters in joining visually to make words and lines.' [49]

nagmbur

g t

◂ Swift's name, and to a certain extent some of its shapes, were inspired by Unger's favourite bird, the swallow-like swift.

▿ Swift 2.0, issued in 1998.

▿ Cyrano, made for Hell in 1989, was shown in the 1990 *Encyclopedia of Typefaces*, but remained unpublished.

During the work on Hollander Unger also made sketches for a semibold version which never materialized. He rejected the design but later took it up again as a point of departure for a new line of thought which would lead to his first best-selling typeface – *Swift*.[50]

Swift was designed as a new newspaper typeface; after an informal but thorough survey, Unger had concluded that the market could use one. He had also studied historical precedents; in a 1981 article he described the experiments conducted in the 1930s for Linotype by W.A. Dwiggins, one of the past masters whom Unger greatly admires. Swift is characterized by a certain sharpness and angularity which remain intact even under the difficult conditions of fast web-fed presses and coarse newsprint. But the typeface also has a high-spirited dash expressed in its generous curves. Hence the name: the swift, a swallow-like city bird related to the hummingbird, is the acrobat of the Dutch skies.

While the serifs in Hollander are linked to the stems by a supple curve and are distinctly cupped, recalling such early twentieth-century classics as Monotype Van Dijck and Poliphilus, these forms have been simplified and sharpened up in Swift. The serifs are wedge-shaped, consisting of pure straight lines. Swift's overall construction has the same no-nonsense quality. The handwriting roots of the roman have not been completely eliminated, yet the letterform has moved away from the stroke of the pen. The way the parts are united does not suggest a flowing movement, as it does even in an unromantic early typeface such as Demos. They seem to be joined with a kind of nuts-and-bolts logic that would become a feature in most of Unger's later type designs. This lends them their trademark clarity and coolness when used in text sizes and makes for a striking presence in large sizes.

Like other typefaces produced for Hell, Swift was leased to the German foundry Elsner+Flake for distribution as a PostScript font. Dissatisfied with the E+F version, Unger later redesigned the typeface and digitized it with the help of the Visualogik company in 's-Hertogenbosch. This new version, Swift 2.0, is distributed by Unger.

Another look at low resolution

Towards the mid-1980s, the typographic letterform was again threatened by a new piece of hardware. The new machine, the laser printer, was not only meant for professionals, but also for use in home and office environments. In view of today's superfine results, it is hard to imagine what a 300 dpi print (with no 'optical correction') looked like in 1986: the letterform became a crumbly blotch which, if the machine had been badly adjusted, was further deformed by clots of toner. Suddenly a new mission awaited the type designer: to think out typefaces that could not be messed up under these conditions no matter what. Bigelow and Holmes made their *Lucida* ('lucid, clear'), Erik Spiekermann his *Officina* ('workshop'). Unger, too, felt naturally attracted to the problem. His renewned involvement with low resolution resulted in two very different typefaces: *Oranda* and *Amerigo*.

Oranda (the Japanese word for 'Holland') was the outcome of an assignment from Océ, a Dutch manufacturer of printers where Unger was adviser between 1983 and 1986. It is a slab serif and in that respect belongs in the same category as, say, *Rockwell* and *Memphis*, typefaces which in the Vox classification are called 'mécanes' because of their machine-like character. Yet in spite of its sturdy proportions – Unger has called it his 'most solid' design – Oranda lacks such a mechanical appearance. As Unger has written, it was vaguely based on typewriter faces to cater to Océ's clients in the office market; but Unger took that model in a different direction, mixing in

Swift

Regular *Italic* **Bold** *Italic* **Extra Bold** *Italic* SMALL CAPS *ITALIC* **BOLD** *ITALIC* Doch al het overige is advokaterij, haspelen van geleerden onderling, oorzaak tot meesmuilen voor het toeschouwend publiek, welks gezond verstand er zich steeds zwijgend tegen verzetten zal, dat ter wille eener zoo schamele vischvangst zooveel water troebel wordt gemaakt.

abcdefghijklmnopqrstuvwxyz
ABCDEFGHIJKLMNOPQRSTUVWXYZ
1234567890 &£$.,:;!?"'

abcdefghijklmnopqrstuvwxyz
ABCDEFGHIJKLMNOPQRSTUVWXYZ
1234567890 &£$.,:;!?"'

abcdefghijklmnopqrstuvwxyz
ABCDEFGHIJKLMNOPQRSTUVWXYZ
1234567890 &£$.,:;!?"'

abcdefghijklmnopqrstuvwxyz
ABCDEFGHIJKLMNOPQRSTUVWXYZ
1234567890 &£$.,:;!?"'

49 Gerard and Marjan Unger, 'Dutch landscape with letters', in *Gravisie* 14, Utrecht 1989. See also Max Caflisch, 'Die Hollander, eine neue Schriftfamilie', in *Typographische Monatsblätter* no. 2, 1987, pp 1–12.

50 The genesis of Swift was extensively described by Max Caflisch in 'Swift, eine neue Zeitungsschrift', in *Typographische Monatsblätter* no. 4, 1987, pp 1–16.

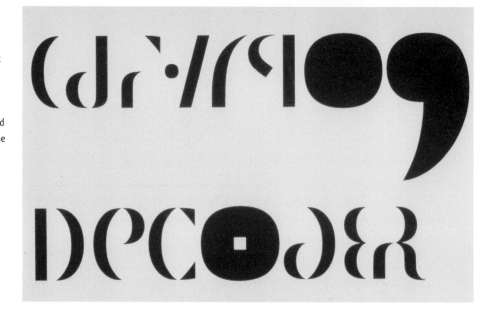

▾ Early sketch of Amerigo, the first typeface Unger designed for Bitstream. Published in 1986.

▾ Amerigo (1986); Argo (1991).

▸ Made as a contribution to FontShop's experimental typographic magazine FUSE, Decoder is a do-it-yourself kit rather than a typeface. In was published as part of FUSE 2 'Runes' (1991).
To create Decoder, Unger used a series of shapes based on the Amerigo letters.

hamburgevios

hamburgevios

Amerigo

Regular *Italic* Medium *Italic* **Bold** *Italic*
Ook onafhankelijk van haar weldadig karakter, is de typografie zulk eene vernuftige uitvinding geweest, blijk gevend van zulk een opgeklaard verstand, zulk eene praktische vaardigheid, zulk een fijn gevoel van de behoefte des tijds, dat hij zeker gaat, die a priori elke overlevering verwerpt, welke aan de spits dier ontdekking een stumpert plaatst.

Argo

Light *Italic* Regular *Italic* Medium *Italic* **Bold** *Italic* **Black** *Italic* SMALL CAPS LIGHT *ITALIC* REGULAR *ITALIC* **MEDIUM** *ITALIC* **BOLD ITALIC** **BLACK ITALIC** Daar het *odisse quos laeseris* sedert de dagen van het oude Rome niet op-gehouden heeft eene menschelijke eigenschap te zijn, bemerkt men reeds uit de voorrede, dat het werk vooral hierom met zoo veel verve, zoo veel hartstogt, inzonderheid zoo overijld geschreven is.

◄ Art work designed by Unger for an office building in Amsterdam. Spanning seven storeys, the work consists of seven times three silk banners indicating the numbers of the floors. The work was executed in collaboration with the silk-screen artist Nanda Laas.

▼ Delftse Poort, a single alphabet designed for the signage and lettering of the office building of the same name, close to Rotterdam Central Station, 1991. Referring to the building's two striking towers, Unger split the letters in two wherever possible, creating a kind of stencil type.

Delftse Poort

abcdefghijklmnopqrstuvwxyz

elements of classical roman forms and ending up with an attractive hybrid that shows some affinity with Eric Gill's *Joanna*. The upright italic of Joanna can be regarded as a precedent for the two most beautiful Orandas, the condensed and bold condensed versions. They have the proportions of a roman, but some characters – like a, e and g – have an italic structure. Océ never made much use of Oranda; the typeface was eventually licensed through Bitstream.

Amerigo, designed around the same time as Oranda, is named after Amerigo Vespucci, the explorer who lent his name to an entire continent. It was in fact the first typeface with which Unger crossed the Atlantic. Bitstream, the type foundry created in 1981 by Mike Parker and Matthew Carter, had asked Unger to have a look at *Optima* by Hermann Zapf. This elegant glyphic face, with its subtly waisted verticals, was immensely popular in America in the 1980s, but became a caricature of itself when printed on a 300 dpi laser printer. Parker asked Unger to design a similar typeface which could stand rough handling. 'I could see no mileage in simply imitating Optima,' wrote Unger; what did interest him was to find 'an extension of the class that the Vox classification calls "incises".' [51] Unger researched forms which differed from Zapf's design in a major way. 'While Optima is wide and round, I chose a much narrower overall image. While Optima has long ascenders and descenders, I opted for a relatively large x-height.' Amerigo, the first typeface which Unger drew for a type foundry instead of a hardware manufacturer, turned out to be one of his most remarkable designs. The toughness typical of most Unger designs is incorporated in letterforms that vaguely resemble Roman inscriptions but are also more bird-like than Swift. Although Amerigo has never become as popular as Optima in, say, cosmetics packaging, it has been put to a wide array of uses. In the United States, Amerigo is often used as a television typeface (for which it seems to have a natural talent), starring in some high-profile programmes.

Thanks to Unger's craftsmanship, both Oranda and Amerigo successfully survived the low-resolution era. With his redesigns of the magazines *Adformatie* and *HP/De Tijd*, Unger himself showed that Oranda could do a fine job in magazine design.

The dazzling technological evolution of the 1980s had led to a veritable massacre in the printing business. Many functions within the press and printing process simply disappeared. Dozens of companies stood by helplessly while the expertise and reputation on which their success had been built for decades – or centuries – became virtually useless. One-time competitors sought each other's support and merged. Hell, Unger's main customer, merged with Linotype, originally an American company, but now almost exclusively German. Both firms have since been subsumed by the Heidelberg group. At the new firm of Linotype-Hell AG there was no room for a type designer of Unger's calibre, and he was offered a generous handshake in 1989; the new type design *Argo*, financed by Hell, was his. Unger decided to license this type family, his 'Swift sanserif', to the Dutch Type Library (DTL).

Oranda used in the masthead of *Adformatie* as redesigned by Unger in 1989.

▼ *Oranda* was originally designed as a corporate typeface for Océ, a Dutch hardware manufacturer. It was eventually licensed to Bitstream and published in 1987.

Oranda

Regular *Italic* **Bold** ***Italic*** **Bold Condensed**

Over de feestviering van 1823 kan ik niet medespreken; maar dit kan ik getuigen, dat die van 1856 niet geweest is eene openbaring van nationale eenheid, maar van de goedhartigheid eener provinciestad.

51 Text on Unger's website www.gerardunger.com

▸ Sketch for Paradox, a contemporary typeface inspired by the work of the eighteenth-century punchcutter François-Ambroise Didot, published in 1999.

▾ Gulliver was designed to be the most economical newspaper typeface in the world. To demonstrate its legibility at very small point sizes, Unger designed a miniature book containing parts of Jonathan Swift's original *Gulliver* story, 1993.

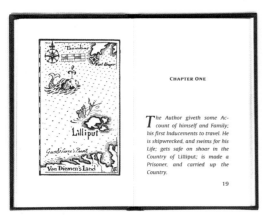

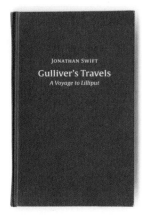

The world's most economical typeface

Ever a pragmatist and tireless problem-solver, Unger discovered a new opportunity in the market for typefaces. A new, economical newspaper typeface was needed. 'There is an evident tendency in newsprint to use larger type. If you compare daily newspapers printed in the late 1940s with today's pages, there is an amazing difference. Designing a newspaper always means: making the most of the space available. Therefore tricks are being invented to save space, like narrowing the type by electronic scaling, which generally speaking does not improve legibility.' Was there any room left for manoeuvre? Unger felt that the problem was 'a tasty nut to crack'.[52] By stretching the well-known qualities of his romans – generous counters, a large x-height, striking details – a little further, he managed to come up with 'the world's most economical printing type'. In an investigation published in the *Gulliver* brochure, Unger compared Gulliver to *Times*, another typeface known to be very thrifty. The results were remarkable. When setting texts of equal optical size, Gulliver saves 14% while at the same time being more agreeably readable.

Gulliver, issued in 1993, was the first typeface marketed by Unger himself. Among those he sold it to – at a professional price – were *Der Tagesspiegel* (Berlin), *Berlingske Tidende* (Denmark) and a number of Dutch dailies and publishers. One of them wrote to Unger saying that he had earned back the typeface within a year on saving paper and printing costs. It was a high point in Unger's career when *USA Today*, America's largest-circulation newspaper, decided to adopt Gulliver from early 2000 onwards.

Reading and writing; Paradox

Not only has Unger become somewhat of a public figure as a type designer, he has also become known as an author of succint essays and books. Writing in a language that is at once poetic, witty and technically precise, he manages to reach an audience that is far wider than the circle of graphic designers who use his typefaces. Between 1989 and 1990 the daily magazine *Trouw* published a series of light-hearted columns about letterforms, which were later published by De Buitenkant, Amsterdam, in a volume simply called *Letters*. He regularly publishes articles about the technical and historical aspects of type design in the international trade press.

In 1997 he published his most ambitious book so far: *Terwijl je leest* ('While you read'). In a loosely structured sequence of short chapters Unger explains how type design works and how he thinks, or assumes, that letterforms cooperate with the reader. In the book, Unger continuously zooms in and out, from everyday rituals to the details of type, from serifs and counters back to the noise of the street. *Terwijl je leest* is also a candid self-portrait of a pragmatist and a rationalist to whom each design is, first and foremost, the solution to a problem but who also manages to word his views on designs, processes and human behaviour in a surprisingly imaginative way.

Habegnsv26
Habegnsv26

Terwijl je leest is also a very well-made book. Designed by Unger himself, it served as a test-lab for a typeface issued by the Dutch Type Library in 1997: *Paradox*. The typeface is based on a design for a bookface named Diderot, made around 1975, but never completed. Of all Unger's typefaces, Paradox comes closest to being a revival. In a lecture at the TypoBerlin 2000 conference, Unger presented the results of his extensive reseach concerning the origins of the Didone or modern face, concentrating on the work of François-Ambroise Didot (1730–1804) and his punchcutter Louis Vafflard.

Taking his cues from that lecture and the article it spawned, [53] Frank E. Blokland, the font's publisher, further investigated Paradox's pedigree in his introduction to a type specimen booklet. Blokland argues that the model that Paradox owes most to is the *Romain du Roi* designed for the French royal printing office and cut by Philippe Grandjean between 1694 and 1702. Referring to the style of type design which forms a bridge between 'old face' and 'modern face', Blokland calls Paradox 'the "transitional" in Unger's body of work'. Yet one should be cautious not to emphasize too strongly the typeface's relationship with eighteen-century models. As Unger has said, 'the paradox of Paradox is that I am unable to make a revival, yet have allowed myself to be inspired by type design in the eighteenth century.' [54] In other words: Paradox is as contemporary and personal a face as any of Unger's other designs.

Taking Paradox as a starting point, Unger designed yet another newsface in 1999–2000. *Coranto* was made with the latest developments in printing technology in mind. As Unger wrote, 'Today, newspapers are not merely a matter of cheap grey paper, thin ink and super-fast rotary printing, and type design no longer has to focus on surviving the mechanical technology and providing elementary legibility. Now there is also room to create an ambience, to give a paper a clearer identity of its own; there is scope for precision and refinement. At the same time it is more delicate than either Swift or Gulliver and demands a higher standard of printing.' [55]

Highways and city streets

In the mid-1990s, Unger was commissioned to redesign the alphabet of the small-format road signage in Holland, the so-called 'hand-pointers'. For decades, the signage typeface had been the same as the one used by the United States Federal Highway Administration – the alphabet that inspired Tobias Frere-Jones's *Interstate* (1993–94). The client, the Dutch motoring organization ANWB, wanted the new typeface to be more economical and more legible without being conspicuously different from its predecessor – so as to avoid unneccessary and possibly hazardous surprises. Unger embraced the challenge. 'Although this type is read very differently from most of my designs ... it became apparent once again that enlarging the counters improved legibility.' [56] With minor references to the old alphabet, the letterforms were completely redesigned.

Coranto
Ambience and legibility

CORANTO IS OPEN, CLEAR, SHARP, LIVELY AND WARM — AN INVITATION TO THE READER

A new generation of text faces for newspapers has become possible thanks to improved technology. Newspaper production still demands a lot of letter forms, but advanced printing brings out details better and makes typography more appealing to readers. This means that ambience plays a growing part in reaching and keeping newspaper readers. **Ambience is now at least as important as legibility.**

Although newspapers today are better printed than ever, legibility continues to be vital because of the added pressure of time on readers' attention from other media. But even if there's less time for the paper, readers still tend to want more information, rather than less. And even with less time for the paper, most readers seem to be reading just as much as before. Probably they read faster than in the past by reading more selectively, by skimming or by skipping over parts of the text, and so on.

Coranto can both make your newspaper more legible and give it more atmosphere. *Coranto* has a generous x-height, but ascenders and descenders still manifest themselves clearly and thus keep the appearance of words and line structure varied. Verticals widen slightly at top and bottom. Serifs, which merge fluidly with verticals, are large but taper off to relatively fine ends. Counters are large, so that the letter forms are very open: it is this that makes *Coranto* so legible.

NEWSPAPER NEWS

52 Jan Middendorp, 'Gulliver in Drente', in *Items* vol. 16, no. 5, August 1997, p 66.

53 G. Unger, 'The Types of François-Ambroise Didot and Pierre-Louis Vafflard. A further investigation into the origins of the Didones', in *Quaerendo*, vol. 31, no. 3, 2001.

54 Jan Middendorp, 'Echte Ungers: beetpakken en meeslepen', in *Items* 2, April 1998, p 26.

55 Text on Unger's website www.gerardunger.com

56 Gerard Unger, 'A type design for Rome and the year 2000', in *Typographhy Papers* 3, 1998, p 61.

While Unger designed the ANWB typeface as a 'subcontractor' for the Leyden industrial design firm n|p|k (the designers of the new road signage), the roles were reversed in the next project. Unger won the assignment, then called in n|p|k. The job was one of the most remarkable of his entire career: the design of an information and signage system for the celebrations of the Holy Year 2000 in Rome, an event that was expected to attract 20 to 25 million visitors. What made the assignment extremely interesting to Unger was the requirement that a new typeface be designed as the central element of the information system. 'A specific type face, … a modern one for the third millennium (and not at all a philological *repêchage*), but in some way related to the tradition of the city.' [57] Thus the brief of the organizers, the *Agenzia Romana per la Preparazione del Giubileo*. Rome is very probably the only European city that boasts an uninterrupted two-thousand-year tradition of road signage. So designing a typeface for Rome was both a prestigious and a delicate job, perhaps, Unger wrote, 'the typographic equivalent of taking coals to Newcastle.' [58]

The brief, which explicitly asked for a contemporary typeface, suited Unger well, as he is 'not an enthusiastic supporter of twentieth-century revivalism'. [59] He set out to make a pragmatic, versatile typeface – a 'real Unger' which, somehow, also had to communicate Roman-ness. In other words: a blond design with a Latin heart. For *Capitolium* Unger chose to take as his starting point the work of the sixteenth-century writing master Giovan Francesco Cresci – notably a lower case alphabet which Cresci drew to accompany the classic roman capital. For some time, Unger played with the idea of making the alphabet into a sanserif – lowercase with initial capitals – tapping into twentieth-century signage tradition. Yet in Rome classic capitals are still the norm, even for contemporary street signs. Eventually, Unger reconciled readability and tradition by choosing an in-between solution: a brisk seriffed roman of classical proportions, to be used in lowercase with capitals. After several rounds of improvements and refinements, Unger finalized Capitolium: an unorthodox signage alphabet with a companion version for use in print. Although the project did not plan for the type to be set in caps-only, the capitals would work perfectly in this way: in their sober stateliness, they recall Jan van Krimpen's hand-drawn titles. The design team worked around the clock, managing to meet the extremely tight deadline; unfortunately the organizing committee of the 2000 Jubilee did not succeed in implementing the information system. Parts of it were used for signalling single sites, but the street signage system envisioned by Unger never materialized. For Unger, this was disappointing but by no means a disaster. It simply meant he had been paid to design an interesting typeface of a sort he might never have made without this assignment; from 2002, when the copyright went back to him, Capitolium was marketed by Unger himself.

In the subsequent years the Rome project yielded two more typefaces. *Vesta* (2001) was developed from the sketches for a sanserif signage typeface made during the early phase of the project. Vesta is Unger's most 'literary' sans: high in contrast, with a wide, rather square oval as the basic form of the round characters, it breathes clarity and openness. As with Gulliver (but even more extremely so) Unger managed to come up with a design that allows for heavy horizontal scaling without losing its character; his own specimen sheet shows samples of electronic condensation and expansion from 87.5% to 115%.

In 2003, while this book was going to press, Unger was working on a newspaper version of Capitolium. He had found that changing tastes have led to the need for an elegant newsface with a classic touch.

The typeface Capitolium was designed as part of the signage system for the celebrations of the Holy Year 2000 in Rome, developed in cooperation with the design firm n|p|k, 1998.

Vesta, based on an idea for a sanserif type for the Holy Year. Published in 2001.

San Giovanni in Laterano
Pantheon
Colosseo

Vesta

Light *Italic* Regular *Italic* Medium *Italic* Semibold *Italic* **Bold** *Italic* **Extrabold** *Italic* **Black** *Italic* Dit is voorwaar geen geringe verdienste; en het getuigt van zeldzame geestkracht, in een reeds eindeloos gerekt debat over eene afgezaagde en onbelangrijke kwestie, weder leven te kunnen storten.

57 Unger, 'A type design for Rome…' (cit.), p 61.

58 Ibid., p 63.

59 Ibid., p 61. See also Jan Middendorp, 'Design olandese per l'anno duemila', *Druk* 001, summer 1999, pp 8 – 9.

Letters from The Hague

Experimental screen alphabet by Frank E. Blokland, c. 1982. 'New typesetting techniques require new typefaces fit for the possibilities of these techniques. If one chooses to adapt typefaces from the metal era for this purpose, one needs to realize that, in order to obtain the same result as with letterpress printing, the design will have to meet new requirements that can be the opposite of the old ones. Although in some cases it can undoubtedly be rewarding to adapt typefaces designed for letterpress, designing new typefaces is a better option. The more, the better, as every face has its own typographic limitations. For the typographer there are never too many typefaces.'

Nieuwe letters

Nieuwe zettechnieken vragen om nieuwe letters afgestemd op de mogelijkheden van die technieken. Wanneer men letters uit het loodtijdperk hiervoor wil aanpassen moet men rekening houden dat om hetzelfde resultaat als bij boekdruk te bereiken de nieuwe aan de letters te stellen eisen tegenovergesteld kunnen zijn aan de oude. Hoewel het niet te ontkennen is dat het in een aantal gevallen de moeite waard is om voor lood ontworpen letters aan te passen, is er nog meer voor te zeggen om vooral nieuwe letters te ontwerpen. En hoe meer hoe beter. Iedere letter heeft tenslotte zijn typografische beperkingen. Het aanbod van letters kan de typograaf dan ook nooit groot genoeg zijn.

Gerrit Noordzij's school of letters

In Gerrit Noordzij's classes, practical work and theory have always been inextricably linked. Photographs taken by Jan Willem Stas, head of the KABK Type & Media course, during a workshop Noordzij gave in Kampen in November 2000, some ten years after his retirement as a full-time teacher.

Until the early 1980s, the Department of Graphic and Typographic Design of the Koninklijke Academie van Beeldende Kunsten (KABK, Royal Academy of Fine Arts) in The Hague seemed to be a school like any other, producing respectable book typographers as well as designers capable of doing sound corporate identities. When typefaces designed by KABK students began to be published around 1983, it gradually dawned on the outside world that the Academy prepared students for an occupation which few people knew existed – that of type designer. With the advent of desktop computing and the globalization of digital typographic culture, fonts by former students of the Royal Academy quickly conquered the international design world. Type designers from the 'school of The Hague' provided the new technology with useful tools and ideas.

The man who single-handedly brought about this small miracle was Gerrit Noordzij, who began teaching at the KABK in 1960, and from 1970 onwards developed an ambitious 'letter programme' for design and art students. I use the word 'letter' – as opposed to the more specific *type, lettering,* or *writing* – because this word in Dutch has all these meanings at once, and it is the term Noordzij prefers, even when writing in English, to define his field. As explained on pp 150 ff., there is no essential difference for Noordzij between handwriting and printing type: 'typography is writing with prefabricated letters.' Noordzij's clear theory about the construction of letterforms provided his students with a sharp tool to analyse and criticize existing alphabets as well as their own.

The letter programme was never actually meant as a curriculum for training type designers. The following is a fragment from Noordzij's text for *Dossier A-Z 73,* a file on 'Education in Letter Forms' prepared for the 1973 ATypI conference. It was quoted in a 1996 article by Frank E. Blokland, who pointed out that Noordzij's synopsis of type education at the KABK had remained valid to date. 'This programme [does not have] the ambition of producing highly qualified type designers. It has a modest place in the course of graphic design at the Koninklijke Academie, The Hague. This programme should make our students independent of trends in typography. They will have a notion of the problems that arise from enlarging letters, from making letters three-dimensional, from changing colours and printing techniques, etc. For advanced studies in letterforms the programme should provide a solid foundation.'[1]

Besides being a type designer, writer and letter carver, Noordzij is also a respected book typographer and graphic designer. These are the disciplines in which many of his former graphic design students from the 1970s excel. During that decade, no KABK graduate chose to be a type designer. This was, at least in part, due to outside circumstances. The reigning fashion in graphic design – 'functionalism' inspired by Swiss typography – did not call for a great variety of new typefaces. Type production in the Netherlands had practically ground to a halt, and the international type world was a virtually impregnable fortress. Young type designers from The Hague were to be instrumental in changing that situation.

Lida Lopes Cardozo Kindersley

When interviewed for this book in her Cambridge workshop, Lida Lopes Cardozo (1954) gave a succinct description of Gerrit Noordzij's lettering class – making clear why he left such an indelible impression on many of his students, and why others disliked him intensely. 'He came into the classroom, took a piece of chalk, broke it and wrote "Gerrit Noordzij" on the blackboard – he knows no modesty, of course. But he wrote his name with the authority of the maker. And you thought: I too will be able to do that one day. Then he made you fumble for weeks with a little pen and self-made ink, until you finally achieved something – a real victory. There were no tricks, you just had to do it a lot. You could see that he had, too. He had the thumb of a book-binder, there was power in it. Beautiful. If you liked the work, you could lose yourself completely in it. And Noordzij would give everything he had. But if you did not feel like it, he did not feel like doing anything for you either. He was very methodical. Everything was built up from theory. Gerrit made me realize that I was a stone carver. But he also gave me enough theoretical baggage for the rest of my life.'[2]

Having graduated from the Royal Academy in 1976, Lopes Cardozo – who, in spite of her Mediterranean name, is as Dutch as a milkmaid – went to visit David Kindersley in his workshop. At that point, Kindersley was just over sixty, and a monument in the English typographic landscape. From 1933 to 1936 he had been an apprentice at Eric Gill's workshop in Pigotts, where Gill's right hand man Laurie Cribb had taught him the art of letter-carving. After the war, he set up his own stone carving shop near Cambridge, but was also interested in technology, devising a system for optical letter-spacing system that won him a consultancy at Letraset.

Lida Lopes Cardozo wanted an apprenticeship but instead was hired by Kindersley to make slides of his work for a series of lectures – photography being one of the disciplines taught to design students at the KABK. 'For two months I was given private lectures about his work, and I got to know it really well. Just before he left on his lecture tour of the States, he took me aside for a whole day to teach me about letter-carving. When I took him to the airport, he simply said: "Well, if you're still here in two weeks, see you then." I stayed, naturally.'

Lopes Cardozo had made her first steps in letter-carving with Noordzij, but Kindersley's approach was completely different. 'Noordzij is very strict, which was fine at the time. When you are a student, it's great when somebody tells you what to do. David gave you a lot more liberty when it came to creating letterforms. So after those four years of very precise, calligraphy-based type education, I was encouraged to explore a whole new range of letterforms. But I think I never got rid of the Noordzij quirk.'

Cardozo and Kindersley soon realized they were kindred spirits. They struck up an intensive working relationship, co-wrote a book called *Letters Slate Cut*, and became partners in 1981. They married five years later and had three sons. In addition to the stone carving work, they published several more books under the imprint of Cardozo Kindersley Editions (occasionally in collaboration with De Buitenkant, Amsterdam). After Kindersley's death in 1995, Cardozo took charge of the workshop which, after a short period of confusion, continued to flourish.

As in Kindersley's day, the lettering styles used at the Cambridge workshop show great variety; assistants and apprentices are encouraged to develop their own style. But in Cardozo's own work it is the italics that stand out – the workshop is famous for them. Cardozo's italics are elegant and light, as if they were not painstakingly carved but nonchalantly written with a magic quill. If the Noordzij influence is visible anywhere in her work, it is here.

Maxim of the Dutch navy commander Piet Hein, carved by Lida Lopes Cardozo, 1988.

1   Mathieu Lommen and Peter Verheul, *Haagse Letters*, Amsterdam 1998, p 12.
2   All quotes taken from an interview with Lida Lopes Cardozo, 1999.

The Group

Emilida

I do not eat an apple
the way I eat a pare
so reason not the feeling
the two do not compear

When tomorrow comes
think tomorrow's thoughts

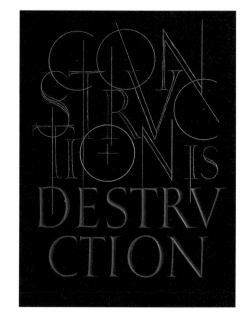

Her one digital typeface, *Emilida*, also started out as an Italic. It was commissioned by Timothy Guy Design for the music company EMI as a corporate typeface. Cardozo: 'EMI wanted the company mentioned in the name. So I said: I want mine in, too.' Hence: EMI-Lida. The font was drawn by hand, then digitized by Eiichi Kono of ITA Kono Design in Reading. Emilida italic is an elegant, traditional humanist cursive with no frills. Rather light in colour, it works very well as a medium-sized headline face, but also makes agreeable reading in short texts, as shown in publications of the Cardozo Kindersley Workshop. While the italic shows some influence of the Noordzij teachings, the roman – which was made later – is very English: an alphabet in the classic Gill-Kindersley tradition. With its cupped serifs, diamond-shaped dots and overall sharpness, it is more detailed and interesting as a display face than, say, the digital versions of Gill's *Perpetua* (Monotype) and *Golden Cockerel* (Dave Farey for ITC). Yet it is probably too light and narrow to be a successful text face, unless used at 14pt or more.

Lida Lopes Cordozo has never given much thought to the sources of her letterforms. 'Some British specialists have photographically enlarged showings of Emilida and discussed its forms. Creating letters to me is a mysterious process which I have no theories about. What counts is that the next form, the next stone, must be even more beautiful than the last.'

Rudy Vanderlans and Emigre

The first Noordzij student to make a name for himself internationally was Ruud van der Lans or, as he called himself after emigrating to the USA, Rudy VanderLans (1955). Having graduated in 1979, Vanderlans worked at several design studios in Amsterdam and The Hague before moving to Berkeley, California to study photography. Here he met a fellow expatriate, Slovak-born designer Zuzana Licko, who became his wife and working partner. Vanderlans started a magazine called *Emigre*, which began as a rather anarchic art magazine but soon became a forum for new ideas in graphic design and type design.

Immediately after the release of the Apple Macintosh in 1984, this machine became the twosome's favourite tool. As interesting and effective fonts for the Mac were lacking, Licko began designing custom fonts for the magazine. On the strength of the showings in *Emigre*, demand for the fonts began to grow. Licko and Vanderlans then created the Emigre Graphics font library, arguably the most trendsetting type collection of the early digital era. Although many type designers contributed to *Emigre*, Zuzana Licko remained its central figure.

Vanderlans himself only designed three font families in the Emigre collection. Two constructed typefaces, *Variex* and *Oblong*, were co-designed with Zuzana Licko. Oblong is drawn on a strict rectangular grid using only straight lines of equal width. The design of Variex is rather ingenious. It consists of three weights defined by the same centre lines; the various weights are obtained by changing the thickness around this axis. This means that both the x-height and the alignment may vary. Variex plays with these variations; the axes of a character are in the same position in all three weights, so characters can be layered to form multicoloured or outline letters.

Suburban is VanderLans's only solo performance as a type designer. He wrote: 'I imagine, like many designers who design their first font, that my goal, too, was to incorporate into one design all of those components from other typefaces that I've always enjoyed. In my case, these were script faces, in particular hand-lettered script faces, such as the ones you might find on the jersey of your local softball team. However, in order to create a typeface with a slightly wider applicability than a hand-drawn script, many of the forms had to be simplified and many script features had to be stylized. The final alphabet, therefore, is a combination of fairly rational, geometric shapes sprinkled throughout with whimsical and calligraphy-inspired characters. Designing Suburban also functioned as catharsis, an opportunity that allowed me to disprove (at least to myself) some of the basic notions I had learned in art school regarding traditional type design. My type design teacher would call Suburban a 'vermicelli' font, a typeface lacking the necessary visible contrast and stresses between counters and strokes and/or optical corrections to make it a 'successful' typeface. All valid notions, but by no means the only route to legibility and/or beautiful type.'[3] The teacher whom Vanderlans refers to is obviously Gerrit Noordzij.

When asked for a contribution to a Noordzij tribute – *Het primaat van de pen*, a booklet about Noordzij's work as a teacher[4] – Vanderlans was a little more generous. He wrote a short text which became the blurb on the volume's back cover: 'I won't be able to come up with any decent writing regarding Noordzij. I must say, though, honestly, that Noordzij is a very, very distant memory for me (was it 23 years ago?). Although, at the same time, any wisdom regarding type that I carry with me must have come from him.'

▲ Variex (1988) by Zuzana Licko and Rudy Vanderlans is a constructed stroke design built around the letters' centre lines.

◄ Cover by Armand Mevis and photographer Jodokus Driessen of *Emigre*'s 'Dutch issue' (Winter 1993). Guest editors were Mevis, Vincent van Baar and Gerard Forde.

▼ Vanderlans's *Suburban* (1994) was a reaction to his education in The Hague.

Suburban

Light **Bold** Dit alles is mogelijk, denkbaar, en zelfs, als men in aanmerking neemt welke ongezellige en onpraktische schepselen er plegen te groeien uit lieden, die levenslang overdezelfde zaak zitten te peinzen, waarschijnlijk.

3 Rudy Vanderlans in *Refining Obsolescence*, a catalogue introducing Platelet, Whirligig and Suburban, Berkeley 1994.

4 *Het primaat van de pen*, The Hague 2001.

Letters] and international relations

From the early 1970s, Gerrit Noordzij contributed to international magazines and meetings, and corresponded about his theories with his peers abroad. This naturally enriched his letter programme, because students received first-hand information about developments in the international type world.

When a small group of graphic design students in 1977–78 showed interest in the new digital type design technology, they were invited to one of the world's most advanced type laboratories, Peter Karow's company URW Software & Type in Hamburg. Using logarithms originally written for shipbuilding, URW had developed Ikarus, a revolutionary programme for describing characters by means of outlines. Petr van Blokland was one of the graphic design students who spent several weeks in URW's basement, inventing ways of interpolating Bodoni and Garamond to test Gerrit Noordzij's theories. Being a self-taught computer programmer and hardware developer, Van Blokland took serious interest in Ikarus's structure and remained in contact with URW. Several years later he wrote the first version of IkarusM, the Apple Macintosh version of URW's font software, which is still in use today.[5]

In 1980 a new group of type enthusiasts made itself heard. Frank E. Blokland proposed to his fellow students Jelle Bosma and Albert-Jan Pool to start a 'letter club' of aspiring type designers.[6] Noordzij welcomed the initiative: 'The letter club would offer my fanatics a critical climate simply by bringing them together; among each

◄ *Letters]* (1986) was the first publication of the Royal Academy's 'type club'. Designed by Jelle Bosma.

► Unfinished typeface, designed collectively by the Letters] group during an ATypI working seminar in Hamburg, 1985. The typeface was drawn on a 512 × 512 pixel grid, then scanned for Scangraphic's Scantext system.

Hausmann raum sommer seegang monogramm Irgan regenbogen barbara morgen gera Hummer rom Heber sauer Iberammergau bauer summe roman magen sorgen neuerer garbe Imen maus Homer georg I fen farbe Hafen auf

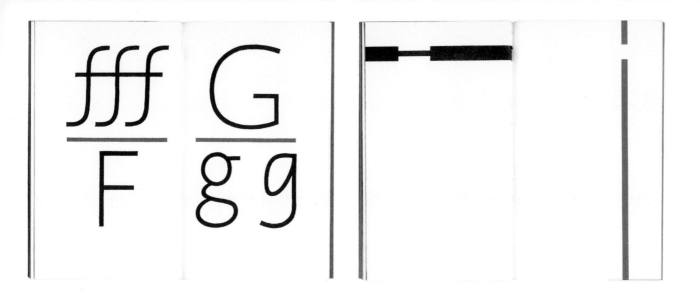

^ Page by Peter Matthias Noordzij
from *Letters] & techniek* (1990),
the working group's last
publication. On this page,
the behaviour of metal type is
demonstrated by comparing
it to a potato stamp.

↗ Two spreads from the booklet
26 Letters] (1987): F and G by
Marie-Cécile Noordzij-Pulles
and H and I by Henk van Leyden.

other they would not be outsiders any more.'[7] The members of the group met to exchange ideas and criticize each others' designs; as the group grew over the years and its members ventured into the real world, its activities became more pronounced. Young type designers in the early 1980s had only a minor chance of having their type designs accepted by one of the large type foundries. User-friendly, affordable software for font production was not yet available, and the production of new typefaces was a costly affair; the type establishment was not inclined to take many risks. The members of the letter club exchanged the experiences they had with type manufacturers, gave each other access to the contracts proposed by these companies, and assisted each other in the production of fonts and lettering projects.

In 1986 the group was finally given a name: Letters] ('letters bracket'), and produced its first publication, a catalogue published on the occasion of an exhibition of their work held in the Museum of the Book in The Hague.[8] Gerrit Noordzij arranged another exhibition to take place during the yearly ATypI conference in Basle, thus putting his 'fanatics' firmly on the map of the international typographic elite. By then, the group consisted of the founding members Blokland, Pool and Bosma plus Petr van Blokland, Henk van Leyden, Peter Matthias Noordzij (son of Gerrit) and his partner Marie-Cécile Noordzij-Pulles. Four of the members already had typefaces published, or in preparation for publishing, with international companies; a fifth, Henk van Leyden, had designed a custom font for the Rotterdam transport system. Two more publications saw the light. Peter Matthias Noordzij edited and designed the playful booklet *26 Letters]*, with contributions by all members, including newcomers Just van Rossum, Luc(as) de Groot, Bart de Haas and Peter Verheul. The group's final sign of life was *Letters] & techniek*, a collection of illustrated essays about various technological aspects of type design. It took three years to make the booklet; apparently, for most of its members Letters] was not a necessity any more – it had accomplished its mission. As Noordzij phrased it: '[they] had been accepted as colleagues on a world-wide level: the Hague type designers firmly hold their ground in the international professional discourse.'[9]

5   Information based on conversations and e-mail correspondence with
    Petr van Blokland and Frank E. Blokland.

6   Cf. Mathieu Lommen, 'De werkgroep Letters]' in *Haagse Letters* (cit.), pp 19–24.

7   Ibid., p 19.

8   *Letters]*, The Hague 1986.

9   Quoted in Mathieu Lommen's 'De werkgroep Letters]' (cit.).

Henk van Leyden: hanging figures on the buses

The first of Noordzij's students who landed an assignment to design a custom type-face was Henk van Leyden (1960). His internship at Vorm Vijf, a leading corporate design studio in The Hague, was turned into a fulltime job when a new typeface was needed for the Rotterdam public transport system (RET). The studio was designing a new signage system which would mainly be adopted in and around the underground stations. Because of the varying lighting circumstances, it had been decided that light boxes would be used. Existing sanserifs proved hard to read when used for the backlit, white-on-grey lettering; Van Leyden's proposals for a dedicated typeface proved a much better option when tested in the same circumstances. 'When we proposed the idea to the client,' says Joop Ridder, one of Vorm Vijf's founders, 'the RET replied: "Sure, if you say so. We can offer you 3000 guilders [less than 1500 euros or dollars] for the typeface." So that's what we did it for. We simply loved the idea of having our own alphabet in the metro.' [10] The RET letter was designed and implemented in 1983 and has been in use ever since. It is a low-contrast sans with a humanist construction; its short extenders make sure it takes up little vertical space. Thanks to its open counters and relative lightness, its forms are left intact by the back lighting; there is also a slightly bolder version for front lighting. One of its most remarkable features is that is has mediaeval or 'hanging' numerals, in accordance with its humanist character; for years Rotterdam was one of the few, if not the only city where buses were numbered with such a degree of sophistication.

Henk van Leyden planned to use the RET letter as basis for a full-fledged typeface, but never found the time. After five years at Vorm Vijf he set up shop with his brother Gé. Their studio named (i-grec), parentheses included, was one of the first in Holland where the Macintosh played a central role; it has specialized more and more in design for screens. Van Leyden has remained fascinated by type, and has occasionally designed letterforms for logos. He is still convinced that the RET alphabet could make a useful sanserif; it is his intention to eventually extend it and issue a complete font family. [11]

Henk van Leyden (at Vorm Vijf, The Hague), typeface for the Rotterdam transport authority RET, 1983. Two alphabets were made: one for backlit signs, and a slightly bolder one for frontlit signs.

The typographic systems of Petr van Blokland

Most members of the study group Letters] have explored the correlation between type and digital technology, and made contributions to both. But Petr van Blokland (1956) was a pioneer – even in his student days. He went to high school in the early 1970s; and while other whizz-kids of his age were soldering radio parts, he taught himself programming and built his own computer from do-it-yourself kits. Petr van Blokland, like his younger brother Erik, inherited his inquisitiveness and creative thinking from his parents, Rokus van Blokland and Corry Mobach.[12] In the late 1940s the two of them studied in The Hague with Paul Schuitema and Gerard Kiljan, the pioneers of Dutch functionalism; Rokus went on to teach, both in The Hague and at the new Academy of Industrial Design in Eindhoven. The Van Bloklands are the designers of Sio Montage, Holland's most popular construction toys, and amongst them shared the tasks of teacher, inventor, illustrator, industrial designer and graphic designer.

At the Royal Academy, Petr (originally 'Peter') van Blokland took part in Gerrit Noordzij's writing classes with interest, but also challenged his teacher with proposals to combine his self-developed digital technology with Noordzij's typographic system. Noordzij, who regarded computer technology as a possible ally in demonstrating the validity of his theories, struck up an intense correspondence with his student. Models invented by Noordzij were tested, fine-tuned and expanded by Van Blokland.[13]

To Noordzij's dismay, many colleagues in the 1970s saw his historical and theoretical research as somewhat of an anachronism, a return to pre-modern tradition. Thanks to the experiments of students like Van Blokland, it gradually became clear that Noordzij's ideas were much more universal than most of his peers assumed, and even gave aspiring designers somewhat of an intellectual head start when embracing new technologies.

VijfZeven, or the blessings of contrast

Van Blokland's *VijfZeven* ('FiveSeven') type family is a case in point. The VijfZeven design started as a student project in Van Blokland's last school year. It was 1978, and the very first desktop computers were hitting the market; hardware manufacturers were coming to grips with the limitations of the available technology. Monitors were black-and-white (or black-and-green) and had extremely low resolution. Manufacturers tried to solve the problem by using monoline matrix fonts, in which the strokes of a simplified sanserif typewriter alphabet were represented by dots. In Noordzij's writing classes Van Blokland had learnt that the contrast within characters is an essential aspect of legibility. He set out to demonstrate that this insight was valid even at the lowest possible resolution, with characters measuring five by seven pixels.

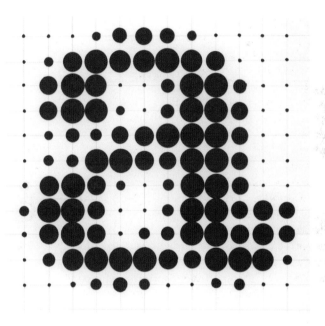

Petr van Blokland, screen matrix study for the electronic reproduction of letterforms, late 1970s.

10 Interview with Joop Ridder.

11 Based on information provided by Henk van Leyden in conversation and by e-mail.

12 Cf. Jan Middendorp, '*Ha, daar gaat er een van mij!*', Rotterdam 2002, pp 20–22; Erik van Blokland, 'Sio Montage', in *Druk* 012, 2002, pp 18–23.

13 Information provided by Petr van Blokland in conversation and by e-mail.

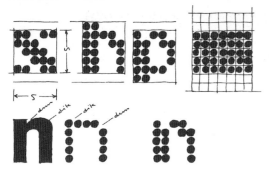

Van Blokland designed the screen font VijfZeven (1978) as a student, arguing that contrast enhances legibility even at the lowest possible resolution.

Vijfzeven
Ultra Light Light
Medium **Bold Black**
Screen *Italic*

◁ Around 2000 VijfZeven was further developed and released as a family consisting of sixteen styles.

▽ Buro Petr van Blokland + Claudia Mens used Productus, the sanserif companion to Proforma, to design the Vlietland hospital's corporate identity. A special font was created to be able to automate the design of forms.

Noordzij, when publishing his students' work in a 1983 goodwill publication of the printer Lecturis, wrote: 'Superficially considered, contrast (the difference between thick and thin) is a bonus added to the simple contrastless basic form of writing. In reality, diminishing contrast is a way of complicating the initial simplicity. Even more superficially considered, it does not matter how you look at it. This is the kind of 'vision' to which we owe the illegible texts on screens. The limited possibilities of a coarse matrix are restricted even further when using type with no contrast. Petr van Blokland shows that the possibilities of a 5×7 matrix can be made better use of if contrast is maintained as much as possible in the type design.'[14] Through the years, VijfZeven has been further developed as a kind of side project. It is now available as a high-resolution font family of seven weights, created by varying the size of the 'pixels' (which are now the round building-blocks of a normal outline font). As all weights have the same width, the fonts can be layered, creating a surprising effect of depth. There is also a set of italics, plus a rough and 'sphere' variety, which seem to simulate lack of sharpness on a screen.

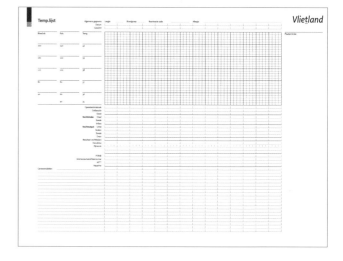

The studio as model

After graduating from the Royal Academy, Van Blokland worked briefly as a graphic designer with Studio Dumbar (The Hague) and Total Design (Amsterdam); in 1980 he set up his own studio with his wife, interior designer and colour specialist Claudia Mens. He simultaneously studied Industrial Design at the Delft University of Technology. This enabled him to further sharpen his ideas about how to structure the work and, in his own words, how to 'design the design process'.[15]

Van Blokland likes to solve complex problems by creating typographic systems which help to structure information. This type of work occurs mainly in corporate design projects that involve a lot of developing work; such projects are usually commissioned by large institutions and executed by large agencies. In order to be competitive in that sector with their six-man studio, Van Blokland and Mens have set up a rather unique structure – a model of rational thinking. All overhead tasks, except for picking up the phone, are computerized. Every document created in the studio, be it a memo, layout, spreadsheet, image or typeface, is part of a central server which is continuously fed and referred to by the individual designers. This enables the small group to take up large projects, while retaining the flexibility of a small think-tank. For two decades, Buro Petr van Blokland + Claudia Mens has worked for ING Group, one of The Netherland's largest bank companies; they designed and implemented the corporate identity of the insurance company Nationale Nederlanden, for which they developed the Helvetica-based font family NNSans; created a system for the automatic layout of Hotelplan travel guides; designed an XML-based website for a television station; and were involved in dozens of corporate identity projects.

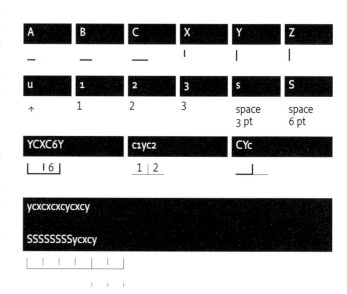

Proforma

Besides the custom typefaces developed or modified for his clients, Petr van Blokland has designed two major typeface families: *Proforma* and *Productus*, a roman and its companion sanserif, both published by the Font Bureau in Boston.

Proforma has a long history. In the heyday of Letters], Van Blokland invited Frank E. Blokland (not related) to collaborate with him on the design of a typeface commissioned by Purup Electronics in Lystrup, Denmark. After they drifted apart, Petr van Blokland completed Proforma; Frank Blokland took the design into a different direction and made *Documenta*.

A sister company of Purup Graphics, one of the largest forms printers in Denmark, Purup Electronics had developed a laser-based forms system which was sold successfully throughout the industry. Purup wanted a typeface especially for typesetting forms. One consequence of this 'specialization' was that the typeface was given a wide range of weights (five in the Purup version) that are relatively close. The reason for this is that the design of forms often makes use of white type on a coloured background: in order to give negative type the same optical weight, especially on uncoated paper, it is necessary to use a slightly heavier font.

Much attention was given to the technical circumstances under which Proforma was to be reproduced. Van Blokland wanted the typeface to have the subtlety of a traditional typeface while optimally reproduceable on medium-resolution imagesetters. The subtly curved stems of oldstyle fonts he replaced with vertical stems with straight-lined swellings at the top and bottom; at small sizes the effect is that of a 'classic' face, at large sizes one sees a contemporary yet elegant solution. In both cases the slanted lines minimize the 'staircase effect' in 1200dpi output or lower.

Van Blokland made the working drawings by hand, then digitized the typeface using Ikarus M, the Macintosh version of URW's type design software which he had helped develop. The brochure that he edited and designed for the 1988 release of Purup Proforma contains a few maxims that summarize his typographic credo. 'It is harder to design a straightforward typeface than an extravagant one ... The same bottom line that applies to typography also applies to typefaces: when no one notices, the aim has been accomplished.'[16]

The typographic world was impressed by Proforma, as well as by Van Blokland's efforts to reconcile computer technology and typography rooted in tradition. In 1988, at 32, he was given the Charles Peignot Award of the Association Typographique International (ATypI).

purup electronics

PE Proforma®

Hamburgefonstiv
Hamburgefonstiv
Hamburgefonstiv

Petr van Blokland

**hhbjlotwy
mursveai
ßAapfcfi**

Schetsen vet

Schetsen vet

▲ Type specimen of the first version of Proforma, designed for the Danish company Purup as a dedicated font for forms, 1988.

◄ Early sketch of a joint design by Frank E. Blokland and Petr van Blokland, which would be developed into Proforma by the latter and Documenta by the former.

14 Gerrit Noordzij, *Letters in studie*, Eindhoven 1983, p 24.

15 From a lecture held at the first International Conference on Typography and Visual Communication, Thessaloniki, June 2002; published on Van Blokland's website www.petr.nl, 2002.

16 Proforma specimen, Purup Graphics, 1988.

◀ During the various editions of TypeLab, daily newspapers were produced; often with unpublished fonts such as Just van Rossum's black roman Dispose (used in the masthead with Erik van Blokland's FF Kosmik).

▼ The extended and partly redesigned Proforma family as published by the Font Bureau, Boston, in 1994. Below: Deforma, a one-weight 'corruption' of Proforma, 1999.

▽ Productus, the sanserif companion to Proforma, was released by the Font Bureau in 2001.

TypeLab

Having been awarded a prestigious prize by the ATypI, Petr van Blokland became a respected member of that organization. Yet ATypI in the late 1980s and early '90s was still a rather elitist, industry-dominated association, whose yearly conferences consisted mainly of lectures *ex cathedra*: 'one-way traffic', according to Van Blokland. He and his good friend David Berlow, co-founder of the Font Bureau, thought it was time for a change. In 1993, when the ATypI conference was being held in the Antwerp Holiday Inn, they planned a coup. Without much preparation, they organized the first edition of TypeLab in the conference's lunchroom, with the consent of the main sponsor, Agfa, and to the dismay of the ATypI establishment. TypeLab was set up as an informal meeting where attendants could converse, compare notes, get hands-on experience of type design software and jot down improvised typefaces. It was a great success, and many conference attendants spent a lot of time at Typelab. The effect was immediate. For a number of years, TypeLab was continued as an official counterpart of the ATypI conferences. It hosted informal events such as lettering classes, demonstrations and public interviews. During the events, the daily newspaper published by TypeLab, edited and designed by Berlow and others, functioned as an informal log as well as a playground for type designers.

In 1996, the ATypI conference was hosted by the Royal Academy in The Hague (KABK), where Van Blokland now was a teacher. By then the two events had virtually fused into one. Many participants did not even realize that they were in fact attending two conferences at the same time.

FB Proforma

Ultra Light *Italic* Light *Italic*
Book *Italic* Medium *Italic*
Semi Bold *Italic* **Bold** *Italic*
SMALL CAPS ULTRA LIGHT *ITALIC*
BOOK *ITALIC* **SEMI BOLD** *ITALIC*
BOLD *ITALIC*

Deforma Book

FB Productus

Book *Italic* Medium *Italic* **Semi Bold** *Italic*
Bold *Italic* **Black** *Italic* De straatjongens
en de burgers wedijverden in sarkasmen ten
koste van den ijzeren Louw; de heeren rookten Costersigaren, de dames snoepten
Costerbanket, en elk hield zich overtuigd,
dat in den grond der zaak het geheele feest
alleen bestemd was, een genoegelijken laatsten levensdag te bezorgen aan den ouden
heer De Vries.

Proforma and Productus at Font Bureau

After Purup had been acquired by the Lego Group in 1991–92, copyrights to Proforma returned to Van Blokland. He reworked the family, drawing more supple italics and adding an ultra light version plus small caps for all weights, and reissued Proforma at the Font Bureau. The new version of Proforma was nominated for the 1995 Rotterdam Design Award, a prestigious triennial competition for all design disciplines. The jury report called it 'eminently suitable for the design of forms' and 'also extremely beautiful'.[17]

Early on, Van Blokland had planned to design a sanserif companion to Proforma. This branch of the family was initially announced as *Prolinea*; shortly before the release in 2001 the name was changed into *Productus*. The name refers to the 'ductus change', the term Van Blokland uses for the straight-lined widening of the stems – a design principle which is a unique feature of Proforma and also defines the shapes of Productus. Now that low-resolution output and economy of memory are

Vlietland

▸ The logo of the Vlietland Hospital made with Productus, 2001.

▾ All design work within Van Blokland's studio is automated, using an XML/XSLT web server based on the Python scripting language.

▾ Generating accented characters by using a Python script in RoboFog.

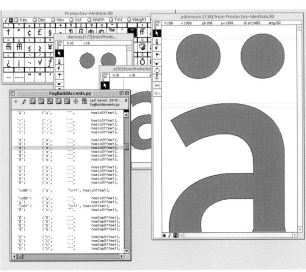

no longer relevant in the way they were ten years ago, another advantage of the ductus change principle becomes apparent: using straight lines to suggest curves makes for better shapes in small sizes on screens – pixels are automatically distributed more regularly along the outlines.

Van Blokland described Productus as 'an answer to the current straight typefaces of the mainstream [by this he probably means popular sanserifs such as *Interstate* and DIN], but also to today's arbitrariness and illegibility. Productus is a sanserif, too, but possesses just enough refinement to make typography even more interesting.' Productus is open yet narrow, business-like yet lively. It was designed as a complete family in order to make it a viable candidate for corporate identities. The Van Blokland + Mens studio uses it for its own house style and documents, as well as the identity designed for the Vlietland hospital (2000).

Robofog: scripting type design

For many years Petr van Blokland has researched the possibilities of rationalizing and automating type design. He built the first Mac version of Ikarus with URW, and worked on an extended version named Pika ('Parametric IkarusM'). In close collaboration with Just van Rossum and Erik van Blokland, his brother, he then developed RoboFog. 'The best ideas from Pika went into RoboFog. Starting with an application that already works makes it possible to get to the point quicker. RoboFog is the result of type designers trying to build the tools they've always wanted.' [18]

RoboFog started its life as a custom version of Fontographer 3.5 programmed by Steven Paul for the Font Bureau in Boston. Petr van Blokland suggested including a scripting language that would allow Fontographer functions to be automized; Just van Rossum joined the project, bringing in Python, the object-oriented scripting language developed by his brother Guido. Erik van Blokland became involved in testing and requesting new features.

After demonstrating RoboFog to type designer friends and colleagues, it became clear that other people were interested in using the software as well. For several years RoboFog was sold on a subscription basis, providing buyers with continuous support and updates of what was now one of the most powerful font editors around. In April 1999, the world's RoboFog users gathered in The Hague for Robo-Thon, an intimate three-day conference on the possibilities of the program. But RoboFog's career was brought to a halt by outside factors. The Fontographer code on which it was based was too old to be ported to Mac OS X. A new, powerful application called FontLab had appeared on the market, which better met the high requirements of OpenType font production. Development of RoboFog was discontinued and its makers focused their attention on an extension of FontLab called RoboFab, which on the LettError website is described as 'a toolkit for scripting and programming with fonts and glyphs, inside and outside of FontLab'.

The work on Python scripting has also brought new developments to Petr van Blokland's studio. In 2001 – 02 he wrote an application called xpyth:, a Python-based XML/XSLT web server, which has become the studio's central tool. (XML and XSLT are document description languages similar to the internet's HTML, but more sophisticated.) At the Van Blokland + Mens studio, xpyth: enables designers to perform tasks such as design and layout in a web browser environment, using the same source for every possible output – and throwing most design software except PhotoShop out of the window. Furthermore, the server is used for project management and administration, and as a database, editorial system, web server, generator of scripted images, etc. In 2002, it was made commercially available. The studio has also used xpyth: to develop a patient information system for a group of hospitals and health insurance companies. The system, called *InfoDoc*, enables doctors and medical specialists to create personal websites for their patients allowing them to check information at home. *InfoDoc* was developed by The Health Agency, a new company co-founded by Van Blokland.

17 Jury Report of the 1995 Rotterdam Design Award.

18 Published on the website www.petr.nl, 2001.

Albert-Jan Pool: no nonsense

Albert-Jan Pool, imaginary
licence plates showing OCRF.
FontShop International, 1995.

A founding member of the work group Letters], Albert-Jan Pool (1960) studied at the KABK in The Hague for six years, but never graduated.[19] The year after leaving the Academy he landed a job at Scangraphic, where he worked as type director from 1987 to 1991. Scangraphic is a hardware manufacturer in Wedel (near Hamburg, Germany) which at the time made typesetting equipment with its dedicated Scangraphic fonts description system. Pool had become acquainted with the company through its type consultant Volker Küster, the designer of *Today Sans*, whom he had met at ATypI meetings. 'Scangraphic gave me a unique opportunity to get a job in the type industry. There were hardly any possibilities in the Netherlands at the time. Foreign companies like Monotype and Berthold were going through a difficult phase, and in the States there was mainly a lot of thieving and revivalling going on. But Scangraphic was doing nicely, and because their library of about 1000 fonts consisted of bitmap characters which all had to be converted to Ikarus outlines, there was a hell of a lot of work to be done.' He called in the help of his fellow student Jelle Bosma. 'Hundreds of fonts have gone through our hands. It was fascinating and extremely instructive to see how all these type designers had found different solutions to the same problems. Furthermore, we had to compare the scans made at Scangraphic with the outlines bought from our main supplier, URW. Which gave us an interesting view of how colleagues at Hell, Purup, Letraset, ITC, Berthold, Linotype and Monotype – all of whom URW had done digitizing jobs for – had made working drawings of the exact same typefaces, and extended the fonts with new characters.'

Revivals and originals at URW
Albert-Jan Pool left Scangraphic to become type director at URW Software & Type, where he was engaged in the management of type design and production. From the early 1980s onwards, URW's Ikarus lab had provided digitizing service for the world's type foundries. The company was also building its own type library, producing versions of many classic and contemporary typefaces, as well as a few original designs, notably URW *Antiqua* and *Grotesk* by Hermann Zapf, *Alcuin* by Gudrun Zapf von Hesse, and URW *Linear, Imperial* and *Mauritius* by Pool himself.
Both Linear and Imperial were based on what Pool calls 'generic outlines' from the URW archive. These outlines were part of a plan to develop software for automatically generating type designs, by adding serifs, varying widths, etc. The project was brought to a halt, but Pool skilfully recycled the basic designs into two extensive families, with the help of URW's technical man Achaz Reuss. He calls Imperial a 'Roman Sans'; in fact, with its heavy vertical stress it might even be called a 'serifless modern face' – a Bodoni Sans, so to speak. Linear also has vertical stress, but almost imperceptibly so. It is therefore akin to certain nineteenth-century grotesques, although its atmosphere is bookish rather than industrial. What makes the two

▾ Hand-rendered logo for the Rotterdam machine factory and shipbuilding firm Piet Smit jr. BV (mid-1980s). The asymmetrical serifs were inspired by the construction of the Carolingian Minuscule. Taking this logo as a starting point, Pool began designing a typeface called Kadanz. Due to lack of time it was never finished.

Sketches for an unfinished humanist sanserif, mid-1980s.

The quick brown fox jumps over the lazy dog

Piet Smit jr bv

URW Imperial

Medium **Extra Bold Ultra Bold**

URW Linear

Medium **Extra Bold Ultra Bold**

URW *Mauritius*

Regular

⌃ Pool based Linear and Imperial (1994) on 'generic outlines' from the URW archive; Mauritius (1994) was a variation on Marigold.

▸ Detail from Albert-Jan Pool's type classification as published in the 1996 type catalogue issued by (URW)++ Design & Development.

families fun to play with is the fact that they come in five different widths, from extra narrow to extra wide. This was in fact current URW practice: several oldstyle faces, such as *Garamond* and *Baskerville*, received the five-width treatment, being given horrendous oblique romans for italics. But in Pool's faces this all seems to make much more sense.

Pool designed one more typeface for URW, an italic script called *Mauritius*. The typeface is not completely original; it was based on Arthur Baker's *Marigold*, one of the standard TrueType fonts on HP printers at the time. URW's client Fujitsu wanted a similar, if not identical font for their own printers. Albert-Jan Pool decided not to clone Marigold but use its proportions and basic shapes to draw a simpler typeface with spirited details. He had hoped for a chance to further develop the design into a more original script, but the work came to a halt when URW Software & Type folded in 1994.

The next year Pool started up his own studio, Dutch Design in Hamburg. One firm to become his client was (URW)++ Design & Development, the company founded as a continuation of URW by former staff members.

Type classification and type criticism

A significant achievement during Pool's Scangraphic and URW years was the compilation of two type catalogues for both firms. The second of these was a two-volume type specimen published in 1996 by (URW)++, for which Pool conceived the type classification and wrote a lengthy introduction. His classification deserves some attention. Pool points out the two main factors by which typefaces can be distinguished from one another: the amount and direction of contrast, and the shape (or absence) of the serifs. This is not new – in fact, his naming of typefaces closely follows the conventions of BSA (British Standard Association) in English and of DIN (Deutsche Industrienorm) in German. But there are some subtleties that betray the influence of Gerrit Noordzij's classification, which is much simpler and mainly

19 information and quotes based on e-mail correspondence with Albert-Jan Pool.

Branding with Type (Adobe Press, 1995), the translation of *Typen machen Marken mächtig*, a group project by Albert-Jan Pool, Ursula Packhauser and Stefan Rögener. The English edition was edited by E.M. Ginger.

OCR-F

Light **Bold** Ook onafhankelijk van haar weldadig karakter, is de typografie zulk eene vernuftige uitvinding geweest, blijk gevend van zulk een opgeklaard verstand, zulk eene praktische vaardigheid, zulk een fijn gevoel van de behoefte des tijds, dat hij zeker gaat, die a priori elke overlevering verwerpt, welke aan de spits dier ontdekking een stumpert plaatst.

DIN

Light *Italic* Medium *Italic*
Bold *Italic* **Black** *Italic*
0123456789 0123456789
Condensed Light Medium **Bold** **Black**

based on the type of stress within the character: the contrast derived from either the broad-nibbed pen or the pointed pen.[20]

Referring to the importance of contrast, Pool adds two main groups: Roman Sans and Linear Serif. 'Applying these names, we would like to distinguish typefaces more than just on the basis of whether serifs are present or not. Equally important, we feel, is the level of the thick-to-thin contrast. You will find *Britannic* and *Souvenir Gothic*, for example, under the Roman Sans heading whereas usually you would find them under Linear Sans or specified as a Roman Serif variant.'[21] The new categorization is a worthy endeavour, and especially useful when looking to combine contrasting fonts with similar constructions. In some respects, however, it is exaggeratedly detailed.

In the same year, 1995, another publication to which Pool had made an important contribution saw the light of day. Its alliterating German title *Typen machen Marken mächtig* literally means 'Typefaces make brands powerful'; a translation of the book, published in the same year by Adobe Press, was entitled *Branding with Type*. The book was a group project, written by Ursula Packhauser, designed by Pool and published by Stefan Rögener. Conceived by the three of them, it offers a witty and irreverent view of the way companies use type as part of their image-building – or don't. It argues convincingly for a conscious and professional use of typography in advertising and corporate design. Design school teachers made the book required reading. To the dismay of many, the English version of the book became unavailable when Adobe discontinued its publishing activities.

No-nonsense: OCR-F and DIN

In the early 1990s trendy graphic designers began using industrial and computer typefaces for aesthetic purposes. They did so as a reaction to the overdesigned 1980s style, but also as an alternative to the grunge fashion, which was wearing out rapidly. In order to obtain an 'undesigned' look, they started using engineers' types such as OCR-A, *Pica*, and the DIN *Schriften*.

In 1994 Albert-Jan Pool shared a taxi with FontShop's Erik Spiekermann on their way to San Francisco airport after the ATypI conference. Spiekermann knew that Pool was out of work due to URW's recent bankruptcy, and proposed to involve him in some type projects he had in mind. Pool: 'Spiekermann said: If you want to make some money off your type designs, look into those no-nonsense faces like OCR and DIN. He invited me to come and see him in Berlin about this. I was honoured, of course.'

Spiekermann's first proposal was to rework and expand OCR-B, designed in the late 1960s by Adrian Frutiger for ECMA, the European association of computer manufacturers, as a more human successor to their very robotic OCR-A. At first Pool considered the idea 'rather nonsensical': 'After all, Frutiger had also designed Univers, which can be considered as the typeface from which OCR-B had been derived. How could it make sense to "improve" OCR-B?'[22]

Yet this is what he set out to do, and the result is admirable. OCR-F is a balanced little family, with added light and bold weights. Pool also added oldstyle figures, which seems a very Dutch thing to do in an 'industrial' typeface. The look of the face was consciously ambiguous: 'The true non-monospaced-but-not-proportionally-spaced-look was created by adapting the typeface to a coarse width-grid of about 12 units to the Em square. Characters like m, w and M and W were kept rather narrow, and of course i and I were allowed to keep their serifs.'

Having completed FF OCR-F, Pool began working on his second FontFont, FF DIN. This family was based on the famous DIN-*Mittelschrift*, the German 'Autobahn' alphabet which has dominated signage in Germany for decades, both on roads and on public buildings. Pool considers DIN-Mittelschrift to be 'probably the most non-designed typeface ever made'. It is a typical engineers' design, constructed with strokes of equal width, all curves drawn with a compass. This has resulted in 'a spotty typeface with quirky letterforms, as can especially be seen in the characters a, e and s. Compared with characters with less strokes, such as b, d, p, q, o and n, they appear rather black.'[23]

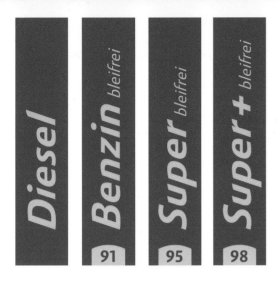

As it was precisely its primitiveness which had made DIN popular in the first place, the best option seemed to be to make the typeface more generally usable by improving the typographic quality of the design while maintaining its overall appearance. To that end, the weight of the horizontal strokes was reduced, and the curves more subtly drawn. The medium weight of FF DIN is close to the original weight of DIN Mittelschrift; as it gives a rather dark appearance in small-size body text, a new and lighter 'regular' version was added. In all, the family has five weights, each with an 'Alternate' cut that offers oldstyle figures, circular dots and oblique terminals on some characters.

Since its release in 1995, FF DIN has become one of the most popular FontFonts. Together with the Font Bureau's *Interstate* – based on the American highway font – it has become a fetish of contemporary graphic design, just like the 'Swiss' sanserifs Helvetica and Univers were twenty-five years ago. FF DIN is increasingly used for book typography and other sophisticated genres of printed matter; so the italics released in 2000 were a welcome addition. A condensed version was published simultaneously.

Pool's corporate types

In 1998 Albert-Jan Pool's Hamburg studio Dutch Design merged into FarbTon Konzept + Design, a versatile agency for corporate design and communication. Their work on corporate identities has resulted in a number of custom typefaces. The first of these was *Jet Set Sans* for the gasoline brand Jet, commissioned in 1997 by the Hamburg agency Syndicate Brand & Corporate. Influenced by geometric 'sci-fi' headline faces such as *Handel Gothic*, it is a sturdy sanserif whose bold italic version makes the Jet gas stations stand out. The corporate font DTL *Hein Gas* was based on DTL *Nobel*, the redesign by Fred Smeijers and Andrea Fuchs of a modern classic from the Amsterdam Type Foundry. Pool designed this narrow version of the font in close consultation with its publisher, Frank E. Blokland's Dutch Type Library, for whom he had acted as German representative in the early years. To furnish the campaigns of the left-wing political association Regenbogen with a more human and friendly typography, a computer-smooth *Letter Gothic* bold was modified into 'a coarse and honest typewriter font' by giving it rugged edges and firm serifs.

JetSet

Regular *Italic*
Medium *Italic*
Bold *Italic*
Condensed Bold

Hein Gas

Regular *Italic*
Bold *Italic*
Headline

˄ Jet Set Sans, a corporate typeface for the gasoline brand Jet, commissioned by the Hamburg agency Syndicate Brand & Corporate in 1997.

◂ DTL Hein Gas, based on DTL Nobel. The narrow version was designed by Pool as a custom-made corporate typeface. In a second phase, Hein Gas Headline was developed to give more 'human warmth' to the gas company's communication.

20 (URW)++ *FontCollection*, Hamburg 1996.

21 Ibid., part 1, p 32.

22 Quoted from the *Readme* files with FontFont release 14, FontShop International 1995.

23 Quoted from the *Readme* files with FontFont release 15, FontShop International 1995.

Jelle Bosma: behind the scenes

Anonymous design of a DGG
album cover using Bosma's
WTC Cursivium. This reissue:
1994.

When type became hip in the early 1990s, several Hague type designers became household names in the lecture and conference circuit. Jelle Bosma remained behind the scenes, and never acquired anything near star status. Yet the typefaces he contributed to – by co-designing, redesigning, improving or hinting them – are probably sitting on more harddisks worldwide than the types of all other Hague designers put together. Some are system fonts used by millions.

At the Royal Academy Jelle Bosma was a versatile and talented student. He was interested in photography and illustration, and was the first graphic design student to design a corporate identity with a self-made font. He even designed a typeface which was made as a computer program, enabling consecutive weights to be generated automatically – an early form of 'multiple master'. However, Bosma never graduated. In his final year, when he was supposed to start his mandatory internship, he was contacted by the World Typeface Center (WTC) in New York, who wrote that they accepted a typeface he had submitted, called *Cursivium*. Instead of graduating, Bosma chose to work on the pencil drawings required for production. 'I thought: hey, I've got work. That was the point of studying, wasn't it?' [24]

Cursivium is a humanist slab serif, quite an unheard-of idea at the time. Early twentieth-century slab serifs, such as *Rockwell*, *Memphis* or *Stymie*, have geometric proportions and an industrial feel; hence the name 'mecane' in the Vox classification. Their italics – Gill's *Joanna* being the obvious exception – were mere oblique romans. Influenced by Gerrit Noordzij's theories and writing classes, Jelle Bosma and Peter Matthias Noordzij simultaneously (but unbeknown to each other) developed a new concept in early 1983. Both Noordzij's *Caecilia* and Bosma's Cursivium have traditional proportions rooted in handwriting, but projected onto the firm, low-contrast lines of a slab serif or egyptian. Cursivium does not have a roman in the strict sense. It is an upright italic, while Cursivium Italic is a slanted version of the same form with a few calligraphic elements added.

Jelle Bosma now regards Cursivium as 'a sin of his youth'; but he sees no point in rejecting it. 'I think it was even more radical than Caecilia, but Matthias's design clearly had more potential. I also just dashed it off as soon as WTC had accepted it, while Caecilia was worked on for several more years.' Cursivium was produced by WTC's technical department via hand-cut copies in ulano film, and released in 1986 for Linotronic 300 Imagesetters. It never became widely popular. 'It has certainly been used a couple of times,' says Bosma drily. 'I think Deutsche Grammophon Gesellschaft did a few CD covers with it.' WTC ceased its publishing activities years ago. The fate of Cursivium is unclear; apparently a PostScript or TrueType version was never published.

ZO IS ER BIJ-
VOORBEELD
DE KWESTIE
VAN DE INTER-
RLINIE VAN D-
E TEKST HIER
IN HET MIDD-
EN NEERGEK-
ALKT (MET DIE

Oh, mijn hemeltje, wat nu? Hier klopt niets van. Een bespot- ting van de wetten van de TYPOGRAFIE!

SLIERTEN ERA-
AN VAST). NAU-
WE LETTERSPATI-
E TROUWENS.
BOVENDIEN
WORDT DE
TEKST OP EEN
HINDERLIJKE
WIJZE AFGEBR-

Indien die er zijn.

◄ Jelle Bosma's cartoons, doodles and hand-written improvisations show his playfulness and weird sense of humour.

▾ Drawing of Cursivium, 1982.

▾ The complete WTC Cursivium as shown in the *Modern Encyclopedia of Typefaces*, 1990. Forlane, published by Scangraphic in 1991.

ijk*łmt*

abcdefghijklmnopqrstuvwxyz
ABCDEFGHIJKLMNOPQRSTUVWXYZ
1234567890 &£.,:;!?''

abcdefghijklmnopqrstuvwxyz
ABCDEFGHIJKLMNOPQRSTUVWXYZ
1234567890 &£.,:;!?''

abcdefghijklmnopqrstuvwxyz
ABCDEFGHIJKLMNOPQRSTUVWXYZ
1234567890 &£.,:;!?''

abcdefghijklmnopqrstuvwxyz
ABCDEFGHIJKLMNOPQRSTUVWXYZ
1234567890 &£.,:;!?''

Scangraphic and Forlane

With Frank E. Blokland, who had graduated from the KABK in 1982, Bosma founded a small company called Script Design, which specialized in font production. The firm did some serious international prospecting, but the business was hit by recession and potential clients like Letraset stopped accepting type designs from third parties. Bosma took on a full-time job at Scangraphic, the Hamburg manufacturer of typesetting equipment where Albert-Jan Pool was coordinating font production. Scangraphic obtained most of its font outlines from URW, also in Hamburg, whose Ikarus lab provided type digitizing service for many large players in the European type community. In the years Bosma spent in Hamburg, the Scangraphic system was gradually replaced by PostScript, and many fonts had to be adapted a second time. Bosma remembers working on many well-known ITC and Letraset fonts, as well as two typefaces Gerard Unger had originally designed for Hell, *Demos* and *Hollander*.

Working for Scangraphic enabled Bosma to design his first full-fledged type family, and supervise its production from start to finish. Named after an eighteenth-century Venetian folk-dance, *Forlane* is a spirited text face with a strong, rather vertical stress and squarish shapes – Bosma calls it 'neo-rococo'. Although Forlane resembles Mendoza's *Photina* in some aspects, Bosma did not look at past or present models. 'I'm not the kind of person who travels to Italy to photograph a pretty inscription and bases a typeface on it. I chance upon an interesting form when doodling – like the r of Forlane – and I decide I'd like to do something with it.'

Like other Scangraphic families, Forlane has a series of separate headline fonts, more pronounced in contrast and more sharply detailed than the fonts for body type. This makes it a very complete typeface, with its three weights, small caps and mediaeval figures. Unfortunately, its publisher never took much trouble to promote the font; the headline fonts were not even marketed at all. Bosma remembers receiving a sales slip 'on which they admitted owing me 3.50 German marks of royalties.' To add insult to injury, FontShop's 1998 FontBook, the bible of type, credits Bosma's creation to the wrong designer. The typeface is still available, from a new incarnation of Scangraphic as well as the Elsner+Flake foundry, but its existence has gone unnoticed by most. If any forgotten typeface deserves a second chance, it is Forlane.

Bosma at Monotype

In early 1992 Bosma was hired by Monotype Typography as a 'typographic consultant'. Initially, his main task was to supervise large-scale font projects; given that much of these concerned standard fonts produced for the Windows™ operating systems, he was introduced to the finer points of Microsoft typography at the Redmond Headquarters. Among the system fonts he helped domesticate is *Impact*, a standard font on most desktops.

Forlane

Roman *Italic* Medium *Italic* **Bold** ***Italic***
SMALL CAPS MEDIUM Headline *Italic* Toen de heer De Vries in 1856 kommandeur van den Nederlanschen Leeuw geworden was, hoopten de verstandige lieden dat het tijdperk van het costergesnoef voor goed gesloten zou zijn.

24 Based on an interview and e-mail correspondence with Jelle Bosma.

Bosma can be regarded as the main designer of the Nokia corporate font family, as the family was based on a bitmap face designed by him; the serif version was almost entirely his work.

ଅଆଇଈଉଊରୠଏଐଓଔକଖଗଘ
ଙଚଛଜଝଞଟଠଡଢଣତଥଦଧନପଫ
ବଭମଯରଲଳଶଷସହଡ଼ଢ଼ୟୱ
୦୧୨୩୪୫୬୭୮୯

Throughout the 1990s Bosma did not design a single new roman typeface. Recently, however, he coordinated the design of a corporate font family for Nokia. The large family, which consists of sanserif, serif and display sub-families, was designed by an international team including Erik Spiekermann, Robin Nicholas and Carl Crossgrove; but Bosma can be regarded as its main designer, as the family was based on a bitmap face designed by him; the serif version was almost entirely his work.

Bosma owes most of his international reputation to the more technical work he has done for Monotype: he is one of the world's type gurus when it comes to fine-tuning the mechanics of digital fonts. His speciality is hinting – providing a font with codes which help create bitmaps for optimum screen legibility at specific point sizes. He has also become a specialist in non-Western typefaces, designing and optimizing anything from Arabic and Tamil types to a syllable script for native Canadian languages.

Hinting is a highly specialized task; in a recent interview, Bosma guessed that there are about 25 expert-level hinters worldwide, subtly adding 'This number may exclude those that hint at expert-level without being an expert.' [25] As for the time it takes to hint a font: it is a question which is almost impossible to answer. 'Hinting is a rather open ended commitment. I like to compare it to the computer game Tetris: You can play to improve your score, but you can never win. One tries to make the font as good as one can, but there are always too many characters at too many sizes with too many pixels to get all the pixels right. Therefore the most honest and accurate answer is: The time it takes me for an average font is all the time that I have until the deadline is reached.'

To facilitate these production tasks, Bosma has written a program called FontDame, a tool for automating the production and hinting of TrueType and OpenType fonts. Spending roughly a third of his time on programming, Bosma has developed FontDame into a complex piece of software. It is even used as a design tool for creating so-called 'stroke fonts', a system that is mostly adopted for complex non-Western scripts.

Although his original typefaces have virtually disappeared and his name will not ring a bell with the average graphic designer, Bosma is more than happy with his current position. 'I am well-known among those who were and are involved in creating today's and tomorrow's type technology. Not as the designer of Forlane, but as the person who can hint their system fonts, and make an Indian version if necessary. That is more than most people can hope for.' [26]

⌃ Inuit syllable script.

⌃ Characters for Indian Oriya typeface developed by Bosma.

▸ Devangari typeface. The line of characters on top shows the smooth outlines for high resolution. The lines below show bitmap fonts for different sizes.

⌄ Screen shot of the program FontDame, conceived and written by Jelle Bosma.

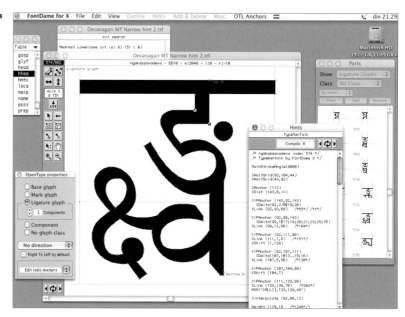

Frank E. Blokland and DTL

Among the Hague type designers of his generation, Frank E. Blokland (1959) epitomizes the designer as organizer, combining the qualities of the craftsman-technician and the negotiator-businessman. As initiator and secretary of Letters], he brought together ten people who would play a key role in a discipline which hardly existed in the Netherlands at the time. After graduating in 1982 he became an independent type designer, and was among the first of his group to sell a typeface. While exploring the production possibilities of digital technology, he continued to practise traditional crafts such as stone carving and calligraphy. Throughout the 1980s, he received assignments for monumental lettering, of which the Homo Monument in Amsterdam (1987) and the Bulthuis Monument in Bergum (1986, for the Dutch PTT) stand out. He wrote the book that accompanied a successful television course in calligraphy aired in 1991 and presented by Gerrit Noordzij[27]. He remained active as a writer, contributing opinionated articles to Dutch and international trade magazines. In 1990 Blokland created his current company, *Dutch Type Library* (DTL), the first and largest publisher of digital type in the Netherlands. Not only did DTL issue a collection of high-quality new text faces and superb revivals, the company also published a number of compact historical studies and organized seminars. DTL's latest new activity is the production and distribution of type design software: FontMaster, developed with German partner (URW)++ Software & Development GmbH, is marketed as a state-of-the-art tool for professional font production.[28]

House number carved by
Frank E. Blokland, mid-1980s.

Early typefaces

Upon graduating in 1982, Frank E. Blokland founded the company Script Design with former fellow student Jelle Bosma, and negotiated type design assignments with long-established companies such as Letraset. It was soon decided that the company did not have much of a future, due to a lack of business experience as well as unrest in the type market which made potential clients stop buying new work.

Blokland's first opportunity to sell a typeface came in 1984 when Chartpak, an American manufacturer of office stationery, held a competition for a new display type for transfer sheets. The next year, Chartpak published Blokland's *Bernadette*, a rather wide, sturdy roman which Blokland later said he regarded as an exercise: 'I designed Bernadette in a rather short time. I wanted to see if I was able to develop a product-oriented typeface.'[29] Although he was not totally unhappy with the result, and Bernadette was quite original at the time, the designer now considers it immature. There are more alphabets on which Blokland worked in the mid-1980s that have subsequently disappeared. *Berenice*, designed in Blokland's final year at art school, was a personal view of the modern-classic roman based on handwriting, much in the Van Krimpen tradition. Although a complete digital version was made, it remained unpublished, as did *Beatrice* (1985), an interesting step forward in the idiom of Dutch-style open-counter romans.

25 Both quotes are from an interview by Andy Crewdson on his now defunct
   website *Lines and Splines*, 2002.

26 Interview with Jelle Bosma.

27 Frank E. Blokland, *Kalligraferen, de kunst van het schoonschrijven*, TELEAC book, 1990.

28 This article is largely based on interviews and e-mail correspondence
   with Frank E. Blokland, 1997–2003; additional information from texts
   by Frank E. Blokland on the website www.dtl.nl.

29 'De letterklanken van Frank Blokland', in *Qwerty* 1 (1989), pp 10–13.

Speciaal met zijn hoofd hamerde de stoffige querulant bijzonder krachtig welgeteld vijf psalmen in oude berijming op de xylofoon.

Cellini was an alphabet of capitals designed for the Amsterdam Homomonument (a monument to homosexuals who have been the victims of war and intolerance); Blokland later began designing its lowercase, published as *Orfeo Roman* in a magazine article. In 1991 the German firm Scangraphic offered Blokland a lucrative deal to complete the typeface, but folded soon afterwards. An early type study for the Homo Monument resulted in a wide italic display face called *Bacchus* (1987). World Typeface Center, the New York company that had issued Jelle Bosma's *Cursivium*, was interested in publishing Bacchus and commissioned Blokland to design a matching roman; however, the publisher did not survive the advent of PostScript.

In the mid-1980s Frank Blokland was asked by a fellow-member of Letters], Petr van Blokland (not related), to assist him in the design of a typeface for small sizes. The sketches which resulted from this request were soon taken in different directions by the two designers, resulting in two rather different typefaces: Frank Blokland's DTL *Documenta* and Petr van Blokland's *Proforma*.

The evolution of Documenta

The first Documenta drawings date back to 1986. Blokland drew the typeface as a sort of reaction to his earlier attempts – determined to obtain the professional level he was aiming at and which he felt his other alphabets had failed to reach.[30] 'When designing a new typeface I have never relied on an historical model,' Blokland said in 1996. 'This is the reason why it took quite some time before I made a typeface that I was completely happy with.'[31] Documenta was that typeface.

Documenta was designed with openness and clarity in mind: a typeface made for long texts in small point sizes. Blokland: 'I wanted a very lucid form from which, in spite of the classical theme, all archaisms have been barred. Of course, there are historical features in Documenta, but that is because these features are in the latin script itself. It has serifs, it has arches, so it is inevitable that elements from the past slip in. But you can see my hand in Documenta, as in Bacchus and Cellini. In fact, I find these historical links quite interesting; it is a challenge to add something new within those conventions. There has never been a typeface I admired so much that it robbed me of the desire to create something new.'[32]

Documenta makes for pleasant reading; its roman is both neutral and contemporary. The italic had initially been drawn as a classical, subtly sloped, rather narrow alphabet with obvious traits of humanist calligraphy. It underwent several changes and ended up as something rather unusual; contrary to custom, the lowercase italic is slightly wider than the roman. This anomaly does not make the italic too conspicuous; it lends extra clarity to the typeface, especially in small sizes.

While other young type designers from The Hague and Arnhem experimented with the new Ikarus digitizing system from Hamburg's URW, Blokland decided to digitize Documenta the hard way: by drawing it on the screen of his Macintosh, pixel by pixel, with a program called Fontastic. It took him several years to complete the family, which included some weights (like an extra-bold and a swash alphabet) which the current vector version would lack for many years to come.

MacDocumenta, as the bitmap family was called, worked well in Quark XPress 2 and was first used in 1989 in a publication designed by Blokland;[33] the next year it was used in *Letters] en techniek*, the final publication by the work group Letters]. Of course, a bitmap font has several disadvantages over a vector-defined font: it takes up more memory, and cannot be scaled to a larger point size than the size it was drawn for. For Blokland, the experiment was the most direct way of digitizing his fonts for use

ABCDEFGH
IJKLMNOPQR
STUVWXYZ

Before Gutenberg equiped the scholar with the accuracy of type the task of duplicating manuscripts without variance was impossible. Connoisseurs in the fifteenth century deplored the new mass production of books but men of letters eagerly hailed the printing press as a method of disseminating knowledge in permanent form & the earliest printed books soon rivalled in beauty as they superseded in economy the fine manuscripts of their day

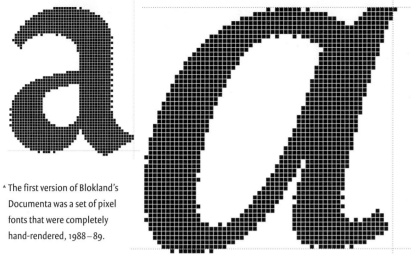

▴ The first version of Blokland's Documenta was a set of pixel fonts that were completely hand-rendered, 1988–89.

▸ Early sketches of Documenta.

on the Macintosh. And, as he wrote in *Letters] en techniek*: 'An advantage of designing type in the form of bitmaps is that the shape you see on the screen is actually what you are designing. [In the case of a vector description] the screen only gives an interpretation of what the typesetting machine will produce.' [34]

At the time when *Letters] en techniek* was being produced, Blokland was already working on the typeface's definite vector version, which progressed rather quickly thanks to the existing meticulous bitmaps. He now had a clear picture of how he wanted this and subsequent typefaces to be produced and marketed, making it possible to create his own foundry, Dutch Type Library or DTL, in 1990.

Originally in Zoetermeer, near The Hague, DTL is now based in 's-Hertogenbosch, where Blokland runs the company with his wife, Noortje Blokland-Pulles.

Creating a library

From the onset, Frank Blokland envisaged his collection as a type library with a clear programme. DTL focuses on text faces, with a preference for versatile, large families. Blokland has a strong aversion to typefaces that are derivative or nonchalantly made; in his articles in the trade press he often fulminates against what he perceives as lack of professionalism among type designers and publishers. He has pointed out that most large type libraries – companies that were once known for their professional rigour – now shy away from investing in serious design projects and bring out almost anything that is offered to them. Conversely, DTL's typefaces are exceptionally well made. Blokland encourages his designers to submit their fonts as semi-finished products, so that fine-tuning and production can be done in-house.

Blokland also wanted the DTL collection to be historically and conceptually sound. 'As a type foundry you need to have a clear and well-structured programme. Each new typeface you publish must have an added value: there should be no overlaps with very similar typefaces within the library. If you produce revivals, it is crucial that they bring something new to the market, too.' [35]

In the first decade of its existence, DTL did an exemplary job in realizing such an ambitious programme. Step by step, a collection was developed representing each period or style from 1500 to the present. *Nobel*, *Argo* and *Caspari* were three twentieth-century sanserifs from three different generations; Documenta was a modern traditional roman, followed in 1996 by a more calligraphic variation on the same theme, Elmo van Slingerland's *Dorian* (> p 202).

The adding of Gerard Unger's Argo to the Dutch Type Library was an important step for Blokland's company. In 1991, shortly after creating DTL, Blokland had founded another firm together with his former trainee Gerard Daniëls: the ambitiously named type production studio Type Unlimited International (TUI). One of the projects TUI took on was the production of Gerard Unger's newsface *Gulliver*. Being a specialist typeface for a limited market, Gulliver was to be sold by Unger himself. Yet

DTL Documenta

Regular *Italic* **Medium** *Italic*
Bold *Italic* SMALL CAPS
D SMALL CAPS TITLING CAPS
Sans Regular *Italic* SMALL CAPS

30 Sander Neijnens, *De onweerstaanbare letter*, self-published booklet, 1996.

31 Ibid., p 14.

32 Ibid., pp 14–16.

33 *De jaren zestig. Actie, kunst en cultuur in Leiden* (a book about the 1960s in Leyden). Blokland's display face Bacchus was used on the cover.

34 *Letters] en techniek*, Zaltbommel 1990, pp 49–50.

35 interview with Frank E. Blokland.

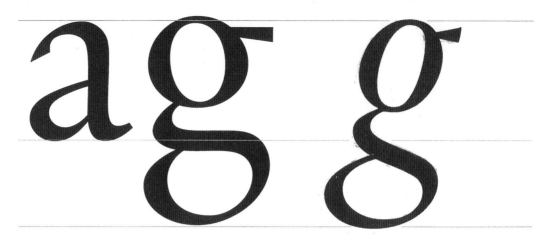

DTL VandenKeere-Italic   datum: –   –1995   tekenaar: ©1995 by Dutch Type Library

DTL VandenKeere

T Regular SMALL CAPS
D Regular *Italic* D Medium D Bold
SMALL CAPS

DTL Fleischmann

T Regular *Italic* T **Medium** *Italic*
T **Bold** *Italic* SMALL CAPS
D Regular *Italic* D Medium *Italic*
D **Bold** *Italic* SMALL CAPS
ch ct ffi ſſ ſh sp th *gg ch ct ffi ſſ ſh sp th*

his previous typeface, the sanserif *Argo*, did not yet have a home. Originally created for the hardware company Hell, Argo had been given back to its designer at the Linotype-Hell merger; Unger had then taken it to URW. In agreement with URW it was decided that the newly founded Dutch Type Library would be a better context for Argo, and DTL took over production. Thus Blokland's new foundry hit the market in 1992 with a winner – the sanserif companion to Unger's bestseller *Swift*. Argo was followed in 1993 by Blokland's own Documenta, Caspari and Elzevir by Gerard Daniels (> p 201) and the Nobel revival by Fred Smeijers and Andrea Fuchs (> p 242). In 1994–95 two remarkable revivals were published. DTL *VandenKeere*, designed by the DTL studio, was based on Hendrik van den Keere's *Paragon Roman* from c. 1575 (*Reale Romaine* in Plantin's 1585 specimen), punches of which are preserved in the Plantin-Moretus Museum in Antwerp. Professor H. Vervliet called it 'one of the truly outstanding designs originating in the Low Countries'.[36] The one-weight type was reworked into a family with separate text and display fonts – a very usable, bright alternative to *Garamond*. As Van den Keere had cut no italics, the italic to DTL Vanden-Keere was based on the *Ascendonica Cursive* by Van den Keere's predecessor as supplier of punches to Plantin, François Guyot, while new italic capitals were designed using Van den Keere's roman capitals as a starting point. DTL also planned to produce a revival of another Van den Keere type, one of his texturas; Matthew Carter was asked to design the font. It was announced (but not shown) as DTL *Flamande* in a 1996 German-language brochure[37]; it is due to come out in 2004.

The other revival was DTL *Fleischmann*. Ten years ago, nobody was particularly interested in eighteenth-century typefaces. So it was a stroke of great inspiration when, in late 1992, Frank Blokland commissioned the German type designer Erhard Kaiser (1957) to design a large family of text faces based on the work of Johann Michael Fleischman (> p 27). The eighteenth century has since come back in vogue (think of Matthew Carter's *Fenway*, Gerard Unger's *Paradox* and Fred Smeijers's *Arnhem*), but Kaiser's type family still stands out as an extraordinary performance. Kaiser – a type designer trained in the Eastern German tradition headed by Albert Kapr – studied all of Fleischman's romans as they had been reproduced in the 1806, 1825 and 1953 Enschedé specimens available to him at the Deutsche Bücherei Leipzig. Convinced that 'the conservation and careful reconstruction of the most valuable historical typefaces has nothing to do with nostalgia'[38], he tried to capture the *Zeitgeist* of the eighteenth-century Netherlands in a versatile type family of twelve weights, each equipped with an impressive arsenal of ligatures and alternate characters. Two complementing faces were distilled from Fleischman's twenty-four romans: a display version which uses the rococo gestures and curtsies to full effect; and a pleasant text face which, although simpler, does not shy away from picturesque detail.

The Jan van Krimpen project

The work of Jan van Krimpen has always been an important source of inspiration to Frank Blokland. He has issued several publications examining the connections between Van Krimpen and the English-speaking type world: in 1994 DTL and URW jointly published a booklet by Mathieu Lommen entitled *Jan van Krimpen & Bruce Rogers*[39]; shortly afterwards, Blokland co-edited an issue of *The Monotype Recorder* subtitled *The Dutch Connection* and dedicated to the collaboration between Monotype and Dutch type designers Jan van Krimpen and Chris Brand.

One of the contributors to the *Monotype Recorder* issue was Huib van Krimpen, son of Jan. Huib van Krimpen (1917–2002) was a gifted typographer in his own right, who worked in the Dutch tradition of modern-classic typography of which his father had set the norms. Yet he was an independent thinker, and as an author on typographic matters largely surpassed Jan van Krimpen in productivity, didactic talent and wit. He edited and commented on his father's writings in a way that was surprisingly critical. For instance, here is what he wrote about his father's *Monotype Memorandum*: 'Stylistically the text suffers from Jan van Krimpen's usual laborious prose, although the tone is less pompous than in some other pieces.'[40]

From 1986 onwards, Frank Blokland established a good personal and working relationship with Huib van Krimpen. They discussed the possibility of publishing a full-size facsimile of all of Jan van Krimpen's drawings of typefaces. When Huib van Krimpen found the drawings of *Haarlemmer* (1938), which had long been thought lost, at Monotype, he agreed to sell them to Blokland. The Haarlemmer typeface had remained unfinished, partly due to wartime circumstances, partly because it was judged a failure by its author (> p 61). Blokland argued that it was feasible and defendable to give the typeface a second chance, interpreting it from the drawings, the way Enschedé's punchcutter Rädisch had done with *Lutetia*, *Romanée* and other Van Krimpen designs. Blokland says that 'the Monotype version was too poor to be taken as reference. There was no reason to adopt the 18 unit system of the Monotype typefounding machine. The drawings were not literally digitized but interpreted, resulting in a typeface which corresponds as much as possible with the concept developed by Jan van Krimpen.'

In a letter to Huib van Krimpen, Blokland described the pleasure with which he embarked on the job. 'I find it relatively easy to enter into Jan van Krimpen's idiom; To me the rather wide italic was the main reason to revive this design: all Jan van Krimpen's italics are narrow, which can prove troublesome in the smaller sizes. I find the Haarlemmer italic unique and definitely a gain.'[41]

Blokland went on to design *Haarlemmer Sans*, a delicate humanist sanserif based on the Haarlemmer proportions, initially produced as a corporate font for the Rotterdam Museum Boijmans Van Beuningen. Like the sanserif version of Blokland's own Documenta, Haarlemmer Sans is still a small family which lacks a bold version; the main reason being, in all probability, that Blokland has been too involved in matters concerning type production and distribution to focus on his own designs. The Van Krimpen project was continued with the publication of two more typefaces. *Romulus* (2003) has been produced in agreement with Monotype, its original publisher. A digital version of *Sheldon*, Van Krimpen's idiosyncratic Bible face, has been in preparation since the mid-1990s and will be released in due course.

Preserving the near and distant past

Frank E. Blokland and his firm have made font production their specialization. This has made them an ideal partner for type designers who have a great talent for drawing letterforms but need outside expertise to produce workable, harmonic fonts. Chris Brand was one such designer. His *Albertina* had been produced for phototypesetting by Monotype in 1966, in a way that Brand was less than satisfied with, and has long been unavailable.[42] From 1993 onwards, DTL took up production of the digital Albertina, to which Brand made considerable contributions before his death in 1998. Albertina became the official face of the Royal Library in Brussels, the institution it had once been named after. In 1998, after consulting with (URW)++, DTL's partner in Hamburg, the European Union selected the typeface as its corporate

▼ DTL Haarlemmer (1995) is a new interpretation of Jan van Krimpen's original drawings for Haarlemmer. Haarlemmer Sans (1996) is its sanserif companion, designed by Frank E. Blokland.

▼ DTL Romulus was first presented in late 2003.

DTL Haarlemmer

Regular *Italic* **Medium** *Italic*
Bold *Italic* SMALL CAPS
Sans Regular *Italic* SMALL CAPS

DTL Romulus

T Regular *Italic* T **Medium** *Italic*
T **Bold** *Italic* SMALL CAPS
Display Poster SMALL CAPS

36 H.D.L. Vervliet, *Sixteenth-century Printing Types of the Low Countries*, Amsterdam 1968, p 252.

37 DTL Schriftenübersicht, May 1996.

38 Erhard Kaiser, *Schriftmuster der DTL Fleischmann*, 's-Hertogenbosch/Leipzig/Hamburg.

39 The book was also the first publication set in the definite version of the digital Documenta.

40 *The Monotype Recorder*, New Series, vol. 9, 1996, p 1.

41 Ibid., p 19.

42 According to Frank Blokland, Chris Brand has always maintained that Albertina was originally meant to be produced for Monotype hot metal line-casting machines.

DTL Fell, drawing for digitization with URW's Ikarus. The program is now incorporated in the FontMaster software jointly developed by Dutch Type Library and (URW)++ Software & Development GmbH.

typeface after a series of tests. The availability of a Greek version (drawn by Brand himself) was one of the deciding factors. A Cyrillic version was released in 2001.

The Fell project is a revival of a totally different kind. Unpublished to date, DTL Fell is based on an investigation into the famous Fell types, which John Fell, bishop of Oxford from 1675 until 1686, bought in the Netherlands and bequeathed to Oxford University Press. The English Roman and Italic in this collection are Dutch types ('English' is a body size, c. 12pt) which may have been bought from Abraham van Dijck, son of Christoffel. The DTL revival will in part be based on seventeenth- and twentieth-century books printed in the original Oxford Fell types. (> p 26)

When the Tetterode company hived off its type foundry, Frank Blokland obtained the right to digitize and market the Dutch typefaces designed for the Amsterdam Type Foundry. So far, this possibility has not been made much use of. DTL brought out Nobel – but that particular revival had been the initiative of two outside designers. A revival of Sjoerd de Roos's *Hollandse Mediaeval* was announced in a 1996 type specimen, but has been abandoned.

New faces: Paradox, Unico and Prokyon

During the past five years, DTL has published several more new typefaces by Dutch and foreign designers. Gerard Unger's *Paradox* – a personal interpretation of the late eighteenth-century style – is dealt with on pp 172 – 173. In 2002 DTL published a handsome little type specimen for Paradox, with a text by Frank E. Blokland.

DTL Unico (2000) is a new typeface by Michael Harvey (1931). Harvey, who was initially inspired by the work of the Dutch-German designer Helmut Salden, is one of the great innovators of the English lettering tradition. Typefaces by Harvey include *Ellington*, *Strayhorn*, *Braff* (Monotype); *Mezz*, *Andreas* and *Conga Brava* (Adobe). Most of these fonts are display alphabets based on the unique lettering styles which Harvey used in many of the 1500 or so book covers he has designed. Unico is an exception in that it has been conceived as a family of text fonts, developed in close collaboration between Harvey and Blokland. Like all other DTL typefaces, Unico is well-made and balanced: round and open, with subtle vertical stress. Yet it lacks some of the dash and swing of Harvey's other work. Perhaps the designers judged it necessary for a book face to be better behaved; but it may also result from the fact that the design by the jazzman Harvey passed through the somewhat homogenizing filter of the DTL studio – where the soundtrack is Bach rather than Bird.

In 2002 DTL published *DTL Prokyon* by Erhard Kaiser. Having been conceived immediately after Kaiser's *Fleischmann*, it is a completely different typeface. *Prokyon* is a rationalist sanserif based on what its designer calls 'Formreduktion' of the lowercase m and n – in other words, the elimination of the top serifs which in grotesques betrays their origin in the written letter. The idea is not completely new: it is visible in Hans Reichel's typefaces *Barmeno/Sari* and *Dax*, as well as in Gerard Unger's *Delftse*

DTL Fell

Regular *Italic* **Medium** *Italic*
Bold *Italic* SMALL CAPS ctffffifhſt
asesisusffiskſhſp *asesisusffiskſhſp*

DTL Paradox

Regular *Italic* Medium *Italic*
Bold *Italic* **Black** *Italic* SMALL CAPS

DTL Unico

Regular *Italic* Medium *Italic*
Bold *Italic* SMALL CAPS
абвгедҗзий АБВГЕДҖЗИЙ

DTL Prokyon

Light *Italic* Regular *Italic*
Medium *Italic* **Bold** *Italic*
SMALL CAPS

Poort; but the way in which the principle has been consistently adopted throughout the alphabet lends a special crispness to Prokyon's lowercase, as do the subtle curvatures of v, w, x, y and z. In large sizes, some quirky details show up – notably the top serif to the g, an anomaly in the otherwise clean-shaven font – whereas the rhythm in text sizes is even and pleasant. Prokyon is clearly not a *Dutch* typeface, but precisely for that reason is a valuable and innovative addition to the DTL library.

FontMaster

The font digitizing tool preferred by most Dutch designers of Blokland's generation was Ikarus, developed by URW's Peter Karow, and adapted for Macintosh computers by Petr van Blokland. Ikarus was pioneering software – the first to define letters as scalable outline forms – but as a product it was surpassed by cheap easy-to-use software such as Fontographer, which encouraged type designers to work directly on screen, or tweak existing data, while Ikarus is basically a tool for processing drawings that exist on paper.

In the mid-1990s, URW's successor (URW)++ Software & Development GmbH became an important business partner to DTL. Their working relationship enabled technicians at URW to use their skill for developing a new set of type design tools. Partly based on software developed at URW for font production on a SPARC workstation (under Solaris and Sun operating systems), FontMaster was developed 'with the experienced user in mind' and works on both Mac OS and Windows-based systems. Originally developed for exclusive use at the DTL studio, DTL FontMaster was made publicly available in 2002. The application is sold as a modular set of seven utilities: BezierMaster (a module for designing and editing letters in bezier format); BlendMaster (an interpolation tool); ContourMaster (for testing and correcting outlines); DataMaster (for generating and converting font formats), IkarusMaster (to edit the IK format); KernMaster (for generating and editing kerning pairs) and TraceMaster (for scanning and auto-tracing letters and logos).

Gerard Daniëls: Elzevir and Caspari

For about three years, Gerard Daniëls (1966) was Frank Blokland's business partner in the type production studio Type Unlimited International, whose clients included Gerard Unger, Mannesmann, Scangraphic and Monotype Typography. During that same period, in the early 1990s, Daniëls was also involved in the design of some of the first DTL typefaces.

Work on DTL *Elzevir* began in 1992 with a research of possible seventeenth-century models. Blokland was convinced that the current digital version of Monotype Van Dijck was virtually useless, and the world could use a better Van Dijck. It was decided not to take one single original as a starting point, but to put together a collection of types attributed to Van Dijck and distil them into a loose interpretation of the famous punchcutter's work. Although for Daniëls the job was an assignment – Blokland's initiative, not his own, and a revival too – he felt that in the process of finding the right shapes, the perfect combinations of details, he had sufficiently appropriated the design to call DTL Elzevir (1993) *his* typeface.[43]

Caspari (1993) was a more personal project. Daniëls had begun the typeface in 1989, when still a student at the KABK. Caspari was produced some years before Documenta Sans and Haarlemmer Sans were issued, and was therefore the first humanist sanserif in the DTL collection. It can be situated somewhere halfway between Gill Sans and Syntax, but its openness and simplicity lend it a typically Dutch quality. It also has beautifully shaped oldstyle figures and powerful real italics, which most sanserifs lacked at the time. Caspari is equipped with medium, bold and black weights, and is therefore the most extensive DTL family in its genre.

In 1995 Daniëls took over the Hague branch of the former typesetting company Eduard Bos and started up his own design and service bureau. Type Unlimited International was discontinued and Daniëls's type designing activities ground to a halt. Yet the plans to develop condensed and compressed varieties of Caspari are still

DTL Elzevir

Regular *Italic* Book *Italic* Medium *Italic* **Bold** *Italic* SMALL CAPS *ACKMQ* OPEN CAPITALS ct st ffi ft e *ases ct sp tt*

DTL Caspari

Regular *Italic* Medium *Italic* **Bold** *Italic* **Black** SMALL CAPS абвгед **абвгед**

43 Information supplied by Gerard Daniëls in an interview.

alive. DTL also holds an option on an interesting (but unfinished) family of romans and slab serifs called *Chirocco*, somewhat reminiscent – because of its square forms – of Hermann Zapf's *Melior*. An alphabet of beautifully drawn upright italics, named *Giacometti*, never advanced beyond its first, one-weight incarnation.

Elmo van Slingerland, calligrapher and type designer

When Elmo van Slingerland (1964) arrived at the KABK in 1989, he already had several years of training behind him. In the Graphic School of his native Rotterdam he had graduated as a paste-up artist and draughtsman. He had already discovered his love of and talent for letterforms, and had been attending several calligraphy workshops by the likes of Claude Mediavilla and Jovica Veljovic. He had even designed a printing typeface – 'very clumsy', he specifies. His choice to enrol in the Academy's typographic department – where Gerrit Noordzij was entering his last year as a teacher – was an informed one: he knew that the KABK was the place to be for an aspiring type designer.[44]

After graduating with honours in 1993, Slingerland set up the graphic design studio Ampère in Gouda. Since then, he has divided his time between three types of work: graphic design, type design, lettering and calligraphy. His versatility as a lettering artist is remarkable. His logos and signs cover a wide range of styles and atmospheres, each of which he seems to capture almost effortlessly. Van Slingerland was soon admitted into that small, worldwide circle of enthusiasts of the written letter, and his work has been shown in international exhibitions and magazines.

For several years, Elmo van Slingerland was a part-time assistant in the DTL studio. Among the projects he participated in were the small caps for Gerard Unger's Argo, published in 1995. His main project was his own typeface which came out in 1997 as *DTL Dorian*. The typeface was based on sketches made when Van Slingerland was still a student at the KABK. Frank Blokland commissioned him to work out the alphabet into a full-fledged font family, and monitored its design. Dorian was made to work well both in small sizes and as a headline face: its smart, subtle details, which are clearly rooted in the designer's penmanship, lend it a lot of character when used in large sizes; its low contrast and even appearance make for agreeable reading even at 8 pts or less – sizes at which the details do not impose themselves. The italic is both delicate and readable; drawn with the calligrapher's verve, restrained by the graphic designer's critical eye and sense of function.

DTL Dorian

Regular *Italic* **Medium** *Italic*
Bold ***Italic*** **Black** ***Italic***
Heavy ***Italic*** SMALL CAPS

PrinsWijn

Ratelband Research Institute

Erigeron mucronatus
Fuchsia paniculata
Gardenia augusta
Heliconia rostrata
Ismene festalis
Jacaranda
Kalanchoe manginii
Laurus nobilis

Peter Matthias Noordzij
and The Enschedé Font Foundry

Like his father Gerrit, Peter Matthias Noordzij has insight in letterforms, a keen eye for detail and a critical mind. He is also an extremely independent thinker, which has enabled him to map his own career, instead of following in Gerrit Noordzij's footsteps. Yet his father's teachings must have influenced him from an early age. When he and his elder brother Christoph were at elementary school, their father decided it would be a good idea to field-test his revolutionary ideas about the pedagogics of handwriting by giving writing lessons to children. So in addition to his position at the KABK, he became a part-time teacher in the village school. His sons quickly got used to it, says Peter Matthias Noordzij, 'and when Christoph and I went to study at the Academy, he simply was there again. I have never experienced this as limiting in any way.' Gerrit Noordzij's teaching method called for a particular kind of sensibility. 'He has invented a useful theory which helps you get a grasp of letterforms and fathom the endless possibilities of the craft. Those who understood him well could make very quick progress. But in every class there was only a handful of students who really appreciated and made sense of what he was doing.' [45]

In 1983 Gerrit Noordzij edited a booklet entitled *Letters in studie* ('Studying letterforms') in which the new generation of Dutch type designers was presented to the outside world for the first time. It featured work by Arnhem students like Fred Smeijers and Martin Majoor, as well as alphabets by students from Breda and Enschede, but it was the students and graduates of the KABK who stole the show. A double page in *Letters in studie* is devoted to the sketches for a new typeface which Peter Matthias conceived in his third year and which in due course would become PMN *Caecilia*.

Caecilia: an unprecedented confrontation

Caecilia, or *Academic*, as it was initially called, was the first typeface to successfully reconcile certain principles from the tradition of type design that were held to be incompatible. In his design Noordzij examined the possibilities of combining the idiom of the low-contrast *slab serif* or *egyptian* with the humanist letterforms suggested by handwriting. Gerrit Noordzij's translation principle, which traces back old-style type to the broad-nibbed pen, obviously served as a guideline. But whereas many students adopted this insight in classic-looking alphabets with a strong calligraphic streak, *Academic* brought about an unprecedented confrontation – as did Jelle Bosma's *Cursivium*, conceived at exactly the same time.

In Academic/Caecilia, as in Cursivium, the italic was the key to the solution. Instead of an oblique roman, it is a separate design which echoes humanist handwriting in showing 'a smooth transition from the upstroke into the stem' and because 'the Academic's italic is narrower than the roman' (Peter Matthias Noordzij). Unlike Bosma's design, Academic had a real roman, and the overall typographic sophis-

Peter Matthias Noordzij, early sketch of the typeface that would become PMN Caecilia, made during his third year at the Royal Academy.

44 Based on a conversation and e-mail correspondence with Elmo van Slingerland, 1998–99; additional information in Elmo van Slingerland, 'Vallen en opstaan', *Sciptores* vol. 9 no. 2, 1994, pp 10–11, and Michael Clark (ed.), *Scripsit*, vol. 19, no. 2.

45 Quotes taken from conversations with Peter Matthias Noordzij.

the quick brown fox jumps over a lazy dog

tication of an accomplished text face. It took over a year to further develop the design, which was presented as a graduation project in 1984.

Noordzij Jr. was convinced that his type deserved to be published. 'I had put a enormous lot of time into it and realized that I had found a solution to a problem that no-one had been able to solve before. Now in those days, you totally depended on the goodwill of the big type foundries. There was no question of digitizing a font yourself; the equipment you needed cost hundreds of thousands of guilders. I said to myself: if nobody is interested, on the basis of the material available, in producing and publishing that thing, I will choose a different trade.'

During an ATypI conference in London, drawings of Academic were shown as part of a small exhibition. Peter Matthias Noordzij met with type designer and Linotype consultant Adrian Frutiger, who immediately decided that the typeface qualified for publication. The specialists at Linotype, however, were less easily convinced. At their request Noordzij designed test words in a light and a bold version, which then were commented on and redrawn a couple of times. Meanwhile several companies – Bitstream, Monotype, ITC – were showing interest in the typeface. Finally, after almost a year of negotiations, an agreement was signed with Linotype in September 1986.[46] Noordzij asked Peter Verheul, a fellow member of the group Letters], to assist him in making the first seies of working drawings of the complete alphabet. Though production began just two months later, the family would take several years to complete. This was not only due to the designer's perfectionism, but also to the fact that Noordzij had found an ideal partner within Linotype: Werner Schimpf, head of the 'Schriftenatelier' (type workshop). Their collaboration was a decisive factor in Caecilia's ultimate success. Schimpf challenged Noordzij to question his assumptions and made valuable suggestions for subtle improvements. The italics, for instance, were slanted by 1 to 2 degrees more to distinguish them better from the roman (which in itself is slanted by 0.5 degrees); the serifs were made less heavy and the weights were adjusted. The outcome was an extensive family in four weights, from light to heavy; at Noordzij's insistence small capitals and mediaeval figures were included for all weights. As the work proceeded it became necessary to give the face its definite name. 'Academic' did not seem such a good idea after all. *Claudius* was already taken, *Gaudium* was rejected because of the association with Frederic Goudy. Finally, Noordzij proposed the current name, as a tribute to his colleague and wife Marie-Cécile Noordzij-Pulles. PMN *Caecilia* was released by Linotype in 1991.

The Enschedé Font Foundry

By the time Caecilia came out, Peter Matthias Noordzij was already involved in another monster project: digitizing Bram de Does's typeface *Trinité*, a task that would ultimately lead to the establishment of The Enschedé Font Foundry.

PMN Caecilia

Light Italic Roman *Italic* **Bold** *Italic*
Heavy *Italic* SMALL CAPS LIGHT ITALIC
REGULAR ITALIC **BOLD ITALIC**
HEAVY ITALIC Hij is geen afgekoeld dweeper, geen scepticus geworden idealist, geen *esprit revenu*, zooals de Franschen zeggen, maar een warm gebleven omgekeerde, een ongeloovige opgevuld met bekeeringsijver, een apostel in de huid van een renegaat, en daardoor meestentijds een *fanfaron de radicalisme.*

Paul Valéry
Het kerkhof
bij de zee

▾ Drawing of a Trinité glyph,
marked for Ikarus digitization.

⅄ Production of the digital
Romanée showing enlarge-
ments of the soot proofs and
printed matter of the Romanée.

Working for Enschedé in Haarlem, Bram de Does had designed his face between 1978 and 1982 for the imagesetters manufactured by the Swiss company Bobst/Auto-logic. When photocomposition was gradually replaced by digital equipment, Trinité – one of the most interesting Dutch typefaces of the twentieth century – was in danger of extinction. Noordzij talked about the matter to De Does, whom he knew superficially. 'I found De Does's work extremely intriguing. He had made a typeface which was in no way compatible with my father's theoretical principles, but which I admired immensely. I suggested Bram could do the digitizing himself with Ikarus M, but he was reluctant to get acquainted with yet another technology. So when Enschedé agreed on the digitization, Bram asked me for the job; that seemed a nicer idea than working with some firm in Switzerland.'

Digitizing Trinité, a complex design as well as a large family, took nearly two years. During the final round it became clear that Trinité's future was still uncertain. 'When we asked Enschedé what their plans were,' says Noordzij, 'the answer was not very satisfying. They simply wanted to put Trinité on the list of typefaces available for typesetting. So I made a kind of expense-profit analysis: how much would it cost to have two people work full-time on a project for almost two years, and what did they think could be made from composition jobs done with the typeface? I had the impression that the face was, more than anything, a matter of prestige to them. I believed that one ought to look at it from a more businesslike point of view: you can earn back your investment by licensing fonts.'

The time was ripe for a radical change at Enschedé. The firm had outgrown its location in the Haarlem city centre, where it had resided for 250 years. The printing office was to be moved to newly built premises on the outskirts of the city; the management decided not to take along the old typefounding machines and discontinue the production of metal type. Peter Matthias Noordzij tried to convince them that the new version of Trinité could be the beginning of a new life as a publisher of digital fonts. His ideas were not given a very warm reception. But when Noordzij ventured to propose an alternative solution in the shape of a small-scale foundry of which he would be the principal, the reactions were unanimously positive. Thus the type foundry of Joh. Enschedé en Zonen, set up in 1743, was continued by The Enschedé Font Foundry (TEFF), a one-man company run from Noordzij's home office on a river dike in the central Netherlands.

Building a library

TEFF officially has the right to market digital versions of the typefaces in Enschedé's former letterpress library – including most of Jan van Krimpen's types. So far, this possibility has not been made much use of. This is mostly a result of Noordzij's uncompromising perfectionism; besides, he is convinced that investing time and money in the creation or revival of a typeface can only be justified when it effectively fills a void – when it is 'necessary' from the typographer's point of view.

There is also the question of copyrights. For instance, TEFF has acquired the right of use of Jan van Krimpen's designs for Enschedé. But in some cases it has to share this right with Monotype, while most copyrights are owned by the Van Krimpen estate. This has not led to actual problems but it has created a somewhat hazy situation. Notably, the Dutch Type Library of former fellow-student Frank E. Blokland has acquired the rights to revive two Van Krimpen typefaces, collaborating closely with Monotype and with Van Krimpen's son Huib van Krimpen (who died in early 2002). This combination of factors is a reason why TEFF has taken up only one Enschedé revival so far: Jan van Krimpen's *Romanée*, his most elegant typeface according to many. *Romanée* was digitized by Peter Matthias Noordzij and Fred Smeijers. A preliminary version of it was used (by Martin Majoor) as early as 1995 in *Adieu Æsthetica en Mooie Pagina's*, a book that accompanied an exhibition of Jan van Krimpen's work at the Museum of the Book in The Hague. The definitive version of the digital *Romanée* is still in preparation.

It is no exception that considerable time passes between a TEFF typeface's first use and the moment it becomes generally available as a font family. *Lexicon* by Bram de Does made its debut in the twelfth edition of the *Van Dale* dictionary (1992), to be

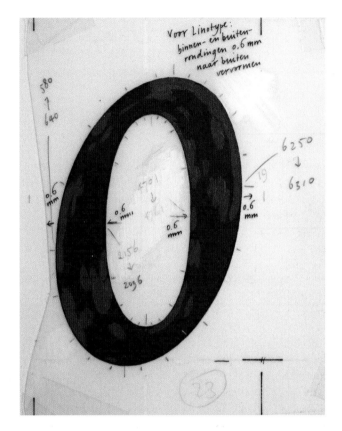

46 Extensive information about the design and production of Caecilia in Max Caflisch, 'Eine neue Egyptienne: die PMN Caecilia', in *Typografische Monatsblätter*, Heft 5, 1993.

Romanée
Romanée

ABCD abcdefghijklm

ABCD *abcdefghijklmnopq*

published three years later; in 1997, TEFF and De Buitenkant issued a Lexicon specimen, beautifully designed by Marie-Cécile Noordzij-Pulles. Fred Smeijers's Van den Keere revival *Renard* also needed a long incubation period. Originally designed in 1992 and first used in Smeijers's *Counterpunch* in 1996, the face was finally published in the fall of 2001. This, too, was due to Noordzij's relentless quest for quality. 'A typeface is not released until it is finished. It is possible that a graphic designer or a client informs us that he would like to use a typeface for a specific end. In that case, knowing the precise requirements, we may decide to make a dedicated version for that particular use. We know the point sizes in which the type will be used, and therefore what precision and amount of details are needed. A typeface marketed as a finished font must be able to do a whole lot more. The user must be able to adopt it in very large or very small sizes without being disappointed. In this respect I demand a lot from a type design.'

In addition to the Romanée revival, the company's most important type project for the coming years is probably the production of Gerrit Noordzij's typefaces. Unlike Bram de Does, Noordzij Sr. has digitized his own typefaces on the Macintosh. This was done purely for the designer's own use, so that any imperfections could be solved in the typography and typesetting. As 'final editor' Peter Matthias Noordzij has a complex task: each font must be brought in line with TEFF's quality criteria without touching on the designer's vision. At times, the collaboration has led to passionate discussions. At the moment of this writing, a number of Gerrit Noordzij fonts are in preparation. According to Peter Matthias Noordzij, 'Gerrit Noordzij has been as productive and versatile a type designer as, for instance, Frutiger, but due to circumstances nothing was ever published. Now this will finally happen.'

The Enschedé Font Foundry is more than a type foundry: it is also a typographic design studio. Van Dale, the publisher of Holland's most renowned dictionaries, is still one of their main clients. In the dictionaries made for Van Dale, type customizing is often used as a means to optimize the automatic typesetting of the books. The designers hired by the TEFF studio – Paul van der Laan, Bas Smidt, Simone van Rijn and Jacques Le Bailly – are typographers as well as type designers. As in the earliest days of printing, the production of type and the design of printed matter are brought together in one integrated process.

wezen vereert ⊚ *persoon* ⊚ *dienaar* ⊚ *afgodendienaar, zon-aanbidder* ② iem. die een ander het hof maakt ⊚ *bewonde-raar* ♦ een stille aanbidder²

¹aan·bie·den [wk ww, bood aan, aangeboden] ① (van zaken) zich vertonen, zich voordoen ⊚ *voorkomen* ② ⟨Belg.⟩ zich melden

aan·dacht [de] ① bewuste, gerichte belangstelling ⊚ *ge-hoor* ⊚ *afwezigheid* ⊚ concentratie, exposure, extraversie, mede-leven, toewijding

aan·dui·ding [de (v)] ① dat waardoor men aanduidt ⊚ AAD, ADD, beschermingsfactor, DDD, *functieaanduiding, omschrij-ving, vingerzetting, vocalisatie, wegaanduiding* ② het aandui-den ⊚ *betekenis* ⊚ *denotatie* ⊚ *adres, vintage* ③ ⟨Belg., niet alg.⟩ benoeming ⊚ *aanstelling*

aan·een [bw] ① aan elkaar vast ♦ woorden aaneen schrij-ven

²aan·ha·ken [onov ww, haakte aan, aangehaakt, -king] ① (van schaatsenrijders) de rechterhand in de op de rug gehouden linkerhand van een voorganger leggen en zo meerijden ⊚ *schaatsen* ② ⟨sport⟩ aansluiting vinden, bv. bij een groep renners ⊚ *aansluiten* ⊚ *aanpikken*

¹aan·ha·len [ov ww, haalde aan, aangehaald] ① (ook abs.); haalde aan, aangehaald] (een mens, dier) vleiend naar zich toe halen ⊚ *liefkozen* ⊚ *knuffelen, kroelen* ② (ook abs.) [haalde aan, aangehaald] citeren ③ *aantrekken, verstevi-gen* ④ (iets moeilijks) beginnen ⊚ *zich belasten met* ⊚ *zich iets op de hals halen* ♦ de /broekriem*/buikriem/ aanha-len³; de teugels aanhalen³; de vriendschapsbanden aan-halen³ met iem.

aard·kun·de [de (v), -kundig, -kundige] ① wetenschap die de bouw en de ontwikkelingsgeschiedenis van de aard-korst bestudeert ⊚ *geologie* ⊚ *agrogeologie, fotogeologie, pa-leontologie, sedimentologie, seismologie, tektoniek, vulka-nologie*

bed [het, ~den] zie ook **bedding** ① slaapmeubel voor mensen, met matras en toebehoren ⊚ *ledikant, legerstede, nest, sponde* ⊚ *bedstee, bovenbed, boxspring, brits, couchette, eenpersoonsbed, gipsbed, harmonicabed, hemelbed, hoogslaper, huwelijksbed, kooi, kraambed, logeerbed, onderbed, opklapbed, stapelbed, stretcher, strobed, tweepersoonsbed, twijfelaar, verlos-bed, vouwbed, waterbed, wieg, ziekbed, ziekenhuisbed* ② plaats in een verpleeginrichting ③ leger van wild ④ onderlaag van een weg ⊚ *ondergrond* ⊚ *kiezelbed, rijsbed, stortebed* ⑤ afgeperkte en/of verhoogde plaats in een tuin, waarop bloemen of gewassen gekweekt worden ⊚ *perk* ⑩ bed-ding van een rivier ⊚ *rivierbedding*

¹a [de] ① 100 m² ⟨are⟩

²a [de, a's, a'tje] ① de eerste letter van ons alfabet ② zesde toon van de diatonische en tiende toon van de chromati-sche toonladder, uitgaande van de grondtoon c ⊚ *muziek-noot* ♦ de A¹ van Anna; wie a¹ zegt, moet ook b zeggen wie eenmaal met iets begonnen is, moet daarmee door-gaan; van a¹ tot z geheel en al

a- ① niet- ⟨voor uitheemse grondwoorden⟩ ♦ asociaal, atechnisch

à [vz] ① ⟨tussen zeker getal en een hoger getal om een hoe-veelheid ongeveer te bepalen⟩ ② per eenheid ⟨bij prijs-aanduidingen⟩ ♦ 20 a¹ 25 minuten; 5 meter à² 6 euro, is 30 euro

A4'tje [het, A4·tje, ~s] ① vel papier met het formaat 210 × 297 mm

aai /jelsløtˈʌl/ [de (m), ~en] ① liefkozing waarbij men met de hand over de huid strijkt ⊚ *streling* ♦ iem. een aai over zijn bol geven

aai·baar·heids·fac·tor [de (m.)] ① ⟨scherts.⟩ mate waarin een mens of dier geschikt is om geaaid of geknuffeld te worden ⊚ *graad*

aai·en [aaide, geaaid] ① zacht met de hand over iets heen

Christoph Noordzij, Collis and Thalys

Like his brother Peter Matthias, Christoph Noordzij considers himself first and foremost a typographer and book designer. The design of a new typeface to him is not an autonomous process – it is triggered by a well-defined personal need or, as was the case for the *Thalys* typeface, a precise commission.

When designing book jackets and posters for the publisher Van Oorschot and other clients, Christoph Noordzij felt the need for a typeface which could easily be used in reverse printing: a typeface with a 'classic' look, low contrast and relatively short ascenders and descenders. The alphabet he designed for this purpose was initially named *Collage*, after his design company: the name was later changed into *Collis*. It was immediately used on several book covers; Christoph Noordzij was so pleased with his design that he decided to make it the starting point for an entire family. The chance to develop it further came when Theologischer Verlag Zürich, a Swiss publisher of religious books, commissioned him to design the *Neue Zürcher Bibel*.

This 'Zurich Bible' is not one book, but a large series of editions of the Bible or parts of it, intended for different markets, from schools to the scholarly community. Each title was to be published in a one-column layout as well as a space-saving two-column layout; each was to be produced in several formats, from pocket to pulpit size. These variants would not be made by simply enlarging or reducing a standard layout, but were to be separate designs. The content, too, was variable, as the editions for a young or large public had sparse comments and the scholarly editions were amply annotated. There were to be 120 volumes in all, produced with automated typesetting based on one single copy file, coded to generate text files for each level of readership.

'Given the complexity of this assignment', wrote Christoph Noordzij, 'it was inevitable that the typeface chosen would have to be customized; but we might face copyright problems when working with an existing typeface. I therefore chose to rework the beta version of Collis – which had proved to work well in small point sizes – into a dedicated Bible font.' [47]

The definite version of Collis has the basic qualities needed for a bible face – it is robust and space-saving. It also has some features specifically designed for the automated production of a German-language Bible. Accented uppercase characters are slightly smaller than standard uppercase characters, so that leading is less influenced by the frequent use of the Umlaut (Ä, Ö, etc.) in German. As the official German grammar, the Duden, forbids the use of ligatures in composite words (such as a fi ligature in Schiffingenieur), it was necessary to design an f with – as Noordzij puts it – 'too short a flag'. In order to have complete control over the many numerals used in an annotated Bible, several different kinds of figures were included. One of the most remarkable things about Collis is that, despite the complexity of the job it was designed for, it has remained a one-weight family – be it equipped with small caps, italics and swash capitals. For typographers who can live without bolds, Collis is one of the clearest and most harmonious book faces around.

The other three typefaces designed by Christoph Noordzij are custom display alphabets. They were commissioned from him by Jelle van der Toorn Vrijthoff, then a senior designer at Total Design (renamed Total Identity).

When Al-Futtaim, a trading company in Dubai, needed a replacement for its 1970s logo by Wim Crouwel, a dual alphabet was designed as a basis for new trademarks. Noordzij designed the Western version – a sturdy upright italic with asymmetric serifs – whereas a matching Arabic set was designed by Mamoun Sakkal.

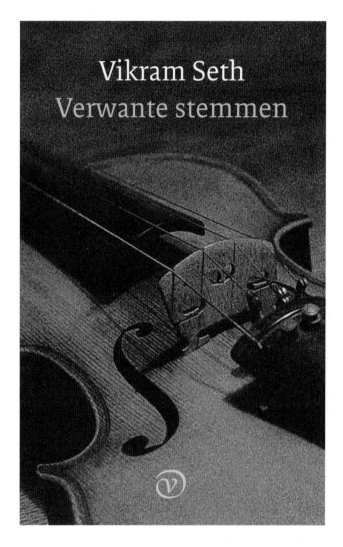

Christoph Noordzij, book cover designed with the Collis typeface, 2003.

47 E-mail to the author. This article is based on information provided by Christoph Noordzij, Jelle van der Toorn Vrijthoff and Peter Matthias Noordzij, in person, by phone and by e-mail.

A corporate identity for the Chocolate Museum in Cologne, Germany, an initiative of Stollwerck chocolate manufacturers, was a perfect alibi for making typography based on an old Dutch tradition: chocolate letters. (> p 32)

The assignment for the Thalys alphabet initially consisted solely of a logotype design. The logo was part of Total Design's entry to a competition for the visual identity of an international highspeed train. Noordzij: 'When the train's name was changed during the preliminary design process, Total Design was confronted with an impracticable situation. In order to stay ahead of the competition – TD were pitching against a number of renowned European design firms – it was necessary to be able to produce a new logo quickly, and adapt it to stationery, signage, a train model, etc. So it was decided to draw an entire alphabet and set of figures, which allowed for logos to be designed instantaneously.'

The caps-only Thalys alphabet has conspicuous, asymmetric serifs which literally give the logotype wings. The slant given to the characters enhances the sense of speed. The vignette of a woman's profile, designed by Total Design's Monique Coffeng, was slightly adapted to incorporate certain shapes of the alphabet, notably the O and Q. The idea of drawing a complete alphabet may have won Total Design the assignment. 'When the train's name had finally been established, all other agencies had to get back to work on new logos. As Total Design had nimbly skipped that part of the process, they could concentrate on filling in the rest of the concept using the ready-made logotype.'

Although Christoph Noordzij has designed several logotypes and custom display alphabets, his main activities are in editorial design. He runs his studio Collage in the Northern village of Aldeboarn, where he collaborates with his wife and business partner Nina Noordzij-Everts. In their book designs and cover designs for the Van Oorschot publishing house in Amsterdam – an ongoing assignment which Collage has gradually taken over from Gerrit Noordzij – he has made ample use of his own Collis, as well as typefaces by other Hague designers.

Collis

Roman *Italic* EXPERT ROMAN *ITALIC*
Swash *Roman Itálic* Doch des te meer licht valt op Gutenberg's beéld, die hier voor het eerst in 1434 áls maintzer uitgewékene te Straatsburg optreedt, zich reeds in 1439 áldaar in een proces met een géldschieter gewikkéld ziet, steeds voortgaat de patricische industrieél te zijn, waarvoor men hem van het begin af leert kennen, onafgebróken vervúld is met de gedachte aan eene kostbare uitvinding, in wier exploitatie door verschillende kapitálisten géld gestóken wordt.

Collwerck

ABCDEFGHIJKLMNOPQRSTU
VWXYZ
abcdefghijklmnopqrstuvwxyz
1234567890
fh fj ff fk fb ffh ffj ffi ffb

LettError, or the ghost in the machine

By the end of the 1980s, the personal computer – and specifically the Macintosh – had become the type design and production tool par excellence. For type designers who had used other methods before, the new process brought about important changes. The new medium changed the way decisions were made and tasks were distributed. Nevertheless most designers regarded the computer as a tool to do the same job in a different way. Yet the Mac can do a lot more than calculate and remember the positions of curves and points. It is a computing machine with a relatively open architecture: every software developer can teach the beast new tricks. Few designers ever reach this level of familiarity with the insides of their machines. More often than not, they tend to adapt their ideas to what the standard software can and will do. [48]

Just van Rossum (1966) and Erik van Blokland (1967) did not settle for that. In their hands, the Mac became a typographic magic box. By asking lucid questions, proposing adventurous alternatives, inventing modifications to existing software and playing typographic games with boyish open-mindedness, LettError helped digital type come alive, both on paper and on screen.

'Working apart together' would be an apt description of their partnership. Both work from their respective homes, and even when both living in The Hague they never shared a studio. Today, many of their conversations take place via a personalized e-mail server. Van Rossum and Van Blokland have been each other's sounding boards and sternest critics. Under the joint label of 'LettError' they have been challenging the habits and assumptions of the typographic mainstream. Yet they are not a team in the traditional sense. Both have their own clients; the typefaces they have designed betray different sensibilities. The only typefaces that were co-signed by both are their well-known 'intelligent' typefaces *Beowolf* (1990) and *Twin* (2003).

When they became design students at the Hague Royal Academy (KABK), Just and Erik each had ample computer expertise. In fact, they are part of the first generation that got a chance to grow up with the home computer. Van Rossum recalls that in 1981 his father bought a Sinclair ZX81, the kind of pre-PC desktop computer you hooked to your television screen. 'Programming in Basic was about the only useful thing it let you do. This turned out to be the perfect way of mastering the computer's principles.' Van Blokland: 'For both of us, learning how to use computers was a very natural thing. We were both professed into the Mac before it was introduced at art school.'

The beginning of a beautiful friendship

Van Rossum had enrolled at the KABK in 1984, a year before Van Blokland. He knew Petr van Blokland's reputation as a typographic computer wizard, but did not meet Petr's younger brother Erik until Gerrit Noordzij grabbed them both by the arm in

Erik van Blokland, shopfront of the LettError website, 2002.

48 This article is based on several interviews and informal conversations with Just van Rossum and Erik van Blokland. It contains fragments of an early piece: 'Graven in bits & bytes. De letterterreur van Erik van Blokland en Just van Rossum', in: *Items* vol. 15 no. 2, 1996, and of an article in the LettError book: Erik van Blokland and Jan Middendorp, 'Why? Tools.' in Els Kuijper (ed.), *LettError*, Nuth 2000.

JustLeftHand

ErikRightHand

JvR EvB

^ The digitized handwriting of Just van Rossum and Erik van Blokland, marketed together as FF Hands (1990), epitomize the pair's attitude to type: personal, playful and professional.

▶ ErikRightHand as used on a German milk carton.

▾ Just van Rossum was co-designer of Erik Spiekermann's Officina Serif (1990). Rossum Book (1990) and Juniper (1989) are both unfinished and un-published text faces by Van Rossum. FF Brokenscript (1990) is his slightly ironic view of blacklettter.

Officina Serif
Roman *Italic* **Bold** *Italic*

Rossum Book
Roman *Italic*

Juniper

Brokenscript
Bold Rough Condensed Rough

the school corridor, introduced them to each other and said: 'I think the two of you ought to talk.' Thus Noordzij's (possibly apocryphal) version of the story.

Their first joint project took place in 1988, when a group of Hague students were commissioned to create the signage for an exhibition in Amsterdam entitled 'The Netherlands as design, now'.[49] Erik and Just convinced Apple Computers to sponsor the exhibition and provide the means for creating the lettering on a Mac. It was one of the first KABK projects in which the computer was used. By the time they prepared their graduation projects, the Mac Plus had become part of their toolbox.

Hand-made sketches and drawings would, however, continue to be an important element of their work. Both Van Rossum and Van Blokland are able draughtsmen. Van Blokland's witty Typoman cartoons and animations are a running gag in their international lectures; Van Rossum's drawings show his talent for creating stark, simple images with a strong personality. It is this natural ability to translate ideas into images that makes even their most experimental and irreverent typefaces – some of which seem ready-made copies of existing alphabets, but have in fact been subtly adapted to their idiosyncratic but acute aesthetics – such a joy to watch. This is also true of their handwriting, which was digitized into two complete fonts and successfully marketed by FontShop as *JustLeftHand* and *ErikRightHand* (1990).

Like the other designers in this chapter, they were influenced by Noordzij's theories about printing type as a form of writing. Noordzij's analysis, says Van Rossum, 'was a way to recognize how other designers work, and to understand why typefaces from a particular era have certain shapes. It questions traditional classifications, which are too often based on outward appearances. According to his system, *Gill Sans* is more akin to *Bembo* than to most other sanserifs; this analysis can clarify a lot of things.' Which is not to say that they uncritically followed Noordzij's examples.

After graduating in 1988, Just van Rossum was given a work placement at Erik Spiekermann's MetaDesign in Berlin. His first major assignment was to finish Spiekermann's new typeface *Officina*. According to Van Rossum, his task consisted mainly in 'cleaning up curves and removing some idiosyncracies that, after my stern Hague education, hurt my eyes.' Impressed with his trainee's skills, Spiekermann soon hired Van Rossum as a paid employee and credited him as co-designer of *Officina Serif*. When Van Blokland graduated the next year, he too was invited to join the ranks at MetaDesign. In Berlin, their collaboration hit it off in a big way. Then as now, they seldom worked jointly on a single project. After an initial brainstorm session, tasks are allocated and each goes his own way. Yet many concepts are the product of their continuous interaction. 'There are many ideas that cannot be credited to one or the other,' they specify.

The beauty of random behaviour

One such idea was the concept of 'randomfonts' that was hatched in Berlin. The basic idea is simple. A font is a piece of software instructing a printer to perform a task, so it should be possible to randomize the output by adding a new set of instructions. At the 1989 ATypI conference the idea of the randomfont was presented in a little newspaper called *LettError* – the first time the name of their joint venture was used. To understand the principle of randomfonts, an elementary understanding of PostScript is necessary. PostScript is the (programming) language that was developed by Adobe for communication between computers and printers. PostScript fonts are typefaces specifically digitized for this language. They are drawn by means of vector outlines; only in the printer or image processor is the type translated into

◄ The LettError booklet presented at the 1989 ATypI conference was the first publication on which Just van Rossum and Erik van Blokland collaborated.

▲ Example of Beowolf output at a high degree of distortion: each letter is different.

▼ Beowolf (1990) is a 'random-font' with a built-in function to change the outlines while printing. Beo Sans (1992) is a sanserif based on the same principle.

a shape of the right size, made up of black dots. Each PostScript glyph is defined by a number of instructions: draw a line from point A to B (lineto), then draw a curve to C (curveto), etc. Van Blokland and Van Rossum 'hacked' PostScript by adding a new function named 'freakto': draw a line or curve to a random point near B. The random principle was then adopted to a classic roman typeface called *Kwadraat* (no relation to Fred Smeijers's *Quadraat* family) which Van Blokland had designed as a school project. The result was *Times New Random*, later renamed *Beowolf*, a typeface that changes while it is being printed. No two shapes are identical. What you see is not what you get: the shapes on the screen do not change. Based on the same principle, Van Rossum would later design two sanserif versions: *Beo Sans Hard* and *Beo Sans Soft*. Beowolf was conceived as a personal reaction to the total perfection that had been achieved by sophisticated revivals such as *Adobe Garamond*. 'It is the kind of perfection that has been striven after for five centuries,' says Van Blokland. 'But now that we have reached that point, something seems to have been lost.' Beowolf was an attempt to regain the liveliness of letterpress by digital means. Van Rossum and Van Blokland admit they found the letters that resulted from their experiments too ugly to be taken seriously. But the enthusiasm of their colleagues at MetaDesign encouraged them to look at the type as a marketable product.

In 1990, FF Beowolf was the very first typeface released by FontShop; it helped establish FontShop's name as a foundry to be reckoned with, and marked LettError's

Beowolf

R21 R22 R23 Doch al het overige is advokaterij, haspelen van geleerden onderling, oorzaak tot meesmuilen voor het toeschouwend publiek,

Beo Sans

R11 Soft **Bold** R12 Soft **Bold** R13 Soft **Bold** R21 Hard **Bold** R22 Hard **Bold** R23 Hard **Bold** welks gezond verstand er zich steeds zwijgend tegen verzetten zal, dat ter wille eener zoo schamele vischvangst zooveel water troebel wordt gemaakt.

49 'Nederland nu als ontwerp', Beurs van Berlage, Amsterdam 1988.

 LettError on the history of Trixie

LettError on the history of Trixie

the trixie files

THE TRUTH IS IN HERE

^ One of Erik van Blokland's Typoman comics, 1994.

▸ Trixie's capital X became a star in her own right by playing a major role in the original logo of the television series *The X Files*. A parody of a famous image from the series was seen on the LettError website (c. 1997) announcing *The Trixie Files*, the story of how Trixie came about.

▾ The four variants of Erik van Blokland's FF Trixie (1991), plus three of the 'found' alphabets from Van Rossum's package FF InstantTypes (1992).

Trixie

Light Text extra Cameo

Stamp Gothic

DYNAMOE

FLIGHTCASE

breakthrough in typographic circles. Several months later the FontFont label was introduced with the release of yet more Dutch typefaces by Max Kisman, Martin Majoor, Peter Verheul and LettError.

Type as idea

Beowolf was followed by a series of typefaces of impressive variety – some commissioned, most of them issued in the FontFont library. During the first half of the '90s, hardly any LettError typeface was created for purely aesthetic reasons, or as a problem-solving device. Each design was the illustration of a idea or principle – a demonstration that things could be done in a different way. Not surprisingly, many of these inventions have been taken up by other designers. However, their success did not just depend on the newness of the idea; it was also based on the quality and thoroughness of the design.

Take FF *Hands*, the handwritten fonts that became one of the early bestsellers of the FontFont library. These fonts were probably the first of their kind; other type designers, such as the American Chank Diesel, have digitized hundreds of handwritings since. Yet the unselfconscious elegance of *ErikRightHand* and *JustLeftHand* (Just van Rossum being left-handed) have charmed graphic designers ever since; the fonts ended up in such disparate places as a Sting album cover and posters of the right-wing Christian Democratic party in Germany.

Trixie (1991) was probably even more influential. The real Trixie was a friend in Berlin, Beatrix Günther, who owned an old typewriter of unspecified make. To Erik van Blokland, its letters were the archetype of the old-fashioned, seasoned typewriter type.[50] He digitized its output in various grades of muckiness. As printers around 1990 could only handle only relatively small font files, a fair amount of editing by hand had to be done in order to minimize the number of outline points. *Trixie Text* – a less detailed version of *Trixie Plain* – was added as a convenient compromise for body copy. After a slow start, FF Trixie was increasingly adopted by graphic designers to signify irreverence, informality and youth and became one of the archetypes of 'the vernacular' in typography. So did *InstantTypes* (1992), a package of five 'ready-made' fonts that Van Rossum created from found material, including a children's stamp box (FF *Stamp Gothic*), a strip from Dymo lettering pincers (FF *Dynamoe*) and stencil lettering from shipping boxes (FF *Flightcase*).

Some of the LettError font names – such as the 'Gothic' used for the Stamp typeface – betray a tongue-in-cheek approach to the conventions of typography. Yet, contrary to numerous derivatives that have been published in low-budget font collections more recently, their treatment of ready-made type is just as thorough as that accorded to any of their more serious fonts.

Of the two, Van Rossum seems to be most interested in the design of functional text typefaces. His sanserif additions to the Beowolf family, *Beo Sans Hard* and *Beo Sans Soft*,

◄ The five weights of Advert Rough (1992) are carefully spaced for layering.

▼ The 'Flipperfont' Kosmik (1993) has three versions of each character which are automatically alternated

▼ Schulschrift (1992) comes with a program called Scripter to create a smooth script combining alternate characters and joints.

▷ Corporate font family for the GAK, an administration agency of the Dutch government, designed by Just van Rossum in 1996–98.

work well in a more conventional context. His attractive sanserif FF *Advert* has been used in body text on CD packaging and music magazines but was also chosen for the logo of the Dutch airline company Transavia. *Advert Rough* is a more experimental typeface derived from it. Developed around the same time as Neville Brody's *Blur*, Advert Rough plays a similar game with softened renderings of the letterform. Unlike Blur, its weights – going from light to black – are carefully spaced for layering. Van Rossum also designed a classically proportioned seriffed roman called *Rossum*. It was shown at the 1989 ATypI conference as ITC Rossum but was never actually issued; used as a text font for the *LettError* book published in 2000, it worked very well in a small point size.

With the typeface *Kosmik*, Erik van Blokland brought into practice a new digital invention: the 'flipperfont' principle. A tiny program included in the font makes sure that the printer chooses one of various available versions of each character (three in Kosmik). Unlike Beowolf's random output, the different shapes of each flipperfont character have been established by the designer. Kosmik was based on the hand-drawn letters Van Blokland uses for his comic strips and reflect their playful, yet precise style. To demonstrate the liveliness that can be achieved with Kosmik, LettError produced an animation in which the letters rock, shake and jump. Like the other LettError clips, the Kosmik demonstration is both playful and meaningful. According to Van Blokland, 'the ideas behind Kosmik or Beowolf can be explained more effectively with moving images'. In 2002, an OpenType version of Kosmik was released which flippers even more effectively thanks to the possibility of using automatic 'context-sensitive' character selection in programs such as Adobe InDesign.

Van Rossum's font *Schulschrift* (German for 'school script') has built-in intelligent behaviour as well. Each of the fonts contains joints of different lengths and positions; there is also a set with alternative letter shapes. With these extra tools, a plausible connnected script can be created. FF Schulschrift comes with a small program called *Scripter*, which automatically converts a selected text fragment to flowing cursive schoolchildren's handwriting using these 'spare parts'. Another FontFont credited to him, FF *Schulbuch*, was a digital remake of two German schoolbook sanserifs, commissioned from him through FontShop. According to Van Rossum, 'anyone could have done that job'; he prefers not to regard it as part of his body of work.

Custom typefaces

Having acquired a certain renown with the FontFonts they had released in rapid succession, both Van Blokland and Van Rossum were commissioned to produce custom typefaces. Studio Dumbar in The Hague invited Just van Rossum to design a font family for their corporate identity of the GAK, the Dutch government agency responsible for the administration of national insurance. Taking Tobias Frere-Jones' *Interstate* as a point of departure, Van Rossum gave the design a friendlier and less technical look, notably by creating subtler, lighter joints.

Van Blokland was invited to design a set of custom fonts for the London headquarters of MTV Europe.[51] His contact there was designer John Critchley, director of the music channel's print department, which was involved in the design and production of merchandising, stationery, and press and PR kits. A serious competition had been held for the main assignment, a screen font to be used exclusively by MTV-UK in captions and subtitles. The new font was meant to enhance the channel's individuality, and Van Blokland's *Critter* was designed to meet this brief: its shapes, although regu-

Advert
Light **Bold** **Black**

Advert Rough
One, Two, **Three**, **Four**, **Five**

Kosmik

Flipperfont aaa bbb ccc ddd eee fff ggg hhh

Schulschrift A
Schulschrift B
Schulschrift C

GakSans
Light *Italic* Regular *Italic*
Bold *Italic* **Black** *Italic*

GakSerif
Light *Italic* Regular *Italic*
Bold *Italic*

50 The Trixie story is told on the LettError website, www.letterror.com/foundry/trixie

51 For Van Blokland's MTV typefaces, see Jan Middendorp; 'Bizar! Degelijk! Parmantig! Erik van Blokland ontwierp Critter-font voor MTV', in *Items* vol. 16 no. 6, 1997.

NewCritter

Plain *Italic* **Bold** ***Italic***

Salmiak

Plain *Italic*

lar and straightforward, are also rather unorthodox and immediately recognizable, with extremely small capital heights for accommodating the all-cap acronyms which are so frequent in today's youth culture. *Critter* was originally a family of only two weights, plain and bold, roughly built on a 50 by 50 unit grid for better readability at coarse screen resolution. Having been designed for MTV under an exclusive five-year contract, Critter was published as a commercial font in 2000 after substantial revisions and with added italics under the name *New Critter*. A font especially created for MTV's print department was *LettError Doodle*. It is a set of quirky sketches which can be layered in different colours by means of a specially written random generator. Using this program, Van Blokland created a doodled map of Europe, a king-size colour print of which was used to decorate a wall at MTV's London headquarters.

One little-known custom typeface by Erik van Blokland is *Utrecht*, a font specially designed to be used as perforated letters. It was commissioned by the Amsterdam designer Irma Boom for her famous SHV book (1995), a memorial volume for a private holding company and one of the most complex book designs in recent history.

Historical studies

Van Blokland and Van Rossum are best known as the makers of irreverent, cutting-edge font families such as Beowolf or the InstantTypes series. However, their work is based on a thorough study of and keen interest in the history of type; and some of their typefaces reflect this interest more directly.

In 1990, FontShop published Van Rossum's FF *Brokenscript*. It is a study in Fraktur, or blackletter, possibly inspired by Gerrit Noordzij's extensive writings on the subject. Another historical exercise is *Bodoni Bleifrei* (1993) concocted by the LettError duo during a typography workshop at the Hochschule der Künste in Hamburg. 'The venue was the printing office of the HdK, computers next to lead type. We found a typeset page for a Bodoni specimen: a printed page as well as the lead type. Both were scanned and produced as digital fonts, and we called it *Bleifrei*, German for unleaded. Years went by. Then we opened our own online shop and rummaged through the digital attic to find nice things we'd forgotten about. We added one more weight, and built a special LayerPlayer (MacOS only) to make the layering of the fonts easy.'

Van Blokland's latest addition to the FontFont library was also, to a certain extent, a revival. FF *Zapata* is based on various wide slab serifs, often called 'antique', from the era of metal and wood type. In the late nineteenth and early twentieth centuries, especially in North America, these antiques were widely used as display faces, on posters, official documents and in advertisements. As Van Blokland wrote, 'Every antique was another interpretation. In the same tradition, FF Zapata is an antique, but not a digitization of one particular version. ... FF Zapata is an ideal typeface for filling pages if you don't have much to say, or it can be very loud if you have a point to make.'[52] Needless to say, FF Zapata is one of Van Bloklands' favourite fonts when it comes to promoting LettError fonts, some of which are now directly available from their website.

One of these products is LTR *Federal*, a typeface which, like Zapata, is inspired by nineteenth-century Americana; to be more precise, it bears a strong resemblance to the lettering used on US currency. However, LettError stipulates, 'it is not possible to create counterfeit money with LTR Federal. The typefaces ... are not photographic reproductions of actual currency.'[53] To recreate the shading and hatching effects found in nineteenth-century lettering, as well as on dollar bills, Van Blokland invented Digital Engraving: a combination of programming and type design. With the 22 Federal fonts comes the program LayerPlayer, which helps the user to assemble layers of type, choose the optical size of the shading effects and select style and colour. Federal is a typical example of LettError thinking: a mind game born out of a personal fascination, developed into a tool with which any designer can create impeccable pastiches of the kind of typographic wizardry which once required great skill and painstaking work.

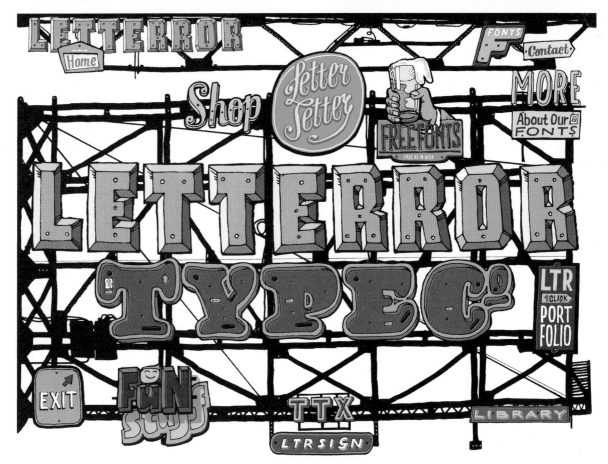

Opening page of the 2003 LettError website. Hand-drawn by Erik van Blokland, it shows his fascination with American-style display type.

Both FF Zapata (1997) and Federal (2000) are based on nineteenth-century American lettering styles. Federal comes with an extensive set of shadows and hatching styles, plus scripting software for rendering 'digital engraving'.

Zapata

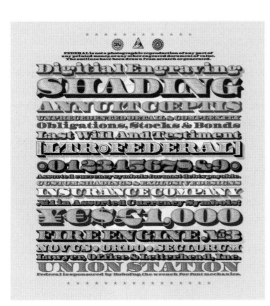

Designers as programmers: why?

In 2000 LettError received the Charles Nypels Award, a Dutch (but internationally applicable) prize for innovation in typography. The book published on that occasion (*LettError*, edited by Els Kuijper) gives ample insight into LettError's ideas about the way designers can make use of the hidden possibilities of digital tools. The following paragraphs are a synthesis of these ideas – they are based on the article 'Why? Tools', written by Erik van Blokland with the present author.

Van Rossum and Van Blokland argue that software is a commercial mass product, and is therefore not made for individuals but for a target group with hypothetical wishes and demands. If that target group turns out to have unfulfilled desires, extra functions are added with an upgrade, provided that there is enough interest. You can do everything with a program as long as there are enough people who want to do the same thing. But as it is precisely the task of designers (graphic, industrial or type designers) to discover new possibilities, in their case the use of a computer can be more of a handicap than an advantage.

In the past you were successful if you could make what was in your mind's eye with your own hands. Now there is a danger that designers will only function properly if

52 *FontFont 20 Release notes*, April 1997.

53 Text on the Federal page of the letterror.com website, 2003.

their creativity does not exceed the potential of their computer. In the long run this leads to a monotonous computer-driven uniformity.

An alert designer may have questions or problems which the software is incapable of solving. This can be frustrating. Should the designer begin to have doubts about his or her capacities? On the contrary: it simply means that the people who devised the program did not take the designer's idea into account, so it is a relatively new idea. It is not a bad thing for a designer to have new ideas.

Artisans of the past were rarely satisfied with tools as they found them in the shop. They always had the tendency to personalize their tools by honing them, converting them or expanding them. It must be possible to do something similar with software.

Right from the start, LettError found it logical and fun to solve design problems with self-developed or modified software. They had, of course, the big advantage of having had an early interest in the workings of the computer. But even designers without a whizz-kid past can now do their own programming, provided they are given the right tools for the job. Python, for instance, a programming language that was developed by Guido van Rossum (Just's brother) is internationally recognized as an easy-to-learn and powerful language for addressing the computer. More and more designers are using it for programming without much prior knowledge.

Parametric design

An interesting aspect of honing one's own digital tools is the opportunity to automate part of the creative process. A design usually starts with a series of sketches, a vague visualization of possibilities that gets the selection process going – the choice between good and mediocre solutions. As long as you're sketching on a napkin, the marks can mean whatever you like them to. But if your very first visualization is already computer-rendered, as is common nowadays, ideas are fixed with millimetre precision and dead straight lines. The design takes on finality when it should be time for flexibility.

There is an alternative: programming-assisted design. In this case possible solutions are neither sketched by hand nor directly drawn on the computer. The designer indicates the ingredients and the margins, and asks the computer to think up a series of variables, taking certain rules into account. In other words, to vary certain parameters at random. The computer itself will not begin designing, so it cannot be accused of interfering with the creative process. It does what a computer is best at doing: working out the consequences of possible decisions very quickly. Fully informed, the designer selects the most attractive, the handiest or the best solution from a range of alternatives. The designers themselves determine how complex they want this process to be, how long they want to postpone the definitive decisions.

A practical application of this kind of automated design is LettError's Stamp Machine. It produces an infinite variety of post stamps of a fixed size, based on parameters or margins with respect to colour, layout and fonts. One could, in fact, imagine a future in which the barcode stickers which in some countries are replacing stamps, will in turn be replaced by unique, custom-made LettError stamps. Van Rossum and Van Blokland have used similar guided random processes to design calendars, advertisements and type specimens.

Design machines and experiments

The endless LettError experiments have resulted in many more typographic inventions, some very useful, others mere play, and some slightly disturbing.

The program that is most like a typeface is *BitPull*. With characteristic politically incorrect humour, LettError recommends BitPull as a device that 'does to typography what pitbulls do to little girls'. A program called BitPuller is used to convert text into outlined building blocks distributed across a bitmap grid. When linked to one of the specially designed BitPull fonts, these forms are transformed back into legible text, to be used in a program like XPress, InDesign, Illustrator or Freehand. As each of the blocks forming a letter or sign is treated by the layout program as a single character,

LettError's Stamp Machine is one of several programs or scripts for automatically generating layouts on the basis of a given number of options. This page was created for a special The Hague issue of FontShop Benelux's *Druk* magazine, 2000.

many features used to format text – spacing, setting on curved paths, etc. – will influence the 'layout' of the letterforms. BitPull is especially recommended for animation.

LettError developed several scripts and extensions to work with BitPull, such as a randomized font which varies the position and shape of the pixels; this font, called *BitPull-VariRound* shows round pixels that vary in size when printed on a PostScript printer. Another variation was the *Doormat* version designed by Van Blokland as a headline font for the Dutch magazine *MediaMatic*.

LettError's *RobotFonts* are also bitmap fonts; here it is writing the code of filters which is the determining creative act, not the type design. A simple bitmap font called *Python Sans* is interpreted, and often heavily distorted, by a small program; filters are disposable and are thrown away once the font has been created. The process is guided by the designer, but he cannot predict the precise result.

The design of 'conventional' type can be automated as well. Van Rossum and Van Blokland made major contributions to *RoboFog*, developed by Petr van Blokland using the scripting language Python. RoboFog is a type design program based on Fontographer, in which many functions are scripted, allowing the designer to work faster and more precisely. RoboFog is dealt with more extensively in the section on Petr van Blokland's work.

A rather scary experiment, conducted by Erik van Blokland with New York type designer Jonathan Hoefler, is Filibuster. It started out as a parody of the thousands of professional-looking, database-driven websites that flood the internet hoping to sell, well, anything. Each of these sites is doctored to suggest serious businessmanship and a solid company behind it. The Filibuster site (built in 1999 – 2000) showed that such a website can be a mere facade, an empty shell. The program generated plausible web pages using a set of key words and product shots; on close inspection the pages contained absolutely nothing. Inspired by Peter Bilak's QuickEssay, a script for generating theoretical jargon, Van Blokland then developed Filibuster into a language generator that makes random choices from a list of given words and has been taught enough grammatical rules to come up with a convincing – or at least confusing – piece of prose. Filibuster's main message is that appearances, both on the internet and in print, must be mistrusted; that the apparent credibility of dot-coms as well as academic writing may have been created by applying a simple set of clichés. The filibuster.org website was active between 2000 and 2002, but was discontinued when Hoefler and Van Blokland found that the joke had worn off.

Type and copyright

GifWrap was a small application written by LettError in the early days of the World Wide Web. It was a simple solution for setting web page headlines in the font of one's choice by building words from single-character gif images. GifWrap, a script to be used with the text and code editor BB Edit, automates this process. The program was not just a handy tool, it was also a modest political statement. Like many other type designers, Van Rossum and Van Blokland are concerned about the practice of embedding fonts in internet pages or public PDFs; they fear that typefaces will be up for grabs.

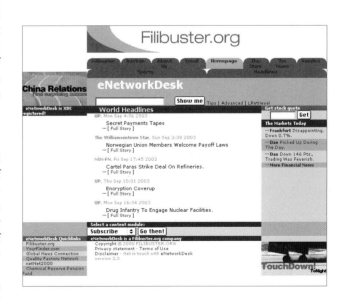

Their concern about copyrights is understandable. Although they are two of the most versatile and influential type designers of their generation, Van Blokland and Van Rossum have never had more than an average income from licensing their typefaces. It has been estimated that for every legal copy of Trixie, between 30 and 50

ꟻE WEАΤHEꞄ
NE Weather

Twin (2003) was selected from six proposals for a typeface to represent the character of the 'Twin Cities' Minneapolis and St. Paul. It is not one single typeface but a set of 800 characters from which a choice can be made by the user or by feeding the software with outside factors, such as the weather.

copies sit on designers' hard disks without having been paid for. In LettError's case, this is a painful paradox. Thanks to the irreverent nature of their work, they have become immensely popular among design rebels and students; it is precisely this group that seldom thinks of actually buying the fonts they work with. An article that Erik Spiekermann once wrote for *Wired* was entitled 'Just van Rossum and Erik van Blokland would be rich and famous if everyone who used their typefaces paid for them'. The Random Twins – as Spiekermann has lovingly labelled them – have indeed become famous and have won awards; but they earn much of their daily bread by designing print, code and websites rather than new typefaces.

Twin, a typeface that can't make up its mind

In the rare cases when a typeface design is both a paid commission and a license to experiment, conditions are perfect for generating something really remarkable. This was the case with LettError's 2003 joint project *Twin*, a typeface for the Twin Cities.

Can a typeface communicate the unique character of a city? In June 2002 the University of Minnesota Design Institute (UMDI) invited six design teams to propose an answer to that question. LettError: 'The brief indicated that the typeface should reflect the characteristics of the cities. This was a problem because we had never visited Minneapolis before (or left the airport). How to make a typeface for a city we had never seen – or worse yet: how to make a typeface for any city? Rather than to come up with one particular style, we wanted to try out an idea about a system that could collect ad hoc typefaces based on a large characterset. The "Panchromatic Hybrid Style Alternator". This frightened the jury and the project was selected.'[54]

Twin was presented in June 2003 during TypeCon, a yearly conference organized by the Society of Typographic Aficionados (SoTA), which that year took place in Minneapolis as part of the Twin Cities Design Celebration. Twin is an interactive typeface: it changes according to the variables that the user chooses. During their presentation at TypeCon, LettError made the font react to a microphone that registered the audience's shouting. Twin even made the *New York Times*.[55]

Instead of forcing one particular style upon a diverse group of people, Twin is a machine that allows each individual to generate letterforms appropriate to the occasion. LettError drew as many alternatives for each character as they could find – over 800 different designs in all – using the possibilities of OpenType technology. When playing with the controls, each image is generated afresh, which makes it possible to look up environmental factors of the Twin Cities, such as the weather, and incorporate them in the letterforms.

In its own weird way, Twins sums up the qualities inherent to most of LettError's work: unconventional thinking, a playful view of typographic conventions, and user-friendliness. After the presentation, Erik Spiekermann wrote: 'I think the Random Twins deserve as many medals as this industry has to give. They are great designers, great programmers, and – most importantly – they haven't lost their sense of humour. Wacky and wonderful.'[56]

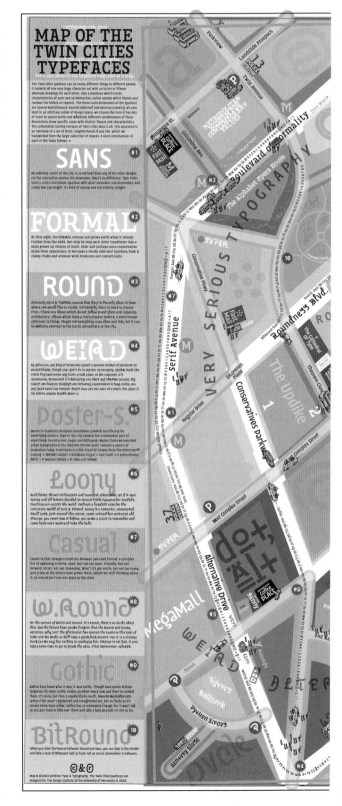

The two sides of Luc(as) de Groot

Lucas – or Luc – de Groot (1963) is full of contradictions. He is the designer of *Thesis*, which at the time of its release in 1994 was the most extensive digital family ever made, and a very thorough typeface indeed. Then he also created about a dozen Thesis spin-offs, many of which are deliberately sloppy, ugly or illegible. The text typefaces which make up the bulk of his output are neither adventurous nor idiosyncratic: they were designed to modestly serve a precise purpose. Yet his lectures are often shamelessly personal, and usually contain some erotic cartoons from his diaries, several of which have been published. During his career as a designer at corporate design agencies he seemed to be quietly looking for a place to concentrate on type. Yet at thirty-six he found himself the owner of two companies: FontFabrik, a small studio for custom type design, and LucasFonts, the foundry that produces and sells De Groot's typefaces. In Luc(as)'s career, the frivolous and the serious, the boyish and the businesslike have always gone hand in hand.

After graduating from the Royal Academy in The Hague, De Groot freelanced for a year. He worked for Studio Tint, a small design firm co-founded by Huug Schipper, who had been his teacher at the Academy. Among the jobs De Groot did for Tint were several book covers, hand-lettered with great precision in a condensed sans which could only have been developed under the influence of Gerrit Noordzij. Another studio he worked for was Studio Dumbar, which in 1987 commissioned him to design an intermediate weight of *Frutiger*, the Dutch PTT's corporate typeface. This assignment and the research involved led to his 'Interpolation Theory', a formula for calculating in-between weights.

From 1989 to 1993 De Groot worked at BRS Premsela Vonk in Amsterdam, which at the time was the largest corporate design agency in the Netherlands. Up to then, all of his type design and lettering projects had been made by hand; at BRS he became Mac-savvy. Among the many projects De Groot was involved in, one assignment stands out: the corporate identity of one of the Netherlands' largest governmental bodies, the Ministry of Transport, Public Works and Water Management (Verkeer en Waterstaat). His main contribution to the identity was the Ministry's logo and the sub-logos for its departments, based on a typeface designed for the occasion.[57]

Parenthesis and the logo font

The Ministry typeface was based on an idea by two designers in the team, Edo van Dijk and Edo Smitshuijzen, whose briefing to De Groot included a sample of Frutiger's *Glypha* with some of the serifs cut off. De Groot kept the idea of the half-serif, but for the internal structure reverted to an earlier alphabet of his, *NarsDesis*, drawn around 1987–88 as a school project – an italic which also happened to have asymmetrical serifs.

The Ministry's logos were set in a roman, slightly slanted at a 2.5° angle to suggest dynamism. As there was no need for a corporate typeface, the designers were asked

54 Text published on the LettError website, July 2003. The other designers invited were
   Peter Bilak (> p 292), Gilles Gavillet and David Rust (Optimo), Sybille Hagmann
   (Kontour), Conor Mangat (Inflection), and Eric Olson (Process Type Foundry).
   At TypeCon 2003, the Design Institute presented a book documenting the project:
   Metro Letters, edited by Deborah Littlejohn.

55 Matthew Mirapaul, 'Is It About to Rain? Check the Typeface', *New York Times*,
   24 July 2003.

56 Spiekermann's post to the ATypI mailing list, 24 July, 2003.

57 Article based on conversations and an e-mail correspondence with Luc(as) de Groot,
   as well as texts published on the LucasFonts website and in FontFont *Readme* files.

Ministerie van Verkeer en Waterstaat

Directoraat-Generaal Goederenvervoer

narsdesis Ministerie van Verkeer en Waterstaat

▲ The logo for the Ministry of Transport, Public Works and Water Management and, below, its two sources: a sketch of a semisans by Edo van Dijk and Edo Smitshuijzen (right), and De Groot's art school project NarsDesis (left).

▶ Hand-rendered sanserif for the back cover of *Babylon Hotel*, a collection of short stories by Bart Chabot. Designed by Luc(as) de Groot when working at Studio Tint, The Hague, 1988.

▼ Hand lettering for the cover design of *De beste Nederlandse en Vlaamse verhalen van het jaar*, Amsterdam 1989. Made at Studio Tint, The Hague.

Vier Verhalen

Gesundheit Macht Krank

Tranendal BV

Babylon Hotel

Eur-O-Rama

Nederlandse verhalen van het jaar

to simply provide thirty-six EPS files for correspondence and in-house desktop publishing. It is typical of De Groot's practical mentality and determination that he did come up with a font after all. A 'clever typeface' allowed the user to create the Ministry's Dutch-language logo by typing A-B-C-D, the first department by typing E-F-G-H, etc. The bold, italic and bold-italic text styles were linked to the English, French and German versions of these logos.

Berlin, MetaDesign and Thesis

Erik Spiekermann, the founder and creative director of the Berlin studio Meta-Design, was permanently on the lookout for young specialists to assist in the design and implementation of corporate typefaces and corporate identities; he had decided that the best ones were to be found in Holland. In 1991 he went to visit Luc(as) de Groot, still at BRS Premsela Vonk. De Groot recalls: 'Spiekermann said: "Why don't you come to Berlin? MetaDesign is a great little studio and you'll be making more money, too." I was flattered, but I decided to stay at the Amsterdam agency for another two years. However, if you wanted to grow within BRS you were supposed to eventually take charge of a team and attend many meetings with customers; that was not my cup of tea. I realised that Meta was probably the only agency in Europe where I could continue to specialize in type design and high-end corporate typography. I went to show my work and was invited to start right away.'

It was the beginning of a strange and decisive period in De Groot's life. During working hours, he had a large variety of tasks at MetaDesign: he expanded Spiekermann's Meta typeface into a larger family; he customized corporate typefaces; he developed templates for scientific magazines, and designed printed matter. Having to work with other people's typefaces all the time, he became convinced that most had flaws or were not equal to the complex demands of a large corporate identity. He decided that there was room for a specialized type family, and that now was the time to design it. '... all the ingredients were available: pencils to do fast and rough sketches, intelligent type design software, ten years of experience and exercise, a big computer monitor and a high resolution laser printer for immediate decisions; a lively after wall metropolis [*sic*: the Berlin wall had come down a few years earlier, JM], inspiring surrounding designers, willing to do beta-testing, and a type distribution centre next door.' [58] This last phrase refers to FontShop, the face's original publisher, located in the same building as MetaDesign.

The new typeface's starting point was *Parenthesis*, the logo font designed at BRS. Initially De Groot concentrated on the original half-serif. The genesis of a more ambitious plan was a question of serendipity rather than calculation. 'One boring night I cut off all the serifs. Well, there weren't too many and suddenly I had a sanserif typeface. A few days later colleagues spotted some printouts and asked me

a rens brownfix jumps oven the

if they could use it for a proposal. ... The client was interested and wanted to see more. So I made a semibold, bold and italic in the following nights.' [59]

Thesis grew over a period of a year and a half, mostly in the evening hours, during the weekends and holidays. De Groot's private life was virtually non-existent: he spoke little German and hardly knew anybody outside work. 'For quite some time, Thesis was the most important thing in my life. It was a kind of substitute for a relationship.' [60] Every version of the typeface was immediately tested by his colleagues at the studio, who followed its developments with great interest. 'Without MetaDesign it would have been a lot more difficult to finish the typeface. Designing type is basically a very lonely activity, but the studio's atmosphere helped me to work up the discipline that was necessary.'

When Thesis was finally released in the FontFont series, it made history as the largest ever digitized font family, with three sub-families (sanserif, serif and semi-sans), eight weights (from extra light to black), plus italics, small caps and expert sets for each weight; a total of 176 fonts.

'Parenthesis' was the working name throughout the design process, but FontShop made it clear that, because of the lengthy suffixes, the font names would be too long. So it became Thesis. On the eve of the final presentation to FontShop, De Groot invented even shorter names for two of the sub-families: TheSans and TheSerif. He suggested that Thesis or TheSis should remain the name of the original half-serif, but this was seen to be puzzling. After a survey among colleagues, TheMix was chosen as font name for this hybrid version.

In the texts published at the time of its release as well as the lectures he was soon invited to give, De Groot pointed out that Thesis was a very apt name because 'the typeface is based on theories'. These theories are twofold. For the construction of the letterforms Gerrit Noordzij's translation theory was the guiding principle – in other words, there is a diagonal stress of the kind found in handwriting with the broad-nibbed pen. Yet in Thesis the difference between thick and thin has been reduced to an absolute minimum, so that the stress or contrast has become almost imperceptible – but still it is vital for the overall image. This can be demonstrated by reversing the lowercase characters. The diagonal stress suddenly appears to be much stronger, and very unnatural: the letters seem to fall over.

The other theory is De Groot's own 'interpolation theory' developed years earlier when freelancing in The Hague. It presupposes that an optically correct intermediate weight between two extremes (such as light and black) is not calculated by a linear formula, i.e. by taking the average, 'but somewhat below the middle.' De Groot invented a scientific-looking formula to quantify this insight. [61]

Thesis was designed to be a 'total solution to corporate needs', and was beta-tested simultaneously by three design groups. After its release, it became almost immediately successful; this was at least in part due to a brochure-and-poster that De Groot

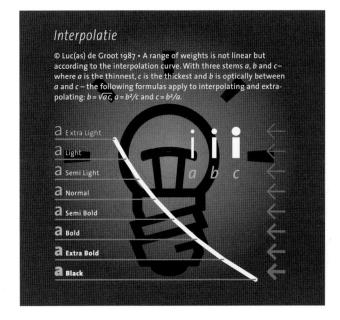

Interpolatie

© Luc(as) de Groot 1987 • A range of weights is not linear but according to the interpolation curve. With three stems *a*, *b* and *c* – where *a* is the thinnest, *c* is the thickest and *b* is optically between *a* and *c* – the following formulas apply to interpolating and extrapolating: $b = \sqrt{ac}$, $a = b^2/c$ and $c = b^2/a$.

a Extra Light
a Light
a Semi Light
a Normal
a Semi Bold
a Bold
a Extra Bold
a Black

a b c

↑ De Groot developed his interpolation theory when designing an intermediate weight of Frutiger for Studio Dumbar in 1987. According to this formula, the optically correct intermediate font between two extremes is created by calculating a stroke weight somewhat below the average.

↑ Sketch for humanist sanserif, late 1980s.

58 *Type design*, text published on the lucasfonts.com website, 2002.

59 From a text written by De Groot on the occasion of the FF Thesis release, 1994. The unpublished text, which outlines his career and design principles, was made available to journalists and other people interested in De Groot's work.

60 Quotes in this paragraph from Jan Middendorp, 'Zinnelijk plezier', in *Items* vol. 14, no. 3, 1995, pp 60 – 61.

61 Cf. www.lucasfonts.com/lucasfnt/infos/fredtemp/interpol.html (2003).

apegosagvug ansgdireajde

AaBbCcDdEeFf

◄ Sketch for a seriffed roman, late 1980s.

▼ Example showing the relationship between TheSerif and TheSans.

▼ When FF Thesis came out in 1994, it was the largest digital family available. TheSans Mono and Mono Condensed followed in 1996.

TheSans ExtraLight	TheMix ExtraLight	TheSerif ExtraLight	TheSansMono ExtraLight
TheSans ExtraLightItalic	*TheMix ExtraLightItalic*	*TheSerif ExtraLightItalic*	*TheSansMono ExtraLightI*
THESANS EXTRALIGHTCAPS	THEMIX EXTRALIGHTCAPS	THESERIF EXTRALIGHTCAPS	TheSansMono Light
THESANS EXTRALIGHTCAPSITALIC	*THEMIX EXTRALIGHTCAPSITALIC*	*THESERIF EXTRALIGHTCAPSITA*	*TheSansMono LightI*
Expert ★ 0123₄₅₆₇→℞〜	Expert ★ 0123₄₅₆₇→℞〜	Expert ★ 0123₄₅₆₇→℞〜	TheSansMono SemiLight
ExpertItalic ✳ 0123₄₅₆₇↗ℓ〜	*ExpertItalic ✳ 0123₄₅₆₇↗ℓ〜*	*ExpertItalic ✳ 0123₄₅₆↗ℓ〜*	*TheSansMono SemiLightI*
TheSans Light	TheMix Light	TheSerif Light	TheSansMono Normal
TheSans LightItalic	*TheMix LightItalic*	*TheSerif LightItalic*	*TheSansMono NormalI*
THESANS LIGHTCAPS	THEMIX LIGHTCAPS	THESERIF LIGHTCAPS	TheSansMono SemiBold
THESANS LIGHTCAPSITALIC	*THEMIX LIGHTCAPSITALIC*	*THESERIF LIGHTCAPSITALIC*	*TheSansMono SemiBoldI*
Expert ★ 0123₄₅₆₇→℞〜	Expert ★ 0123₄₅₆₇→℞〜	Expert ★ 0123₄₅₆₇→℞〜	**TheSansMono Bold**
ExpertItalic ✳ 0123₄₅₆₇↗ℓ〜	*ExpertItalic ✳ 0123₄₅₆₇↗ℓ〜*	*ExpertItalic ✳ 0123₄₅₆↗ℓ〜*	***TheSansMono BoldI***
TheSans SemiLight	TheMix SemiLight	TheSerif SemiLight	**TheSansMono ExtraBold**
TheSans SemiLightItalic	*TheMix SemiLightItalic*	*TheSerif SemiLightItalic*	***TheSansMono ExtraBoldI***
THESANS SEMILIGHTCAPS	THEMIX SEMILIGHTCAPS	THESERIF SEMILIGHTCAPS	**TheSansMono Black**
THESANS SEMILIGHTCAPSITALIC	*THEMIX SEMILIGHTCAPSITALIC*	*THESERIF SEMILIGHTCAPSITALIC*	***TheSansMono BlackI***
Expert ★ 0123₄₅₆₇→℞〜	Expert ★ 0123₄₅₆₇→℞〜	Expert ★ 0123₄₅₆₇→℞〜	TheSansMonoCon ExtraLight
ExpertItalic ✳ 0123₄₅₆₇↗ℓ〜	*ExpertItalic ✳ 0123₄₅₆₇↗ℓ〜*	*ExpertItalic ✳ 0123₄₅₆↗ℓ〜*	*TheSansMonoCon ExtraLightI*
TheSans Normal	TheMix Normal	TheSerif Normal	TheSansMonoCon Light
TheSans NormalItalic	*TheMix NormalItalic*	*TheSerif NormalItalic*	*TheSansMonoCon LightI*
THESANS NORMALCAPS	THEMIX NORMALCAPS	THESERIF NORMALCAPS	TheSansMonoCon SemiLight
THESANS NORMALCAPSITALIC	*THEMIX NORMALCAPSITALIC*	*THESERIF NORMALCAPSITALIC*	*TheSansMonoCon SemiLightI*
Expert ★ 0123₄₅₆₇→℞〜	Expert ★ 0123₄₅₆₇→℞〜	Expert ★ 0123₄₅₆₇→℞〜	TheSansMonoCon Normal
ExpertItalic ✳ 0123₄₅₆₇↗ℓ〜	*ExpertItalic ✳ 0123₄₅₆₇↗ℓ〜*	*ExpertItalic ✳ 0123₄₅₆↗ℓ〜*	*TheSansMonoCon NormalI*
TheSans SemiBold	**TheMix SemiBold**	**TheSerif SemiBold**	**TheSansMonoCon SemiBold**
TheSans SemiBoldItalic	***TheMix SemiBoldItalic***	***TheSerif SemiBoldItalic***	***TheSansMonoCon SemiBoldI***
THESANS SEMIBOLDCAPS	**THEMIX SEMIBOLDCAPS**	**THESERIF SEMIBOLDCAPS**	**TheSansMonoCon Bold**
THESANS SEMIBOLDCAPSITALIC	***THEMIX SEMIBOLDCAPSITALIC***	***THESERIF SEMIBOLDCAPSITALIC***	***TheSansMonoCon BoldI***
Expert ★ 0123₄₅₆₇→℞〜	Expert ★ 0123₄₅₆₇→℞〜	Expert ★ 0123₄₅₆₇→℞〜	**TheSansMonoCon ExtraBold**
ExpertItalic ✳ 0123₄₅₆₇↗ℓ〜	*ExpertItalic ✳ 0123₄₅₆₇↗ℓ〜*	*ExpertItalic ✳ 0123₄₅₆↗ℓ〜*	***TheSansMonoCon ExtraBoldI***
TheSans Bold	**TheMix Bold**	**TheSerif Bold**	**TheSansMonoCon Black**
TheSans BoldItalic	**TheMix BoldItalic**	***TheSerif BoldItalic***	***TheSansMonoCon BlackI***
THESANS BOLDCAPS	**THEMIX BOLDCAPS**	**THESERIF BOLDCAPS**	TheSansCondensed ExtraLight
THESANS BOLDCAPSITALIC	***THEMIX BOLDCAPSITALIC***	***THESERIF BOLDCAPSITALIC***	*TheSansCondensed ExtraLightItalic*
Expert ★ 0123₄₅₆₇→℞〜	Expert ★ 0123₄₅₆₇→℞〜	Expert ★ 0123₄₅₆₇→℞〜	TheSansCondensed Light
ExpertItalic ✳ 0123₄₅₆₇↗ℓ〜	*ExpertItalic ✳ 0123₄₅₆₇↗ℓ〜*	*ExpertItalic ✳ 0123₄₅₆↗ℓ〜*	*TheSansCondensed LightItalic*
TheSans ExtraBold	**TheMix ExtraBold**	**TheSerif ExtraBold**	TheSansCondensed SemiLight
TheSans ExtraBoldItalic	***TheMix ExtraBoldItalic***	***TheSerif ExtraBoldItalic***	*TheSansCondensed SemiLightItalic*
THESANS EXTRABOLDCAPS	**THEMIX EXTRABOLDCAPS**	**THESERIF EXTRABOLDCAPS**	TheSansCondensed Normal
THESANS EXTRABOLDCAPSITALIC	***THEMIX EXTRABOLDCAPSITALIC***	***THESERIF EXTRABOLDCAPSITA***	*TheSansCondensed NormalItalic*
Expert ★ 0123₄₅₆₇→℞〜	Expert ★ 0123₄₅₆₇→℞〜	Expert ★ 0123₄₅₆₇→℞〜	**TheSansCondensed SemiBold**
ExpertItalic ✳ 0123₄₅₆₇↗ℓ〜	*ExpertItalic ✳ 0123₄₅₆₇↗ℓ〜*	*ExpertItalic ✳ 0123₄₅₆↗ℓ〜*	***TheSansCondensed SemiBoldItalic***
TheSans Black	**TheMix Black**	**TheSerif Black**	**TheSansCondensed Bold**
TheSans BlackItalic	***TheMix BlackItalic***	***TheSerif BlackItalic***	***TheSansCondensed BoldItalic***
THESANS BLACKCAPS	**THEMIX BLACKCAPS**	**THESERIF BLACKCAPS**	**TheSansCondensed ExtraBold**
THESANS BLACKCAPSITALIC	***THEMIX BLACKCAPSITALIC***	***THESERIF BLACKCAPSITALIC***	***TheSansCondensed ExtraBoldItalic***
Expert ★ 0123₄₅₆₇→℞〜	Expert ★ 0123₄₅₆₇→℞〜	Expert ★ 0123₄₅₆₇→℞〜	**TheSansCondensed Black**
ExpertItalic ✳ 0123₄₅₆₇↗ℓ〜	*ExpertItalic ✳ 0123₄₅₆₇↗ℓ〜*	*ExpertItalic ✳ 0123₄₅₆↗ℓ〜*	***TheSansCondensed BlackItalic***

has designed and printed at his own expense and had distributed all over Germany. MetaDesign used Thesis in the new logo of the city of Berlin – TheSans, TheMix and TheSerif mixed in one word. TheSans became the standard typeface of one of the German national TV channels, and was generally adopted as one of Germany's new favourite building blocks for corporate identities. TheMix, having been introduced in a special issue of *Wired* magazine, found favour among trendy art directors, but was also chosen as the corporate typeface of the Belgian police. The Thesis clan was later expanded with a condensed version, a monospace for setting code, several alternate sets and a Thesis-based typewriter font.

Dirty and rough

While designing Thesis, Luc(as) de Groot sometimes took an evening off from the serious work, only to design more typefaces. These designs, though often based on the Thesis proportions, were of a completely different nature. Using an impressive array of programs and filters, Thesis was deconstructed, mutilated, undressed or boiled by its designer. Other 'fun fonts' (the term used by De Groot) were based on hand-written lettering or were designed directly on screen. Many of these fonts premiered in the early issues of the Dutch magazine *Blvd*, designed by the Rotterdam group Hard Werken. De Groot, when visiting that studio shortly before the first *Blvd* was to be printed somewhere in 1993, had left behind a floppy disk with newly created fonts. Chris Haaga, an American designer working at Hard Werken, decided to redesign the magazine using these unpublished typefaces.

Some of them were subsequently issued by FontShop. This is the case of FF *Jesus Loves You All* (1995), a small family of iconoclastic fonts in which the Thesis skeleton has been given 'an agitated crown-of-thorn-like complexity'. This description is by J. Abbott Miller, the author-designer of the book *Dimensional Typography* (1996) in which he presents *Rhizome*, a delightful three-dimensional 'secularised adaptation', which 'exchanges nature for religion and interprets the prickly silhouettes of *Jesus Loves You* as a botanical motif.' [62] FF *Nebulae* also took Thesis as a starting point. Its forms seem to dissolve into a fading pattern of bubbles. The four 'weights' or degrees of dissipation can be layered, using different colours or hues, to obtain spectacular effects as well as greater legibility. *Bolletje wol* ('ball of wool'), published in 1996 as part of FontShops' 'Dirty Faces' series, is an alphabet whose characters look like variations of 'cat's cradle', the game played with a loop of thread.

Many other dirty and destructive alphabets did not make the FontShop collection. Their names speak volumes: *Drekkig* ('dungy'), *Modderig* ('muddy'), *ErgLelijk* ('very ugly'), *NietGek* ('not too bad'), *Verschrompelfont* ('wrinkle font'). Apart from these

Modderig 7 rented nights in thi
Drekkig Feedback raged in m
RipRIP offending stack o
SilverSurrogate When Hiro hit the switch
Gozijer got deeply pissed aka
BlubBlub Vieze vissekop
OldGouda rotte stinkkaas
Origasmi I never visited Japan
Purrie 25 liter Groentesoep
Generation 41 lightyrs away
Cosmos grows milkyway gardens
tandrad De snelle fiets
SpikeLee push just one button
Nebulae

◁ In his book *Dimensional Typography* (1996) the writer-designer J. Abbott Miller presented Rhizome, a three-dimensional adaptation of De Groot's font Jesus Loves You 'as a botanical motif'.

△ Many 'fun fonts' made by De Groot throughout the 1990s were based on Thesis. Most of these typefaces remain unpublished.

62 J. Abbott Miller, *Dimensional Typography* (a KIOSK report), New York 1996, p 51.

Sit on ME!

Punten Straight
Punten Extremo
Punten Rondom

alfalfabetje

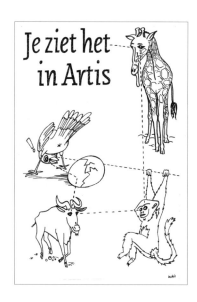

Je ziet het in Artis

MOVE ME

A AA F FF J JJ
C CC G GG L LL
D DD H HH Z ZZ

quickly produced, grungy fonts, De Groot drew – either by hand or on the computer – several alphabets based on various styles of hand lettering; fonts that have names like *Alfalfabetje*, *Aquarelkwast* ('water colour brush') and *Hand & Feet*. *Punten* is a series of three hand-drawn slanted romans with sharp points or spikes. Of these, *Punten Rondom* ('spikes all around') is a font that De Groot has claimed to be his favourite. In it, each character is entangled by its own swashes – almost a parody of the seventeenth-century mannerist calligraphy that his teacher Gerrit Noordzij is so fond of. For some years during the 1990s, De Groot's informal fonts were made available through a small Amsterdam firm run by his sister, The Types. LucasFonts is now gradually including these adventurous or ironic display faces in its collection.

De Groot's funniest contribution to digital typography is an alphabet called *F Move Me* MM, published in 1994 in FUSE 11, the Pornography issue of the experimental typographic magazine edited by Neville Brody and Jon Wozencroft. Each character is an erotic cartoon, vaguely based on an uppercase letterform. The typeface is a one-axis Multiple Master font: on one end of the axis is the drawing, on the other a serious-looking capital letter. De Groot used these extremes to create hilarious little animations in which the letter morphs into a sexually explicit drawing.

Polemics

In late 1997, three years after publication, Thesis was the subject of a fierce polemic in the German press. In an article in the trade magazine *Page*, Max Caflisch, one of the grand old men of Swiss typography, accused Thesis of plagiarism. He claimed that Thesis was to a large extent an imitation of PMN *Caecilia* by Peter Matthias Noordzij, pointing out resemblances between Noordzij's typeface – developed between 1983 and 1991 – and De Groot's TheSerif. Caflisch – who had written a lengthy presentation of Caecilia for the Swiss magazine *Typographische Monatsblätter* – was convinced that De Groot had consciously used certain ideas that were unique to Caecilia.[63]

Page offered De Groot a chance to react to Caflisch's arguments in the same issue. Although his tone was rather sarcastic, many of his objections to Caflisch's view made sense. De Groot drew attention to the example of Jelle Bosma's *Cursivium*, a typeface developed along the same lines as Caecilia, at the same school and during the same period. According to De Groot, Cursivium shows that 'the idea to make a slab serif with no contrast, based on writing with the broad-nibbed pen, did not come from Peter Matthias, nor from Jelle, nor from me, but from "our father" Gerrit Noordzij.' Noordzij Sr. had outlined a scheme of parameters which formed a virtual space in which to fit 'all the typefaces in the world'. 'He added', wrote De Groot, 'that some corners of this space were still empty.' To add weight to this argument he showed one of his early student projects, made when both Academic (the later Caecilia) and Cursivium were still in preparation, with 'improvised lettering' exploring the idea of a slab serif with a humanist cursive construction. De Groot has always maintained that when it was pointed out to him that these ideas were too close for comfort to Academic, he took his projects in a different direction, concentrating mostly on sanserif. Made many years later, Thesis – according to De Groot – is an independent interpretation of Gerrit Noordzij's theories, having a more pronounced contrast ('translation', i.e. derived from the broad-nibbed pen) than either Caecilia or Cursivium.

De Groot's arguments did not convince everyone. In the subsequent issue of *Page*, the polemic was continued, quoting the opinions of Peter Matthias Noordzij,

Erik Spiekermann, Adrian Frutiger and Cynthia Hollandsworth. Spiekermann, of course, defended De Groot, argueing that in an environment as intense as the KABK, it is inevitable that designs by students have similar characteristics. Having monitored the development of Thesis from close by, Spiekermann described how TheSerif was a final addition to a family first designed as a semi-serif and a sanserif. This, however, did not counter Peter Matthias Noordzij's assertion that the skeletons of the two designs are 'too similar'.

Caecilia and Thesis have many traits in common; but a lot of these traits are propelled by an inner logic based on Noordzij's theories. It is not unthinkable that Caecilia was an unconscious influence at some stage of Thesis' development, but then again: the results are different, as is the behaviour of both typefaces in daily use. While Caecilia works smoothly as a text typeface, TheSerif, as De Groot himself has repeatedly pointed out, is mainly successful as a headline face. In other words: they *look* different, in the way that Helvetica and Univers look and behave differently even if in detail many solutions are similar.

Custom Faces at Meta and FontFabrik

As a type director at MetaDesign, De Groot designed and modified many typefaces for exclusive use by the agency's clients; he participated in the development of FF Transit, a variant of Frutiger developed for Berlin public transport. For another MetaDesign client, Volkswagen cars, he designed *Volkswagen Copy* and *Headline* (1996), based on Futura. His most original achievement in this field was the spirited headline face designed for the Brazilian newspaper *Folha de São Paulo*. *Folha* differs from his other original typefaces in that it has strong vertical stress.

De Groot left MetaDesign in late 1996 to found FontFabrik, a studio specializing in the design and modification of custom fonts; MetaDesign remained a client. He made *Elletura*, a subtly redrawn *Futura* with spectacular Extra Light and Hairline version for use at very large sizes. The *Bell South* corporate font, a set of geometric serif and sanserif fonts, was developed in collaboration with Roger van den Bergh of Van den Bergh/Gilliatt/Campbell, New York. In 2001 De Groot designed a new headline face for *Le Monde*, which was named *Floris Newspaper* after his son. Floris is a continuation of Folha: it has vertical stress, narrow forms and a somewhat rectangular oval as a basic shape. The family is now much larger. It comes in seven weights, from Extra Light to Black. Its Regular works well as a condensed text face.

LucasFonts

De Groot's decision, in 1999, not to extend his five-year licensing contract with FontShop International (FSI) and start his own foundry, came as somewhat of a surprise. There were several reasons for De Groot's move. Producing and publishing his typefaces on his own account would mean that he could act more swiftly and would have total control over production, advertising and PR; but there were also financial motives. Like many type designers, De Groot realized that a self-published typeface would bring him considerably higher proceeds per font sold; unlike many of his peers, De Groot had the business instinct as well as the relations with international distributors needed to make his venture into a success. He also had several unpublished typefaces waiting to be released. This enabled him to start up LucasFonts with a collection of half a dozen new type families, plus Thesis and Nebulae.

Most of the new typefaces had originally been commissioned by corporate clients, either directly from FontFabrik or via MetaDesign and other studios. *Spiegel* and *Taz* were designed, respectively, for the weekly *Der Spiegel* and the daily *Tageszeitung/Taz*; *Sun Sans* was developed for Sun Microsystems and later adapted for a left-wing weekly called *Jungle World*; and *Agrofont*, which was renamed *Corpid*, was originally designed for Studio Dumbar's identity of the Dutch Ministry of Agriculture, Nature Management and Fisheries. Having licensed his fonts on short-term exclusivity contracts, De Groot could now market them to the general public. The only case in which this did not work was Folha. In the April 2000 *Newspaper* – its first type specimen – LucasFonts announced the release of LF *Folha Serif*, but the face had to be withdrawn after some legal skirmishes with MetaDesign's then financial director.

▾ Folha was designed as a headline typeface for the Brazilian daily *Folha de São Paulo* (1994). The typeface which De Groot produced for *Le Monde* and subsequently expanded to build the Floris family can be regarded as a continuation of Folha.

▿ De Groot's foundry LucasFonts published its first type catalogue in 2000.

63 Max Caflisch, Luc(as) de Groot, 'Henne oder Ei', in *Page* 10, 1997; Antje Dohmann (ed.), 'Schriften vor Gericht', in *Page* 01, 1998.

ABhamburgefnstickdalp

ABhamburgefnstickdalp

Corpid

Corpid, originally called Agrofont, was part of the corporate identity designed by Studio Dumbar for the Dutch Ministry of Agriculture, Nature Management and Fisheries. Before the overhaul, the Ministry's house typeface was Frutiger. As the Ministry wanted to equip all its computers with the font, it faced an expensive operation, having to purchase a massive multiple user license. De Groot: 'Studio Dumbar suggested that it would be more interesting to produce a new font to replace Frutiger. It would give the Ministry a unique and strong identity.' [64] He agreed to do the job for less than the Frutiger license would have cost.

The regular weight of the typeface had to be similar to Frutiger in weight, width and colour. Respecting these restraints De Groot managed to come up with a distinctly different design. In a short article published on the LucasFonts website, De Groot explains that his main objective was to make the characters more interesting and contemporary by 'getting tension all over the font'. Tension, he continues, 'is how the inner curve relates to the outer curve. I tend to put a bit more diagonal contrast into the fonts. Even in a very neutral, sans serif font like this, it brings a bit of a humanistic, calligraphic touch.' As with Thesis, the 'diagonal contrast' refers to Gerrit Noordzij's analysis of letterforms.

The six fonts needed (three weights, plus italics) were finished in a relatively short time. It was the production of the screen fonts for use in the office environment that turned out the most time-consuming part of the job. After having made a standard conversion to TrueType, using autohinting, the fonts looked 'horrible' on screen. It took De Groot two years to provide his client with a satisfying manually hinted set of fonts. 'When I thought it was pretty good I sent it off to the ministry. ... They had it tested by ergonomics people and they said, "*Arial* is still better". Arial is a built-in PC font which is always taken as a comparison, and the reason is that a few guys at Monotype spent months hinting Arial, so it's perfect in all sizes. If you want to make a font that is as good as Arial, it really takes a long time.' De Groot now claims that Agrofont/Corpid works better than Arial in many display sizes, because – like Frutiger – its forms are more open: it is much harder to confuse characters like a and e, or 6 and 8, when viewed in low resolution.

Corpid was made publicly available at the start of LucasFonts in 1999. The weight range was expanded with Light and Black versions; each weight was equipped with small caps and a Condensed series.

Sun Sans and TheAntiqua

In developing Sun Sans, De Groot worked with Chris Haage, art director at Sun Microsystems. The two had met in 1993 when the latter was working on *Blvd* magazine at the studio Hard Werken in Rotterdam. 'Sun wanted a display face that was typical of a headline style in an American newspaper, that is, rather condensed and heavy. Chris had interestingly bizarre ideas and the process took a long time. He showed me two reference examples of fonts that I would never have given a second look.' [65] In response to the brief, De Groot decided to put aside the contrast principles which had guided him in his earlier designs. Sun Sans, though similar in atmosphere to Thesis or Corpid, shows no traces of the diagonal stress derived from the broad-nibbed pen. 'Designing Sun Sans was quite a struggle,' says De Groot. 'I had to invent completely new principles.' Whereas earlier designs were rational step-by-step processes in which decisions could be verified against Noordzij's analysis of the

Corpid was designed to replace Frutiger (shown in black). While retaining the global proportions of Frutiger, De Groot changed the construction, giving the new typeface (shown in red) a subtle 'diagonal contrast', referring to Gerrit Noordzij's analysis of letterforms.

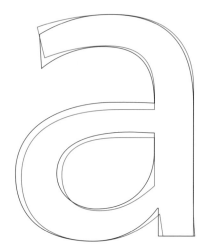

▾ TheAntiqua – 'Antiqua' is German for 'oldstyle' – was designed as a classical book face compatible with Thesis.

The Antiqua

Extra Light *Italic* Normal *Italic*
Bold ***Italic*** **Black *Italic***
CAPS EXTRA LIGHT **NORMAL**
BOLD **BLACK**

▾ Sun Sans, originally designed
as a corporate typeface for
Sun Microsystems.

⅄ Taz, originally made for the
German daily *TaZ*, is now the
foundry's second largest
type family.

23 Streamline Wizards
vaterschaftsanalyse
Federal Bureau closed
PHARCYDE /2MCS LEFTFIELD
Honululu *& the Supersurf*
EDMUNDSCHE STOIBERUNG
Electronic Bodhidharma
ARRONDISSEMENT DE NEUCHÂTEL
A tener encuenta durante la manipulacion

Hair04 AaBbCc *Aabcdefg*
Hair06 AaBbCc *Aabcdefg*
Hair09 AaBbCc *Aabcdefg*
Hair14 AaBbCc *Aabcdefg*
Hair21 AaBbCc *Aabcdefg*
UltraLightAaBb *Aabcdefg*
ExtraLight AaB *Aabcdefg*
Light AaBbCcD *Aabcdefg*
SemiLight AaB *Aabcdefg*
Regular AaBbC *Aabcdefg*
SemiBold AaB *Aabcdefg*
Bold AaBbCcD *Aabcdefg*
ExtraBold AaB *Aabcdefg*
Black AaBbCc *Aabcdefg*
UltraBlack Aa *Aabcdefg*

letterform, Sun Sans was much more intuitive, with 'nothing but trial and error to get the subtle weight differences in character strokes to harmonize with each other.' As a seriffed text face to go with Sun Sans, De Groot proposed a typeface which he called *TheAntiqua Sun*; it was in fact an adaptation of an existing design – still unpublished at the time – named TheAntiqua. 'Antiqua' is the generic German term for Oldstyle; and as the prefix suggests, the typeface is part of the larger Thesis family.

After Thesis had been published, De Groot watched with growing concern how graphic designers began using its seriffed versions TheSerif and TheMix for setting long texts, even entire books. Convinced that nothing beats a classically proportioned roman for legibility in small point sizes, he set out to design an oldstyle companion to Thesis – a rather cumbersome process, as De Groot still felt insecure about traditional romans. The Sun version, a simple family of six cuts, was the first to be finalized; later a different version was made for the daily *Taz*. The LucasFonts catalogue now features the complete TheAntiqua family (under the name *TheAntiquaB*) alongside the smaller custom-built series.

In TheAntiqua, the Thesis proportions have been combined with the conventions of the renaissance roman. Its wedge-shaped serifs are short and solid, its contrast is low; when looking for a precedent among modern classics, Plantin probably comes closest. Yet TheAntiqua's rather wide and 'uncalligraphic' italics don't seem to relate to any such historical model. TheAntiqua is as robust and inconspicuous a text face as one might wish for; but its unpretentiousness may also be considerd a drawback. From a designer as imaginative as Luc(as) de Groot, one might hope for a more spirited roman to see the light of day some time in the future.

Spiegel Sans and Taz

Der Spiegel is Germany's largest illustrated weekly. For it, De Groot designed an interesting sanserif which has been marketed as Spiegel Sans. Its romans are based on the proportions and forms of American early twentieth-century types such as *Franklin Gothic* and *News Gothic*; yet in its openness and in some details it has a distinct Hague touch. This becomes most evident in the Condensed Italic (the only italic in the family): it is not a sloped roman, like most other 'gothic' italics, but a real italic, with a one-eyed a and g, a rounded e and descending f.

Taz (formerly *Tazzer*) was commissioned by the German daily *Tageszeitung* (also known as *TaZ*). The newspaper wanted to get rid of its 1970s look and needed a contemporary headline typeface which in colour and power would match its predecessor, *Futura Bold Condensed*. The headline face was developed with space-saving in mind: it was narrow and had short extenders, as well as a small cap height. For setting longer texts in sanserif, De Groot designed *Tazzer Text*: 'a wider cut, with a two-storey a, which allows text columns to be set very efficiently.' The text version had a hybrid italic – halfway between a calligraphically inspired italic and a sloped roman – because 'a real italic has characteristics of handwriting, which we thought were unsuitable for this newspaper.'[66]

Since its inception as a no-frills newsface Taz has been further developed; the two versions have since merged into one extensive type family. In late 2003 LucasFonts presented *Taz III*. The new version has 15 weights, including 'hairline' variants in five degrees of lightness, and alternative a's for all weights. Designed to support OpenType technology and equipped with many special ligatures and diacritics for Central European languages, Taz III is announced as being 'future-proof'.

64 *Corpid™ Info*, article published on the lucasfonts.com website, 2002.

65 *Info Sun*, article published on the lucasfonts.com website, 2002.

66 Luc(as) de Groot, 'Taz', in Van Rixtel/Westerveld, *Letters*, Eindhoven 2001, pp 90 – 93.

The unprecedented letterforms of Peter Verheul

Peter Verheul has always been in close contact with Just van Rossum and the Van Blokland brothers, but he is not as interested as they are in the technicalities of the computer. The Macintosh is an important tool to him – for type design, graphic design and for composing music – but it is just that: a tool, mostly used for production. Much of the creative work is done by hand; sketches on paper are regarded as crucial in the preparatory phase. Verheul is an able draughtsman, having done numerous illustrations and hand-lettering jobs. He has also engraved letterforms in glass, which was to him 'a way of making the letters palpable'. Although he is a champion of old-fashioned craftsmanship, his type designs are by no means conventional. They show, in fact, a certain idiosyncracy which is striking in the context of the Hague school of type design.

As a student at the KABK, Verheul was a classmate of Just van Rossum. Apart from sharing a passion for the electric guitar, the two of them had, as Verheul puts it, 'a healthy competition' going between them – for instance, they challenged each other to take part in the Morisawa Awards type design competition when still students. Together they worked as interns at the hardware manufacturer Océ, where Fred Smeijers, Jeanne de Bont and Henk Lamers were employees at the time. It was also Van Rossum who established the contacts which led to Verheul's first foreign assignment: an internship with the London studio Banks & Miles, where he participated in the design of the *Johnston Underground* revival for London Transport (*New Johnston*), for which he drew the extra bold roman and the italic – a job he looks back at with some reserve.

Van Rossum, Verheul and Bart de Haas were the last KABK students to become members of the working group Letters]. Verheul's contacts with this group, most members of which had become professional type designers by then, was decisive for his later career. He assisted Peter Matthias Noordzij in the production of PMN Caecilia for Linotype in 1998; from 1991, he worked at Petr van Blokland's studio. Since 1996 he has run his one-man graphic design studio.[67]

The type sheets; Adetro and Illuster

Peter Verheul is as prolific a type designer as any of the Hague Academy graduates mentioned in this chapter. Yet during the first fifteen years of his designing career, only two of the dozen or so typefaces he designed were commercially released. Verheul's alphabets are made first and foremost for his own use. From the onset he aimed to create printed matter and electronic publications with self-designed typographic material. But although many of his fonts have not (and will not) become commercially available, he did issue two modest type specimens. Published in 1992 and 1993, these *Typesheets* on A4 format showed a remarkably versatile body of work and led to several publications in trade magazines.

Peter Verheul, *Typesheet*, 1993.

Illuster

The oldest typefaces shown in the *Typesheets* are *Adetro* (1987) and *Illuster* (1988), both dating back to his student days, both unpublished and both quite well-made. Adetro is a humanist sanserif with slightly thickened terminals; type historian Mathieu Lommen therefore placed it in the category of *glyphic* typefaces or *incises*, examplified by Herman Zapf's *Optima* or José Mendoza's *Pascal*. For some time, Linotype showed interest in the typeface and offered to digitize it, but this was never carried through. Illuster is a beautifully drawn outline alphabet with a subtle shading effect; its cheerful, round forms are related to those of Verheul's more recent *Versa* – the typeface used for the present book.

Newberlin and Sheriff

While working at Banks & Miles in 1989 Verheul had begun to design *Newberlin*, the unorthodox calligraphic font which would become his first published typeface. Newberlin was quickly sketched on paper, then immediately drawn in Fontographer. Despite Verheul's predilection for manual work this was the logical thing to do, as Newberlin consists completely of straight lines, joined by sharp corners. Its forms are rooted in the traditional renaissance italics Verheul had studied and practised in Gerrit Noordzij's writing class; yet the self-imposed limitations of the angular shapes have resulted in something completely different and unique. Verheul had designed the alphabet for his personal use, but when he faxed it to Just van Rossum, who was working at Meta Design in Berlin at the time, the studio's neighbour FontShop turned out to be very interested in publishing it. Van Rossum, who was experimenting with filters, provided alternative rough versions of both weights.

FF Sheriff was published as a FontFont five years after Newberlin, although its first version dates back to 1989. Sheriff – the name refers to the type's sturdy (slab) serifs – is part of the first batch of text faces conceived by the computer-literate generation. Like its contemporaries – *Caecilia, Quadraat, Scala* – Sheriff is rather dark in colour and low in contrast. This common trait was a conscious reaction to the way in which certain famous historical types – from *Bembo* to *Perpetua* – had eroded and thinned in their transition from lead type to photocomposition to digital formats. Sheriff is as unusual a design as Newberlin. In large sizes it looks quirky, almost awkward; in small sizes it is regular and clear, and makes for agreeable reading, holding up under adverse circumstances.

'I wanted to make a workhorse typeface,' says Verheul. 'A narrow, economic face to accommodate a lot of text in small magazine or newspaper columns. At the same time I had in mind a specific kind of construction.' The design's point of departure, he explains, was the shape of the n, in which the arch is joined to the stem at a straight angle. All other forms were derived from this principle. Although the italic has certain features of a 'real' italic, such as the one-eyed g and the single storey a, Verheul found it was not calligraphic enough to be called thus; he therefore came up with *Sheriff Italian*.

Unpublished typefaces

Verheul's *Typesheets* show several alphabets which have remained unpublished to this day; the 1993 sheet specifies 'All types in this little specimen are provisional versions'. In fact, one of the reasons why Verheul left many of his type designs unpublished is the amount of time and hard work that goes into the completion of fonts and the production of high quality final versions. As they are, these faces are good enough for personal use, and that is what their function has been so far.

Adetro
roman *italic*

Newberlin
Regular *Regular Rough* **Bold** ***Bold Rough***

Sheriff

Roman *Italian* **Roman Bold** *Italian*
De kwestie der uitvinding is eene kaatspartij van verwijten geworden; en terwijl het vroeger heette, dat Gutenberg en de Duitschers in meer dan één zin letterdieven geweest waren, vernemen wij thans, dat de Costerianen zelven, te beginnen met Junius en Scriverius, te vervolgen met Meerman en Koning, te eindigen met De Vries en Noordziek, tot de klasse der domkoppen, der kwakzalvers, der boerenbedriegers, en der letterkundige schavuiten behooren.

67 This article is based on several conversations with Peter Verheul. Additional information: Carla Wieske-Roomer, 'Peter Verheul. Tegen rek- en strekoefeningen', in *Graficus* 50, 1991, and Mathieu Lommen, 'Peter Verheul: een Haags letterontwerper', in *Bulletin Stichting Drukwerk in de Marge*, no. 21, 1993, pp 10–14.

Hanset   Hanset
Hanset   *Hanset*

 Euromodel

Nardy

cadavre

exquis

Rosebu*d*

⟨0⟩ ⟨20⟩ ⟨35⟩ ⟨50⟩ ⟨75⟩ ⟨100⟩ ⟨125⟩

Haganum (formerly known as *Discus*) is a typical 'Hague' roman of the Noordzij school, and perhaps this is precisely the reason why it has never been published. Had it been completed earlier, it might have been a very welcome addition to the spectrum of available book faces, with its firm triangular serifs and supple, rather upright italic. *Bumper*, also known as *Pumper*, has been described as 'a pumped-up sanserif'. 'The bold varieties of many typefaces,' Verheul explains, 'are not very interesting; they are simply bold. I think that each weight of a typeface has possibilities for specific qualities, other than the weight itself.'

This single alphabet design is based on the logo of a model agency; Verheul challenged himself to design an extremely heavy, yet elegant alphabet. The condensed roman *Fishbone* was also made for a precise purpose: Verheul created it for the lettering of a CD by that American group – not the original design, but his own copy. The alphabet was drawn as a parody of the all-too-easy grunge faces which were becoming fashionable at the time. Making fun of the type description lingo used to describe such novelties, he called it 'an informal, bad, useless typeface; you can also say that it has a nonchalance in its character.' [68] *Ornamenta* is an exception among the typeface of the Hague school: like Bram de Does's *Kaba Ornament*, it is a small collection of compatible abstract forms which can be combined to create a great variety of ornaments. And like Kaba, *Ornamenta* plays a smart game with positive and negative versions of the same basic shapes.

A typeface for Goethe

In 1997 Verheul was invited to design a book for the Stichting De Roos, an association of bibliophiles which since 1946 has produced an exquisite collection of limited-edition illustrated books. The volume of fragments from Johann Wolfgang Goethe's diaries was to be illustrated by Dik Klut, a versatile Hague illustrator. As there was ample time to realize the assignment, Verheul decided it would be a good idea to design a new alphabet for the occasion. *Rosebud*, named after the rose in the association's name, was designed in four weights, from regular to black. It is an italics-only face strongly rooted in handwriting with the pointed pen. Most capitals, as well as the lowercase d, have small swashes; the varying angles of the slope make it an extremely lively, agile typeface. The fact that the typeface was custom-made for a precise goal is revealed by the small height of the uppercase characters: this is very suitable for a collection of poems printed in German, as all nouns in that language are written with a capital. The rose ornament Verheul drew as a vignette for the title page was subsequently adopted by the Roos foundation as its new logo.

a nerkotsyb lmigfjzxvw œfiœHflfc,.

◄ OurType Versa started out in 1994 as Nardy, an italic display face.

▼ From 1998 Verheul set out to expand Nardy into a full-fledged text type called Versa. After it had been chosen for the present book, many more styles were added, including a sanserif, a condensed sans and a wide headline version.

Versa

Light *Italic* Regular *Italic* **Semi Bold** *Italic*
Bold *Italic* **Black** *Italic* SMALL CAPS
LIGHT *ITALIC* OPEN REGULAR *ITALIC*
OPEN **SEMI BOLD ITALIC** OPEN
BOLD ITALIC OPEN **BLACK ITALIC**
OPEN
Extended Light *Italic* Regular *Italic*
Semi Bold *Italic* **Bold** *Italic*
Black *Italic* SMALL CAPS LIGHT
REGULAR **SEMI BOLD** **BOLD** **BLACK**

Versa Sans

Light *Italic* Regular *Italic* **Semi Bold** *Italic*
Bold *Italic* **Black** *Italic* SMALL CAPS
LIGHT *ITALIC* REGULAR *ITALIC*
SEMI BOLD *ITALIC* **BOLD ITALIC**
BLACK ITALIC
Condensed Light *Italic* Regular *Italic*
Semi Bold *Italic* **Bold** *Italic* **Black Italic**
SMALL CAPS LIGHT *ITALIC* REGULAR *ITALIC*
SEMI BOLD *ITALIC* **BOLD ITALIC**
BLACK ITALIC
Extended Light *Italic* Regular *Italic*
Semi Bold *Italic* **Bold** *Italic*
Black *Italic* SMALL CAPS LIGHT
REGULAR **SEMI BOLD** **BOLD BLACK**

Versa, from display to text

Verheul's largest type project so far is *OurType Versa*, the typeface used for this book. First conceived in 1993 as a rather bold italic headline face, it was subsequently extrapolated to create lighter and extra bold weights. The italic's main feature is its voluptuous, undulating aspect, brought about by the bowed verticals; 'in fact, there is not a straight line in sight,' Verheul wrote.[69] The original *Nardy* appeared occasionally as a headline face, used by Verheul himself or borrowed from him by colleagues, but its designer felt the design had more potential. From 1998 he set out to expand the design into a full-fledged text type. A roman was derived from the italic. Verheul wrote: 'Naturally, the italic has determined the roman to a large extent. Parameters such as weight, x-height and extender length were adopted from it. At an early stage I did try – as I always do – to keep open as many options as possible. The italic's rather organic dynamism led to interesting forms in the roman lowercase, notably the d, a, e and n. However, these dominant forms undermined the roman's stability, thus causing its waggling forms to be incongruous with the more balanced italic.' Adjustments were made to create a more regular image: the counter of the lowercase e was made symmetric, stopping the character from falling over; and the n was stabilized by straightening its stems.

The most remarkable feature of the Versa roman is the shape of its serifs. In the italic, the typeface hardly has serifs: the terminals are naturally thickened, as if painted with a round brush. For the roman, the designer conceived an unusual, asymmetric, speedboat-shaped serif which in small point sizes makes Versa almost look like an *incise* or *glyphic* – a hard-to-define but very legible hybrid.

The decision to use Versa for the present book has been crucial in the further structuring of the type family. In order to be able to accommodate a lot of information in the narrow columns of the captions, it was decided to design a narrow sanserif, from which a more 'regular' sans – not needed for this book – was then derived. Extra fonts were designed for particular purposes: a wide version for titles, and a slightly bolder roman for the 7pt running texts at the foot of the page. Finally, a special set of superior numerals, halfway between lining and 'hanging', was added.

Publications

In 1991, three years after graduating from the KABK, Verheul became a teacher of type design at the same school. He is now one of the permanent teachers of the school's postgraduate Type and Media course. In connection with this position, Verheul co-edited and/or designed several publications which deal with type education at the KABK. In 1996 De Buitenkant in Amsterdam published *Haagse letters* (Hague letterforms), edited by Verheul and Mathieu Lommen. The book was launched to coincide with the ATypI Conference which the Royal Academy hosted in The Hague in late 1996. In typographic circles, the book has achieved the status of a classic: a small but

68 Mathieu Lommen, 'Peter Verheul' (cit.), p 12.

69 Peter Verheul, 'Nardy, van display- tot tekstletter', in Van Rixtel and Westerveld, *Letters*, Eindhoven 2001, pp 78–81. This book also contains Verheul's article 'Een visie op letterontwerpen vanaf 1900', a personal view of a century of (Dutch) type design.

0123456789

0123456789

indispensable overview of type education and production in the Hague tradition. Part of it is a type specimen of virtually all typefaces – from student projects to the faces released by major foundries – rooted in Gerrit Noordzij's school of type design. *Special characters from The Hague*, published in 1998, is a trilingual booklet produced to promote the KABK's postgraduate course Type Design & Typography (later: Type & Media) at home as well as abroad. Written by the department's head Anno Fekkes and edited by Mathieu Lommen, the booklet presents the various aspects of type education, as well as work by the teachers. It was one of the first publications in which Verheul's Nardy was showcased as a text face.

Gerrit Noordzij's teachings were the subject of *Het primaat van de pen* ('The Primacy of the Pen'), edited by Fekkes, Lommen, Verheul and Jan Willem Stas, and published in early 2000 on the occasion of the Gerrit Noordzij exhibition in the KABK. The booklet was the result of a workshop given by Noordzij in November 2001 to KABK students. It was designed by Peter Verheul and Bart de Haas – the latter had been a fellow member of the Letters] group in the 1980s. This collaboration proved successful, and the same team was asked to work on the design of the present book.

Letters from Arnhem

Fred Smeijers, Sloane, c. 1996. Unpublished typeface of four variants exploring the transition from a typographic italic to a formal cursive. Smeijers: 'The idea was not mine, but Fournier's. By replacing only a few characters from one of his typographic italics with a more flowing form, Pierre Simon Fournier created a plausible imitation of formal classicist handwriting. With Open Type we will be able to develop this concept further.'

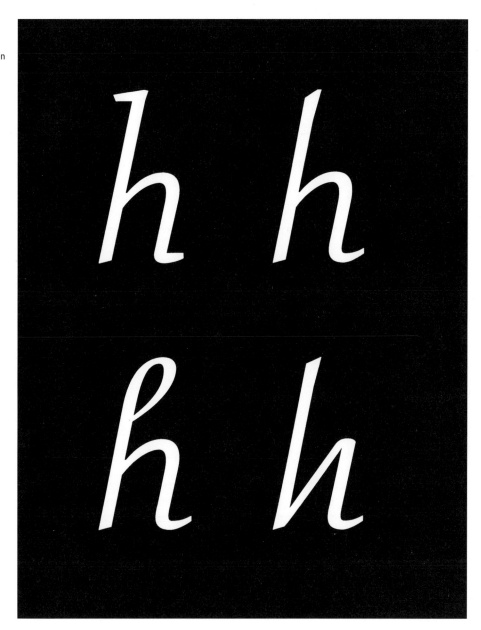

Type design and dissidence

Unlike the Royal Academy in The Hague, the Arnhem Art Academy never developed a programme concerned with the creation of type or letterforms. Yet the school has yielded some of the country's best-known type designers, so that Arnhem – the largest city in the eastern Netherlands – is often regarded as the second 'alphabet city' after The Hague. This is largely the merit of a handful of individuals.

Evert Bloemsma, Martin Majoor and Fred Smeijers all graduated from the Arnhem Academy in the early 1980s. As type designers they are largely self-taught; in art school their decision to focus on letterforms met with considerable resistance from certain teachers. The fact that Majoor and Smeijers sought inspiration in traditional crafts such as calligraphy and letter-carving was barely tolerated in the rather rigidly modernist atmosphere of the Academy where only two teachers, Alexander Verberne and Jan Vermeulen, stimulated these interests.

Another type designer who had close connections with these two teachers is Julius de Goede, a student of an older generation who rebelled against the dominance of modernism at the Arnhem Art Academy by embracing realist illustration; he later became a calligrapher. Among the Arnhem graduates who have published less conventional typefaces, Roelof Mulder – originally a painter and sculptor – and Alex Scholing stand out; both have been inspired by the work of their fellow Arnhemmers, notably Smeijers and Majoor.

▹ Scala Sans specimen, FontShop 1993. Concept by Martin Majoor, design by Jaap van Triest, another graduate of the Arnhem Art Academy.

▹ Fred Smeijers, corrected proof settings of Quadraat Sans Italic. FF Quadraat Sans was published in 1996 by FontShop International.

The justification of Evert Bloemsma

Few typefaces have been as long in the making as *Balance* by Evert Bloemsma (1958).
A preliminary version of the design was presented at his 1981 graduation exhibition
at the Arnhem Academy; eleven years would pass before FF *Balance* was released as
part of FontShop's FontFont type library. To a large extent, this lengthy incubation
period was due to practical circumstances. Just like other faces created during the
1980s, *Balance* went through a rather troublesome series of reworkings, from the
hand-drawn design, via digitization for a high-end typesetting system, to the final
form in PostScript. But Balance's long design period also reflects its maker's personality. Evert Bloemsma is one of the more thoughtful of the current generation
of type designers. He is a thinker who makes the highest demands on his own work
– not just at the levels of technicality and readability, but also conceptually. He has
set himself the task of inventing new forms which, although rooted in tradition,
contribute something really new to the spectrum of letterforms. The three typefaces
he has created so far – Balance, *Cocon* and *Avance* – amply meet these ambitions. They
are workmanlike and well-conceived, in addition to being original and of their
time. The three types are also very different from one another.

Bloemsma has explained his principles in several lectures and articles. One of his
basic assumptions is the changing relationship which designers and users have
with technology. In the graphic design field as well as the household, technology has
become increasingly invisible, hidden behind user-friendly interfaces and plastic
coverings. Similarly, letters have been separated from the technical constraints of
their representation. 'Tradition, manufacturing, functioning and material can hardly be seen as constraining factors for defining a formal expression any more,'
Bloemsma wrote. 'In this sense the designer is left to his own devices. Where can he
find the clues for connecting the commonplace with the miraculous?' Bloemsma
believes that transplanting old insights to a new age is generally of little use. 'We live
in a world which only ten years ago could be regarded as science fiction,' he wrote in
1997. 'This fact must, of course, be expressed in type.'[1]

Bloemsma's explorations of letterforms for new technologies are informed by a
wide interest in other media. In his lectures, he has drawn parallels between letters
and the design of buildings, domestic appliances, bicycles and cars. For several
years, he worked as an architectural photographer, participating in a number of
projects, including the creation of an exhibition and photo book about Le Corbu-
sier's Chandigarh project in India.

A delicate Balance

During his studies at the Arnhem Academy Bloemsma was fascinated by 'Swiss
typography' – the approach to graphic design which in the Netherlands was labelled
'functionalist'. For the project *Opvattingen over typografie* (Opinions on Typography, a
box of diverse publications issued by the Arnhem Academy in 1984) he conducted an

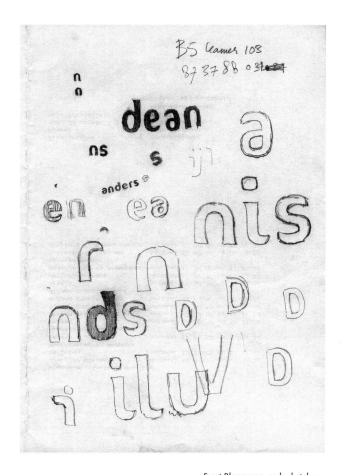

Evert Bloemsma, early sketches
of FF Cocon, c.1997.

1   Evert Bloemsma, lecture held during the CiType seminar, Karel de Grote Hogeschool,
Antwerp, October 1997 (unpublished).

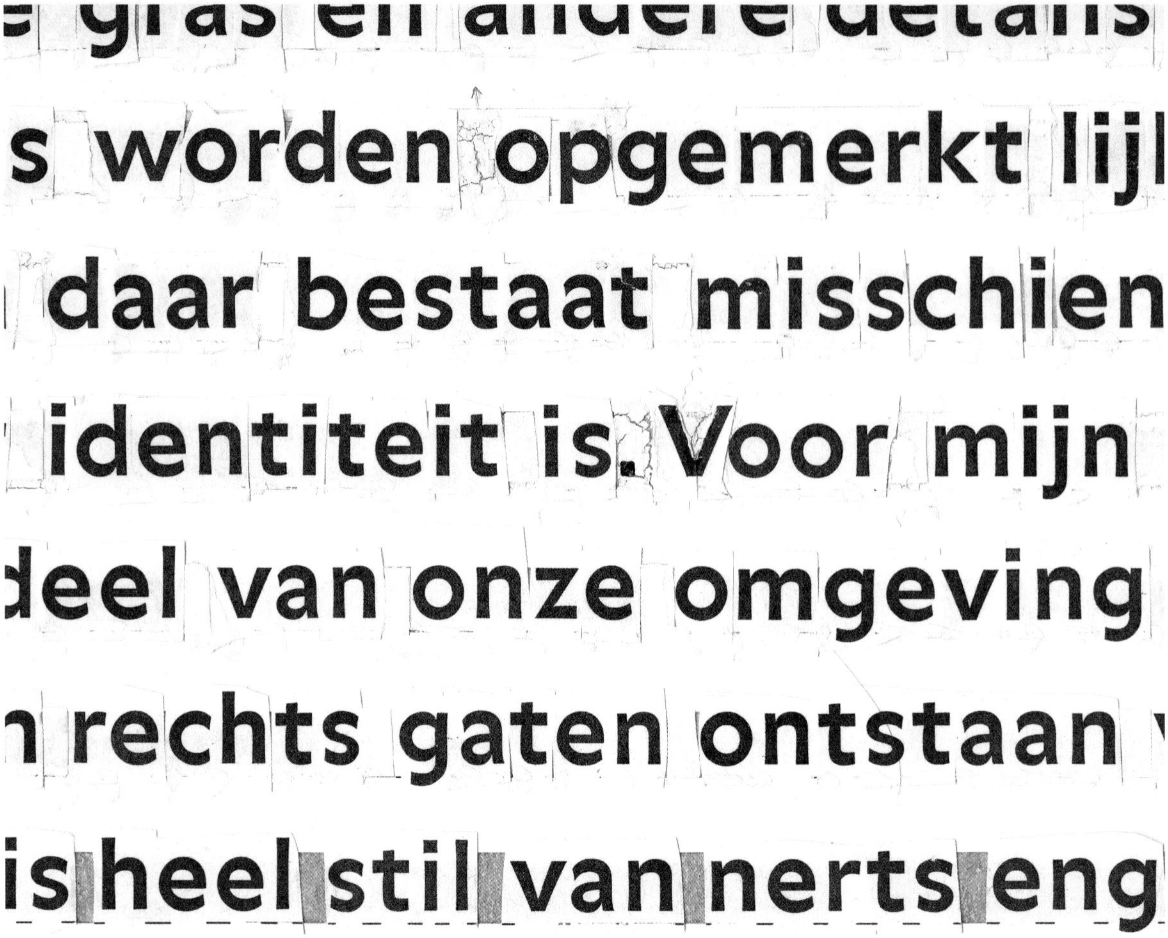

s gras en andere details
s worden opgemerkt lij
daar bestaat misschien
identiteit is. Voor mijn
deel van onze omgeving
n rechts gaten ontstaan
is heel stil van nerts eng

▸ Paste-up proof of the earliest version of Balance, 1981.

▾ In FF Balance, all weights have equal width, so that the user can decide to substitute one weight for another at the last moment.

Une ligne a *toujours la même longueur* quelle que soit la graisse de la LETTRE.

Une ligne a *toujours la même longueur* quelle que soit la graisse de la LETTRE.

Une ligne a *toujours la même longueur* quelle que soit la graisse de la LETTRE.

Une ligne a *toujours la même longueur* quelle que soit la graisse de la LETTRE.

Balance

Light *Italic* Regular *Italic*
Bold *Italic* **Black *Italic***
SMALL CAPS LIGHT *ITALIC*
REGULAR *ITALIC* **BOLD *ITALIC***
BLACK *ITALIC*

extensive interview with Wim Crouwel, the best-known representative of that persuasion. Given Bloemsma's interest in modernist typography, it followed that his first typeface was to be a sanserif: his opinion at the time was that there was no place for serifs in the era of new technologies.

Yet the typefaces nearest his heart were not *Univers* and *Helvetica*, those impeccably cold Swiss faces which functionalist designers had embraced emphatically. In spite of his fascination with rational thinking, Bloemsma had a penchant for the nonconformist, the Latin, the elusive. He admired, for instance, the types of Roger Excoffon, the quintessential French type designer. He was intrigued by Excoffon's *Antique Olive*, a typeface which still enjoys popularity in Latin countries, in spite of – or perhaps because of – its eccentricity. Antique Olive has two unusual features which Bloemsma adopted in his Balance: it is top-heavy – subtly sturdier at the top than at the base – and it has an 'inverted stress', where the horizontals are heavier than the verticals.

It is typical of Bloemsma that he has taken much trouble to rationalize and justify, after the fact, his intuitive predilection for such unusual proportions. 'Experience has taught us that bodies which are heavier at the bottom than at the top stand firmer on the ground and fall over less easily. Therefore, perhaps, these proportions give a sense of safety, security and continuity. Proportional relations like these can be found in most printing types of past centuries. But is this idea really applicable to

Letters from Arnhem

Uso dell'asciugatrice:
Non asciugare capi di lana
Risparmiare costi d'energia

type? Aren't letters simply printed on paper? They are not affected by gravity, are they? There is no functional reason for the classic proportions of letterforms. In fact, recognizability and readability largely depend on the top half of most characters. So perhaps enhancing this half can have a positive effect on readability.'[2] The objective of improved readability is also used to explain *Balance*'s other unusual feature: the stressing of the horizontals. This 'inverted contrast' leads the eye along the lines of text and thus attempts to compensate for the absence of serifs, which have a similar function.

Even though Balance has been designed with the reader in mind, it is nevertheless a typeface with unorthodox shapes. This is not necessarily problematic and it makes the typeface an interesting alternative to *Univers* or *Frutiger*. It is clearly part of the same modern tradition, but it is more idiosyncratic and more contemporary – without looking anything like the many 'humanist sanserifs' which have recently been published.

Bloemsma tried in vain to sell the first versions of Balance to a number of well-known international foundries (several of which, as he subtly pointed out in a lecture, have now folded or been taken over): Berthold, Linotype, Purup, Monotype and ITC. In 1986 he was given the opportunity to digitize the font using the Ikarus system developed by his then employer, URW in Hamburg, though their publication of the font was not an option. Finally, in 1992, the PostScript version of Balance was completed and that same year it was published as part of the FontFont library. FF Balance – a well-equipped family with four weights, small caps and two sets of figures – was not an immediate success. Designers are not easily convinced of its usability until they see it applied in an interesting way. Since its publication, however, interest has steadily risen as some remarkable books employing the typeface have appeared both in Europe and North America.

Cocon: extremely sans

Bloemsma's second typeface, FF Cocon (1998) was also published by FontShop. Like Balance, Cocon questions conventional principles of type forms. It tackles an aspect which is part and parcel of the tradition of type design, to the extent that it is hardly noticed any more: the origin of letterforms in writing. 'Type designers should beware of unthinkingly adapting and repeating accepted conventions. Typography is full of traditions, and is therefore a field full of designer pitfalls. Before getting to work, you must be aware of all those conventions passed down to us, otherwise you won't succeed in adding something substantial.'[3]

In the first sketches for Cocon, Bloemsma made an attempt at erasing every trace of handwriting, arguing that even an 'industrial' typeface such as *Helvetica* contains many references to writing in its stems and terminals. Bloemsma realized that it was more complicated than expected to eliminate these elements, yet retain a convincing, natural-looking result. An initial experiment with a letterform with completely straight terminals proved unsuccessful. Finally, he let in a calligraphic element through the back door: the terminals of the stems and extenders were given an elegant asymmetrical rounding, creating the suggestion that the characters were drawn with a (round) brush. These ingenious curves seem to have a practical function as well: they propel the eye forward from left to right, an effect similar to that of FF Balance's unconventional stress.

When writing about Cocon, Bloemsma has described it as a 'serious typeface', apparently referring to the many hours of experimentation that went into the design, as

2   Bloemsma, CiType lecture (cit.).

3   Interview with Evert Bloemsma.

Espace qu'on a parcouru
avant quelqu'un, distance
qui en sépare.
*Espace qu'on a parcouru
avant quelqu'un, distance
qui en sépare.*
**Espace qu'on a parcouru
avant quelqu'un, distance
qui en sépare.**
***Espace qu'on a parcouru
avant quelqu'un, distance
qui en sépare.***

◁ Evert Bloemsma's FF Avance
was published by FontShop
International in 2000.

▽ Avance was developed over a
series of drastic reworkings of
the initial concept, sketched in
1996. The early straight-lined
version (bottom) appeared to
tumble backwards. The letters
were therefore subtly slanted
and the strokes were given
curved, more organic shapes.

▽ FF Legato, 2004.

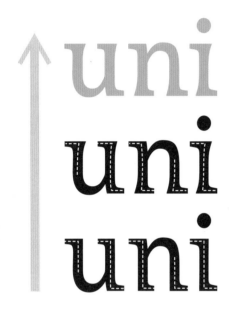

Legato

Light *Italic* Regular *Italic* **Semibold** ***Italic***
Bold ***Italic*** SMALL CAPS LIGHT *ITALIC*
REGULAR *ITALIC* **SEMIBOLD** ***ITALIC***
BOLD ***ITALIC*** Tot hiertoe is geen enkel
bewijs geleverd, dat hetzij achter de
herberg van den schepen Lourens Janszoon
te Haarlem, hetzij achter de werkplaats van
den kaarsemaker Coster aldaar, zich eene
drukkerij bevonden heeft.

well as the wide spectrum of possible uses. In large sizes Cocon is a display face with
unusual details, in small sizes it remains surprisingly readable. In spite of its claims
to seriousness, Cocon is a family of seductive, voluptuous fonts – suited for anything
from packaging to the design of an architecture book, for which it has already been
used. In 2001 Cocon was expanded with an italic – which the first release lacked – and
a compressed version, in addition to the condensed.

Avance: no dead lines

Like Cocon, Bloemsma's third typeface FF Avance (2000) offers an expedient to guide
the reader's eye in a forward direction. This is realized by means of sturdy serifs
which point to the left at the top and to the right at the base of each character.
Creating a serif or semi-serif font was quite a step for Bloemsma, whose work was
guided by the principles of functionalist aesthetics. While he had long been convinced that contemporary type design was incompatible with serifs, he has embraced a less dogmatic stance in recent years, having decided that serifs can help
a typeface to be read more easily and thus enhance its functionality.
Bloemsma's initial source of inspiration for Avance was Adrian Frutiger's *Icone*, published by Linotype in 1980, and currently unavailable as a PostScript font. Icone is a
hybrid between a incised or 'glyphic' face and a semi-serif: the small, triangular serifs protrude on both sides of the stem, but are subtly asymmetric. Bloemsma's first
sketches followed this model rather closely, and he even corresponded with Frutiger to ask his permission to take up the idea. Later, the triangular shape was abandoned for a horizontally stressed, curved form which is more distinctly asymmetric.
Although for its designer it was a somewhat speculative experiment, Avance is quite
a successful design; more so, in fact, than its initial model. In small point sizes it is
virtually indestructible – a kind of *Century Schoolbook* for the twenty-first century.
When used in bigger sizes, the typeface appears to possess a stiff kind of swing; it
becomes clear that it is almost completely constructed with curved forms. Perhaps
the latter is the main constant in Bloemsma's typefaces, so that all of his small but
sophisticated body of work can be regarded as a tribute to his teacher Jan Vermeulen, whose dictum 'a straight line is a dead line' has been a guiding light to Bloemsma throughout his career.

Custom type and Legato

Unlike Fred Smeijers and Martin Majoor, Bloemsma does not regard himself as a
graphic designer or typographer. Apart from his position as a teacher of typography
at the Breda St. Joost Academy, all his work is directly related to type design. In recent years Bloemsma has devoted much of his time to fine-tuning existing typefaces, doing hinting work for Monotype and customizing fonts for clients of Font-
Shop Benelux. Among the typefaces designed for specific clients, there is a sanserif
text face for schoolbooks for the publisher Wolters Noordhof. Recently Bloemsma
developed an Open Type font based on the cursive *Normschrift* (standard script) central to the writing method published by the *Broeders van Liefde* (Friars of Charity) of the
Flemish city of Ghent. Using Open Type's possibilities to automatically select alternate characters according to context, he obtained a natural, hand-written look.
At the moment of this writing, Bloemsma has resumed his explorations of the conventions of type design. In mid-2003 the FontFont type board accepted his proposal for a new sanserif, which was then developed over the subsequent months. The
new typeface will be called *FF Legato* – a name that does not refer to actual 'connections' between characters, but to an internal tension that enhances the cohesion of
the word. In Legato Bloemsma examines the traditional notion of diagonal contrast
or stress, unlinking that stylistic feature from writing with the broad-nibbed pen.
The shapes of Legato's counters seem to contradict the outside curves, making the
letterforms more interesting and, paradoxically, more coherent. As in his earlier
designs, Bloemsma's speculations have again led to the creation of a typeface that is
not only original and fresh, but also possesses great clarity and usability. Bloemsma
is convinced that Legato is his best typeface to date.

Fred Smeijers: from punches to pixels

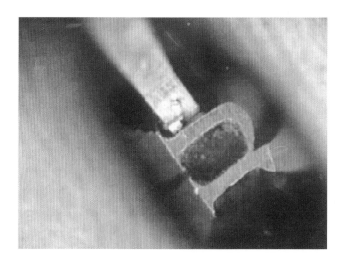

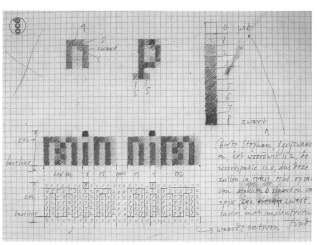

^ Fred Smeijers, drawing for a
grey-scale screen font, made
at Océ, c. 1988.

‡ Still from a video made during
a punchcutting demonstration
by Fred Smeijers, c. 1996.

Many older typographers, type designers and typesetters have witnessed the advent of digital typography with suspicion and, sometimes, panic. Where could they look to gain an understanding of the behaviour of vectors and bitmaps? In the mid-1990s, Fred Smeijers (1961) came up with a surprising and interesting answer: by studying the punchcutters of the sixteenth century. In his book *Counterpunch: making type in the sixteenth century, designing typefaces now* (1996) Smeijers builds a bridge between the past and the present. He makes it clear that there are fewer differences between type production in those early stages of 'the craft' and digital type design than we are inclined to think. And he shows that an awareness of traditional techniques and an understanding of digital technology are not mutually exclusive. Smeijers's varied oeuvre of typeface designs, too, is proof of his wide interests and limitless curiosity. Besides classically inspired book typefaces such as *Quadraat* and *Renard* he has drawn everything from bitmap and grey-scale fonts for use on screens to logos for kitchen utensils.

Smeijers's fascination with the typographic tradition developed during his studies at the Academy of Fine Arts in Arnhem. With his fellow student and roommate Martin Majoor he explored the disciplines that have nurtured type design throughout the centuries, from writing with a quill to carving letters in stone; simultaneously the two students experimented with the first digital font editors. Their first experience with type production came when their guest teacher Nico Spelbrink had a look at the italic alphabets drawn in Alexander Verberne's writing classes and proposed that they justify them on a unit system. Smeijers wrote: 'This imaginary production process made it possible for us to look at our own letters in relation to typographic measurements', and compare '[their] performance with real typefaces.' [4]

After graduation both Smeijers and Majoor were hired by Océ in Venlo, a Dutch manufacturer of printing and photocopying hardware. From 1986 to 1990 Smeijers worked in the Industrial Design section of the company's Research & Development department. Like Gerard Unger before him, he took part in the design of fonts for early laser printers, which often meant working with existing typefaces that had to be radically adapted to obtain an acceptable result. Océ engineers repeatedly approached Smeijers with questions about the specifics of type design, for which he did not have easy answers. For instance, he found it difficult to explain why a resolution of 300 dots per inch – which at the time was the norm for laser printers – was not sufficient to accurately represent the details of letters. Smeijers decided to return to the source: the mostly forgotten techniques of primordial type design.

In his book *Counterpunch* Smeijers describes how, over the course of dozens of visits to the Plantin-Moretus Museum in Antwerp, he examined its rare collection of early typographic material in order to reconstruct the daily practice of sixteenth-century

4 Fred Smeijers, *Type Now*, London 2003, p 127.

Early sketches for Quadraat
Italic, taking written letterforms
as a reference.

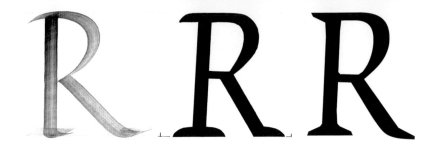

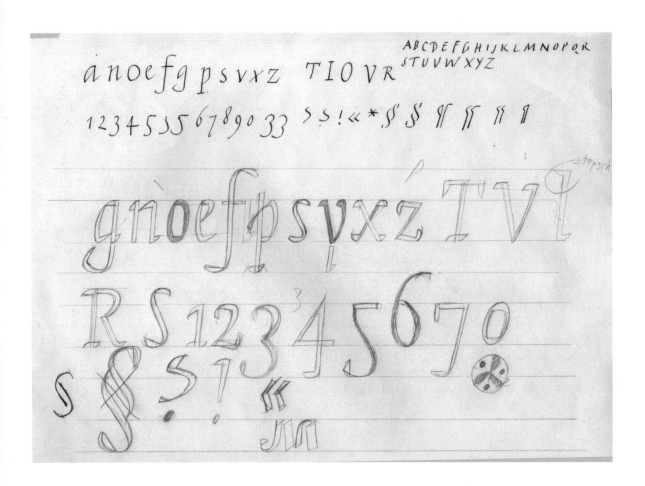

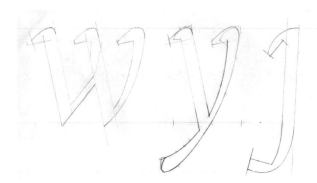

punchcutters. He set out to teach himself their craft with the help of books and by carefully studying the original instruments. He was also unexpectedly aided by the expertise of his father, a former metal worker who had cut seals used to print cigar bands. Smeijers observed that the soft steel used for the punches allowed for very fine detailing. While making minuscule shavings, Smeijers discovered that even the slightest tooling had an effect on the character's image. He proceeded to photograph and measure the shavings using an electron microscope, making the refinements of old printing type quantifiable and measurable – and thus intelligible to the engineers at his firm.

Smeijers's punchcutting experience was instrumental in helping formulate his ideas about contemporary type design. 'Since the advent of the desktop computer,' says Smeijers, 'designers have become used to looking at their drawings on a large screen. This fosters the tendency to approach letterforms in a very rational way. One tends to view them with a mundane kind of logic: are they *tidy* enough? Cutting punches has taught me what it is like to work at actual size – which is extremely small. I realized that today's freedom, the possibility of seeing characters on a large screen, takes away much of the nerve. Seen at large size, unusual forms look very rugged, very impudent. In the Plantin-Moretus Museum I had the chance, day after day, to scrutinize unique historical material, letter shapes which still are a measur-

◄ Sketches of the comma of Quadraat Sans.

▾ Sketches of the Quadraat Sans Italic ampersand, with the published version printed in red, c. 1994.

▾ Following the publication of the FF Quadraat core family in 1992 and Quadraat Sans in 1996, Smeijers designed several display versions of the typeface, partly based on earlier lettering jobs done as a member of the Quadraat studio and Het Lab.

ing stick for quality. I encountered many quirky details which do not strike the eye at small point sizes but do give the letter a certain liveliness.'[5]

An early outcome of these discoveries was *Quadraat*, a book typeface with classical proportions but very contemporary and idiosyncratic details. The FF Quadraat core family was published at FontShop in 1992, followed by *Quadraat Sans* and its *Condensed*, as well as *Quadraat Display* and *Headline*. Simultaneously with *Quadraat Head* (2000) Smeijers published *Quadraat Mono*, a code-friendly monospaced version which is so elegantly drawn that it surpasses its functionality and can be used (perhaps with some negative spacing) as an interesting headline face.

As a book face, Quadraat is flamboyant without being obtrusive. It is relatively economical and retains its legibility and rather dark colour even at small point sizes. Combined with the sanserif and headline varieties, it has become a favourite with designers of typographically complex publications, from books and magazines to arts listings. Like *Scala*, *Sheriff* and many other recent Dutch fonts, Quadraat's figures follow the traditional typographic forms: oldstyle or hanging figures are default, while Quadraat even has a series of special-size lining figures to accompany the small caps.

Like many of his peers, Smeijers has felt the need to justify *Quadraat* by explaining, in writing and in interviews, why it was necessary for him to design yet another typeface. From these statements it becomes clear that Smeijers approaches a new type design from the point of view of the type user – the typographer. 'You want to design the typeface that is missing from your typographic palette,' he says. The original impetus behind Quadraat was Smeijers's need for a typeface 'somewhere in between *Plantin* and *Times*': lighter than the first, darker than the second. In retrospect, of course, Quadraat was so original (and so good) that it did not have to be justified in this way, but the need to do so was understandable at a time when creating new book faces was still an uncommon ambition for young designers.

During the development of Quadraat, Smeijers allowed non-specialists to influence his decisions by taking informal surveys similar to the 'focus group' pre-tests set up by marketers and product developers. 'I would simply draw various options and ask for the opinion of a bus driver, the dentist, my mother. Look here a minute, I'd say, this word and that: do you see a difference? Which do you like best? I realized that normal people notice differences just like any typographer, but lack the means to express it.'

Boekblad and Nobel

Smeijers's subsequent typefaces were the result of external rather than personal demands. *Boekblad*, his first typeface after Quadraat, was a headline font for the magazine of the same name – 'Book Paper', a trade monthly for booksellers – for which Smeijers's studio Quadraat designed the template in 1993. 'I made some characters

Quadraat

Regular *Italic* **Bold** ***Italic***
SMALL CAPS *ITALIC* **BOLD ITALIC**

Quadraat Sans

Regular *Italic* **Bold** SMALL CAPS
Condensed Regular *Italic* **Bold Italic**

Quadraat Display

Italic **Bold Italic**
Sans Semi Bold **Sans Black**

Quadraat Headliner

Light *Italic* **Bold Italic**

Quadraat Sans Mono

Regular *Italic* **Bold Italic**

5   Quotes based on several interviews held with Fred Smeijers, 1997–2000.

▼ Nobel, a revival of a 1930s typeface from the Amsterdam Type Foundry designed with Andrea Fuchs. The typeface was brought out by Dutch Type Library, but Nobel Open, Nobel Shadow and Nobel Ornaments remained unpublished.

▸ Boekblad, Smeijers's first typeface after Quadraat, was a headline font for the magazine *Boekblad* – 'Book Paper', a trade monthly for booksellers – for which Smeijers's Quadraat studio designed the template in 1993.

Boekblad De uitvinder der boekdrukkunst kan verstoken zijn geweest van muzikaal gevoel zowel als van financieel beleid.

NOBEL OPEN
NOBEL SHADOW

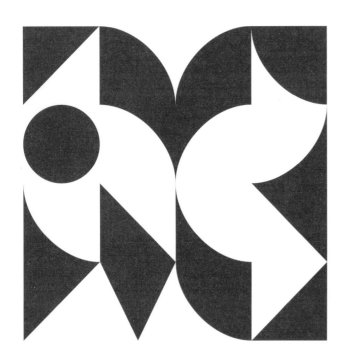

for display just for fun, which we inserted among other proposals,' Smeijers wrote ten years later.[6] 'To my surprise these were taken rather seriously, resulting in my first custom-made typeface.'

While a teacher at the Arnhem Academy, Smeijers was approached by German student Andrea Fuchs, who wanted to create a revival of *Nobel*, Sjoerd de Roos's reworking of *Berthold Grotesk*. While detested by the post-war functionalists, *Nobel* intrigued a younger generation of designers, who were charmed rather than annoyed by its ambiguity. Fuchs – who had no ambitions as a type designer – had found Nobel as a foundry type in the school's printing shop and wanted to use the typeface on her computer. Smeijers guided Fuchs through the first steps of a digital design, then warmed to the task and became a co-designer. Both of them spent considerable time researching and combining models from the many versions of Nobel published over the years by the Amsterdam Type Foundry. When the designers considered publishing the font after completion in 1993, it became clear that Tetterode – the company that continued the business of the Amsterdam Type Foundry – had recently sold the copyrights to the typeface to Frank E. Blokland's Dutch Type Library. DTL agreed to publish the new digital version. Smeijers and Fuchs also designed two alphabets of decorative capitals, an interesting set of ornaments and a 'wood type version', from which Fuch's life partner Just van Rossum derived a Type3 font with a built-in random wobble function, *WiebelNobel*. As DTL did not have much interest in these more frivolous varieties, they have remained unpublished.

Renard, a tribute to Hendrik van den Keere; Romanée

In 1996, Smeijers's book *Counterpunch* was delivered by the printer just in time for the annual ATypI conference in The Hague. For the *TypeLab* newspaper produced daily during the conference, the book's publisher and editor Robin Kinross wrote an account of how *Counterpunch* was made.[7] He described how the various jobs involved in its production – author, editor, designer, publisher – were initially divided between Smeijers and himself, until Françoise Berserik and Peter Paul Kloosterman stepped in as designer/co-editor and co-designer respectively. One of the reasons why the team had to be expanded was the fact that Smeijers had decided to design a new typeface for the book. Appropriate to *Counterpunch*'s contents, the font was a revival of one of the types cut by Hendrik van den Keere, the sixteenth-century punchcutter from Ghent who, as Kinross wrote, is 'a hero of the book'.

Renard is an interpretation of the *Canon Romain* (or 2-line Double Pica Roman, approximately 44 pts) cut around 1570 for Christophe Plantin in Antwerp, who at that time ran one of Europe's largest printing houses and was Van den Keere's main client. The typeface, shown in Plantin's folio specimen of circa 1585, was cut in a large size for display setting. A typical application would have been the text of a hymn in a choir-book, which would then be placed in front of the choir for all singers to read.

Agefilaus. Alio quodam laudante rheto-
rem hoc nomine, quòd mirificè res
exiguas verbis amplificaret: Ego,
inquit, ne futorem quidem arbitrer
bonum, qui paruo pedi magnos in-
ducat calceos. Veritas in dicendo
maximè probanda est : & is optimè
dicit, cuius oratio congruit rebus,
ex quibus petéda est orationis qua-
litas potius, quàm ex artificio.

◀ Hendrik van den Keere's
Two-Line Double Pica Roman
(*Canon Romaine*, c. 45 pts.),
c. 1570. The specimen was
photographed in the Plantin-
Moretus Museum by Fred
Smeijers, who used this type
as a model for his *Renard*.

▼ First specimen of Renard,
designed at Het Lab and published as an insert of *Hollandse
Hoogte* no. 23/24, 1997.

To enhance legibility the typeface was rather condensed, with a large x-height and dark overall colour.

Fred Smeijers wrote about his design: 'Renard belongs to the broad category of Garamonds but occupies a unique place among them. The roman descends – unlike some other Garamonds – from a clearly traceable historical origin. In other words: it's from a good pedigree with decent papers. Next to that it's the only Garamond which can rightfully claim to be "Flemish". Not only because of its roots, but certainly due to its almost Breughelian features.'[8] As Van den Keere never cut a complete italic, *Renard*'s italic is a new design, made in the spirit of the period. Smeijers did a mental exercise, trying to imagine Hendrik van den Keere's situation at the time when a hypothetical italic could have been created. Smeijers: 'Van den Keere ran one of the world's first specialized type foundries. As a privileged supplier to Plantin, he could take a close look at his competitors' material. I am sure he would have wanted to emulate the best italic available. Which, at that moment, was Granjon's *Ascendonica Cursive*. Matthew Carter based *Galliard*'s italic on that typeface, but I find it too monotonous. It think Van den Keere would have given it more of a rhythm, which is what I have tried in Renard Italic.'[9]

Renard, named after the smart fox that is the star of a famous Flemish mediaeval satire, was released by The Enschedé Font Foundry in 1998. In a departure from contemporary thinking about type families, Renard is limited in its range of styles. There is no 'bold' to accompany the regular. Instead, there are two lighter weights: Renard No. 2 and Renard No. 3. Renard No. 2 is intended as a headline face with Renard No. 1, while Renard No. 3 can serve as a 'light' variant.

If Renard was a reinterpretation of a design from the distant past, *Romanée* is a revival in the true sense of the word. In 1995, Martin Majoor designed *Adieu aesthetica & mooie pagina's!*, a book that accompanied a Jan van Krimpen exhibition held in The Hague. Majoor, knowing that The Enschedé Font Foundry had plans for a digital Romanée, enquired if an acceptable version had already been produced. Peter Matthias Noordzij replied that this was not the case, but agreed to design a provisional version in collaboration with Smeijers. 'So then', Smeijers wrote, 'we rolled up our sleeves and got the typeface done for that book.'[10] Romanée has since been further developed by the TEFF studio.

The Arnhem project

The Werkplaats Typografie ('Typography Workshop') is a postgraduate course in typographic design in Arnhem led by Karel Martens and Wigger Bierma. It differs from other, similar courses in that it takes on 'real' assignments – usually at a rather high level – which are executed by the participants. One such job was the redesign of the *Nederlandse Staatscourant*, a daily newspaper published by the Dutch government. Fred Smeijers was invited by Karel Martens to join the Werkplaats team as a consul-

6 Smeijers, *Type Now* (cit.), p 98.

7 *TypeLab*, 25 October 1996; republished on the Hyphen Press website.

8 Fred Smeijers, quoted on the website of The Enschede Font Foundry, www.teff.nl [2001].

9 Quoted in Jan Middendorp, 'Een 21ᵉ-eeuwse lettersnijder' in *Items*, vol. 17, no. 6, October 1998, pp 20–25.

10 Smeijers, *Type Now* (cit.), p 101.

The Arnhem type family was published in 2002 by Smeijers's own type foundry OurType. It comes in two text versions: Normal and Blond, the latter a font of a slightly lighter colour. Arnhem Fine, a more subtly detailed face, is the headline version.

Unpublished trial issue of the governmental newspaper *Nederlandse Staatscourant*, in a new design by the Werkplaats Typografie Arnhem (1999). Smeijers developed a custom-made type family which came to be called Arnhem.

Arnhem

Blond *Italic* Normal *Italic* **Bold** *Italic*
Bold *Italic* SMALL CAPS BLOND *ITALIC*
NORMAL *ITALIC* **BOLD** *ITALIC* **BLACK**
ITALIC Om van geen mogelijke karakterfeilen te gewagen, – eigenzinnigheid, hoog-
moed, ongeduld, een losbandig leven, –
de uitvinder der boekdrukkunst kan verstoken zijn geweest van muzikaal gevoel
zowel als van financieel beleid, kan geen
slag hebben gehad met menschen om te
gaan, kan door zijne eenzelvigheid, met
zeker besef van verstandelijke meerderheid
gepaard, zich in allerlei wespennesten
gestoken, en dien ten gevolge niet slechts
de voordeelen, maar ook tijdelijk den roem
van zijn arbeid verbeurd hebben.

Arnhem Fine

Normal *Italic* **Bold** *Italic*

tant in the choice of typeface and other type-technical matters. It was soon suggested that Smeijers should design a new typeface, made to measure for the brief. One of the rather classical designs he had been working on lately seemed to be a suitable point of departure.

The original aim was to use the new type only for headlines. When a trial version was tested, the results were promising: the wt team liked the serious, sophisticated look. Smeijers was asked to design matching text fonts, as the headline fonts were meant for large sizes only and lacked the sturdiness needed for legibility in body text. During 1998–99 the font family was tested several times in the new design, up to the point when a 'real' newspaper was printed using the new typeface, which by then had been nicknamed *Arnhem* after the Werkplaats's location. The choice was also a practical one: Arnhem appears at the top of the font menu, right under *Arial*, and so Arnhem has kept its name.

In his type designs Smeijers has always tried to be both innovative and respectful of conventions, achieving a balance between traditional proportions and inventive details. 'The constant fight to achieve this balance is what keeps me going. … In this perspective, it might seem improbable that I would design a typeface that belongs to the tradition of typical newspaper or journal faces, such as *Excelsior* or *Imprint*. The freedom for personal interpretation [in the Arnhem typeface] seems to be too little. But I think that we were able to succeed in making a text typeface with this degree of 'sparkle', because the Arnhem project was rather loosely defined at the start.'[11]

Although Arnhem has the clarity of *Excelsior* and similar news faces designed for legibility, it lacks the nineteenth-century personality of these designs. If there is a historical reference, one should perhaps look for it one hundred years earlier: in the sharp, sparkling types of Fleischman and, more importantly, Rosart. In fact, Arnhem's wide, round Italic has many traits in common with Rosart's *Italiques*, a modern-style italic which he issued alongside his more calligraphic, narrow *Cursyfs* (> p 29); it is the same style which Matthew Carter refers to in his *Fenway* italic. Smeijers himself denies any direct link with these models, but does see a connection between the concept of the headline font and the *Romain du Roi*.[12]

The *Staatscourant* project was eventually cancelled, apparently for lack of determination on the client's side. In 2002 the Arnhem typeface became commercially available. In its final form the headline version is called Arnhem Fine; because of its fragility, it is recommended that it is not used in sizes smaller than 14 points. The text typeface, on the other hand, is rather dark in colour. As this strong presence may be disturbing 'in larger sizes or when setting poetry', a slightly lighter weight called 'Blond' was designed. Smeijers: 'The blond is in no way to be considered as a light version. Rather, the blond is an alternative regular weight. In fact, one might consider the Normal just as a "brunette".'[13]

abcdefghijklmnopqrstuvwxyz &
1234567890 (.,!?)-@-{\}-[/]*
ABCDEFGHIJKLMNOPQRSTUVWXYZ

abcdefghijklmnopqrstuvwxyz &
1234567890 (.,!?)-@-{\}-[/]*
ABCDEFGHIJKLMNOPQRSTUVWXYZ

◄ Smeijers designed Philips Script, an attractive script font in two weights to be used for Philips product names.

▼ Following his work on Philips screen fonts, Smeijers received a commission to design a number of logos for Philips cosmetic devices, starting with Philishave. The Cellesse logo became the starting point of an alphabet used to design subsequent logos like Natura and Profile.

Type for machines

Smeijers's historical studies and book faces are only one aspect of his activities. The work he did in the 1990s for the Visual Communications department of the Philips company was of a completely different nature. Smeijers's connection with the hardware manufacturer began when Jeanne de Bont of Philips Design (formerly a colleague of Smeijers at Océ) asked him to lend a hand in the production of screen fonts. The initial small set later grew into the *Philips Screen Font Family*, which has remained in use to date. In 1995 Dingeman Kuilman, head of graphic design, asked Smeijers to redesign the logo for Philishave electric razors. This was followed by a series of related logotypes for other cosmetic devices and their packaging; finally Smeijers decided to draw a complete alphabet with which to make new logos. With the kitchen appliances, things were handled in a similar way. As new product names were to be launched in quick succession, it was decided to design an alphabet right from the start. *Philips Script* is a simple yet attractive script font in two weights, used for the product names on Philips kitchen appliances from 1996 onwards.

For Smeijers's book types as well as for these display fonts, handwriting has always been an important reference. This is not true of his most technologically complex specialization: the development of screen fonts for clients like Philips, Mannesmann and his first employer Océ, which still hires him occasionally for expert jobs. With these fonts there is no question of supple curves or subtle details. The fonts that Smeijers tackles are purely technical constructions, usually developed for the displays of office machines or audiovisual equipment. They are typefaces made for specific texts viewed on miniature screens. For a period of time he also drew bitmap fonts for ordinary computer screens. In the early Océ days, Smeijers helped develop the principle of grey-scale fonts – a kind of anti-aliasing. This work resulted in three worldwide patents. 'To solve a complex technical problem by way of a typeface,' says Fred Smeijers, 'that's what I love to do.' [14]

Ladyshave
Natura
Philishave
Profile

PHILIPS   Cellesse

Fresco – a fresh look at the book face

In 1998, when this author interviewed Smeijers for *Items* magazine, the article was accompanied by the first showing of a new typeface called *Fresco*. The completed font family was formally introduced to the public three years later, when the designer published a short article in the multi-author volume *Letters*. Fresco is not a revival or reinterpretation but a wholly new family with two varieties: a serif and a low-contrast sanserif, both in 4 weights. In the *Items* interview Smeijers described it as 'a classic typeface with contemporary features; clear and robust yet with a hand-made feel, calligraphic without being dusty.' [15]

In the autumn of 2002, the complete Fresco family was presented in *Druk*, the magazine published by FontShop Benelux. Less outspoken and unusual than, say, Martin Majoor's *Seria*, Smeijers's new typeface looks inconspicuous and modest in small

11 Unpublished text by Fred Smeijers and the Werkplaats Typografie Arnhem.

12 E-mail to the author, August 2002.

13 See note 11.

14 Middendorp 1998 (cit.), p 22.

15 Ibid., p 24.

Fresco

Light *Italic* Normal *Italic* **Bold** *Italic*
Black *Italic* SMALL CAPS NORMAL *ITALIC*
BOLD *ITALIC* Dit alles is mogelijk, denkbaar, en zelfs, als men in aanmerking neemt welke ongezellige en onpraktische schepselen er plegen te groeien uit lieden, die levenslang over dezelfde zaak zitten te peinzen, waarschijnlijk.

Fresco Sans

Light *Italic* Normal *Italic* **Bold** *Italic*
Black *Italic*
SMALL CAPS NORMAL *ITALIC*
BOLD *ITALIC*
Condensed Normal *Italic* **Bold** *Italic*
Black *Italic*

sizes. Only in large showings do the remarkable details, especially the asymmetric serifs and terminals, stand out. Smeijers's aim was to make a contemporary roman which – although it is part of the age-old tradition of the seriffed book face – does not refer to any ancient model and thus avoids the 'literary' feel of most renaissance-inspired text typefaces; this makes Fresco well-suited for advertising and magazine typography.

Like Quadraat, Fresco comes with an accompanying sanserif. If Quadraat Sans was a rather literal translation of Quadraat – mimicking its classical look by preserving some of the contrast between thick and thin – *Fresco Sans* has not been derived as directly from the roman it accompanies. It is rather cool and business-like, but still has the elegance and readability of a humanist sanserif; it will work best in rather informal publications which still require clarity, such as magazines and arts listings.

OurType, a new venture

The specimen in *Druk* magazine was part of an extensive section dedicated to a new type foundry called OurType, a joint venture of Fred Smeijers and Rudy Geeraerts, the owner of FontShop Benelux. For several years, Smeijers had been looking for alternative ways to publish his typefaces and have more control over their context, presentation and positioning. Being distributed worldwide by FontShop Benelux through the FontShop network, OurType has great visibility while giving Smeijers the creative freedom as well as the immediacy he has always wanted.

At the introduction of OurType in late 2002, four type families were presented: Arnhem, Fresco and two typefaces that had not been heard of before: *Sansa* and *Monitor*. Sansa came into existence as a private font – an unpretentious contemporary sans for correspondence, suited for faxing, photocopying and on-screen reading. As the designer gradually needed more weights, the font grew into a four-weight family – from light to black. Sansa is extremely simple and is closer to a constructed design than any other Smeijers typeface. Monitor is a set of two fonts, initially developed as screen fonts for a Dutch hardware manufacturer. The high-resolution version was based on the proportions of the screen font. Created to solve a particular technical problem, Monitor belongs to the same group of optically indestructible sanserifs as Matthew Carter's *Verdana*; but in its proportions and in the detailing of the curves it somehow betrays its Dutch origins.

Among the typefaces that may be part of future OurType releases is *Custodia*, designed in 2002 for two typographer friends, Wigger Bierma and Ingo Offermans. In its present form, Custodia is a single weight family, consisting of a roman, an italic and small caps. Its flavour is distinctly seventeenth-century Dutch.

A reward and a manifesto

In 2001 Smeijers's activities as a type designer, typographer, researcher and writer won him the Gerrit Noordzij Award, an international prize for type design and typography. A retrospective exhibition to celebrate the award opened at the Royal Academy in The Hague in October 2003, simultaneously with the presentation of the 2003 Gerrit Noordzij Award to Erik Spiekermann. During the ceremony Smeijers's new book *Type now, a manifesto/Work so far* was also presented.

Type now sums up Smeijers's view of type design: a strong commitment to craftsmanship and historic consciousness, balanced by an equally firm belief in originality. In the essay Smeijers fulminates against the 'font tweakers' who modify other people's typefaces (or even their own) by changing a few curves or by using the 'mix' function of font design software and present the result as a new typeface. At the end of his manifesto Smeijers proposes a new 'code of conduct' to put an end to what he perceives as a fast deterioration of values and standards.

While Smeijers is uncompromising when it comes to principles and skill, his view of his craft is unprejudiced and open. Being among the most versatile type designers in the Netherlands, he sees no contradictions between the very diverse aspects of his work. He realizes that studying classical book faces is an activity for specialist scholars, but also knows himself to be firmly connected to the here and now through his other work. 'Perhaps filing and shaving steel is kind of unworldly,' he says, 'but pixels are not. A better-made screen font may cause fewer secretaries to get a headache.' Even though the medium is a different one, Smeijers regards digital technology as a continuation of sixteenth-century practice. 'My historical work is not only a kind of archaeological research, it is also a way of talking with my predecessors. Granjon and Hendrik van den Keere were exercising the same craft, and so there are overlaps. Those are what I am looking for.'[16]

Custodia

Normal *Italic* SMALL CAPS *ITALIC* Als weleer ter plaatse aanwezig opmerker kan ik verzekeren, dat het standbeeld op de Groote Markt te Haarlem, in Julij 1856, om zoo te zeggen door niemand als eene ernstige zaak beschouwd is. Noch bij den hoogeren, noch bij den middenstand, noch onder handwerkslieden, de laatsten sterk vertegenwoordigd door deputatiën van drukkersgezellen uit de stad en van elders, openbaarde zich de geringste geestdrift.

◄ In 2001–02 Smeijers was invited by Eric Kindel at the University of Reading to participate in a project to reconstruct early stencil lettering. Stencil cut by Smeijers, stencilling done by Kindel.

▲ Custodia (2002), a one-weight typeface that breathes a seventeenth-century atmosphere.

16 Middendorp 1998 (cit.), p 25.

Martin Majoor: innovating tradition

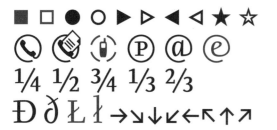

Of the many typefaces conceived in the Netherlands in the first few years of desktop type design, FF *Scala* found the largest and widest audience. It was an immediate success among book designers both at home and abroad. In the Netherlands, it was the most-used contemporary typeface for books listed in the yearly Best Books catalogues for several years. It was the first font family of its generation to be used for the complete typographic restyling of a major Dutch newspaper, *Algemeen Dagblad*. And it became the preferred titling face of Germany's high-profile art book publisher Taschen, as well as the corporate typeface of KLM Royal Dutch Airlines. Scala epitomizes many qualities typical of twentieth-century Dutch type design: clarity, simplicity and an innovative yet historically conscious approach.

Martin Majoor (1960) enrolled at the Arnhem Academy in 1980, the same year as Fred Smeijers. Those early years were crucial to Majoor's development as a type designer. Majoor and Smeijers and a few fellow students shared a fascination with the tradition of type design and lettering. As described earlier, several teachers were rather hostile towards what they regarded as an unmodern, even reactionary interest. But in 1981, when Majoor and Smeijers saw the graduation exhibition by Evert Bloemsma, who presented his typeface *Balance* alongside his panoramic photographs, they realized it must be possible to take up type design as part of their curriculum. In his final year, Martin Majoor designed his first typeface, *Serré*, borrowing the name (French for 'narrow') from the writings of Pierre Simon Fournier. He later described this narrow slab-serif as 'a preliminary study for Scala'.[17]

Immediately after graduation, Majoor landed a job at the Research & Development department of the hardware manufacturer Océ, where he was soon joined by Smeijers. In producing digital typefaces for Océ laser printers, they soon learned that many existing type designs were virtually useless when exposed to the harsh circumstances of primitive digital and laser technology. More often than not, subtly drawn, high-contrast characters lost their serifs and thin strokes when used on screens or early 300 DPI printers. These conditions led Majoor to favour robustness and durability in his first mature typeface.

FF Scala: custom-made

His chance to work on this type presented itself in 1988, when Majoor became an assistant designer at Muziekcentrum Vredenburg, a large concert venue in the centre of Utrecht. This job was part of a scheme which allowed (or obliged) conscientious objectors to work for two years in the social or cultural field instead of joining the army. Vredenburg's design department, headed by Jan Willem den Hartog, had been one of the first to introduce the Apple Macintosh for the in-house production of all publicity material. As none of the sixteen fonts available for PageMaker at the time offered the small caps and oldstyle figures which Den Hartog thought necessary for good typography, Majoor was invited to design a new, exclusive typeface as

Scala

Regular *Italic* **Bold** *Italic*
SMALL CAPS *ITALIC*
BOLD ***ITALIC***
Condensed Regular **Bold**

Scala sans

Regular *Italic* **Bold** *Italic*
SMALL CAPS *ITALIC*
BOLD ITALIC

◂ FF Scala (1991) and its sanserif companion (1993).

▾ Sketch for Scala, c. 1988.

⟆ Drawing of Serré, a 1983 art school project which Majoor later regarded as a preliminary study for Scala.

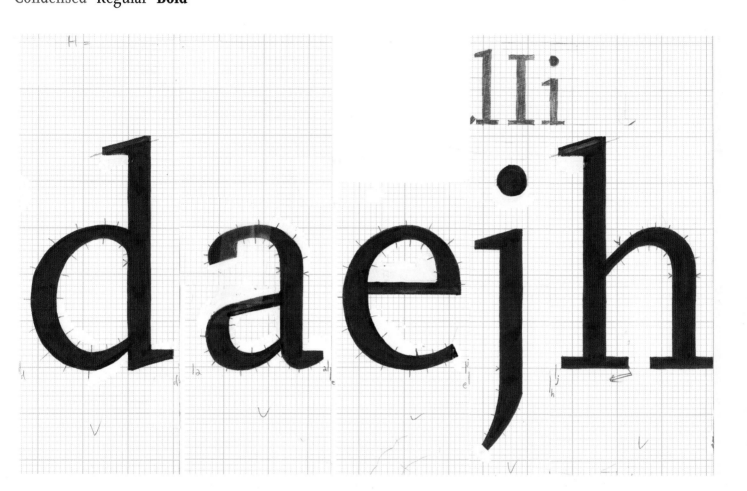

part of his day job. Thus Scala became one the first original font families designed for the Macintosh to possess many qualities of a classic book face. Simultaneously, its sturdiness and clarity made sure that the face held up even when faxed or photocopied. 'This was the main reason why I used those straight serifs. Some people have noted similarities with Eric Gill's *Joanna*; yet for me the forms were not based on an historical model, but on practical considerations.'

When Erik Spiekermann began looking for typefaces to add to his newly-founded FontFont collection, Scala was an obvious candidate. Having agreed on a year's exclusive use by Vredenburg, Majoor was soon able to license the face to FontShop International, where it became a long-lasting best-seller.

What turned Scala into one of the most versatile and influential FontFonts was Majoor's decision to add a companion sanserif series. The idea was not new. Jan van Krimpen's *Romulus* sanserif (1930s) had been an early attempt at coupling a modern-classic roman with a low-contrast humanist sanserif. Although it was never developed beyond the design stage, Van Krimpen's concept influenced type designers of subsequent generations; Majoor, who designed and co-edited a book about Van Krimpen, certainly fell into this category. *Scala Sans*, published in 1993, translates Scala's properties and proportions to the sanserif format by reducing the contrast to almost a monoline. Yet the typeface's calligraphic qualities remain intact. At that time, the best-known sanserifs – *Univers, Frutiger, Syntax* – all had sloped romans for

17 Quotes and additional information based on several interviews held with Martin Majoor.

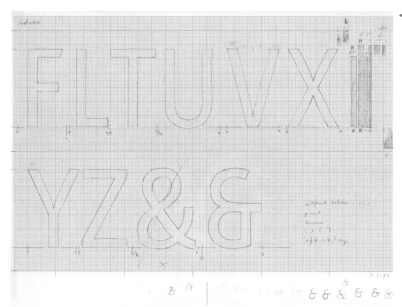

Typeface for the PTT telephone directory. This text page printed in rotary offset. 08-04-1994. © Martin Majoor

◄ Sketches for Telefont List, 1993.

▼ Test printings of Telefont list, trying out the possibilities to compensate imperfections in printing technology by using ink traps and spikes, none of which proved necessary, 1994.

▼ Telefont Text in use on a KPN phonebook CD.

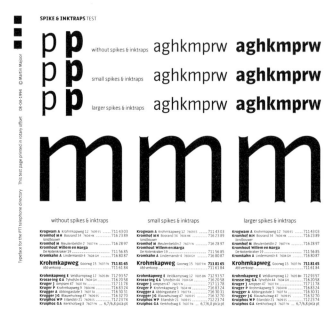

SPIKE & INKTRAPS TEST

p **p** without spikes & inktraps aghkmprw **aghkmprw**

p **p** small spikes & inktraps aghkmprw **aghkmprw**

p **p** larger spikes & inktraps aghkmprw **aghkmprw**

m m m

without spikes & inktraps	small spikes & inktraps	larger spikes & inktraps
Krogwam A Krohmkapweg 12 76091S 711 43 03	**Krogwam A** Krohmkapweg 12 76091S 711 43 03	**Krogwam A** Krohmkapweg 12 76091S 711 43 03
Kromhof M H Bosrand 34 7604 HK 716 23 89	**Kromhof M H** Bosrand 34 7604 HK 716 23 89	**Kromhof M H** Bosrand 34 7604 HK 716 23 89
landbouwer	landbouwer	landbouwer
Kromhof M Meulenbeldln 2 7607 FN 716 28 97	**Kromhof M** Meulenbeldln 2 7607 FN 716 28 97	**Kromhof M** Meulenbeldln 2 7607 FN 716 28 97
Kromhout Willem en Marga	**Kromhout Willem en Marga**	**Kromhout Willem en Marga**
De Notenkraker 19 ....711 56 85	De Notenkraker 19 ....711 56 85	De Notenkraker 19 ....711 56 85
Kromkahn A Lindemanstr 4 7604 GH 716 80 87	**Kromkahn A** Lindemanstr 4 7604 GH 716 80 87	**Kromkahn A** Lindemanstr 4 7604 GH 716 80 87
Krohmkapweg Goorwg 15 7607 FN **711 81 65**	**Krohmkapweg** Goorwg 15 7607 FN **711 81 65**	**Krohmkapweg** Goorwg 15 7607 FN **711 81 65**
Afd verkoop 711 61 84	Afd verkoop 711 61 84	Afd verkoop 711 61 84
Krohmkapweg E Veldkampswg 12 7605 BN 712 93 57	**Krohmkapweg E** Veldkampswg 12 7605 BN 712 93 57	**Krohmkapweg E** Veldkampswg 12 7605 BN 712 93 57
Krosse ing G A Tyhofsln 44 7604 GH ...716 20 58	**Krosse ing G A** Tyhofsln 44 7604 GH ...716 20 58	**Krosse ing G A** Tyhofsln 44 7604 GH ...716 20 58
Kruger J Ampsen 47 7607 FN 717 11 78	**Kruger J** Ampsen 47 7607 FN 717 11 78	**Kruger J** Ampsen 47 7607 FN 717 11 78
Kruger P Krohmkapweg 9 7604 HK 716 83 24	**Kruger P** Krohmkapweg 9 7604 HK 716 83 24	**Kruger P** Krohmkapweg 9 7604 HK 716 83 24
Krugger A Abbingastate 3 7607 TA 716 30 31	**Krugger A** Abbingastate 3 7607 TA 716 30 31	**Krugger A** Abbingastate 3 7607 TA 716 30 31
Krugger J G Blauwhulswg 47 76091S ...716 32 70	**Krugger J G** Blauwhulswg 47 76091S ...716 32 70	**Krugger J G** Blauwhulswg 47 76091S ...716 32 70
Kruiphos W P Eilandstr 21 76091S 712 23 74	**Kruiphos W P** Eilandstr 21 76091S 712 23 74	**Kruiphos W P** Eilandstr 21 76091S 712 23 74
Kruiphos G A Kerkhofswg 8 7607 FN ... 6,7/6,8 pica pt	**Kruiphos G A** Kerkhofswg 8 7607 FN ... 6,7/6,8 pica pt	**Kruiphos G A** Kerkhofswg 8 7607 FN ... 6,7/6,8 pica pt

italics; so Majoor's decision to give Scala 'real italics' with a distinctly calligraphic feel was somewhat of a novelty. There had been precedents, notably *Lucida Sans* and *Stone Sans*, but Majoor's solution was more personal and more distinctive. Only Gerard Unger's *Flora*, an upright italic to be used with his *Praxis*, was as innovative and original, but it is a very different sort of typeface. The Scala Sans small caps are also quite successful: they are as elegant and round as Gill Sans caps (and its recently added small caps), as clear as Futura's and as well proportioned as any of them. At the time, Scala Sans was one of the very few sanserif faces with oldstyle figures.

Soon after the complete Scala family had been published, renowned book designers such as Ellen Lupton (USA), Irma Boom (Netherlands) and Gert Dooreman (Belgium) began exploring the possibilities of combining the serif and sans fonts. Majoor is especially proud of the way Lupton used Scala in several of her theory-driven book designs, such as her catalogue of the *100 Show* and in *Design Writing Research* (1996, with J. Abbott Miller). It was in fact Lupton's work which convinced Majoor of the applicability of both Scala varieties in serious book typography. Considering himself a 'new traditionalist' (his own words), he had long been unsure about whether the family was suited to books. He remained extremely critical of designers who used Scala for texts of a 'higher' order, such as Bibles or poetry – the typeface being too business-like, in his opinion – and Majoor would later draw Seria for precisely that purpose.

The phonebook type

Majoor's second major type design was *Telefont*, a family of sanserifs used for the Dutch phone books from late 1994 onwards. For fifteen years, the directories had been produced using a 1977 design by Wim Crouwel and Jolijn van de Wouw (TD) which had been rather controversial mainly for its exclusive use of lowercase *Univers* (at a later stage, more legible figures drawn by Gerard Unger and Chris Vermaas were added). When it became clear that the recently privatized telephone company KPN Telecom wanted a redesign to fit in with their new, consumer-oriented approach, designer Jan Kees Schelvis – who had done the directory's cover for some years – decided to propose something radically different. He talked to Majoor, who at the time was a fellow teacher at the Arnhem Academy. 'We agreed, more or less in jest, that it would be a good idea if Martin made a new typeface for the phone book. I contacted Ootje Oxenaar, the director of KPN's Art and Design department, and introduced Martin to him. Initially Oxenaar hesitated: in the country of Gerard Unger, why should one work with a lesser known type designer? But our presentation convinced him and we were given an assignment to make a preliminary design. Our plan was appreciated because of its user-friendliness and because the layout, typography and type design were totally integrated. Besides, our concept would save space and consequently, money.' [18]

SCALA JEWELS

CRYSTAL DIAMOND
PEARL SAPHYR

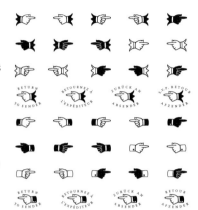

> ▲ Scala Jewels (1996). Of this set
> of ornamented capitals, Crystal
> was based on Rémy Peignot's
> Cristal, and Pearl on Austin Fry's
> Ornamented, retaining the
> Scala proportions and basic
> forms.

> ▸ Scala Hands was released in
> 1998 as part of the FF Scala Sans
> 2 package.

> ▾ Majoor made the first sketches
> of Fuga – later renamed Seria –
> on a Polish napkin, travelling by
> train to Warsaw in July 1996.

Schelvis and Majoor took some time before deciding that a new font was in fact needed. They compared telephone directories from around the world, but could not point out any typographic solution that completely satisfied them.

Majoor therefore designed two font families for exclusive use by KPN: *Telefont List* for the address listings, and *Telefont Text* for the introductory pages. Both consist of regular, italic and bold weights, Telefont Text being the most extended family, equipped with small caps and two types of figures. Throughout the process, Fred Smeijers supplied feedback and assistance. As Telefont List was more dependent on technical requirements, it was designed first; the text fonts were derived from it. 'The basic principles are clarity and readability,' says Majoor. 'To avoid that two characters should be too similar, I sometimes preferred somewhat unconventional forms. The lowercase f, for instance, has a descender, which accounts for a very special look; but it was done mainly to distinguish it from the t. Some characters, such as lowercase a and s, have a small serif in order to get a sharper image – possibly my reaction to the somewhat woolly greyness of the old directories.'[19] For economy's sake, the capitals of Telefont List are unusually small; this is not the case in the text version which, while being innovative, is a more conventional sanserif.

Several versions of Telefont were tried out before deciding on the final design. Tests were done on the necessity of spurs and ink traps, devices to improve readability at small point sizes when using crude printing techniques. For instance, *Bell Centennial* (Matthew Carter, 1978) has become famous for its conspicuous ink traps, which eventually came to be seen by some designers as an aesthetic rather than a technical feature. For Telefont, it was decided that no spikes or ink traps were needed, as typesetting and printing techniques had been greatly improved in the intervening fifteen years.

Scala extensions

Having been immersed in the complex phone guide project for several years, Majoor took up a more playful type project in 1996. He designed *Scala Jewels*, a series of titling capitals inspired by ornamental initials such as Rémy Peignot's *Cristal*, Austin Fry's *Ornamented* and eighteenth-century titling capitals cut by Fournier and Rosart. Two years later, more extensions to the Scala family were introduced. At the request of several designers who needed a narrower set of Scalas for posters and book covers, Majoor drew *Scala Condensed*; a more frivolous addition was the glyph font *Scala Hands*, a set of pointing fingers and fists with a nineteenth-century flavour. Furthermore, Scala Sans was made more suitable for magazine and advertising jobs by adding the '*BlackLight*' – light and black – series.

FF Seria

When writing and talking about the *Seria* design, Majoor has repeatedly pointed out that he finds Scala too much of a workhorse typeface to be appropriate for poetry and other forms of 'refined literature'; he therefore needed to design a font with a more elegant feel.[20] Such considerations are very welcome when they justify the design of yet another typeface; but as a guideline for users they are rather confusing. Poems have been set in typefaces as business-like as Helvetica and Courier and have still come across well; it is not always desirable that a text with a certain stylish sophistication find a typographic form that mimics this. Conversely, a typeface made for poetry may be employed successfully for prosaic purposes. Shortly after its publication, FF Seria was used by Majoor's former boss Jan Willem den Hartog for the newspaper of his own communications agency; the typeface works admirably in this rather down-to-earth context.

18 Telephone conversation with Jan-Kees Schelvis, 2000. On Telefont,
    see also Jan Middendorp, 'Een bruikbaar instrument. Nieuwe vormgeving voor
    het telefoonboek', in *Items* vol. 13 no. 8, 1994.

19 Interview with Martin Majoor.

20 Martin Majoor and Jan Middendorp, *FontFont Focus – FF Seria*, 2001. Text republished
    in Van Rixtel and Westerveld (eds.), *Letters*, Eindhoven 2001, pp 82–85.

▾ First use of Seria, then still
called Fuga, in a volume of
poems designed by Majoor,
1998. The name was changed
for copyright reasons.

Be this as it may, Majoor's personal need for a more 'literary' type was very real when, in mid-1996, he drew the first sketches of Seria – or *Fuga*, as the face was initially called. The place: the train to Warsaw, where he and his wife, Polish composer Hanna Kulenty, spend part of their lives. The date: 25 July, as noted on the paper napkins which Majoor used for want of a notebook.

FF Seria evidently comes from the same designer as FF Scala. It has similar clarity and openness, and was made with the same sensitivity to typographic conventions as its predecessor. 'As in Scala', wrote the young type enthusiast Andy Crewdson on his *Lines & Splines* web page, 'the details of Seria's forms are frequently novel and surprising but the effect at small sizes is harmonious through-and-through.' [21] Like Scala, Seria consists of a serif and a sanserif series and will be available in a large set of weights, from light to black.

There are also some important differences. Seria has extremely long ascenders and descenders and therefore a relatively small x-height. The typeface's proportions are thus related to those of classically inspired romans like Bruce Rogers's Jenson revival *Centaur* and *Trinité no. 3* by Bram de Does. Like Trinité, as well as *Lexicon*, the complete FF Seria will have an alternative set of fonts with shorter extenders.

Seria also possesses an even rarer quality: it comes with two different italics. Besides the almost upright italic it has a 'cursive' with a more pronounced slope. This uncommon feature was the result of a request from the French critic and typographer Hector Obalk, who wanted to use FF Scala for a book about the artist Marcel Duchamp. The complexity of the material – there would be many quotes within quotes – would make it desirable to use two different italics. Wouldn't it be possible, Obalk asked, to design a second, more oblique italic for Scala? This did not seem such a good idea to Majoor; but the option did occur to him to create a completely new typeface with an upright and a sloped italic. It was not possible to finish the typeface in time for the Duchamp book; however, a concept was born.

Seria (then still called Fuga) made its debut in publications designed by Majoor himself: first in a volume of poems for the bibliophile publisher Herik (1998), then in the posters and handouts of Warsaw Autumn 1999, a festival of contemporary music in the Polish capital. The FF Seria type family was presented in 2000 in FontShop's FontFont series. Releases of new weights – including light and extra bold variants, as well as the sloped cursive mentioned above – have been announced.

COLOFON

De gedichtencyclus ANTIDOOD werd door Hester Knibbe aangeboden op verzoek van uitgeverij Herik, Landgraaf. De tekeningen werden gemaakt door Bep Scheeren, Schinnen. De cyclus werd gezet uit de Fuga — een letter van Martin Majoor die haar hier voor het eerst toepast — en gedrukt door drukkerij Econoom te Beek, (L) op 115 g/m² Mellotex mat. Martin van den Berg, Simpelveld verzorgde de afwerking. Deze uitgave kwam tot stand met medewerking van Brand Bierbrouwerij BV, Wijlre; T. Ruijters, Maastricht; NV Koninklijke Sphinx Gustavsberg, Maastricht; Van der Tol, Tuinarchitecten, hoveniers en terreininrichters BV, Amsterdam.

De oplage bedraagt 299 door de uitgever genummerde en door de auteur gesigneerde exemplaren.
Dit is nummer

23

Dit is Seria Cursive Classic.
ABCDEFG abcdefg & 12345

Dit is Seria Cursive Swash.
ABCDEFG &

Dit is Seria Cursive Finito.
abcdefg &

◂ First showings of Seria Cursive,
2002 (to be released).

Scholing's Engines

Until recently, Alex Scholing had published one single typeface: FF *Engine*, issued in the FontFont library in 1995. Engine was his first attempt at type design, and came about almost by chance; if the FontShop type committee had not accepted his proposal and urged him to work out a font family, he might have abandoned designing type altogether. But Engine was also made too eagerly and published too quickly – Scholing was almost immediately dissatisfied with it. During the past seven years, alongside his daily work as a graphic designer, he has developed his initial design into a more mature and more usable font family, provisionally called *EnginePro* and released in autumn 2003 as FF *Roice*. Scholing: 'EnginePro has been my study project and love baby. If the original Engine was a vehicle for the design ideas I had at a specific moment, EnginePro was my self-appointed teacher.' [22]

As the name suggests, Engine is a rather mechanically drawn font constructed with rounded lines, circular shapes and curious little serifs. Being neither a real text face nor an obvious headline face, it is hard to pinpoint. It even confused the editors of the 2000 FontFont catalogue, who put FF Engine in the 'hand-written' category – where it evidently does not belong. Although it is original and carefully drawn, the overall image is somewhat unbalanced; for instance h, n, m and u are very wide compared to the rather condensed a and g, and the numerals are not very powerful. These beginner's mistakes have been amended in Roice. The result is an unorthodox but very usable and readable text face in five weights, which Scholing has already used to set an entire book.

Scholing wrote: 'I have always preferred the deviant over the accepted. Of course the problem is that type functions thanks to acceptance. I am now convinced that *everything that is readable must be a typeface* and, conversely, that *a typeface does not have to meet any other condition than to be readable*. Once you have grown fully aware of the implications of this idea, it becomes incomprehensible that most typefaces made today pursue stylistic conventions, not readability – contrary to what many type designers

▲ Nuclear Type, an unpublished display variety of Engine/Roice, is designed to be layered to dazzling effect.

▼ Scholing used his Carrera, a 'streamlined' variant of Engine, in a brochure for Glasurit enamel paints.

21 Andy Crewdson, [no title], published on the *Lines and Splines* website, 2002; see also Crewdson's 'Seria's motives', in *Druk* 013-014, 2002, pp 49–51.

22 All quotes from e-mails by Alex Scholing to the author, 2003.

▼ FF Engine (1995) and FF Roice, formerly NewEngine (2003), compared at equal point size.

▸ Scholing's unorthodox campaign for the image CDs distributed by FontShop Benelux won him a Certificate of Typographic Excellence in the 2000 TDC competition.

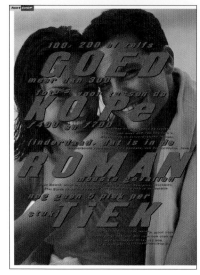

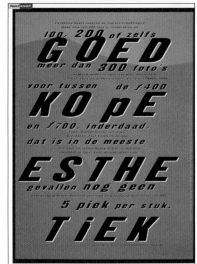

Roice

Light *Italic* Regular *Italic*
Medium *Italic* **Bold Italic**
Black Italic CAPS LIGHT ITALIC
REGULAR ITALIC MEDIUM ITALIC
BOLD ITALIC **BLACK ITALIC**
De uitvinder der boekdrukkunst kan geen slag hebben gehad met menschen om te gaan, kan door zijne eenzelvigheid, met zeker besef van verstandelijke meerderheid gepaard, zich in allerlei wespennesten gestoken hebben.

Engine

Light *Italic* Regular *Italic*
Bold Italic SMALL CAPS ITALIC **BOLD**
De uitvinder der boekdrukkunst kan geen slag hebben gehad met menschen om te gaan, kan door zijne eenzelvigheid, met zeker besef van verstandelijke meerderheid gepaard, zich in allerlei wespennesten gestoken hebben.

try to make us believe. So for the most part, my struggle took place on that cutting edge: stylistic unconventionality versus readability.'

Just how unconventional Scholing is as a graphic designer is shown by series of ads he made for FontShop Benelux, catering to the Dutch and Belgian market. The ads, meant to promote the collections of royalty-free images distributed by FontShop, were conceived, written and designed by Scholing. The campaign focused on the idea of cheapness; headlines like 'cheap romance' and 'cheap aesthetics' were laid out over full-page pictures in distorted bold capitals – an extremely slanted and stretched FF *Kipp* (by Claudia Kipp) – that danced above and below the baseline. The campaign was awarded a Certificate of Typographic Excellence in the 2000 Type Directors Club competition, 'despite the fact', Scholing wrote, 'that I knowingly and willingly trampled two basic typographic rules: never skew type and never stretch type.'

Scholing has designed several display typefaces based on Engine/Roice. *Compressor* is a narrow Engine variant, with short ascenders and descenders; *Condensor* has the same construction but is slightly wider. *Carrera* is a 'streamlined' version in which the letters are connected by a baseline which is a little wobbly under the word spaces. The more elaborate variety is *Nuclear Type,* a set of equal-width fonts of increasing boldness with corresponding outline faces, designed to be layered. All of these fonts are as yet unpublished.

Scholing's new type project may be his most ambitious to date. Intrigued and inspired by the work of Fred Smeijers and Martin Majoor, he has begun to research the outer limits of the most conventional kind of type – the seriffed roman. One of the fonts he has created as part of this research is called *TypoBrutto*. In his own words, 'an attempt to make a seriously usable text face in as crude a way as possible, as a reaction to the many over-designed and way too smooth serif types available today. Letterforms, weights and serif forms of TypoBrutto are rather irregular and inconsistent, but proportioning of the basic forms is given considerable attention.' As this sample text progresses its point size decreases and gradually the font's quirky irregularities fade into a lively, readable overall image. 'Remember that real serif type is sloppy,' Scholing says.

Roelof Mulder: speed is what we need

Roelof Mulder, two paintings shown in his 1988 self-published catalogue *Speed is what we need*. The lettering is based on Crillee Extra Bold Italic.

In the mid-1980s Roelof Mulder (1962) was a promising young sculptor. He made polished, abstract forms, mostly of painted wood. In retrospect it would be easy to say that these objects already possessed a strong graphic quality. What is more telling is that Mulder published two self-designed booklets about his work during that same period. The second one, dating from 1988, is especially remarkable. By then, Mulder's art had advanced: the sculptures had made way for paintings in enamel on wood – combinations of words, signs and patterns reminiscent of advertising. The booklet in which he presented these works, *Speed is what we need*, was ahead of its time. With its clear-cut shapes, strong contrasts and ironic use of logo-like textbites, it was techno avant la lettre. About five years later, when global graphic trends had caught up with Mulder's visual intuition, he realized what he may have known all along: that he was a graphic designer.[23]

Coincidentally, two of the first graphic projects he worked on resulted in the design of a typeface. Both were created in collaboration with colleagues from the small Arnhem design community.

In 1992 Mulder was asked to design an issue of the artists' magazine *Real Time*: 50 by 70 centimetres, 20 pages, no text allowed. He asked his famous colleague Karel Martens to collaborate. 'Mulder is an agreeably unorthodox thinker,' said Martens in an interview, 'so I liked the idea of working with him.' Martens and Mulder looked for a way to get around the 'no text' rule, '... to make letters which are not letters ... I thought language had to have a place in there somewhere. That's how *Starface* came about. Martin Majoor helped us produce it, and in no time we had a complete alphabet ... It was for laughs, but it was also a statement about what a letter really is – a code, a key for transmitting information.'[24] Each of the glyphs in Starface shows the face of a famous actor; some zoom in on details (an eye, a mouth, a hand with a gun). The typeface, or face-type, was first shown in *Emigre* 25 – the *Made in Holland* issue (1993) – in a layout based on a classic Berthold specimen.

One of Mulder's first serious book designs was a catalogue for an artists' group called Oceaan. As a reference to the lettering on ocean steamers or luggage Mulder wanted to use a stencil font, and decided to make one himself. With the help of Martin Majoor a sturdy uppercase alphabet was designed which worked admirably. The catalogue won Mulder the first Rotterdam Design Prize (1993).

Three years later, Mulder expanded the single alphabet into a complete display type in five variants: light, regular, bold, rough and outline. It was first announced as *Ocean* but, to avoid name conflicts, was issued by FontShop as FF *Offline* (1996). Offline is a rather narrow, constructed sanserif in which the horizontal lines running through the letterforms create a distinctive rhythm. Monotony is avoided by subtle interruptions, e.g. in the lowercase e, v and w, and uppercase A and E. In spite of its simplicity and constructed character, Offline has a human touch to it.

23 This article was largely based on information supplied by Roelof Mulder in several informal conversations, as well as in e-mails to the author.

24 Karel Martens interviewed by Max Bruinsma in *Items* vol. 15, no. 6, October 1996.

normal
regular
normal

normal
chiaro tondo
normal

ROELOF MULDER / KAREL MARTENS
1992
M.T.I.
FOR EMIGRE

(5 P) 10 20 30 40

(6 P) 10 20 30

(7 P) 10 20 30

(8 P) 10 20

(10 P) 10 20

(12 P) 5 10 15

(14 P) 5 10 15

(18 P) 5 10

14 p
16 p
18 p
20 p
24 p
28 p
32 p
36 p

◄ Starface by Karel Martens and Roelof Mulder. Original artwork for the 'Made in Holland' issue of *Emigre*, 1993.

▼ Superstripe, an unpublished typeface designed in 1994–1995.

⅄ Advertisement for FF Offline designed by Mulder for FontShop Benelux, 1998.

Roelof Mulder is grafisch ontwerper. De FF Offline is zijn eerste niet illegaal uitgebrachte letter. Een unieke en complete letterfamilie waarmee volgens geruchten de nieuwe versie van de Bijbel zal worden opgemaakt.

FF Offline light FF Offline regular FF Offline bold FF Offline outline FF Offline rough

LIGHT REGULAR BOLD OUTLINE ROUGH

strange new experiences

for those who already know what time it is

10:05:96AM
UP IN THE FANTASY WORLD
beyond the limits of time and dimension

HEAVEN IS HOT

FF Offline

In 1994–95, simultaneously with Offline, Mulder developed a typeface called *Super-stripe*. Here, too, the letterforms are sliced by white lines. The effect, especially in the oblique, is that of pace and urgency. Superstripe – a rather daring display face of limited legibility – was proposed to FontShop's type board, who asked for a more extensive family. Attempts were made at an unstriped and a condensed variety, but the project was never completed and Superstripe was not released.

Since the mid-1990s, Mulder has worked for clients in the fashion industry, such as Diesel, Daniel Poole and Takeo Kikuchi, and designed numerous magazines and books. As art director of the design magazine *Frame* in 2001–2003, he occasionally used his own typefaces; it has been one of the few places to see Superstripe in use.

Julius de Goede, writing master

When asked why he began designing typefaces on the computer, Julius de Goede's reply is surprising: 'Because I wanted to get rid of the ink stains on my hands.'[25] Strictly speaking, Julius de Goede (1944) belongs to a generation of designers that precedes Bloemsma, Majoor and Smeijers. Yet his first published typefaces are of a later date than theirs. Before emerging as a type designer, De Goede had had a successful career as a graphic designer, illustrator and author of calligraphy books. It was as a kind of by-product of his activities as a teacher and writing expert that his fonts came into being. They are, almost without exception, script types directly derived from handwriting.

Julius de Goede graduated from the Arnhem Academy of Fine Arts in 1967. An eager and quick-witted student, he had become friends with his teacher of typography, Jan Vermeulen, who proposed setting up a joint studio. Thanks to Vermeulen's fame in the publishing world, their ironically named *Adviesbureau voor Visuele Kommunikatie* ('Consulting agency for visual communication') was immediately in business, enabling De Goede to design hundreds of book covers within the first few years. To De Goede's surprise, Vermeulen left all the work to him; eventually they drifted apart.[26] By that time De Goede had become a freelance illustrator, making realistic drawings for large-circulation magazines such as *Panorama*, *Pep* and *Nieuwe Revu*.

As fashions changed and De Goede saw the number of assignments decline, he decided to professionalize his writing skills, hoping to turn them into a source of income. He enrolled in a correspondence course of formal writing with a qualification to educate future teachers. Having voiced his dissatisfaction with the way the course was structured, he was promptly invited by the publisher, the reputable Leidse Onderwijs Instellingen (LOI, 'Leyden Education Institute'), to develop a calligraphy course himself. De Goede wrote the course under the supervision of Alexander Verberne – a teacher of writing and typography at the Arnhem Academy – and for fifteen years gave weekend courses at the LOI, 'mostly to elderly ladies'.

In 1982 he published his first calligraphy manual, followed by some 20 books on the subject. Thanks to a profitable contract with the German book club Weltbild, the sales of his German books exceeded those of the ones written for the Dutch market. By the mid-1990s De Goede had sold 400,000 copies of his German-language books, which probably made him the best selling Dutch author in Germany.

In the early 1990s Malmberg, a publisher of educational books, invited him to contribute to the text and layout of a new writing method for elementary schools. De Goede had been co-author and calligrapher of a similar project at Wolters-Noordhof publishers in 1978 – 82. This time he proposed that Malmberg use computer-generated handwriting instead of writing each example by hand. On De Goede's advice, the publisher bought Scripter, a small piece of software written around 1990 by Just van Rossum to accompany his typeface *Schulschrift*, a standard script for German elementary schools (> p 213). Van Rossum and De Goede adapted Scripter to work with De Goede's newly designed script.

While the teaching method was being developed, De Goede came up with another proposal. He saw a great discrepancy between the kind of connected script which young children were taught to write, and the printing types that were used to teach reading. 'I have always thought it would be advisable to establish a link between these two. Having made a connected script for the computer, I then proceeded to design a cursive printing typeface for teaching children to read.' The idea, however, was never implemented by Malmberg. The schoolbook typeface became *Julius Primer*, one of six typefaces by De Goede issued in 2000 – 01 by Agfa-Monotype.

▲ *De mooiste kalligrafische alfabetten* (The Most Beautiful Calligraphic Alphabets). One of around thirty calligraphy books written by Julius de Goede, 1988.

25 Quotes taken from a conversation with Julius de Goede.

26 Julius de Goede, *Gedachtig aan Jan V.*, self-published brochure, Utrecht 1993.

Dit moet je doen:
Pak de pan. Snijboon erin.
Spruitje erbij. Pel de sinaasappel.
Partjes in de pan. Pak de pruimen.
Prak de peren. Pak de perziken.

◄ Reproduction from *Schrijfactief*, a writing method for young children co-written and typeset by Julius de Goede. The writing was simulated with a digital font, joining the characters in a natural way using Just van Rossum's Scripter software.

▼ Typefaces by Julius de Goede. Arian is unpublished; the remaining fonts were released between 2000 and 2003 by Agfa-Monotype (Creative Alliance) and Linotype Library.

Each of De Goede's script types is derived from a specific handwritten model. Two of the Monotype fonts were based on friends' informal handwriting. *Xander* is the handwriting of typographer Alexander Verberne, with whom De Goede corresponded intensively for many years. Choosing the most neutral characters from Verberne's letters, and carefully adapting them to be used in different combinations, De Goede obtained a plausible and very recognizable digital version of Verberne's handwriting. He used the same method in digitizing the handwriting of the illustrator Phile van der Veen. That font is named *Amadeo*, the Latin translation of Van der Veen's Greek Christian name, Théophile.

Three of the Monotype script fonts are historical scripts: *Rudolph*, a Fraktur; *Uncia*, an uncial; and *Augusta Cancellaresca*, a cursive chancery script. Each is a fairly simple, straightforward digital version of traditional calligraphy; Augusta has many interesting alternate characters, ligatures and swashes. Julius Primer, the schoolbook face, has an affinity to Rosemary Sassoon's typefaces made for that purpose, but is less formalized: the spontaneity of handwriting is still palpable in the printing type. This is also the case with *Gaius*, his latest published script which was brought out by Linotype in 2002 as part of the Take Type 4 package. Gaius, a cursive script, seems to be less polished than other, comparable typefaces such as *Zapfino* and *Poetica*. Like these typefaces (with which De Goede was not familiar) Gaius offers a large range of characters, including special swashes for beginnings and endings of words and a set of upright capitals, in order to create text which resembles real calligraphy.

Besides the scripts, Julius de Goede has designed a small number of book faces, but so far nobody has been interested in publishing them. *Arian*, named after his father and his son, is a contemporary traditional text face; possibly inspired by Scala in its proportions, but more conventional in its details; as could be expected, the italic has a beautiful handwritten quality. De Goede uses his text faces occasionally ('out of vanity,' he says, smiling) for the interiors of the books he designs and typesets – mostly simple, straightforward text-only books. 'I am realistic enough to know that I will never make book faces that are as special as Scala. I am not in that league. I often feel that I am just a sincere amateur who is merely playing around.'

Arian
Regular CAPS *Alt Italic*

Linotype Gaius
Regular *Bold* *beginning* *end*

Julius Primary
Light *Italic* Regular *Italic*
Bold *Italic*

Amadeo
Alternate *Bold*
SMALL CAPS **BOLD**

Xander
Alt *Bold* SMALL CAPS **BOLD**

Augusta
Regular *Cancellaresca alt*
Schnurkl *Swash alt*

Digital lettering and type

Donald Beekman, *#100* of
Beeldinstituut De Volkskrant,
a forum for artists and designers
in the arts section of the
Dutch daily *De Volkskrant*.
Beekman used his page as a
free advertisement for his fonts.
15 May 2003.

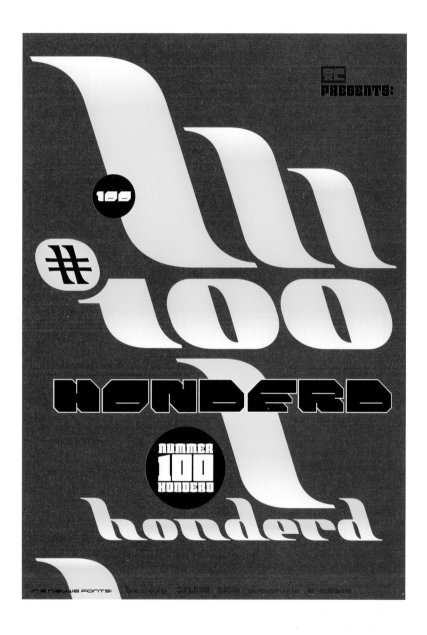

Personal alphabets in the digital age

During the past half-century, type production has gone through more changes than during the five hundred preceding years. When it comes to the accessibility of the trade, the biggest changes have happened since 1985. Thanks to desktop typography and the availability of affordable type design software, the step from drawing letterforms to making them into a workable typeface has become very small indeed – any student can learn the basic principles in less than a day. This has led to a major shift in the status of typefaces.

In the past, as we saw in previous chapters, many custom-made hand-drawn alphabets never became printing typefaces – not because the designer lacked the ambition to go public with his letterforms but because of the undemocratic structure of the type world. One had to be either well-acquainted, lucky or extremely focused to get type designs accepted for production by a type foundry – and there were only a few of them around. Many lettering artists and typographers did not even bother.

With a Mac on every graphic designer's desk, to take an alphabet to the font stage has become an almost negligible step. It is true that producing a full-fledged font family that functions impeccably under any circumstance is still an involved task for specialists, which requires hundreds – even thousands – of hours; but digitizing a relatively simple display alphabet for one's own use is a piece of cake. This implies that the letterforms that designers make for their own lettering jobs or even for text typography will now find their way into useable digital fonts much sooner. Whether these fonts are made for in-house use only or are eventually perfected, standardized and marketed, is just a matter of organization.

The first half of this chapter deals with designers whose fonts originate in the alphabets they have created in order to give their own graphic work a unique identity. Needless to say, most of these fonts are display alphabets, not text type.

The second part focuses on the new generation of type designers who are in some way linked to the Royal Academy in The Hague. Here, the number of text typefaces designed for general use is significantly higher.

▲ Catelijne van Middelkoop, *Hey Dutchie!*, student project made with a custom alphabet, Cranbrook Academy, 2002.

▼ Max Kisman: Poster for Paradiso's 1991 Tegentonen Festival of experimental music. Designed using the typeface Jacque and custom lettering.

The irreverent faces of Max Kisman

In the mid-1980s Max Kisman (1953) was among the very first designers in Holland to recognize the graphic potential of desktop computers. Before embracing the Macintosh, he designed a series of stamps on the Commodore Amiga, an instrument that he continued to use to create animations for Dutch television. He was one of the first to design lettering and display typefaces that explored the graphic possibilities and limitations of early personal computers, instead of adapting old forms to a new technology. Yet his earliest alphabets were created without electronic means: they were manually cut – not in steel, but in red masking film.[1]

Cutting letters for Vinyl

Kisman was part of a small group of designers and photographers who, from the early 1980s onwards, were associated with the Amsterdam alternative music, art and theatre scene and had a strong impact on its graphic look. Kisman first made a name for himself as the art director and designer of *Vinyl*, an independent music magazine founded in 1980. In many respects *Vinyl* was the Dutch equivalent of *The Face*, the London magazine famous for its Neville Brody design. Having been created as a kind of fanzine for the new wave in pop/rock, *Vinyl* also explored other fields, such as performance, art and fashion. And like *The Face,* its publishers wanted the magazine's design to be as exciting as its subject matter. Kisman and his design partner Ronald Timmermans were not as radical as Brody, but at times they were almost as ambitious in their aspiration to redefine magazine design.

Kisman soon began developing his own letterforms. Pre-press for offset printing around 1983 was a matter of cutting and pasting, and custom lettering had to be hand-drawn or cut out of the red adhesive film used for masking negative offset film – which was the technique Kisman used. This laborious, and sometimes physically painful working method accounts for the relative simplicity of his early letterforms. One of his most complete early types can be found on the cover of the January 1985 *Vinyl* and on the inserted *Post-'84 Poster*. It is an uppercase alphabet constructed exclusively with straight lines and 45° diagonals, and is reminiscent of certain 1920s Art Deco types. Kisman acknowledges this formal relationship, but feels he has 'less affinity with Art Deco than with De Stijl and Bauhaus'. The choice to construct letterforms with straight lines was, above all, a time-saving decision. The alphabet was shown in 1990 as *ZwartVet* ('BlackBold') in an *Emigre* article by Ellen Lupton and J. Abbott Miller, who labelled it 'neo-modernist'.[2] It was later completed with a lowercase and digitized.[3] A similar face in two weights was called *Traveller.* Both typefaces remained unpublished until 2003, when Kisman released a large number of typefaces in his new collection Holland Fonts.

The system of cutting letterforms out of masking film was also used in a series of silk-screened posters for the Amsterdam Tegentonen ('Countertones') event, a festival of experimental sound and music held in the Paradiso venue. The Tegentonen posters have become classics; following the one-off letterforms created for these posters, Kisman also designed the Tegentonen alphabet, a quirky geometric font which never got beyond the prototype stage.

Kisman, an energetic and opinionated person with a anarchic attitude towards typographic tradition and anything solemn, did not limit himself to 'form-giving'. As a teacher at the Rietveld Academy he was outspoken and loyal, surprising his students by buying their work at graduation exhibitions. As an art director at *Vinyl*, he ventured into writing more than once. In 1986 he provided himself with a platform for airing his unorthodox opinions on typographical matters: with the artist Peter

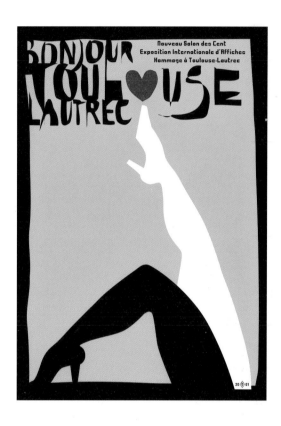

Max Kisman, poster designed as a contribution to *Le Nouveau Salon des Cent – Ode to the poster designer Henri de Toulouse-Lautrec,* 2001. The typography is a combination of digital type and freehand digital lettering.

1   This chapter is partly based on notes prepared by Max Kisman for this book. See also the untitled interview in *Emigre* 15, 1990, pp 4–7.

2   Ellen Lupton and J. Abbott Miller, 'Type Writing', in *Emigre* 15, 1990, pp I–VIII.

3   The complete Zwartvet was shown in Peter Bil'ak's self-published booklet *Illegibility*, 1995.

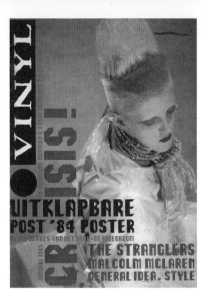

Mertens and a group of like-minded friends and colleagues who called themselves The Ambassadors of Aesthetics he founded *TYP/Typografisch Papier*, a magazine which still exists today in the form of a website. Besides being a place for presenting informal reports on typographic research, provocative statements and in-jokes, *TYP* was also a visual laboratory. Kisman experimented with free-form lettering of the kind that, in a more finished state, would later result in the typeface *Cutout*.

Pioneering the Macintosh

After leaving Vinyl in 1987, Kisman became art director of a new Dutch-American magazine called *Language Technology/Electric Word*, which would later develop into *Wired*. Along with Rudy Vanderlans's *Emigre* magazine, *LT/EW* was one of the first publications entirely produced on the Macintosh. Kisman's work for the magazine resulted in his first digital fonts, the headline face *LTtype* and *Scratch*. These were soon followed by the more experimental *TTtype* – a minimalist single-case alphabet consisting solely of straight lines – and *Squares*, an 'abstract' font of squares and diamonds of various sizes that could be used to generate patterns.

As a type designer Kisman reacted to the functions and properties of desktop computers and early graphic design software in a way that was radically different from that of many – slightly younger – type designers educated in The Hague and Arnhem. For most of them, the computer became a tool to produce basically traditional fonts that could, in theory, have been similarly realized with other means. Kisman, on the other hand, allowed the technology itself to suggest new possibilities and new forms, much like Emigre's Zuzana Licko in California. Repetition, the fast construction of geometric forms, cut-and-paste, freehand drawing: all these standard functions of the Macintosh were explored by Kisman and were used to design pages, illustrations, animations and typefaces.

Kisman saw type design as something other than a utilitarian craft rooted in convention. To him, typefaces were creative statements; but this did not exclude functionality and communication. 'With custom-designed typefaces,' he said in 1990, 'you can give a specific identity to a product. That is why and how I design typefaces. … The characters in my designs aren't always meant to be readable in the traditional sense. Sometimes they are abstract graphic symbols, used for identity purposes only. But they will always remain communication elements. The concept of communication is based on an agreement, it is a code that we have learned to decipher. When we exclude "functional" communication, by abstract graphic symbols you can create other forms of communication based on visual impressions, rhythm and expression. And that's what identity is about.'[4]

ZwartVet

abcdefghijklmnop qrstuvwxyz

Traveller

Regular **Bold**

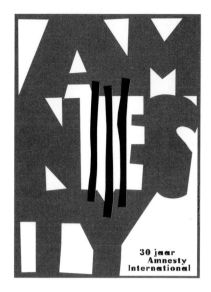

Published by FontShop

Thanks to his presence in Dutch and international magazines, Kisman's work had not gone unnoticed. In 1990, Erik Spiekermann approached him with a request to license typefaces to the newly founded FontFont collection. Formerly, Kisman had not been very enthusiastic about the prospect of making his typefaces available to other designers. However, he found FontShop's interest in his work 'very flattering' and it renewed his enthusiasm for type design. There was much work to be done, as none of his custom alphabets had been drawn up as a complete character set. Kisman found time to do this work during a sojourn of well over a year in Barcelona. Among the earlier custom fonts completed and digitized for the FontFont library were FF *Rosetta*, FF *Vortex*, FF *Scratch* and FF *Cutout*, all based on the display alphabets originally designed (some digitally, some with masking film) for posters and magazines. Rosetta – formerly *LTtype* – is probably the most sophisticated of these fonts, the only one that was issued as a four-member family. It had begun its career as the standard headline typeface in *Language Technology/Electric Word*. When designing it Kisman 'was seeking a form which could be constructed relatively simply, would offer possibilities for modification (extending, compressing) and would nevertheless retain a certain elegance in appearance.' Although it now looks slightly dated, Rosetta has certainly succeeded in this respect. The main criticism could be that the regular and bold weights are not very well matched though in 1990, as Kisman wrote to the author, 'requirements were not so high yet in that respect'.

Kisman also set out to design new typefaces directly on the computer screen. FF *Network* was a homage to early bitmap technology. 'With the improvement of screen and printer quality,' Kisman wrote, 'the low resolution charm of the original bitmaps got lost. Network is an aesthetic attempt to recreate this charm by creating an image which refers to the screen, to basic computer technology, to "cyberspace".' [5] Another typeface which originated in the Barcelona days (and nights) is FF *Jacque*, a face which looks as if it had been drawn by hand but was, in part, directly created on the screen. As described in an amusing account written for the trade magazine *Compres* by his colleague Chris Vermaas, FF Jacque was Kisman's reply to a request from that magazine to explain what his favourite typeface was; Kisman couldn't think of one. Vermaas: 'Well then, make it!'.[6]

The font that Kisman is proudest of is FF *Fudoni*, another face that was born in Barcelona. Being an irreverent mixture of Futura and Bodoni, it was one of the very first typefaces which used the Macintosh's cut-and-paste function to ironize tradition. Kisman: 'In the same way that early 1980s music videos with pixelated images made me realize that computers might play a role in my work, hip hop and digital sound sampling inspired me to create collages in typefaces. During that same period, software became available to open existing typefaces and manipulate them. I was exploring the two extremes: serif and sans. I found the combination with classically shaped serifs unattractive, so I decided on two geometrically shaped typefaces. Futura and Bodoni, in combinations which were almost randomly chosen. ... It was a period in which the appreciation of typography was going through a fundamental change. Fudoni was originally created for a special edition of *TYP*, precisely to illustrate that breakthrough in thinking about type and typography.'

Scratch

abcdfghijklmnopqrst uvwxyz

Rosetta

Regular *Italic* **Bold** *Italic*

Kisman

Cutout Vortex Network Scratch

Fudoni

Fudoni One Two **Three**

4   Interview in *Emigre* (cit.), p 6.
5   This quote and following taken from e-mails to the author, 1999–2002.
6   Chris Vermaas, 'Liever heimwee dan Holland', *Compres*, 19 February 1991.

◄ Logotype of Kisman's online type foundry, 2002.

► Kisman's ᴘᴘ Jacque (1991) is a script face drawn directly on the screen.

Jacque

Slim **Regular** **Fat** *De bakersvertelling van Junius omtrent den kuijeren-den grootvader, die op eene wandeling in den Haarlemmer Hout uit beuken-schors een alfabet voor zijne kleinkinderen sneed, heeft, voor zoover ik mij herinneren kan, nooit elders dan in de kinderkamer gehoor gevonden; en werd zij eene enkele maal in gezelschappen van volwassenen voorgedragen, dan moest.*

Bebedot

Blonde **Black**

Interlace

Single **Double**

Submarine

Extra Light Light **Regular** **Bold**
Extra Bold

Pacific

Standard Light **Bold** Standard Serif Light **Bold**
Classic Light **Bold** Serif Light **Bold** Sans Light **Bold**

BFRIKA

Kisman is aware that the idea to assemble letterforms from various different type-faces was used in certain poster designs in the 1960s, but Fudoni was possibly the very first commercially released typeface to adopt this principle. This was also why it took some time to be published, as FontShop first had to research the possible legal implications. Since its debut in 1991, the Fudoni principle has been copied countless times. A 1998 Linotype release, based on the same idea, was shamelessly called *Futoni*. 'Bodura' would at least have been a more original name.

Kisman left Barcelona in late 1991 to work as a designer of animations and station identifications for the Dutch ᴠᴘʀᴏ television. This change marked the end of a pro-lific period as a type designer. His interest in letterforms made way for a deep suspi-cion of the way typographic experimentation was absorbed by the mainstream and deprived of its sharp edges. In 1995, he wrote in an e-mail interview with Slovak designer Peter Biľak: 'Too much I see now is somehow related to what I did years ago. Of course I recognize some very good designs but to me the revolution is over and repetition began a while ago. There is no meaning in type design, all is decora-tion. ... More important at this moment is to redefine graphic design.' [7]

Kisman in the Bay Area

Kisman continued to redefine his own commitment to graphic design on a regular basis. In the mid-1990s he moved to San Francisco to work as a designer for *HotWired*, the internet version of the monthly technology magazine *Wired*. After *HotWired* de-creased its investments, Kisman found other clients in the Bay Area, from the San Francisco Opera to FontShop ᴜꜱᴀ. For the latter, he edited and designed the online magazine *Tribe*. He continued contributing to ᴛʏᴘ, and wrote illustrated columns for the Dutch design magazine *Items*. In the Bay Area, as in Amsterdam, Kisman works energetically at bringing together designers and artists to exchange experiences and develop joint projects. In October 2003, he organized the one-day conference 'Spaced Out, Black Holes in Typography'. When FontShop decided to stop investing in *Tribe* after two issues, Kisman continued it on his own website, inviting colleagues from around the globe to contribute. For issue #03 (2003) he put together *Frisco Remix*, a sample font with the contributions of thirty-four Bay Area designers, illus-trators and letter artists.

In late 2002 Kisman's type designing activities entered a new phase, when he an-nounced the opening of his own online type foundry, Holland Fonts. The first re-lease consisted of 15 font families – some dating back to the mid-1980s, others very recent. Among the older typefaces that have now been made available for the first time are Zwartvet and Traveller. The relatively new fonts include *Submarine*, a family of five weights with square forms and cut corners; and *Pacific*, a narrow display face whose basic version is a ᴅɪɴ-like sanserif from which four more styles and 'atmos-pheres' were derived. These newly published faces seem to indicate a slightly more pragmatic attitude to type, moving away from the idiosyncracies of Kisman's earlier letterforms. At the same time other recently published fonts, such as the tribal-style *Bfrika* and the experimental *WeLoveYou*, show a remarkable continuity in relation to the early work. While the circumstances may have changed, Kisman's ideas are as playful as ever.

◄ Selection of typefaces published as part of the first releases by Kisman's foundry Holland Fonts, 2002–2003.

► Early work: cover designed with custom type for *Language Technology*, the magazine that later became *Wired*, 1988. LTtype, the font used for the quote 'Put your lips...', was published in 1991 as ᴘᴘ Rosetta.

Put your lips
together and blow

Jeanne de Bont and Henk Lamers: ongoing research

Having worked together for over a quarter century, Jeanne de Bont (1954) and Henk Lamers (1956) are among the Netherlands' least known typographic pioneers. They have probably created dozens of typefaces, some of which are audaciously experimental. Yet without exception, these alphabets have remained unknown or anonymous, either because they were the outcome of in-house assignments for one of the large companies they worked for, or because they were part of personal music, film or book projects. De Bont and Lamers have never felt the need to issue any of their typefaces as commercial fonts.[8]

Henk Lamers and Jeanne de Bont graduated in the mid-1970s from a printing school (*Grafische* MTS) and were both hired by a small advertising agency as junior designers. Eager to find a more challenging job, the couple began puting together a portfolio of their own projects – investigations and designs done without a client. Many of these projects were related to type design. Inspired by Wim Crouwel's work, the couple made a typeface called *Alpha*, which owed much to Crouwel's postage stamp alphabet (the future *Gridnik*). For their own stationery, they designed a more complex constructed alphabet with unorthodox asymmetrical serifs which they call *Briefpapierfont* ('Letterhead font'). One of the most ambitious self-created projects was the redesign of the Dutch traffic signs – a totally fictitious assignment which yielded a set of professional-looking proposals that, again, betrays the twosome's predilection for the functionalist idiom.

Total Design and early digital work

When, in 1979, Total Design had an opening for a graphic designer, they managed to step in together. TD was then at its peak, and more or less in the process of redesiging the Netherlands according to functionalist standards. Apart from the work done for the studio, Lamers and De Bont developed a series of side projects that were presented as silk-screens in 1983 in designer Pieter Brattinga's Amsterdam gallery. Among these designs were a stencil alphabet – showing, again, a strong affinity to Crouwel's lettering work – and lamps decorated with specially made type. Around the same time, the couple created *Dialoog*, one of the first Dutch experiments in computer graphics, developed with the help of the electronics department of Delft University of Technology. In *Dialoog*, abstract signs resembling a coded script were generated simultaneously with music programmed by Lamers.

Having invested in their first computer – a Pearcom, an early pre-Mac Apple clone – Lamers and De Bont began programming alphabets in Basic. 'Type,' says Jeanne de Bont, 'was more or less the only thing you could design with a machine like that.' These desktop experiments resulted in a self-produced digital alphabet that was used to set an entire article – on the outer edge of legibility – in a 1982 issue of the design magazine *Items*.

Océ and Philips

In 1984 Gerard Unger introduced De Bont to Océ, a manufacturer of office hardware for which Unger worked as typographic consultant; Lamers, having done some work for the company as a freelancer, asked to be hired as well in order to have a firmer grip on the projects. To Océ, a large company struggling to come to terms with the growing impact of digital technology, their unique combination of typographic and technological expertise was priceless.

After De Bont and Lamers had joined the Research & Development department, pioneering projects in the field of pre-PostScript screen and printer typography took

◄ Fictitious redesign programme for the Dutch traffic signs. Late 1970s.

▼ Océ 6000 was probably the first digital design and layout system developed in the Netherlands. Fonts and screen design by De Bont and Lamers, mid-1980s.

⩒ Specimen of the typeface Alpha, strongly inspired by Wim Crouwel's lettering work. The alphabet gave De Bont and Lamers an opening at Philips, where they were invited to design a keyboard typeface.

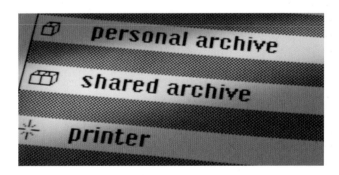

7   Peter Bil'ak, *Illegibility*, Slippery Rock University, Pennsylvania, 1995.

8   This text was based on an article written by Fred Smeijers and Jan Middendorp, 'Forever Young', in the FontShop Benelux magazine 96#3, 2003, pp 2–5. Henk Lamers and Jeanne de Bont provided information by e-mail and in conversation with the authors.

shape. As the technologies evolved – the company even developed its own page lay-out software – new digital types were constantly needed. Lamers and De Bont contributed by designing new bitmap fonts, but were also instrumental in hiring two of the country's most promising young type designers: Martin Majoor and Fred Smeijers.

After-hours, Lamers and De Bont experimented with digital animation (in this field, the Commodore Amiga ruled). This new interest grew into a proper job after they had joined Philips Design – De Bont in 1992, Lamers four years later. At Philips, the electronics company that invented the Compactcassette and the CD, new consumer goods are developed on a daily basis. Designing user-friendly interfaces for digital equipment as well as websites and CD-ROMs became the core of their activities. It was now possible to integrate their side projects into the work done for the company. Philips Design also welcomed lectures and exhibitions born out of the couple's personal interest in specific aspects of typography, technology or the arts. Thanks to their trailblazing investigations into digital design for screens, De Bont and Lamers have moved on to Philips's Strategic Design department, where they now work as design researchers. Yet apart from futuristic-looking interfaces and devices they still design the odd logotype as well.

Parallel to the Philips projects, Henk Lamers and Jeanne de Bont made a name for themselves producing computer/video animations, appearing at venues such as the Toronto Digital Image Festival and the York Independent Film Festival. Lamers's music projects keep a somewhat lower profile, and are only issued on self-produced CDs in very limited runs. In 2003 the double CD *Five Acres of Independence* was brought out as a joint project with Peter Verheul, the co-designer of the present book. Two other type designers were involved as well: both Just van Rossum and Donald Roos appeared as guest musicians.

Most sound and multi-media projects as well as the events that Lamers and De Bont organized at Philips included print work, from posters to CD packaging. Many of these designs were made with custom-made fonts, as were the goodwill publications produced in the mid-1990s with the printer Lecturis. It would be a tough job to compile a complete inventory of the typefaces Lamers and De Bont have created over the years. What is shown on these pages is only the tip of the iceberg.

◄ *Five Acres of Independence*, poster for a self-published double CD featuring music by De Bont and guitarist-type designer Peter Verheul, 2003. The typeface used is Lamers and De Bont's Vogue, based on an old hot metal face from the Intertype catalogue.

▾ *BobsLife* was part of a series of goodwill publications written and designed by Lamers and De Bont and sponsored by Lecturis printers. It was made with a custom typeface called Bobster.

◄ *Don't Come The Raw Prawn With Me Mate!* is an eight-minute film about a radio journalist's travels in Australia. The poster and packaging were designed with a custom stencil alphabet named Road.

▸ The typeface Nicolas is a historical study based on Griffo's type used in *Hypnerotomachia Poliphili* by Aldus Manutius.

What still remains of the visual language of the cla[s]
lost it entirely? Have things improved or deteriorate[d]
old visual language reactivated as soon as anything[?]
visible? Given the 20th century reverence for techno[logy]
we still able to produce stylish things? What does c[?]
have to contribute to history? Where are elements o[f]
found in today's cultural expressions?

Donald Beekman, smart drugs & rock'n'roll

In 1999 FontShop International published a large series of display faces by Donald Beekman. Their precision and quality showed that they were the work of an accomplished designer; but Beekman's name was virtually unknown in the typographic world. Stylistically his typefaces have nothing in common with the exponents of the Dutch typographic tradition that have been so vital for the image of the FontFont library – pragmatic and tailored for legibility under diverse circumstances. Beekman's fonts are adventurous, imaginative and only usable in very specific contexts: they are logos made into alphabets. Their musical roots are evident; in fact, Beekman likes to refer to his style as 'global techno'.[9]

Born in 1961, Beekman entered the music scene at thirteen, playing guitar and bass in various rock and funk bands. In the 1990s he was the founder of two recording bands – hip hop act Bonecrushin' and the more trippy Backbone Soundsystem – as well as the music label Illy Noiz. For over twenty years, he has produced graphic work relating to the Dutch music world. 'I must have designed hundreds of logos for up-and-coming bands. For free, because it was fun to do.'[10]

Beekman studied graphic design at the Rietveld Academy, and was soon fascinated by type design; but he got stuck when an uncompromising typography teacher refused to accept his unorthodox proposals. Fortunately, the system allowed him to switch to the audio-visual department and still attend selected typography classes. In the same period, Beekman was deeply involved in the Amsterdam music scene as one of the initiators of an organization called GRAP (meaning 'joke', but in fact an acronym for GroepenRaad Amsterdamse Popmuziek – Group Council for Amsterdam Pop Music), which looked after the interests of the capital's bands. Many of the musicians and managers with whom he worked in the early days have made a career for themselves and have become paying clients.

Beekman has conceived the promotion and packaging material for a succession of record labels, bands and music events. He designed stacks of twelve-inch record covers for dance acts; this has enabled him to experiment with self-designed letter-

◄ Donald Beekman, hand-out for an open air festival organized by the Amsterdam rock music council GRAP, 2001. Custom lettering is combined with an early version of Beekman's typeface Monodon.

◄ Poster for a mini festival of cover versions of the Dolly Parton song *Jolene*, organized by GRAP in 1987. 'Wild West' letterforms photocopied from books on American wood type.

---

9 'Readme' text of the FontFont 25 release, FontShop International, October 1999.

10 All quotes from an interview with the designer. Additional information: Piet Schreuders, 'Echt zo: BAF! Donald Beekman', in *Qwerty* no. 1, 1989.

Most of Donald Beekman's FontFonts originated in logos and custom lettering on posters and packaging.

▼ The packaging and posters for the 'smart drug' Stargate became the FF Stargate font (1999, part of the FF Backbone package).

▲ Tsunami was designed for the music label of the same name.

▶ FF Totem is based on this 1996 poster for the Amsterdam club Mazzo. Both fonts were published in 1999 as part of the FF Backbone package.

MAZZO'S INDIAN SUMMER

SEPTEMBER 1996
WARM GLOBAL GROOVES
EVERY FRIDAY IN MAZZO

MAZZO ROZENGRACHT 114 | AMSTERDAM
T 020.6267500 | F 020.6263382
OPEN 23:00 - 05:00 HRS | TICKETS FL.15

forms, combining them with repetitive patterns and ornaments. Legibility was of secondary importance; his clients wanted an attractive and immediately recognizable image which could also be achieved with pure form and colour.

Beekman's debut as a designer of digital typefaces was the package FF *Backbone* (1999). It consists of half a dozen very diverse fonts, some of which come in several varieties. Backbone was the outcome of ten years of work in the music world: each of the alphabets started out as a logo for a band, record company or event. FF *Stargate* is an exception; it also began as a logo, but for a different kind of product. It was first used in his branding work for a company called Conscious Dreams, a distributor of legal 'smart drugs'. Stargate is one of the company's many brandnames – a 'herbal XTC'. Working for this client has enabled Beekman to make some of his most outrageous designs. 'On a global level,' he says, 'there aren't very many designers who are in a position to conceive campaigns for mind-expanding drugs.'

Simultaneously with the Backbone package, FontShop issued FF *Beekman*, a typeface of square forms for which the first sketches were made around 1983. It refers to experiments carried out in the early twentieth century. Like Van Doesburg's 1919 alphabet, the Beekman fonts can be expanded and condensed 'without losing their face' (according to the readme files published at the release). When Beekman first drew these alphabets, he was hardly aware of these historical precedents: they were simply an exercise in spartan, flexible letterforms.

Digital lettering and type

Armada

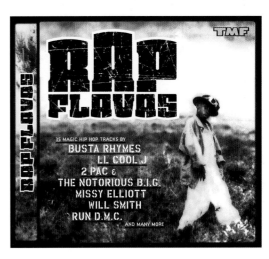

▲ The Armada logo was designed with the font Breeze East, 2003.

▼ FF Beekman can be stretched both ways, 1999.

▲ FF Automatic was originally a logo for a music production company, 1999.

▼ FF Droids and FF Stargate were part of the Backbone package, 1999. Noni (Wan and Too), based on Thai lettering, was issued in 2000.

▲ FF Flava (2003) has four versions designed to be combined into compact headlines and ready-made logos.

▶ An example of this was the first use of the Flava alphabet on the packaging of the *Rap Flavas* CD.

BEEKMAN

LIGHT ITALIC
REGULAR ITALIC
BOLD ITALIC
STRETCHED
STRETCHED

DROIDS
REGULAR
ABCDEFGHIJK
LMNOPQRSTU
SANS
ABCDEFGHIJKL
MNOPQRSTUVW

STARGATE
ABCDEFGHIJKLMNOP
QRSTUVWXYZ
1234567890?!&

NONI WAN
ABCDEFGHIJKLMNOPQRS
TUVWXYZ 1234567890?!&

NONI TOO
ABCDEFGHIJKLMNOPQRS
TUVWXYZ 1234567890?!&

It was Max Kisman, a designer of some of the earliest FontFonts and an occasional partner of Beekman in one-off projects, who had advised him to contact FontShop. Beekman had dozens of custom alphabets sitting on hard disks, all drawn as outline shapes in FreeHand; so producing a package of full-fledged fonts seemed easy. Beekman was flabbergasted when he received the FontFont character list, specifying some 250 glyphs to be drawn for each font. Making the FontFonts became a time-consuming learning process. Beekman realized that some of his more fantastic forms could be impractical when used outside their original contexts. 'Some fonts had shapes for S and 5, Z and 2 which could hardly be distinguished from each other. Some were constructed according to a set of rules which completely fell apart when I tried to adapt them to the shape of a Ç or an accented letter. A nightmare!'

Four years into his type designing career, Donald Beekman has contributed several more exotic display fonts to the FontFont series. FF *Noni* was inspired by local lettering photographed on two trips to Thailand. FF *Imperial* is based on the eerie aesthetics of 'gothic' youth culture. FF *Manga* refers to Japanese scripts. Although Beekman managed to steer clear of the corny Chinese restaurant atmosphere that similar alphabets often offer, in is hard to imagine these picturesque fonts being used in a way that is not anecdotal, or ironic.

FF *Flava* (2003) is very different in this respect. Flava is a very usable heavy slab serif, based on several sources – from *Aachen Bold* to lettering found in a 1920s poster. It was first used on the cover of a hip hop compilation entitled *Rap Flavas*; Beekman calls Flava his 'ultimate hip hop font'. It comes in four varieties with alternating square and round tops and bottoms, meant to be combined with very little leading.

In 2003 Beekman was approached by two emerging German type foundries with offers to licence the unpublished fonts shown on his website. Die Gestalten, a Berlin publisher of art and design books and gadgets, published Beekman's *Breeze*, a script-like constructed italic with versions leaning left ('*West*') and right ('*East*'). Stefan Claudius from the Essen foundry Cape Arcona issued *Monodon*, a family of squarish sanserifs consisting of five weights. Monodon was initially a monospaced font (hence the name) reminiscent of Wim Crouwel's *Gridnik*, but was later taken in a different direction, becoming more idiosyncratic and more contemporary.

Despite the impressive output of the last few years, Beekman still does not consider himself a 'real' type designer. 'I don't think I could ever design a text typeface,' he says. 'My attention span is far too short.'

René Knip: the magic of the sign

When designing a logo and corporate identity for the Dutch fashion chain Anna van Toor, Knip provided a complete alphabet to be used for creating typographic shop decorations, 1999.

Since the replacement of metal type by less tangible technologies, the final appearance of letterforms has escaped the designer's control. A digital letter is a virtual stain which lends itself to being blown up, deformed or filled with colour; it can never be sure of its future context or the material in which it will eventually be realized. There are a few exceptions: in some cases, where digital type design meets lettering and maybe art, letters are brought to their definitive state by their maker, to the point where they have become an immutable object. These are the kind of letters than René Knip makes.[11]

Not for print

René Knip (1963) has been designing alphabets for fifteen years, but none of them has been made publicly available. He makes ample use of the Macintosh, yet this does not imply that his letterforms are meant to become digital fonts. Knip has conceived virtually all of his alphabets for specific uses, defining their material, size and colour. He has designed a typeface for enamel shields; a set of numerals cast in aluminum; another that was die-cut in a paper calender block of 365 pages – a different shape for each day of the year. He designed an alphabet called *Laundry Sans*, which is only available as green plastic letters to be hung on a line. An alphabet used by the HEMA department stores was exclusively made for red and blue ceramic tiles. Laundry Sans and the HEMA typeface are not meant to be printed. 'They are environmental alphabets,' says Knip. 'They are not supposed to be used for typesetting.'
To clarify his view on type, he adds: 'When looking at a landscape, I like to single out forms which have a strong graphic character, such as trees and fences. To me, a letter is like a form that rises up from the background.'
Even when designing printed matter, René Knip likes to play with the dimensional and physical character of letterforms. The BNO Books (the bi-annual guides of the Association of Dutch Designers) which he designed in 2000 for BIS Publishers are a case in point. Each of the seven books was conceived as an object with its own volume and colour, and metal foil lettering specially designed to reflect the nature of each design discipline. Knip had previously used metal foil to add a suggestion of dimensionality to the printed matter made for the Amsterdam Oude Kerk – a church in the red light district that has been turned into a cultural centre and which for several years housed Knip's studio. The exuberant ornamented typeface created for this client was drawn with a felt-tipped pen on paper in one go and then scanned into the computer. Knip's ultimate spatial lettering was designed for a recent invitation card for a furniture shop: die-cast out of a sheet of transparent plastic, the text is literally made of air.
In addition to Atelier René Knip, his graphic design studio, Knip recently created a new venture with his brother Edgar, who specializes in product development. Gebroeders Knip (Knip Brothers) design and produce 'graphic objects' in which letterforms and numerals are part of the structure. Products include a 'company clock' made of cast aluminum, and a cast iron fire basket which can be read like a poem. The brothers are working on a modular typographic lamp whose text can be modified by the user by changing the moveable metal cut-out letters.

Chris Brand as mentor

René Knip's fascination with letterforms began at an early age – before he could read or write. 'I was the youngest, so my brothers could read and write before me. I copied their writing without knowing its meaning. That feeling has stuck in my

Digital lettering and type

mind forever: a fascination for the magic of the sign.' Knip's alphabets are inspired by a wide array of sources, including architects' lettering from the early twentieth century and vernacular type from India, Greece and North Africa.

Although his alphabets show a strong understanding of letterforms, they do not betray Knip's background – a thorough training in the writing and drawing of classically inspired letters. At the St. Joost Art Academy of Breda his teacher was Chris Brand, a master of the humanist cursive and the designer of *Albertina* (> p 144). To René Knip, Brand became a genuine mentor; he was one of the privileged students who were invited to Brand's home for advanced private lessons. 'Chris Brand', says Knip, 'taught me to see the finer points in typographic design. He was able to show you where there is tension in a script and where it is weak. He had a great eye for typographic white space. He talked about "firm white" or "hazy white"… He showed me how to balance form and counterform so precisely that the "white" begins to vibrate.'

Working according to Chris Brand's method – making very precise four-centimetre-high pencil drawings – Knip designed a book face as a study project. 'But I have never sought contact with the world of conventional typography. I often find these people too picky, too deadly serious. Though I do understand why that is: typographic tradition is about fractions of millimetres – about legibility criteria for phone books. I prefer to take typography to the street. There is more room for play there. I am fascinated by the anonymous designs of people who have decided to express something with letterforms. The power of letters is their transparency: beyond their meaning as a sign, there lies enormous graphic, pictorial or ideographic power. Therefore I also like letterforms which stand alone. I made huge block prints of single characters: an "a" whose only role is to be "a". Shouting it out loud.'

Knip is fascinated by the environmental potential of letterforms, as well as the use of type in architecture. He regrets the facility with which people order plotted computer lettering when a typographic problem in a public space needs solving. 'I find those solutions too flat. A lot of feeling for dimensionality has been lost. The street has become a no man's land in which I try to make amendments. And I don't mind if it's not one hundred per cent historically correct. Most of the forms I use come from flea markets anyway.'

The Bridge type and IJburg

All the same, Knip does pay attention to precise historical models. He has borrowed certain forms from Art Deco typography: the lettering on Amsterdam School buildings or the hand-drawn book covers of Fré Cohen, whose 1930s lettering shows a great affinity for that school. At Studio Anthon Beeke, where Knip worked in the early 1990s, Knip digitized the Amsterdam Bridge Alphabet. A typical architect's type of the Art Deco era, it was drawn for the City's technical department, possibly by

Fenceless, a project conceived by René Knip for the 2003 exhibition 'Armour, the Fortification Of Man' at Fort Asperen, a nineteenth-century fortress. The work was a metal fencing based on hand-written lines of text. The exhibition was curated by trend watcher Li Edelkoort.

Gebroeders Knip (Knip Brothers) is a company run by René and Edgar Knip. The brothers design and produce 'graphic objects' such as lamps, clocks and this fire basket.

Keepsake of the manifestation 'Labyrint van de toekomst' (Labyrinth of the future) organized by the Bouwfonds (Building Fund), Amsterdam 1999.

11 An early, Dutch-language version of this article appeared in *96#1*, 2003. Based on conversations with René Knip. Additional information: Ewan Lentjes, 'René Knip. Hinken op twee liefdes', *Items* vol. 18 no. 1, 1999, pp 22 – 29.

Knip's 2003 calendar for the Amsterdam printing firm Calff & Meischke was an ingeniously designed and brilliantly produced piece of work, with a different die cast for each of the 365 pages. It won the first prize with distinction in that year's national calendar award.

ZEEBURG

ALEXANDRINE TINNEHOF

ABCDEFGHIJKLMNOPQRSTUVWXYZ

▲ Alphabet and street sign conceived for IJburg, a newly built Amsterdam neighbourhood that is part of the Zeeburg riverside district, 2003.

▶ Each of the seven volumes of the *Dutch Design Guide 2000* has a separately designed cover with custom lettering appropriate to the discipline covered in that book.

▼ The alphabet for the printed matter of the Amsterdam Oude Kerk (Old Church) was hand-drawn with a felt-tipped pen, then digitized, 1998.

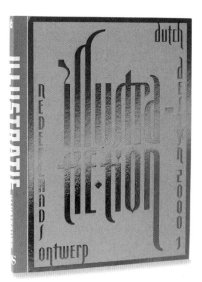

▸ Laundry Sans, an alphabet designed to be produced as green plastic letters to be hung on a line. First used as part of the exhibition 'Mooi Maar Goed', 1999.

▾ The HEMA alphabet for the chain of department stores of that name was executed as blue and red ceramic tiles for exclusive use in the HEMA restaurants and cafés, 1997.

ɤ Inktpot, alphabet for lettering the floors of the NS (National Railways) headquarters, 2002.

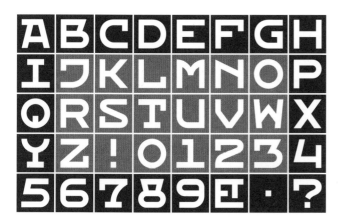

Anton Kurvers (> p 75). Knip cleaned up the Bridge Alphabet for use in floor lettering in the basement of the Amsterdam Concertgebouw; Studio Anthon Beeke used his 'dirty' digital version in a series of type-only posters for the Toneelgroep Amsterdam (Amsterdam Theatre Company).

Being a true revival, the Bridge Alphabet is an exception in Knip's body of work. His own alphabets and sets of numerals are more personal and contemporary; often their forms are influenced by the technique used. The new typeface for street signs in the Amsterdam IJburg district is a case in point. Still in preparation at the time of this writing, it is inscriptional, supported by historical references yet very contemporary. It is a rectangular typeface, but has round angles because of the milling technique that will probably be used for removing the excess aluminium. Should the production technique change, the typeface's appearance will change accordingly.

Interior design

Many of Knip's commercial environmental projects were conceived in cooperation with Merkx + Girod, an interior architecture company. One of the projects Knip has participated in was the corporate design of the fashion chain Anna van Toor; the brief was to make a typeface which suggested that the shop 'had always been there'. Merkx + Girod also designed the restaurants of HEMA, one of the largest department store chains in the Netherlands. In these restaurants, Knip's red-and-blue tile alphabet was used both for signposting and as a decorative element. Yet the alphabet was not conceived with the project in mind: prototypes had already been produced when HEMA came along. The same was true for Laundry Sans, the green plastic 'hanging letter' which became an eye-catcher for 'Mooi Maar Goed', an exhibition of contemporary Dutch graphic design (Stedelijk Museum, Amsterdam 1999). 'Such alphabets are designed without making concessions. They start out as autonomous projects; if it then turns out that they can be adopted within a project, you have an ideal situation.'

LUST: the process as product

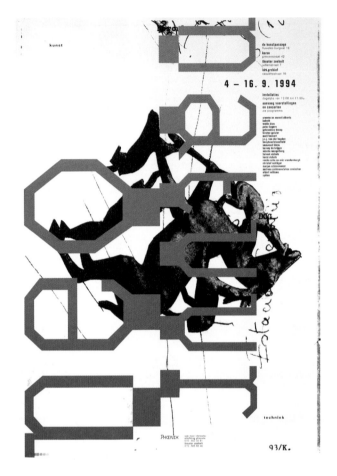

LUST was the title of the 1995 graduation project by Jeroen Barendse (Dutch, 1973) and Thomas Castro (American, 1967) at the Arnhem Institute for the Arts (formerly the Academy of Fine Arts). It became the name of their studio when, the next year, they set up shop in The Hague with a small government grant.[12] In those early days, when LUST was a duo, they wrote ambitious manifestos which made it clear that they were not just the next client-driven design studio; that they were not interested in style and problem-solving, but in defining concepts and ideas. 'LUST designs and philosophy do not emerge from style but from interpretation and conceptualization of the assignment. We are mainly interested in CONTEXT and ASSOCIATION.' It was perhaps a way of encouraging the right future clients and directing the wrong ones towards the competition: 'Many of our ideas are based on the process – to the extent that sometimes the process becomes the final PRODUCT.'[13]

In 1999 Barendse and Castro were joined by Dimitri Nieuwenhuizen (1971), a specialist in interface design and interactive design. Working for a diverse selection of culturally informed clients – architects, theatre and music festivals, the PTT, the City of The Hague – LUST has found a balance between personal research and public service. Their designs, both for print and for the screen, are functional in that they communicate the client's message; yet the language they speak is their own. The work invites the user to look for hidden meanings, and even question design itself. Thus, all the work created by the studio is part of an all-encompassing research project, of which Castro wrote back in 1995: 'No one interpretation of LUST is correct. Your conclusion is just as valid as ours. LUST is, after all, personal ...'[14]

One element that has helped shape the studio's individualistic idiom is the self-designed type. Most of the typefaces designed by Barendse and Castro belong to the early years of their collaboration and show influences of grunge fashion and deconstruction theory. Almost ten years later, most of these fonts look dated; one could also say that they perfectly express the spirit of the early 1990s. *LUST Gothic* (based on DIN *Mittelschrift*) and *LUST Incidenz* (a redrawn grotesque) look amateurish and un-

▲ Poster designed by Thomas Castro using the Blockbuster font by Jeroen Barendse, 1994. At the time Castro was working at the Barlock studio, co-founded by Vincent van Baar.

▶ Blowout by Thomas Castro, one of the earliest LUST fonts.

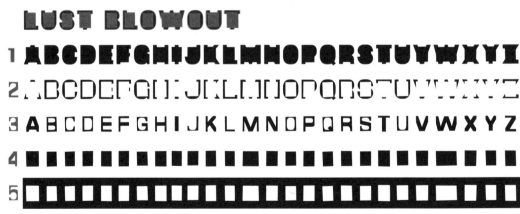

▼ Temporary typography designed by LUST for the De Volharding building, The Hague, on the occasion of the annual Architecture Week. Specially designed bitmap faces were produced as adhesive vinyl lettering. A lowercase font called

LUST Pop was used in 1998 (left); the 1999 font was LUST Pong (right). Built in 1927–28 by the architects J.W.E. Buijs and J.B. Lürsen, De Volharding was originally lettered in a similar manner.

▼ Die-cut posters for the International University Theatre Festival, Amsterdam 2000. The typeface used is the monospaced font LUST Pure.

▼ Studio 'Bits&co', signage for New Metropolis, Amsterdam 2002, film transfer on glass. Seen in perspective, visitors can read the words to a traditional Dutch game for teaching children to read: *Aap Noot Mies...*

finished; but the imperfections were deliberately built in. The letters of Jeroen Barendse's *Blockbuster* sit on big squares that extend beneath the baseline; their square skeletons with skewed corners recall Wim Crouwel's *Gridnik*. Castro's *Blowout* family is the most conceptual of the LUST typefaces: it plays a challenging game with letterforms cut out of squares and vice-versa, exploring the outer edges of recognizability.

These LUST fonts were initially distributed as freeware on a diskette which carried the admonition 'abuse wisely'. As Thomas Castro explained to *Emigre* magazine, that phrase expressed the excitement of being part of a process whose result is as yet unknown. 'The great thing about designing type [is] to see the different ways a designer uses or abuses the typefaces that we so carefully designed. I take ultimate care that the curves, the kerning, the color, everything, is in perfect harmony, or sometimes in perfect discord, with each other, when along comes a designer who uses my typeface in a surprising way. That is the moment I cherish, because whether my typeface is used well or badly, the designer using it is taking part in the total design process that began when I designed that typeface. It's a visual dialog.' [15]

The early typefaces are now distributed by the London outfit FontWorks, as is LUST *Pure*, a simple yet sophisticated one-weight monospaced font. Most recent typefaces were designed to be used in graphic and multimedia designs by the studio and have not been marketed. Several were made for architectural projects. For several years LUST took part in the Week of Architecture organized by Wils & Co Architectural Platform in The Hague, designing and producing spectacular lettering for the famous De Volharding building with custom bitmap fonts. A more recent project also used bitmapped letterforms in an architectual setting: a glass wall in the New Metropolis museum, Amsterdam, carries a seemingly abstract bitmap pattern which, when read at a sharp angle, spells out the words to the traditional Dutch *leesplankje* or reading plank. Here, as in other LUST projects, the letterform is not just a solution, it is also a challenge – an invitation to participate in a game of form and meaning.

12 This article is partly based on information supplied by Jeroen Barendse, Thomas Castro and Dimitri Nieuwenhuizen in conversation and by e-mail.

13 Type specimen printed as part of Barendse and Castro's graduation project, Arnhem Institute for the Arts, 1995.

14 Ibid.; republished on the LUST website, www.lust.nl

15 'An interview with LUST' [by Rudy Vanderlans?], in *Emigre* 45, winter 1998, pp 50–58.

Hunters and collectors

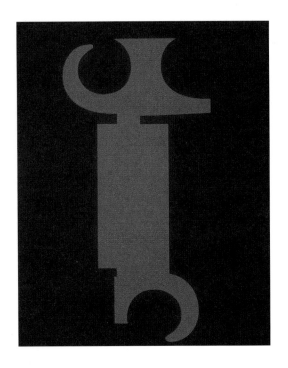

With the advent of digital typography came the possibility of using existing type-faces and vernacular lettering as material for new fonts. In the Netherlands, the number of type designers who playfully manipulate or appropriate the letterforms found on the street, in wastebins or on harddisks, is limited compared to those who design completely new text and display faces. These are a few of the most interesting.

Marianne van Ham: type as art

Based in Utrecht, Marianne van Ham (1963) has always had an artist's approach to typography. One of her projects at art school was a sort of reverse type specimen in which, step by step, she deconstructed *Helvetica* and its counterforms until the letters melted into pure image. Another study of counterforms resulted in a font called *Tussen Bodoni* ('In-between Bodoni', c. 1990), which seems almost legible but can only be used to compose abstract texts.

Her work as a graphic designer, although it does not gravitate towards the abstract like these type projects, is equally conceptual. A programme of the Theater aan de Werf festival in Utrecht, designed in cooperation with SYB, was structured on the basis of the entrance prices, 'because that is an aspect of theatre that is usually stashed away'. Figures seem to be ever-intriguing to her. As a form of season's greetings, friends and colleagues were presented with her *Jaarverslag 1997 in cijfers* (1997 Annual Report in figures). The small booklet contains nothing but figures, a mixture of forms and counterforms embedded in repetitive patterns of lines and circles, accompanied by short captions such as 'Estimated IQ' and 'Age in years'. She has also designed autonomous sets of numerals: *Fresh Numbers* – a name quoted from a Shakespeare sonnet – is a montage of letter parts, taken mainly from Bodoni shapes. *Dubieuze Getallen* (Dubious Numbers, c. 1992) is a project consisting of several sets of numerals which through their form express the ambiguity of figures.

▲ Abstract composition made
with Bodoni counterforms.

▶ Double page spread from
Van Ham's student project
*The Origin of Species;
Helvetica revisited*, 1993.

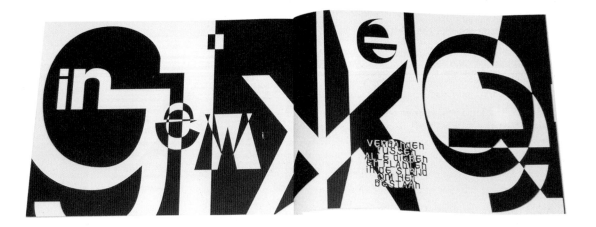

Digital lettering and type

Double Dutch

Smooth Bitmap *Ware de schrijver minder haastig geweest met het uitgeven van een onderzoek, welks elementen nog naauwlijks in zijn eigen geest naar eisch bezonken konden zijn, hij zou zijn boek niet slechts van allerlei zonden tegen den goeden smaak gezuiverd, maar zich ook minder overdreven voorstellingen gemaakt hebben omtrent de waarde zijner resultaten als geheel.*

Marianne van Ham's only typeface to be commercially available was also constructed using sampled material from several Bodonis. Each glyph in FF *Double Dutch* (1992) is the result of a juxtaposition of the roman and the italic of the same character – both in slightly distorted versions. It is the kind of procedure that has become commonplace in 'grunge' type design; but Double Dutch is more readable than most and has a sense of childlike joy about it. It is also the only published typeface made by a female Dutch designer (!).

Van Ham has made one more complete alphabet: a college project called *Universal Handwriting* (c. 1989), 'universal' because it was made by as many hands as possible. Based on photographs she took of hand-written and hand-painted notes and signs she came across in the street, each character was distilled from a different message written by a different person.

The anarchy of Ko Sliggers

Around 1980 Ko Sliggers (1952) was one of the iconoclastic young designers who contributed to what has become known as the 'Dumbar style'. After two years at Studio Dumbar, Sliggers worked as an independent designer, became a professional cook, switched back from food to design, producing challenging visuals at Studio Anthon Beeke and VBAT Advertising and in 2002 set up a one-man studio in a tiny village called Lalleweer in the northern province of Groningen.

In recent years, several of Sliggers's graphic designs were made with self-designed typefaces; in 2003 he began marketing these fonts via a website. Although he was trained by Chris Brand at the St.Joost Academy in Breda, Sliggers is not part of the Dutch tradition of literary, historically inspired type design. Like most of the other designers in this chapter, he creates fonts as a by-product of his graphic designs in order to give the work an unmistakable typographic identity. Sliggers's work has always stood out for its energy and unconventionality. His posters (for various theatre companies and, while working at Beeke, for the Holland Festival) show an anarchic attitude, a tendency to make some noise to interfere with the message. Type – notably destructive, 'grungy' type – is an effective means to create such noise.

Sliggers's typeface *Ko* was developed for the text posters of the 1997 Holland Festival. Like Barry Deck's *Template Gothic*, it is based on letterforms created with a lettering stencil, but the result is totally different in feel: intentionally sloppy, and directly referring to the vernacular use of lettering stencils by suggesting different pen thicknesses. Thus *Ko Light* has become an outline font, as the thin penstroke does not fill up the letterform.

The *Etalage-script* (literally: 'Shop window script') is based on an early twentieth-century stencil used by a local farmer to letter his wheat bags. A version with

15 This article is based on an interview with Marianne van Ham.

16 Information supplied by Ko Sliggers in e-mails to the author, 2003.

▶ Staple (2003) comes in three weights, complete with 'real' italics.

↙ Etalage-script and Ariënne, used for a graphic designer's stationery; left, the original stencil used by a local farmer.

ariënne boelens

grafisch ontwerper

Van Oldebarneveldstraat 116   3012 GV Rotterdam

T   010 213 57 06   info@arienneboelens.nl

F   010 240 95 15   www.arienneboelens.nl

klojoritueeltje
mosterdpatatten
moules d'anvers
dislexmsprroest
magischtyppetje
& * ( ) #€$%+={ }[ ]?

painted-in counters was called *Ariënne*, after the graphic designer for whom it was made. Sliggers's most recent – and possibly most interesting – typeface is *Staple*, a complete font family based on the forms that can be created by bending and folding staples. Not being too dogmatic about this concept, Sliggers has managed to create a pleasant, slightly irregular monoline with proportions reminiscent of, say, *Letter Gothic* but with quite original shapes.

Mark van Wageningen's Russian deconstructivism

The development of Mark van Wageningen (1969) as a type designer is typical of his generation. Having graduated from the Amsterdam Rietveld Academy in 1994, his early typefaces were derivative and grungy; but his interest in letterforms deepened and culminated in an extensive family of constructed typefaces, *Gagarin*, still expanding at the time of this writing.

Van Wageningen's motives for making type are those of a restless graphic designer who wants new and unusual alphabets to give his book jackets, magazines and posters a more personal touch. He began selling his fonts because fellow designers asked for them, and because he enjoyed playing around with their packaging and specimens. Several of them were later licensed to international foundries.

The first font issued was a graduation project called *Stavba* (1994). Van Wageningen described it as 'a laserprinter print-out of *Futura Bold*, each letter cut up in a consistent manner and the pieces pasted up again and returned to the computer.' *Cerny* (1995) looks equally destructive, but was not derived from an existing typeface. Using a technique practised by fellow Amsterdammer Willem Sandberg, Van Wageningen tore each character out of black paper, then digitized the result without much alteration.

Cerny, a rough-and-tumble caps-only alphabet with no counters, is an amusing experiment of limited use. It was judged interesting enough for inclusion in the Take-Type 2 collection published in 1998 by the Linotype Library. Two more fonts by Van Wageningen were on that CD: *Laika* and *Sjablony* (from *sjabloon*, the Dutch word for stencil). Of his 'rough' fonts, the stencil type *Zkumavka* is the most interesting. It has rather original forms that are vaguely reminiscent of 1920s display lettering, and is surprisingly legible in smaller point sizes. Zkumavka dates from 1995 but was not published until 2002, when it was released by 2Rebels in Montreal.

Van Wageningen was first brought into contact with 2Rebels by FontShop Benelux. He had long been playing with the idea of a typeface family structured in an unusual way. In an article presenting the Gagarin family, he wrote: 'Compared to a real family, a typographic family is usually a rather dull show. Where is the criminal nephew? Where is the uncle who knows all kinds of tricks? A type family usually

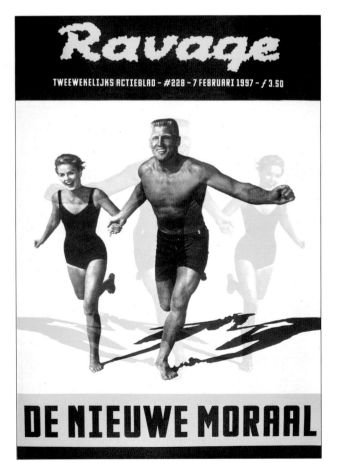

Digital lettering and type

Gagarin Family

ANNA **Boris** *Christa* Dmitri
Elena Fjodor Gregor **HEKTOR**
Igor Jouri **Leonora** **Magda**
Ossip Petrov

◄ Gagarin family, published by
2Rebels, Montreal, 1998–2003.

▶ Mark van Wageningen, self-
published type specimen, 1998.

↕ Magazine cover using Gagarin
and hand-rendered logo, 1997

goes from roman to italic and from thin to thick … These boring series allow very limited space to the individual freedom of their members. … The Gagarin family is a real family, like life itself, in good times and bad times.' [17] This last phrase is a reference to a well-known Dutch TV soap.

As his font names indicate, Van Wageningen is fascinated by Russian culture, especially by Futurism and Constructivism. Gagarin is the first typeface for which he has actually taken clues from that period: it is partly based on the geometric principles apparent in the lettering of Rodchenko and the Stenberg brothers and copied in a lot of vernacular lettering from the Soviet era. Each variant is drawn on the same simple grid. The basic fonts are rectangular, with rounded angles; some are roughened or blurred. The structure of the family is an open system, allowing for foreign influences. When Van Wageningen wanted to add two 'female' Gagarins with a more calligraphic streak, he invited a young Flemish designer named Nele Reyniers to participate in his project. Being left-handed, she incorporated the inversed stress of a left-handed broad-nibbed pen in her two contributions to the Gagarin family, *Leonora* and *Magda*. A serif version of Gagarin drawn by Reyniers is on its way.

Martijn Oostra and the fascination of the ordinary

Martijn Oostra, who studied at the Arnhem Institute for the Arts, now runs a graphic design studio in Amsterdam. Oostra is also an artist, photographer, and publicist – but first and foremost he is a collector. He saves printed matter that is distributed door-to-door; he picks up obscure handouts in bars; he takes home a traffic sign now and then. Most importantly, he has taken thousands of pictures recording the weird and wonderful details of urban life. Oostra has immortalized the unintentional graphic poetry of building sites and mobile toilets; of parked cars and neglected shop windows. There is no graphic manipulation. The design is in the framing and the context – for although this is autonomous photography, Oostra likes to present it in design magazines.

Oostra's typefaces, issued by Montreal's 2Rebels foundry, are also collections of mundane items reproduced in a new context. *Blackmail* (1996) is a variation on the well-known theme of the ransom letter. Oostra's alphabet happily alternates positive and cameo characters and has some very recognizable letters for Dutch readers – e.g. the ones taken from the mastheads of two major dailies. *Ericssome* (after the electronics company of almost the same name) was made in 1999 for the headlines and diagrams of a magazine article on mobile phones. It was later issued as a commercial font but was soon surpassed by FontShop's FF *Call* (made by Ignaszak, Kister and Scheuerhorst), a wide selection of mobile phone alphabets covering almost all available brands. *Educational* is like a schoolbook font for the children of the grunge generation; its Pi-font has a number of distorted traffic signs. Both Educational fonts were based on stamps made decades ago for didactic purposes. Designed a few years before Ko (> p 277), Oostra's *Mould* family seems to be based on the exact same lettering template as Ko Sliggers's typeface. *Tsjecho* is a digitized version of letterforms used in former Czechoslovakia for lettering shop windows. Finally, *WiresAndPlanks* is the only Oostra font whose forms were newly designed. It is a kind of stencil face whose parts are held together by, well, wires. [18]

▲ Martijn Oostra, Blackmail,
released by 2Rebels in 1997.

↕ Oostra's typeface Tsjecho was
based on the die-cut paper
letters used in former Czechoslovakia for lettering shops.

▶ Oostra used his font Ericssome
in this poster for a story-writing
contest in the city of Almere.

17 Mark van Wageningen in 'De familie Gagarin', *Druk* 012, summer 2002.

18 Information supplied by Martijn Oostra in e-mails to the author, 2002–03.

The Hague, the new generation

Gerrit Noordzij retired from his teaching post at the Koninklijke Academie van Beeldende Kunsten (KABK) in The Hague in 1990. Many of his students have since been teaching typography, type design or writing at that school: type designers Frank E. Blokland, Peter Matthias Noordzij, Peter Verheul, Just van Rossum, Petr and Erik van Blokland; graphic designers Huug Schipper, Jan Heijnen and Dick Visser.

As in Noordzij's day, graphic design students are familiarized with letterforms through writing classes; lettering and type design are included in the curriculum, but are by no means its main ingredient. As former student Paul van der Laan has noted, 'in The Hague, type design is not taught as a separate discipline, but is regarded as part and parcel of graphic design. You can only judge the type you design if you also use it. This approach makes sure that designing type is about more than just "form", because "function" is equally important.' [19]

Postgraduate course 'Type and Media'

In the mid-1990s the KABK's graphic design and typography department decided to emphasize the Academy's tradition in type education by setting up a one-year post-graduate course in type design and typography. Many European art schools carry similar programmes, but the course in The Hague is one of two courses (the other one being the MA course at the University of Reading) specialized in type design. To emphasize the fact that ample attention is given to the use of type in the digital realm – and also as a political move – the course was renamed Type and Media in 2000, although the curriculum still includes hand-rendered lettering and stone carving. The postgraduate course is attracting an international student population, with graduates from art schools across Western and Eastern Europe and the Americas. [20]

▲ Overview of the 2003 graduation exhibition of the post-graduate course 'Type and Media' at the Koninklijke Academie van Beeldende Kunsten (KABK – Royal Academy of Arts), The Hague. The 2003 graduates were from Portugal, France, Germany, Lithuania, Mexico and the Netherlands.

▸ Specimen of LD Spaghetti Bolognese, the first complete display font by the Letter-dispuut (Donald Roos and Onno Bevoort).

Digital lettering and type

Con form: the class of '96 – '97

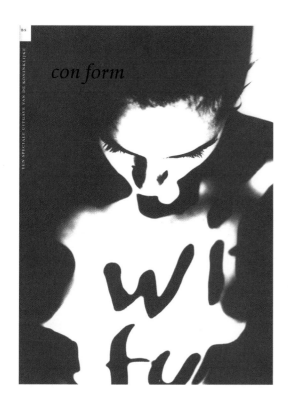

Although many students from the regular four-year course of graphic design at the Royal Academy of Arts (KABK) are now mainly interested in electronic media and conceptual projects, there have been occasional outbursts of enthusiasm for type design. This was the case in 1996, for instance, when a group of KABK students spontaneously organized themselves to publish a collective presentation of their type designs. This publication, a brochure titled *Con form*, was presented to the participants of the 1996 ATypI conference in The Hague, hosted by the KABK. The brochure was in part a reaction to the ample attention given to the more established Hague type designers in the book *Haagse Letters*, published on the same occasion. The group of students and recent graduates who put together *Con form* wanted to make clear that a younger generation was waiting in the wings; and that they, too, had a professional attitude towards type. Among the initiators of the projects were Bas Smidt, Jesse Skolnik and Paul van der Laan; participants who published their lettering and type designs included Hannes Famira, Eyal Holtzman, Jacques Le Bailly, Martijn Rijven and Martin Wenzel.

About half of the twenty or so students who showcased type in *Con form* found work as graphic designers and are not likely to return to letterforms; but a surprising number has managed to make type design a part of their professional activities.

Martin Wenzel and Profile

Born and raised in Berlin, Martin Wenzel (1969) was a neighbour of MetaDesign and FontShop in the early 1990s: he was employed at the typesetting company CitySatz in the same building. Thanks to the informal contacts established with FontShop's Jürgen Siebert he immediately had a publisher on finishing his typeface FF Marten, designed after-hours. Published in 1991, FF Marten is a typical first typeface. 'Since I had never been taught how to do it,' wrote Wenzel, 'I started intuitively drawing geometric shapes and angles ... very modular.' [21] There is more to FF Marten than this; the 'Grotesque' version with its asymmetric joints already embodies a first step from geometry to a more sophisticated view on curves.

What Wenzel really wanted was to be able to design a text typeface. His friends in the field of type design pointed out that the Hague Academy was the best place to learn how to do that. From 1993, he was a student at the KABK evening school of graphic design, while continuing to design and publish experimental typefaces.

His subsequent FontFonts show his eagerness and talent in exploring a wide range of styles and design problems. He drew a small family of classically proportioned text faces built with irregular straight lines – the kind of procedure used by Vojtech Preissig in his *Preissig* typeface. Wendel's FF *Rekord* (1994) has striking details and an irregularity all of its own; but at small point sizes it works admirably well, giving an impression of liveliness rather than chaos. FF *Primary* (1995) is based on an earlier design called *Daela*, a narrow, rather calligraphic typeface made of straight lines only. Primary incorporates some of the lessons learnt at the KABK: for instance, the

Marten

Regular CAPS Grotesque CAPS

Primary

Book **Bold** Round book **Bold**

PrimaryStone

Rekord

Book *Italic* CAPS **Black**
(Symbols) ⬡⬡⬡⬡⬡⬡⬡⬡

▲ The A4 brochure *Con form*, published on the occasion of the 1996 ATypI conference in The Hague. Cover photography by Bas Smidt.

◀ Wenzel's early FontFonts: FF Marten (1991), FF Primary (1995) and FF Rekord (1994).

19 Note on Van der Laan's website type-invaders.com.

20 Anno Fekkes (ed. Mathieu Lommen), *Special characters from The Hague*, Royal Academy of Art, The Hague [2000]. *Out Now. Examenwerk 2003*, KABK, The Hague 2003.

21 'How to get from a to a' in *Druk* 010, autumn 2001, p 37. Additional information supplied by Martin Wenzel in conversation and by e-mail.

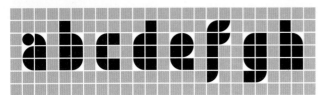

TrinitéSans?

▾ FF Profile (2000) and a folder designed by Wenzel as part of a corporate identity for Dinostor, a manufacturer of servers and software for network-attached storage.

▴ Trinité Sans? only exists as a question: the hypothetical typeface has not been developed beyond this test word.

Profile

Light *Italic* Regular *Italic* Medium *Italic*
Bold ***Italic*** **Black *Italic*** SMALL CAPS LIGHT *ITALIC*
REGULAR *ITALIC* **MEDIUM** *ITALIC* **BOLD ITALIC**
BLACK ITALIC Ook onafhankelijk van haar weldadig karakter, is de typografie zulk eene vernuftige uitvinding geweest, blijk gevend van zulk een opgeklaard verstand, zulk eene praktische vaardigheid, dat hij zeker gaat, die a priori elke overlevering verwerpt, welke aan de spits dier ontdekking een stumpert plaatst.

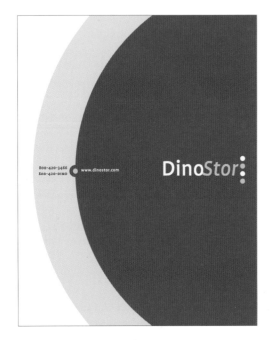

800-420-3466
800-420-DINO   www.dinostor.com

DinoStor:

◂ Letters made (by the author) with Wenzel's InTegel; the basic shapes are the same as those used in several experiments by the modernists and their heirs, so the results are rather similar.

▾ The alphabet set in Schirft.

diagonal contrast derived from writing with the broad-nibbed pen is more outspoken than in Daela. An ingenious variety is the 'three-dimensional' *Primary Stone*, with which one can simulate letters chiselled into stone by layering the four fonts (bottom-left-right-top) and giving them different shades of colour.

Another variation on *Daela* was created for the 'Code' issue of the experimental typographic magazine FUSE: *Schirft* turns the characters of the original face upside-down and inside-out, creating a new version of the alphabet that needs some training to read. *InTegel* is a font he designed for another issue of FUSE – 'Tegel' being Dutch for 'tile' as well as the name of Berlin's largest airport. Like Unger's FUSE font *Decoder*, it is a series of modules that allow the user to create his or her own characters. Among Wenzel's other type experiments is *TrinitéSans?* (question mark included), an incomplete font which tentatively explores the possibilities of creating a companion sanserif to Bram de Does's much admired original.

The text typeface that Martin Wenzel had gone to The Hague for was five years in the making. Having done the first drawings in 1995, he achieved 'the fluidity and definition' he was looking for by 2000, when the typeface was published as FF *Profile*. The family went through several name changes: it was announced as *Dialogue*, and was called *Media* before that – both names had to be dropped for copyright reasons. The name stills lives on in *MediaPigeons*, an (unpublished) amusing attempt to mix the sanserif with seventeenth-century mannerist writing.

FF *Profile* is a humanist sanserif in the Dutch tradition exemplified by *TheSans* and *Productus*. But Wenzel managed to steer clear of these kindred designs by inventing his own internal logic, and finding a balance between the straightforwardness of, say, Spiekermann's FF *Meta* and the calligraphic verve that is part and parcel of the Hague style. As an introduction to the Profile specimen in FontShop's *FontFont Focus* series, Wenzel wrote the following 'recipe': 'Take – metaphorically speaking! – the forms of classical typefaces based on writing with a broad-nibbed pen (for example a Garamond). Then carefully reduce the contrast within the character shapes – the difference between the thick and the thin – to a minimum. Simultaneously reduce the serifs so far that only a little detail will remind us that they were here once.' This way of approaching the sanserif should liberate us from 'the closed, heartless, oversimplified shapes of all sorts of Helveticas' and result in 'designs that have become more vivid as well as more legible.'[22] Shortly after its release Profile won an award at the 2000 Type Design Competition of the Type Directors Club (New York).

Martin Wenzel is now working part-time at Petr van Blokland's studio where he customizes typefaces and designs websites. In The Hague he runs his home studio under the name of Martin+. He is currently working on a typeface called *Monda*, which is 'based on writing with the pointed pen': the Hague way of saying that it will be a typeface in the modern or Didone style with vertical stress. Although, according to the designer, 'Monda is not sure yet what she wants to become', he envisages 'a font that applies the typical openness of a renaissance face to a classicist design.'[23]

Paul van der Laan, a versatile talent

Among the initiators of the 1996 *Con form* project, Paul van der Laan (1972) is probably the most prolific type designer. His lettering and type designs show a great variety in styles and modes, from Van Krimpen revival to low-resolution screen font. All are firmly based on handwriting in the KABK tradition – although some seem to belong to a completely different, hi-tech world.

Having graduated in 1997, Van der Laan became a graphic designer and web designer at the Hague company 5D. Simultaneously he started participating in type design projects by The Enschedé Font Foundry (TEFF), run by his former teacher Peter Matthias Noordzij. Helped by his experience in media design he also built TEFF's efficient and original website.

In order to specialize further in type design, he quit his day job after two years and went back to school, enrolling in the KABK's postgraduate course in typography and type design. Having graduated a second time in 2000, Van der Laan became an independent graphic designer, sharing a workspace called Lokaal 0.11 with other graphic designers as well as interaction designers and programmers. Van der Laan tries to work with his own typographic material as much as possible. 'With each new assignment', he wrote, 'I ask myself if any of my own typefaces can be used for it. If the answer is no, it is time to start working on a new typeface.'[24]

During his year as a postgraduate student, he scored with a display face originally designed for a friend's stationery. Early 2000, *Rezident* received a Silver Award in Linotype's International Type Design Competition and was subsequently included in the Linotype TakeType 3 font package. Rezident looks at the properties of letters written with a broad-nibbed pen or flat brush, and takes them into a new realm – the techno age. The heavy strokes with rounded oblique extremes almost seem to be a parody of the diagonal stress found in italic writing, while the heavier weights also hint at blackletter. This interest in blackletter is confirmed by some of Van der Laan's later lettering experiments, notably for 'Fraktur[ed]', an activity that was part of the 2000 ATypI conference in Leipzig.

Van der Laan's first full-fledged text typeface was *Flex*, presented in 2000 as his graduation project of the postgraduate course in type design and typography. Flex is a typical humanist sanserif in the Hague style, and bears some resemblances to Petr van Blokland's *Productus* or Martin Wenzel's *Profile*. Yet the concept for Flex differs from these workhorse faces in that it focuses on research, not functionality. Besides a full range of weights, Van der Laan 'wanted to give the typeface different appear-

Flex

Regular *Italic* **Medium** *Italic* **Bold** *Italic*
Extra Bold *Italic* De associatie wierp, gelijk het heette, geen of te weinig winsten af; Fust eischte het voorgeschotene terug, onder eede verklarend dat hij die gelden bij anderen opgenomen en er rente voor betaald had; Gutenberg kon de in pand gegeven werktuigen niet lossen; pers en materialen werden het eigendom van Fust, die zich associeerde met Peter Schöffer, Gutenberg's leerling en als technicus zijn meester.

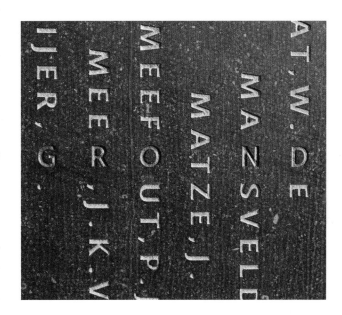

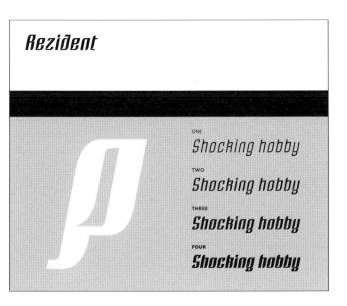

◀ Van der Laan's first published font, Rezident, won him a Silver Award in the 2000 Linotype International Type Design Competition.

▲ Detail of a monument to the victims of the struggle for independence of the Dutch East Indies (Indonesia) between 1945 and 1962. Westbroekpark, The Hague, 2002. Design: Gert Dumbar and Jesse Skolnik with Van der Laan's typeface Flex.

▴ The Book version of Flex, Van der Laan's graduation project at the Type and Media course, 2000.

22 'How to get from a to a' (cit.), pp 38–39.

23 E-mail to the author, 2002.

24 Van der Laan on the website of the Raad voor Cultuur (cultuur.nl/jaarverslag). Additional information supplied by Paul van der Laan in conversation and by e-mail.

▾ Feisar (2000) was made as a custom font for the veejay application Resolume, developed by Van der Laan's colleagues at Lokaal 0.11. The screen font was designed first, the print version was derived from it.

↘ Duiker Grotesk (2002) is a signage alphabet for the converted school by the architect Jan Duiker in The Hague-Scheveningen, where Van der Laan's studio is based.

Feisar

Bitmap Bold
Venom Class
Vector Class
Rapier Class

ances as well.' [25] He experimented with a serious and a more playful version that share one 'skeleton' but have different details, allowing the mood of the typography to change according to the message. The difference between the two varieties lies mainly in the terminals, which are straight in the 'serious' version, and rounded off in the playful variety. Flex has not been published, but has been in regular use since its completion.

Although not part of his graduation project, the font *Outbox* was another result of research done during his one-year type design course. Outbox is a typeface for personal e-mails, based on the designer's handwriting but adapted to a coarse pixel grid. On his website *type-invaders.com*, Van der Laan published an entertaining account of how the typeface evolved through a playful process of trial and error. He describes how he went through a series of alternatives – including slab serif, italic and swash versions – only to arrive at a slightly more extended version of his initial design. At the current state of technology it is not yet possible to embed a personal font with text e-mails. As Van der Laan wrote on his website, 'All that's left now is to wait for the software to catch up.'

Feisar, too, is a typeface made with low-resolution screens in mind. It was initially drawn as a bitmap typeface for the veejay application Resolume, created by two interaction designers based at Lokaal 0.11. For the bitmap version, Van der Laan managed to pack a maximum of dynamism and high-tech cool in a minimum of pixels. For the high-resolution variant, these coarse forms were translated into a three-weight monoline family which, with its smart alternation of straight and curved lines, conveys a feel of 1970s nostalgia and sci-fi optimism simultaneously. Feisar has been made available at Kombinat Typefounders, a web-based foundry owned by former fellow student Hannes Famira.

Van der Laan's third font for low-resolution screen display was *Decaf*, a bitmap face designed for a LCD display of a coffee machine. The machine was designed by N|P|K Industrial Design, the company that also collaborated with Gerard Unger on several large-scale projects. As the machine is sold throughout Europe, the Decaf character set has an ample collection of diacritics to cover all languages.

Working at Lokaal 0.11 has led to a completely different, historically inspired type project. The studio's location is a splendidly restored modernist school built in 1931 by the architect Jan Duiker (1890–1935). For the lettering, signage and graphic identity, Van der Laan designed a sanserif alphabet of capitals based on Art Deco lettering. 'Initially the idea was to use Futura, whose current versions I think lack character. I proposed to design a new typeface that showed the same intention as the building's restructuring: a functional design that is respectful of the past.' By an

DUIKER GROTESK

ABCDEFGHIJKLMNOPQRSTUVWXYZ

PAARDERENNEN OP DUINDIGT
WESTLANDSCHE AARDAPPELHANDEL
VLIEGEN OP YPENBURG
DUIKERS DERDE AMBACHTSSCHOOL
ROTTERDAM-IJMUIDEN
FABRIEK VAN OPTISCHE INSTRUMENTEN
HOTEL „OUD GELDERLAND"

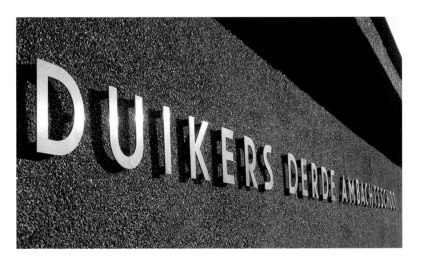

DUIKER GROTESK

KAPITALEN - OPEN KAPITALEN

extraordinary coincidence House Industries, an American foundry Van der Laan has worked for on several occasions, presented *Neutraface* around the time when *Duiker* was completed. *Neutraface*'s display version, based on lettering by the architect Richard Neutra, is very similar in feel to Duiker – yet both typefaces were developed independently of one another. During 2003, Van der Laan worked on another project that involved the revival of architectural lettering. For the reconstruction of the pre-1940 departure hall of Schiphol Airport, built as part of the Aviodrome aviation museum in Lelystad, he designed three typefaces based on the hall's original lettering. Having chosen Van der Laan's Flex as its corporate typeface, the Aviodrome also commissioned him to design a special version of Flex for signage.

Currently, Van der Laan's time is split between graphic, multimedia and type design. He is a part-time member of the TEFF studio, working on revivals of types by Jan van Krimpen and Gerrit Noordzij. He has also participated in TEFF's dictionary designs for Van Dale publishers. As a personal project, he has embarked on a digital revival of Jan van Krimpen's great italic *Cancellaresca Bastarda*.

Bas Smidt, typographer

Bas Smidt (1971) was also one of the initiators of *Con form*. The booklet showed two designs by Smidt of well-made traditional text faces, which he decided not to pursue – they were obvious school projects and lacked a voice of their own. His lettering work published in the same brochure was more original: joyous, bold display alphabets that showed their calligraphic origin without looking old-fashioned or conventional. A logotype for a painter, designed in the same period with a custom-made, playful 'pointed-pen letter' or modern face, has the same qualities. Several of Smidt's teachers greatly appreciated their student's talent, both as a type designer and a typographer. He worked as an intern at Frank E. Blokland's Dutch Type Library and was then hired by Huug Schipper's Studio Tint, the firm that has also employed Luc(as) de Groot and Peter Verheul. During the past six years he has been working for The Enschedé Font Foundry, where he is involved in type design and production and has also contributed greatly to the studio's output of book designs. He now regards himself as a typographer – a user of type – rather than a type designer. Drawing original letterforms has become a marginal activity, usually limited to a logo or a few characters – such as the name of his new-born son on a birth announcement. This shift of focus has meant that Smidt's plans for new typefaces have been suspended without much regret.[26]

Outbox Twelve

Regular **Bold** Onwaarschijnlijk daarentegen is het, dat de man, die de boekdrukkunst uitvond, niet zou geweest zijn een werktuigkundige in de gestalte van een geletterde, een fysicus met de eigenschappen van een filosoof, maar bovenal en in de eerste plaats toegerust met het bijzonder talent, hetwelk de eenen tot veldheeren, de anderen tot dichters, nog anderen tot uitvinders maakt.

Céci ijréa rdzij

▲ Paul van der Laan's Outbox was made as a font for sending personalized e-mails – anticipating the technology that will make this possible, 2000.

◄ Bas Smidt, study for an unfinished 'house typeface' for the typographer-illustrator Cécile Noordzij, 1997.

◄ Bas Smidt, logo for a publisher of legal textbooks, designed at The Enschedé Font Foundry.

◄ Calling card for an artist, using custom lettering.

Sander ten Napel

KUNSTSCHILDER

25 Paul van der Laan, *Flex*, self-published specimen, 2000.
26 Information supplied by Bas Smidt in conversation and by e-mail.

Jacques Le Bailly, the Baron von Fonthausen

Jacques Le Bailly (1975) was still a student at the KABK when he was offered his first professional type design jobs. As as intern at Linotype (Bad Homburg, Germany) he collaborated on the Syntax project, contributing to the new extended version of Hans-Eduard Meier's type family. Linotype then asked him to help design Euro glyphs for the Linotype Library. In all, Le Bailly designed some 300 Euros.[27]

During the months at Linotype Le Bailly made his first sketches for what is still a work in progress to date: a straightforward, functional book face provisionally called *TyPress*. Working in Germany allowed him to take some distance from the Hague model; if TyPress betrays its origins, it is by its generic character – openness, a contemporary look at tradition, and usability – rather than by using a specific idiom. The family, consisting of some 30 styles, is still unpublished.

Between 1999 and 2003, Le Bailly lived in Berlin, where he worked at Moniteurs graphic design studio and later as an independent graphic designer. For Moniteurs he redrew the studio's corporate font: Alexander Branczyk's *Monako*, a typeface based on Apple's monospaced system font *Monaco*. The resulting variant, called *Monyako*, is elegant and friendly, the technical character of the original having been softened by gentle curves, and readability improved by careful spacing. Le Bailly also drew a bold and a monospaced version.

While the typefaces mentioned above are adequate, well-made fonts for daily use, Le Bailly's other projects are more outrageous. He is an able draughtsman: the display faces he has made as personal research projects (or school assignments) show a strong illustrative and playful quality, as well as a subtle sense of humour. When asked to design a monospaced font as a student, he did not come up with the obvious modified typewriter alphabet, but made *Sardines*: an amusing parade of heavy-weight characters crammed into squares. *D-Day* is a novelty display font, also dating back to the Academy days. 'A parody of *Clarendon*,' according to its designer, with rather silly swashes added for extra charm. It will be made available at Lineto, the Swiss type foundry run by Stephan Müller and Cornel Windlin that has already commissioned several custom designs from Le Bailly.

His most original project – and, paradoxically, the one that most obviously shows the influence of the 'Hague school' – is a family of display faces with the working name *Ballpoint* that has been in the making since 2000. When it was first shown, it existed in one rather heavy weight only. 'I often begin by drawing fat characters,' wrote Le Bailly. 'After having defined the basic form, I then draw the lighter weights.' Ballpoint wants to convey 'the informality of handwriting, combined with the strict-

▼ TyPress (working name), unpublished text typeface.

▽ Monyako, corporate font for the Berlin studio Moniteurs, 2000.

▽ D-Day, a Clarendon with swashes (unfinished).

▽ Jacques Le Bailly's Bic/Ballpoint is an experiment with forms that resemble ballpoint pen writing. Letters were sketched closely together in order to arrive at interesting new solutions. When the first digital version proved 'overdone' (left, top), the concept was redefined (bottom).

(TyPress)

Regular *Italic* **Bold** CAPS DIK
Onwaarschijnlijk daarentegen is het, dat de man, die de boekdrukkunst uitvond, niet zou geweest zijn een werktuigkundige in de gestalte van een geletterde, een fysicus met de eigenschappen van een filosoof, iemand op de hoogte en meer dan dan op de hoogte van de middelbare beschaving zijns tijds.

Monyako
Regular **Bold**

D·Day
Abcdefghijklmnopqrstuvwxyz

Digital lettering and type

► Fettnies, a bitmap font especially designed for simulating a sales slip needed for his graduation project (1998); Le Bailly couldn't help adding small caps and making four kinds of numerals.

► Le Bailly's solution for a monospaced font, made as an art school project, 1997.

► Logo for the Baron von Fonthausen, 2002.

Page from Eyal Holtzman's website letterpress.nl showing Joël, the typeface that later became the starting point of Kristal (see next page).

ness of a text face.'[28] Having arrived, at first, at forms that were too simple and rigid, Le Bailly used negative spacing to form words that look like massive blocks of type. This effect led him to design a new, more irregular version which is beautifully drawn and surprisingly legible. Other weights are in the making.

After his return to the Netherlands in 2003, Jacques Le Bailly was hired by The Enschedé Font Foundry, where he is involved in the production of typefaces. Le Bailly is also the man behind the Baron von Fonthausen, a fictitious character who during 2002–03 had his own website; plans for a magazine, either printed or online, have been temporarily suspended for lack of time.

Eyal Holtzman: an Eastern feel

Born in Israel, Eyal Holtzman has been living and working in the Netherlands since 1991. Although he was trained at the KABK, his typefaces do not show a Noordzij influence. They have a Central-European rather than a Dutch feel to them, and recall the work of Czech designers such as Vojtech Preissig and Oldrich Menhart.

Holtzman briefly worked for the Petr van Blokland + Claudia Mens studio and The Enschedé Font Foundry (TEFF), but has remained somewhat of an outsider. He now works mostly as a teacher and a painter. Though he is an accomplished type designer, none of his faces has been published. This is a pity, as they are among the most original alphabets produced in the Netherlands.

Holtzman (Haifa, 1969) enrolled in the KABK to train as a graphic designer (with a special interest in illustration); his talent for drawing letterforms was spotted early on by his teachers. Yet he never felt completely at ease with the pragmatic, utilitarian approach to type advocated at the school. 'To me,' he says, 'a letterform is like a painting in black and white. Like any painting, a letter needs to have an intrinsic harmony. But it also has a bunch of friends with which it must harmonize in order to form a large exhibition of pictures. Of course, every character must be recognizable in order to be legible. But then again, the same thing goes for portraits.'[29] This view does not imply that Holtzman's approach to type is conceptual or 'artistic'; he has always chosen to operate within the conventions of the alphabet, rather than use the letterform as a trigger for experimentation. It makes sense. As a painter, he paints portraits; a genre in which self-expression must be balanced with convention. As a type designer, his approach is similar: very personal, driven by form rather than function, but by no means iconoclastic.

During his art school years Holtzman explored a wide variety of letterforms, several of which found their way into digital fonts – ranging from *RainBirds*, based on a found Art Deco type (which can be identified as the 1929 *Stadion* by E. Grundeis) to a trendy all-caps font with blurred edges called *Sexshop*. Yet his most promising fonts were text faces which were not based on any model or fashion but were pure invention, tapping into an idiom that no other type designer working in the Netherlands has ever used.

27 Jan Middendorp, 'Jacques, de Euroman', *Druk* 007, winter 2000–01, p 50;
   Jacques Le Bailly, 'What are you doing at the moment?', *Druk* 007, winter 2000–01,
   pp 48–49. Additional information supplied by Jacques Le Bailly by e-mail.
28 Le Bailly, 'What are you doing …' (cit.).
29 Conversation with Eyal Holtzman.

Staring *Italic*

^ Staring, a revival of a nineteenth-century book face, named after a Dutch poet from that era.

ɣ Holtzman's graduation project Jerusalem (1996) consisted of Latin and Hebrew alphabets, designed to create a harmonic combination without sacrificing each script's singular character.

Jerusalem was Holtzman's graduation project at the KABK's postgraduate course in type design. His self-imposed problem was how to reconcile the Hebrew and the Latin script within one typeface. He argued that both scripts are strongly calligraphic, and based on writing with the broad-nibbed pen, but that there are few examples, if any, of a successful combination of the two. 'One of the reasons for this', he wrote, 'is that in Hebrew the horizontals are heavier than the verticals, whereas in the Latin script it is the other way around.' [30] He disapproved of a solution like *Lucida Hebrew*, in which the Hebrew alphabet has been adapted to the roman by reducing the contrast to almost a monoline: it is too wide and too light in colour. Holtzman's proposal – prompted by the suggestions of his teacher, Peter Matthias Noordzij – was not to focus on details and formal correspondences, but to look at the overall behaviour and colour of the typefaces in a text. This resulted in a Hebrew alphabet which is slightly more flowing – less squarish – than most, combined with a sturdy, expressive seriffed roman. Jerusalem was never taken up again after its first presentation.

Joël, a book face begun during art school, was later developed into a small but well-equipped family. Joël seems to speak a formal language all of its own. It has the feel of a seriffed roman but lacks bottom serifs in many places; it has straight strokes and edgy curves, but looks supple rather than stiff. The italic owes some of its sharpness and dash to Matthew Carter's *Galliard Italic* but is not derivative of it.

The work on Joël spawned many new insights which found their way into a new typeface called *Kristal*. This work in progress is clearly a continuation of Joël, but while the earlier typeface was an exploration into unknown territory, Kristal has been conceived as a more conventional and usable text typeface. The vertical accent of the rather long ascenders is compensated by the large, wedge-shaped serifs which put the characters firmly on the baseline. Although the typeface has some built-in irregularities and idiosyncracies – such as the pointed endings of j, k and y, or the quirky flag of the r – the overall image is fresh rather than exuberant. Kristal has separate fonts for text and headlines, as well as a set of open capitals. Its weakest point is the italic: it is perhaps too picturesque for daily use (it shows similarities to Menhart's *Manuscript*, although Holtzman seems to have been unaware of this precedent) and has been designed in one weight only.

Having a sharp eye for detail, Eyal Holtzman has worked on several revivals of pre-1900 foundry typefaces. One is called *Staring*, after the nineteenth-century Dutch writer of that name. Based on the typeface used in the introduction to an edition of Staring poems, it is a typical Didot-like textface used in post-1850 industrial printing

Jerusalem

Book Latin *Italic* SMALL CAPS Ook onafhankelijk van haar weldadig karakter, is de typografie zulk eene vernuftige uitvinding geweest, blijk gevend van zulk een opgeklaard verstand, zulk eene praktische vaardigheid, zulk een fijn gevoel van de behoefte des tijds, dat hij zeker gaat, die a priori elke overlevering verwerpt, welke aan de spits dier ontdekking een stumpert plaatst.
Thchćtćlćkffśtśhffifjśkfflślftfu
ABCDEFGHIJKLMNOPQRSTUVWXYZ1234567890
שנבגקכעיןוחלרצממספרדאוהסטז

Kristal

◄ Kristal, a typeface still under development.

► Holtzman's unpublished Rosart revival, made for TEFF, and the original model.

Thin Regular SMALL CAPS *Italic* **Bold** **Black** OPEN CAPS Head SMALL CAPS
Ware de schrijver minder haastig geweest met het uitgeven van een onderzoek, welks elementen nog naauwlijks in zijn eigen geest naar eisch bezonken konden zijn, hij zou zijn boek niet slechts van allerlei zonden tegen den goeden smaak gezuiverd, maar zich ook minder overdreven voorstellingen gemaakt hebben omtrent de waarde zijner resultaten als geheel.

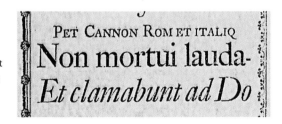

PET CANNON ROM ET ITALIQ
Non mortui lauda-
Et clamabunt ad Do

Rosart Two-Line
English-Bodied

and is similar to *Torino* by Alessandro Butti (1908). As the original was badly printed with worn-down type, many characters were designed anew to correspond with the overall feel of the text, rather than copying specific showings.

The opposite is true for Holtzman's latest revival project, an experimental digitization of the *Two-Line English-Bodied* roman by Jacques François Rosart made for TEFF. The model is shown as *Petit Cannon* in a specimen in the Enschedé Museum, an original of very high quality. Contrary to the position he had taken with the Staring project, Holtzman tried 'to stay as invisible as possible' and remain very close to the original. The Rosart project has remained unfinished.

Martijn Rijven: type for illustration

Although he never got to publish a font, Martijn Rijven has remained a type enthusiast. Among his school projects was a book face that showed some affinity to Proforma; yet his real interests lay elsewhere: in comics and graffiti. Rijven is an able illustrator, specializing in outline drawings that may recall American 1940–50s comics or Japanese manga, and which are often combined with letterforms of his own making. Many of Rijven's clients are in the music business: he has drawn logos for bands, made websites for record companies and created animated graphics to be used by veejays at parties.[31]

Rijven's typefaces – all of which have been made strictly for his own use – are display fonts with a tongue-in-cheek approach to tradition. *Frigidaire*, which started out as a logo for a rock band, is an ultra bold italic which can be layered, so that it has an instant outline that can be coloured separately. *Bastard* was named after a Thai manga comic and is based on the Thai typography used in that book, translated into latin characters. It, too, comes in two layers for outline and fill. By using negative spacing the inline letterforms can be made to touch, while the outlines form a dense background. The typeface *M4* came about when working on the visual identity for a metal band called Motherfed (from the Dutch *moddervet*, 'extremely fat'). In the designer's words, it has 'that clean cold futuristic feel the kids like so much these days'. *Bitscream*, originally designed as a headline face for a magazine, parodies the look of a low-resolution TV screen. Finally, *Dense* was deliberately made to look 'blunt and stupid'. Rijven gave himself three hours to design it, but finds himself still using the font today. 'Whether or not you think that's a good idea,' he once wrote, 'is up to you.'[32]

Unpublished alphabets by Martijn Rijven.

▲ Frigidaire is meant to be used in layers and with negative spacing.

◄ Dense was made to look 'stupid and blunt'.

↗ The M4 alphabet.

▼ Logo for a tattoo artist, made with custom lettering.

30 Jerusalem specimen, published as part of Holtzman's graduation project.

31 Information supplied by Martijn Rijven in conversation and by e-mail.

32 Note on Rijven's website boltgraphics.com.

Underware: a good time with type

dirty brown pazta

◄ New script face by Underware, as yet unreleased.

▼ The Dolly booklet designed by Wout de Vringer, 2001. Illustration by Edgar Kober.

▼ Dolly, 2001.

Dolly

Regular *Italic* SMALL CAPS **Bold** Om van geen mogelijke karakterfeilen te gewagen, de uitvinder der boekdrukkunst kan verstoken zijn geweest van muzikaal gevoel zowel als van financieel beleid, kan door zijne eenzelvigheid, met zeker besef van verstandelijke meerderheid gepaard, zich in allerlei wespennesten gestoken, en dien ten gevolge niet slechts de voordeelen, maar ook den roem van zijn arbeid verbeurd hebben.

Underware, a graphic design studio and type foundry based in The Hague, Amsterdam and Helsinki, is typical of a relatively new phenomenon in the design trade: a small-scale studio consisting of a handful of individuals who collaborate while located many kilometres apart. Underware also represents the kind of open-minded mentality which allows designers to be serious about their work yet playful in finding original ways to present it; eager to work with their hands in an old-fashioned craftsy way yet equally clever at using digital technology.

Bas Jacobs (1976, Dutch) and Akiem Helmling (1971, German) met as students of the one-year postgraduate course in type design and typography at the KABK in 1998 and soon struck up a close working relationship. In 2001 Sami Kortemäki (1975), a fellow student who had gone back to his native Helsinki after studying in The Hague, was taken on board. In 2002 Underware was joined by Portuguese Hugo Cavalheiro d'Alte (1975), a 2000 graduate from the course.[33]

The first typeface published by Underware was *Dolly*, based on Jacobs's graduation project at the KABK type design course. In a way, Dolly is the quintessential Dutch book face: at once traditional and contemporary; even and comfortable at small point sizes and full of lively details at close range; based on handwriting but not conspicuously so. Its limited range of weights may be regarded as a drawback: besides the three regular styles (roman, italic and caps) there is only a bold roman that is, in fact, an extra-bold. But Dolly has managed to turn its limitations into an advantage. Many graphic designers seem to be attracted by this uncomplicated family structure which, of course, comes with a modest price as well.

For the font's initial distribution Underware developed a unique and daring system based on honesty and honour. A charming booklet showing Dolly in a series of stylistic pastiches was sold at a modest price; it came with a free CD containing a full version of the typeface. The user was supposed to pay for the typeface only if he or she decided to actually use it. The perfect distribution system – in a perfect world. Apparently it has worked fairly well: requests for licenses have poured in steadily ever since the first presentation at the 2001 ATypI conference in Copenhagen.

Dolly, far from being cloned like the homonymous sheep, has a long and splendid pedigree: it has assimilated elements from the best of recent Dutch book faces. *Sauna*, on the contrary, is a typeface that does not look familiar at all. Based on a college project by Sami Kortemäki and completed in close collaboration with the other Underware members, it is a peculiar amalgam of seemingly incompatible styles and features. Its juxtaposition of straight angles and smooth curves is vaguely related to solutions proposed by W.A. Dwiggins, Gerard Unger or Fred Smeijers, but the result is totally different; in the black weight Oz Cooper's *Cooper Black* comes to mind. Due to its wide basic shapes, its rounded terminals and informal appearance, Sauna has a warm and friendly feel. It will look striking when used for large-scale lettering. The regular weight, though rather thin, is perfectly legible at small sizes. Therefore Sauna, a display typeface in shape, also functions well when used for body text. Thanks to its large collection of ligatures and swashes it lends itself to creating eye-catching typography with a sense of humour.

Like Dolly, Sauna was first presented in a self-published booklet with a font CD included. Not only was the specimen created by one of the country's best-known designers, Piet Schreuders, it also had a built-in gimmick. In reference to the font's name and Finnish origin, the publication was produced with special heat and moisture resistant paper. Some texts, written by contributors from the design world, were printed with invisible ink that only reveals its secrets at sauna temperatures.

Digital lettering and type

Read naked

◄ Read naked, type specimen for
► Sauna, 2002. Designed by
Piet Schreuders, printed on
special heat and moisture resistant paper.

▾ Sauna, 2002.

▿ Unibody 8, 2003.

▿ Hand-painted lettering on a
boat, 2001.

Aptly titled *Read naked*, the booklet was first presented at Typo Berlin 2002 in an actual sauna temporarily installed in an art gallery window.

There are two more Underware typefaces that can be considered Finnish rather than Dutch. *Ulrika* is a custom font designed for a Finnish film and video production company named Proidea Ltd. Inspired by the illustrations made for the firm's corporate identity, Ulrika is a one-weight display face of bold conical shapes, wider at the top than at the bottom. The result is at once friendly and confident. *Stool*, a customized typeface for the Finnish printing house Salpausselän Kirjapaino Ltd., is a humanist sanserif that bears some resemblance to Scala Sans.

Underware's daily work is by no means exclusively focused on type design: books, posters and websites are part of their daily practice. Hand-lettering is another, less frequent aspect: Jacobs has painted the names of several boats. As a by-product of the web-designing work Underware developed a screen font called *Unibody 8*. The idea behind Unibody is that anti-aliasing (smoothing type outlines by adding greyscale pixels) is not always the best way to improve screen legibility. At small sizes, a dedicated pixel font may do a better job. Hence Unibody 8, meant to be read as a sharp, aliased image at size 8 pts. The typeface follows the underlying grid of squares. The solutions are typical examples of Hague thinking: strong contrast in the bold weight for improved legibility, an upright italic instead of a sloped one, so that jagged diagonals are avoided. The best news is that Unibody has been made available as freeware, downloadable from the Underware website.

An important aspect of Underware's activities is teaching. Underware has given workshops at art schools and during conferences worldwide. These workshops are made public in real time (or almost) on a special website that Underware has set up for the purpose. Colleagues accross the typographic community are invited to comment on the assignments that are shown online. This site – typeworkshop.com – also contains a section called *Type basics*, containing valuable guidelines for aspiring type designers. Another forum for workshop results, and for questions related to teaching, is the magazine *pts.* (as in 'points'). Designed by students of the schools that have hosted the Underware workshops, it is an unpredictable, ever-changing low-budget magazine that is, in its own modest way, a very personal contribution to the Dutch type culture.

Sauna

Regular *Italic* **Bold** *Italic* **Bold Italic**
SMALL CAPS *Italic Swash* **Bold** **Black**
Italic Swash Ligatures: Ch Ct Sk St ffl fj ll Qu Th
Door het aannemen van dien betoogtrant heeft hij op zijn boek den kleingeestigen polemischen stempel gedrukt, en zichzelven veroordeeld te konkluderen, in plaats van tot een waardig en historisch feit, tot het eenigszins kwâjongensachtig advies, een stedelijk museum op te ruimen.

Unibody 8
Regular Italic Bold
Black SMALL CAPS

33 Information provided by Bas Jacobs and Akiem Helmling in conversation with the author; additional information: underware.nl

Peter Biľak and Typotheque

Eureka

Roman *Italic* Medium **Bold** CAPS

Eureka Sans

Light *Italic* Regular *Italic* Medium *Italic*
Bold *Italic* **Black** *Italic* SMALL CAPS LIGHT
REGULAR MEDIUM **BOLD** **BLACK** Doch al het overige is advokaterij, oorzaak tot meesmuilen voor het toeschouwend publiek, welks gezond verstand er zich steeds zwijgend tegen verzetten zal, dat ter wille eener zoo schamele vischvangst zooveel water troebel wordt gemaakt.

Throughout history, Dutch typography has been enriched by the advent of foreign craftsmen and designers who, for various reasons, established themselves in the Netherlands. Like Fleischman or Schlesinger before him, Slovak designer Peter Biľak brought with him a sensibility and a tone of voice that is distinctly different from what the Dutch are used to.

Peter Biľak (1973) studied graphic design in Bratislava and type design in Paris; he came to the Netherlands in 1997 for a one-year postgraduate course at the Jan van Eyck Academy in Maastricht, and stayed. He set up a design studio in The Hague where he also runs Typotheque – a web-based foundry that publishes his typefaces and those of his colleague and life partner Johanna Balušíková. Besides designing books, magazines, posters and on-screen publications, Biľak has curated exhibitions and written numerous articles, introducing new Dutch design to the Czech and Slovak public, and was the co-founder of the design magazine *dot-dot-dot*.

Biľak admires the straightforward approach to problem-solving that is standard procedure in the Netherlands, but his is a more intellectual viewpoint. He makes a point of questioning the basics of graphic design. His writings have a greater degree of abstraction and are more theoretical than those of most Dutch typographer-writers. His critical thinking is coupled with a sharp sense of humour and a taste for mystification: he satirised the pretensions of academe by presenting QuickEssay, a program for generating theoretical texts, and *Euroface*, a 'scientific', blurred alphabet for highway signage that is supposed to become sharper when viewed at high speed. An important contribution to the typographic community is the *Articles* section on the website typotheque.com where critical writings on graphic design and typography, often by well-known authors, are re-published.

When making his first fonts at the Academy of Fine Arts & Design in Bratislava, each design was a personal investigation of a specific period or technology. *Craft* is mediaeval woodcut simulated by making manual linocuts of each letter and digitizing the result; *Atlanta*, a parody of the coarse cathode ray tube typography of the 1970s; and *Masterpiece*, a distorted parody of copperplate script. Having presented an early version of Craft to FontShop International, Biľak was invited to complete it as a family; subsequently, several of his typefaces were issued as FontFonts in 1994–97.

Biľak began designing his first text face, *Eureka*, when studying at the Atelier National de Création Typographique in Paris in 1995–96. The face premiered in a self-published booklet entitled *Transparency*, an essay on the state of contemporary typography and type design. FF Eureka was published by FontShop in 1998, followed by *FF Eureka Sans* in 2000. Eureka was designed with Slovak and other Central-European languages in mind. It has long ascenders to accommodate the many diacritic signs of these languages in a visually harmonious way. It works well, although the long extenders, wide letterspacing and sloped e-bar make Eureka look rather quaint.

With *Fedra*, his most mature typeface to date, Biľak has consciously moved away from the idiosyncracies of his earlier fonts. Fedra Sans was designed for the Paris agency Rudi Baur Integral Design as the corporate typeface of a German insurance company. The brief for the typeface was to 'de-protestantize Univers'. The assignment came at the very time when Biľak had decided to do something about what he saw as Eureka's shortcomings; now he had the opportunity to make a completely new typeface instead of reworking it. When the client was swallowed up in a merger, Biľak decided to finalize and publish the new sanserif on his own. When his computer and back-up system were stolen shortly before the release date, this too turned out to be a blessing in disguise, allowing him to take another look at the

HOLY COW

WHITE **BLACK**

Jigsaw

Light Stencil

▸ Fedra Sans (Typotheque, 2001).
Fedra Serif (2003). This version
(A) has short ascenders and
descenders; Fedra Serif B has
longer extenders, 2003.

◂ Biľak's Holy Cow and
Balušíková's Jigsaw were both
published by Typotheque in
2003.

ʓ Fedra Greek, 2003. As with the
seriffed version of Fedra, Greek
and Cyrillic are not simply
expanded versions of the same
font, but designed from scratch.
Biľak claims that his non-latin
versions have in turn influenced
their Latin starting point.

Fedra Sans

Light *Italic* Book *Italic* Normal *Italic*
Medium *Italic* **Bold Italic** SMALL CAPS LIGHT
BOOK NORMAL **MEDIUM BOLD** De onder-
stelling, dat één van hen, of beiden, het bedrijf
van drukker zullen hebben uitgeoefend in het
geheim, ten einde aan de goegemeente
ongemerkt voor veel geld …

Fedra Serif A

Book *Italic* Normal *Italic* Medium *Italic*
Bold Italic SMALL CAPS BOOK NORMAL
MEDIUM BOLD … boeken in plaats van
handschriften te kunnen slijten – het stil-
zwijgend aannemen van dergelijk vroom
bedrog getuigt van weinig inzigt in het
karakter eens uitvinders.

---

design and get rid of any remnants of the original brief. The result is a robust sanserif text face that has borrowed features from both the (Dutch-style) humanist sanserif and the functionalist sans à la Univers; its unusual details, like the hanging f, square dots and charming wide small caps, give it a likeable personality.

When setting out to design a companion seriffed roman, Biľak decided it should not be derived directly from the sans: a new interpretation of the original idea, resulting in an independent yet compatible typeface seemed like a bigger challenge. Biľak has called Fedra Serif a 'synthetic' and 'polyhistorical' typeface. 'Polyhistorical' because it borrows from various historical sources and periods at once. 'Synthetic' because seemingly contradictory construction methods are combined within one typeface design: chirographic (i.e. based on writing), drawn, modular, geometric. Andy Crewdson, in his contribution to the Fedra specimen, cites the work of Gerard Unger, with whom Biľak has exchanged ideas on several occasions. As Biľak wrote in an early draft of the specimen: 'Fedra does not invent anything radically new, but rather builds on earlier discoveries and hopefully contributes its tiny bit towards the definition of contemporary type design.'

Both Eureka and Fedra have grown steadily over the years. The monospaced versions of both typefaces are interesting display faces in their own right. The latest addition to the Fedra family is Fedra Sans Alt, a 'normalized' variety in which some peculiarities of the original version, such as the descending f and square dots, have been replaced by more anonymous variants. Biľak also developed Greek and Cyrillic versions of Fedra, in keeping with his long-term interest in multi-lingual typography, Apart from the extended Fedra family, the Typotheque library contains a number of display fonts. *Holy Cow*, a monolinear design based on the circle, is more playful than most geometric designs. *Champollion*, made at the Atelier National de Création Typographique, was inspired by the errors of a laser printer in the school's workshop. Finally, *Jigsaw* is the only published typeface by Johanna Balušíková. It is a youthful yet somewhat stiff monolinear sanserif that comes with an interesting stencil variant. Typotheque has announced new fonts to be released.

Biľak calls Fedra Serif 'poly-historical'. While the overall design is as rigorously planned as the Romain du Roi, the more playful details refer to other periods. The varying angles of the italic show an influence of Garamond and contemporaries.

Fedra Serif A Greek

Η *Fedra Serif A* είναι μια ανισόπαχη γραμματοσειρά χαμηλού κοντράστ με πατούρες και αποτελεί μέρος μιας οικογένειας γραμματοσειρών που περιλαμβάνει επίσης παραλλαγές όπως η ισόπαχη χωρίς πατούρες (*Sans Serif*) και η ισόπαχη με χαρακτήρες σταθερού πλάτους (*Monospace*). Αντί να αναζητά έμπνευση στο παρελθόν, η *Fedra Serif* είναι μια σύγχρονη, πολυσύνθετη γραμματοσειρά όπου η αισθητική και τεχνολογική πλευρά της είναι συνδεδεμένες. Η *Fedra* συνδυάζει φαινομενικά αντιφατικούς τρόπους σχεδίασης σε μια απόλυτα, όμως, αρμονική γραμματοσειρά. Οι ανθρωπιστικές της καταβολές (*χειρόγραφος ρυθμός*) ισορροπούν με τον ορθολογικό σχεδιασμό (*τραχύς κάνναβος στην οθόνη του υπολογιστή*).

Η *Fedra Serif* διαθέτει 4 βάρη, πλάγια, μικρά κεφαλαία και σέτ ειδικών χαρακτήρων (*experts*) για κάθε βάρος και τρία διαφορετικά συστήματα αρίθμησης (*ανισοϋψείς αναλογικοί, ισοϋψείς αναλογικοί καθώς και αριθμοί σταθερού πλάτους*), ενώ εκτός από μονοτονικό, είναι διαθέσιμη και σε πολυτονικό σύστημα. Η γραμματοσειρά διατίθεται επίσης σε δύο διαφορετικές εκδοχές με διαφορετικά ύψη των ανωφερών και κατωφερών στοιχείων. Η εκδοχή Α ταιριάζει στις αναλογίες της *Fedra Sans*, με μεγάλο ύψος πεζών (*x-height*) και μικρά ανωφερή. Η εκδοχή Β έχει αυξημένο κοντράστ και επιμηκυμένα ανωφερή, γεγονός που την κάνει ιδανικότερη για εκτυπώσεις υψηλής ανάλυσης ή χρήση σε μεγαλύτερες στιγμές γραμμάτων. Ο συνδυασμός αυτών των παραλλαγών έχουν σαν αποτέλεσμα μια γραμματοσειρά ικανή να δώσει λύσεις σε περίπλοκα τυπογραφικά προβλήματα.

Fedra Book *Italic* CAPS
Fedra Normal *Italic* CAPS
Fedra Medium *Italic* CAPS
Fedra Bold *Italic* CAPS

aáàâãāăåâàβγδ
εéêéêĕčėèzçηηήή
ηηηῆῆ̂θιìíῖ̈́ἷ̈́ι
ῒ̈ικλμνξοòóôõðð
ōͬρρφροτυϋύῦϋϋͮ
ῦ̈ϋῦϋῦϋ̈φχψωώῶ
ῶ̈ῶ̈ώ̈ῶ̈ϛϛʒ

34 Information provided by Peter Biľak in interviews and by e-mail; additional information: typotheque.com. Several interviews with Biľak are archived on this site.

Aa Bb Cc Dd Ee Ff Gg Hh
Ii Jj Kk Ll Mm Nn Oo Pp
Qq Rr Ss Tt Uu Vv Ww Xx
Yy Zz 0123456789 (:ʼ;@?)

‒A ʾB CC ƆD ƎE ꟻF ꓢG ‒H
II ,J ＜K ꟻL I MI IIN CO ƆP
ꓹQ ꓜR ꓢꓢ ꓔT ꓴU VV V ꓥX
ꓥY ꓜZ C 01234456789 :ʼ;

SEXY·QUA·LIJF
DOCH·BANG·VOOR
HET·ZWEMPAK

Emma Book
Emma BookItalic
Emma Normal
Emma NormalItalic
Emma SemiBold
Emma SemiBoldItalic
Emma Bold
Emma BoldItalic
Emma UltraBlack
Emma UltraBlackItalic

Type and Media, two cases: Kloosterman and Van Rosmalen

The KABK's postgraduate course Type and Media addresses two aspects of type design: the craftmanship of writing, drawing and carving on the one hand; the digital production and processing of typefaces on the other. This is a combination that comes naturally to many young type designers, yet students often decide to favour one aspect over the other in their graduation projects.

The work of two Dutch Type and Media graduates of the class of 2002 is a case in point. Both had considerable professional experience before going back to school. Peterpaul Kloosterman was a partner in Quadraat and Het Lab, two Arnhem studios of which Fred Smeijers was also part in the 1990s; Pieter van Rosmalen is an independent designer who already had made dozens of fonts for his own use when he enrolled in the postgraduate course to deepen his knowledge about designing book typefaces. The two 'self-willed elder youngsters' (Kloosterman) chose to work on two opposing aspects of type.

Peterpaul Kloosterman (1965) is enamoured with the traditional and artisanal side of type design. His projects were guided by 'the conviction that it is necessary to master the craft before you can develop type design any further'. *Primo*, designed as part of his graduation project, is a glyphic or 'incise', a typeface whose curved strokes and flared terminal refer to the shapes of carved letters. As Kloosterman wrote, it also has the 'irregular regularity' typical of a well-made inscription. Primo is not an accomplished typeface, but a good start for a new take on a genre which, after *Optima*, *Pascal* and *Amerigo*, has not yielded many type designs of any importance.

Perm, Kloosterman's second offering, was even more directly related to the act of stone carving: it is designed for use in inscriptions. Kloosterman started out by carving letterforms – a process with a steep learning curve, performed under the guidance of his teachers Françoise Berserik and (his former business partner) Fred Smeijers. Having developed some dexterity in stone carving, the next step was to design a stencil alphabet for drawing simple letterforms on the stone. Kloosterman developed an ingenious alphabet with detached letterparts, allowing each letter to be drawn with a maximum of two stencils.

Unlike most other aspiring type designers who enrol in the Type and Media course, Pieter van Rosmalen (1969) had already designed a large number of fonts, of which more than twenty are available at GarageFonts. Most of these are constructed alphabets, made with straight lines only or based on a simple grid.

An admirer of Bram de Does's work, Van Rosmalen went back to school after having worked as a graphic designer for eight years, because he wanted to know more about

CARABUS — CARABUS GRANULATUS L.

This seventeen to twentythree millimeters long beetle is found in Europe and eastward as far as eastern Siberia and Japan. Its colour is bronze to metallic green or black. Most individuals have reduced hind wings, but in some they are fully developed. It is found in farmlands, grasslands and forests, in lowlands as well as high up in the mountains. It feeds mainly on other insects. The beetles hibernate during winter and reproduce the next year. The female lays about forty eggs in a small hollow in the ground. The adult beetles can be seen from April to September. The larvae live underground.

al capone is one of the most recognized names in american history. alphonse was born to neapolitan immigrants gabriel and teresa. his surname, originally caponi, had been americanized to capone. the capone family included james, ralph, salvatore (frank), alphonse, john, albert, matthew, rose and mafalda. capone was proud to be an american:

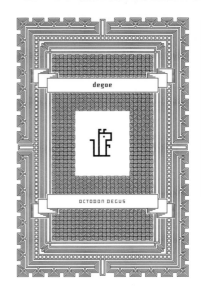

designing text typefaces. However, for his graduation project at the KABK's Type and Media course Van Rosmalen made two typefaces that have little to do with traditional book typography: *Remote*, 'an anonymous sanserif' that looks like a Dutch variant of *Folio*; and *Capibara*, an idiosyncratic pixel-based font family. Of these two Capibara – named after a species of large rodent that roams the *llanos* of Venezuela – is the most original. Although it is strictly geometric and very rigid, it has enough typographic subtleties to make it (almost) acceptable as a text font. Capibara was presented in a booklet entitled *Heer van het gras* ('Lord of the grass', the translation of the word *capibara*) The booklet has delightful illustrations of various rodents, all pixel-based like the font's characters. What is intriguing and amusing about the typeface is the staggering number of ligatures and ornaments – there is probably no other pixel font that has as many.

Some of Van Rosmalen's most interesting projects are as yet unpublished. There is a type family called *Alterego*, drawn on a tight grid of horizontal and vertical lines; and *Carabus*, a friendly slab serif with shapes borrowed from the italic. His most accomplished conventional typeface is a large family of business-like sanserifs called *Emma* that was adopted by TelDesign, the Hague's oldest design company, as their corporate font.

The Sociable Type Society

Although they were regular students at the KABK's Graphic Design Department and not at the Type and Media course, Onno Bevoort (1976) and Donald Roos (1978) soon fell in love with letterforms. They struck up a close friendship and working relationship and in 1997 created a two-man typographic society called Het Letterdispuut. The name is an ironic take on the customs of university students: *dispuut* means 'fraternity'. The English name they came up with – The Sociable Type Society – also indicates that this brotherhood should not be taken too seriously. However, Bevoort and Roos are certainly serious about type.

After graduating in 2001, Onno Bevoort became assistant to Fred Smeijers and was later hired by a design studio in The Hague; Donald Roos worked at Petr van Blokland's company and subsequently opened his own studio in Amsterdam. After hours, work on collaborative type projects has continued. Numerous display alphabets have been conceived, few have been finalized. The one typeface ready for publication is an outrageous script-like font called *Spaghetti Bolognese* (> p 280). This high-contrast italic has joints which laboriously wind from one character to the next. In addition to being an experiment in creating joined characters, the font is also a wonderful joke. More serious and more generally usable typefaces are in the making.

In 2003 Donald Roos, working together with the Hague designer Robert-Jan van Noort and coached by Erik van Blokland, created the typographic portal site type-base.com. The site aims to become one of the web's most trustworthy sources on type and typography.

⌃ One of the fonts from Pieter van Rosmalen's extensive Alterego series (unpublished).

⌃ Pages from the Capibara specimen *Heer van het gras* ('Lord of the grass'), Pieter van Rosmalen, 2002. Pages composed with Capibara Ornaments.

▾ *Letters at work*, a project of typographic sculptures by Onno Bevoort and Donald Roos, 2001.

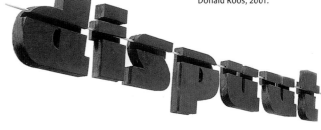

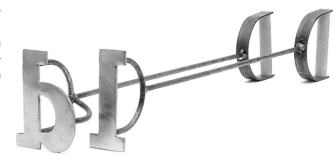

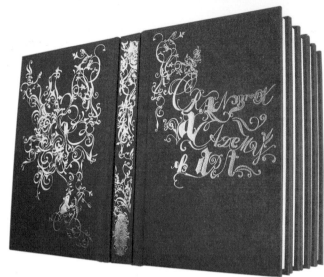

Catelijne van Middelkoop: exuberance at Cranbrook

As a graphic design student at the Royal Academy (KABK) in The Hague, Catelijne van Middelkoop (1975) envied her colleagues in the fine arts department, who were allowed to create things that were simply beautiful. She was bothered by the constant demand that graphic design be justified in terms of functionality and efficiency. Although she diligently took in the lessons of Frank E. Blokland, Matthias Noordzij and Peter Verheul, she ultimately felt that her own approach to typography – her desire to explore ornament and decoration – was not very welcome in The Hague or, for that matter, the Dutch scene. On the advice of Jan Willem Stas, the head of the KABK's Type and Media course, she went to the States and enrolled at the Cranbrook Academy of Arts after graduating in The Hague in 2000.

When she and and her partner Ryan Pescatore Frisk were invited to teach 'Graphic Language' at a Detroit technical school, Van Middelkoop decided to do as she had been taught: 'to begin at the beginning and enter the high-tech computer room armed with broad-nibbed and pointed pens.' Teaching became a way to rediscover the roots of graphic design, exploring ancient sources such as *The Universal Penman* by George Bickham and John Baskerville's gravestone designs. Her new-found joy in writing and drawing letterforms led to the exuberant design of Cranbrook's *Graduate Studies Catalogue* as well as a picturesque graduation project: hand-drawn, machine-produced gravestones for Cinderella and other fairytale heroines.

Catelijne van Middelkoop discovered that historical consciousness is embedded much more profoundly in American arts education than in the Dutch schools, where teachers and students seldom look beyond the 1920s avant-garde. At the same time she felt that she, too, had something to offer – the craftsmanship of writing and drawing by hand is more developed in The Hague than in most American schools. The fonts and lettering that Van Middelkoop created during the past few years are proof of this successful transatlantic cross-fertilization.

Having returned to the Netherlands, Van Middelkoop and Pescatore Frisk created Dialog Nouveau, an initiative aimed at 'the investigation of typographic subculture, graphic pluralism and subsequent typographic development' or, in other words, 'active typographic anthropology'. Central to these activities will be a website due to be released in spring 2004; the site will also be a showcase and a point of sale for new typefaces.

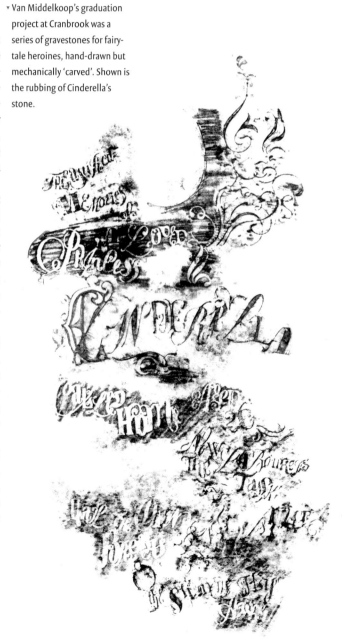

Special projects

Poster for the Rotterdam Luxor Theatre, designed by L5 concept design management with the custom-made Luxor fonts, 2001.

Custom alphabets and outsider projects

Most of the alphabets described in this book are the work of professional type designers and lettering artists – people to whom designing letterforms is or was either their core business or a specialization within their design practice.

This chapter discusses typefaces with different origins: one-off projects made by individuals or groups for special occasions; typefaces made to prove a point or solve a problem by people who have not since returned – or may never return – to type design again; and a few unpublished or unfinished typefaces by professionals who were once, or are still, aspiring type designers. This collection is by no means exhaustive; the catalogue of experimental alphabets by designers, architects, artists and technicians is virtually endless. The remarkable special projects included here were selected based on the qualities of their letterforms, the circumstances surrounding their conception, or the unusual approach of their creators.

NEN 3225: instead of DIN

NEN 3225 is the serial number of a standard issued by the Nederlands Normalisatie Instituut (Dutch Standardization Institute) in 1962. The standard consists of two sets of models of alphabets and numerals to be used for public lettering: a 'roman' (seriffed) type and a sanserif.

During the German occupation, the Central Standardization Office (supervised by the occupying forces) asked a number of large Dutch corporations if it would be feasible to standardize public lettering on the basis of the German standard DIN 1451. A rather crude series of anonymous alphabets designed on a coarse grid of squares, that early DIN alphabet was ugly as well as despicable to patriotic Dutchmen – a symbol of German oppression. In 1944, a commission of specialists was assembled consisting of Jan van Krimpen, Sem Hartz, G.W. Ovink, the architect C. Wegener Sleeswijk, a notary and type specialist named H.C. Warmelink, and N.A.J. Voorhoeve of Philips, and presided over by H.G.J. Schelling, an architect at the National Railways. They did not bring out a statement until well after the liberation. The DIN standard was rejected; in a preliminary report presented in 1950, the commission judged that it would 'inflict immeasurable damage to our typographic art'.[1] When the final results were presented in 1962, the commission explained that the letters and numerals of the DIN model were judged to be inefficient because 'by striving for too strong a similarity between the shapes of the respective characters, the characteristic differences which are the basis of clarity are blurred so that clarity diminishes.'[2] Instead of the sort of 'rationalized' alphabets developed in many other countries by engineers and architects, the group came up with two traditional, distinctly typographic typefaces. The commission wrote that they were 'well aware of the fact that the shapes proposed are more difficult to produce than those established in DIN 1451, where they have been squeezed into a straitjacket for simple reproducibility', but that reproducibility alone should not be a reason to accept inferior aesthetic standards.

The seriffed type is vintage Van Krimpen. Strong in contrast, with classical proportions and subtle details – including oldstyle numerals, several ligatures, a tailed Q and a long J – it is a book face rather than an alphabet for signage. Van Krimpen's main source of inspiration was Roman lettering; in fact, the NEN 3225 manual recommended it especially for stonecarving. Because of its relative inefficiency, the typeface never found wide acclaim.

⌃ Condensed sanserif capitals of the NEN 3225 standard alphabets, designed c. 1958 at the Dutch Railways' drawing office.

▸ The capitals and lowercase of the bold sanserif show a strong influence from Johnston's Underground alphabet and Gill Sans.

ABCDEFGHIJKL
MNOPQRSTUV&
WXYZPRNHUM

Roman of the NEN 3225 standard alphabets, based on drawings by Jan van Krimpen. With its ligatures and descending J and Q it is a typeface for typography rather than signage. Note the wide alternates for N, H, U and M. Designed before 1957, first presented in 1962.

ʏ Sloped sanserif of the NEN 3225 standard alphabets.

Zabcdefghijklm
nopqrstuvwxyz
ff,fbfhfifjfkflffiffl?
II234567890 . ;!

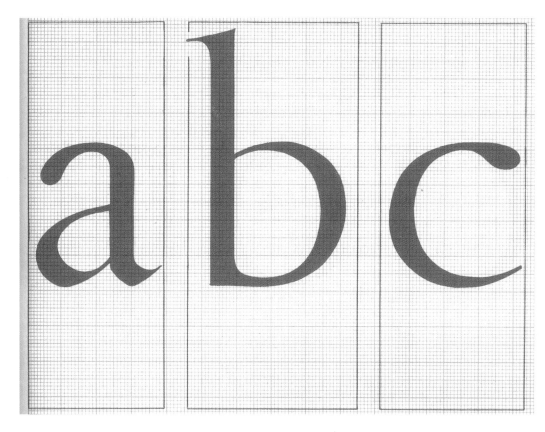

Gerrit Noordzij has argued that the roman alphabet was also flawed because Van Krimpen was not very interested in lowercase romans. Van Krimpen's drawings for lowercase faces, according to Noordzij, 'breathe reluctance'. Noordzij is convinced that the harmony of their final form was largely the merit of Enschedé's punch-cutter, P.H. Rädisch. 'The roman 36,101 of the standardization document NEN 3225 shows what happened if Van Krimpen had to cope without Rädisch's assistance.' [3]
The sanserif was more generally adopted, notably in the new street signs of several cities (including Amsterdam) and on the Dutch licence plates. Largely designed at the drawing office of the National Railways, the typeface followed the English model of the 'humanist sanserif' as pioneered in *Johnston Underground* and further developed in *Gill Sans*. The NEN 3225 sans was designed as a versatile family in three weights – light, regular and bold – with a sloped roman and a condensed variant for the regular weight. The models were published as easily reproducible samples, with suggestions on how to extend the family: 'by interpolating the *bold upright* and the *light sloped sanserif* it is possible to construct a *bold sloped sanserif*; or *light narrow capitals* from plates 14 – 19 and 53 – 56 [the normal light and the narrow regular].' [4] This open approach, which may not always have resulted in superb lettering, heralded a method of interpolation that has become daily practice in digital type design.
The official digital version of the NEN 3225 alphabets has been made available at the type production company Visualogik in 's-Hertogenbosch.

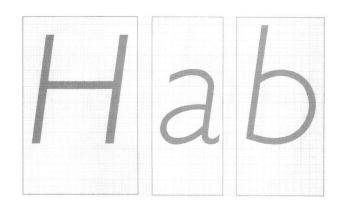

1 Quoted in K. Sierman et al., *Adieu aesthetica en mooie pagina's*, The Hague/Amsterdam/ Haarlem 1995, p 61.

2 Nederlands Normalisatie Instituut, NEN 3225, The Hague 1962.

3 Gerrit Noordzij, 'De meester van het monogram', in *Helmut Salden, Letterontwerper en boekverzorger*, Rotterdam 2003, p 110.

4 NEN 3225 (cit.).

All Pootjes glass products were made with the same mechanically drawn monolinear alphabet, designed by Pim Pootjes in the 1940s.

Pootjes glass

During the 1950s and '60s thousands of shop windows and entrance doors throughout the Netherlands were adorned with small black or coloured glass plates extolling the virtues of the shop's products and service. All of these signs used identical lettering, mechanically painted in white (and occasionally black) opaque ink. They were produced by one firm: Pootjes, a family business in the town of Hilversum. Texts could either be chosen from a catalogue of generic slogans, or were custom-produced in the workshop.

The system had been designed by Pim Pootjes, the firm's principal during the postwar decades. At the time of this writing in 2003, Pim Pootjes was 81 and living on his daughter's cheese farm on the isle of Terschelling. When interviewed by telephone he was not sure about the date of his invention; he probably developed it in his mid-twenties, during the Second World War. The Pootjes glass typeface is an Art Deco-style constructed monoline alphabet; it has some alternate swash characters and makes a sparse use of lines for decoration. Pim Pootjes designed a hand-operated machine (displayed at the Goois Museum in Hilversum) for producing the glass plates, which had to be handled with double care: the glass was breakable, and the ink was not waterproof. In spite of these drawbacks, the popularity of Pootjes glass was phenomenal – it was a famous brand name and a mark of distinction for quality shops. The glass plates and their unadorned yet charming lettering provided Dutch retailers with a kind of collective corporate identity. Even the printing workshop of Bram de Does's father had a Pootjes plate showing the opening hours.

The Pootjes company became De Haan in the 1980s, having been taken over by relatives. The firm tried to transfer the typeface to a computer-operated plotting system but the new version of Pootjes glass did not catch on. The De Haan firm is now a regular lettering company using existing digital typefaces.

Special projects

Petronius

abcdefghijklmnopqrstuvwxyz
ABCDEFGHIJKLMNOPQRSTUVW
1234567890
(&$.,;:"'"-!?¢%/*)

◄ The regular roman of the Petronius typeface, presented by J.H. Moesman in 1969. The prints in the Museum Meermanno, The Hague, lack the uppercase X, Y and Z.

▼ J.H. Moesman, cover for a self-published catalogue entitled *Moesman*, 1971. The book, which has early showings of Petronius capitals, was printed and co-published by the Utrecht printing firm Van Rossum, the artist's main partner in the type design project.

Petronius by J.H. Moesman

Johannes Hendrikus Moesman (1909–1988) was one of the most peculiar Dutch artists of the twentieth century. Having discovered Surrealism in 1929, he remained an enthusiastic Surrealist throughout, unlike other Dutch artists who briefly flirted with the movement. Moesman never quit his daytime job at the Dutch Railways, where he had begun working as a lithographic draughtsman at sixteen – a 'totally stupid job' [5] which allowed him to develop his art in relative freedom. His paintings and drawings, imbued with erotic imagery and symbols of death, enjoyed a brief *succès de scandale* in the 1930s. Having been largely forgotten, he was rediscovered by a younger generation after 1980.

Moesman inherited a love of letterforms from his father, a lithographer, calligrapher and collector of printed curiosities. J.H. Moesman had a theory about type design: in his eyes, the work of De Roos and Van Krimpen had limitations because they never managed to free themselves from the monumentality and stiffness of the Roman alphabet carved in stone. Moesman wanted a printing type that was 100% 'written'. In 1969 he presented *Petronius*, a typeface derived from his calligraphy.[6] During the previous years, the alphabet had been tested in collaboration with B.H.J. van Rossum, principal of the now defunct Utrecht printing firm Van Rossum. Petronius capitals were used in the 1971 self-published booklet *Moesman*; in 1975 Moesman edited a specimen entitled *Op engel voeten, à pas de loup* in which the typeface is tested 'in various grades of reduction', showing four styles: roman, italic, narrow capitals and initials. The specimen also contains a showing of a 'simplified arabic' alphabet designed by Moesman. The colophon specifies that 'Petronius is available for limited texts, to be set in a way that is to be approved by me and excluding any kind of modern haste or pressure, at the Layoutzetterij Typo Delvos, Lange Leidsedwarsstraat 103–105 in Amsterdam.' [7] That typesetting firm has now disappeared; I found no information as to the reproduction technique used to set texts in Petronius.

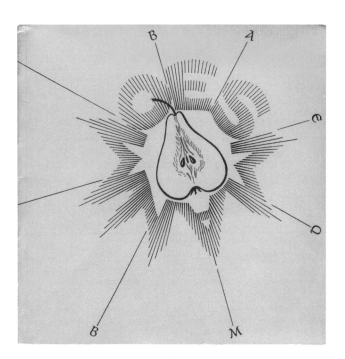

Rudeaux Deluxe, alphabet for a publisher

Rudo Hartman (1945) is one of the eminent book designers who graduated from the Royal Academy (KABK) in The Hague in the 1960s. Hartman was always fascinated by letterforms; yet his type designing activities have remained limited to one alphabet of titling capitals. Its first letter – C – was designed as a logo for the publishing company Contact, one of Hartman's regular clients. Gradually an alphabet of rather spiky roman capitals took shape: each time one of Contact's employees celebrated a special occasion, Hartman gave a drawing of one of his initials as a present. Once the complete alphabet had been drawn, it was digitized by Jacques Le Bailly, a former student of the KABK. *Rudeaux Deluxe* was showcased in a booklet of short poetic texts written, illustrated and designed by Hartman, and published as a keepsake in 1998. The book as well as Hartman's accompanying text – a lengthy press release – suggest that the curves and lines of the graphic sign have an appeal to him that is almost erotic. Apparently, this is true of many typographers and type designers.[8]

ABCDEFGHI
JKLMNOPQR
STUVWXYZ
0123456789&

◄ Rudeaux Deluxe by typographer Rudo Hartman, gradually developed during the 1980s and '90s.

5 J.H. Moesman, 'Ons dagelijks brood en de kunst'; in *Moesman*, a booklet published in 1971 by J.H. Moesman and B.H.J. van Rossum, pp 36–40.

6 C.A. Schilp, 'Moesman ontwierp nieuwe letter', *Nieuw Utrechts Nieuwsblad*, 12 Nov. 1969.

7 *Op engel voeten, à pas de loup*, Editions Surréalistes 'Brumes Blondes' (=Moesman, Schalkwijk), 1975. Quoted in Lane and Lommen, *Dutch typefounders' specimens*, Amsterdam 1998, p 285.

8 Press release accompanying *De F van Fantekast en het vervolg van verder*, The Hague 1998.

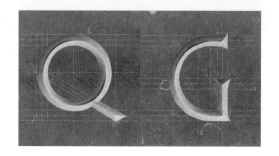

Dom Hans van der Laan's alphabet for stonecarving was designed on a strict grid based on the square and the 3:4 rectangle. All proportions were derived from this principle; the spacing, too, was precisely calculated.

Characters from Van der Laan's alphabet carved in stone for Rosbeek Printers in Nuth, in the province of Limburg where the architect-monk lived and worked most of his life.

Dom van der Laan: letters for stonecarving

Dom Hans van der Laan (1904 – 1991) abandoned his architectural studies to become a Benedictine monk. In the quiet and regularity of monastic life he developed a very personal view of the architectonic space, based on a system of three-dimensional proportions which he called the Plastic Number. Architecture, according to Van der Laan, has a practical as well as an intellectual task: it should make 'the space of nature at one and the same time both habitable and intelligible'.[9] He outlined his theory in lectures and books and put it into practice by designing a number of convents as well as the main building, church, garden, churchyard and furniture of the abbey of Mamelis [10] where he spent most of his life.

To Van der Laan, the alphabet was a form of architecture.[11] His preferred model was the Roman alphabet of monumental capitals or 'early Christian alphabet', as he chose to call it. From 1961 onwards, Van der Laan developed an alphabet of capitals for stonecarving. A series of drawings of single characters made in 1972 was lost; a series of drawings dated November 1982 can be regarded as the definitive version of his alphabet. Van der Laan's system was used for numerous inscriptions carved by monks at the abbeys of Oosterhout and Mamelis.

The alphabet is based on simple proportions: the square and the 3:4 rectangle, which are combined to form the 'basic shapes' (*grondfiguren*). With architectural logic, the letters are ranged into categories according to the shape and direction of the strokes; all proportions, including the space between characters, words and lines, are guided by a strict set of rules.

When compared to other architects' alphabets based on geometric systems, Van der Laan's work stands out for its harmony and intelligence. It is appropriate that it was used for the gravestone of the architect himself, who wrote in 1985: 'The written word is the great monument, the most important monumental form of a society. It takes its shape in inscriptions and in the book.'[12]

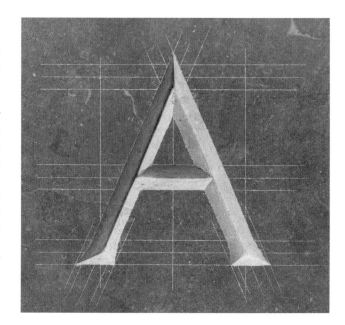

Large Type Library and GLB-16

Jan Tholenaar (1928) is a famous man in the Dutch type world, being the owner of one of the world's most extensive private collections of type specimens.[13]

Until his retirement, Tholenaar was active as a publisher, specializing in co-productions for the Dutch and international market of mostly non-fiction books. One of his initiatives was the *Grote Letter Bibliotheek* (Large Type Library), a collection of books for the partially sighted. Since the early 1970s, hundreds of books have been issued or reissued in this series; it is now continued by Tholenaar's son.

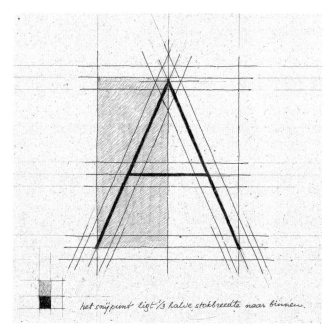

werden vierkant om het gewicht te kunnen tor-
sen en de kalme schoonheid van kracht straalde
hem uit de ogen.
Het was schemerig in het Paleis, schimmelig en
treurig. De jongens lagen op hun bed, lusteloos
en geknakt. Mack staarde omhoog naar zijn bal-
dakijn; hij was er het ergste aan toe van allemaal, want er was geen uitdrukking op zijn

249

◂ Page from a volume in the
Grote Letter Bibliotheek, shown
at true size, 1974.

▾ GLB-16 was a pixel font whose
characters were drawn on sheets
of graph paper, then fed into
the computer numerically.

At the start of the Grote Letter Bibliotheek, Tholenaar decided that a new typeface was needed. Research by Alison Shaw and others had shown that sanserif type was the best option for people with reading difficulties. One constraint that made type-faces like Helvetica and Univers unfit for the job was the need to have the greatest possible difference between a, e and o. Tholenaar set out to draw a new sans. 'It was not my intention, nor was I able, to design an aesthetically satisfying typeface: I was exclusively interested in making an alphabet with optimum legibility for the par-tially sighted.' [14] After a series of tests, he decided that the best size for large type books would be circa 16pt with 3pt extra leading; his letters were to have an x-height of 3 mm and 0.7 mm stroke width and required extra letterspacing.

The characters of GLB-16, as the typeface was named, were first sketched, then drawn on A4 sheets of graph paper. With the help of Nico Beersen at the Amsterdam type-setting firm Infonet, these hand-pixeled letters were then coded by counting the pixels on each line and feeding the numbers into the typesetting machine, making proof settings and changing the numbers until optimum letterforms had been achieved. In 1973, this pioneering work resulted in what must have been the first digital typeface in the Netherlands.

After publishing some 50 books set in GLB-16 (during 1973–74) Tholenaar switched back to *Times New Roman* and later to *Weidemann*. Users found the large sanserif too unorthodox, associating this style with children's books. However, Tholenaar was and still is convinced that his sanserif is among the best typefaces for people with a sight impediment.

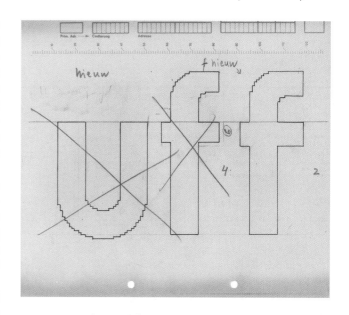

Levanah, a personal investigation

The brochure [15] published in 1993 by Melle Broeksma (1968) to present his typeface *Levanah* should be required reading for aspiring type designers. It records a student project involving extensive research and countless hours of designing and testing, resulting in a typeface that was well-made, very readable and original – but not good enough, according to its maker, to qualify for publication. Levanah has remained in limbo ever since. Its fate exemplifies the self-critical attitude of many young Dutch type designers, who will not publish a face until it is good enough to measure up to the best available.

Levanah was developed between 1991 and 1993, during Broeksma's studies at the Rietveld Academy in Amsterdam. Coached by Gerard Unger and Jan Boterman, Broeksma set out to design a typeface based on historical investigation, studying fifteenth- and sixteenth-century letterforms created by Griffo and Garamond. This was a rather unusual project for a student of the Rietveld Academy – an art school

9 Dom H. van der Laan, *Architectonic Space*, Leiden 1983; quoted in Albert van der Schoot, 'Rationality and irrationality in architecture', in Frans van Peperstraten (ed.), *Jaarboek voor esthetica*, Tilburg 2001, p 205.

10 Near Vaals, province of Limburg, in the southern Netherlands.

11 William PARS Graatsma, Introduction to *Alfabet in Steen*, Nuth 2001.

12 Quoted in *Alfabet in Steen* (cit.), p 12.

13 Cf. Jan Tholenaar, 'Over het verzamelen van letterproeven', in *Hollandse hoogte. Bulletin Stichting Drukwerk in de marge* 23/24, Summer 1997, pp 29–41.

14 Tholenaar in a letter to the author, October 2003.

15 Untitled specimen, written and designed by Melle Broeksma, Amsterdam 1993.

▾ Showings of the regular roman and italics of Levanah, an art school project by Melle Broeksma. The specimen published in 1993 as part of his graduation project showed numerous variants including a bold weight, an upright italic and even a seriffed version.

▾ Drawing for Levanah, as reproduced in Broeksma's self-published specimen.

which, despite the fact that type designer Gerard Unger and type historian Jan Boterman have been long-time teachers, has yielded no other designers of text faces. Broeksma's aim was to design a sanserif with the rhythm, sharpness and legibility of renaissance book faces. After 'un-seriffing' contemporary versions of *Bembo* and *Garamond* as a preliminary study, he drew the first version of *Levanah* by hand. Countless proof settings and test printings on the Rietveld's offset press led to a meticulously spaced font. Its pronounced contrast and subtly flared strokes make it hard to classify, somewhere halfway between a glyphic face and a sanserif.

The Levanah family which Broeksma presented as a graduation project comprised a roman, italic and small caps, with a large number of optically adapted fonts for small point sizes. Among the proposals for further development were bold and intermediate weights, an upright italic and a serif version. Working as a typographic designer, Broeksma regrettably has not had time to develop Levanah any further.

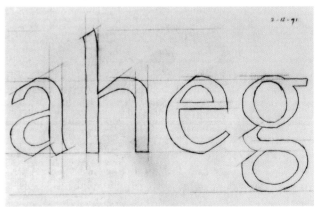

983. LANGE sees the three cases of 'εἰ δέ κε μή in HOMER as particular cases of 'εἰ μή. However, one of these examples, *Il.* α 137, is seen by GOODWIN 179 as an omitted apodosis, «when some such expression as it is *well* or *will be done* can be supplied, or when some other apodosis is at once suggested by the context.», likewise by SCHWYZER II 687 as an example that an apodosis is not expressed, and finally by WAKKER 209-210 as an acute case of 'εἰ … κε' with *coni..* In *Tit. Gort.* VII₄₇ «αἰ δέ κα μὲ» occurs and twice 'αἰ δὲ μέ' in col. VIII (*cf. infra* n. 1013). This points to the fact that both expressions exist alongside each other and that the supplement 'κε' is determined by the *modus*. Cf. *Tit. Gort.* VII₄₇₋₅₂: «αἰ δέ κα μὲ ὀπυίει ἆι ἔγρατται, τὰ κρέματα πάντ' ἔκονσαν, αἴ κ'ἐι ἄλλος, τõι ἐπιβάλλοντι·vac. αἰ δ'ἐπιβάλλον μὲ εἴε, τᾶς πυλᾶς τõν αἰτιόντõν ὅτιμ'κα δἒι ὀπυίεθαι.» – "And if he should not marry her as written, the heiress, holding all the property, is to marry the next in succession, if there be another; might there be no groom—elect, she is to be married to whomsoever she wishes of those who ask from the tribe." and *s.* n. 983.

Loek Schönbeck's Elyade

Published in 1998, *Sunbowl or Symbol* by Loek Schönbeck (1949), an Amsterdam historian of ancient philosophy, is a 500-page book about Heraclitus's conception of the sun. Wanting to make sure that the complex book would be in every respect as magnificently produced as he envisaged it, Schönbeck decided to personally design and publish it; as he found no typeface which had perfectly balanced Greek and Latin alphabets, he decided to draw and digitize a complete font family himself.

The typeface *Elyade*, designed between 1990 and 1998 for *Sunbowl or Symbol*, is the work of an uncompromising perfectionist and individualist. Schönbeck set out to single-handedly revolutionize the typography of highly complex philosophical/philological texts. Besides his ambition to create optimum compatibility between Greek and Latin alphabets, he also wanted letterforms as interesting and lively as the types used in the books printed by Aldus Manutius in fifteenth-century Venice – strongly believing that in that respect he could outdo most contemporary Aldus and Garamond revivals. Schönbeck's unique do-it-yourself approach won him one of 1998's Best Dutch Book Awards.[16]

Schönbeck has written extensively about his motives and method in designing Elyade, partly in reaction to two short, scathing reviews by Frank E. Blokland in the trade press. Schönbeck related that both his original drawings and his corrections to early proof settings were made in Venice, bent over the original Aldine pages. He argued that in order to fully appreciate the way Elyade's Latin alphabet was adapted to harmonize with the Greek, one has to 'undogmatize the laws of form' – meaning, apparently, to set aside the rule that characters have to relate to each other in a regular, predictable way, which Schönbeck assumes underlies all of today's historically inspired type design.

The ultimate test of any typeface is in the eye of the reader. And to this reader's eye, Schönbeck's effort is not without merit, but immature. The brilliant idiosyncracies of the original Aldine forms have been translated into undulating details which do indeed make the romans blend in nicely with the Greek script; but the overall colour in text sizes is rather weak, and some of the type's frills attract too much attention. There are recent examples of how undogmatic thinking about form can lead to fascinating typefaces that possess the historically inspired irregularity Schönbeck has striven for, yet make for pleasant reading – from Fred Smeijers's *Renard* to the complete works of Prague type designer František Storm. Yet it is those designers' talent and expertise that has turned interesting ideas into great type. In the case of Elyade, the result is too self-conscious and, literally, too meagre to be in that league.

◄ Elyade was designed by Amsterdam philosopher Loek Schönbeck because he found no typeface in which Latin and Greek letterforms were really compatible.

▼ Published in 1998, Schönbeck's dissertation *Sunbowl or Symbol* was designed by the author, who typeset it in his own typeface.

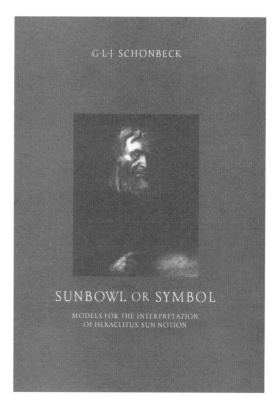

G·L·J· SCHÖNBECK

SUNBOWL OR SYMBOL

MODELS FOR THE INTERPRETATION OF HERACLITUS' SUN NOTION

16 G.L.J. Schönbeck, *Sunbowl or Symbol: Models for the Interpretation of Heraclitus' Sun Notion*, Amsterdam 1998.

◄ Text sample of Oneliner from the brochure *Total Identity. One goal. Multiple strategies*, 2002.

▼ Detail of a presentation panel about Total Identity's corporate typeface Oneliner, 2002.

Aad van Dommelen: a Oneliner for Total Identity

Founded in 1963, Total Design (TD) has long been the Netherlands' most influential graphic design firm. In the 1980s the company went through several crises and management changes, losing its pole position as the unrivalled champion of Dutch functionalism. But TD survived and kept redefining itself. In 2000, the firm changed its name to Total Identity, a name chosen to underline its expertise in all aspects of corporate communication, branding and 'reputation management'.

Although during the 1960s and '70s Wim Crouwel and, to a lesser extent, other TD designers drew display and signage typefaces to enhance the identity of certain clients, the firm never made an alphabet for itself; nor did TD ever develop a text face. So when Total Identity's Aad van Dommelen set out to design a corporate face for the studio, to be used in headlines as well as text, it was an absolute first.

Type design was not new to Van Dommelen (1956); as a classmate of Petr van Blokland he was among the first students of Gerrit Noordzij to explore vector-based digitizing techniques at URW in Hamburg. However, Total Identity's corporate font *Oneliner* is his first full-fledged type family.

As explained in a text he wrote on the typeface, the design method was rather unusual – and not at all ' Hague school'. In order to come up with a typeface that was 'no-nonsense' as well as 'original … sophisticated and innovative' (the brief asked for all this and more) Van Dommelen conceived it as a monoline sans built around a central skeleton – optical corrections were made only in the last stage of the design. The didactic panel shown on this page is more or less self-explanatory.

For the sake of practicality, the capitals were drawn so small that no separate set of small caps was needed; numerals have been designed as table figures only. Oneliner has a lot in common with DIN, from which it took part of its inspiration. But it surpasses DIN in naturalness and, despite its no-frills construction, builds rather elegant text pages.[17]

design

The letters are drawn in one line, thus not in contours, as is usually the case. This has consequences for the shape: a curvature that's too sharp immediately results in an ugly outside form.

design

The weight of the typeface can be altered by changing the line width.

design

The horizontal parts of the characters have the same width as the vertical parts. However, they appear to be too heavy – this is an optical effect. To compensate for this effect, the characters are made 15% taller.

design

Now the lines are converted into contours. These characters have the same stroke width everywhere.

design

The characters are then reduced to their original height. This doesn't effect the vertical parts, only the horizontal. They are now thinner, which has the effect of making the type look more harmonic.

design

The resulting drawings now have to be retouched by hand – the contours are far from ideal and in spite of the bended stems, the connections are too cluttered. The middle part of the 's' has been slimmed, but it should be heavier instead – and so on…

Special projects

Standard, wide and condensed
version of the Luxor alphabet
by Maurice Blok at L5.
The alphabet is used for
signage, printed matter and
on-screen publications, 2001.

Luxor, a Rotterdam typeface

In April 2001, the new Luxor Theatre opened on the *Kop van Zuid* ('South Head'), an extraordinary site on the Rotterdam harbour front. Designed by Australian architect Peter Wilson, the spectacular red building was built to replace a run-down old theatre in the city centre. Its somewhat ship-like forms are accentuated by a giant column that lights up at night, showing the theatre's name in condensed, rectangular capitals. That lettering is part of the integrated typography designed by the Rotterdam company L5 concept design management. A new type family called *Luxor* was designed by L5's Maurice Blok as a central element of the theatre's corporate identity.[18]

The Luxor typeface is a robust constructed alphabet, designed to represent the character traits for which Rotterdam is famous: straightforwardness, workmanship and toughness. The simple structure of its letterforms makes it an extremely flexible alphabet that can be stretched vertically and horizontally; the different widths are combined to create typographic compositions in various degrees of legibility. Within the building, the basic square version of the alphabet makes for loud, sturdy signage, adding to the theatre's unique personality.

17 Article based on material prepared for this book by Aad van Dommelen.
18 The Luxor project is extensively covered in Frans Happel, *Het nieuwe Luxor theater*, 010 Publishers, Rotterdam 2001.

► According to Neijnens, good shirt numbers are seriffed, semi-bold and designed with a clear contrast between thick and thin. This is the improved version of his shirt numbers, King III.

123 4567 890

⌐ The King's figures in use. Jaliens (2) runs after Shoukov (9) to congratulate him with his goal against De Graafschap. *Photo GéVé Multimedia/ Geert van Erven*

Neijnens's football numerals

The typographer Sander Neijnens (1957) is the author of a booklet about the Dutch Type Library; on his website he has published articles on aspects of everyday typography, such as license plates. Another phenomenon that has caught Neijnens's eye was the lettering – or numbering – of sport shirts. In a self-published article, Neijnens argued that the most common styles chosen for shirt numbers (such as the square forms of the well known *Superstars* and *ITC Machine*) are unfit for their task because the forms are too similar and therefore make it hard to recognize the players. According to Neijnens, good shirt numbers are seriffed, semi-bold and designed with a clear contrast between thick and thin.

To prove his point he designed a set of classically proportioned Dutch-style figures. The soccer team Willem II from Tilburg agreed to use Neijnens's shirt numbers during the 2002–2003 season as they were seen to be easier to identify at a distance than the previous ones. Having observed the performance of his *King's figures* from the stands, the designer proposed an improved set, *King III*, which has not yet been implemented. Neijnens will publish a booklet on the design of shirt numbers, with special attention for striped shirts, in 2004.

How refreshing. How Heineken.

The Heineken logotype is one of the world's best known beer identities. It is a known fact that the current version was, at least in part, conceived by Alfred Henry (Freddy) Heineken (1923–2002), who was advertising manager during the postwar decades. Freddy Heineken was the father of the logo's 'laughing e', demanding a cheerfully sloped cross-bar when supervising the restyling of the 1930s–'40s fatface logotype. As the company's CEO during the 1970s and '80s, he managed to turn his family name into a global brand.

In 1999 the Heineken logo became the starting point of an extended type family developed by the Amsterdam design firm Eden (formerly BRS Premsela Vonk). Eden designer Earik Wiersma first made *Horizon*, an eight-weight type family based on the logo; Eden then invited independent type designer Luc(as)de Groot – a former staff member of BRS – to complete and optimize the typeface. The result, an eleven-weight family of serif and sanserif variants, was presented as *Heineken Sans/Heineken Serif* in September 2000. With its unmistakable early-1900s influences, the new corporate typeface epitomizes the Dutch word *gezellig*, meaning 'cozy, homely, social', while the sans adds a touch of modernity – evoking everything the Heineken name stands for.

▾ *Heineken Sans/Heineken Serif, a corporate type family of eleven weights. The final version of the typeface was designed by Luc(as) de Groot in 2000 for the Amsterdam design company Eden.*

☆ **Heineken Serif**

Regular *Italic* **Bold** ***Italic*** Market research in France shows that young adults perceive the bottle as beautiful, modern and stylish.

☆ **Heineken Sans**

Regular *Italic* **Bold** ***Italic*** **Black** ***Italic*** The sensation of coldness and weight make the bottle attractive, together with its originality and freshness.

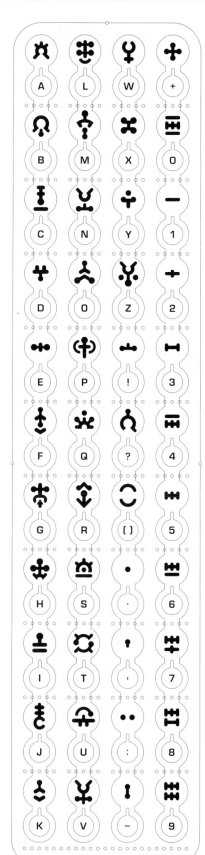

◀ Breaking the code: explanation of the signs of the Swip alphabet by Swip Stolk, 2002.

▶ Keepsake by Stolk, made with the Swip alphabet. Client: ID Laser, a specialized firm for electronic die-cutting with which Stolk has worked for many years, 2003.

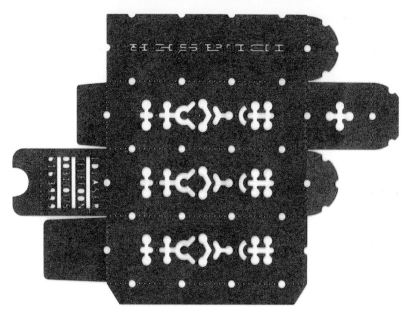

Swip, a code from outer space

No graphic designer in the Netherlands has been as consistent, and as consistently innovative, as Swip Stolk. For four decades he has constantly reinvented himself and his art, keeping abreast of the latest design and production technology. But he has also used the same characteristic stylistic features throughout his career: an ironic use of ornamentation and of centred, 'solemn' layouts; typography in boxes. He has remained a draughtsman, despite his digital tools: he draws new ornaments where others just use clip-art or pick a dingbats font; he modifies existing type, honing it until it perfectly fits his design. So when Stolk comes up with a new typeface, it is bound to be something truly original, yet immediately recognizable.

Swip is not an alphabet, it is a code. As Stolk has said, it may just as well have been transmitted to us from outer space. The signs represent letters, but they also stand for concepts: w=woman; g=god, etc. Of course, the font works differently in every language. Stolk's alphabet premiered in the Italian-made worldwide magazine *Stile*; the readers received a decoding card to help them figure it all out.

The Swip font takes the alphabet one step beyond the conventions of written language, into a realm of myth and play. Maybe it is just an isolated game; maybe it is a symptom of a new era in typography, one in which signs and codes are shared across cultures and enjoyed for the sake of their visual power and suggestiveness.

DECODE CARD E·13·12·2002
ONLY FOR ENGLISH
Decode Card R·28·04·2002 Russian • Decode Card A·24·08·2002 Arabic
Decode Card L·06·13·2002 Latin • Decode Card J·66·27·2002 Japanese
Decode Card C·16·19·2002 Chinese • Decode Card S·25·19·2002 Spanish
These codes are not available

'A slow start is a sign of wisdom'. Showing of an alphabet by J.L.M. Lauweriks, published in J. van Leeuwen's *Letterboek voor den teekenaar en ambachtsman*, 1907.

Bibliography

A note on Dutch names

Many Dutch family names begin with *de* ('the'), *van* ('of/from') or *van de(r)*. As the preposition or article is regarded as secondary, it is ignored in alphabetical listings. For instance, Sjoerd de Roos is listed as 'Roos, Sjoerd de'. As for the use of capitals in these names, the rule (in Northern or Netherlandish Dutch) is the following: when the family name is preceded by a first name or by initials, the interjection is written in lowercase. When the family name stands alone, an initial capital is used. For instance: 'Sjoerd de Roos was a socialist but Van Krimpen was not.' This system is used throughout this book.

General bibliography

Aldus, *Allemaal Flauwekul*. De Buitenkant, Amsterdam 1989

Fernand Baudin, *L'Effet Gutenberg*. Edition du Cercle de la Librairie, 1994

John D. Berry (ed.), *Language Culture Type. International type design in the age of Unicode*. ATypI/Graphis, New York 2002

Peter Biľak, 'Contemporary Dutch graphic design: an insider/outsider's view', in HD, *New Dutch graphic design*, ACTAR, Barcelona 2001

Frank E. Blokland, Robin Nicholas and Steve Matteson (eds.), *Monotype Recorder, New Series no. 9*. Dutch Type Library, 's-Hertogenbosch 1996

Alexander Branczyk et al., *Emotional Digital. A sourcebook of Contemporary Typographics*. Thames & Hudson, London 1999

Pieter Brattinga and Dick Dooijes, *A History of the Dutch Poster 1890–1960*. Scheltema & Holkema, Amsterdam 1968

Kees Broos and Paul Hefting, *Grafische vormgeving in Nederland. Een eeuw*. 3rd edition, ATRIUM-ICOB, Alphen a/d Rijn 1999

Max Caflisch, 'Hoogtepunten van het letterontwerpen in Nederland' in *Gravisie 14*. Van Broekhoven-Bosch, Utrecht 1989

Sebastian Carter, *Twentieth century type designers*. Trefoil Publications, London / Gaade Uitgevers, Veenendaal 1987

Dick Dooijes, *Wegbereiders van de moderne boektypografie in Nederland*. De Buitenkant, Amsterdam 1988

Geoffrey Dowding, *An Introduction to the History of Printing Types*. The British Library, London / Oak Knoll Press, New Castle 1998

Leonie ten Duis and Annelies Haase, *The World must Change. Graphic Design and Idealism*. Sandberg Instituut, Amsterdam 1999

Ron Eason and Sarah Rookledge, *Rookledge's International handbook of type designers: a biographical directory*. Sarema Press, Carshalton Beeches 1991

Friedrich Friedl, Nicolaus Ott, Bernard Stein, *Typography, when, who, how*. Könemann, Cologne 1998

Kees Gnirrep et al., *Een punt voor typografie. De Typografische Bibliotheek in de Universiteitsbibliotheek Amsterdam*, Tetterode, Amsterdam 2001

M.H. Groenendaal jr., *Drukletters. Hun ontstaan en gebruik*. De Technische Boekhandel / H.Stam, Amsterdam 1944

M.H. Groenendaal, *Nederlandse drukletters / Dutch Printing Types*. Amsterdamse Grafische School, Amsterdam 1960

Steven Heller and Philip B. Meggs (eds.), *Texts on type. Critical Writings on Typography*, Allworth Press, New York 2001

W. Pincus Jaspert et al., *The Encyclopaedia of Typefaces*. Blandford, London 1970

Robin Kinross, *Modern Typography. An essay in critical history*. Hyphen Press, London 1992

Manfred Klein, Yvonne Schwemer-Scheddin, Erik Spiekermann, *Type & Typographers*. SDU Uitgeverij, 's-Gravenhage (The Hague) 1991

Karel Kuitenbrouwer, Koosje Sierman, *Over grafisch ontwerpen in Nederland: een pleidooi voor geschiedschrijving en theorievorming*. 010, Rotterdam 1996

John A. Lane and Mathieu Lommen, *Letterproeven van Nederlandse gieterijen / Dutch typefounders' specimens*. De Buitenkant, Amsterdam 1998

Martijn F. Le Coultre and Alston W. Purvis, *A Century of Posters*. V+K Publishing, Blaricum 2002

Ruari McLean, *The Thames and Hudson Manual of Typography*. London 1980

Jan Middendorp and Amy Ramsey (eds.), *FontFont in Nederland*. FontShop Benelux, Zwijnaarde 1998

Jan Middendorp, '*Ha, daar gaat er een van mij!*'. Stroom hcbk / Uitgeverij 010, Rotterdam 2002

Stanley Morison, *First principles of Typography*. Academic Press, Leyden 1996

Stanley Morison, *Letter Forms; Typographic and Scriptorial*. Hartley & Marks, Vancouver 1997

Stanley Morison, *A Tally of Types, with additions by serveral hands and with a new introduction by Mike Parker*. David R. Godine, Boston 1999

James Mosley, *The Nymph and the Grot. The Revival of the Sanserif Letter*. Friends of the St Bride Printing Library, London 1999

Frans van Mourik, *Beeldschermtypografie*. Lecturis, Eindhoven 1998

G.W. Ovink, 'Anderhalve eeuw typografie in Nederland', in *Anderhalve eeuw boektypografie 1815–1965*. Thieme, Nijmegen 1965

Alston W. Purvis, *Dutch Graphic Design 1918–1945*. Van Nostrand Reinhold, New York 1992

Robert van Rixtel and Wim Westerveld (eds.), *Letters. Een bloemlezing over typografie*. Veenman drukkers, Ede / [Z]oo Produkties, Eindhoven 2001

Geert Setola and Joep Pohlen, *Letterfontein*. Fontana, Roermond 1997

Jürgen Siebert, Erik Spiekermann and Mai-Lihn Thi Truong, *Font Book*. FontShop International, Berlin 1998

Richard Southall, 'A survey of type design techniques before 1978', *Typography Papers 2*. University of Reading 1997

Kees Thomassen (ed.), *Lood en oud ijzer*. 25 jaar Stichting Drukwerk in de Marge, 2000

Walter Tracy, *Letters of Credit. A View of Type Design*. David R. Gordine, Boston 1986

Marian and Gerard Unger, 'Hollands landschap met letters', in *Gravisie 14*. Van Broekhoven-Bosch, Utrecht 1989

Maximilien Vox, *Nouvelle classification des caractères*. Ecole Estienne, Paris 1954

Lawrence W. Wallis, *Modern Encyclopedia of Typefaces 1960–90*. Lund Humphries, London 1990

Printers and punchcutters

Fernand Baudin and Netty Hoeflake, *The Type Specimen of Jacques-François Rosart. Brussels 1768*. Van Gendt & Co, Amsterdam 1973

P. van Boheemen et al., *Het boek in Nederland in de 16de eeuw*. Museum Meermanno / Staatsuitgeverij, 's-Gravenhage 1986

Christopher Burke, *Paul Renner. The Art of Typography*. Hyphen Press, London 1998

Max Caflisch, 'Christoffel van Dijck, An outstanding punch-cutter', *Type, A Journal of the Association Typographique Internationale*, vol. 1, no. 1, 1997

Harry Carter, *A View of Early Typography*. New edition with an introduction by James Mosley. Hyphen Press, London 2002

Colin Clair, *A History of European Printing*. Academic Press, London/New York/San Francisco 1976

B.P.M. Dongelmans et al., *Boekverkopers van Europa. Het 17de-eeuwse Nederlandse uitgevershuis Elzevier*. Walburg Pers, Zutphen 2000

John Dreyfus (ed.), *Type Specimen Facsimiles 1–15*. Bowes & Bowes and Putnam, London 1963

Charles Enschedé, *Typefoundries in the Netherlands from the fifteenth to the nineteenth century*. English translation with revisions and notes by Harry Carter, Stichting Museum Enschedé, Haarlem 1978

Just Enschedé, *Enschedé aan het Klokhuisplein*. De Vrieseborch, Haarlem 1991

Frederic W. Goudy, *Typologia; Studies in Type Design & Type Making*. University of California Press, Berkeley/London 1977

György Haiman, *Nicholas Kis, A Hungarian punch-cutter and printer*. Jack W. Stauffacher / The Greenwood Press, San Francisco 1983

S.L. Hartz, *The Elseviers and their contemporaries*. Elsevier, Amsterdam/ Brussels 1955

Horst Heiderhoff, 'Zur Rehabilitierung der Nikolaus Kis', in *Die Original-Janson-Antiqua*. D. Stempel AG, Frankfurt am Main 1983

Lotte Hellinga-Querido and Clemens de Wolf, *Laurens Janszoon Coster was zijn naam*. Joh. Enschedé & Zonen, Haarlem 1988

Wytze Gs Hellinga, *Copy and Print in the Netherlands. An Atlas of Historical Bibliography*. Amsterdam 1962

Frans A. Janssen (ed.), *Fleischman on Punch-cutting*. Spectatorpers, Aartswoud 1994

Jan van Krimpen, *Het huis Enschedé 1705–1953*. Joh. Enschedé en Zonen, Haarlem 1953

John A. Lane, *The Enschedé Type Specimens of 1768 & 1773. Introduction and notes* [to] *Proef van Letteren, Welke gegooten worden in de Nieuwe Haarlemsche Lettergieterij van J. Enschedé, 1768* (facsimile). Stichting Museum Enschedé / The Enschedé Font Foundry / Uitgeverij De Buitenkant, 1993

Douglas C. McMurtrie, *The Brothers Voskens and Their Successors*. Chicago 1932

Douglas C. McMurtrie, *Over de uitvinding van de boekdrukkunst* (transl. of chapters x and xi of *The Book*, New York 1937). Brandt & Proost, Amsterdam 1940

Francine De Nave and Leon Voet, *Museum Plantin-Moretus Antwerpen*. Musea Nostra / Ludion, Brussels 1989

Pieter F.J. Obbema, Marja C.Keyser et al., *Boeken in Nederland. Vijfhonderd jaar schrijven, drukken en uitgeven*. Grafisch Nederland 1979

G.W. Ovink, 'Dutch Chocolate Letters', Typographica 15, pp 26–32

Herbert Simon, *Introduction to Printing. The craft of letterpress*. Faber and Faber, London/Boston 1968

Fred Smeijers, *Counterpunch. Making type in the sixteenth century, designing typefaces now*. Hyphen Press, London 1996

S.H. Steinberg, *Five Hundred Years of Printing*. New edition, revised by John Trevitt, British Library, London / Oak Knoll Press, New Castle 1996

Daniel Berkeley Updike, *Printing Types. Their history, form and use. A study in survivals*. 2nd edition, Harvard University Press, Cambridge 1951

H.D.L. Vervliet, *Sixteenth-Century Printing Types of the Low Countries*. Menno Hertzberger & Co., Amsterdam 1968

H.D.L. Vervliet and Harry Carter, *Type Specimen Facsimiles ii*. The Bodley Head, London 1972

H.D.L. Vervliet, *Post-incunabula and their Publishers in the Low Countries*. Martinus Nijhoff, The Hague/Boston/ London 1979

Reinventing Tradition

Guus Bekooy a.o. *Philips Honderd. Een industriële onderneming*. Zaltbommel 1991

Jan P. Boterman (ed.), *Zilvertype corps 15*. De Buitenkant, Amsterdam 1994

Ernst Braches, 'Bookfaces by G.W. Dijsselhof in the 'nineties', *Quaerendo* vol. 2, no. 1, 1972

Ernst Braches, *Het boek als Nieuwe Kunst; een studie in Art Nouveau*. Oosthoek, Utrecht 1973

Yvonne Brentjens, *Dwalen door het paradijs. Leven en werk van G.W. Dijsselhof (1866–1924)*. Waanders, Zwolle / Gemeentemuseum, Den Haag 2002

Wim Crouwel, 'Onderkast in Nederland' *Bulletin Drukwerk in de Marge*, no. 18, 1990

Peter van Dam and Philip van Praag, *Stefan Schlesinger 1896–1944. Atelier voor reclame*. Uniepers, Abcoude 1997

C. van Dijk, *Alexandre A.M. Stols 1900–1973, uitgever/typograaf*. Walburg Pers, Zutphen 1992

Dick Dooijes, *Sjoerd H. de Roos zoals ik hem mij herinner*. Rijksmuseum Meermanno-Westreenianum / Museum van het Boek, 's-Gravenhage (The Hague) 1976

Dick Dooijes, *Over de drukletterontwerpen van Sjoerd H. de Roos*. Bührmann-Ubbens Papier, Zutphen 1987

John Dreyfus, *The Work of Jan van Krimpen. A record in honour of his sixtieth birthday*. Joh. Enschedé en Zonen, Haarlem / W. de Haan, Utrecht 1952

Jan Engelman et al., *In Memoriam Charles Nypels*. Lettergieterij Amsterdam et al., Amsterdam 1953

Sjoerd van Faassen, *W.L. & J. Brusse's Uitgeversmaatschappij 1903–1965*. Uitgeverij 010, Rotterdam 1993

Jan Feith, 'Over Pieter Das', *De bedrijfs-reklame*, vol. 2, nr. 1, 1917

A.M. Hammacher, *Jean François van Royen 1878–1942*. D.A. Daamen / A.A.M. Stols, 's-Gravenhage (The Hague) 1947

Sem Hartz, 'Sjoerd Hendrik de Roos', in *Essays*, ed. by Mathieu Lommen, Klein Kapitaal / Serifpers, Amsterdam / Spectatorpers, Aartswoud 1992

Paul Hefting, *Royal PTT Nederland NV, Art & Design – Past & Present*. PTT, 's-Gravenhage (The Hague) 1992

Magriet Knol, *Klaas van Leeuwen 1868–1935*. Drents Museum, Assen 1988

Huib van Krimpen, 'Type design in the Netherlands and the Influence of the Enschedé Foundry', *Fine Print*, vol. 15, no. 4, 1989, pp 189–197

Jan van Krimpen, *On Designing and Devising Type*. The Typophiles, New York 1957

Jan van Krimpen, *A Letter to Philip Hofer on Certain Problems Connected with the Mechanical Cutting of Punches*, ed. by John Dreyfus. Harvard College Library, Cambridge / David R. Godine, Boston 1972

Jan van Krimpen, *Memorandum*. De Buitenkant, Amsterdam / Dutch Type Library, 's-Hertogenbosch 1996

K. van Leeuwen, *Letterboek voor den teekenaar en ambachtsman*. G. Schreuders, Bennekom/D.Bolle, Rotterdam 1907

Letterproef der Lettergieterij 'Amsterdam' voorheen N. Tetterode. Amsterdam [1916]

Lettergieterij 'Amsterdam' voorheen N. Tetterode, *Choice of modern types; Urval av Tidsenliga Stilar*. Amsterdam [c. 1951]

Kurt Löb, 'Deutschsprachige Gestalter als Emigranten', *Philobiblon* vol. 33, no. 3, September 1989

Mathieu Lommen, *De grote vijf. S.H. de Roos - J.F. van Royen - J. van Krimpen - C. Nypels - A.A.M. Stols*. Bührmann-Ubbens Papier, Zutphen 1991

Mathieu Lommen, *Jan van Krimpen en Bruce Rogers*. Dutch Type Library, 's-Hertogenbosch / URW, Hamburg 1994

Gerrit Noordzij, *De actualiteit van het Romulus projekt*. Self-published brochure, 1992

G.W. Ovink, *De ontembare lettergieter*. Nederlandse Vereeniging voor Druk- en Boekkunst, 's-Gravenhage 1947

G.W. Ovink and Huib van Krimpen, *Jan van Krimpen. Tentoonstelling van zijn ontwerpen; letters en boeken*. 's-Gravenhage / Antwerpen / Brussel 1967

G.H. Pannekoek, *De verluchtiging van het boek*. W.L. & J. Brusse, Rotterdam 1927

Etablissements Plantin, *Spécimen de caractères 'Plantin', Supplément*. Brussels [c.1932]

M.R. Radermacher Schorer, *Bijdrage tot de geschiedenis van de renaissance der Nederlandse boekdrukkunst*. G.H. Bührmann's Papiergroothandel, Amsterdam 1952

Sjoerd H. de Roos, *Typografische geschriften*. Ed. by Sjaak Hubregtse; intr. by Jan P. Boterman. SDU Uitgeverij, 's-Gravenhage (The Hague) 1989

Jean François van Royen 1878–1942. Museum Meermanno-Westreenianum, 's-Gravenhage (The Hague) 1969

Stefan Schlesinger, *Voorbeelden van moderne opschriften voor schilders en tekenaars*. NV Kosmos, Amsterdam 1939

Koosje Sierman, 'De Libra van S.H. de Roos, een uitmiddelpuntige', TYP vol. 2 no. D, July 1988

Koosje Sierman et al., *Adieu Aesthetica & Mooie Pagina's! J. van Krimpen en het 'schoone boek'*. Museum van het Boek, 's-Gravenhage / De Buitenkant, Amsterdam / Museum Enschedé, Haarlem 1995

A.A.M. Stols, *De toegepaste kunsten in Nederland: Het schoone boek*. Interbook, Schiedam 1979 [first printing 1935]

A.A.M. Stols, *Het werk van S.H. de Roos. Een bijdrage tot de geschiedenis van de herleving der Nederlandsche boekdrukkunst*. n.v. Lettergieterij 'Amsterdam', voorheen N. Tetterode, Amsterdam 1942

Manifestations of the New

Carel Blotkamp (ed.), *De vervolgjaren van De Stijl 1922–1932*. L.J. Veen, Amsterdam/Antwerp 1996

Mechteld de Bois, *Chris Lebeau 1878–1945*. Drents Museum, Assen / Frans Halsmuseum, Haarlem 1987

Kees Broos, *Piet Zwart 1885–1977*. Van Gennep, Amsterdam 1982

Kees Broos, *Architekst*. Lecturis, Eindhoven 1989

Kees Broos, *Mondriaan, De Stijl en de Nieuwe Typografie*. De Buitenkant, Amsterdam / Museum van het Boek, 's-Gravenhage (The Hague) 1994

Martijn F. le Coultre, *Wendingen 1918–1932*. V+K Publishing, Blaricum 2001

Peter van Dam and Philip van Praag, *Fré Cohen 1903–1942*. Uniepers, Abcoude 1993

Peter van Dam and Philip van Praag, *Amsterdam gaf het voorbeeld*. Uniepers, Abcoude 1996

Titus M. Eliëns et al., *Kunstnijverheid in Nederland 1880–1940*. V+K Publishing/ Inmerc, Bussum 1997

Gerd Fleischmann et al., *Bauhaus Typografie, Drucksachen, Reklame*. Oktogon, Stuttgart 1995

Steven Heller and Louise Fili, *Dutch Moderne*. Chronicle Books, San Francisco 1994

Els Hoek (ed.), *Oeuvrecatalogus Theo van Doesburg*. Centraal Museum, Utrecht / Kröller-Müller Museum, Otterlo / THOTH, Bussum 2000

Toos van Kooten (ed.), *Bart van der Leck: 'een toepassend kunstenaar'*. Kröller-Müller Museum, Otterlo 1994

Arthur Lehning and Jurriaan Schrofer, *i-10, de internationale avant-garde tussen de twee wereldoorlogen*. 's-Gravenhage (The Hague) 1963

Dick Maan, *De Maniakken. Ontstaan en ontwikkeling van de grafische vormgeving aan de Haagse academie in de jaren dertig*, Lecturis, Eindhoven 1982

Dick Maan and John van der Ree, *Typo-foto*, Veen / Reflex, Utrecht / Amsterdam 1990

Dick Maan, 'Zo moet de wereld zijn' (on Jac. Jongert), *Druk* 008, Spring 2001

Hans Oldewarris, *H.Th. Wijdeveld, Art Deco design on paper*. Museum Meermanno, 's-Gravenhage (The Hague) / 010 Publishers, Rotterdam 2003

Paul Overy, *De Stijl*. Thames & Hudson, London 1991

Alston W. Purvis, *Dutch Graphic Design 1918–1945*. New York 1992

Piet Schreuders, 'Amsterdamse Eselsbruggen. Een ijzeren alfabet', *Qwerty*, vol. 2, no. 2, 1990

A.S.A. Struik and Marja Keyser, *Nederlandse industriële boekbanden*. Universiteits-bibliotheek, Amsterdam 2000

Jan Tschichold, *The New Typography*. transl. Ruari McLean, Berkeley/Los Angeles/London 1998

Nic. H. M. Tummers, *J.L. Mathieu Lauweriks, zijn werk en zijn invloed*. G. van Saane, Hilversum 1968

Gijs van Tuyl, Marlene Müller-Haas, *Bart van der Leck, Maler der Moderne*. Kunstmuseum, Wolfsburg 1994

N.J. van de Vecht, *Onze letterteekens en hun samenstelling*. W.L. & J. Brusse, Rotterdam 1930

Metal type, the final years

Dick Dooijes, *Over drukletters en het ontwerpen daarvan*. Amsterdamse Grafische School, Amsterdam 1959

Dick Dooijes, *Mijn leven met letters*. De Buitenkant, Amsterdam 1991

S.L. Hartz in de grafische wereld. Rijksmuseum Meermanno-Westreenianum, 's-Gravenhage (The Hague) 1969

Sem Hartz, *Essays*, ed. by Mathieu Lommen. Klein Kapitaal / Serifpers, Amsterdam / Spectatorpers, Aartswoud 1992

Lettergieterij Amsterdam, *Internationale catalogus van drukletters*. Amsterdam 1968

Mathieu Lommen, *Letterontwerpers. Gesprekken met Dick Dooijes, Sem Hartz, Chris Brand, Bram de Does, Gerard Unger. Met een voorwoord van John Dreyfus*. Joh. Enschedé en Zonen, Haarlem 1987

Lettertypen van Lettergieterij en Machinehandel vh N. Tetterode-Nederland bv, Tetterode-Nederland / Stam, Amsterdam [c. 1979]

Painters and penmen

Hermanus Berserik, *Overzichtstentoonstelling schilderijen, grafiek, tekeningen*. Self-published catalogue, 1973

Bibeb, *Sandberg*. Thieme nv, Nijmegen 1969

Simon Carmiggelt, foreword to *Bertram: Bijna zonder woorden*. Amsterdam 1956

C. van Dijk, *Alexandre A.M. Stols 1900–1973, uitgever/typograaf*. Walburg Pers, Zutphen 1992

Dick Dooijes, *Helmut Salden*. Nijmeegs Museum voor Schone Kunsten, 1965

Julius de Goede, *Gedachtig aan Jan V.* self-published brochure, Utrecht 1993

Jelle Kingma (ed.), *Susanne Heynemann, typografe*. Museum Meermanno, 's-Gravenhage (The Hague) / Universiteitsbibliotheek, Groningen 1998

Reinold Kuipers, *Gerezen wit. Notities bij boekvormelijks en zo*. Querido, Amsterdam 1990

Ank Leeuw-Marcar, *Willem Sandberg, portret van een kunstenaar*. Meulenhoff, Amsterdam 1981

Kurt Löb, *Exil-gestalten. Deutsche Buchgestalter in den Niederlanden 1932–1950*. Gouda Quint, Arnhem 1995

Mathieu Lommen, *Helmut Salden 1910–1996, zijn boekomslagen en vignetten*. Amsterdam 1998

W.J. Rozendaal, 'Bij de afwezige: Bertram Weihs', in *Bertram Weihs, Grafisch Werk*. 's-Gravenhage (The Hague) 1959

A.L. Sötemann, *Querido van 1915 tot 1990*. Querido, Amsterdam 1990

Katja Vranken et al. (eds.), *Helmut Salden, letterontwerper en boekverzorger*, Uitgeverij 010, Rotterdam 2003

Nicolaas Wijnberg, *Van de hoed en de rand*. Venlo-Antwerp 1997

Jan Wolkers, Hans van Straten a.o., *Leven in letters. Over Jan Vermeulen*. Gelderse Cahiers, Arnhem 1992

Functionalism and geometry

Bibeb, *Jurriaan Schrofer*. G.J. Thieme NV, Nijmegen 1972

Evert Bloemsma, 'Interview met Wim Crouwel'. Brochure published as part of the package *Opvattingen over typografie*. KAA (Arnhem Art Academy), Arnhem 1984

Hughues Boekraad, 'Lines. about the designer Wim Crouwel', *Affiche 7*, September 1993 (Dutch version published, with modifications, in Huyghen and Boekraad 1997)

Ben Bos and Wim Crouwel, *Benno Wissing*. BNO, Amsterdam 1993

Kees Broos, *Ontwerp: Total Design / Design: Total Design*. Reflex, Utrecht 1983

Kees Broos and David Quay, *Wim Crouwel Alphabets*. BIS Publishers, Amsterdam 2003

Max Bruinsma, 'Wim Crouwel interview', *Items 5/6*, December 1993

Wim Crouwel, *New Alphabet*, Steendrukkerij de Jong, Hilversum 1967

Wim Crouwel, *Ontwerpen en drukken. Over drukwerk als kwaliteitsproduct*. Gerrit Jan Thiemefonds, Amsterdam 1974

Frederike Huygen and Hugues Boekraad, *Wim Crouwel, Mode en module*. Uitgeverij 010, Rotterdam 1997

Paolo Palma, *New Alphabet. Wim Crouwel e la tipografia sperimentale*, self-published, Urbino 2003

Helmut Schmid (ed.), *Typography today*. Seibundo Shinkosha Publishing Co. Ltd., Tokyo 1980

Jurriaan Schrofer, *Letters op maat*. Drukkerij Lecturis, Eindhoven 1987

Jurriaan Schrofer, *Zienderogen*. Gerrit Jan Thiemefonds, Amsterdam 1988

Gerard Unger, *A counter-proposal*. Steendrukkerij de Jong, Hilversum [1968]

Dingenus van de Vrie (ed.), *Benno Wissing*. Museum Boijmans Van Beuningen / NAi Uitgevers, Rotterdam 1999

[Benno Wissing and Hartmut Kowalke] *Geprogrammeerde belettering Ahoy'*. Total Design, Amsterdam 1970

A graphic counterculture

Paul Hefting, 'Te veel om op te noemen. Notities over het werk van Joost Swarte', in *Joost Swarte*. Plano, Amsterdam 1987

Steven Heller, 'Past Perfect. The lettering of Joost Swarte', *U&lc*, vol. 26, no. 2, Fall 1999

Martin Kaye (text by Jan de Jong), *Facade AlphaBets et Cetera*. De Buitenkant, Amsterdam 1985

Ewan Lentjes, 'Joost Swarte, bricoleur typographique', *Items 6*, December 2001 / January 2002

Piet Schreuders, *Lay In – Lay Out (En Ander Oud Zeer)*. 2nd printing, revised and extended, De Buitenkant, Amsterdam 1997

Han Steenbruggen (ed.), *Swip Stolk, Master Forever*. Groningen/Gent 2000

Printing types for a changing technology

Fernand Baudin, *Chris Brand*. Koninklijke Bibliotheek van België, Brussels / Academie voor Beeldende Kunsten Sint Joost, Breda 1996

Frank E. Blokland, 'Schoonschrijven als basis voor letterontwerpen. Chris Brand, letterontwerper en kalligraaf', *Compres*, 6 March 1996

Frank E. Blokland and Antoon de Vylder, *Chris Brand & Willem Elsschot*. Breda / Antwerp 1996

Ernst Braches, *De tragedie van NEN 2296*. Mercator, 1984

Max Caflisch, 'Die Hollander, eine neue Schriftfamilie', *Typografische Monatsblätter*, no. 2, 1987

Max Caflisch, 'Swift, eine neue Zeitungsschrift', *Typografische Monatsblätter*, no. 4, 1987

Max Caflisch, 'Bitstream Amerigo von Gerard Unger', *Typografische Monatsblätter*, no. 3, 1989

Max Caflisch, 'Die Schriftfamilie Trinité' in *Typografische Monatsblätter*, no. 6, 1994

Bram de Does, *Romanée en Trinité; Historisch origineel en systematisch slordig*. De Buitenkant, Amsterdam / Spectatorpers, Aartswoud 1991

Bram de Does (text by Mathieu Lommen), *Lexicon*. De Buitenkant, Amsterdam 1997

Hans Kessens, 'Chris Brand en zijn letters', *Brabants Dagblad*, 1 July 1967

Kurt Löb, 'Chris Brand: In Love with 26 Signs', *Gebrauchsgraphik* no. 10, 1973

Matthieu Lommen (ed.), *Bram de Does. Catalogus bij de tentoonstelling van zijn letterontwerpen, grafische ontwerpen & ornamentiek*. Universiteitsbibliotheek, Amsterdam 1999

Matthieu Lommen (ed.), *Bram de Does, letterontwerper en typograaf*. De Buitenkant, Amsterdam 2003

Jan Middendorp, 'Echte Ungers: beetpakken en meeslepen', *Items 2*, april 1998, pp 22–26

Jan Middendorp, 'Design olandese per l'anno duemila', *Druk 001*, summer 1999, pp 8–9 (on Unger's Capitolium)

Gerrit Noordzij, 'Broken Scripts and the Classification of Typefaces', *The Journal of Typographic Research*, vol. IV, no. 3, 1970, pp 213–240

Gerrit Noordzij, *The stroke of the pen*. Koninklijke Academie van Beeldende Kunsten, Den Haag (The Hague) 1982

Gerrit Noordzij, *De streek. Theorie van het schrift*. Van de Garde, Zaltbommel 1985

Gerrit Noordzij, *De staart van de kat. De vorm van het boek*. GHM, Leersum 1988

Gerrit Noordzij, *Letters kijken* (calendar 1995). Bankiva Groep, Leersum 1994

Gerrit Noordzij, *Vergeetboek. De expansie van het boek in zijn ontwikkeling van leesboek tot naslagwerk, van rol tot rom*. Colofon, 's-Gravenhage (The Hague) 1995

Gerrit Noordzij, 'Het primaat van de pen' in Ton Croiset van Uchelen and Hannie van Goinga (eds.), *Van pen tot laser. 31 opstellen over boek en schrift aangeboden aan Ernst Braches*. De Buitenkant, Amsterdam 1996

Gerrit Noordzij, 'Reply to Robin Kinross', *Typography papers 2*, University of Reading 1997

Gerrit Noordzij, *De handen van de zeven zusters*. Van Oorschot, Amsterdam 2000

Gerrit Noordzij, *Letterletter. An inconsistent collection of tentative theories that do not claim any other authority than that of common sense*. Hartley & Marks, Vancouver 2000

Hans Rooseboom, 'De stokken en staarten van Chris Brand', *De Stem*, 4 March 1996

Bavo H.J. van Rossum, Gerard Unger, *Gulliver, the world's most economical printing type*. Bussum, undated

Gerard Unger, *Kijk… je kunt er mee lezen en schrijven*. Gerrit Jan Thiemefonds, Amsterdam [1979]

Gerard Unger, *Letters*. De Buitenkant, Amsterdam 1994

Gerard Unger, 'Moderne Incunabelen' in Ton Croiset van Uchelen and Hannie van Goinga (eds.), *Van pen tot laser*. De Buitenkant, Amsterdam 1996

Gerard Unger, *Terwijl je leest*. De Buitenkant, Amsterdam 1997

Gerard Unger, 'A type desing for Rome and the year 2000' in *Typography Papers 3*, University of Reading, 1998

Letters from The Hague

Frank E. Blokland, Jelle Bosma et al., *Letters]*. The Hague 1986

Frank E. Blokland et al. (foreword by Huib van Krimpen), *Letters] & techniek*. Koninklijke Van de Garde, Zaltbommel 1990

Max Caflisch, 'Eine neue Egyptienne: die PMN Caecilia', *Typografische Monatsblätter*, no. 5, 1993

Max Caflisch, Luc(as) de Groot, 'Henne oder Ei', *Page 10*, 1997

Michael Clark (ed.), *Scripsit*, vol. 19, no. 2

Antje Dohmann (ed.), 'Schriften vor Gericht', *Page 01*, 1998

Anno Fekkes (Mathieu Lommen, ed.), *Special characters from The Hague. Postgraduate course in type design & typography*. Royal Academy of Art, The Hague 1998

Erhard Kaiser, *Schriftmuster der DTL Fleischmann*, 's Hertogenbosch/ Leipzig/Hamburg, undated [c. 1999]

David Kindersley and Lida Lopes Cardozo, *Letters Slate Cut. Workshop philosophy and practice in the making of letters*. Cardozo Kindersley Editions, Cambridge 1990

Robin Kinross, 'Type as Critique' in *Typography papers 2*, 1997

Robin Kinross, 'Interview with Gerrit Noordzij', Van Rixtel/Westerveld 2001

Els Kuijper (ed.), *LettError*, Rosbeek, Nuth 2000

Christian Küsters, 'Love letters', *Graphics International 50*, 1997 (on Luc(as) de Groot)

Ewan Lentjes, 'Hinken op twee liefdes', *Items 1*, maart 1999 (on René Knip)

Mathieu Lommen, 'Peter Verheul, een Haags letterontwerper', *Bulletin Stichting Drukwerk in de Marge*, 21 [1993] pp 10–14

Mathieu Lommen and Peter Verheul, *Haagse Letters*, De Buitenkant, Amsterdam 1996

Mathieu Lommen et al. (red.), *Het primaat van de pen. Een workshop letterontwerpen met Gerrit Noordzij*. Koninklijke Academie van Beeldende Kunsten, Den Haag (The Hague) 2001

Lida Lopes Cardozo, *The Cardozo Kindersley Workshop. A guide to commissioning work*. Cardozo Kindersley Editions, Cambridge 1999 (1st printing 1996)

Jan Middendorp, 'Zinnelijk plezier', *Items* vol 14, nr 3, 1995 (on Luc(as) de Groot)

Jan Middendorp, 'Graven in bits & bytes. De letterterreur van Erik van Blokland en Just van Rossum', *Items* vol. 15 no. 2, 1996

Matthew Mirapaul, 'Is It About to Rain? Check the Typeface', *New York Times*, 24 July 2003 (on LettError)

Sander Neijnens, *De onweerstaanbare letter*, self-published, 1996 (on Frank Blokland and DTL Documenta)

Gerrit Noordzij, *Letters in studie*, Lecturis, Eindhoven 1983

Albert Jan Pool, 'URW++ Type Classification' in (URW)++ *FontCollection*, Hamburg 1996, pp 25–63

Albert-Jan Pool, *FontFont Focus: FF DIN*, FontShop International, Berlin [2000].

Elmo van Slingerland, 'Vallen en opstaan', *Sciptores* vol. 9, no. 2, 1994

Poul Søgren, 'PE Proforma, the first typeface for forms' in *PE Proforma*, Purup Electronics, Lystrup 1988

Erik Spiekermann, 'Just van Rossum and Erik van Blokland would be rich and famous if everyone who used their typefaces paid for them', *Wired*, July 1995

[Rudy Vanderlans], 'An interview with LUST', *Emigre 45*, Winter 1998

Hans Vonk, 'De letterklanken van Frank Blokland', *Qwerty 1*, 1989

Letters from Arnhem

Evert Bloemsma, 'Balance, Avance, Cocon', in Van Rixtel/Westerveld (cit.)

Andy Crewdson 'Seria's motives' in *Druk 013-014*, 2002

Antje Dohmann, 'Serifen wider Willen', *Page 5*, 2000, pp 60–62 (on Bloemsma's Avance. Republished in Dutch in *Druk 005*, summer 2000)

Julius de Goede, *Gedachtig aan Jan V.*, self-published brochure, Utrecht 1993

Robin Kinross, 'Counterpunch: how the book was made', *TypeLab Krant*, ATypI/Typlab, The Hague 1996. Republished on the hyphenpress.co.uk website

Martin Majoor and Jan Middendorp, *FontFont Focus: FF Seria*, FontShop Benelux, Zwijnaarde 2001

Martin Majoor, 'My type design philosophy', *tipoGráfica*, no 53, 2002. Republished on typotheque.com

Jan Middendorp, 'Een bruikbaar instrument. Nieuwe vormgeving voor het telefoonboek', *Items 8*, 1994 (on Telefont by Martin Majoor)

Jan Middendorp, 'Een 21e-eeuwse lettersnijder', *Items*, vol. 17, no. 6, October 1998, pp 20–25 (on Fred Smeijers)

Jan Middendorp, *FontFont Focus No. 8: FF Avance*, FontShop International, Berlin [2000]

Roelof Mulder, *Speed is what we need*, self-published, Arnhem 1988

Fred Smeijers, *Counterpunch. Making type in the sixteenth century, designing typefaces now*. Hyphen Press, London 1996

Fred Smeijers, *FontFont Focus No. 2: FF Quadraat*, FontShop International, Berlin [1999]

Fred Smeijers, 'Fresco', in Van Rixtel/Westerveld 2001 (cit.)

Fred Smeijers, *Type Now, a manifesto. Plus Work so far*. Hyphen Press, London 2003

Lettering and Type Design in the Digital Age

Peter Biľak, *Illegibility*, self-published, Slippery Rock, Pennsylvania, 1995 (includes interview with Max Kisman)

Peter Biľak, *Transparency*, Academy of Fine Arts & Design, Bratislava 1997

Peter Biľak, *FontFont Focus No. 8: FF Eureka*, FontShop International, Berlin [2000].

Paul van der Laan et al., *Con form*. KABK, Den Haag (The Hague) 1996

Ewan Lentjes, 'René Knip. Hinken op twee liefdes', *Items*, vol. 18, no. 1, 1999

Ellen Lupton and J. Abbott Miller, 'Type Writing', *Emigre 15*, 1990

Jan Middendorp, *FontFont Focus: Constructs*, FontShop Benelux, Zwijnaarde [2002].

Jan Middendorp, 'René Knip en de magie van het teken', *96#1*, 2003

Piet Schreuders, 'Echt zo: BAF! Donald Beekman', *Qwerty* no. 1, 1989

Fred Smeijers and Jan Middendorp, 'Forever Young', *96#3*, 2003 (on Lamers and De Bont)

[Rudy Vanderlans], 'Max Kisman', *Emigre 15*, 1990

Chris Vermaas, 'Liever heimwee dan Holland', *Compres*, 19 February 1991

Martin Wenzel and Della Riney, *FontFont Focus No. 5: FF Profile*, FontShop International, Berlin [2000]

Special projects

Dick Adelaar and Her de Vries, '*Beste Vriend! Vuile Ploert!*'. Het surrealisme van J.H. Moesman in werken op papier. Centraal Museum, Utrecht 1998

Frans Happel, *Het nieuwe Luxor Theater Rotterdam*, Uitgeverij 010, Rotterdam 2001

Rudo Hartman, *De F van Fantekast en het vervolg van verder*, The Hague 1998

Edsco de Heus, Aad van Dommelen et al., *Total Identity*, BIS, Amsterdam 2003

William PARS Graatsma and Cor Rosbeek, *Alfabet in Steen*, Rosbeek, Nuth 2001

J.H. Moesman and B.H.J. van Rossum, *Moesman*, Utrecht 1971

[J.H. Moesman], *Op engel voeten, à pas de loup*. Editions Surréalistes 'Brumes Blondes' [J.H. Moesman, Schalkwijk] 1975

Nederlands Normalisatie Instituut, NEN 3225, 's-Gravenhage (The Hague) 1962

C.A. Schilp, 'Moesman ontwierp nieuwe letter', *Nieuw Utrechts Nieuwsblad*, 12 November 1969

Jan Tholenaar, 'Over het verzamelen van letterproeven', *Hollandse hoogte. Bulletin Stichting Drukwerk in de marge 23/24*, Summer 1997

Index of names

Index of typefaces

Credits

This book has been made possible by the generous support
of the Mondriaan Foundation and the Prins Bernhard
Cultural Foundation.

Mondriaan Stichting

Prins Bernhard
Cultuurfonds
geeft cultuur de kans

Compilation and text: Jan Middendorp
Editorial assistance and index: Catherine Dal
English text edited by: John Kirkpatrick, with thanks to
Andy Crewdson
Graphic design: Bart de Haas and Peter Verheul
Typeface: OurType Versa by Peter Verheul
Cover typeface: OurType Fresco Sans by Fred Smeijers
Printed by: Die Keure, Bruges

About the author

Born in The Hague, the Netherlands, Jan Middendorp is a self-taught
graphic designer and writer living and working in Ghent, Belgium.
From 1999 to 2002 he was the art director and editor of *Druk*, a type
magazine published by FontShop Benelux; he is currently an editor
of FontShop's magazine *96*. He writes for the Dutch design magazine
Items and has contributed many articles on typography, design and
dance to other magazines including *Typographic, Typographische
Monatsblätter* and *Ballett International*. He wrote *'Ha, daar gaat er een van
mij!'* (2002), a chronicle of graphic design in The Hague since 1945,
and wrote and designed the award-winning book *Lettered, typefaces and
alphabets by Clotilde Olyff* (2000).

About the type specimens

The text used for type specimens throughout this book is from
'Jonker Johan Von Gutenberg', an essay from 1871 by the Dutch
writer Conrad Busken Huet (1826 – 1886). In it, the author wipes
the floor with those who claim that one Laurens Janszoon Coster
of Haarlem is the inventor of printing. But the myth proved
indestructible. The website that republished the article
– an electronic library of Dutch-language literature – is called
Project Laurens Janszoon Coster. *(http://cf.hum.uva.nl/dsp/ljc/)*